Lecture Notes of the Institute for Computer Sciences, Social Informatics and Telecommunications Engineering 587

AF148026

The LNICST series publishes ICST's conferences, symposia and workshops.
LNICST reports state-of-the-art results in areas related to the scope of the Institute.
The type of material published includes

- Proceedings (published in time for the respective event)
- Other edited monographs (such as project reports or invited volumes)

LNICST topics span the following areas:

- General Computer Science
- E-Economy
- E-Medicine
- Knowledge Management
- Multimedia
- Operations, Management and Policy
- Social Informatics
- Systems

Abdoulaye Sere · Oumarou Sie · Rashid A. Saeed
Editors

Towards new e-Infrastructure and e-Services for Developing Countries

15th International Conference, AFRICOMM 2023
Bobo-Dioulasso, Burkina Faso, November 23–25, 2023
Proceedings, Part I

 Springer

Editors
Abdoulaye Sere ⓘ
Nazi BONI University
Bobo-Dioulasso, Burkina Faso

Oumarou Sie
New Dawn University
Ouagadougou, Burkina Faso

Rashid A. Saeed ⓘ
Taif University
Taif, Saudi Arabia

ISSN 1867-8211   ISSN 1867-822X (electronic)
Lecture Notes of the Institute for Computer Sciences, Social Informatics
and Telecommunications Engineering
ISBN 978-3-031-81569-0   ISBN 978-3-031-81570-6 (eBook)
https://doi.org/10.1007/978-3-031-81570-6

This Springer imprint is published by the registered company Springer Nature Switzerland AG
The registered company address is: Gewerbestrasse 11, 6330 Cham, Switzerland

If disposing of this product, please recycle the paper.

Preface

It is with immense gratitude and excitement that we extend a warm invitation to all participants, researchers, professionals, and enthusiasts who joined us at the 15th International Conference on e-Infrastructure and e-Services for Developing Countries (AFRICOMM 2023). This distinguished conference, organized by the European Alliance for Innovation (EAI), took place from November 23–25, 2023, at the esteemed Sissiman Hotel in Burkina Faso.

The success of AFRICOMM 2023 in Burkina Faso was made possible through the collaborative efforts of numerous individuals, and we would like to extend our heartfelt thanks to all involved. A special thanks is extended to EAI for their instrumental role in the conference organization. Their dedication to advancing research and innovation has been crucial in bringing together diverse perspectives and expertise to address the unique challenges and opportunities in the development of e-Infrastructure and e-Services within the African context.

Success would also not have been possible without the dedication and hard work of the local committee, the technical program committee, authors, and reviewers. Their commitment to ensuring the highest standards in research and innovation greatly contributed to the rich and diverse program of the conference.

Special thanks to Sidi Mohamed Galiam Ouedraogo, the Director General of Electronic Communications (DGCE/MTDPCE/Burkina Faso), for his visionary talk to the young African researchers, are also extended to Alain Mille from Universitaires Sans Frontières, for his thought-provoking keynote address on "Intelligence Artificielle en Afrique : pour quel développement?" (Artificial Intelligence in Africa: for which development?). His insights into the role of artificial intelligence in the African context sparked meaningful discussions and added significant value to the conference.

We express our sincere appreciation to Pascal Urien, a distinguished professor at Télécom Paris, for his captivating keynote presentation on "Building Trust with secure elements and open technologies: crypto device use cases." His expertise shed light on critical aspects of cybersecurity, contributing to the broader conversation on digital trust and security. The conference, set against the backdrop of Burkina Faso's rich cultural heritage, provided a dynamic forum for researchers, academics, industry experts, and policymakers to share insights, discuss challenges, and propose innovative solutions for the development of e-Infrastructure and e-Services in developing countries.

Africa, with its rapidly evolving landscape in Information and Communication Technologies (ICT) and Telecommunications, is in great need of events such as AFRICOMM 2023. These conferences play a crucial role in bridging the gap between technological advancements and the unique challenges faced by the continent. They serve as platforms for collaboration, knowledge exchange, and the exploration of solutions tailored to the specific needs of African nations. As we reflect on the conference's success, we extend our gratitude to the organizing committee, sponsors, and all those who played a pivotal role in making this conference a reality. Your dedication and contributions have laid the foundation for a digitally empowered and sustainable future. We eagerly anticipate your continued engagement and participation in future editions of AFRICOMM, as we collectively strive to explore ideas, innovations, and partnerships for the advancement of e-Infrastructure and e-Services.

Rashid A. Saeed
Abdoulaye Sere

Organization

Steering Committee

Rashid A. Saeed   Taif University, Saudi Arabia

Organizing Committee

General Chair

Rashid A. Saeed   Taif University, Saudi Arabia

General Co-chairs

Oumarou Sie   Université Aube Nouvelle, Burkina Faso
Théodore Marie Yves Tapsoba Université Nazi Boni, Burkina Faso

TPC Chair and Co-chairs

Sere Abdoulaye   Université Nazi Boni, Burkina Faso
Yahya Hamad Sheikh   State University of Zanzibar, Tanzania
Abubakar Bakar Diwani   State University of Zanzibar, Tanzania
Abdi Talib Abdalla   University of Dar es Salaam, Tanzania
Borlli Michel Jonas Somé   Université Nazi Boni, Burkina Faso

Sponsorship and Exhibit Chair

Seydou Golo Barro   Université Nazi Boni, Burkina Faso

Local Chair

Mesmin Dandjinou   Université Nazi Boni, Burkina Faso

Workshops Chair and Co-chairs

Malo Sadouanouan	Université Nazi Boni, Burkina Faso
Tounwendyam Frédéric Ouedraogo	Université Norbert Zongo, Burkina Faso

Publicity and Social Media Chair

Telesphore Tiendrebeogo	Université Nazi Boni, Burkina Faso

Publications Chair

Tiguiane Yélémou	Université Nazi Boni, Burkina Faso

Web Chair

Pasteur Poda	Université Nazi Boni, Burkina Faso

Technical Program Committee

Rashid A. Saeed	Taif University, Saudi Arabia
Sere Abdoulaye	Université Nazi Boni, Burkina Faso
Sallam Osman Fageeri	University of Nizwa, Oman
Bharat S. Chaudhari	MIT World Peace University, India
Osama Rayis	Africa Technology City, Sudan
Idowu Diyaolu	Obafemi Awolowo University, Nigeria
Tounwendyam Frédéric Ouedraogo	Université Norbert Zongo, Burkina Faso
Kennedy Ronoh	Strathmore University, Kenya
Pragasen Mudali	University of Zululand, South Africa
Mahmoud Abdulwahab Alawi	Karume Institute of Science and Technology, Tanzania
Namatovu Hasifah Kasujja	Makerere University Kampala, Uganda
Emmanuel Eilu	Uganda Christian University, Uganda
Abdi T. Abdalla	University of Dar es Salaam, Tanzania
Kalum Priyanath Udagepola	Scientific Research Development Institute of Technology, Australia
Ayodeji O. Oluwatope	Obafemi Awolowo University, Ile-Ife, Nigeria
Arsène Sabas	Canadian Nuclear Safety Commission, Canada; Institut de Mathématiques et de Sciences Physiques, Benin

Nikola Djuric   University of Novi Sad, Serbia
Olasupo Ajayi   University of the Western Cape, South Africa
Ousmane Sadio   Universite Cheikh Anta Diop, Senegal

Contents – Part I

Wireless Networks

E-health

Cybersecurity and Privacy

Contents – Part II

Ontology, Data Preparation

**Responsible Artificial Intelligence for Sustainable Development in
Africa (workshop)**

Digital Economy, Digital Transformation, e-Government and e-services

Digital Identity Frameworks: A Review

Sthembile Ntshangase$^{(\boxtimes)}$, Samuel Lefophane, Tanita Singano, Daniel Shadung, Nthabiseng Mokoena, and Sthembile Mthethwa

Information and Cyber Security Centre (ICSC), Council for Scientific and Industrial Research, Pretoria, South Africa

{sntshangase,slefophane,tsingano,dshadung4,nmokoena, smthethwa}@csir.co.za

Abstract. Government organisations from various countries worldwide including the South African government, are working towards employing digital identity to solve identity challenges such as, identity theft, individuals lacking identity etc. The use of digital identity has demonstrated promising outcomes to overcome these challenges while maintaining security and privacy of individuals. However, it is crucial to use appropriate governance frameworks to ensure proper handling and issuance of digital identities. Hence, this paper presents a review conducted to determine and understand various frameworks that have been proposed and implemented by other countries. This review contributes by guiding South African organisations, researchers, and decision makers towards understanding which frameworks are currently being used and which framework/s can be considered when developing a South African based governance framework that will ensure interoperability in digital identity systems.

Keywords: Digital Identity · Governance Frameworks · Security · Trust · Privacy

1 Introduction

The issue of identity has been prevalent for a long time and according to the World Bank (2016) 1.5 billion people cannot, at the time of the report, prove their identity [1]. This study was recently updated, and at the end of 2022 the statistics indicated that under 850 million people around the world do not have an official identity (ID) [2]. This invisibility has significant implications for a range of development outcomes that depend on delivering services to people or on them being able to access services. Identity plays a huge role by allowing individuals to exercise their rights and responsibilities fairly and equally in a modern society [3]. Identity is crucial to social inclusivity whereby individuals can now access essential services. In the past, identity has been in physical formats, however, with the rise of the Internet and the Fourth Industrial Revolution (4IR) characterised by digitisation has ushered in a new era of *"digital identities"* [4]. This was further exacerbated by the COVID-19 pandemic, where individuals and organisations were forced to adapt to new ways of conducting business.

A. Sere et al. (Eds.): AFRICOMM 2023, LNICST 587, pp. 3–18, 2025.
https://doi.org/10.1007/978-3-031-81570-6_1

Presently, with billions of globally connected devices such as, computers, smart-phones, cameras, supermarket scanners, payment systems, etc.; petabytes of data are now generated and consumed hourly to provide services. Technology is ingrained in even the smallest of devices and is connecting everything, making it a part of our daily life [5]. When making use of services offered by the evolving technology, one option for authenticating, identifying, and verifying a person is to use digital identity. Digital identity is the transformation of physical identities into a digital format to enable three functions, namely the digital identification of individuals, their authentication at various access points, and their authorisation to perform specific actions or access specific services [3]. These functions are critical for a digital identity model to reach its full potential and demonstrate its benefits. The following presents some of the benefits of digital identities that include:

- Privacy Protection: Mobile solutions can allow users to control, share, and easily authenticate their credentials to access various online services. This lessens the chance of unwanted information exchange and data breaches.
- Global Identity Trust: Individual's credentials can be instantly verified, regardless of geographical location or cross-border limitations, through the establishment of universal digital identity framework of trust.
- Smart City Access: Digital identity can be used to increase engagements (with government, public and private organisations) and efficiency in accessing smart cities.
- Inclusive Growth: It can increase economic growth by reducing the number of people worldwide who are excluded in financial and governmental services due to lack of identity documents that can be proven.
- Interoperability: Users can share their digital identities across various platforms, services, and organisations without being tied to a specific identity provider. This eliminates the need for multiple accounts by enabling consumers to access various online services with a single digital identity.
- Customer Trust & Regulatory Compliance: The use of digital identity contributes towards improving organisations Know Your Customer (KYC) strategy and provides efficient customer onboarding, reducing manual verification processes and ensuring compliance with the requirements for regulation.

Even though a digital identity is required for a wide variety of services some are online, and some are physical, there is no "one-size-fits-all" approach towards implementing IDs and access systems [6]. While an increasing amount of personal and critical business information is collected and available online, provisions must be made to ensure security of sensitive data. There is a growing movement among government bodies for the adoption of a digital identity framework that allows users to provide alternative forms of IDs to access key services. This requires creating a digital identity framework to complement and/or act as an alternative to physical documents such as passports or ID cards [7].

Thus, as the South African government is also in a process of adopting digital identity for their services, it is vital to ensure that they adjust to the new era and are not left behind in these new developments. This paper presents the review conducted to determine existing digital identity frameworks, and the major components in those frameworks that can assist South African government towards developing a secure and universal digital identity system. The remainder of this paper is organised as follows. In Sect. 2 an overview and different models of digital identities is provided. Section 3 presents work done towards developing digital identity frameworks. Section 4 summarises identified digital identity frameworks, and discussions. Finally, in Sect. 5 conclusions are drawn and future directions are presented.

2 Overview of Digital Identities

Digital identity has been defined in various ways, but according to the International Telecommunication Union (ITU) digital identity is defined as a "representation of an entity in the form of one or more attributes that allow the entity or entities to be sufficiently distinguished within context" [8]. The Australian Digital Transformation Agency refers to it as "safe, secure and convenient way to prove who you are online, to access online services" [5]. In THALES view, it is "a set of validated digital attributes and credentials for the digital world, similar to a person's identity for the real world" [9]. Based on the National Institute of Standards and Technology (NIST), it is the "unique representation of a subject engaged in an online transaction." They further clarify that; a digital identity is always unique in the context of a digital service but does not necessarily need to uniquely identify the subject in all contexts [3]. This may mean that "accessing a digital service may not mean that the subject's real-life identity is known" which presents another aspect for digital identities [9]. All these definitions are almost the same, however, other aspects are introduced like the uniqueness introduced by NIST. In our view, digital identity can be defined as a unique and/or detailed digital representation of a subject in a form of attributes and credentials for digital services/context.

2.1 Digital Identity Ecosystems/Architecture Models

Digital identities have evolved tremendously over the past few years. The fist model being a *centralised model* whereby a single *entity* establishes and manages identities in a centralised storage [3]. This model forces users to be dependent on the organisation that holds their data. This approach also centralises cyber risks making it easier for cyber attackers to succeed as they are only required to attack one central point. Regardless, this model is still widely used due to its simplicity and convenience.

To address some of the issues presented by centralised models, a *federated model* was introduced which consists of a group of organisations that have established trust amongst each other. In the group, one organisation becomes the main player known as the Identity Provider (IDP), which holds the user's data. The user can access services offered by other organisations in the group through the IDP, thus introducing the concept of Single Sign-on (SSO). This approach introduces power aggregation whereby more power resides with the IDP; hence, it becomes vulnerable to single point of failure.

Data silos are the main challenge with the previous models. As a solution a *decentralised model* was introduced with the aim of removing silos and IDP's and move towards a user centric approach (where users have full control over their data). Consequently, introducing the concept of *Self-Sovereign Identity (SSI)*. This model is still in its initial stages and still requires efforts towards establishing its governance model.

Therefore, this research aims to study some of the governance models, frameworks or policies that have been established in other countries and propose a framework/s that would be ideal when developing a South African based framework. This is crucial for a successful implementation of a digital identity ecosystem.

2.2   South Africa's Digital Identity Roadmap

Just like any other country, South Africa's journey has evolved and with that imple- mentation of various digital identity programs was experienced as depicted in Fig. 1 below.

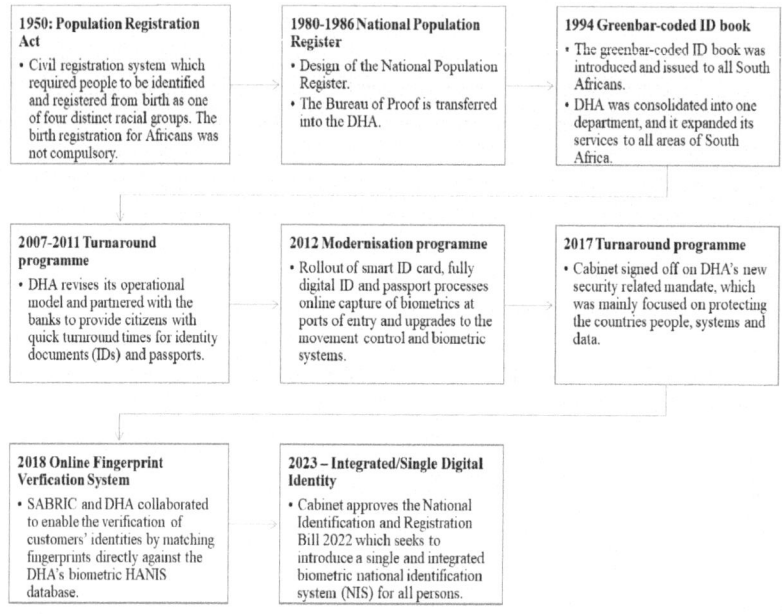

Fig. 1. South Africa's Digital Identity Roadmap.

South Africa is still a developing country and with that, it is still lagging in terms of digitisation and digital identity. However, the efforts made since the COVID-19 pandemic are essential towards the realisation of this in the country. This can be observed through the recent approval of the National Identification and Registration Bill of 2022 [10]. As it stands, the country could lean on the experiences of other countries that have successfully implemented this, but there are many considerations that must be acknowledged as this is pursued for a successful implementation in South Africa's context. According to Imprivata's digital identity maturity assessment categorisation, South Africa can be classified as *Phase 1: Initial* [11]. The five phases of digital identity maturity are depicted in Fig. 2 below.

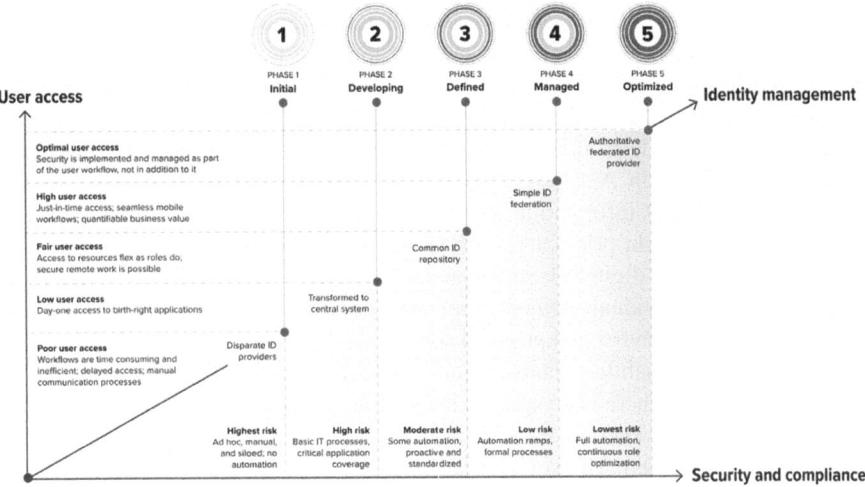

Fig. 2. Five phases of digital identity maturity.

3   Literature Review

3.1   International

This review focuses on digital identity frameworks proposed internationally by countries who are leading the digital identity space, specifically, [12] countries which are members of the Digital Identity Working Group, namely, Australia, Canada, Israel, New Zealand, Singapore, and European countries such as Finland, the Netherlands, and the United Kingdom (UK).

Australian government introduced the Trusted Digital Identity Framework (TDIF) which [13] as of August 2023, has thirteen policies which sets out the requirements that applicants must meet to achieve authorisation. The requirements presented in this framework includes Digital identity accreditation process, Functional Requirements which covers, Fraud control, Privacy, Protective Security, User Experience, Technical Testing, and Functional Assessments. Other requirements are Role Requirements which includes Common Role, Identity Service Provider, Credential Service Provider, Attribute Service Provider, and Identity Exchange. Additional requirements are Federation onboarding and Maintaining accreditation.

In Canada, the government introduced Pan-Canadian Trust Framework (PCTF) which was developed with a purpose of meeting the current and future Canadian digital identity ecosystem innovation needs by verifying trust of services and networks [14]. The PCTF includes ten components that should be considered when implementing a digital identity framework, which is; authentication, credentials, digital wallet, notice & consent, trust registries, verified person, verified organisation, assurance maturity model, glossary, and model. In addition, Canada's digital identity ecosystem is provided in [15] which is the integrated authentication and intermediary licensing model. This model includes four main elements of the ecosystem: An individual who seeks to provide identification to perform a digital transaction or interaction. The dependent section which involves an organisation, individual, or system that requires access to an authority institution. An authority institution incorporates a certified, recognised, or trusted institution which provides warranty arrangements (related to credit or identity information) for dependent institutions.

In New Zealand, a Digital Identity Services Trust Framework was first introduced in 2021 and accepted in April 2023 [16]. It establishes rules to protect the privacy and security of people's information when shared within the trusted environment. This framework includes eight principles, such as the rights and needs of people and other entities involved in the digital identity system, governed by the Privacy Act. Inclusive of any entities and individuals without compromising security or privacy. Secure digital identity systems in the cyber and physical space. It is inclusive of Māori's perspectives, which caters for sustainability, interoperability, openness, and transparency.

In Singapore, [17] there is no specific legislation or framework for National Digital Identity presented. However, there are related legislations put in place to create Decentralised identifiers (DIDs). The key legislative acts include: The Public Sector (Governance) Act, which governs the management of data including personal data protection and data sharing. The Personal Data Protection Act, which provides a baseline standard of protection for personal data by the private sector in Singapore. Other legislations that support this act includes the Banking Act and Insurance Act. It governs the collection, use, disclosure, and care of personal data in Singapore—which is of vital importance to both privacy and trust in a digital identity ecosystem. The National Registration Act, which enables Singapore to retain a high-quality, high-coverage foundational ID system upon which Singpass is reliant. The Electronic Transactions Act, which is the key legal basis for Singpass by establishing trusted certification authority services in Singapore. It focuses on the facilitation of electronic transactions through the recognition of electronic signatures and records.

In Europe, digital identity regulations were introduced as described in [18], towards the development of the European Self-Sovereign Identity Framework (ESSIF) presented in [19] which incorporates digital identity ecosystem on the old regulations. These regulations provide an EU-wide framework for public electronic identities which ensures that any citizen or residents can have access to a secure European e-identity. These regulations include the following requirements to make-up the digital identity framework: objectives of the EU Digital Identity Wallet, roles of the actors of the DID ecosystem, wallet's functional and non-functional requirements, compliance with related standards, frameworks, and legislations, security, privacy, and trust.

Countries that are adopting the EU DID framework includes Finland, Netherlands, UK, and Israel. Finland, is still working towards self-sovereign identity frameworks, aligning with the EU Commission [12]. Finland is pursuing an ambitious schedule to introduce sovereign identity wallets like EU, to be available for people to provide various attributes, such as vaccination certificates, by 2023. Similarly, Netherlands has also been active in the development and participation in the electronic identification and trust services (eIDAS) regulation to create interoperable digital identity initiatives across the EU [12].

The UK's digital identity and attributes trust framework was developed to let individuals use and reuse their digital identities [20]. The trust digital identity framework provides a set of rules that different organisations should follow. These includes legislation, standards, Good Practice Guides (GPGs) which are used to ensure products and services are inclusive, privacy and data protection, fraud management and security are highly considered. In addition, presented requirements are Privacy and data protection; Legal, technical and policy; Security; Both physical and cyber; Communications security (COMSEC); Fraud monitoring; Legal, policies and procedures for fraud management; Fraud reporting; Intelligence and fraud analysis; Sharing threat indicators ('shared signals').

In Israel, a system based on The International Organisation for Standardisation (ISO) standards was proposed and is anticipated to support future mutual recognition and interoperability [12]. Additionally, Israel is exploring compatibility with eIDAS standards and other international partners.

Other international research works includes work by researchers in [21] from the UK who proposed an open digital identity framework and architecture. This framework contributes to promoting the implementation of identity architectures while satisfying limitations that are considered important to the protection of human rights. The authors recommended a combination of strong technology such as Distributed Ledger Technologies (DLTs) and considerate policies shall be considered to promote and ensure the implementation, deployment, and the use of digital identity technology.

Another framework was introduced in Germany to improve security under the KYC theme [22]. Firstly, an eKYC architecture was proposed which involves three primary parties: the customer (holder), a bank (verifier), and an issuer (the same bank, another bank, or any third party trusted by the verifying bank, such as a government agency). The customer is the KYC subject and defines the centre of the architecture. The advantage of this framework is that customers manage their digital identity through user agents by creating and storing DIDs and cryptographic keys in their digital wallets. In addition, users can collect credentials, create backups, and manage permissions.

In [23], NIST provides a digital identity framework with four main components, namely; governance and administration (which includes compliance and risk mitigation of the DID system), identity management (this includes approved or qualified identity provider information and support and management of the DID system), authorisation, (may include roles and responsibilities for involved parties and individuals, policies and other regulation involved, data security and privacy, and identity assurance), last component is authentication and access (which is about access control, multifactor authentication, etc.

In [24] a DID framework was proposed for managing data in the department of health. Also, to provide Information Technology (IT) and security leaders with a toolkit to drive their Identity and access management (IAM) strategy. It addresses key governance principles for developing the DID ecosystem, related to required administration, identity management, authorisation, access, and authentication.

In 2018, the ITU from Switzerland reported a comprehensive report that contributes to the development of DID frameworks, the Digital Identity Roadmap Guide [8]. This guide presents guidelines covering the required design, development, and implementation of digital identity framework. In 2019, [25] authors presented a survey of digital identity architectures and their applications, focusing on the use of emerging standards introduced by the World Wide Web Consortium (W3C) to ensure interoperability and portability throughout the SSI stack.

3.2   Africa

In the African context, research was conducted on aspects related to the state of digital identity in ten countries [26]. The project focus was on local foundational ID systems in countries such as Ghana, Kenya, Lesotho, Mozambique, Nigeria, Rwanda, South Africa, Tanzania, Uganda, and Zimbabwe. This research considered parameters set by an Evaluation Framework for Digital Identities (the 'Framework'), that was developed by the Centre for Internet and Society (CIS) with the purpose of assessing the alignment of digital identity systems for compliance with international rights and data protection norms. By using this Framework, the selected countries evaluated certain aspects of the existing governance and implementation mechanisms of digital identity in their respective and unique contexts. Moreover, the African Union Commission is currently working on a continental initiative to develop an interoperability framework for digital ID [27]. Amongst others, it draws efforts its mandate from the Digital Transformation Strategy (DTS) for Africa (2020–2030), which emphasises the importance of digitised legal identification mechanisms in the continent.

In 2019 [28] Nigerian organisation Secure Identity Alliance (SIA) initiated a programme for Open standards Identity APIs (OSIA) to develop a digital identity framework. This framework involves three main principles, sovereignty, technology neutrality, and privacy by design. The first principle (sovereignty) is about enabling ability of governments to choose what their ID solution will be, and which components are required in the digital identity ecosystem. The second principle promotes the value of deployed legacy technologies to be preserved, and freedom for governments to choose technology of their choice according to their needs. The third principle emphasize the importance of incorporating privacy by design on digital identity ecosystems while complying to legislations related to data privacy and security and enabling citizens to control access to their digital identity.

In South Africa, a case study and roadmap analysis were conducted by [29]. The findings showed that South Africa defined five important requirements for a DID system to meet: Identity management system and existing infrastructure, Frameworks and policies, Digital identity scheme administrator and committed stakeholders, Government endorsement and participation and the role of the private sector and Interoperability which involves the standardisation of the identity management infrastructure. Additionally, there are guiding principles to be considered when developing a DID system, categorised into three pillars, namely, inclusion, design, and governance. Inclusion encompasses principles to ensure universal coverage, and to remove barriers to access and usage of IT. Design involves values corresponding to establish a robust, unique, and secure programme, to create a platform that is interoperable, to use open standards and ensure technology neutrality, to plan for financial and operational sustainability and to protect user privacy and control. Lastly, governance involves principles to safeguard data privacy, security, and user rights through a comprehensive legal and regulatory framework, to establish clear institutional mandates and accountability, and to enforce legal and trust frameworks.

To our knowledge there has not been any research work conducted on comparing existing governance frameworks with the aim of learning from presented experiences to develop a country's governance framework. Thus, this paper presents a review of existing frameworks.

4   Digital Identity Frameworks

This section presents identified frameworks from the literature review conducted and presented in Sect. 3, and the results are presented in Table 1. To assess the identified frameworks, an assessment criterion has been defined.

4.1   Evaluation Criteria

According to [7], there are cross-cutting principles, which, collectively, can assist in the development of a progressive and holistic National Digital Identity Framework. These principles are:

- Vision and mission – set out goals to pursue, and how to achieve these goals.
- Comprehensiveness – all-encompassing understanding and analysis of the overall digital environment, considering the country's context, circumstances, and priorities.
- Social inclusiveness - should be developed such that its services cater for a community of users, with specific focus to vulnerable individuals and minority groups.
- Economic and social prosperity - should foster economic and social prosperity and maximise the contribution to sustainable development and social inclusiveness.
- Fundamental human rights - should respect and be consistent with fundamental human rights and values.
- Resilience - should enable an efficient risk management approach and ensure an appropriate level of resilience.
- Trust, privacy, and security - ensures adequate security measures are in place for maintaining information security, privacy and improve trust among users and stakeholders.
- Sustainability and cost optimisation - should be developed considering the economic sustainability of the system.
- Flexibility and scalability - must accommodate for efficient updates or modification when necessary.
- Interoperability - to ensure the ability of different systems to exchange information and queries.
- Speed of deployment - should follow a swift roll-out schedule.
- Identity as a platform - should foster the development of digital ID as a platform, so that users can plug it into any domain and use it.
- Uniqueness of IDs - ensures that people can get only one digital identity.
- Robustness and future-proofing technology – these include technologies and systems used for the creation of digital identities.
- Data quality - should serve as the base for other programmes of national importance; it is thus critical that steps are taken to ensure data quality at multiple levels.

These guidelines provide a great guide to when developing a framework focusing both on technical and non-technical aspect. Therefore, to assess these identified frameworks and to achieve a minimum viable digital identity framework, the following Assessment Criteria (AC) was followed:

- *AC-1*: Does it support the SSI model? As there is a shift towards SSI it vital for the framework to support SSI implementations to align for future developments.
- *AC-2:* Does it support Interoperability? This is critical to ensure that the system can exchange information with different systems even on an international level.
- *AC-3:* Does it support DID framework/ecosystem?

4.2 Discussion

From the high-level assessment criterion defined in Sect. 4.1, we can compare all the frameworks and discover the most suitable framework/s to learn and derive from their experiences and expertise. It is worth noting that some frameworks have not specified other requirements due to either being architectures which therefore cannot specify for example model types. These are represented by "not specified" in Table 1. Out of the eleven identified frameworks, Table 1shows that, when compared against the assessment criterion; ESSIF, SSI4Web, PCTF, eKYC meets all the three requirements. These findings shows that Canada, Europe, and Germany are part of the countries that are leading Digital Identity, thus South Africa and other countries can learn from them.

The New Zealand Digital Identity Services Trust Framework is the secondary candidate for investigate and learn from especially because they have implemented and are about to roll out in 2024 [33]. Although for now it does not specify the use of DID ecosystem, it might support it in the future when the South African framework is drafted and implemented. The NIST digital identity framework [23] which focuses mainly on governance and administration, identity management, authorisation and authentication and access, will be beneficial in the development of the framework.

Other findings reveal that although other countries have adopted the use of digital identity, there is still more work required to address the support of SSI model to align for future developments, and to for the framework to support Interoperability to enable a secure information exchange with different systems even on an international level. These frameworks are presented in countries such as Nigeria (OSIA digital identity framework [28]), UK Government's Digital Identity and Attributes Trust Framework [30], The African Union (AU) Develops a Draft Interoperable Digital ID Framework for Africa [27], Digital identity framework [24, 31] originated in the United States, Australian Trusted Digital Identity Framework (TDIF) [13], and a Decentralized Digital Identity Architecture [21] from the United Kingdom.

It is worth noting that, Africa is also investing towards this topic whereby the AU has developed a draft Interoperable Digital ID Framework for Africa. Once it is finalised and agreed upon, it would make things easier especially the interoperability aspect of digital identities. Additionally, other frameworks are system or sector based like the TDIF which focuses on accreditation, thus limits the adoption of this framework. With the advancement towards SSI based solutions, it is vital to consider frameworks that cater for such, like ESSIF and SSI4Web (which also adds the aspect of password-less).

Table 1. Identified Digital Identity Frameworks.

Framework	Description	AC-1	AC-2	AC-3
OSIA digital identity framework [28]	An open standard set of interfaces (APIs) that enables, seamless connectivity between building blocks of the identity management ecosystem – independent of technology, solution architecture or vendor	Does not define the workflow between modules nor the architecture on any ID management solution	Yes	Not specified
UK Government's Digital Identity and Attributes Trust Framework [30]	Establishes a governance and oversight function and develops proposals to remove legislative and regulatory blockers to the use of secure digital identities and establish safeguards for citizens	No	Yes (plans to)	No
The African Union (AU) Develops a Draft Interoperable Digital ID Framework for Africa [27]	Proposes different models of the Identity Credentials such as Digi-tally signed credentials or digital wallets aimed at empowering citizens to have control over their personal data, while maintaining privacy and security	Not specified	Yes	Not specified

(*continued*)

Table 1. (*continued*)

Framework	Description	AC-1	AC-2	AC-3
Digital identity framework [24, 31]	Addresses key governance principles for developing the DID eco-system, related to required administration, identity management, authorization, access, and authentication	Not specified	Not specified	Yes
Trusted Digital Identity Framework (TDIF) [13]	Sets out requirements that applicants must meet to achieve accreditation. The accreditation framework and process ensure that all identity providers meet strict rules and standards for usability, accessibility, privacy protection, security, risk management, fraud control and more	Not specified	Yes	No
European Self-Sovereign Identity Framework (ESSIF) [19]	Implements a generic and interoperable SSI framework, defining the necessary specifications and building support services and capabilities that will allow citizens to control their digital identity	Yes	Yes	Yes

(*continued*)

Table 1. (*continued*)

Framework	Description	AC-1	AC-2	AC-3
Self-Sovereign Identity (SSI) Framework for the Web (SSI4Web) [32]	Integrates SSI for providing web services in a secure password-less manner with much more user control and greater flexibility	Yes	Yes	Yes
A Decentralized Digital Identity Architecture [21]	Defines a set of fundamental constraints that digital identity systems must satisfy to preserve and promote privacy as required for individual sovereignty. Authors proposed a decentralized, standards-based approach, using a combination of DLT and regulations, to facilitate many-to-many relationships among providers of key services	Not specified	Not specified	No
Pan-Canadian Trust Framework (PCTF) [14]	Designed to meet current and future Canadian digital identity ecosystem innovation needs by verifying trust of services and networks	Yes	Yes	Yes

(*continued*)

Table 1. (*continued*)

Framework	Description	AC-1	AC-2	AC-3
Germany framework for digital identity Know Your Customer (KYC) [22]	Presents an Electronic Know Your Customer (eKYC) architecture involving three primary parties: holder, verifier, and an issuer	Yes	Yes	Yes
New Zealand Digital Identity Services Trust Framework [16]	First introduced to establish rules to protect the privacy and security of people's information when shared amongst organisations in the trusted environment	Yes	Yes	No

5 Conclusion

In this digital age, the use of digital identities will increase exponentially and with that the need to have governance frameworks in place to control how these identities are issued, maintained, and authenticated. This provides opportunities for researchers and decision-makers to study the trend of governance frameworks. This is crucial for South Africa as currently; centralised models are utilised for identities. The country is making formidable strides in closing existing gaps of citizens lacking identities and moving towards social inclusion, as well as moving towards digitisation. However, the country is still at the initial stages of digital identities. The goal of this study was to understand what other countries have done towards developing governance frameworks for digital identities, specifically developed countries as they are already ahead with digitisation. In understanding these frameworks, we can draw conclusions and work towards, defining a framework or combination of frameworks suitable for South Africa.

In this study, we investigated existing literature on digital identity frameworks worldwide, eleven frameworks were identified and compared against a defined assessment criterion. While this list is not exhaustive, it paints a picture of the existing gap especially in Africa and paves a way for South Africa to develop its own framework, learning from these existing frameworks. We hope that our review will help guide the field in providing clarity and advance the field. Digital identity models have moved from centralised to decentralised and due to their new/evolving nature, it is vital that we keep abreast of any improvements. With the high-level assessment criteria presented in this study, and there is a possibility for change in future as the field gains traction. Hence, it is vital to remain updated with these improvements.

References

1. Clark, J., Diaphasia, A., Casher, C.: 850 million people globally don't have ID-why this matters and what we can do about it. World Bank Blogs   (2023);. https://blogs.worldbank.org/digital-development/850-million-people-globally-dont-have-id-why-matters-and-what-we-can-do-about. Accessed 16 Aug 2023
2. The World Bank. (2019, August). Inclusive and trusted digital ID can unlock opportunities for the world's most vulnerable. World Bank, Who We Are, News (2019). https://www.worldbank.org/en/news/immersive-story/2019/08/14/inclusive-and-trusted-digital-id-can-unlock-opportunities-for-the-worlds-most-vulnerable. Accessed 16 Aug 2023
3. Preukschat, A., Reed, D.: Self-sovereign identity. Manning Publications (2021)
4. Ndung'u, N.S., Signé, L.: Capturing the fourth industrial revolution: a regional and national agenda. (2020)
5. Digital Transformation Agency. Digital Identity. Digital Transformation Agency (2023, July 3). https://www.dta.gov.au/our-projects/digital-identity. Accessed 16 Aug 2023
6. Kiourtis, A., et al.: Identity management standards: a literature review. Comput. Inform. 3(1), 35–46 (2023)
7. I. Fernmelde-Union. Digital identity roadmap guide (2018)
8. International Telecommunication Union, Digital Identity Roadmap Guide (2018). https://www.itu.int/pub/D-STR-DIGITAL.01-2018. Accessed 20 Jul 2023
9. Thales. Digital Identity Trends – 5 forces that are shaping 2023. Thales Group (2021). https://www.thalesgroup.com/en/markets/digital-identity-and-security/government/identity/digital-identity-services/trends. Accessed 16 Aug 2023
10. Department of Home Affairs. National identification and registration bill: Draft. South African Government. https://www.gov.za/documents/national-identification-and-registration-bill-draft-18-apr-2023-0000 Pierucci, Federico, and Valeria Cesaroni. "Data Subjectivation-Self-sovereign Identity and Digital Self-Determination." Digital Society 2.2 (2023). Accessed 16 Aug 2023
11. Imprivata. Digital identity maturity assessment. https://www.imprivata.com/assess. Accessed 20 Aug 2023
12. DGX (Digital Gov Exchange) Digital Identity Working Group. "Digital identity in response to covid-19." Digital Transformation Agency (2022)
13. Australian Government. Trusted Digital Identity Framework (TDIF) | Digital Identity. https://www.digitalidentity.gov.au/tdif. Accessed 20 Jul 2023
14. The Digital Identification and Authentication Council of Canada (DIACC). Trust Framework. Digital ID Authentication Council of Canada, April 2023. https://diacc.ca/trust-framework/. Accessed 17 August 2023
15. Rasouli, H., Valmohammadi, C., Azad, N., Abbaspour Esfeden, G.: Proposing a digital identity management framework: a mixed-method approach. Concurrency Comput. Pract. Experience 33(17), 62–71 (2021)
16. Hon Dr D. Clark.: Digital Identity Services Trust Framework bill - New Zealand legislation (2023). Available at: https://www.legislation.govt.nz/bill/government/2021/0078/latest/LMS 459583.html?src=qs Accessed 17 August 2023
17. World Bank. National Digital Identity and Government Data Sharing in Singapore: A Case Study of Singpass and APEX. World Bank (2022)
18. European Commission. The Digital Services Act: Ensuring a safe and accountable online environment. European Commission (2022, October). https://commission.europa.eu/strategy-and-policy/priorities-2019-2024/europe-fit-digital-age/digital-services-act-ensuring-safe-and-accountable-online-environment_en. Accessed: 20 July 2023

19. Du Seuil, Daniel. European Self Sovereign identity framework (2019)
20. Department for Science, Innovation and Technology, Department for Digital, Culture, Media & Sport, and Warman M. "UK digital identity and attributes trust framework alpha v2 (0.2)" (2023). https://www.gov.uk/government/publications/the-uk-digital-identity-and-attributes-trust-framework/the-uk-digital-identity-and-attributes-trust-framework. Accessed 16 Aug 2023
21. Zwitter, A., Cooper, N., Zambrano, Goodell, R.G., Aste, T.: A decentralized digital identity architecture," Frontiers in Blockchain| www.frontiersin.org 2(17), 1–19 (2019)
22. Schlatt, V., Sedlmeir, J., Feulner, S., Urbach, N.: Designing a framework for digital KYC processes built on blockchain-based self-sovereign identity. Inf. Manag. 59(7), 103553 (2022)
23. National Institute of Standards and Technology. NIST Special Publication 800–63BNIST Special Publication 800–63B Digital Identity Guidelines Authentication and Lifecycle Management (2022). NIST Special Publication 800–63B. Retrieved July 20, 2023, from https://pages.nist.gov/800-63-3/sp800-63b.html, https://identitymanagementinstitute.org/nist-digital-identity-summary-and-update/
24. Imprivata, Digital identity framework | https://www.imprivata.com/digital-identity-framework. Accessed: 20 July 2023
25. Avellaneda, O., et al.: Decentralized identity: Where did it come from and where is it going? IEEE Commun. Stan. Mag. 3(4), 10–13 (2019). https://doi.org/10.1109/mcomstd.2019.9031542
26. Research ICT Africa, & Spuy, A. van der. Ria releases 10 country reports on Digital ID framework. Research ICT Africa (2021). https://researchictafrica.net/2021/11/09/ria-releases-10-country-reports-on-digital-id-framework/. Accessed 16 Aug 2023
27. The Lawyers Hub, The AU Develops a Draft Interoperable Digital Id Framework for Africa, https://lawyershub.org/blog/The_Au_Develops_A_Draft_Interoperable_Digital_Id_Framework_For_Africa_30. Accessed 20 July 2023
28. Nigeria National Identity Management Commission (NIMC). Unlocking the ID Ecosystem with OSIA: A universal interoperability framework for innovation, competition, and sustainability (2022). OSIA. Retrieved July 20, 2023, from https://secureidentityalliance.org/osia
29. Razzano, G.: Digital Identity in South Africa: Case study conducted as part of a ten-country exploration of socio-digital ID systems in parts of Africa. Research ICT Africa (2021). https://researchictafrica.net/publication/digital-identity-in-south-africa-case-study-conducted-as-part-of-a-ten-country-exploration-of-socio-digital-id-systems-in-parts-of-africa/. Accessed 16 Aug 2023
30. UK digital identity and attributes trust framework alpha v1 (0.1) - GOV.UK, https://www.gov.uk/government/publications/the-uk-digital-identity-and-attributes-trust-framework/the-uk-digital-identity-and-attributes-trust-framework. Accessed 20 July 2023
31. Cairns, K., Wright, W.: The Imprivata digital identity framework: A guide for IT leaders in healthcare. Imprivata (2022)
32. Ferdous, M.S., Ionita, A., Prinz, W.: SSI4Web: A Self-sovereign identity (SSI) framework for the Web. In: International Congress on Blockchain and Applications. Cham: Springer International Publishing (2022)
33. Burt, C.: New Zealand digital identity trust framework law passes. Biometrics News. https://www.biometricupdate.com/202303/new-zealand-digital-identity-trust-framework-law-passes. Mar 30, 2023

Cloud Adoption in Low Resource Settings: A Case Study of Higher Education Institutions in Uganda

Alex Mwotil[1]([⊠])[iD], Benjamin Kanagwa[1], Aminah Zawedde[2],
Thomas E. Anderson[3], and Engineer Bainomugisha[1]

[1] Makerere University, Kampala, Uganda
{alex.mwotil,benjamin.kanagwa,baino}@mak.ac.ug
[2] Ministry of ICT and National Guidance, Kampala, Uganda
[3] University of Washington, Seattle, USA

Abstract. Cloud computing has experienced substantial growth in the past decade, and it is projected that the global public consumption of cloud services shall persistently soar to annual unprecedented levels. This growth has prompted significant investments by cloud providers in infrastructure and service portfolios, highlighting the increasing relevance, reliance and adoption of cloud solutions. However, research on cloud adoption reveals notable disparities between developed and developing economies, emphasizing the importance of understanding contextual trends, barriers and opportunities. In this study, we focus on higher education institutions in Uganda and conduct surveys from readiness, implementation and usage dimensions. Our findings indicate that 88% of the institutions are in the early stages of cloud adoption, representing infancy in this context. Additionally, the results provide key inputs in our novel attempt to define a cloud adoption assessment tool for higher education institutions in low resource settings. Finally, and based on our research, we offer recommendations to improve assessment scores and foster increased cloud adoption within these settings.

Keywords: cloud · adoption · higher education · developing economies · low resource settings · assessment

1 Introduction

Cloud computing revolutionizes the way Information and Communications Technology (ICT) resources are accessed and utilized, offering flexible on-demand access to a comprehensive size and range of infrastructure, software, platforms, storage, and applications through network-based provisioning [1] [2]. From

Government of Uganda through the Makerere University Research and Innovation Fund (RIF).

A. Sere et al. (Eds.): AFRICOMM 2023, LNICST 587, pp. 19–38, 2025.
https://doi.org/10.1007/978-3-031-81570-6_2

Infrastructure as a Service (IaaS) to Anything as a Service (XaaS), the evolution of cloud computing has brought about a paradigm shift, transforming daily online operations [3]. This transformation has empowered organizations and individuals to leverage a diverse range of cloud services, enhancing productivity, efficiency and innovation [5]. The cloud has become an integral part of modern technology ecosystems, driving digital transformation and reshaping how we work, collaborate and interact online [4]. With application domains spanning big data computing, health, private sector, government, artificial intelligence and education [8], the global cloud market is projected to grow at an annual rate of over 21.3% by 2024 [6]. Public and private cloud providers have made substantial investments to enhance their service offerings, driven in particular by potential gains en masse. As of 2023, Amazon Web Services (AWS) plans to launch five new global data centers [10], signifying ongoing investment in its cloud infrastructure footprint. Other major public cloud providers like Microsoft Azure and Google Cloud are adopting similar strategies with billion-dollar investments in data center infrastructure. These efforts reflect their anticipation of increased demand and adoption of cloud services. This signifies the relevance of cloud adoption studies for all business domains, regardless of the operational environment.

Public cloud infrastructure in low resource settings is limited due to strategic positioning of cloud providers in demand-intensive locations. Cloud regions, which are geographical locations where cloud providers operate physical data center infrastructure, play a crucial role in determining the quality and availability of cloud services. Out of the 127 operational regions across major cloud providers like AWS, Microsoft and Google, only three regions are located in Africa, representing only 2.4% of the total [33]. Additionally, there are currently no available cloud regions in other African countries, outside South Africa. The connectivity and data center power challenges of these settings haven't helped the cause, further affecting adoption of cloud services. One of the most recent approaches in software development and deployment that leverages cloud computing principles and technologies to build and run applications is cloud-native. It involves designing applications specifically for deployment in cloud environments, taking advantage of the scalability, flexibility, and resilience offered by cloud platforms [13,15]. Ideally, cloud-native application development and deployment principles are a best fit for low resource settings. This is because applications can easily move, for example, between unreliable resource pools. In addition, the lightweight nature of the applications provides for optimized resource utilization in a rather erratic, constrained and unpredictable environment. Gaining an understanding of the current state of cloud computing and cloud-native technologies in low resource contexts is paramount to its adoption.

Cloud Adoption in Higher Education Institutions

In the field of education, the cloud has found extensive use in collaboration, storage, learning management systems, gaming, mobile computing, data analytics, online libraries and digital content management [9]. The ubiquitous operation mode of the cloud can support collaboration between and within the institutions. This involves the use of tools such as online cloud drives (Google Drive, OneDrive), video/web conferencing (Zoom, Microsoft Teams) and source code version control systems (GitLab). Cloud infrastructure and applications can also be shared amongst researchers from different institutions collaborating on similar artefacts. Higher Education Institutions (HEIs) can play an important role in driving the advancement, utilization, and adoption of emerging technologies. Grid Computing, a cloud computing predecessor, originated as a research project at the University of California, Berkeley. The evolution of the Internet, now serving as a medium for provisioning and accessing cloud resources, owes much to collaborative research efforts between the Advanced Research Projects Agency Network (ARPANET) and various universities in the United States. In usage, HEIs have requirements for computation-intensive research operations in fields such as Artificial Intelligence (AI), Simulation, and Modeling, and the cloud is the native computing platform. Moreover, the adoption and usage of cloud services in the education sector can have a ripple effect on the wider industry. While the specific needs for cloud utilization may vary, the significance of the cloud transcends the wider economic and geographical divide.

Within the context of developing economies, new research areas emerge. These include cloud adoption trends, edge computing, low resource cloud networks, relationship between adoption and resources, barriers to adoption, cloud service opportunities and use cases. The abundance of research on cloud adoption in various domains (such as SMEs, commercial banks, health, and education) and regions (for example country-specific studies) [8, 28–32] underscores the need for a contextual approach to comprehend the specific factors influencing cloud adoption. In addition, HEIs require comprehensive cloud adoption assessments to guide their future endeavors in the cloud. These assessments can provide valuable direction and insights for institutions as they navigate their cloud adoption journey. Examining practical use cases of cloud technology can offer insights into the state of cloud adoption within HEIs. Our focus in this study is universities in Uganda, and delves into the cloud adoption landscape in this and similar contexts.

Research Questions

This study seeks to answer the following research questions (RQs):

1. *RQ1: What strategies have been employed by higher education institutions in Uganda to facilitate the adoption of cloud technologies?*
2. *RQ2: How are higher education institutions in Uganda utilizing cloud and cloud-native technologies?*
3. *RQ3: What is the current state of research and teaching in cloud-based technologies in higher education institutions in Uganda?*
4. *RQ4: What are the main challenges and opportunities associated with the adoption of cloud technologies in higher education institutions in Uganda?*

We conducted two surveys, over a span of two years, to assess the state of cloud computing and cloud-native adoption in higher education institutions in Uganda. Our research findings provide insights into the current landscape of cloud technology and its future prospects within the context of a developing nation. We identify the challenges and opportunities that exist for enhancing cloud adoption and utilization in this setting. While there have been efforts to establish a standardized maturity model for cloud adoption [19,35], we recognize that its applicability can be subjective and varies across different application domains. This observation aligns with the diverse range of research publications addressing cloud adoption [21–25]. Based on the survey results, we develop a novel cloud adoption assessment tool specifically tailored for HEIs in low resource settings.

Organization of the Paper

The rest of the paper is organized as follows: Sect. 2 provides the related work, Sect. 3 describes the methodology, Sect. 4 details the findings of the study, Sect. 5 describes the cloud adoption assessment tool, Sect. 6 presents our future outlook, and Sect. 7 is the paper conclusion.

2   Related Work

The importance of cloud computing in driving sectoral transformation at the national and regional levels cannot be overstated. Countries and organizations worldwide have recognized the value of cloud technology, transitioning to elaborate cloud usage, as a testament to its significance [6]. Extensive research and industry efforts have been dedicated to exploring cloud adoption in various domains and contexts. These endeavors have yielded frameworks [34], models, strategies, and insights into the challenges, trends, and contextual factors associated with cloud adoption. It is worth noting that disparities in cloud adoption exist between developed and developing economies, with low-income countries often facing greater challenges in adopting cloud technologies [26,27]. Investing in research and higher education has emerged as a promising approach to accelerate cloud adoption [26]. Additionally, public cloud providers have developed adoption frameworks to assist organizations in migration and utilization of cloud services [19].

In the adoption journey of developing economies, unique challenges such as high anticipated costs and network connectivity limitations pose obstacles that hinder the full benefits of cloud services for many users. However, over the past decade, cloud adoption has gained significant research attention. In the case of Ghana and Kenya, organizational challenges and institutional forces (coercive, normative and mimetic) have played a key role in shaping the cloud adoption landscape [28,29]. Despite arguments of stagnation, there have been notable strides in cloud adoption [8], albeit at a relatively slow pace. To gain a better understanding of cloud adoption, it is essential to consider contextual and sector-specific use cases. In this regard, the education sector holds particular significance as it serves as a primary provider and pipeline for technical resources, research artefacts, expertise and a consumer of cloud compute and storage services.

Researchers have investigated the adoption of cloud computing in higher education institutions located in low income countries. In the Philippines, slow internet connections and limited awareness of cloud computing have been identified as factors negatively impacting adoption [30]. Similarly, in Malawi, technological challenges (such as operational skills), organizational factors (including management support), and environmental factors (such as high bandwidth costs) have influenced cloud adoption [31]. Similar studies have been conducted in Kenya, where researchers examined the barriers to cloud computing adoption in higher learning institutions and proposed recommendations. The identified barriers include concerns related to data security and confidentiality [32]. Our work in adoption goes further to assess the state and readiness of institutions for cloud-native technologies. Additionally, we advance a novel cloud adoption assessment tool for institutions in these settings.

In Uganda, cloud adoption has attracted research attention across various sectors, including SMEs, commercial banks, health, and education. Researchers, such as Onayemi et al., have employed the Diffusion of Innovations Theory (DIT) to assess the gradual change and identify challenges in cloud adoption for SMEs, highlighting future uncertainties as a major barrier [21]. Kasse et al. emphasize the overall recognition of cloud computing by SMEs and propose a validated framework to enhance its adoption [25]. Mpanga et al. focused on lower government agencies in Uganda, using an Enterprise Resource Planning (ERP) system as a motivating use case to explore the contextual adoption of cloud-based systems [22]. Mugyeni discussed the potential benefits of cloud computing for commercial banks and suggested adoption strategies along with a system deployment scenario [23]. The adoption of cloud-based eLearning platforms in higher education institutions is also examined in a study by Etengu et al., where the authors proposed a framework to deliver education activities and resources through the cloud [24]. While Service Oriented Architectures (SOA) are often compared to cloud-native approaches, it is important to assess institutional capabilities and requirements to drive this forward. Moreover, our focus is on exploring adoption within the intersection of perception, practical usage and trends in higher education institutions.

3   Methodology

3.1   Data Collection

In Uganda, there are 53 universities accredited by the Uganda National Council for Higher Education (UNCHE) [16] - a government entity tasked with regulation of higher education institutions and constituent programmes. Of the total, 9 are public (government-funded) and 44 are private institutions. These institutions run various degree and diploma programmes to approximately 200,000 registered students in Uganda. The institutions are located in all the 4 regions of the country (East, West, Central and North) with the central accounting for over 50%. Government institutions are entitled to the National Backbone Infrastructure (NBI) [17] - an optical fiber network that connects all major towns in the country. The NBI project is expected to cumulatively cover 3,156 km across the country with the current completion at 82%. The research and Education Network for Uganda (RENU)[1] connects over 66% of the universities (public and private) to a single national network providing upstream connectivity and other collaboration services to support research and education.

In this study, we conducted two surveys to investigate cloud adoption from both visionary and applied perspectives. The first survey, conducted in 2021, aimed to assess the preparedness and current state of institutions regarding cloud migration across various domains using the AWS Cloud Adoption Framework [19]: Applications and infrastructure, business (need for cloud migration), people (cloud-related roles), process (workflows), operations (governance), and security (secure cloud transactions) [18]. The strategic alignment of these domains is crucial for enabling organizations to derive maximum benefits from cloud services. The survey would further provide a baseline understanding of cloud to an institution, implications on business processes and adoption challenges. In the second survey, we set cloud-native application development and deployment and associated DevOps practices as the median bar to evaluate the current state of cloud and institutional readiness to adapt to its dynamism. The level of research and teaching in cloud and associated technologies is further explored. The latter parts of the survey determine the cloud-native adoption challenges and opportunities for institutions to leverage.

To conduct the two surveys, we developed and validated an online questionnaire that was distributed via email to participants representing ICT operation teams in all the 53 higher education institutions in the country. The survey comprised a combination of quantitative and qualitative questions to gather detailed insights and provide for open-ended views. The participants primarily consisted of ICT technical personnel working in systems and network support departments. Since the teams within each institution are relatively small, targeted sampling was preferred as the most suitable approach. The administrative divide between institutional management and the operations support teams is minimal, enabling a strong likelihood of capturing management viewpoints directly from the support staff. In order to gather comprehensive data and improve response rates, face-to-face interviews were conducted alongside the questionnaires. These interviews served as a means to seek further guidance and gather additional perspectives as deemed necessary by the research team.

3.2   Data Analysis

A total of 26 institutions provided responses to the survey and subsequent analysis was done. To ensure privacy, unique identifiers were assigned to the

---

[1] https://renu.ac.ug/.

institutions, as stated in the questionnaire preamble. The responses were categorized and recorded using a simple naming scheme: [Category][Question Number][Response]. The respondents included ICT departmental heads/managers, network and systems administrators, systems analysts, IT and planning officers, eLearning coordinators and technicians. Due to the manageable number of responses, a manual walk-through procedure was employed for each institution and responses mapped to a Google Sheets template. Additionally, textual analysis was conducted on the open-ended questions to identify relevant keywords related to the research domain. The closed questions such as those requiring option selection were numerically coded, for example, Yes - 1, No - 0 and Maybe (or not sure) - 3. In Sect. 4, we provide a detailed report of the findings.

3.3   Limitations

The response rate, accounting for 49.1% of the total institutions, may not present a complete view of the current state. However, it is important to highlight that the representation of public institutions in the responses is 100%. The respondents from institutions encompass a diverse range of roles, including managerial and support staff, which may introduce bias in certain question responses. It is worth noting that in smaller institutions, similar personnel often perform multiple roles. The timing of the first survey coincided with the end of the COVID-19 pandemic, which may have affected the response rate and influenced the responses themselves due to the lingering impact of the pandemic. The research team conducted physical interviews across the country, where possible, for additional information.

4   The State of Cloud Adoption in Low Resource Settings

The state of cloud adoption in low resource settings can be established from different perspectives including the adoption strategies, its relevance and use cases in an educational environment, management of supporting infrastructure and integration of evolving cloud technologies. We present our survey findings in the next subsections, aligned with research questions in Sect. 1:

4.1   RQ1: Cloud Adoption Strategies

Overall, cloud adoption in higher education institutions in Uganda is still in its early stages. There is a variation in the understanding of cloud computing and its significance among different institutions. However, each institution tends to utilize some form of cloud service to enhance its business processes. While there are instances of cloud use within these institutions, the absence of formal adoption structures, such as business cases (39% of the institutions), indicates lack of comprehensive plans and strategies for cloud adoption. For example, in our first survey, one of the institutions had expressed no intention to adopt cloud services. However, in the follow-up survey, progress was observed as the institution was using IaaS and SaaS cloud services. It is noteworthy that most institutions (61%) that identified business needs for cloud adoption subsequently developed business cases to support their transition to the cloud. This signifies a positive shift towards recognizing the benefits and relevance of cloud technologies in enhancing institutional operations. On the downside, less than 40% of the institutions had assigned personnel to lead the cause for cloud adoption with a meagre 26% having formulated any change management plans.

Data security and privacy are major barriers to cloud adoption, as highlighted by the survey results. While a majority of the institutions (57%) have an understanding of secure cloud operations, the number of institutions with personnel certified in cloud security is quite low at 4%. Moreover, a majority of institutions (over 85%) lack documented plans or methodologies for cloud security. In addition, the role of institutional management is important in driving adoption strategies, development and implementation of security policies. The survey results, however, reveal that a higher number of institutions (74%) have not obtained leadership approvals for creating security policies or guidelines, suggesting a potential lack of managerial support. The persisting challenges in security, coupled with the disconnect between management and security practices, may hinder the progress of cloud adoption. It is essential for all stakeholders to actively engage in the adoption process, enabling informed decision-making and shaping the future direction of cloud adoption.

HEIs have taken various approaches to cloud adoption, ranging from use of local infrastructure to cloud-native solutions. From the results, one institution is exclusively using public cloud services for its business processes. However, for most institutions, the initial step involves virtualizing existing local infrastructure using open source tools like Proxmox[2]. By virtualizing their infrastructure, these institutions can optimize resource utilization, although it may come at the expense of potential failure points. To ensure improved availability, resources can be clustered to provide redundancy. The next phase may involve establishing a local private cloud, which requires expertise in setting up and administering the different components that form a "cloud" environment. Achieving high availability necessitates additional investment in resources located in diverse locations, as well as a robust supporting network. As an example, one institution has implemented an OpenStack[3] cloud that spans two sites. 61.1% of the institutions use collocation services with 75% in-country, 8.3% out-country and 16.7% either option. The government of Uganda through the Ministry of ICT & National Guidance and its agency, the National Information Technology Authority (NITA-U)[4], RENU and Raxio Uganda[5] are the prevalent collocation service providers that institutions use. NITA-U serves government Ministries, Departments and Agencies (MDAs) including public higher education institutions. The final stage of cloud adoption involves leveraging either a public or private cloud

---

[2] https://www.proxmox.com/en/.
[3] https://www.openstack.org/.
[4] https://www.nita.go.ug/.
[5] https://www.raxiogroup.com/.

service provider to host certain institutional services. This transition may eventually involve incorporating cloud-native principles for orchestrating and managing services deployed in the cloud. The process typically follows a pipelined approach with controlled operations to ensure smooth integration and operation within the cloud environment.

4.2   RQ2: The State of Cloud and Cloud-Native

Cloud Relevance and Cost 'Myths': HEIs in Uganda are using cloud services for a range of applications and operations. From eLearning systems to disaster recovery management, the cloud is gaining traction. Other key use cases include storage, real-time communication, collaboration tools, and institutional management systems. One of the notable advantages of cloud adoption is high system availability, which enhances resilience. In contrast, locally hosted deployments often face challenges such as limited resources, equipment theft, power fluctuations, and restricted bandwidth, leading to service access issues. These are typical challenges of a low resource environment. The survey results indicate that cloud adoption brings about cost reductions in infrastructure management, including the purchase, maintenance, and management of equipment. However, there are differing views on the overall costs associated with cloud adoption and maintenance. While many believe that the cloud offers cost advantages, especially in terms of managing infrastructure, users remain skeptical with concerns about potential long-term costs and the fear of being locked into services that could become expensive in the long run. In settings with highly restrictive ICT budgets, the cost dimension becomes a significant hindering factor to cloud adoption.

Despite cost and access barriers, HEIs consider cloud adoption as integral to supporting institutional operations. The cloud's high system availability ensures continuous access to critical services such as learning management systems and communication platforms, minimizing downtime and disruptions. Scalability and elasticity are additional advantages, allowing institutions to easily adjust their computing resources based on changing demand. During peak periods, such as enrollment or exam seasons, institutions can scale up resources to accommodate increased workloads. Conversely, they can scale down during periods of lower demand to optimize resource utilization and cost efficiency. Cloud-based disaster recovery solutions offer reliable data backup and recovery mechanisms, enabling institutions to protect against data loss caused by hardware failures, natural disasters, or other unforeseen events. Moreover, cloud-based collaboration tools and real-time communication platforms foster seamless teamwork and knowledge sharing among students, faculty, and staff, irrespective of their physical locations. These tools enhance learning and administrative processes by facilitating effective collaboration and communication.

Cloud-Native: Cloud-native refers to an advanced utilization of cloud technology that leverages containerization for streamlined application development and deployment. In this approach, developers encapsulate applications into microservice abstractions, which are executed as containers, enabling portability across different platforms with similar run-time environments. By incorporating principles and practices of Development (Dev) and Operations (Ops), cloud-native solutions significantly enhance product-to-market timelines, reducing them by up to 30% and yielding additional cost savings in production [20]. Moreover, containerization enables more efficient resource optimization, particularly important in resource-constrained environments. However, it is important to acknowledge the collaborative effort required among development teams to implement new application features. The cloud-native approach necessitates a focus on local development efforts and a dedicated team responsible for the application's lifecycle. Conversely, proprietary software may not offer the required customization flexibility to align with this paradigm.

Among the respondent institutions, 55.6% have locally developed software systems, while the remaining half primarily rely on proprietary software. This poses challenges in implementing and managing cloud-native development and deployment concepts. For institutions with local development, software releases are predominantly manual and vary in frequency, ranging from a few weeks to quarters, with minimal updates to application functionality. Only 16.7% of the institutions employ some form of Continuous Integration/Continuous Deployment (CI/CD) tools in their software release cycles, with Docker, Github, and Jenkins being the most commonly used. Regarding application containerization, most institutions have future plans to integrate it into their Proof of Concept (PoC), development, testing, and production environments, as depicted in Fig. 1 and Table 1. However, over 72% of the institutions currently do not utilize application containerization for the majority of their application requirements. The reasons for this limited adoption or deployment include lack of capacity and skills, complexities in networking and service discovery, storage management issues, and challenges related to vendor and legacy system support.

Table 1. The state of Cloud-Native in HEI in Uganda

Stage	Current Use (%)	Future Plan (%)	No Plan (%)
Proof of Concept	11.1	61.1	27.8
Development	16.7	44.4	38.9
Testing	16.7	44.4	38.9
Production	16.7	50.0	33.3

4.3   RQ3: Applications, Learning and Research

Most higher education institutions in Uganda are using some form of cloud service with private or on-premise cloud deployment models the most prevalent

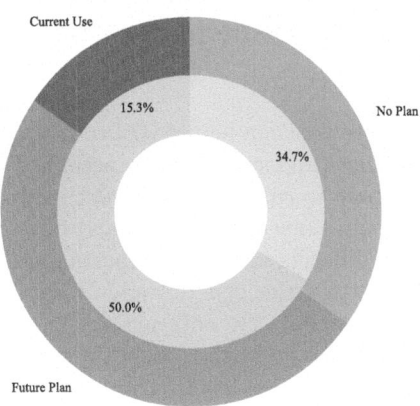

Fig. 1. The state of cloud-native in higher education institutions in Uganda: Less than 16% of the institutions are using any form of cloud-native technology and over 30% have no immediate or long-term plans.

(44.4%). 61.2% of the respondent institutions use a hybrid cloud (private, community and/or public) as supporting infrastructure for their services. On the public cloud, Google Cloud Platform (GCP) is widely used with 66.7% of the respondents with Microsoft Azure a distant third with 11.1%. The community cloud with 22.2% of the institutions is provided by the Government of Uganda and RENU. The main cloud service model used by institutions (83.3%) is Software as a Service (with example software applications including Google email, Google Apps for Education, Zoom, Learning Management Systems, CRM, ERP). Infrastructure as a Service (IaaS) - a form of cloud computing where a resource pool is provisioned as a virtual machine (VM) or instance with an operating system and optional prebuilt packages - closely follows at 72.2%. The VMs are either reserved or provided on-demand to run a set of workloads.

The study revealed that 46.2% of the participating higher education institutions in Uganda have incorporated cloud computing as a dedicated course unit within their undergraduate or graduate programmes. This inclusion is particularly prominent in disciplines such as Computer Science, Software Engineering, Information Technology, and Information Security. The subject content of these courses varies among institutions, but generally encompasses fundamental aspects of cloud computing. Despite the presence of cloud computing courses, research on cloud systems within these institutions is relatively limited. This can be attributed to the infrastructure constraints prevalent at the institutions. However, it is worth noting that research in other fields, such as Artificial Intelligence (AI), heavily rely on the infrastructure provided by cloud platforms. Integration of cloud computing into academic curricula highlights the recognition of its importance and the need to equip students with the necessary knowledge and skills in this evolving field. While research in cloud systems may be hindered by infrastructure access, the cloud requirements for computation-intensive operations in these settings are paramount.

5   Cloud Adoption Assessment for Higher Education Institutions

A cloud adoption assessment tool can help a HEI to track maturity and progress in adopting cloud technologies and supporting practices. The tool should use key indicators of the HEI domain to capture the current state of adoption of a technology. There are a number of maturity models and frameworks that have been developed [19,36,37] with differing levels of complexity, generalization and applicability. For a specific context, the generic models require significant amount of rework as the target is mainly the enterprise. There have also been advocacy efforts for a more holistic approach to developing a standardized adoption model from a consumer perspective [35]. However, the cloud has been dynamic with incorporation of new and advanced technologies, and a universal maturity model would most likely be obsolete within a few years of use. The assessment tool should also be contextual as domain differences exist, for example in computing resource concentration. Maturity models mostly define five stages of the adoption journey from none to extensive and optimized usage of cloud services. Nonetheless, we extend these stages analogized by planting practices in a tropical region dominated by the agricultural sector. The findings of the survey provide key inputs to the development of this tool as shown in Fig. 2.

1. **Pre-season Stage:** During the pre-season, which is marked by uncertainties in the agricultural cycle (weather, production costs, harvest, demand and eventual product prices), institutions face similar challenges in their cloud adoption journey. While they may possess basic knowledge of cloud computing, they are hampered by concerns about adoption and the potential challenges that lie ahead. As a result, there are no immediate or future plans to transition their services or infrastructure to a cloud-based solution. These institutions rely on on-premise infrastructure and predominantly utilize monolithic applications. In some cases, cloud adoption may be deemed irrelevant to their foreseeable needs.

2. **Seed Stage:** Akin to planting seeds in fertile soil (the odds are very much in favor of the farmer), this phase represents the initial stage of cloud adoption in institutions. They recognize the potential benefits of cloud technologies and begin to explore their capabilities. The opportunities presented by the cloud outweigh the adoption barriers they may face. Activities during this phase include conducting feasibility studies and researching cloud service providers to lay the foundation for future adoption. Institutions may also run experimental applications in the cloud to gain hands-on experience. Management becomes supportive of the cloud proposition, and there is a strategic direction for cloud adoption. The on-premise data center infrastructure undergoes virtualization (IaaS), resulting in improved utilization of available compute resources. To bridge the education and industry demands, cloud computing modules can be incorporated into the curriculum.

3. **Sprout Stage:** In the Sprout stage of cloud adoption, institutions witness the value of growth and development in their cloud adoption efforts. They

begin migrating critical workloads to the cloud, leveraging the benefits it offers. Technical personnel acquire the necessary skills to effectively manage and administer cloud resources, ensuring smooth operations. To overcome local power challenges and enhance availability, institutions take advantage of collocation services, which provide reliable infrastructure and minimize disruptions. Additionally, some institutions make substantial investments in setting up local cloud infrastructure, tailoring the cloud environment to their specific needs. The students learn how to develop applications that can leverage cloud service models, enabling them to experience the power of the cloud.

4. **Mature Stage:** The institutions have established strong roots, much like a mature and thriving plant in the African environment. They have achieved a high level of maturity in their cloud adoption journey, encompassing various aspects of cloud technology. Institutions widely utilize cloud deployments, embracing the flexibility and scalability they offer. They adopt cloud-native architectures, leveraging microservices, containers, and serverless computing to build resilient and agile systems. Governance frameworks are in place to ensure compliance and security measures are enhanced to protect data and systems. For on-premise clouds, the infrastructure is distributed, enabling efficient resource allocation and workload management. Disaster recovery and business continuity plans are documented and regularly tested to ensure their effectiveness in case of disruptions. The technical teams within institutions are more structured, with a strong focus on collaboration between Development (Dev) and Operations (Ops). DevOps principles and practices are ingrained in the institutional culture, promoting collaboration, automation, and continuous improvement. Overall, in the Mature stage, institutions have established robust cloud architectures, implemented governance frameworks, enhanced security measures, and embraced DevOps practices, enabling them to fully leverage the benefits of cloud technologies and drive innovation.

5. **Harvest Stage:** Like a bountiful harvest in an agricultural cycle, the institution has fully integrated cloud technologies into its ecosystem. This stage represents a mature and thriving cloud environment, characterized by several key aspects. Firstly, the institution has established strong cloud partnerships and collaborative relationships. It actively engages with other institutions, industry leaders, and cloud communities to share best practices and knowledge gained from its own experiences. This collaborative approach fosters a culture of continuous learning and improvement within the cloud community. Secondly, the institution has achieved optimized performance, scalability, and cost-efficiency controls in its cloud environment. It has fine-tuned its cloud infrastructure and processes to ensure optimal utilization of resources, seamless scalability to meet demand fluctuations, and cost optimization strategies to maximize value. Furthermore, the institution's contributions to the cloud community and its sharing of best practices are notable. Cloud providers recognize the institution's expertise and value its contributions. As a result, they may provide grants, credits, or other forms of support to further the institution's research and innovation in the field of cloud computing. The institution may drive advancements, influences industry trends, and contributes to

the overall growth and development of cloud technologies. Its expertise and thought leadership have a meaningful impact on shaping the future of cloud computing.

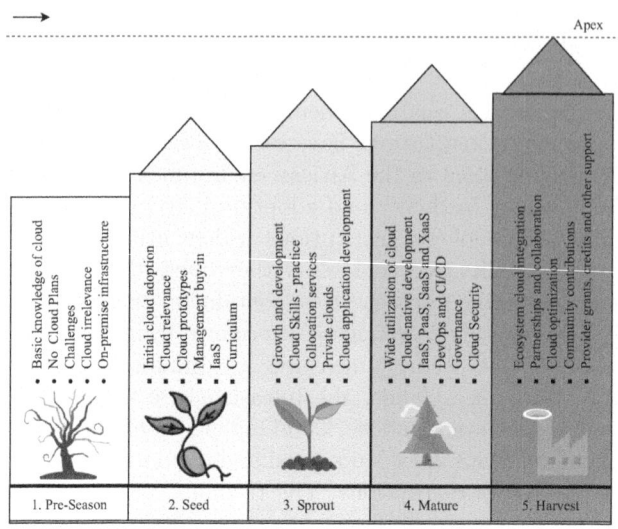

Fig. 2. A Cloud adoption assessment tool for higher education institutions in developing settings. In the pre-season, the institution has no cloud plans and the harvest phase involves the institution as part of the cloud ecosystem.

Based on the survey results from 26 higher education institutions in Uganda and using the phases defined in Sect. 5, the current state of these institutions can be determined. We develop an adoption matrix from Fig. 2 and generate the assessment of each institution and shown in Table 2. *I - Institution, CxxT - Institution Code (where xx is a numeric identifier and T is the institution type which is either G for public or R for private), P1 - institutional plans for cloud, P2 - business need for cloud, SE1 - institutional cloud prototypes, SE2 - relevance and support for next stage, SE3 - management support and involvement, SE4 - use of IaaS and/or SaaS and virtualization, SP1 - growth and development in the cloud, SP2 - real (production) application workloads on the cloud, SP3 - collocation and/or use private clouds, SP4 - research, teaching and learning in cloud computing, M1 - wide utilization of cloud technologies, M2 - the use of cloud-native and DevOps practices, M3 - demonstrated use of XaaS in the cloud, M4 - governance structures on cloud administration, H1 - Grants on use of cloud services, H2 - Optimized usage of cloud resources, H3 - community support in the use and development of cloud services, H4 - partnerships and collaborations with cloud providers.* The score range breakdown is as follows: Preseason (0 - 1), Seed (3 - 6), Sprout (7 - 10), Mature (11 - 14) and Harvest (15 - 18). The overall results are presented in Fig. 3.

Table 2. Cloud adoption assessment of HEI in Uganda

I	Pre		Seed				Sprout				Mature				Harvest				Total
	P1	P2	SE1	SE2	SE3	SE4	SP1	SP2	SP3	SP4	M1	M2	M3	M4	H1	H2	H3	H4	
C01G	1	1	1	1	1	1	1	0	0	0	–	–	–	–	–	–	–	–	7
C02G	0	0	–	–	–	–	–	–	–	–	–	–	–	–	–	–	–	–	0
C03G	1	1	1	1	1	1	1	0	0	0	–	–	–	–	–	–	–	–	7
C04G	1	1	1	1	1	1	1	1	0	0	–	–	–	–	–	–	–	–	8
C05G	1	1	1	1	1	0	–	–	–	–	–	–	–	–	–	–	–	–	5
C06G	1	0	–	–	–	–	–	–	–	–	–	–	–	–	–	–	–	–	1
C07G	1	1	1	1	1	1	1	1	1	1	1	1	0	0	–	–	–	–	12
C08G	1	1	1	1	1	1	1	1	1	1	1	1	0	0	–	–	–	–	12
C09G	1	1	1	0	0	0	–	–	–	–	–	–	–	–	–	–	–	–	3
C10G	1	1	1	1	1	1	1	1	1	1	1	1	0	0	–	–	–	–	12
C11G	1	0	–	–	–	–	–	–	–	–	–	–	–	–	–	–	–	–	1
C12G	1	1	1	1	1	0	–	–	–	–	–	–	–	–	–	–	–	–	5
C13R	1	1	1	1	1	1	1	1	0	0	–	–	–	–	–	–	–	–	8
C14R	1	1	1	1	1	1	1	1	0	0	–	–	–	–	–	–	–	–	8
C15R	1	1	1	0	0	0	–	–	–	–	–	–	–	–	–	–	–	–	3
C16R	1	1	1	1	1	1	1	1	1	0	–	–	–	–	–	–	–	–	9
C17R	1	1	1	1	1	1	1	0	0	0	–	–	–	–	–	–	–	–	7
C18R	1	1	1	1	1	1	1	0	0	0	–	–	–	–	–	–	–	–	7
C19R	1	1	1	1	0	0	–	–	–	–	–	–	–	–	–	–	–	–	4
C20R	1	1	1	1	0	0	–	–	–	–	–	–	–	–	–	–	–	–	4
C21R	1	1	1	1	1	1	1	1	1	1	1	1	1	0	–	–	–	–	13
C22R	1	1	1	0	0	0	–	–	–	–	–	–	–	–	–	–	–	–	3
C23R	1	1	1	1	1	1	1	0	0	0	–	–	–	–	–	–	–	–	7
C24R	1	1	1	1	0	0	–	–	–	–	–	–	–	–	–	–	–	–	4
C25G	0	0	–	–	–	–	–	–	–	–	–	–	–	–	–	–	–	–	0
C26R	1	0	–	–	–	–	–	–	–	–	–	–	–	–	–	–	–	–	0

The largest number of institutions (34.6%) are in the sprout stage, experiencing growth and development attributed to the use of cloud services, with real application workloads in the cloud, utilization of collocation services and private clouds, and potential involvement in cloud computing research. The next significant number of institutions (30.8%) are in the seed stage, having a business case supported by governance, at least one production service in the cloud, and relying on virtualized infrastructure. A smaller percentage of institutions are in the preseason (15.4%) and mature (11.5%) stages, with no institutions currently at the harvest stage or close to it, which represents an advanced level of maturity, with a symbiotic relationship with a cloud provider, actively monitoring and optimizing cloud operations for service delivery and cost efficiency.

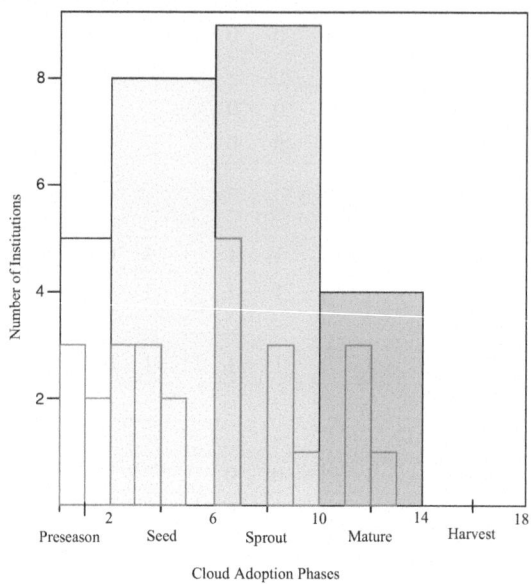

Fig. 3. The survey results of higher education institutions in Uganda in their cloud adoption journeys using the model in Sect. 5. The mini bar-plots represent the distribution of the institutions at each phase.

6   RQ4: Cloud Adoption Outlook

Cloud adoption in higher education institutions in developing economies is hindered by several challenges. The major inhibiting ones being the high costs associated with *cloud commitment* and concerns regarding data privacy, security and sovereignty. With the enactment and expected enforcement of data residence laws in many countries, institutions are cautious about large-scale migrations to the cloud. Compounding the problem is the sparse distribution of public cloud service providers in these settings, further limiting the options available. Additionally, network partitions can isolate institutions from cloud services due to unreliable local and upstream connectivity. The limited infrastructure in terms of bandwidth availability and high costs pose further challenges. There is a disconnect between service availability, connectivity, data center power and other operational issues and how the cloud can or should bridge the gap. The location of the consumers of a service can influence its placement at the cost of availability and quality of service. If there is a local connectivity challenge to a remote cloud service, then there is an availability challenge to the local users - this may not necessarily affect the remote users. If there is a local data center operational or system issue, there is still an availability challenge to both local and remote users (including multi-campus institutions). One approach that can be explored is in the federation of available compute infrastructure at the different institutions to create a diverse, more available and bigger edge-like resource pool. The institutions that desire to collaborate shall be expected to meet local connectivity requirements. Government nation-wide fiber expansion programmes and RENU campus interconnection can provide the federation network. Software abstractions to interface with this resource pool can be explored.

Despite the connectivity challenges in higher education institutions, there is indicative progress in adoption of cloud technologies. There is a pressing need for increased awareness and comprehensive training programs to cater users at various levels of expertise. Starting from the fundamentals, such as describing the relevance and benefits of cloud-based systems, to addressing concerns regarding security and other barriers, this approach will establish a solid foundation for widespread adoption. It is imperative for institutions to incorporate cloud computing into their curricula, allowing them to tackle research challenges specific to their local context and community in both the medium and long term. This requires playground infrastructure of a cloud provider available to staff and students to reinforce class sessions. Cloud providers offer discounted education pricing which is still high for users in these settings. Given budget constraints in developing economies, further discounts or *diversity* platforms should be explored. GÉANT[6], the pan-European data network for the research and education community, has negotiated over 400 framework agreements with commercial cloud providers with significant discounts to the higher education community in 40 European countries [7].

Cloud adoption by higher education institutions can influence efforts in other business domains. Initiatives focused on digitization encourage and urge organizations to prioritize the utilization of cloud computing services for their IT infrastructure and application deployment. This prioritization is aimed at enabling organizations across various sectors to harness the numerous advantages offered by cloud computing. In Uganda, the attainment of its Vision 2040 [11] is hinged on the use of ICT (and the cloud) [14] to power most development sectors for middle income status. The digital government strategy [12] under NITA-U considers *'aggregation of hardware and software across different government sectors'* as one of the objectives in the desired direction. However, the successful implementation of such agendas heavily relies on the availability of technical resource pools from the research and education sectors. These sectors play a critical role in providing the necessary expertise, knowledge sharing, and innovation required to support and drive the adoption of cloud technologies. Without adequate contributions from the research and education domains, the progress and success of these digitization agendas may be at risk.

---

[6] https://geant.org/.

7   Conclusion

Cloud adoption in higher education institutions in low-resource settings is still in its early stages, despite the numerous benefits it offers, including availability, cost-efficiency, and resource scalability. In Uganda, the adoption of cloud services is seen as a double-edged sword, with most benefits overshadowed by a pessimistic perspective. Some question the relevance of cloud services for institutions that are already grappling with challenges related to local network connectivity and limited ICT budgets. As government strives to improve connectivity by investing in national backbone infrastructure, the rate of cloud adoption is expected to improve. The establishment of new tiered data centers in the country, such as Raxio and the Government National Data Center, will contribute to this progress and provide added value to the ecosystem. To promote a more holistic integration of cloud computing, it is essential to incorporate cloud-related topics into the institutional curriculum. This includes providing cloud training and raising awareness among stakeholders at various levels of expertise and responsibility. Considering the existing staffing gaps and technical limitations, development and use of abstractions that manage cloud infrastructure and services can offer a promising avenue for further research and exploration.

In the wider low resource context, a clear understanding of the current state of cloud adoption in HEIs can be useful. The cloud adoption assessment tool proposed in this paper can provide a baseline, but can be adapted where required. Whereas our case study focused on Uganda, the low compute resource definition extends to most countries or regions in developing economies. The properties of limited or unavailable cloud infrastructure, connectivity and data center power challenges and the skill-set required to develop and operate cloud-based solutions are not particular to Uganda. One of the recommendations that we highlight in the paper on local federation of available resources between institutions can provide an understanding of the ubiquity of cloud resources. In addition, this can ensure a better utilization of available resources especially for tasks that require scalable computing power. Governments, providers and other sectoral entities can play a role in adoption but we believe that the higher education sector can play an even integral role in the chain.

References

1. Dillon, T., Wu, C., Chang, E.: Cloud computing: issues and challenges. In: 2010 24th IEEE international conference on advanced information networking and applications, pp. 27–33, IEEE (2020). https://doi.org/10.1109/AINA.2010.187
2. Liu, F., et al.: NIST cloud computing reference architecture. NIST special publication, pp. 1–28. (2011). https://doi.org/10.1109/SERVICES.2011.105
3. Miyachi, C.: What is "Cloud"? It is time to update the NIST definition?. In: IEEE Cloud computing, vol. 5, pp. 6–11 (2018). https://doi.org/10.1109/MCC.2018.032591611
4. Mirashe, S.P., Kalyankar, N.V.: Cloud Computing. arXiv preprint (2010)

5. Mudialba, P.J.: The Impact of Cloud Technology on the Automation of Businesses 2016 International Conference on Platform Technology and Service (PlatCon), Jeju, Korea (South), pp. 1–4 (2016). https://doi.org/10.1109/PlatCon.2016.7456831

6. Gartner Press Release. https://www.gartner.com/en/newsroom/press-releases/. Accessed 23 Jun 2023

7. GÉANT Cloud Services in Conjunction with OCRE. https://clouds.geant.org/geant-cloud-catalogue/geant-cloud-catalogue-ocre/. Accessed 30 Jun 2023

8. Kshetri, N.: Cloud computing in developing economies. In: Computer, vol. 43, no. 10, pp. 47–55, Oct. (2010). https://doi.org/10.1109/MC.2010.212

9. Agrawal, S.: A survey on recent applications of Cloud computing in education: COVID-19 perspective. J. Phys.: Conf. Ser. (1828), 012076 (2021). https://doi.org/10.1088/1742-6596/1828/1/012076

10. AWS Global Infrastructure. https://aws.amazon.com/about-aws/global-infrastructure/. Accessed 23 Jun 2023

11. Vision 2040. http://npa.go.ug/vision2040/. Accessed 30 Jun 2023

12. Digital Government Strategy. https://www.nita.go.ug/sites/default/files/2022-02/Digital%20Government%20Strategy%20-%20Draft.pdf. Accessed 30 Jun 2023

13. Linthicum, D. S.: Cloud-native applications and cloud migration: the good, the bad, and the points between. In: IEEE Cloud Computing, vol. 4, no. 5, pp. 12–14, September/October (2017). https://doi.org/10.1109/MCC.2017.4250932

14. Mwesigwa, C.: Cloud computing can reshape Uganda's development. In: 2014 IST-Africa Conference Proceedings, pp. 1–8, Mauritius (2014). https://doi.org/10.1109/ISTAFRICA.2014.6880600

15. Kratzke, N., Quint, P.C.: Understanding cloud-native applications after 10 years of cloud computing - a systematic mapping study. J. Syst. Softw. **126**, 1–16 (2017). Elsevier https://doi.org/10.1016/j.jss.2017.01.001

16. The State of Higher Education in Uganda. https://unche.or.ug/wp-content/uploads/2023/06/SHE-Report-2020-21.pdf. Accessed 30 Jun 2023

17. National Backbone Infrastructure Project. https://www.nita.go.ug/projects-service-portfolio/national-backbone-infrastructure-project-nbiegi. Accessed 30 Jun 2023

18. Trivedi, H.: Cloud adoption model for governments and large enterprises. MSc Thesis, Massachusetts Institute of Technology, Massachusetts (2013)

19. An Overview of the AWS Cloud Adoption Framework. https://docs.aws.amazon.com/pdfs/whitepapers/latest/overview-aws-cloud-adoption-framework/overview-aws-cloud-adoption-framework.pdf. Accessed 23 Jun 2023

20. Ebert C., Gallardo G., Hernantes J., Serrano N.: DevOps. In: IEEE Software, vol. 33, no. 3, pp. 94–100, IEEE (2016). https://doi.org/10.1109/MS.2016.68

21. Onayemi, K.K., Bada, J., Kiyingi, F.P.: The diffusion of innovations theory and the adoption of cloud computing technologies by small scale enterprises in Kampala, Uganda (2022)

22. Mpanga, D., Elbanna, A.: A framework for cloud ERP system implementation in developing countries: learning from lower local governments in Uganda. In: ICT Unbounded, Social Impact of Bright ICT Adoption: IFIP WG 8.6", International Conference on Transfer and Diffusion of IT, TDIT 2019, pp. 274–292. Springer International Publishing (2019). https://doi.org/10.1007/978-3-030-20671-0_19

23. Mugyenyi, R.: Adoption of cloud computing services for sustainable development of commercial banks in Uganda (2018). https://globaljournals.org/GJCST_Volume18/1-Adoption-of-Cloud-Computing.pdf

24. Etengu, R., Namwano, S., Galiwango, M.: The Major Challenges of Adapting Cloud-Based E-Learning at Higher Learning in Developing Countries: A Case Study of Uganda (2014)
25. Kasse, J. P., Musa, M., Fatuma, N.: A validated framework for cloud computing adoption by SMEs in Uganda. In: International Journal of Information Research and Review, vol. 12, pp. 1482–1488 (2015). http://www.ijirr.com/sites/default/files/issues-pdf/0711.pdf
26. Samit T., Angan S., Amalendu J.: "Where do countries stand in cloud computing readiness? A country-level analysis of capacity and potential. Journal of Information Technology and Politics (2023). https://doi.org/10.1080/19331681.2022.2163735
27. Global Cloud Ecosystem Index. https://www.technologyreview.com/2022/04/25/1051115/. Accessed 20 Jun 2023
28. Adjei, J.K., Adams, S., Mamattah, L.: Cloud computing adoption in Ghana; accounting for institutional factors. Technology in Society, Elsevier, vol. 65(C) (2021). https://doi.org/10.1016/j.techsoc.2021.101583
29. Oredo, J.O., Njihia, J., Iraki, X.N.: Adoption of cloud computing by firms in Kenya: the role of institutional pressures. In: The African Journal of Information Systems, Vol. 11(3) (2019). https://digitalcommons.kennesaw.edu/ajis/vol11/iss3/1
30. Alimboyong, C.R., Bucjan, M.E.: Cloud computing adoption among state universities and colleges in the Philippines: issues and challenges. In: International Journal of Evaluation and Research in Education, vol. 10, no. 4, pp. 1455–1461 (2021). https://doi.org/10.11591/ijere.v10i4.21526
31. Makoza, F.: Cloud computing adoption in Higher Education Institutions of Malawi: An exploratory study. In International Journal of Computing & ICT Research, vol. 9, no. 2 (2015)
32. Njenga, K., Garg, L., Bhardwaj, A.K., Prakash, V., Bawa, S.: The cloud computing adoption in higher learning institutions in Kenya: Hindering factors and recommendations for the way forward. Telematics Inf. **38**, 225–246. (2019). https://doi.org/10.1016/j.tele.2018.10.007
33. Cloud Infrastructure Map. https://www.cloudinfrastructuremap.com/. Accessed 30 Jun 2023
34. M'rhaouarh, C.O., Namir, A., Chafiq, N.: Cloud computing adoption in developing countries: a systematic literature review. In: 2018 IEEE International Conference on Technology Management, Operations and Decisions (ICTMOD), pp. 73–79 (2018) https://doi.org/10.1109/ITMC.2018.8691295
35. Müller, S.D., Holm, S.R., Søndergaard, J.: Benefits of cloud computing: literature review in a maturity model perspective. In: Communications of the Association for Information Systems, vol. 37, no. 1, pp. 42 (2015). https://doi.org/10.17705/1CAIS.03742
36. Islam, M.M., Rahaman, M.: A review on multiple survey report of cloud adoption and its major barriers in the perspective of Bangladesh. Int. J. Comput. Netw. Inf. Secur. 42–47 (2016). https://doi.org/10.5815/ijcnis.2016.05.06
37. Khan, N., Al-Yasiri, A.: Framework for cloud computing adoption: A road map for Smes to cloud migration. arXiv preprint (2016) arXiv:1601.01608

A Blueprint for South African Public Schools ICT Infrastructure

Wandile T. Mnynadu[1]($\boxtimes$), Alfredo Terzoli[1], and Hlabishi Kobo[2]

[1] Department of Computer Science, University of Zululand, Richards Bay 3886, KwaDlangezwa, South Africa
201860129@stu.unizulu.c.za, terzolia@unizulu.c.za
[2] Council for Scientific and Industrial Research, Pretoria, South Africa
HKobo@csir.co.za

Abstract. In today's digital age, access to quality education is crucial for individual and societal growth. However, many South African public schools lack access to ICT infrastructure, resulting in significant implications for education quality. While efforts have been made by the Department of Basic Education and research communities, a systematic approach that considers the full technology spectrum for these schools is still missing. To contribute to this deficiency, this research paper introduces an innovative ICT infrastructure model in the form of a modular blueprint. The blueprint encompasses the complete technology spectrum, addressing existing operational schooling challenges and fostering a modern technology-based learning environment. The modular design enables incremental deployment, reducing ICT infrastructure underutilization and accommodating budget constraints. Additionally, each module's independence allows for seamless adaptation to evolving schooling challenges. Seven distinct modules are identified and described in this paper, providing a comprehensive framework for addressing ICT infrastructure deployment in South African public schools. To conduct this study, a comprehensive methodology involving research analysis, DBE publications, academic institutions, interviews, and examination of five public schools in the KwaDlangezwa community, KwaZulu-Natal, South Africa, was employed. Utilizing a design science approach, we developed modules as artifacts to be incorporated into the blueprint.

Keywords: ICT4D · ICT infrastructure · South Africa · Education · DBE · e-Learning

1 Introduction

The deficiency of ICT infrastructure significantly hinders the quality of education in South Africa [1]. However, progress in rolling out Information and Communication Technology (ICT) infrastructure and Internet connectivity to public schools has been sluggish [2]. In a draft white paper on e-Education from the Department of Basic Education (DBE) in 2004, former Education Minister Dr. Naledi Pandor highlighted the need

A. Sere et al. (Eds.): AFRICOMM 2023, LNICST 587, pp. 39–52, 2025.
https://doi.org/10.1007/978-3-031-81570-6_3

to deploy ICT infrastructure tailored to Africa's requirements and future development capacity. To address this, the DBE and research communities have initiated projects to assess the effectiveness of specific devices for teaching and learning in South African public schools [2–4]. But these efforts do not yet consider the full technology spectrum that might be beneficial to all South African public schooling contexts such as administration, safety, for example. Guidelines have also been published by the DBE regarding the recommended ICT devices that should be present in both regular and special public schools [5, 6]. However, these guidelines do not address the overall connectivity of the devices or the Internet connection for each public school and the security of the ICT devices and learners.

The ICT for Rural Education Development (ICT4RED) project was part of the Technology for Rural Education Development (TECH4RED) research program initiated by the DBE in collaboration with the Eastern Cape Department of Education, and the Department of Rural Development and Land Reform. The objective of this project was to test and evaluate the suitability of tablets and supporting infrastructure for teaching and learning in 26 rural schools in the Eastern Cape Province. The supporting infrastructure included communication technologies such as Wi-Fi access points, switches, routers, and very-small aperture terminal (VSAT) satellites for each school. This ICT deployment followed a rigid and wholistic approach utilizing the "Earn As You Learn (EAYL) badge system," which ICT4RED developed to assess a public school's readiness to receive ICT infrastructure through assessments and micro-accreditation [2]. This system was developed in response to concerns about underutilization of ICT infrastructure, as also highlighted by [7], but doesn't consider the gradual deployment of the ICT infrastructure into these schools.

The EAYL badge system implemented by ICT4RED allowed the Department of Science and Technology (DST) to enhance their previous paper-based tool and develop the first version of a web-based decision support tool called eReady (www.eready.co.za). This tool enables the assessment of ICT readiness and maturity for schools across five perspectives or work streams, namely, ICT devices, Connectivity, Curriculum and Digital Content Development and Distribution, e-Administration, and Teacher Development and Support. These categories align with the Operation Phakisa ICT in Education presidential program, which aims to accelerate the deployment and integration of ICT infrastructure in public schools [8].

ICT4RED's project attempted to tackle the above workstreams, however from their analysis, ICT device such as tablets are not suitable for replacing a computer lab, due to their total cost of ownership. On the other hand, the project doesn't clearly outline the security measures that can be upheld using ICT. Motivated by the shortfalls of related works in accelerating ICT infrastructure deployments in public schools, focus on the application of ICT devices in the school in general and for connectivity. A similar initiative, Siyakhula Living Lab (SLL), launched in 2006 by Rhodes University and the University of Fort Hare, focused on ICT for Development (ICT4D) in 17 public schools within a rural community in the Eastern Cape Province (siyakhulall.org).

Although the initial endeavors of SLL where to define a model for community internet access to allow for the access of e-Governance service in rural communities. They also deployed computing infrastructure to which the locals would use to access the Internet and the e-Government portal. The computing infrastructure deployed was based on the thin/thick client computing topology and the schools to which housed these computer labs where connect to the Internet via the model that SSL developed know as Broadband Island incorporating fewer VSAT satellites and using WiMAX to connect each school (Fig. 1). This model of connecting the schools to the Internet is more cost effective than deploying VSAT satellites in each school, done by ICT4RED. Having thin/clicks workstations in school is also more cost efficient in terms of total cost of owners in comparison to replacing desktop computer with tablets. Unfortunately, both initiatives focused primarily on ICT devices for computing and connectivity only.

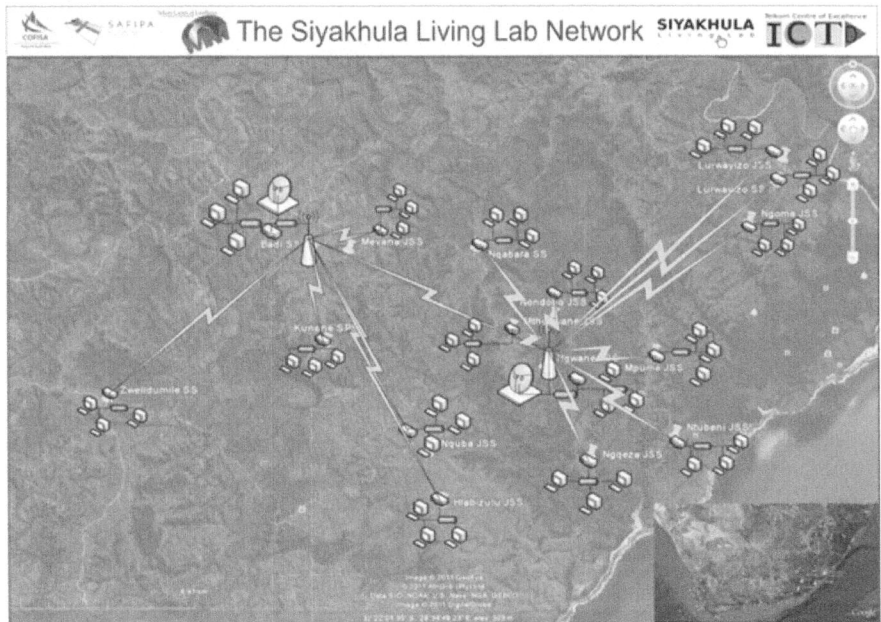

Fig. 1. SLL's Broadband Island

[7] suggests that the DBE should consider individual school contexts when deploying ICT resources to address existing operational challenges in education. This consideration not only reduces the underutilization of ICT infrastructure but also aligns better with budget constraints and avoids overwhelming changes in educational technologies, which may hinder effective ICT infrastructure service delivery planning.

While SLL and ICT4RED focused on ICTs for connectivity and computing, some research efforts have addressed other operational challenges in education, however there is no comprehensive document outlining the complete plan for deploying ICT infrastructure in South African public schools to address these challenges. Hence, a blueprint has been developed to provide an approach for deploying ICT infrastructure, enabling a modern technology-enabled learning environment in South African public schools.

The blueprint encompasses seven modules that can be utilized to address current operational challenges in schools through the implementation of ICT. This modular approach enables the incremental deployment of ICT infrastructure, reducing the overall annual expenditure while avoiding the underutilization of resources. By introducing and integrating ICT gradually into the educational system, the modular structure also simplifies maintenance and accommodates the adoption of new teaching practices and educational technologies. The following sections will elaborate on the motivation and background of this initiative before presenting the details of each module of the blueprint.

2 Motivation and Background

Goal 4 of the United Nations' Sustainable Development Goals focuses on quality education, aiming to "ensure inclusive and equitable education opportunities for all and promote lifelong learning" [9]. The second goal of African Union's aspiration 1 for a prosperous Africa based on inclusive growth and sustainable development, is "well educated citizens and skills revolutions underpinned by science, technology and innovation" [10]. The integration of ICT in teaching and learning is crucial for a country's development and the socioeconomic growth of individuals, leading to an increasing adoption of ICT in educational systems worldwide [11]. ICT in education refers to the utilization of information and communications technology to support, enhance, and optimize the delivery of information. The Department of Basic Education (DBE) captures school infrastructure information and publishes its findings annually through the National Education Infrastructure Management System (NEIMS) [12].

According to the NEIMS report from April 2021, approximately 59.20% (15 600 out of 23,276) of South African public schools do not have computer labs, around 20.35% have internet connectivity for teaching and learning, 92% do not have highspeed internet access, and a mere 2.55% have surveillance cameras, among other infrastructure-related information. Although there is ambiguity regarding the total number of public schools in South Africa (the annual report mentions 22,945 schools [2]), we have chosen to rely on the more detailed results reported by NEIMS. The DBE's e-Education white paper highlights three critical elements that will determine the future effectiveness of ICT as a tool for social and economic development. The first element is cost, emphasizing the need for cost-effective solutions to meet developmental demands and reach remote areas of the country. The second element is sustainability, recognizing that state-of-the-art technology must be sustainable to be worthwhile. Lastly, the efficient utilization of ICTs is crucial for maximizing their impact [1].

This paper is written particularly to allow administrators and decision makers, etc. to make choices based on technical and organizational factors concerning ICT infrastructure in South African public schools or developing countries alike.

3 The Blueprint Design

In contrast to a one-size-fits-all approach, our study focuses on investigating the ICT infrastructure in South African public schools in a modular manner, addressing specific operational challenges and proposing ICT-based solutions. This modular approach allows for independent evolution of each module and facilitates the incremental deployment of ICT infrastructure, considering annual budget constraints and existing implementations in certain schools. The blueprint comprises seven essential modules, each with variations that represent specific functionalities. Consequently, numerous combinations are possible, tailoring the fundamental modules to the unique needs of each school. Thus, different schools may sequence the deployment of the modules differently. The actual implementation of the modules will change overtime, because of the quick technology changes we are witnessing at the moment. However, the modules per se have much longer life due to the way they have been identified, reflecting on the needs of the schools.

The Computer Lab module proposes an efficient computing infrastructure, while the Classroom module encompasses the integration of ICT technologies into teaching and learning processes. The Administration module addresses administrative procedures and suggests improvements, while the Safety and Security module focuses on mitigating safety and security challenges. The Energy Conservation and Power Supply module outlines techniques to conserve energy in relation to the deployed ICT infrastructure. The Communication and Connectivity module describes the school's internal and external network connectivity for communication and internet access. Inherently, the Communication and Connectivity module also acts the module to which other modules are connected and disconnected. Lastly, the Cloud module presents a model for deploying a private community cloud in South African public schools.

To conduct this study, we utilized a methodology involving the analysis of research efforts, publications from the Department of Basic Education (DBE), academic institutions, as well as interviews and analysis of five public schools in the KwaDlangezwa community, KwaZulu-Natal, South Africa. Employing a design science approach, we developed modules as artifacts to be assembled in the blueprint.

4 Modules of Blueprint

4.1 Computer Lab

Schooling Operation Challenges:
According to the DBE (2021), approximately 58% of public schools lack a computer lab. One operational challenge is the theft of computing infrastructure, while another is the maintenance of the infrastructure. Although ICT4RED experimented with the use of tablets in 26 schools, they are not an efficient substitute for a dedicated computer lab due to. In the KwaDlangezwa community, three secondary public schools adopted a common deployment method used in South African public schools, utilizing Microsoft Windows fat clients without a central server [5]. In contrast, SLL conducted tests and proposed the use of thin/thick clients and a central cluster of servers. Linux was chosen as the operating system, and the Linux Terminal Server Project (LTSP) was employed as the enabling software [3]. Thin clients are cost-effective, low resource, and low-power computers with a minimal operating system, while thick clients are similar computers with the ability to process applications locally. By relying on a central server for booting,

the risk of theft is reduced, and maintenance becomes more streamlined since application installation and configuration occur solely at the central servers.

Proposed ICT Solution:
Our proposed ICT solution includes the use of Zero clients, which do not require a minimal operating system and are nonfunctional without a central server (Fig. 2). However, it is important to note that both thin clients and zero clients have limitations when it comes to supporting complex peripheral devices such as projectors, interactive pen technologies (IPTs), or assistive technologies. These limitations need to be assessed on a case-by-case basis [12].

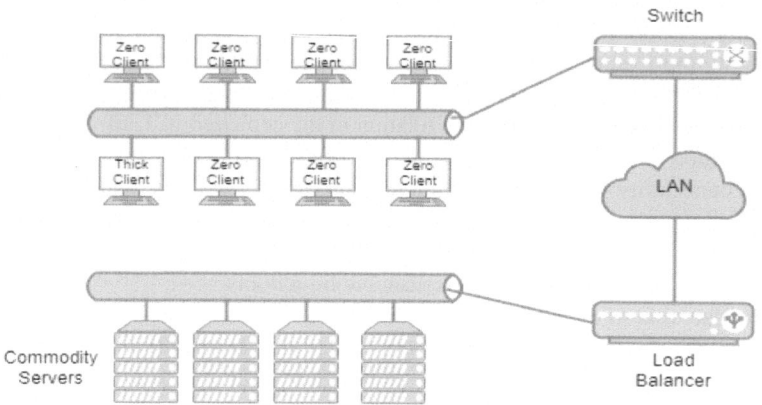

Fig. 2. Computer Lab

Therefore, it may be necessary to utilize thick or hybrid clients for teachers or learners with special needs. The cluster of servers serving the zero/thick clients can be based on Linux. These cluster servers can also be utilized for web caching, local web hosting, and hosting the school's Learning Management System (LMS) [13]. To efficiently distribute the zero-client sessions among the servers, a load balancer is then required.

In terms of transitioning from a fat client computer lab to a thick client computer lab, the school can gradually make the switch as the disks on the computers fail. Subsequently, they can consider transitioning to thin clients when user requirements and expectations exceed the capabilities of the existing hardware. Changing the operating system to Linux can be accomplished using a flash drive.

4.2 Classroom

Schooling Operational Challenges:
The primary and secondary schools in KwaDlangezwa have distinct schooling operations, with teachers visiting learners and learners attending various venues. To enable a more cost effective and enhanced schooling experience for all learners, a classroom is defined as a discipline-specific learning facility. As such, each classroom will be

equipped with 3D-printed artifacts to create an environment conducive to learning a particular subject [14]. The deployment of ICT devices and applications per classroom aims to minimize duplication of efforts, as each classroom will have its own personalized ICT setup while learners share the facilities. ICT devices should be tailored to the specific subjects taught in each classroom, optimizing budget allocation. For instance, subjects like digital art or music composition may require more computing resources compared to language classes and mathematics.

The use of interactive whiteboards (IWBs) in classrooms of developed countries has been extensively studied, highlighting the benefits of this technology for teaching and learning. However, a study conducted by SLL on the use of IWBs in classrooms for selected classrooms of schools in the Easern cape province, revealed certain drawbacks. As an alternative, image processing technology, such as eBeam, was suggested due to its similarity to IWBs but at a lower cost and with greater portability [15]. The eBeam technology involves a receiver placed on the edge of a flat surface, typically a whiteboard, and a radio-wave emitting pen. While the potential applications that can be used in each subject/classroom are extensive, we will outline the main applications that can facilitate teaching and learning in the following section.

Proposed ICT Solution:
IPTs (Interactive Pen Technologies) are portable and can be shared across the school, reducing the overall budget spent on ICT devices for teaching purposes. Therefore, we propose deploying several IPTs that can be shared based on subject demand. Instead of providing VR headsets for each student, purchasing Smart LED projectors is a more cost-effective option. When used with 3D plastic glasses, these projectors can display 3D graphics and support applications like spatial augmented reality (AR) [16]. Additionally, smart projectors can be interfaced with smartphones and support learning outside the classroom.

While web browsers, augmented reality (AR), LMS, 3D printing, artificial intelligence (AI), and word-processing applications are essential for most classrooms [17], accessing them can be done through various devices. LMS is a software application for the administration, tracking, reporting, automation, and delivery of educational courses, etc., [13]. Zero client desktops, smartphones/tablets, or low-cost laptops such as Intel's Classmate PC and Chromebook can be used to access the above-mentioned applications. However, it is important to consider the potential targeting of learners and higher maintenance overhead associated with smartphones/tablets, even though they may be more efficient for applications like AR. The LMS, being web-enabled, should be accessible within the school even without internet connectivity to facilitate the sharing of eLearning resources, as proposed in the computer lab module.

4.3 Administration

Schooling Operational Challenges:
The Personal Administrative Measures (PAM) government gazette outlines the duties and responsibilities of staff members in public schools, including teaching, extracurricular activities, administration, communication, and academic performance [2]. Therefore, the deployment of ICT infrastructure in South African schools should aim to facilitate

these tasks and responsibilities. According to the NEIM's report of 2021, only 30% of public schools in South Africa utilize Internet connectivity for administrative purposes, 93.53% do not have intercom systems, 45.91% have landlines, and 94.55% have access to cellular networks.

The South African School Administration Management System (SA-SAMS), maintained by the DBE, is a school administration and management system that assists educators in streamlining their administrative, management, and governance tasks. It collects teacher and student information, which is then analyzed using an online dashboard called Data Driven Districts (DDD) to visualize overall school performance and other key metrics [18]. However, the system currently relies on manual data entry and lacks support for an Application Programming Interface (API) to facilitate data integration with other applications. This limitation hinders data accuracy and restricts the potential for technological solutions involving the software. A subset of the collected data includes learner registration, results, and progress, as well as attendance records of learners, educators, and non-educators.

A LMS enables students to take assessments and courses, simplifies grading and result collection, and tracks student access and response times during tests or quizzes, aiding in identifying challenging sections [19]. Integrating the LMS with SA-SAMS is crucial for enhancing efficiency and accuracy for the data uploaded into SA-SAMS. In public schools, laptops have already been deployed for teachers to facilitate lesson preparation, mark capturing, teaching, and administrative duties. For a LMS, we recommend using Moodle [20].

Proposed ICT Solution:
To automate class/school attendance registration, we suggest using cost-effective QR codes instead of RFID tags. Teachers/secretaries can scan the QR codes using their smartphones to record attendance, which can then be manually uploaded to SA-SAMS. Alternatively, the data can be automatically uploaded to SA-SAMS' Microsoft Access database (which is used by the current implementation of SA-SAMS) using Java DataBase Connectivity (JDBC) technology, which is free. Considering the limited presence of intercom systems in public schools, we propose deploying Voice-over-IP (VoIP) phones in offices and classrooms, leveraging the existing IP network for easier and more affordable installation. For productivity and document processing, we recommend utilizing the user-friendly and language-supportive LibreOffice, a free and open-source office suite.

4.4   Safety and Security

Schooling Operational Challenges:
In South Africa, communities can be prone to violence, including gang wars and turf wars, which sometimes spill over onto school grounds, endangering the lives of students and teachers. According to the latest NEIMS report, only 3% of public schools have camera surveillance, 5% have alarm systems, 9% have access control measures, and 80% have wire fencing. However, the presence of holes in the fence allows learners to escape from school and invites unauthorized individuals to enter and engage in violent or illegal activities, such as drug dealing.

Additionally, ICT mature nations face challenges such as cyberbullying, cyber-attacks, identity theft, and access to inappropriate internet resources like the dark web or pornography. To address these issues, the ICT guidelines for schools by the DBE recommend segregating administrative computers into a separate virtual network (VLAN) and virtual private network (VPN) from learners and guests. This segregation restricts their access to certain network and internet resources. This best practice should also be considered when public schools adopt IoT devices, which is an inevitable trend.

Proposed ICT Solution:
We propose a cost-effective school monitoring system utilizing Power over Ethernet (PoE) IP cameras and computer vision technology. These cameras offer higher resolution and require fewer units to cover a designated area compared to traditional CCTV systems [21]. To prevent tampering, fixed cameras are recommended.

All camera feeds are streamed to a central network video recorder (NVR), which records the footage for storage. Through machine learning-based computer vision, video analytics can be applied for object detection, tracking, and automatic human action recognition (HAR). This enables the system to identify the presence of ICT devices and monitor crowd behaviour, alerting the school to any potential risks, violence, or missing equipment [22]. Information security policies are essential to regulate and protect sensitive data within educational settings. For this we recommend a Data Loss Prevention (DLP) software maintaining data confidentiality, integrity, and availability, and enforce security policies. It detects and prevents data exfiltration and leakage, mitigating social engineering threats.

We also recommend that that public schools install a patch management system to automate the installation of patches and upgrades throughout the organization, minimizing vulnerabilities and potential data breaches. Essential security controls include firewalls, Intrusion Detection and Prevention Systems (IPS), a remote access server (VPN), honeypots, and monitoring software to ensure network security.

4.5 Energy Conservation and Power Supply

Schooling Operational Challenges:
According to the NEIMS 2021 report, public schools in South Africa have limited access to alternative power sources. Only 2% have generators and 6% use solar energy, while the majority (95%) rely on grid connections. However, 14% of schools face unstable electricity supply. To address this, schools can benefit from using multiple power sources and switching based on grid availability [11].

A study conducted in the Stellenbosch area compared energy usage in schools [23]. It revealed that lighting accounts for a significant portion of energy consumption, especially in underprivileged schools. Upgrading lighting systems to LED lamps can reduce electricity consumption by 26%. Implementing sub-meters for outsourced facilities and installing solar outdoor lighting can further contribute to energy savings [24].

Efficiency strategies in computer labs, such as adjusting brightness, disabling screen-savers, and enabling power management features, can lead to substantial energy savings. A study in a Canadian university found these measures saved significant energy over a six-month period [25].

Projects like ICT4RED have explored alternative power supply systems such as biogas and hydrogen fuel cells. Overall, improving energy efficiency in schools through various measures can help mitigate the challenges posed by limited and unstable electricity supply.

Proposed ICT Solution:
The proposed computer lab models for South African public schools utilize a zero/thick client-server topology with diskless workstations. Thin clients offer over 50% higher energy efficiency compared to fat clients, but server hardware plays a role in determining overall efficiency. Putting thin clients to sleep when not in use can further enhance energy savings. Incorporating energy efficiency strategies mentioned in [25] onto the server serving thin clients is also recommended. Implementing climate control measures in school buildings can reduce energy consumption by computers and technology, especially in hot environments [24].

The ICT infrastructure blueprint for South African public schools includes PoE (Power over Ethernet) devices, which allow for flexible power source alternation and minimize network downtime, Fig. 3. Examples of PoE devices include IP cameras, PoE LED lighting, VoIP phones, and Wi-Fi access points. All four current PoE standards support these devices, with PoE type 4 being the latest and providing a power output ranging from 71.30 W to 100 W. The maximum cable length supported by PoE technologies is 100 m, requiring PoE extenders for devices located beyond this distance. PoE LED lighting, a network-controlled device, can be centrally managed and monitored for energy usage through IT network management software, enabling lighting automation.

We also recommend the use of solar energy as an alternate power source for South African public school ICT infrastructure.

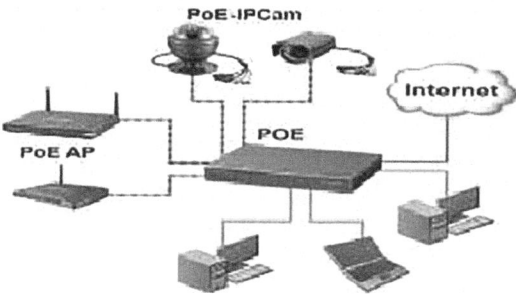

Fig. 3. Example of PoE devices

4.6 Communication and Connectivity

Schooling Operational Challenges:
In South Africa, 96% of public schools have access to a cellular network. However, during power outages, the cellular network service can be slow or unavailable, particularly in deep rural areas. To address this, ICT4RED deployed VSAT satellite dishes in each

school, aligning with the plans of SA Connect for government facilities. This differs from SLL's approach, where VSAT Internet connection is not deployed in each school, offering a more cost-effective solution. Internet access in public schools is capped, and once the cap is reached, it becomes the school's responsibility to provide their own Internet access. SLL uses a model called the Broadband Island, connecting schools to the Internet using multiple technologies. However, this model focuses on the WAN connection, not the internal LAN connecting the ICT infrastructure [4].

Proposed ICT Solution:
We propose an ICT infrastructure deployment using the hierarchical LAN model topology, consisting of three layers [26]. The access layer includes ICT devices and connected switches, while the distribution layer comprises switches connecting the access layer to the core layer (Fig. 4). The core layer connects the school to the Internet, potentially utilizing the Broadband Island model depicted in Fig. 1. Wi-Fi technology is now more accessible and widespread, making it a suitable wireless option for replicating the Broadband Island instead of using WiMAX, as suggested by [3, 4], as it also better facilitates backup routes.

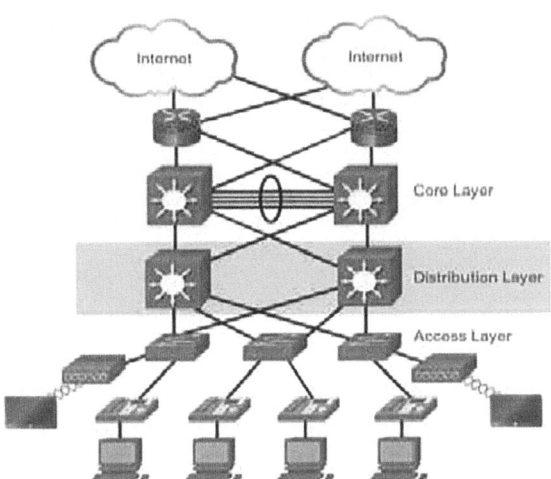

Fig. 4. Hierarchical LAN model

Additionally, we recommend adopting SDN (Software Defined Networking), a novel architecture that reduces data costs by abstracting network functions and requiring fewer network appliances and on-site IT staff [27]. Implementing the ICT infrastructure within SDN would enable the provision of a network abstraction to allow the independent deployment, maintenance, and scalability of the modules [29].

4.7 Cloud

Schooling Operational Challenges:
Cloud computing is a convenient model that provides on-demand network access to

a shared pool of configurable computing resources. It enables intensive computation, multiple applications, and mass storage to be hosted remotely in a data center, accessible by low-powered devices through an Internet connection and a browser [28]. There are four deployment models for cloud computing: public, private, community, and hybrid cloud.

Proposed ICT solution:
We propose a community cloud as a private cloud deployment shared by multiple schools in a community, connected through SLL's Broadband Island. One school within the Broadband Island can host the local cloud infrastructure, providing secure and cost-effective access to private cloud resources for all schools. Cost-effective in a sense that schools need not have an Internet connection. The size of the data center depends on the number and size of schools in the community. The data center can be realized using various technologies, and we recommend OpenStack as the cloud management platform with Linux servers.

5 Conclusion

The goal of this project was to provide a means to accelerate ICT infrastructure deployment in South African public schools. For this goal to be accomplished, it was necessary to understand the schooling operational challenges and how ICT infrastructure in South African public schools can be used to tackle these challenges.

Acknowledgements. The authors thank the educators and principals of the schools that were visited to properly envision an ICT infrastructure that reflects their desired workplace.

References

1. Department of Basic Education (DBE).: Draft white paper on e-Education, Pretoria, South Africa. Available: https://www.gov.za/sites/default/files/gcis_document/201409/267341.pdf (2004).
2. Department of Basic Education (DBE).: Department of Basic Education Annual Report 2021/22, Pretoria, South Africa. Available: https://nationalgovernment.co.za/department_a nnual/404/2022department-of-basic-education-(dbe)-annual-report.pdf (2022)
3. Herselman, M.E., Botha, A.: Designing and implementing an Information Communication Technology for Rural Education Development (ICT4RED) initiative in a resource constraint environment: Nciba school district, Eastern Cape, South Africa, 1st ed.Pretoria, South Africa: CSIR Meraka (2014)
4. Siebörger, I., Terzoli, A., Hodgkinson-Williams, C.: Evolving an efficient and effective off-the-shelf computing infrastructure for rural communities of South Africa. In: Communications in Computer and Information Science, vol. 1236 CCIS, pp. 63–77 (2020)
5. Terzoli, A., Siebörger, I., Gumbo S.: Community 'Broadband Islands' for digital government access in rural South Africa. In: 17th European Conference on Digital Government, Lisbon, Portugal, pp. 204–213 (2017)

6. Department of Basic Education (DBE).: Guidelines for schools ICT Hardware and Specifications, Pretoria, South Africa, Available: https://www.thutong.doe.gov.za/ResourceDownload.aspx?id=47447&userid=-1 (2012)
7. Department of Basic Education (DBE).: Draft National Guidelines for Resourcing an Inclusive Education System, Pretoria, South Africa. https://msmonline.co.za/wp-content/uploads/2021/04/18-Guidelines-for-Resourcing-an-Inclusive-Education.pdf (2018)
8. Munje, P.N., Jita, T.: The impact of the lack of ICT resources on teaching and learning in selected South African primary schools. Int. J. Learn. Teach. Educ. Res. **19**(7), 263–279 (2020)
9. Department of Planning Monitoring and Evaluation.: About Us: Operation Phakisa (2015). Available at: https://www.operationphakisa.gov.za/operations/Education%20Lab/pages/default.aspx
10. Mukhari, S.S.: Teachers' experience of information and communication technology use for teaching and learning in urban schools, University of South Africa, Pretoria (2016). Available: https://uir.unisa.ac.za/handle/10500/22045
11. Gray, J.: The African Union's Agenda 2063: aspirations, challenges, and opportunities for management research, Africa. J. Manag. **2**(1), 93–116 (2016)
12. Department of Basic Education (DBE).: National Education Infrastructure Management System Report, Pretoria, South Africa, Apr. 2021. Available: https://www.education.gov.za/Portals/0/Documents/Reports/neims%20standard%20report%202021.pdf?ver=2021-05-20-094532-570
13. Tollefsen, M.: Thin clients and assistive technology - News - English - MediaLT, Nov. 06, 2022. http://medialt.no/news/enus/thin-clients-and-assistive-technology/692.aspx (2022)
14. Cardellini, V., Casalicchio, E., Colajanni, M., Yu, P.S.: The state of the art in locally distributed Web-server systems. ACM Comput. Surv. (CSUR) **34**(2), 263–311 (2002)
15. Schelly, C., Anzalone, G., Wijnen, B., Pearce, J.M.: Opensource 3-D printing technologies for education: Bringing additive manufacturing to the classroom. J. Vis. Lang. Comput. **28**, 226–237 (2015)
16. Slay, H., Siebörger, I., Hodgkinson-Williams, C.: Interactive whiteboards: real beauty or just 'lipstick'? Comput. Educ. **51**(3), 1321–1341 (2008)
17. Park, M.K., Lim, K.J., Seo, M.K., Jung, S.J., Lee, K.H.: Spatial augmented reality for product appearance design evaluation. J. Comput. Des. Eng. **2**(1), 38–46 (2015)
18. Haleem, A., Javaid, M., Qadri, M.A., Suman, R.: Understanding the role of digital technologies in education: a review. Sustain. Oper. Comput. **3**, 275–285 (2022)
19. Department of Basic Education (DBE).: Call for comments: Amendment of the National Education Information Policy (Government Notice No: 38223), Pretoria, South Africa, Nov. 2014. Available: https://www.education.gov.za/Portals/0/Documents/Legislation/Gov%20Not/38223_21-11_BasicEdu.pdf?ver=2015-01-28-151524-730
20. Burtsev, V.: Adoption of learning management systems at south african learning institutions. In: INTED2021 Proceedings, vol. 1, pp. 10818–10824 (Jan. 2021)
21. Stasinakis, P., Kalogiannakis, M.: Using moodle in secondary education: a case study of the course "research project" In Greece. Int. J. Educ. Dev. Inf. Commun. Technol. (IJEDICT) **11**(3), 50–64 (2015)
22. Schneiderman, R.: Trends in video surveillance give DSP an apps boost. IEEE Signal Process. Mag. **27**(6), 6–12 (2010). https://doi.org/10.1109/MSP.2010.938113
23. Ye, L., Liu, T., Han, T., Ferdinando, H., Seppänen, T., Alasaarela, E.: Campus violence detection based on artificial intelligent interpretation of surveillance video sequences. Remote Sens (Basel) **13**(4), 1–17 (2021)
24. Samuels, J.A., Grobbelaar, S.S., Booysen, M.J.: Light-years apart: energy usage by schools across the South African affluence divide. Energy Res. Soc. Sci. **70**, 101692 (2020)

25. Gibberd, J.: Rapid identification and evaluation of interventions for improved water performance at South Africa schools. In: Smart Innovation, Systems and Technologies, Split, Croatia: Springer Science and Business Media Deutschland GmbH, pp. 173–182 (Dec. 2021)

26. Bishop, A., Fallis, C., Gleason, Maguire, C.B., Vass, T.: University of King's College Energy Audit: A Study of the School of Journalism Computer Labs, Nova Scotia, Canada, Apr. 2013

27. Cisco. Connecting Networks Companion Guide, vol. 1. Hoboken, New Jersey (USA): Cisco Press (2014)

28. Papavassiliou, S.: Software defined networking (SDN) and network function virtualization (NFV). Future Internet $12(1)$, 7 (2020)

29. Mell, P., Grance, T.: The NIST Definition of Cloud Computing National Institute of Standards and Technology Special Publication (NIST SP). Gaithersburg, MD, Oct. 2011

30. Azodolmolky, S., Wieder, P., Yahyapour, R.: Performance evaluation of a scalable software-defined networking deployment. In: 2013 Second European Workshop on Software Defined Networks, Berlin, Germany, pp. 68–74 (2013). https://doi.org/10.1109/EWSDN.2013.18

Re-thinking the Connectivity for Schools Within the Public Education System in South Africa

Tinashe Magwenzi⑩, Alfredo Terzoli⁽✉⁾⑩, and Zelalem Shibeshi⑩

Department of Computer Science, Rhodes University, Makhanda, South Africa
{a.terzoli,z.shibeshi}@ru.ac.za

Abstract. Despite government and industry efforts, internet connectivity in South African public schools located in rural and township areas remains unsatisfactory. What seems to be lacking is a 'virtuous' model for an efficient and practical solution that takes into account all important aspects relating to public schools and maps them into an appropriate network infrastructure. This paper presents a model, re-conceptualising a previous model for school and community connectivity called 'Broadband Island', developed and tested within the ICT4D long-term project known as Siyakhula Living Lab. In this model, schools belonging to an educational Circuit are connected via an overlay built on top of the network provided by a local Wireless Internet Service Provider (WISP). In this model, schools benefit from having access to the Internet efficiently (via statistical multiplexing of the Internet link), through interacting with each other at high speed without crossing the public Internet, as well as sharing common educational resources hosted by the WISP. The WISP, in turn, will benefit from having a solid and well-sized customer in the form of the provincial Department of Education. The community will also benefit because the revenue generated by the local WISP will remain in the community, helping further local economic development. Finally, the reliance on local operators, as opposed to a single, nationwide implementer, mitigates the risk of a single point of failure.

Keywords: School connectivity · Community networks · ICT infrastructures for marginalized areas · Wireless Internet Service Providers (WISPs) · Broadband Island · Private cloud for education · OpenStack · microstack · Software Defined Networks (SDN)

1 Introduction

Education is an integral part of human development and is intrinsically linked to the growth and well-being of a community, including its economy [6]. The right to learn is essential, regardless of socio-economic status or background. However, the less fortunate from low-income families and those living in underdeveloped areas often cannot enjoy such a fundamental right. Delivering quality education,

© ICST Institute for Computer Sciences, Social Informatics and Telecommunications Engineering 2025
Published by Springer Nature Switzerland AG 2025. All Rights Reserved
A. Sere et al. (Eds.): AFRICOMM 2023, LNICST 587, pp. 53–67, 2025.
https://doi.org/10.1007/978-3-031-81570-6_4

especially in low-income areas, primarily relies on the effectiveness of public schools. Many factors contribute to having a functional school, but one that is becoming increasingly important is its Information Communication Technology (ICT) infrastructure and its connection to the public Internet [21].

In this paper, we concentrate on the specifics of providing connection to the Internet to schools in marginalised areas of South Africa, i.e. townships and rural areas, and propose a model that leverages local resources to the benefit of both schools and the community hosting them. The model builds on previous work within a research initiative known as the Siyakhula Living Lab [10] and, in particular, the concept of Broadband Island developed and field tested there [22]. In essence, the Broadband Island is a wireless LAN implemented through WiMAX, an emerging technology at the time - now replaced by outdoor Wi-Fi, connecting schools in a specific geographic area. The Broadband Island was then connected to the Internet by whatever means available, which was a satellite connection in its original realisation within the Siyakhula Living Lab. The conceptualisation of the new model proposed in this paper is the result of more than one and a half years of direct daily experience with a local Wireless Internet Service Provider (WISP).

The paper is organised as follows. We first describe the typical infrastructure of a local WISP and report on the experience of its daily workings. Then we look at the state of the connectivity of public schools within the nearby local community and propose a model that the Education Department may use to provide Internet connectivity leveraging the presence of local WISP, illustrating the benefits for both schools and WISP.

2   Structure of a Typical Local WISP

Broadband connectivity for marginalised communities is mainly through mobile and fixed wireless connectivity [18]. In general, wired links are more robust and reliable, especially in the form of optical fibre, a technology spreading rapidly in South African urban areas. Wired links are costly to install, especially where the population density to be served is low, such as in rural areas or townships, and the area's geography is problematic. Because of that, small ISPs with a local footprint typically make use of wireless technologies that are not only cheaper but faster to roll out and easily deployable in an incremental fashion, shaped by actual demand. As a result, among the various possible technology choices, outdoor Wi-Fi is currently the most commonly used by local WISPs [11].

2.1   WISP Network Infrastructure

WISP networks are often referred to as fixed wireless communication because they connect fixed locations, such as a tower and a building. WISPs make use of the fixed wireless link to provide data communication used for Internet service to homes or businesses. The general structure of a Wireless ISP can be seen in Fig 1. The following description provides a brief overview of the various components and their respective functions.

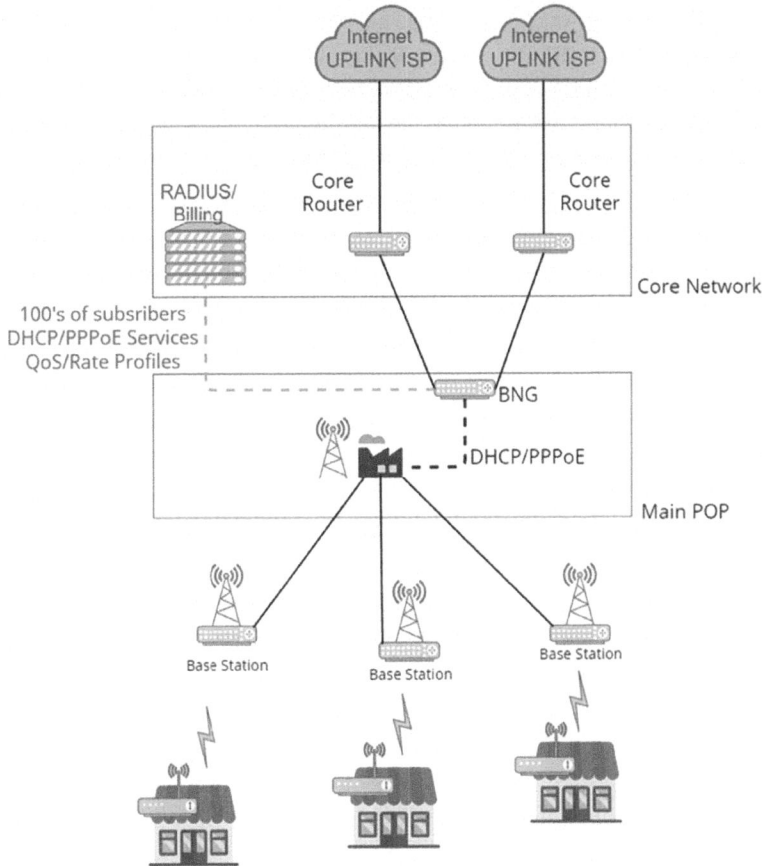

Fig. 1. ISP Network Diagram. Adapted from [1].

Core Network Infrastructure or Backbone: It comprises servers, routers, switches, and related networking equipment. This is where high-capacity data transmissions are supported, and it is where subscribers connect to the Internet.

Billing and Network Management System: This is a software component that tracks and manages the relationship between the customer and the business. It includes billing, customer services, and network management software. It maintains operations and supports customers' inquiries effectively. An example is Splynx, which features Radius to support services such as firewalls or queues to the Border Network Gateway (BNG).

Border Network Gateway (BNG): It provides functions for subscriber management and the allocating of IP addresses. As mentioned earlier, the gateway interacts with the Radius server, responsible for user authorization and termination. Radius server then grants users connectivity using Point-to-Point Protocol over Ethernet (PPPoE) [5] by assigning an IP address giving them access to the Internet. Within the PPPoE's architecture, the authentication and encryption of each user is maintained using the Point-to-Point Protocol, while the Ethernet protocol enables support for multiple users in a LAN. Typically, PPPoE consists of various elements such as servers, clients, hosts, and modems.

Customer Premises Equipment (CPE): This is the equipment located at the subscriber's premises. When the CPE is switched on, a PPPoE session is initiated, and the Radius server is contacted to authenticate and handle the assignment of an IP address. The equipment includes radios, routers, switches, and wireless devices. Customers typically connect to the Internet using the established PPPoE session through wireless devices, such as smartphones or laptops, or a wired one, such as a desktop.

Base Station: This is a hub that serves connectivity within a sub-location. It is the gateway between a cluster of customers' equipment and the backbone network. This is also referred to as the point of presence (POP) within a specific geographical location.

Backhaul Connection: It refers to the connection between base stations and the Internet backbone. It consists of high-capacity wired or wireless links, enabling the WISP to consolidate traffic and deliver high-speed service to subscribers.

2.2 Facilitating Inter-Connectivity in a WISP's Network

The architecture of an ISP network is designed to connect its subscribers with an uplink provider and manage Internet services. Packet flow is shaped and directed by routing devices to forward packets between networks. Routers share routing information using routing protocols. These protocols allow each router to maintain and advertise network links with adjacent routers. They also peer with uplink providers and are configured to advertise specific network prefixes to the public Internet and the ISP peers.

Typically, ISPs use a combination of interior gateway protocols (IGPs) and exterior gateway protocols (EGPs). IGPs exchange network reachability information within the ISP, while EGP exchange information routing information between peered ISPs.

Routing Within the WISP's Network. Routing is essential in an IP network. A router uses the routing table to make decisions. The development of a routing architecture is crucial and ensures that a startup WISP can provide the necessary performance, scalability, and resiliency for its subscribers [17]. Small WISPs commonly use Open Shortest Path First (OSPF) as their interior gateway protocol.

OSPF protocol is defined by RFC 2328 and RFC 5340 for IPv4 and IPv6, respectively [9, 16]. It broadcasts network topology information between neighbouring routers and dynamically calculates the best path for data packets to take [16].

WISP networks usually implement OSPF due to its support for hierarchical organisation. It enables the creation of different areas which facilitate the control of routing within and between different network sections. This approach improves scalability and faster convergence times in case of link failures or other network problems. Additionally, OSPF features to enhance network performance, offering features such as:

- Virtual links to connect non-contiguous OSPF areas
- Route summarising to minimise routing table sizes
- Traffic engineering to control and prioritise different types of traffic

In summary, using OSPF, WISPs can maintain fast and efficient data packet delivery and ensure that customers receive high-quality, reliable Internet service.

External Routing with Other ISP. External Border Gateway Protocol, eBGP [19] is often used in the peering with other ISPs allowing for communication between different autonomous systems (AS). It enables them to exchange routing information seamlessly between their respective networks.

ISPs advertise public network prefixes to other ASes. These ASes can advertise their prefixes to the ISP's network. This ensures that routing information is exchanged efficiently, and the best path for data packets is determined based on various attributes such as network delay, link cost, and the number of hops.

eBGP maintains a globally consistent routing policy, enabling ISPs to efficiently operate their networks and provide the required quality of service to their customers. Furthermore, ISPs can use various attributes, such as route maps and access lists, to define how and when specific routes will be learned and advertised.

Figure 2 shows how a small WISP utilises OSPF and eBGP. Internally, OSPF will map out paths, speeds, and reachability for network subnets. Since links are in the same broadcast domain (Area0), OSPF updates the routing table with the routes to loopbacks (towers) and routes to customers. eBGP is used to exchange routing information between different ASes and allows the filtering of this information.

Provisioning Service to Subscribers. Managing subscribers is a vital part of local WISPs' functions, and they naturally utilise a software framework, such as Splynx [2], designed particularly for Internet service providers and network administrators. Such software is deployed on a server to facilitate user connectivity to the Internet, provide network configuration management, and manage customer relationships. The Splynx framework, for example, includes a Splynx Radius server that supports point-to-point (PPPoE) connectivity between the ISP and consumer.

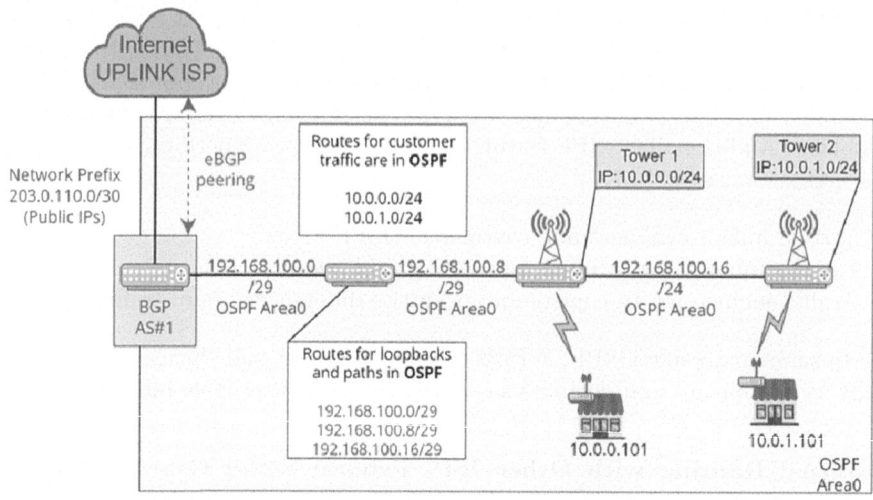

Fig. 2. Routing in an ISP. Adapted from [17]

3   Life Within a Typical South African WISP

In this section, we present one of the author's direct experiences working in a local WISP. Operating in a local WISP presents its own unique set of challenges. Day-to-day operations primarily involve setting up wireless connections, troubleshooting subscriber connectivity, managing network resources, and addressing customer queries and problems. Of course, ensuring proper maintenance is crucial and plays a vital role in delivering a positive user experience.

WISPs span a geographical area and have an influential physical component that therefore requires resources like vehicles and power tools for installation and maintenance. In general, wireless ISPs need to maintain high technical expertise, good communication, good customer service, and a willingness to learn and adapt to issues that may arise in the field.

The following subsections explore the main challenges met while working at a local South African WISP for over one and a half years. As far as we could ascertain, there is no literature on the challenges of small WISPs in South Africa. After widening the scope of the search, we found [12] which details the challenges of rural WISPs in the USA. Interestingly, the challenges reported are not very different from the ones directly experienced by us. We begin by looking at the technical issues, then move to concerns due to load-shedding in South Africa, and conclude by discussing organisational issues. We suggest mitigations for each of the listed points, drawing from our field experience.

3.1   Technical Issues

The challenges faced by each specific WISP may vary depending on factors such as location, network architecture, equipment used, and customer needs. Below are examples of Issues that are generally encountered:

Network Configuration Issues: Configuration changes may cause downtime, typically when a critical update is required. Setting up redundant links ensures service availability during these updates.

Hardware/Software Costs: The cost of obtaining critical hardware or software may be substantial, and deployment of services may be delayed due to budget constraints for acquiring new equipment. We saw that reusing spare old equipment saved us both time and money.

Equipment Failures and Connection Interruptions: Equipment failures at critical locations, like base stations, sometimes cause service disruptions. These failures may be caused by software or hardware faults. Sending messages to notify users about disconnections and scheduled maintenance lessens tension between the ISP and customers while the network is down.

Network Growth: The growth in the number of subscribers means an increase in network resource requirements. Setting a budget for development is necessary to avoid the degradation of the quality of service due to saturation on links. This may mean new equipment to upgrade capacity.

Wireless Limitations: Wireless equipment has limited range and capacity or is affected by environmental conditions. Investing in specialised equipment such as directional antennas, selecting frequencies with lower interference, and using appropriate radio frequency shielding ensures optimum operation.

Technical Personnel Shortage: The shortage of technical personnel may sometimes be unavoidable. Therefore, a proactive approach, such as automating processes, can bring more satisfactory service delivery for users.

Lack of Skills and Knowledge: This can impede the ability to swiftly address technical issues that interfere with the quality of service. Attending training and workshops is valuable and is a way to keep up with current trends and technologies.

In general, there must be sufficient technical force and resources for maintaining and running the network. As a WISP, local or not, it is expected to have high availability 'baked' into the operations as clients expect 24/7, 365 Internet connectivity.

3.2   Experience with Load-Shedding

Load shedding naturally harms the WISP space. Systems must be implemented or established to achieve a round-the-clock connection, as anticipated or desired by the customers. Experiences encountered concerning load-shedding can be summarised as follows.

Increase in Operational Costs: To ensure consistent service delivery, it is necessary to implement additional systems. This includes backup systems, generators, or solar systems. Remote monitoring systems can be expensive, but with the rise of open-source projects and the development of the Internet of Things (IOTs), building in-house solutions can save money and even allow the setting up of equipment tailored to your specific needs.

Battery-based Backup System Failure: Extended power cuts require backup systems to support 6 – 8 hr daily. This places strain on batteries due to an addition in charge cycles and prolonged discharging, meaning that batteries need to be replaced more often. Understanding battery chemistry and system requirements is essential. Specific batteries have limited discharge periods and decrease their capacity during prolonged discharging.

Equipment Failure: Power losses cause damage to electrical appliances and machinery or as a consequence of the sudden loss of power during write cycles. As a result, a device may not initialise properly when the electricity returns, thus causing service interruption.

Incidental Power Interruptions: Faults in power substations sometimes adds to the load-shedding-induced problems.

General Morale: consistent and extended power cuts can cause frustration and de-motivation among employees because of extra hours needed to keep services up. This means travelling to remote sites, re-fuelling generators, additional maintenance, and repairing equipment affected by power cuts.

In general, load shedding has brought an extra concern to deliver service efficiently to customers. To mitigate the impact of load shedding, it is critical to invest in backup power solutions to ensure uninterrupted service delivery to paying customers. Internet service providers need to plan towards a long-term solution to sustain connectivity during power cuts.

3.3   Organisational Issues

Finally, ISPs encounter various operational challenges that arise due to organisational issues. These issues include time management, inadequate resources, and miscommunication, which can potentially decrease productivity. Furthermore, limited awareness of corporate processes and performance can result in inefficiencies, missed opportunities, and a decline in morale. Addressing these challenges is crucial for enhancing the ISP's general productivity, performance, and income. These organisational issues can be reduced by:

– A well-defined strategy that will boost growth and help achieve long-term success.
– Ensuring that teams have the necessary training and resources.
– Making preparations for growth through appropriate budgeting.

4   Connectivity in Schools

We have given an insight into the general WISP operations internally and the issues faced by local WISPs. Let us examine the typical methods by which schools may connect to the Internet. The approaches to Internet connectivity in schools located in township communities may differ depending on the explicit situation. However, some common strategies include employing local community resources that offer free internet access, exploring other networking technologies, or implementing wireless internet connections designed for teaching and learning in rural schools. It is essential to note that specific models and strategies may differ based on the unique requirements and availability of resources in each community.

In theory, schools could subscribe to a service provider enabling Internet connection. But this is not always the case. In the report "Access Denied: Internet Access and the Right to Education in South Africa" we see that there are still a significant number of unconnected schools in townships and rural areas [23].

Even when schools are connected to the Internet, they operate independently of each other, even when they are located in close proximity and are part of the same education 'Circuit'. (In South Africa, a Circuit is the Department of Education's administrative zone demarcated for organising schools close to each other [7]). This is inefficient for several reasons: any communication and sharing of resources among them is routed through the Internet.

As these institutions share similar goals, it would be beneficial for them to be integrated into a single local network, allowing for more efficient communication and sharing of educational resources. The school Internet connection model we present in the next section does precisely this. Building an overlay over the network of a local WISP allows the construction of a specialised network that comprises all schools considered as an education Circuit.

5   Integrating Schools with an ISP

5.1   Broadband Island: Access Efforts for Low-Income Communities

The connectivity model mentioned above expands on the effort initiated by the Siyakhula Living Lab (SLL) to connect the unconnected [10]. As a living lab, the SLL focused on user-centered design in the structure, development, and implementation of Information and Communications Technology solutions that benefit local communities. The core artefact for the connectivity was the "Broadband Island": a high-speed wireless LAN, using WiMAX at its start in 2006, connecting groups of nearby schools [22]. The Broadband Island was connected to the Internet in a way suitable to the context. In the original implementation, in a deep rural area of South Africa in the Mbhashe municipality, the connection to the Internet was accomplished through geostationary satellites. From a technological point of view, WiMAX has been replaced by outdoor Wi-Fi, and Wi-Fi-based local WISPs have appeared and now have multiplied in South Africa. As a result, it was not difficult to see that the best way to implement the concept of Broadband Island in a commercially feasible manner is to rely on such WISPs, as will be detailed in the rest of this paper.

5.2   A Strategy for Fostering Digital Inclusion Among Marginalised Populations

The model we propose in this paper sees its viability through being beneficial to the various actors involved: the schools and, therefore, the Department of Education, on the one hand, and local WISPs, as small, medium and micro enterprises (SMMEs) and related communities, on the other. Schools need connectivity in a special form that transforms their geographical proximity into opportunities for better and more efficient collaboration. The Department of Education, naturally, needs to respond to that need as sustainably and efficiently as possible. For a WISP, presence in a community, i.e., POPs, potentially means an increase in customer base and improved business viability, especially if one of the customers is a large institution with matching finances, such as the Department of Education.

Selecting local WISPs to provide Internet connectivity has significant potential for local economic growth and is aligned with the spirit of the National Development Plan [3]. In particular, such a choice promotes SMMEs, given the fact that the majority of local WISPs are SMMEs. As mentioned in [8], the South African government acknowledges SMMEs for strategic importance in promoting inclusive economic growth, job creation, and its transformation agenda.

In the next subsections, we present our model in more detail, starting with a review of the advantages for the participants in the model and examining the model's key components, significance, and potential impact.

5.3   The Requirements for Integration in the New Model

As mentioned above, in the model, there are two primary participants: the WISP and the schools, each of them with their own needs. Schools aim to have access to information that enriches the student learning experience. Access to the Internet further enables effective communication and collaboration between teachers, students, and parents. Moreover, the Internet allows for the sharing of educational resources, including videos, presentations, and other materials, that complement traditional teaching methods. There are many open-source learning platforms and resources that are found to improve the success of learners, especially for resource-constrained communities. As mentioned in [15], the increase in the growth of users of Khan Academy shows the hunger for quality online learning resources, especially in maths. As a country with a dire need for a solution to the problem of students' maths results, schools will benefit from any form of online or offline resources like Khan Academy.

WISPs, on the other hand, aim to enhance network performance, expand customer reach, and network resiliency, among others. A better and more efficient network means better service delivery and reduced downtimes. For WISPs, the location of their base stations/POP is affected by the proximity to their existing and/or target users, the infrastructure or means for connectivity, the availability of power, and the ease of access. Security is also important.

In general, looking at the requirements for both the WISP and schools, we see that both parties provide something for the needs of the other, and they can benefit from it if they agree to work together. Consider the WISP. They require a location that can provide security, has electricity, is easily accessible, and is strategically positioned near potential users, which schools can provide. On the other hand, schools require connectivity and a local platform for students, teachers, and parents to share educational services.

5.4 Schools/ISP Integration

A collaboration between a WISP and local schools leads to establishing a new Internet infrastructure. This infrastructure enables schools to communicate with each other directly without crossing the public Internet. This can be accomplished by establishing logical connections between the schools, which become part of the WISP's network. The resulting concept is an overlay network, as shown in Fig 3. From the ISP's perspective, the schools are seen as a subnetwork within the network.

The solution we propose employs Software Defined Networking (SDN) to aid in efficiently tracking and configuring network resources, allowing the ISP to effectively manage the complexity and cater to the specific needs of both their customers and the schools. SDN enables the creation of an overlay network that sits atop the existing networking infrastructure. One of the key advantages of SDN is its ability to dynamically adapt the network state based on the specific nature of network traffic, effectively catering to the unique needs of schools and customers.

Implementing an overlay network through a Software Defined Network architecture, such as that commonly used for multi-home visual sharing [14], can further enhance the flexibility, functionality, minimise maintenance and configuration needs while future-proofing the proposed model and enhancing user experience by deploying application services that adapt to changing network traffic requirements. Figure 4 shows the interconnecting between two school networks by leveraging SDN technology. The gateway router receives traffic and enforces decisions based on the traffic engineering rules set by the controller. The traffic is then forwarded accordingly to other routers in the WISP network thereby allowing traffic coordination between schools and the rest of the WISP network.

As part of the school/WISP integration, we propose that the local WISP hosts MicroStack [4], an open-source project with an interesting history [20].

MicroStack allows the schools to deploy a private cloud environment in the local WISP headquarters. It doesn't require costly infrastructure, rendering it a cost-effective solution for schools with tight budgets. Teachers, students and administrators would be able to create virtual learning environments, share resources, and host collaborative spaces where students can work together on projects and assignments. Additionally, using MicroStack, schools can create personal learning facilities, for teachers to provide students with more individualised attention to cater to specific learning needs.

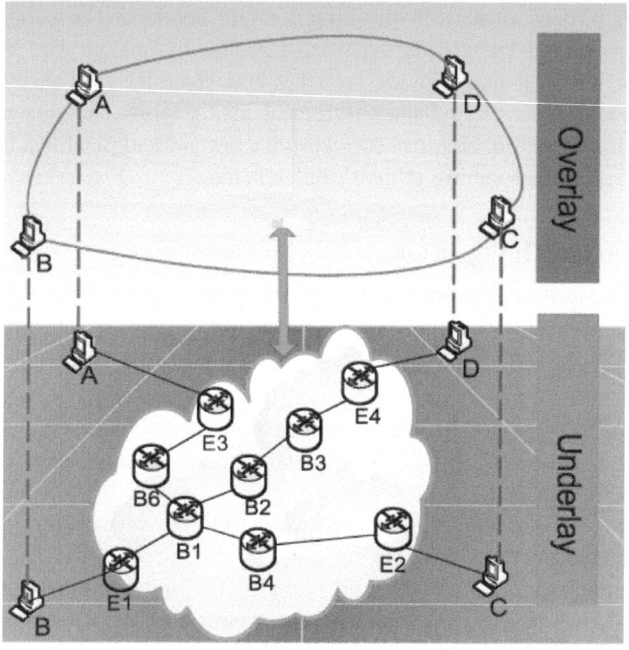

Fig. 3. Overlay Network [13].

5.5   Benefits of School/WISP Integration

The benefits of integrating schools with a local WISP network are many-fold. The main advantage for schools and indirectly for the WISP is the faster and generally more reliable data delivery since all traffic is destined for a local point, such as another school in the WISP's school network overlay. This results in much lower latency for data communication and a better user experience, especially for real-time services such as distributed synchronous video lectures. The architecture, keeping local traffic local and multiplexing the traffic exiting the school network overlay, also reduces the total amount of the traffic on the more costly WISP

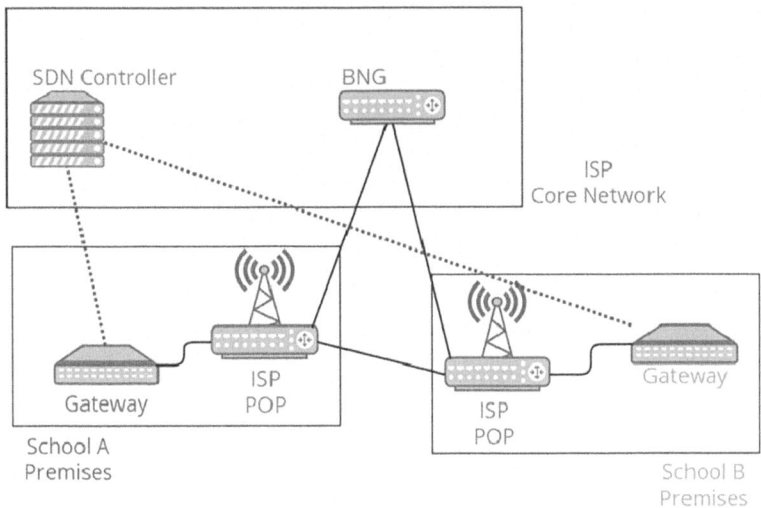

Fig. 4. An SDN-enabled school-networking environment with an SDN Controller connecting to each school gateway. The controller and Gateways coordinate inter-school and intra-school networking, respectively.

uplink to the Internet, allowing the connection of more schools with only a marginal need to increase capacity on that link.

For the local WISP, the partnership with the Department of Education for the management of school traffic will inject capacity, resources, and revenue into its business, directly benefiting the economy of the community of which the schools are part, given the local nature of the WISP. If used effectively, the additional resources gained by connecting schools can enhance the quality of service delivered by the WISP, increasing its stability and capacity to address the earlier-listed challenges. This, in turn, can attract more customers, potentially initiating a 'virtuous circle' that fosters WISP growth and extends connectivity to more homes.

The community itself, of course, will benefit from the presence of a more robust WISP. In particular, such a WISP could potentially increase its points of presence to remote locations to connect remote schools on behalf of the Department of Education, thus making it possible for private homes in that area to connect to the Internet. This would help with the general effort of spreading broadband connectivity in marginalised communities of South Africa.

6   Conclusion

In this paper, we presented a model for Internet connectivity for public schools in South Africa. The model is an evolution of a previous model conceptualised with the Siyakhula Living Lab and proposes the construction of an overlay network for the schools administered by a specific education Circuit in the network of a local WISP. The model might be able to change the unsatisfactory situation of Internet connectivity in public schools, even after more than two decades of attempts by the government to solve the problem.

References

1. The netElastic homepage. https://netelastic.com/elastic-solutions-home/wisp/. Accessed 20 Jun 2023
2. The SPLYNX homepage. https://docs.splynx.com/. Accessed 20 Jun 2023
3. National Development Plan 2030 — South African Government. https://www.gov. za/issues/national-development-plan-2030. Accessed 20 Jun 2023
4. Openstack for the edge, micro clouds and developers. https://microstack.run/. Accessed 18 Aug 2023
5. Carrel, D., Evarts, J., Lidl, K., Mamakos, L.A., Simone, D., Wheeler, R.: A Method for Transmitting PPP Over Ethernet (PPPoE). RFC 2516 (1999). https://doi.org/ 10.17487/RFC2516, https://www.rfc-editor.org/info/rfc2516
6. De Atayde Moschen, S., Macke, J., Bebber, S., da Silva, M.: Sustainable development of communities: ISO 37120 and un goals. Int. J. Sustain. High. Educ. **20** (2019). https://doi.org/10.1108/IJSHE-01-2019-0020
7. Department of Basic Education: The policy on the organisation roles and responsibilities of education districts (2013). https://www.education.gov.za/LinkClick. aspx?fileticket=F4jE1wmNQeA%3D. Accessed 20 Jun 2023
8. Department of Small Business Development: National integrated small enterprise development (NISED) masterplan (2022). http://www.dsbd.gov.za/sites/default/ files/legislation/Government_Gazette_0.pdf
9. Ferguson, D., Lindem, A., Moy, J.: OSPF for IPv6. RFC 5340 (2008). https://doi. org/10.17487/RFC5340, https://www.rfc-editor.org/info/rfc5340
10. Gumbo, S., Thinyane, H., Thinyane, M., Terzoli, A., Hansen, S.: Living lab methodology as an approach to innovation in ICT4D: The siyakhula living lab experience (2012)
11. Hameed, A., Mian, A.N., Qadir, J.: Low-cost sustainable wireless Internet service for rural areas. Wireless Netw. **24**(5), 1439–1450 (2016). https://doi.org/10.1007/ s11276-016-1415-8
12. Hasan, S., Ben-David, Y., Bittman, M., Raghavan, B.: The challenges of scaling wisps. In: Proceedings of the 2015 Annual Symposium on Computing for Development, pp. 3–11. DEV '15, Association for Computing Machinery, New York, NY, USA (2015). https://doi.org/10.1145/2830629.2830637
13. Ijaz, H., Welzl, M., Jamil, B.: A survey and comparison on overlay-underlay mapping techniques in peer-to-peer overlay networks. Int. J. Commun. Syst. **32**, e3872 (2019). https://doi.org/10.1002/dac.3872
14. Jo, J., Lee, S., Kim, J.: Software-defined home networking devices for multi-home visual sharing. IEEE Trans. Consum. Electron. **60**, 534–539 (2014). https://doi. org/10.1109/TCE.2014.6937340
15. Kelly, D.: What do we know about khan academy? A review of the literature and justification for further study (2016). https://doi.org/10.13140/RG.2.1.2462.5044
16. Moy, J.: OSPF Version 2. RFC 2328 (1998). https://doi.org/10.17487/RFC2328, https://www.rfc-editor.org/info/rfc2328
17. Myers, K.: Starting a WISP: guide to selecting a routing architecture (2020). https://stubarea51.net/2020/03/03/starting-a-wisp-guide-to-selecting-a-routing-architecture/

18. Omer, N.: Analysing South Africa's Internet Performance 2022 (2022). https:// researchictafrica.net/publication/analysing-south-africas-internet-performance-2022/
19. Rekhter, Y., Hares, S., Li, T.: A Border Gateway Protocol 4 (BGP-4). RFC 4271 (2006). https://doi.org/10.17487/RFC4271, https://www.rfc-editor. org/info/rfc4271
20. Ruiz, A.: A brief history of MicroStack. Ubuntu (2023). https://ubuntu.com/blog/ k8s-native-microstack
21. Sithomola, T.: The manifestation of dual socioeconomic strata within the south African schooling system. Afr. J. Public Aff. **12**(3), 104–126 (2021). https://doi.org/10.10520/ejc-ajpa_v12_n3_a7, https://journals.co.za/doi/abs/10. 10520/ejc-ajpa_v12_n3_a7
22. Terzoli, A., Siebörger, I., Gumbo, S.: Community broadband islands' for digital government access in rural south Africa (2017)
23. University of Chicago Law School - Global Human Rights Clinic: Access Denied: Internet Access and the Right to Education in South Africa. Global Human Rights Clinic **1** (2020). https://chicagounbound.uchicago.edu/ghrc/1/

Deep Learning Approaches for Object Detection in Autonomous Driving: Smart Cities Perspective

Othman O. Khalifa[1], Hariz Naufal Mohd Daud[1], Elmustafa Sayed Ali[2,3(✉)], and Mamoon M. Saeed[4]

[1] Department of Electrical and Computer Engineering, Kulliyyah of Engineering, International Islamic University Malaysia, Kuala Lumpur, Malaysia
[2] Department of Electronics Engineering, Sudan University of Science and Technology (SUST), Khartoum, Sudan
elmustafasayed@gmail.com
[3] Department of Electrical and Electronics Engineering, Red Sea University (RSU), Port Sudan, Sudan
[4] Department of Communications and Electronics Engineering, Faculty of Engineering, University of Modern Sciences (UMS), Sana'a, Yemen

Abstract. Object detection has been a key feature of autonomous driving. Autonomous driving is believed to be the solution to the hike in accidents. To develop an object detection model for an autonomous vehicle in smart cities, a few methods were identified by research and studies. Deep learning algorithm that uses artificial neural networks to replace brain functions can perform sophisticated computations on large amounts of data. From the various methods and algorithms available, the performance of each model will vary for each study. This study aims to investigate and identify the best algorithm for detecting objects in smart cities based on deep learning. The chosen algorithm, You Only Look Once (YOLOv5) is then used to build an object detection model with a driving dataset in a framework. The performance of the model trained will then be evaluated and the results will be analyzed. One of the performance evaluation metrics included in this study is the Mean Average Precision (mAP) which will be compared to a few other object detection models.

Keywords: Object detection · autonomous driving · smart cities · deep learning · YOLOv5

1 Introduction

Accidents are highly likely to occur every day in our daily lives, generally more than 80% due to human error according to the Malaysian Institute of Road Safety Research (MIROS) (The Sun Daily, 18, February 2015). As autonomous vehicles are a solution, a connection with smart cities with more sensors and instruments results in smarter

A. Sere et al. (Eds.): AFRICOMM 2023, LNICST 587, pp. 68–80, 2025.
https://doi.org/10.1007/978-3-031-81570-6_5

and more intelligent technology [1]. In a smart city, two-way communication between autonomous vehicles and the data from the cities could vastly improve the current mobility and even the vehicles themselves. However, the challenges of connecting the technologies to replace a function of the human brain with the ability to recognize an object and respond to it is something that needs to be considered [2]. The requirements of autonomous driving to be reliable and accurate in detection and recognition lead towards the deep learning application. Deep learning which consists of an artificial neural network is used to replace the ability of humans to process data, initiate decision-making, create patterns and act as much as a human. The development of deep learning is currently reaching a level where they can learn unsupervised from data that is unlabeled or unstructured [3].

2 Methodology

In this research, the latest object detection algorithm of You Only Look Once (YOLO) was trained to detect vehicles. As a computer vision practitioner, the application of the algorithm, data acquisition and data annotation were the focus.

2.1 Objects Design

There were 12 objects focused on this study. As the model was developed for an autonomous vehicle in smart cities, the objects were related to the surroundings and environment of the vehicle. The objects were bikers, cars, pedestrians, stop signs, traffic lights, green traffic lights, green-left traffic lights, red traffic lights, red-left traffic lights, yellow traffic lights, yellow-left traffic lights, and trucks.

2.2 Proposed Algorithm

The usage of convolutional neural networks was chosen because of their simplicity. A range of pre-trained models that can be modified for a variety of tasks are available. They're also readily available, low-cost to compute, and have acceptable performance characteristics [4]. Object recognition systems from the YOLO family have been demonstrated to outperform other target identification algorithms in vehicle detection tests. YOLOv5 has been shown to improve the processing time of deeper networks significantly. When the project expands to larger datasets and real-time detection, this attribute will become more important [5]. YOLOv5 is written in PyTorch in the initial release instead of PJ Reddie's Darknet. With a better-established ecosystem of PyTorch, support for the implementation is simpler while deployment is easier. Even though Darknet is a flexible research framework, due to a smaller community of users and not being for the production environment, it will create some challenges and less-production ready. Besides that, YOLOv5 is used in this research for its fast and accuracy which is a vital factor for detecting objects for autonomous vehicles instantly and precisely.

For the YOLOv5 model, as it is a single-stage object detector, it has three important parts; refer to Fig. 1 like any other single-stage object detector as below:

1. Model Backbone

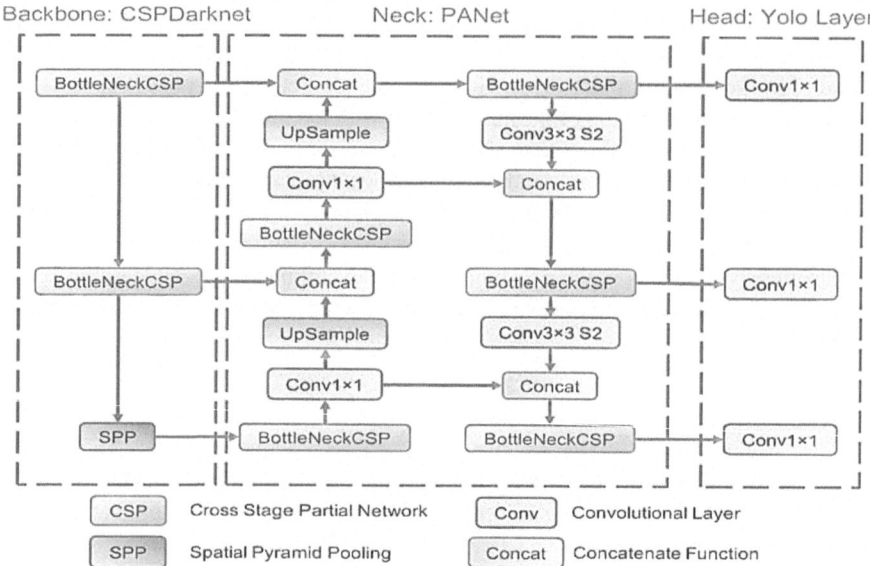

Fig. 1. The network architecture of Yolov5. It consists of three parts: (1) Backbone: CSP Darknet, (2) Neck: PANet, and (3) Head: Yolo Layer.

2. Model Neck
3. Model Head

Model Backbone is mainly used to extract important features from the given input image. In YOLOv5 the CSP—Cross Stage Partial Networks are used as a backbone to extract rich informative features from an input image. CSPNet has shown significant improvement in processing time with deeper networks.

Model Neck is mainly used to generate feature pyramids. Feature pyramids help models to generalise well on object scaling [6]. It helps to identify the same object with different sizes and scales. Feature pyramids are very useful, and help models to perform well on unseen data. Other models use different types of feature pyramid techniques like FPN, BiFPN, PANet, etc. In YOLOv5, the PANet is used as a neck to get feature pyramids. The model Head is mainly used to perform the final detection part. It applied anchor boxes on features and generated final output vectors with class probabilities, objectness scores, and bounding boxes. In YOLOv5 model head is the same as the previous YOLOv3 and YOLOv4 versions [7].

2.3 System Dataset

The Udacity Self Driving Car dataset was used to train YOLOv5, which is a large open-source dataset for object detection, segmentation, and labelling. It is readily available and becomes a choice to save some precious time rather than collecting data and annotating manually [8]. There are nearly 15,000 tagged photos in this collection, with 11 different classes, including cars and trucks. All images are in a resolution of 1920x1200. As a result, YOLOv5 can be used to detect objects as is, or as a starting point for an adjusted model to detect features such as the front and back of the objects.

2.4 Adopted Framework and Tools

Google Colab or Collaboratory, a popular product of Google research provides access for anyone to write and execute arbitrary Python code just by using the browser. It is a purposely built environment and well suited for machine or deep learning, data analysis as well and education. This free-to-use environment is a Jupyter Notebook environment that requires no setup and runs entirely in the cloud. Artificial intelligence and deep learning are a long-life study [9]. The researchers develop and train their models using the Python language. Therefore, all codes were done in Google Colab and were written using Python.

PyTorch is a framework that has two data primitives that enable work with both pre-loaded datasets and your data. The samples and their labels are stored in Dataset, and Data Loader wraps an expected around the Dataset to make it easy to access the samples. To load the Udacity dataset into the environment, PyTorch was used.

Lastly, the visualization tool to provide the measurements and visualizations needed for the deep learning workflow used was Tensor Board. The tool allows the tracking of performance metrics of the model such as accuracy and loss, visualizing the model graph as well as projecting embedding's to a lower-dimensional space [10].

2.5 Training of the Proposed Model

Before the training of the model started, the YOLOv5 repository by Ultralytics Company was cloned into the environment by a few lines of code. Once the cloning process was done, the dependencies such as torch and IPython were installed. Next, the dataset was downloaded and loaded in PyTorch format from the Roboflow website including the YAML file defining the test and train data location. The YAML file then writes the parameters like the number of classes, anchors and each layer [11]. When everything was successfully prepared, the training was initiated at an initial of 50 epochs and gradually increased up to 200 epochs. The training took some time to complete as it depends on the resources of the Graphic Processing Unit (GPU) and Random-Access Memory (RAM) from Google Colab.

2.6 Evaluating the Proposed Model

After a few hours, the training stopped at 200 epochs and Tensor-Board was launched to visualize the performance metrics of the model. A few graphs were shown indicating the Mean Average Precision (mAP), Precision and Recall values as well as losses in box, classification and object. Besides that, the ground truth of the data also was checked to identify potential flaws in the data [12]. From the trained weights, a few video inputs were run as the inference or test for the model. The results will be discussed further in the next section.

3   Results and Discussion

The object detection model was initially trained for 20 epochs and gradually increased over 200 epochs for a better result. It took approximately 3 h and 17 min, efficiently making use of a Python 3 Google Compute Engine Backend (GPU) computing power provided by the Google Colab. During each epoch, the confidence metric improved over time, making detection closer to perfect [13, 14]. Once the training starts, the training images, labels and augmentation effects can be visualized for the ground truth to be observed. Below is the figure; refer to Fig. 2 showing the ground truth training data for the model.

The next figure; refers to Fig. 3 showing the augmented training example from our dataset. The augmentation was done during the pre-processing of the dataset which has the objective of preventing the YOLOv5 network from learning irrelevant patterns from our dataset and essentially boosting the overall performance. It will add slightly modified copies of already existing data to increase the amount of data then lead to a better prediction accuracy [15].

Fig. 2.   Ground truth training data

Through this visualization, it is a vital process to both identify potential flaws in the ground truth labels, as well as to look for insights that will guide the model development. Thus, visualizing the training data is the foundation of every successful deep-learning project [16]. Once the training ended with the visualization and validation of ground truth training data, the performance of the model was evaluated by running some code to launch the Tensorboard. Training losses and performance metrics were saved to Tensorboard and a log file when we trained the model. The results file was plotted as a PNG file after training was completed.

The first metric was the Mean Average Precision (mAP) graph which is a popular metric in measuring the accuracy of a model. It does compute the average precision value for recall value over 0 to 1. Precision measures how accurate are the predictions while Recall measures how well the detector finds all the positives. From the figure below;

Fig. 3. Ground truth augmented training data

refer to Fig. 4, the mAP for intersection over Union (IoU) threshold of 0.5 obtained was initially at 25.08% for 20 epochs training. For 200 epochs, the mAP valued at 60.36% which indicates that the accuracy improves a lot for this model.

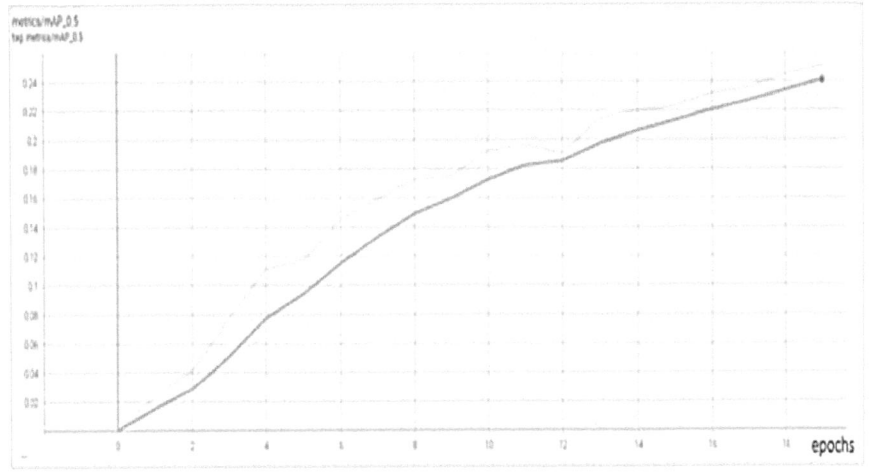

Fig. 4. mAP for IoU of 0.5 for 20 epochs

While for the mAP for the IoU threshold of 0.5 to 0.95; refer to Fig. 5 and Fig. 6, it gave a value of 11.36% for 20 epochs and 30.64% for 200 epochs training. From both mAP graphs, it can be observed that the 200 epochs training showed a smoother and linearly interpolated graph which indicates a better performance of the model. From the precision graphs below; refer to Fig. 7 and Fig. 8, it can be observed that 200 epochs training was more precise in every epoch. However, the graph was a little bit overfitted as the dataset is quite small compared to the training epochs. To overcome this, more data will be needed and prepared in the custom driving dataset in Kuala Lumpur.

Meanwhile, the Recall curves; refer to Fig. 9 and Fig. 10 also seem a little bit overfitted for 200 epochs but overall, the recall curve of 200 epochs was better than the 20 epochs curve.

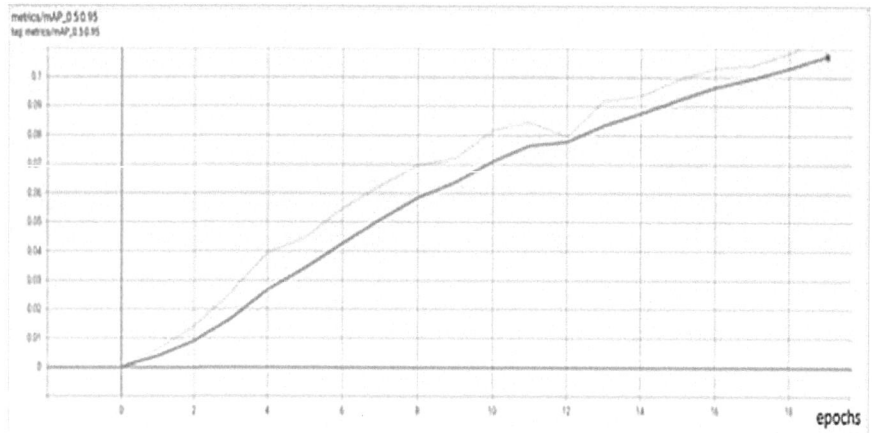

Fig. 5. mAP for IoU of 0.5 to 0.95 for 20 epochs

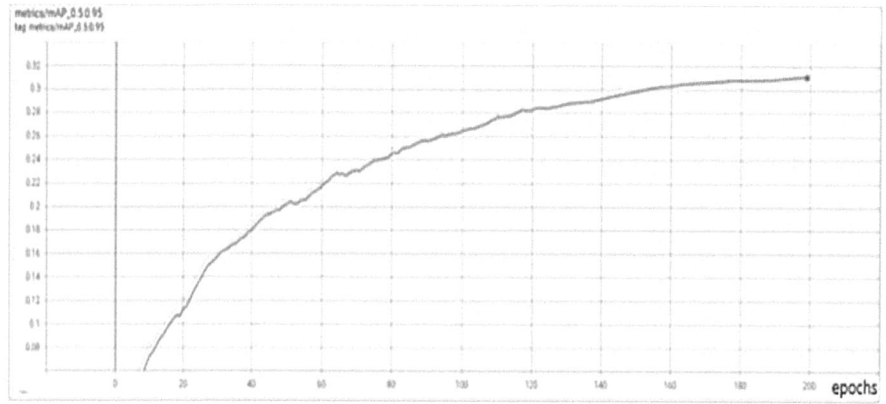

Fig. 6. mAP for IoU of 0.5 to 0.95 for 200 epochs

Comparing both figures, the bounding box loss, classification loss as well and object loss improve a lot as the loss value decreases a lot; refer to Fig. 11 and Fig. 12. The box loss indicates how well the algorithm can detect the centre of the object and how well the predicted bounding box encompasses it. Objectness is a probability measure for the presence of an object in a proposed region of interest. If the objectivity is high, the image window is likely to have an object in it. The algorithm's classification loss indicates how

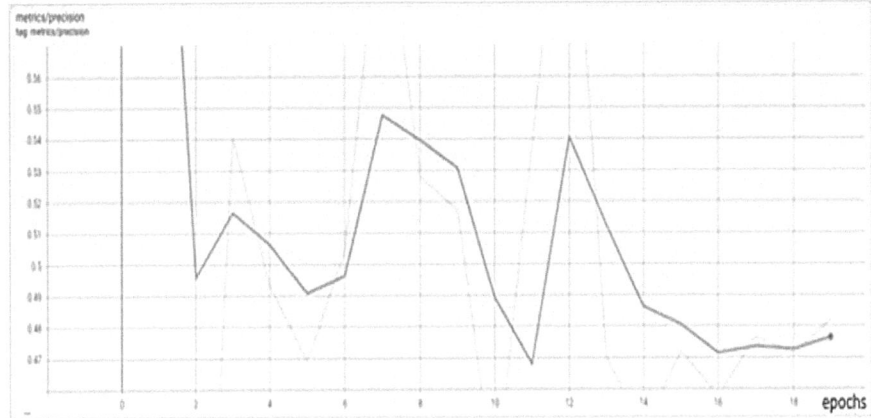

Fig. 7. Precision values for 20 epochs

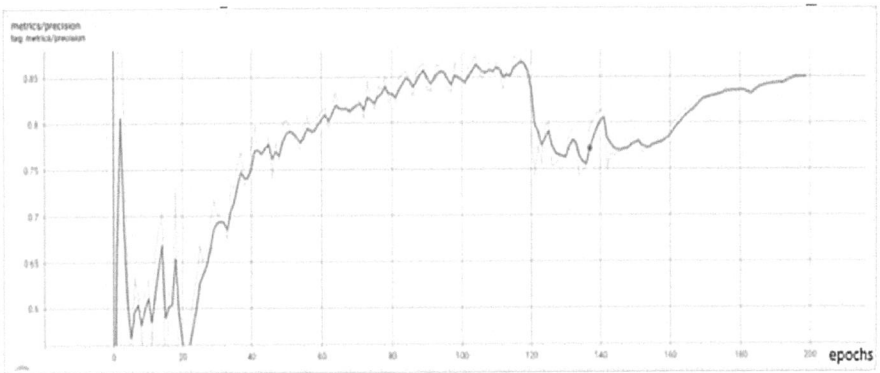

Fig. 8. Precision values for 200 epochs

effectively it can predict the proper class of a given object (Kasper-ulcers et al., 2021). Precision, recall, and mean average precision all improved rapidly before plateauing after roughly 150 epochs. The validation data's box, objectness, and classification losses likewise showed a significant drop until around 150 epochs.

The evaluation on YOLO using real-time data sets is summarized through an example in Fig. 12 and Fig. 13. Here in the first figure; refer to Fig. 13, the biker was successfully detected but it also detects it as a car. As for the cars, some of the cars were undetected by the model. However, in the second trained model; refer to Fig. 14, all the cars and the bikers were successfully correctly detected and true positive. This shows that the accuracy improves and it benefits the purpose of this project to detect objects for autonomous driving.

Based on the evaluation of the models trained, the model with better mAP, Precision and Recall value as well as lower losses of box, classification and object should be used

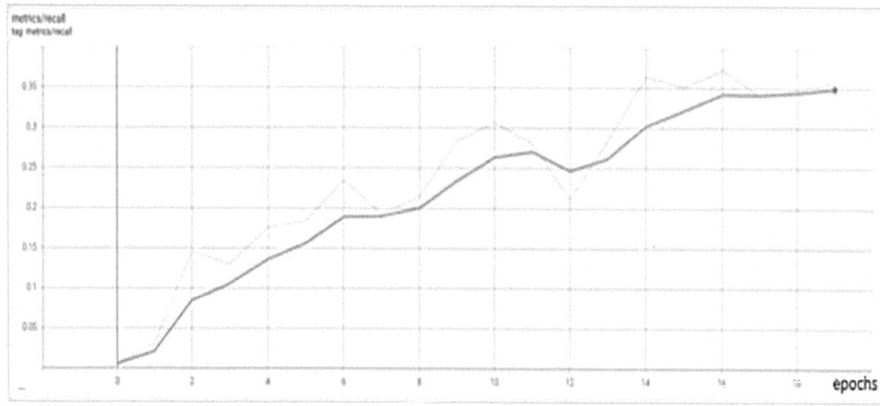

Fig. 9. Recall values for 20 epochs

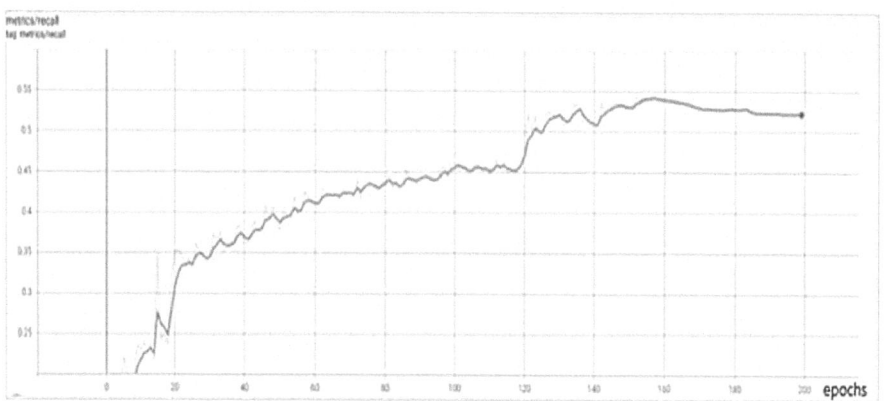

Fig. 10. Recall values for 200 epochs

for object detection model for autonomous driving [17]. With the trained and evaluated model, the object detection model was then compared to some existing solutions (Faramarzi, 2020) [18]. The table below shows the comparison with a model trained for autonomous driving using YOLO. From Table 1 above, it can be concluded that the YOLOv5 network in this study performs well and obtained a better Mean Average Precision compared to the other models trained. Even though the result obtained was improved, room for improvement is still available to increase the accuracy of the model. Besides that, the FPS for the YOLOv5 object detection model was higher than the others. From this comparison, YOLOv5 is a model that is suited for an autonomous vehicle.

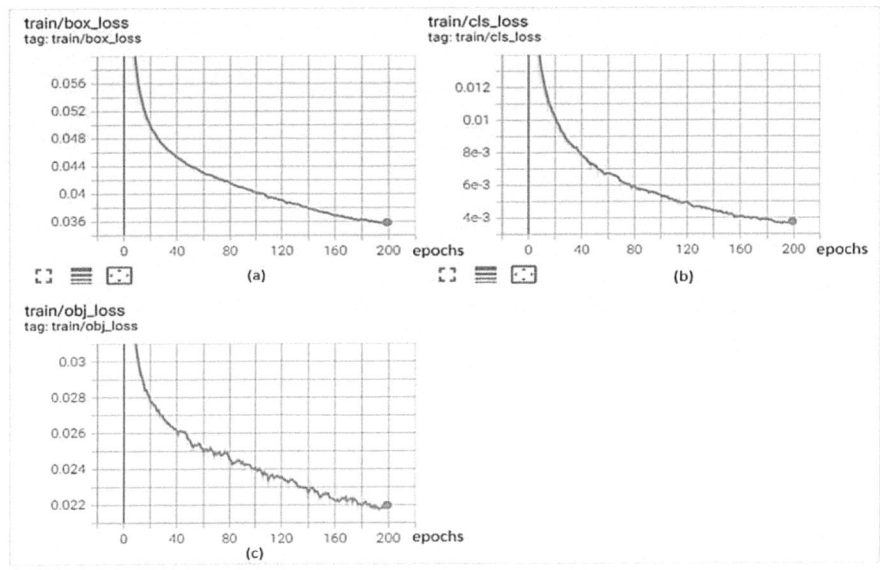

Fig. 11. Losses metrics for 20 epochs

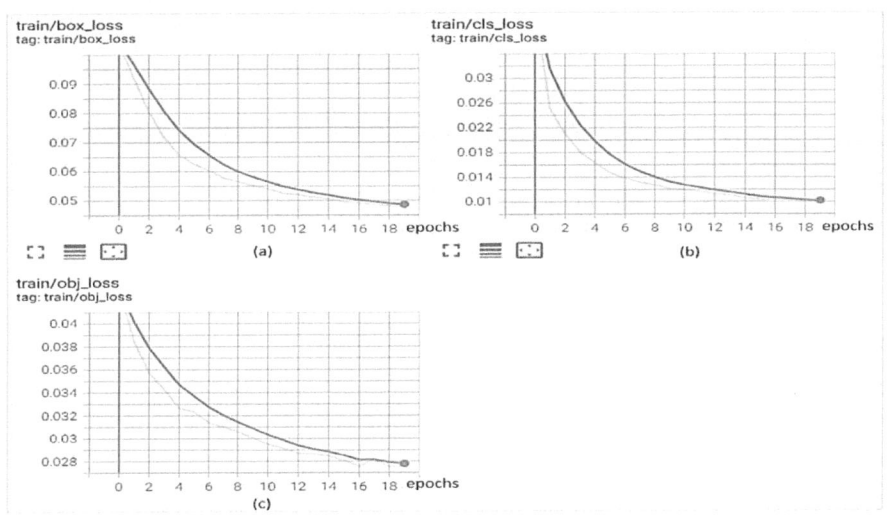

Fig. 12. Losses metrics for 200 epochs

Fig. 13. Inference on 20 epoch's model

Fig. 14. Inference on 200 epoch's model

Table 1. Comparison of YOLO object detection model

Model	Dataset	mAP	FPS
YOLOv2- 608x608	COCO	48.1	40
YOLOv3–608	COCO	57.9	20
YOLOv3	Udacity	28.19	32
YOLOv4	Udacity	41.46	45

4   Conclusion

YOLO is announced as one of the most promising detection systems using neural networks. This study investigates the best algorithm and the development of the object detection model for an autonomous vehicle in smart cities. By performing a comprehensive analysis of the YOLOv5 network over the Udacity dataset, it was discovered that YOLO can achieve 61% precision with 50% recall at 58 frames per second. The results are encouraging and suggest that YOLO is an excellent model for detecting objects required for autonomous driving systems. Further improvements may be made from time to time following the growth of the technology in this decade and improve the speed and accuracy.

References

1. Alatabani, L.E., Ali, E.S., Saeed, R.A.: Deep learning approaches for IoV applications and services. In: Magaia N., Mastorakis G., Mavromoustakis C., Pallis E., Markakis E.K. (eds.) Intelligent Technologies for Internet of Vehicles. Internet of Things (Technology, Communications, and Computing). Springer, Cham (2021). https://doi.org/10.1007/978-3-030-764 93-7

2. Ali, E.S., Hassan, M.B., Saeed, R.A.: Machine learning technologies on internet of vehicles. In: Magaia N., Mastorakis G., Mavromoustakis C., Pallis E., Markakis E.K. (eds.) Intelligent Technologies for Internet of Vehicles. Internet of Things (Technology, Communications, and Computing). Springer, Cham (2021). https://doi.org/10.1007/978-3-030-76493-7

3. Alqurashi, F.A., Alsolami, F., Abdel-Khalek, S., Sayed Ali, E., Saeed, R.A.: 'Machine learning techniques in internet of UAVs for smart cities applications'. J. Intell. Fuzzy Syst. **42**(4), 1–24 (2021). https://doi.org/10.3233/JIFS-211009

4. Arie, L.G., PhD.: The practical guide for Object Detection with YOLOv5 algorithm. Medium (2022, April 1). https://towardsdatascience.com/the-practical-guide-for-object-det ection-with-yolov5-algorithm-74c04aac4843

5. Khan, A., et al.: PackerRobo: model-based robot vision self-supervised learning in CART. Alexandria Eng. J. **61**(12), 12549–12566 (2022).https://doi.org/10.1016/j.aej.2022.05.043

6. Hassan, M. B., Ahmed, E S., Saeed, R.A.: Machine learning for industrial IoT systems. In: Zhao, J., Vinoth Kumar, V. (eds.) Handbook of Research on Innovations and Applications of AI, IoT, and Cognitive Technologies, pp. 336–358. Hershey, PA: IGI Global, 2021. https://doi.org/10.4018/978-1-7998-6870-5.ch023

7. Xu, Q., Zhu, Z., Ge, H., Zhang, Z., Zang, X.: Effective face detector based on YOLOv5 and superresolution reconstruction. Comput. Math. Methods Med. **16**(2021), 7748350 (2021). https://doi.org/10.1155/2021/7748350.PMID:34824599;PMCID:PMC8610656

8. Taye, M.M.: Understanding of machine learning with deep learning: architectures, workflow, applications and future directions. Computers **12**, 91 (2023). MDPI

9. Elmustafa, S.A., et al.: machine learning technologies for secure vehicular communication in internet of vehicles: recent advances and applications. Wiley-Hindawi, J. Secur. Commun. Netw. (SCN) **2021**, 8868355 (2021), https://doi.org/10.1155/2021/8868355

10. Faramarzi, M.: Road Damage Detection and Classification Using Deep Neural Networks (YOLOv4) with Smartphone Images (2020). https://doi.org/10.13140/RG.2.2.21734.65602

11. Gadal, S., Mokhtar, R., Abdelhaq, M., Alsaqour, R., Ali, E.S., Saeed, R.: Machine learning-based anomaly detection using K-mean array and sequential minimal optimization. Electronics **11**, 2158 (2022). https://doi.org/10.3390/electronics11142158

12. Hameed, S.A., et al.: Framework for enhancement of image guided surgery: Finding area of tumor volume. Aust. J. Basic Appl. Sci. **6**(1), 9–16 (2012)

13. Kasper-Eulaers, M., Hahn, N., Berger, S., Sebulonsen, T., Myrland, Ø., Kummervold, P.: Short communication: detecting heavy goods vehicles in rest areas in winter conditions using YOLOv5. Algorithms. **14**, 114 (2021). https://doi.org/10.3390/a14040114

14. Khalifa, O.O., et al.: An IoT-platform-based deep learning system for human behavior recognition in smart city monitoring using the Berkeley MHAD datasets. Systems **10**, 177 (2022). https://doi.org/10.3390/systems10050177

15. Ahmed, K.E.B., Mokhtar, R.A., Saeed, R.A.: A new method for fast image histogram calculation. In: International Conference on Computing, Control, Networking, Electronics and Embedded Systems Engineering (ICCNEEE), pp. 187–192, Khartoum, Sudan (2015)
16. Anatabine, L.E., Elmustafa, S.A., Mokhtar, R.A., Saeed, R.A., Alhumyani, H., Hasan, M.K.: Deep and reinforcement learning technologies on internet of vehicle (IoV) applications: current issues and future trends. J. Adv. Trans. **2022**, Article ID 1947886, 16 (2022). https://doi.org/10.1155/2022/1947886
17. Mansour, R.F., Alfar, N.M., Abdel-Khalek, S., Abdelhaq, M., Saeed, R.A., Alsaqour, R.: Optimal deep learning-based fusion model for biomedical image classification. Expert Syst. **39**(1), 34–54 (2021). https://doi.org/10.1111/exsy.12764
18. Faramarzi, M.: Road damage detection and classification using deep neural networks (YOLOv4) with smartphone images (June 15, 2020). Available at SSRN: https://ssrn.com/abstract=3627382. https://doi.org/10.2139/ssrn.3627382

ICT Infrastructures for Critical Environmental Conditions

Internet of Energy (IoE): A Comprehensive Review of Design, Principles, and Architectural Frameworks

Rania Salih Abdalla[1], Elmustafa Sayed Ali[2,3(✉)], Sara A. Mahbub[3],
Rania A. Mokhtar[1,3], and Zeinab E. Ahmed[4,5]

[1] Department of Computer Engineering, Taif University, Al-Taif, Saudi Arabia
[2] Department of Electrical and Electronics Engineering, Red Sea University, Port Sudan, Sudan
elmustafasayed@gmail.com
[3] Department of Electronics Engineering, Sudan University of Science and Technology,
Khartoum, Sudan
[4] Department of Electrical and Computer Engineering, International Islamic University
Malaysia, Kuala Lumpur, Malaysia
[5] Department of Computer Engineering, University of Gezira, Wad Madani, Sudan

Abstract. Design of energy resources, transmission, distribution, and consumption in network architecture is becoming a challenging energy optimization issue. The demand for power analysis becomes a key pillar in sustainable renewable energy and adaptation to climate change. State-of-the-art technologies can play a vital role in realizing the new architectural design for smart grids and cities. The 4th generation mobile network is considered a critical technology and enabler. The 3GPP standard body is set to a target of 35% of the deployment of the 4G to be Low Power Wide Area (LPWA) network by 2020. LPWA is an Internet of Energy (IoE) structure that can provide a comprehensive stream of energy sector applications. The IoE with intelligent computing tools can dramatically enhance energy efficiency, improve and sustain renewable energy, and diminish energy contamination's ecological effects. This paper reviews the literature on the IoE design principles and architecture models comprehensively. it also explains IoE enabling technologies, including fog computing and various interoperability and data analysis standards.

Keywords: Communications and measurement technology · smart energy systems · smart grid · IoE Computational Tools · IoE Design · IoE Interoperability · IoE Standards · IoE Cyber Security

1 Introduction

The term Internet of Energy (IoE) refers to an electricity solution for power flow and bidirectional information in an internet-style, known as energy internet, and is considered a smart grid extension [1, 2]. IoE evolves into a cloud network in which embedded

A. Sere et al. (Eds.): AFRICOMM 2023, LNICST 587, pp. 83–99, 2025.
https://doi.org/10.1007/978-3-031-81570-6_6

and distributed intelligence power sources communicate with smart grid and mass consumption devices such as intelligent buildings, appliances, and electric automobiles [3, 4].

In IoE, smart metering technology plays a significant fundamental role. With the use of electrical or electromechanical components, its intelligent automation applications enable consumption and energy monitoring, assisting users in managing and optimizing energy resources for both commercial and residential applications, as shown in Fig. 1. This rabid increase of IoE applications in modern life applications and industry led to the innovation of IoE standards, which will be discussed later in this paper and IoE architectures, interoperability, privacy, and security.

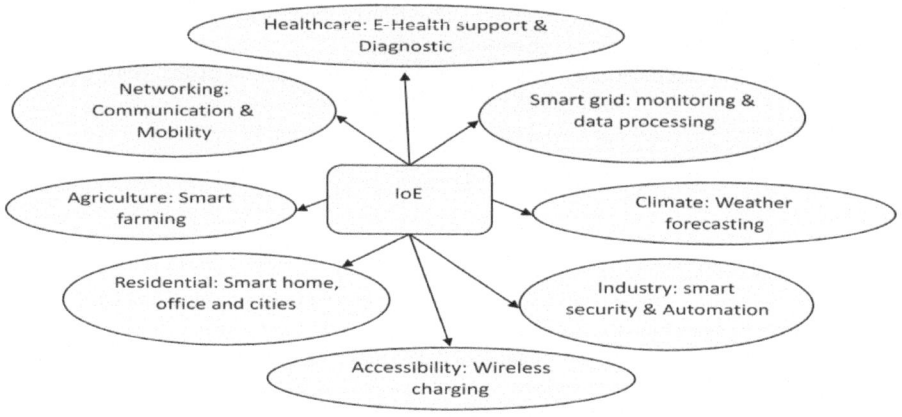

Fig. 1. IoE Applications

2 Internet of Energy Architecture

Traditionally, energy systems deploy generation, transmission, and distribution [5]. Then IoE was invented as an ICT solution to add a communication layer or functionality that integrates all system components in an "end-to-end" fashion while providing other system services [6, 7]. This integration of the IoE platform includes various sectors from system management to data security and development tools. Integrating intelligent end devices, networking, real-time capability, and integrated applications for business and mobile device portals [8]. Technically, to achieve such integration required by the IoE platform proposal, the most practical suitable tactic is the well-known Service-Oriented Architectures (SOA), where networking communication protocols are used to provide service delivery between different system components [9, 10].

2.1 EMS-Based Architecture

An Energy Management System (EMS) refers to the power grid control centre, which takes charge of monitoring and mission management. Besides its essential role in power system operation's safety and stability, it represents a core factor in IoE architecture development [11, 12]. The developed EMS was based on a Sensor and Actuator Network (SANET) that includes HSANET installed at the customer location. At the service provider location, a Data and Service Center (DSC) is installed. Major structure components employed by EMS are shown in Fig. 2, where necessary information infrastructure is represented by the HSANET, which includes a ZigBee-based home sensor network and Zigbee-internet home gateway and control centre.

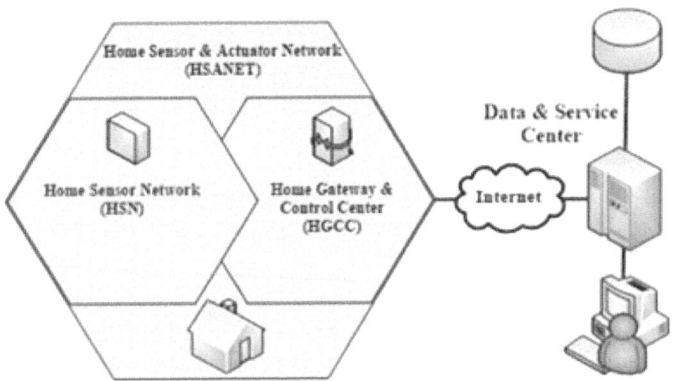

Fig. 2. Basic IoE EMS-Based Architecture

EMS improvement is emerging and reaches all energy grid operation levels from generation to distribution to enable optimal use of traditional or renewable energy sources as in decentralized generation while maintaining system stability and service quality. The architecture above represents a basic form of EMS-based architecture of IoE that was more suitable for centralized energy management. Various developed relative architectures are introduced, especially with decentralized energy generation management, as shown in Fig. 3 [13].

EMS-based IoE architecture's advancement followed different development paths. Architecture involves additional functionality and features such as various energy generation sources, energy storage, enhanced data centres, and smart metering technology. This type of architecture considers decentralized energy generation and management that may include common renewable energy forms like solar and wind; in such architectures, other conditions are also usable such as hydroelectric, geothermal, biomass, etc.

By 2020, more development on EMS-based architecture will be introduced by multiple institutes. The most common one that combines major of these developments is Micro-Service-based EMS architecture [19]. The authors here address significant EMS development factors and express the main facilities and issues with the existing EMS. They also compared their architecture against the service-oriented architecture - Energy Management Systems (SOA-EMS) based architecture from different perspectives [14].

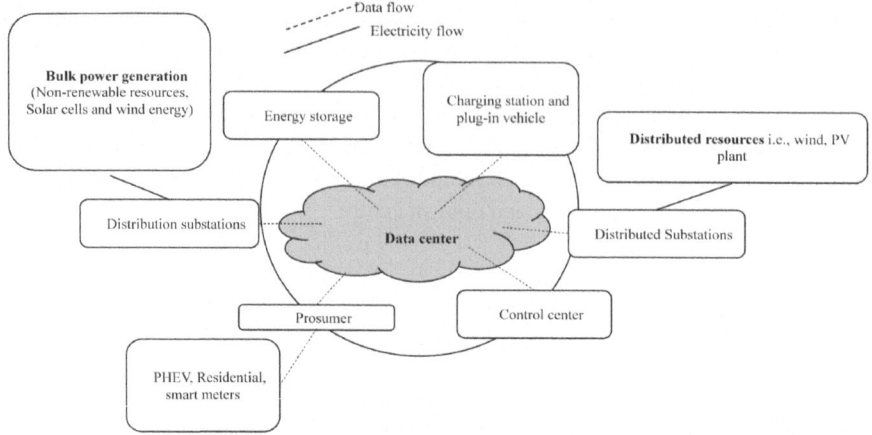

Fig. 3. An advanced EMS-based IoE Architecture

2.2 Fog Based Architecture

The challenge of addressing the optimal use to achieve both operational and business objectives by utilizing companies and customers in distributed energy resources is still an ongoing issue, initiated by the Trans Active Energy (TE) methodology. The Grid-wise Architecture Council (GWAC) defined TE as an electric power system management methodology by uses economic or market-based constructs in generation, consumption, or electric power flow to provide market and control functions jointly [15]. The system connectivity map includes the flow of electrical energy through physical components or points referred to by Transactive Nodes (TN).

TNs are controlled in real-time based on economic impulses or incentives, insurance of control system scalability, which is achieved by the decentralized transactions and information exchange between the TNs [16]. A transactive node uses a Transactive Incentive Signal (TIS), which represents the foretoken transferred electric energy cost. The Transactive Feedback Signal (TFS) represents the forecasted total power flow at a particular transactive node. The balance between supply and demand has been achieved by exchanging transactive signals between the neighbouring transactive nodes. Each TN echoes the system situations among decisions related to the conductance of local assets.

The fog-based IoE architecture shown in Fig. 4 includes three different layers [17]. The first layer is responsible for providing an interface between the power grid and customers through the home gateways, by the transaction of collected energy consumption data. By positioning the Fog nodes at the network edge to function as an energy market server agent on behalf of the retail energy market server of the transactive energy system, the second layer is in charge of giving low latency services to the end consumers. The third layer is responsible for providing a high computing environment and perpetual data storage, by supporting various communication protocols such as HTTP, Constrained Application Protocol (CoAP), and Open Automated Demand Response (OpenADR) alliance [18].

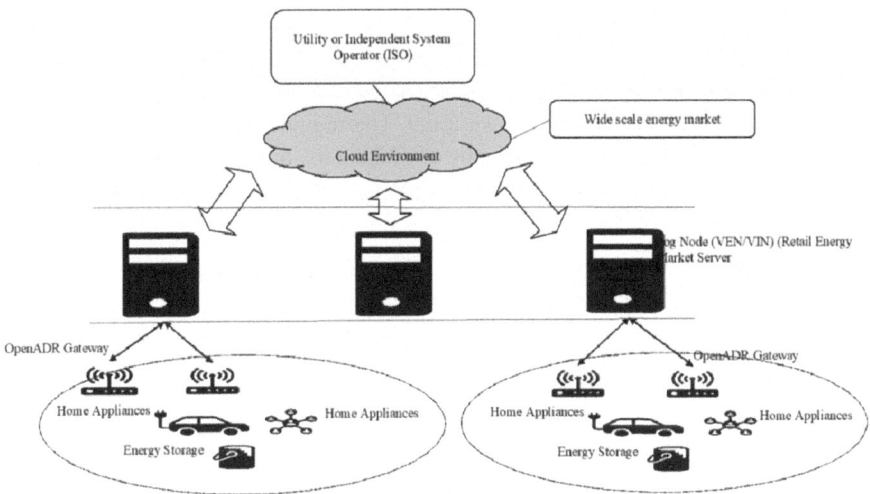

Fig. 4. Fog-based IoE Architecture

3 Hierarchical Context Awareness

Context-aware services are those that provide the user with the most relevant information based on their specific situation, including behavior-based context-aware services. The way that user behavior recognition technology learns behavior is through gathering movement-related data and analyzing it across multiple sensors. One of the key technologies that will drive the next generation of mobile phones is behavior recognition technology [20].

As the mobile phone business evolves, various sensors that are employed in behavioural recognition in mobile phones have been developed. Behaviour recognition technology for mobile phones is constantly evolving. There are several behavioural recognition approaches, the most notable of which being video-based human movement recognition, as well as sensor-based systems [21]. Because of its low power consumption and high accuracy in most wearable contexts, accelerometers are extensively utilised in sensor-based human motion identification.

Such technologies play a crucial role in IoE systems, transforming them into highly dynamic, real-time, resource-constrained, and low-transmission environments. As a result, IoE devices should give real-time behaviour management and reaction service by recognising the local scenario, as well as demonstrate optimal context-aware service by monitoring surrounding situation data such as user, social and industrial experiences [23].

3.1 Hierarchical Context Awareness Engine

Context-aware services are provided by the IoE-based technology depicted in Fig. 5, which monitors user data using smart devices and data from the user's external environment while they are in an IoE environment. This allows for real-time user behaviour study. Two machines are needed for the IoE-based hierarchical context-aware engine: a fast machine and an adequate machine. As an example, the fast context machine hand phone gathers sensing data in order to rapidly assess a user's low-level circumstances; a low-level position is associated with an event. The required sensor data is sent to the server with the event. It offers assistance by evaluating the high-level scenario using the information base on a server equipped with a sophisticated context machine [24].

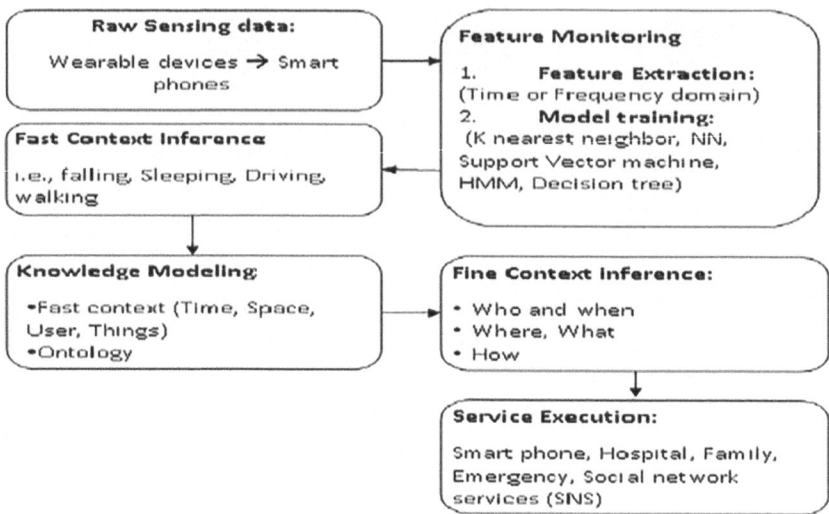

Fig. 5. IoE-based context-aware technology

There are two phases to the context-aware service, which gathers and interprets context information from users of smart devices and then provides relevant services based on the circumstances. It provides sufficient context-knowledgeable assistance for cloud servers and quick context-aware assistance for smart devices.

3.2 Fast Context Awareness Engine

Instant context trigger, ML engine, and service implementer compose the fast context awareness machine. Sensitive data for the smart device is first collected by the machine familiar with the current context when a user asks a context-aware service. At this point, sensor data could come from an internal phone sensor, an IoE sensor attached to a phone, or data gathered from a wearable device. The pre-processed data is gathered, and the ML engine uses the relevant ML algorithm to analyze the data [25].

The identification of user behaviour is facilitated by the process of combining different sensor data. For instance, a mix of weight, touch, and speed sensors in the automobile might be utilised to detect whether or not the user is actually operating the vehicle. Many algorithms in the ML algorithm database can be learned via cloud server-based ML. The real-time context trigger creates an event after evaluating the ML data, and the cloud server uses this event data on a regular basis to deliver enough context-aware service. The event data is kept in the database [26].

The predictive and analytical capabilities used in IoE are consistent with the use of ML algorithms via cloud servers. When these sensors' data is fed into ML algorithms, the algorithms are able to recognize patterns, predict energy consumption, spot any grid problems or inefficiencies, and optimise the distribution of energy [27]. Large-scale data processing can be centralised and scaled with cloud-based ML, which is essential for quickly obtaining actionable insights. Figure 6 shows a flow diagram of the fast context-aware service. Furthermore, real-time context triggers are in line with the Internet of Everything's requirement for quick response and adaptation. Contextual events that require quick responses in IoE applications include abrupt changes in energy demand, weather that affects the output of renewable energy, and system outages. To guarantee continuous and effective energy delivery, these triggers force the system to react dynamically, rerouting energy, modifying loads, or triggering backup devices.

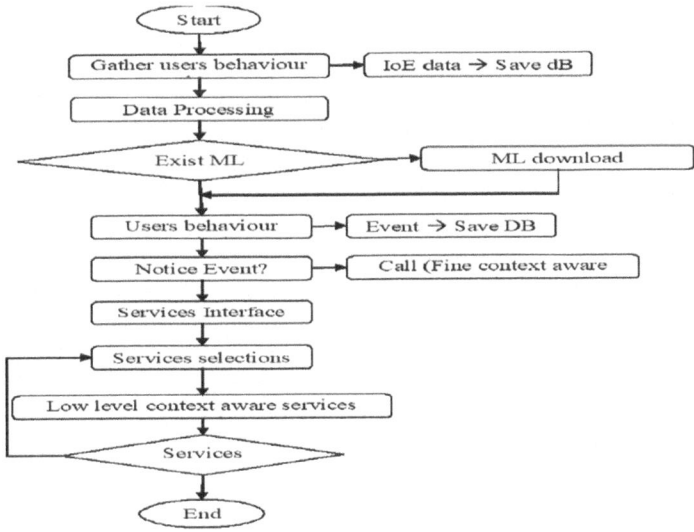

Fig. 6. Fast Context Awareness Service Flowchart

4 Computational Tools for IoE Design

As the development of emerging technology-based systems is rapidly growing and adapting its applications in various real-world fields, data analysis and storage platforms also require a suitable and sophisticated framework to integrate the systems' developments, reliability, and scalability. Especially in real-time applications and such as needed by IoE methodology. Computational environments and tools are found to meet that challenge by enabling more computation and storage capabilities that can affect system performance concurrently [28].

Development in web-based applications represents the main factor behind computation tools development and finds its way into other applications such as networking, communication, healthcare, industry, energy, etc. As mentioned in previous sections, IoE concept occurrence and architecture evolution mainly depend on computational environment growth in cloud computing, fog or edge computing, and the latest emerging technology known as blockchain technology [29]. These technologies use a common principle: the decentralization and distribution of service nodes somehow but may differ in their locations, properties, and functionalities [30].

4.1 Cloud Computing

Cloud computing represents an evolutionary version of computational tools that consists of an improved and reliable management platform for data warehousing, data analysis, and monitoring. Cloud computing providers promise to maintain data availability and reliability of all data-related operations by providing an evolutionary infrastructure that includes multiple ways for data warehousing and data aggregation framework. Moreover, modern developed functionalities that required for emerging applications such as data monitoring and visualization, big data analysis, real-time and low latency processing, and diversity of computation resources [31]. Cloud computing introduced various solutions for service providers by offering four primary services; Infrastructure as a Service (IaaS), Platform as a Service (Paas), Software as a Service (SaaS), and Backend as a Service (BaaS).

Cloud computing upgraded the traditional computation environment by enabling any on-demand and data availability by distributing services into multiple locations from central servers. Where the Virtual Machine (VM) plays the main role of enabling multiple and different computation capabilities on a single hardware, software development plays an essential role in building Application Programming Interfaces (API) for data interaction and management [32]. Additionally, cloud computing offers excellent integration and compatibility with IoT applications and platforms by enabling multiplicity for various IoT platforms and higher system bandwidth capabilities required by IoT applications [33]. The application of cloud computing in IoE introduces more opportunities and solutions in today's challenges between demand and suppliers.

4.2 Fog Computing

Generally, the Fog Computing concept grows with the spreading of IoT applications. It differs from cloud computing by adding a new concept called edge computing, which are major device at an edge between supplier and customer gateways [34]. These edge devices represent the new layer added to bridge terminals with the system computation core as shown in Fig. 7, Fog computing never eliminates cloud computing but represents an evolutionary version that complements cloud computing by adding an edge node. With the growth of Fog computing and its applications in developing systems, IoE is also involved in this development.

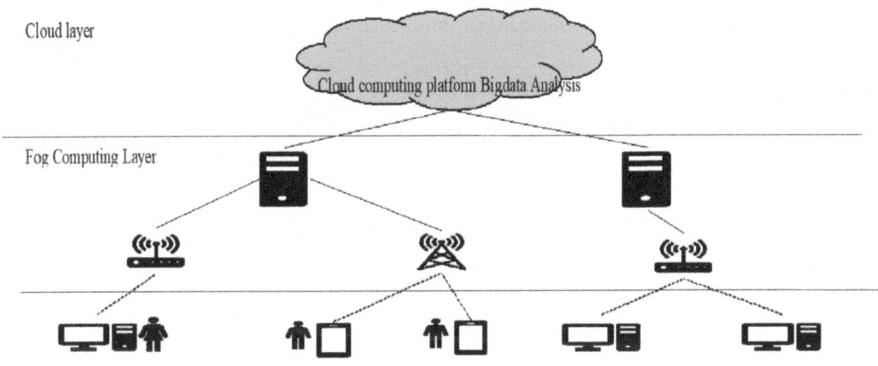

Cloud layer

Cloud computing platform Bigdata Analysis

Fog Computing Layer

Fig. 7. Fog Computation Architecture

5   IoE Standards

Technical instructions and specifications of most ICT applications are standardized by the Institute of Electronics and Electrical Engineering IEEE. To allow the demands and reliability of renewable energy, IEEE has established multiple standards and guidelines to cover ICT aspects across many geographic; and Standards Development Organization (SDO) boundaries for smart energy systems, which are summarized in Table 1.

Table 1. Main IEEE standard for Smart Energy Systems

Standard series	NAME	Description
IEEE 2030	Smart Grid Interoperability	For data flow security, reliability, bi-directional electric power flow and comprise electric cars.
IEEE 1686, IEEE C37.240, and IEEE 1711 series	Cyber Security for Smart Grid	For cyber security in Smart Electronic node Automation and Substation.
IEEE 170X, IEEE 1377, IEEE 2030.5, and IEEE 1901 series	Smart Metering and Demand Response	For smart network grid protocols, intelligent grid profiles, and intelligent metering functionality.
IEEE C37.118, IEC/IEEE 61850-9-3, IEEE 1815, IEEE C37.238, series	Substation Automation	Includes clock protocol, timing work, and electric power system network.
IEEE 2030.1.1	Electric Vehicle Charging	For interface design of electric cars

Table 2. IEEE 2030 standard recommendations and practice guides

Standards	Description
IEEE 2030	Smart Grid Interface with Data Technology Process and Energy Technology for Electric Power System (EPS)
IEEE 2030.1.1	Standard Technical Specifications of a DC Quick Charger and Bi-directional Charger for Use with Electric Vehicles
IEEE 2030.2	The interface of Energy Storage Systems (ESS) combined with the EP Structure
IEEE 2030.2.1	Operation, Design, and Conservation of Energy Storage Systems (ESS)
IEEE 2030.3	Test process for Energy Storage system and equipment Electric Applications
IEEE P2030.4	Draft Guide for Control and Automation Installations Applied to the Electric Power Infrastructure
IEEE 2030.6	Advantage Assessment of Power Grid Consumer Request Answer
IEEE SA - 2030.5™	Ecosystem Steering Committee
IEEE 2030.5	Smart Energy Profile Application Protocol Standard
IEEE 2030.7	Specification of Microgrid Controllers
IEEE 2030.8	Testing of Microgrid Controllers
IEEE 2030.9	Recommended Practice for the Planning and Design of the Microgrid
IEEE 2030.100	Practice for Implementing an IEC 61850 Based Substation Communications, Protection, Monitoring and Control System
IEEE 2030.101	Designing a Time Synchronization System for Power Substations
IEEE P2030.100.1	Draft Monitoring and Diagnostics of IEC 61850 Generic Object-Oriented Status Event (GOOSE)
IEEE P2030.102.1	Interoperability of Internet Protocol Security (IPsec) Utilized within Utility Control Systems

5.1 IEEE 2030 Standard

IEEE 2030 standard is intended to but the roadmap to achieve smart grid interoperability by establishing the Smart Grid Interoperability Reference Model (SGIRM) that models the framework of engineering principles to apply smart grid interoperability upon all-electric power system components. These visions look beyond the year 2030 and predict how the smart grid will evolve for each of these technology-focused areas. The package of the IEEE 2030 standard series includes many recommendations and guides for the design, implementation, and evaluation sectors of smart grid systems, as summarized in Table 2.

5.2 IEEE 802.15.4g

Design consideration of smart grids requires modern solutions for networking and communication operations. WiFi and Zigbee wireless communication were the available suitable standards and demonstrated with some basic smart grid applications. Still, more specifications and procedures are required; the IEEE 802.15.4g standard is developed to meet that requirement. IEEE-802.15.4g describes the standard wireless network platform for intelligent utility service, the structure of IEEE-802.15.4g network standard, as shown in Fig. 8.

5.3 IEEE 21450 and IEEE 21451

International Organization for Standardization and International Electrotechnical Commission ISO/IEC/IEEE 21450 standard provides a common foundation for members of the ISO/IEC/IEEE 21451 series of International Standards to be able to exchange and make use of data. It realizes the functionalities achieved by the Transducer Interconnect Model (TIM) and joint features for TIM-based nodes. It also defines the setups for Transducer Electric Datasheets (TEDS) and the set of instructions to simplify the configuration and control of the TIM and read and write the data used by the system. To enable transmission with applications, TIM, and Application Program Interfaces (APIs) are defined [35].

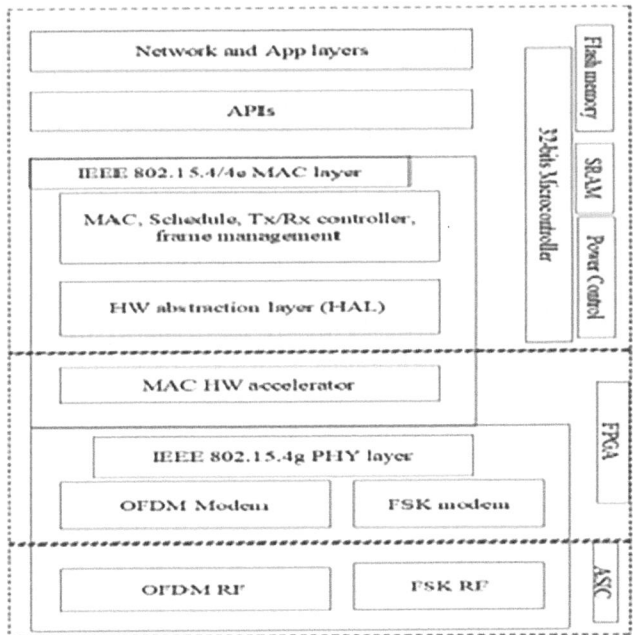

Fig. 8. IEEE 802.15.4G Communication platform architecture

6   IoE Privacy and Security

In critical infrastructures such as smart power grids and IoE, dependability and security are not fully understood yet, and privacy is an additional security objective. The IEEE provides an overview of security issues, strategies, security requirements, risk management, security design, and countermeasures besides the standards and best practice recommendations. Additionally, end-to-end security, security by design, and security in-depth are the most important security concepts that must be included within the conceptual security model.

In the IoE, design security is typically established in relation to the assembly of systems, solutions, and architectures as well as the production of specific goods. The concept of security in depth recognises that no security feature is impenetrable on its own and that the only way to achieve security greater than the sum of its parts is to apply various security controls layered in a concentric manner around assets that are to be safeguarded [36]. Protecting data in a data system from the point of origin to the point of destination is known as end-to-end security. However, full end-to-end security would require all endpoints to support a common control security mechanism [39]. According to IEEE standard recommendations and standards, the IEEE 1686™, IEEE P37.240™, IEEE 1711™, IEEE 1402™, and IEC 62351 series are the best practices for cybersecurity introduced for IoE solutions.

6.1   IoE Cyber Security

Cybersecurity for IoE concerns all procedures and methods of securing communication and networking for data and power flow. According to IEEE, an organization must apply analysis and risk management methods to identify the appropriate solutions to ensure the Distributed Energy Resources (DERs), including related systems and Smart Grids. The security engineer has to understand the data exchange standards to fill the gaps that should be taken into account [37]. The data exchange recommended standards and application programming interfaces that support smart grid technologies and related ISO/RTO services or products based on the data. Demand Response (DR) models are supplied in standard publication documents by the National Institute for Standards and Technology (NIST). The National Electric Sector Cyber Security Organization Resource (NESCOR), Electric Power Research Institute (EPRI), etc. [38]. These recommendations and standards are rich in key functional security regions, various markets, and Critical Infrastructure Protection (CIP) cybersecurity and other pertinent accuracy standards.

6.2   IoE Security Issues

A layer of protection is necessary because the IoE links individuals, information, objects, and processes. Similar to how common equipment are evaluated and rated for conventional attributes like suitability for use, maintainability, etc., IoE items are also subjected to extensive cybersecurity testing. Regulating and establishing common security standards for IoE security is a priority, but the uniform and independent verification of IoE devices' security is still in its early stages.

6.2.1   Threat Modeling

Cybersecurity-related accidents have happened in numerous businesses and sectors, including factories, power grids, water supplies, nuclear facilities, etc., as a result of the expansion of IoT technology [11]. By 2020, the damage climbed by 32%, or $17.7 trillion [22]. Regarding our effort to situate the IoT security challenges inside the framework of a broader architecture that includes more components like people, data, and processes that is, the IoE, many studies have attempted to consider the IoT security issues as an individual problem. Threat-based security analysis of IoT was carried out by particular studies. for example, one study proposed a privacy improvement over Bluetooth Low Energy (BLE) advertising channels. But when taking into account the IoE, this increase is unfeasible and necessitates altering both the protocol and the peripheral. An IoE-driven security mechanism that uses a video camera to detect motion from a visitor while the homeowner is away is reviewed in another study. Home network integrity is crucial for many IoE-based physical security systems, hence maintaining home network security is essential to physical security. Thus, the first step towards improving house physical security is creating a threat model for IoE for homeowners who usually aren't aware of security and privacy problems.

6.2.2   Architecture for Trust Management

IoE is a combination of empowering technologies for Cyber-Physical Systems (CPS), and its structure fits and is compatible with the System-of-Systems (SoSs). The intelligent object is likely to be pervasive, geologically spread, and diverse on the Internet of Energy. IoE clients can create critical associations with other clients and devices in substation networks [40]. IoE can be seen as a node-centric structure where each node or thing, in general, can apply for service from other centric common nodes. It may also offer service for the other utilities and is considered a service provider (SP). In a service-centric Internet of Energy structure, it is compulsory to create a management protocol for trust to assess IoT service providers' reliability and fidelity efficiently and scalable. Indeed, management models for trust are desired since IoE SPs (services providers) may perform maliciously and untruthfully to encourage the IoE nodes to choose them for services on behalf of other SPs (services providers).

Additionally, untruthful IoE service providers may make ballot stuffing, discriminatory and bad-mouthing attacks to disturb the network and control services offered. Thus, it is obvious that the management of trust for service is more than important to defend IoE nodes from malicious SPs. Up to now, there is a huge number of protocols for the management of trust that have been invented for Social, WSN (Wireless Sensor Network), and P2P networks.

7   Internet of Energy Future Trends

IoE enables to collection and organization of the data to simplify the information flow management from single grid edge devices to other grids across the network quickly. In smart grids, IoE presents a principle of smart energy management that helps to keep the network grid stable and balanced in terms of power. In addition, IoE provides smart forecasting to predict future energy demands. It allows to use of cloud-based systems to integrate industry systems and provides a process management of future grids [41]. The cloud-based IoE platforms enable to development of an open interface software for the development of customer-specific applications easily managed in a wide range of grids with new efficient operation utility.

The integration of real things to the internet with smart advanced applications such as grid data management and analytics, distributed energy resource and substation devices management in the IoE network will promise more efficient and sustainable gird than ever before [11]. IoE can manage and operate the smart device processes and data acquisition systems, in addition to interacting with the problem notifications repair and faults occurred i.e. in electric vehicles metering. Moreover, in electric substations, cloud-based IoE applications can automatically asset protection settings and provide advanced services like remote support and security management [42].

Recently, many technologies related to IoE have been taken into consideration, especially in electric power applications. In the USA, an electric power company developed a self-healing grid system to automatically reconfigure itself in case of home power loss. The developed systems can automatically detect, isolate and reroute power in case of fault occurs [43]. In the national UK power grid, a demand-side response company uses a smart balanced supply technology to aggregate energy consumption from across customers' sites. The technology helps to dynamically response to demands and enables consumers to better manage their consumption [44]. In Europe, IoE is dedicated to exploring the business case for IoT in the energy industry.

In the energy industry, IoE offers many benefits in regulating energy usage levels and maximising revenue opportunities. IoE enables to harvest of renewable resources and integrates them with electrical grids as a power generation [103]. Technologies such as AI and blockchain in IoE future applications will build an effective cybersecurity defence mechanism, and provide great security options for data. Moreover, these technologies will help to build the perfect infrastructure for making IoE a blissful reality.

8 Conclusions

The Internet of Energy (IoE) is the integration of Information and Communication Technology (ICT) into the complex web of energy systems. It includes several different types of energy, such as generation, transformation, storage, distribution, and end-device consumption. The IoE's architectural architecture divides the energy network into layers, allowing for seamless connectivity and effective administration across these disparate components. This integration not only simplifies operations, but it also has the potential to transform how energy systems work and interact.

The rapid advancement of ICT has resulted in the introduction of disruptive technologies such as cloud computing, fog/edge computing, and Blockchain, which play critical roles in current internet-based applications. These advancements are critical in developing infrastructure that is not only efficient and reliable, but also secure and adaptable. Their use inside the IoE framework reshapes the traditional energy environment, offering previously unheard-of levels of dependability, security, and adaptability.

Established standards, suggestions, and best practices are critical to IoE's success. These serve as guiding principles for optimal design and deployment, ensuring that interoperability, scalability, and security are fully addressed. IoE implementations that adhere to these benchmarks can accomplish harmonic integration across disparate systems while protecting against potential weaknesses.

This comprehensive assessment emphasizes the importance of IoE in altering energy systems through the integration of ICT and energy components. It emphasizes the mutually beneficial relationship between technical advancement and the aim of efficient, secure, and sustainable energy management. The Internet of Everything (IoE) is a transformative force poised to revolutionize energy systems, opening the way for a more connected, efficient, and resilient future.

References

1. Kafle, Y.R., Mahmud, K., Morsalin, S., Town, G.E.: Towards an internet of energy. In: 2016 IEEE International Conference on Power System Technology (POWERCON), 2016, pp. 1−6 (2016).
2. Dahab, M.B., Ahmed, E.S., Mokhtar, R.A., Saeed, R.A.: Artificial intelligence and machine learning approaches in smart city services. In: Reddy, K., Roy, D., Mishra, T., Hussain, M., (Eds.), Handbook of Research on Network-Enabled IoT Applications for Smart City Services, pp. 339−352 (2023). IGI Global. https://doi.org/10.4018/979-8-3693-0744-1.ch019
3. Hannan, M.A., et al.: A review of internet of energy based building energy management systems: issues and recommendations. IEEE Access 6, 38997–39014 (2018)
4. Keen, M.G., Chin, H.H., Ganapathi, C., Ghazaleh, D., Krogdahl, P.: Patterns: Extended Enterprise Soa and Web Services (Redbooks) (2006)
5. Lyu, Z., Wei, H., Bai, X., Lian, C.: Microservice-based architecture for an energy management system. IEEE Syst. J. 1−12 (2020)
6. Munshi, A.A., Mohamed, Y.A.I.: Data lake lambda architecture for smart grids big data analytics. IEEE Access 6, 40463–40471 (2018)
7. Hassan, M., et al.: BER improvement of cooperative spectrum sharing of NOMA in 5G network. In: 2023 IEEE 3rd International Maghreb Meeting of the Conference on Sciences and Techniques of Automatic Control and Computer Engineering (MI-STA), Benghazi, Libya, 2023, pp. 647−652, https://doi.org/10.1109/MI-STA57575.2023.10169494.M.
8. Yang, D., Wei, H., Zhu, Y., Li, P., Tan, J.: Virtual private cloud based power-dispatching automation system—architecture and application. IEEE Trans. Ind. Inform. 15, 1756–1766 (2019)
9. GridWise transactive energy framework version 1.0 The Grid-Wise Architecture Council, US Department of Energy, Washington, DC, USA 2015.
10. Hassan, M., et al.: NOMA cooperative spectrum sharing average capacity improvement in 5G Network. In: 2023 IEEE 3rd International Maghreb Meeting of the Conference on Sciences and Techniques of Automatic Control and Computer Engineering (MI-STA), Benghazi, Libya, pp. 653−658 (2023). https://doi.org/10.1109/MI-STA57575.2023.10169694.
11. Hasan, M.K., Ahmed, M.M., Musa, S.S.: Measurement and modeling of DTCR software parameters based on intranet wide area measurement system for smart grid applications. In: International Conference on Innovative Computing and Communications 2020, pp. 1139−1150. Springer, Singapore (2020)
12. Khalifa, O.O., et al.: An IoT-Platform-based deep learning system for human behavior recognition in smart city monitoring using the Berkeley MHAD datasets. Systems. 10(5), 177 (2022). https://doi.org/10.3390/systems10050177

13. Forfia, D., Knight, M., Melton, R.: The view from the top of the mountain: building a community of practice with the gridwise transactive energy framework. IEEE Power Energy Mag. **14**, 25–33 (2016)

14. Miglani, A., Kumar, N., Chamola, V., Zeadally, S.: Blockchain for internet of energy management: review, solutions, and challenges. Comput. Commun. **151**, 395–418 (2020)

15. Khan, M.A., Salah, K.: IoT security: review, blockchain solutions, and open challenges. Future Gener. Comput. Syst. **82**, 395–411 (2018)

16. Reyna, A., Martín, C., Chen, J., Soler, E., Díaz, M.: On blockchain and its integration with IoT. Challenges and opportunities. Future Gener. Comput. Syst. **88**, 173–190 (2018)

17. "IEEE Standard Technical Specifications of a DC Quick Charger for Use with Electric Vehicles," IEEE Std 2030.1.1-2015, pp. 1–97 (2016)

18. Saeed, M.M., et al.: A comprehensive review on the users' identity privacy for 5G networks. IET Commun. **16**, 384–399 (2022). https://doi.org/10.1049/cmu2.12327

19. "IEEE Vision for Smart Grid Communications: 2030 and Beyond," IEEE Vision for Smart Grid Communications: 2030 and Beyond, pp. 1–390 (2013)

20. Muni, B.K., Patra, S.K.: FPGA implementation of ZigBee baseband transceiver system for IEEE 802.15.4. In: Advances in Computing, Communication, and Control, Berlin, Heidelberg, 2013, pp. 465–474 (2013)

21. Nurelmadina, N., et al.: A systematic review on cognitive radio in low power wide area network for industrial IoT applications. Sustainability **13**, 338 (2021). https://doi.org/10.3390/su1301 0338

22. IEEE Standard for Local and metropolitan area networks - Part 15.4: Low-Rate Wireless Personal Area Networks (LR-WPANs) Amendment 4: Alternative Physical Layer Extension to Support Medical Body Area Network (MBAN) Services Operating in the 2360 MHz – 2400 MHz Band. IEEE Std 802.15.4j-2013 (Amendment to IEEE Std 802.15.4-2011 as amended by IEEE Std 802.15.4e-2012, IEEE Std 802.15.4f-2012, and IEEE Std 802.15.4g-2012), pp. 1–24 (2013)

23. Ryoo, Kim, S., Cho, J., Kim, H., Tjoa, S., Derobertis, C.: IoE security threats and you. In: 2017 International Conference on Software Security and Assurance (ICSSA), Altoona, PA, 2017, pp. 13–19 (2017). https://doi.org/10.1109/ICSSA.2017.28

24. Memon, I., Shaikh, R.A., Hasan, M.K., Hassan, R., Haq, A.U., Zainol, K.A.: Protect mobile travelers information in sensitive region based on fuzzy logic in IoT technology. Secur. Commun. Netw. **18**, 2020 (2020)

25. Khajenasiri, K., et al.: Design and implementation of a multi-standardevent-driven energy management system for smart buildings. In: Proc.IEEE 3rd Global Conf. Consum. Electron. (GCCE), Oct. 2014, pp. 20–21 (2014)

26. Khajenasiri, I., Virgone, J., Gielen, G.: A presence-based control strategy solution for HVAC systems. In: Proc. IEEE Int. Conf. Consum.Electron. (ICCE), Jan. 2015, pp. 620–622 (2015)

27. Gil-Baez, M., Barrios-Padura, Á., Molina-Huelva, M., Chacartegui, R.: Natural ventilation systems in 21st-century for near zero energy school buildings. Energy **137**, 1186–1200 (2017)

28. Favaro, J.: Strategic research challenges in the Internet of Things. Tech.Rep., p. 6630.

29. Billure, R., Tayur, V.M., Mahesh, V.: Internet of things—a study on the security challenges. In: Proc. IEEE Int. Adv. Comput. Conf. (IACC),Jun. 2015, pp. 247–252 (2015)

30. Blaauw, D., et al.: IoT design space challenges: Circuits and systems. In: Symp. VLSI Technol. Dig. Tech. Papers, Jun. 2014, pp. 1–2 (2014)

31. Cao, J., Yang, M.: Energy Internet—Towards smart grid 2.0. In: Proc.Int. Conf. Netw. Distrib. Comput. (ICNDC), Dec. 2014, pp. 105–110 (2014)

32. Wang, K., Hu, X., Li, H., Li, P., Zeng, D., Guo, S.: A survey on energy Internet communications for sustainability. IEEE Trans. Sustain. Comput. **2**(3), 231–254 (2017)

33. Al-Fuqaha, A., Guizani, M., Mohammadi, M., Aledhari, M., Ayyash, M.: Internet of things: a survey on enabling technologies, protocols, and applications. IEEE Commun. Surveys Tuts. **17**(4), 2347–2376 (2015)

34. Zhang, Y., Weng, J., Dey, R., Fu, X.: Bluetooth low energy (BLE) security and privacy. In: Shen X., Lin X., Zhang K. (eds.) Encyclopedia of Wireless Networks. Springer, Cham (2019). https://doi.org/10.1007/978-3-319-32903-1_298-1

35. Khan., Arsalan, M.H.: Solar power technologies for sustainable electricity generation—a review. Renew. Sustain. Energy Rev. **55**, 414–425 (2016)

36. Al Busaidi, S., Kazem, H.A., Al-Badi, A.H., Khan, M. F.: A review of optimum sizing of hybrid PV–Wind renewable energy systems in Oman. Renew. Sustain. Energy Rev. **53**, 185–193 (2016)

37. . Ayhan., Sağlam, A.: A technical review of building-mounted wind power systems and a sample simulation model. Renew. Sustain. Energy Rev. **16**(1), 1040–1049 (2012)

38. Gvozdenovic, H.B.K., Maassen, W., Zeiler, W.: Roadmap to nearly zero energy buildings. Roy. HaskoningDHV, Eindhoven Univ. Technol., Eindhoven, The Netherlands, Tech. Rep. (2014)

39. Wang, K., Bao, J., Wu, M., Lu, W.: Research on security management for Internet of things. In: Proc. Int. Conf. Comput. Appl. Syst. Modeling(ICCASM), vol. 15, Oct. 2010, pp. V15-133–V15-137 (2010)

40. Ma, Z., Cooper, P., Daly, D., Ledo, L.: Existing building retrofits: methodology and state-of-the-art. Energy Buildings **55**, 889–902 (2012)

41. Salamzada, K.H., Shukur, Z., Bakar, M.A.: A framework for cybersecurity strategy for developing countries: case study of Afghanistan. Asia-Pac. J. Inf. Technol. Multimedia. **4**(1), 1 (2015)

42. Strielkowski, W., Streimikiene, D., Fomina, A., Semenova, E.: Internet of energy (IoE) and high-renewables electricity system market design. Nergies **12**, 4790 (2019). https://doi.org/10.3390/en12244790

43. Shahinzadeh, H., Moradi, J., Gharehpetian, G.B., Nafisi, H., Abedi, M.: Internet of energy (IoE) in smart power systems. In: 5th Conference on Knowledge-Based Engineering and Innovation (KBEI), Tehran, Iran, 2019, pp. 627−636 (2019). https://doi.org/10.1109/KBEI.2019.8735086.

44. Andoni, M., et al.: Blockchain technology in the energy sector: a systematic review of challenges and opportunities. Renew. Sustain. Energy Rev. **100**, 143–174 (2019)

Enhancing Power Efficiency in NB-IoT Networks: PAPR Reduction in SC-FDMA

Désiré Guel[1][✉], P. Justin Kouraogo[1], Boureima Zerbo[2],
and Modeste Dembele[1]

[1] Université Joseph KI-ZERBO (U-JKZ), Ouagadougou, Burkina Faso
guel.desire@gmail.com
[2] Université Thomas SANKARA (UTS), Ouagadougou, Burkina Faso

Abstract. NB-IoT, short for NarrowBand IoT, is a communication standard for long-range connectivity of numerous devices. A key research area in NB-IoT is reducing Peak-to-Average Power Ratio (PAPR).

NB-IoT builds on 4G LTE (Long Term Evolution) and employs Single Carrier Frequency Division Multiple Access (SC-FDMA) in UpLink (UL) to minimize PAPR. To address power amplifier non-linearities, we propose applying the "clipping" technique, borrowing from OFDM.

In this paper, we examine the impact of Clipping Factor (CF) on PAPR reduction and the attenuation factors of Raised-Cosine (RC) filter and the Root Raised-Cosine (RRC) filter on PAPR probability distribution. Our analysis demonstrates a 2.5 dB (33.33%) reduction at a cumulative distribution function of 10^{-3}, with better results when using the Raised-Cosine (RC) filter.

Keywords: Peak to Average Power Ratio (PAPR) · Single-carrier FDMA (SC-FDMA) · Narrowband - Internet of Things (NB-IoT) Networks · Power efficiency

1 Introduction

With the rapid growth of Internet of Things (IoT) devices and their diverse applications, the need for efficient and reliable wireless communication technologies has become increasingly critical [1,2]. Narrowband Internet of Things (NB-IoT) networks [1] have emerged as a promising solution for providing connectivity to a large number of low-power IoT devices. However, power efficiency and performance optimization remain significant challenges in NB-IoT networks.

One of the key components in NB-IoT communication is the Single Carrier Frequency Division Multiple Access (SC-FDMA) modulation technique, which offers advantages such as low Peak-to-Average Power ratio (PAPR) and spectral efficiency. However, the PAPR of SC-FDMA signals even low can lead to power inefficiency and performance degradation, especially in resource-constrained IoT devices [3].

© ICST Institute for Computer Sciences, Social Informatics and Telecommunications Engineering 2025
Published by Springer Nature Switzerland AG 2025. All Rights Reserved
A. Sere et al. (Eds.): AFRICOMM 2023, LNICST 587, pp. 100–112, 2025.
https://doi.org/10.1007/978-3-031-81570-6_7

In this article, we focus on addressing the PAPR issue in SC-FDMA for NB-IoT networks to enhance power efficiency and overall system performance. We investigate various techniques and algorithms for PAPR reduction and their impact on power consumption, spectral efficiency, and error performance. The aim is to provide insights into effective approaches that can mitigate PAPR while maintaining the desired power efficiency and performance levels in NB-IoT networks.

This article is organized as follows. Section 2 provides a brief description of the research methodology used in this study; the aim is to explore effective strategies for reducing PAPR in SC-FDMA signals to enhance power efficiency and performance in NB-IoT networks. Section 3 explores the related works while Sect. 4 decribes the proposed method for PAPR reduction in SC-FDMA and discuses the results obtained through simulations. Finally, Sect. 5 concludes the article and outlines potential future research directions in this area.

2   Research Methodology

The research methodology used in this study, consisted of investigating and analyzing various techniques and algorithms for reducing PAPR in OFDMA systems [3–5]. This has involved conducting an extensive literature review to gather relevant information on PAPR reduction methods.

The research methodology also incorporates the use of appropriate simulation tool Matlab [6] to simulate SC-FDMA systems integrating PAPR reduction techniques for enhancement of power efficiency in NB-IoT Networks.

Also, in this article, we deliberately choose to focus on the "adding signal" techniques for PAPR reduction [7], with a specific emphasis on those that are backward compatible. The selection of "adding signal" techniques is justified by their perceived lower complexity and their ability to meet the primary constraints (power consumption and integration) of an embedded system.

By following this research methodology, the study aims to provide valuable insights into effective strategies for reducing PAPR in SC-FDMA signals, thereby enhancing power efficiency and contributing to the advancement of NB-IoT technology.

3   Related Works

PAPR reduction has already been the subject of research, and several methods have been proposed [3–5,7,8]. However, it is only with the widespread adoption of OFDM modulation [3–5,7,8], due to its use in various telecommunications standards such as LTE, that the issue has become crucial in the literature, given that the signal has a non-constant envelope. In this section, we review different PAPR reduction techniques [8] in OFDM and SC-FDMA systems known as "adding signal" techniques for PAPR reduction [7,8].

While not as straightforward, it has been shown in [7] that various forms of clipping are "adding signal" techniques for PAPR reduction. In fact, any clipping technique can be formulated as an "adding signal" technique [9].

3.1 "Clipping" Techniques Overview

Intuitively, "clipping" is a class of methods that is very easy to understand. It involves reducing the maximum amplitude of a signal to a predetermined threshold by amplitude clipping. This process aims to decrease the power variation of the signal and, consequently, reduce its sensitivity to nonlinearities. However, this procedure degrades the resulting signal and it may not achieve the nominal performance at the receiver. Furthermore, since saturation is inherently a nonlinear element, all the inherent defects of such an element will also be present. Numerous clipping methods have been developed, as evidenced by the works in [10–13].

3.2 "Clipping and Filtering" Technique

This technique has been proposed since the early implementation of terrestrial OFDM (DVB-T) in the late 1990s [10,11]. Therefore, a signal x will be scrambled according to the following formula:

$$f(x) = \begin{cases} x & |x| \leq A \\ Ae^{j\phi(x)} & |x| > A \end{cases} \tag{1}$$

where $y = f(x)$ is the resulting signal, A is the clipping amplitude, the Clipping Factor (CF) is expressed as $\text{CF} = A/\max(|x|)$ and $\phi(x)$ and $\phi(x)$ is the phase of the signal x. "Clipping" as expressed in (1) is a source of distortions (Rise of secondary lobes, interference, etc.).

The articles by L.J Cimini [10,11] can be considered as the reference for this method. They analyze the effects of the previous three points on the power spectral density and the Bit Error Rate (BER). Of course, the BER is degraded by several dB due to clipping noise in the band. In [14], K.R. Panta and J. Armstrong demonstrate that this issue is less significant when the signal traverses a frequency-selective channel. They show that the error rate is predominantly due to subcarriers that are heavily affected by the channel, and in this case, the contribution of clipping noise to the BER is very low. Another analysis of this problem reveals that the degradation in signal-to-noise ratio can be effectively mitigated by using powerful codes such as Turbo codes [12] (though the addition of a Turbo code compromises its backward compatibility nature). A second result in this article states that reducing the PAPR through clipping will be more effective if the OFDM signal is oversampled before clipping.

3.3 PAPR Reduction in SC-FDMA Systems Proposed by MediaTek Inc. [15]

The article proposed in [15] presents an analysis of a PAPR reduction technique for UL NB-IoT based on SC-FDMA. The objective is to study the PAPR reduction offered by this technique and explore potential improvements in the context of UL NB-IoT.

In [15], it is demonstrated that PAPR can be significantly reduced by limiting the number of modulated subcarriers in SC-FDMA and applying temporal windowing of SC-FDMA symbols before band limiting the signal through filtering. Additionally, the application of windowing aids in reducing spectral leakage into the adjacent channel, known as the Adjacent Channel Leakage Ratio (ACLR). However, it has been found that symbol windowing in SC-FDMA has not only positive effects; it could increase InterSymbol Interference (ISI), which could lead to receiver performance degradation in frequency-selective fading channels.

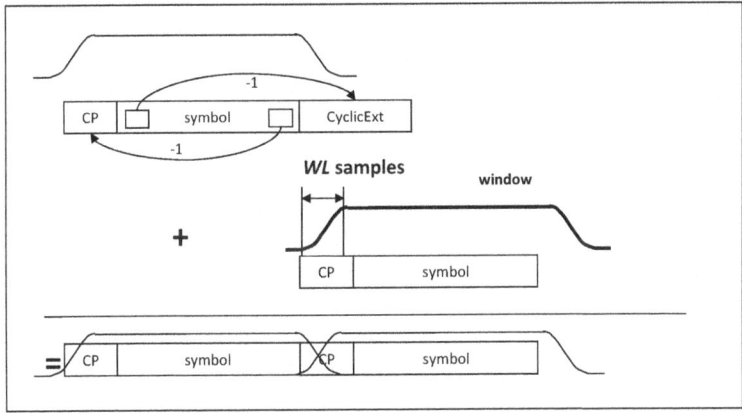

Fig. 1. Windowing of SC-FDMA symbols [15].

As shown in the Eq. (2), the remaining Cyclic Prefix (CP) length can be used for windowing without risking any significant performance degradation of the reception at the eNodeB [15].

$$\text{TotalCPDurationPerSlot} \;+\; 7\text{SC} - \text{FDMAsymbols}/\,(2.5\,\text{kHz subcarrier placing}) \atop = {}^{1}\!/_{2}\;\text{SubFrameLength} = 3\,\text{ms} \tag{2}$$

where
$$\text{TotalCPDurationPerSlot} = 200\mu s/\text{Slot}$$

Consequently, it can be deduced that the minimum duration of the Cyclic Prefix (CP) is $9/320$ kHz $= 28$ μs, which is significantly greater than the typical effective delay spread of standard 3GPP channel models, which generally have a delay spread of less than 5 μs. It is demonstrated in [15] that two samples of the cyclic prefix (CP) length (i.e., the 9th and 10th samples) in SC-FDMA-based NB-IoT uplink are sufficient to account for the multi-path delay spread.

The performance analysis was conducted assuming an uplink (UL) NB-IoT based on SC-FDMA, with a channel bandwidth of 200 kHz occupying 72 sub-carriers with a subcarrier spacing of 2.5 kHz and a guard band of 10 kHz at each end. The subcarriers are indexed from -36 to 35, with 0 corresponding to the

DC (Direct Current) subcarrier at the baseband before the half subcarrier offset as defined in the 3GPP LTE standard. The purpose of the offset is to reduce distortions.

Under the assumption of a sampling frequency Fs = 320 kHz, and the use of a 128-point Inverse Fast Fourier Transform (IFFT) to generate symbols, the cyclic prefix (CP) length is 9 samples, and the overlapping length (WL) characterizing the time window varies from 5 to 7 samples in the simulations. The windowing is illustrated in Fig. 1.

$$IFFT = 320 \,[kHz] \,/180 \,[kHz] \,\times 72 \,[subcarriers] = 128$$

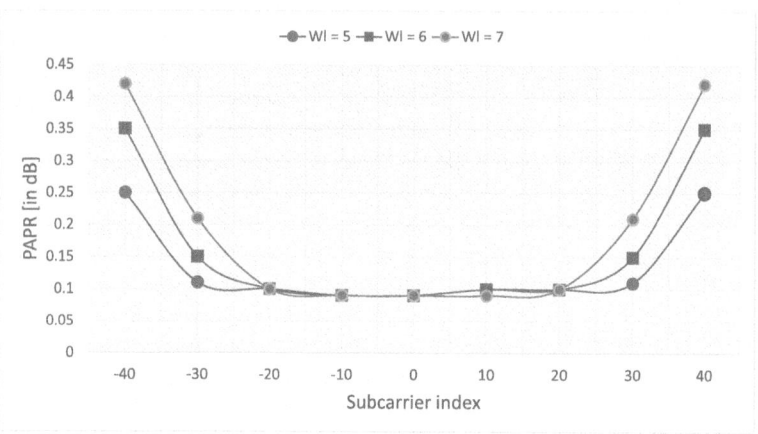

Fig. 2. PAPR [dB] as a function of the subcarrier index of the modulated subcarrier when a single SC-FDMA subcarrier is modulated by BPSK [15].

Figure 2 shows the PAPR statistics obtained as a function of the modulated subcarrier index and the WL parameter when a single SC-FDMA subcarrier is allocated to the mobile and BPSK symbols are used as input. The PAPR results vary across the subcarrier index due to the effects of the pulse shaping filter applied to the IFFT output, which limits the bandwidth.

The green, red, and blue curves represent the PAPR variation for a window length of 5, 6, and 7 symbols, respectively. The effect of windowing is noticeable at the edges where the PAPR values are higher. The longer the window, the less the signal is disturbed and the lower the PAPR. For example, as shown in Fig. 2, the PAPR of the subcarrier with index -36 is 0.25 for a window length of 7 symbols, 0.35 for 6 symbols, and 0.45 for a window length of 5 symbols. The PAPR increases towards the edges of the bandwidth as the window length WL decreases.

This similarity in results between a single subcarrier and two subcarriers modulated by BPSK in SC-FDMA can be explained by the fact that for a BPSK input, the Discrete Fourier Transform (DFT) used as a pre-coding transform leads to multiplexing between the two allocated subcarriers and modulating them by BPSK.

Additionally, it can be observed that SC-FDMA with one or two subcarriers can achieve a low PAPR of approximately 0.5 dB or less. However, the PAPR increases near the edges of the bandwidth compared to its value at the center of the subcarrier.

4 Proposed Method for PAPR Reduction in SC-FDMA

In this section, we present the proposed method for Peak-to-Average Power Ratio (PAPR) reduction in Single Carrier Frequency Division Multiple Access (SC-FDMA) within the context of NB-IoT networks, including the simulation setup and the subsequent discussion of results.

4.1 PAPR Reduction Methodology in SC-FDMA-Based NB-IoT Networks

SC-FDMA can be viewed as an OFDMA scheme where data symbols in the time domain are transformed to the frequency domain using Discrete Fourier Transform (DFT) before undergoing OFDMA modulation. The input binary signals are transformed into complex signals using a baseband modulator in a possible modulation format: BPSK, QPSK, 16-QAM. The functional block diagram of SC-FDMA is illustrated in Fig. 3; it includes the PAPR Reduction scheme.

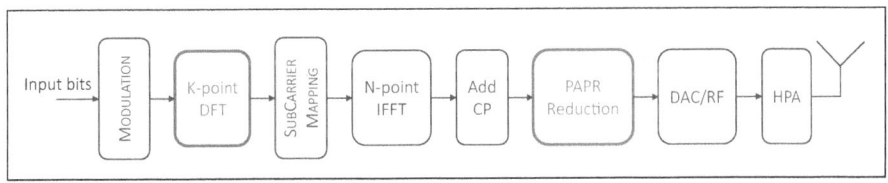

Fig. 3. SC-FDMA Transmitter including the PAPR Reduction Scheme.

In the proposed PAPR reduction technique for NB-IoT networks using SC-FDMA modulation in UL, we have chosen the clipping technique [10,11] for the following reasons: it offers backward compatibility and it has been extensively tested and experimented in OFDM systems [7]. Therefore we analyze the influence of the "Clipping Factor" (CF) on the PAPR reduction gain. To further optimize the reduction of the PAPR, we also studied the impact of the attenuation factor or "Roll-off Factor" (RoF) of two types of transmission filters, namely the Raised-Cosine (RC) filter and the Root Raised-Cosine (RRC) filter.

In SC-FDMA systems, the time-domain signal $x(t)$ can be written as

$$x\left(t\right) = \frac{1}{Q} \times \frac{1}{N} \sum_{k=0}^{N-1} X_k e^{2j\pi \frac{k}{T_s}t}, 0 \leq t \leq T_s, \tag{3}$$

where X_k is mapped data for $k = 0, 1, 2, ..., N-1$, N is the number of subcarriers (IFFT size) and T_s is the OFDM symbol period and $Q = \frac{N}{K}$, where K is the DFT size as shown in Fig. 3.

The PAPR of $x\left(t\right)$ can be defined as

$$\text{PAPR}_{[x]} \triangleq \frac{\max_{t \in [0,T_s]} |x\left(t\right)|^2}{\text{P}_{\text{av}}}, \tag{4}$$

where P_{av} is the average power defined as $\text{P}_{\text{av}} \triangleq E\left\{|x\left(t\right)|^2\right\}$. Note that, it is more useful to consider ξ as a random variable and can be evaluated by using a statistical description given by the complementary cumulative density function (CCDF), defined as the probability that PAPR exceeds ψ_0, i.e., $\text{CCDF} = \text{Pr}\left\{\text{PAPR}_{[x]} > \psi_0\right\}$.

To approximate PAPR in (4) in discrete time-domain, an oversampled version of (3) can be used. In this case, the oversampled time-domain signal x_n can be written as

$$x_n = \frac{1}{Q} \times \frac{1}{N} \sum_{k=0}^{N-1} X_k e^{2j\pi k \frac{n}{NL}}, 0 \leq n \leq NL - 1, \tag{5}$$

where L is the oversampling factor. To better approximate the PAPR of continuous-time OFDM signals, $L \geq 4$ is used to capture the peaks of the continuous time-domain signals. The time-domain samples x_n are NL-point IFFT of the data block with $(L-1)N$ zero-padding. The PAPR computed from the L-times oversampled time domain SC-FDMA signal samples can be defined as

$$\text{PAPR}_{[x]} = \frac{\max_{0 \leq n < NL} |x_n|^2}{E\left[|\text{x}_\text{n}|^2\right]}. \tag{6}$$

4.2   NB-IoT Using SC-FDMA Simulation Setup

The parameters used for PAPR reduction in NB-IoT systems using SC-FDMA are summarized in Table 1. A SC-FDMA system over a bandwidth of 5.10^6 KHz with QPSK and 16QAM modulation is considered.

4.3   Results and Discussion

Figure 4 depicts the CCDF of the PAPR reduced by Clipping Technique with various Clipping Factor (CF) values. Based on the simulation results shown in Fig. 4, depicting the distribution of SC-FDMA PAPR for various clipping factor values, which are summarized in comparison performance Table 2 for PAPR

Table 1. Simulation parameters setup.

Parameters	Values
Sampling frequency Fs	5. MHz
Pulse-shaping filter	Raised-Cosine filter (RC)
	Root Raised-Cosine filter (RRC)
Roll-off Factor (RoF)	0.99; 0.85; 0.6; 0.4
DFT Size	16
Size IFFT	512
Clipping Factor (CF)	0.75; 0.8125; 0.875; 0.9375

reduction, the following observation can be made: The greater the signal clipping (through a low clipping factor), the greater the reduction gain of PAPR. In our example, at a 10^{-3} CCDF (Fig. 4), we observe a PAPR reduction gain of 2.5 dB for a Clipping Factor (CF) of 0.75, whereas it is 0.75 dB for a Clipping Factor (CF) of 0.9375.

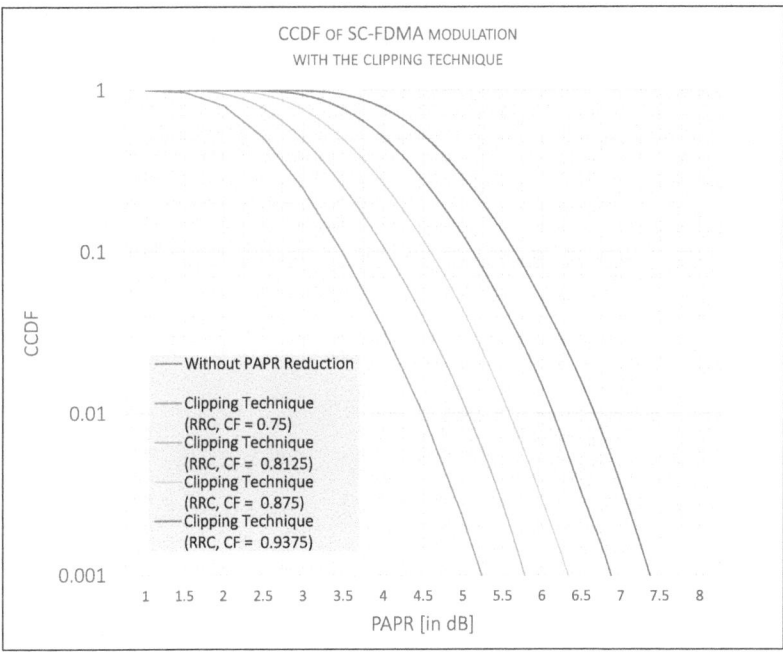

Fig. 4. SC-FDMA PAPR Reduction using Clipping Technique with different Clipping Factor (CF) values.

Table 2. PAPR reduction according to the Clipping Factor (CF).

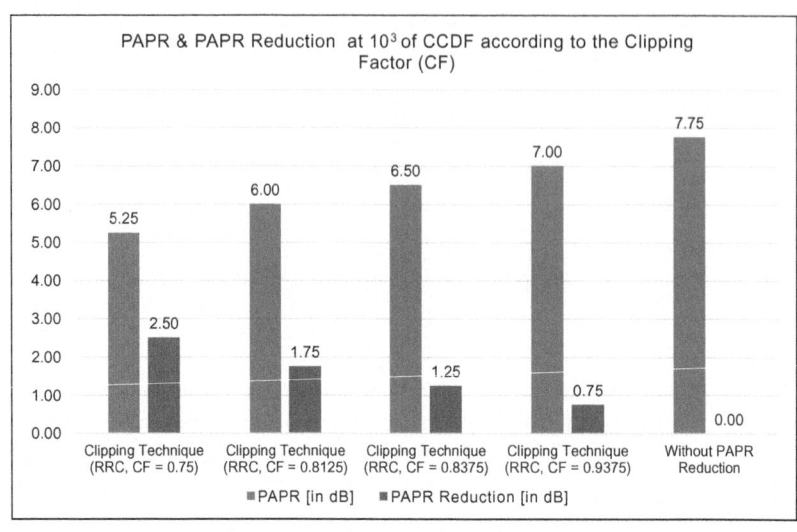

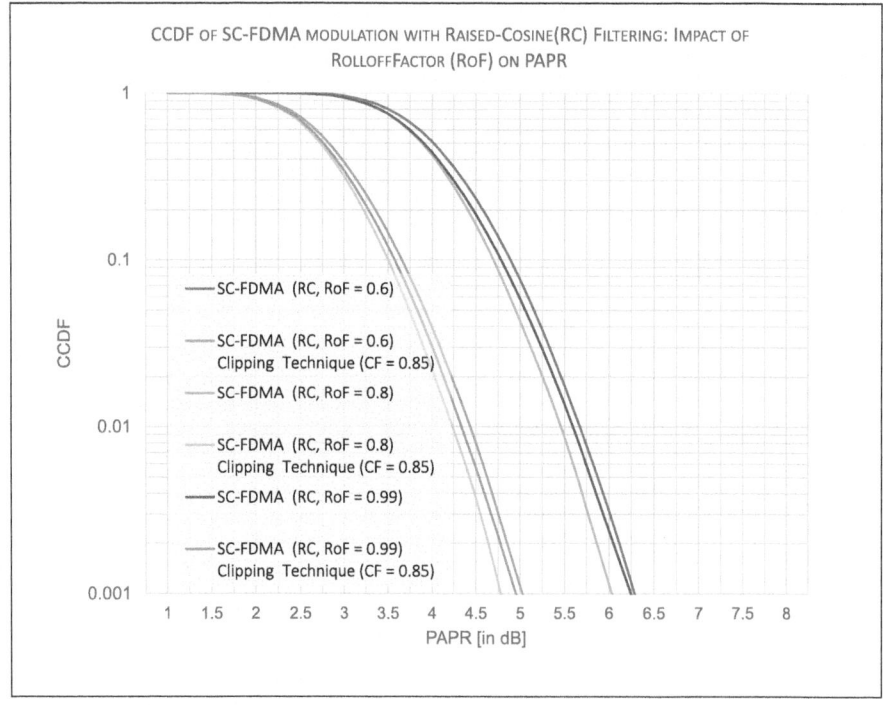

Fig. 5. CCDF of SC-FDMA modulation with Raised-Cosine(RC) filtering Impact of Roll-off Factor (RoF) on PAPR.

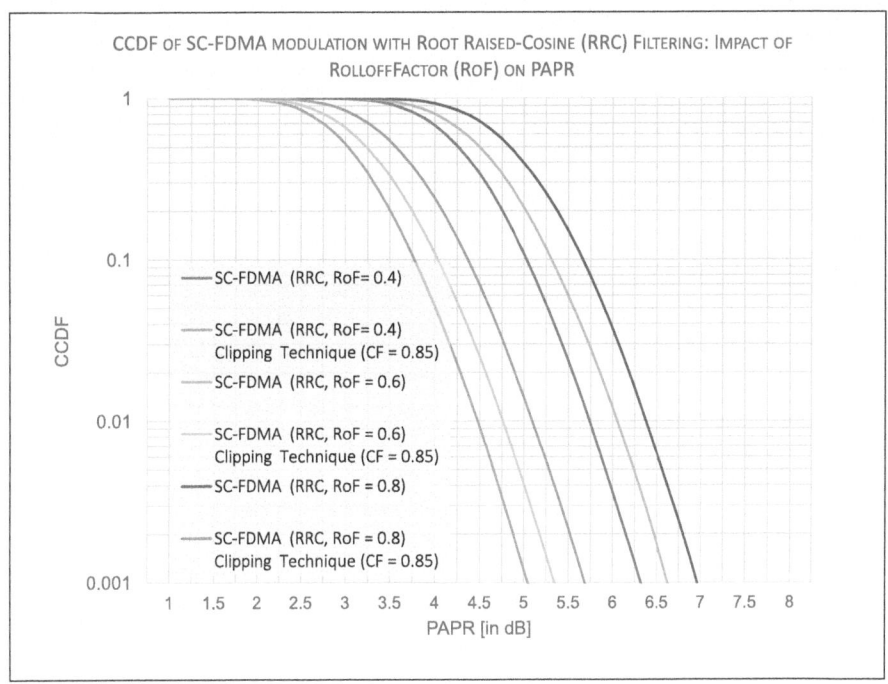

Fig. 6. CCDF of SC-FDMA modulation with Root Raised-Cosine(RRC) filtering Impact of Roll-off Factor (RoF) on PAPR.

In reality, in the SC-FDMA system as well as in most transmission systems, there is a commonly known emission shaping filtering called the transmit filter, which is used to adapt the signal to the propagation channel.

In our case study, we have considered two (02) filters: the Raised Cosine (RC) filter and the Root Raised Cosine (RRC) filter. For each type of filtering, we will analyze the impact of the attenuation factor or Roll-off Factor (RoF), which is a measure of the excess bandwidth of the filter, on the distribution of PAPR. We selected these two filters based on their capability to minimize intersymbol interference (ISI). Figure 5 and Fig. 6 show PAPR reduction performance within SC-FDMA system operating on the one hand with the Raised Cosine (RC) filter and on the other hand with the Root Raised-Cosine (RRC) filter.

The PAPR of SC-FDMA whatever the filtering (RC or RRC filters) increases with the Roll-off Factor (RoF), both in the presence or absence of PAPR reduction techniques (such as clipping). Indeed, as shown in Fig. 5, with Raised-Cosine(RC) filtering, at a CCDF of 10^{-3}, the PAPR of SC-FDMA is 6.00 dB, 6.25 dB, and 6.30 dB for a RoF of 0.6, 0.9, and 0.99, respectively. With a clipping technique using a constant clipping factor (CF) of 0.85, at a CCDF of 10^{-3}, the PAPR of SC-FDMA is 4.75 dB, 4.95 dB, and 5.10 dB for a RoF of 0.6, 0.8, and 0.99, respectively.

In Fig. 6, with Root Raised-Cosine(RRC) filtering, at a CCDF of 10^{-3}, the PAPR of SC-FDMA is 6.25 dB, 6.8 dB, and 7.00 dB for a RoF of 0.4, 0.6, and

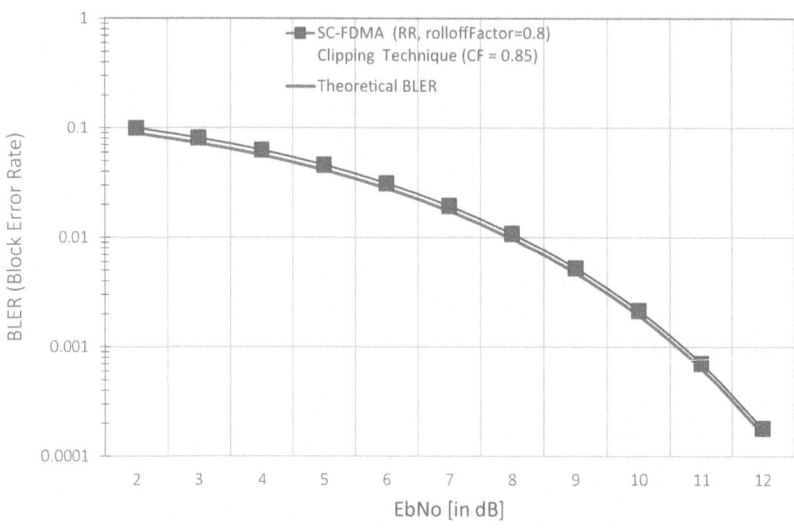

Fig. 7. BLER of SC-FDMA System (RR, RoF = 0.8) using clipping and filtering technique where CF = 0.85.

0.8, respectively. With a clipping technique using a constant clipping factor (CF) of 0.85, at a CCDF of 10^{-3}, the PAPR of SC-FDMA is 5.00 dB, 4.30 dB, and 5.70 dB for a RoF of 0.4, 0.6, and 0.8, respectively.

Raised Cosine (RC) and Root Raised Cosine (RRC) a filtering are used in wireless communication systems including SC-FDMA systems to shape the spectrum of transmitted signals, reducing out-of-band emissions and interference. When the Roll-off Factor (RoF) increases, the rate of transition of the RC or RRC filter becomes steeper, leading to more pronounced peaks in the time domain. This contributes to higher PAPR values, even without considering PAPR reduction techniques as showed in Fig. 5 where RRC filtering is deployed and Fig. 6 where RRC filtering is used.

Figure 7 evaluates the impact of the clipping technique on the performance of the transmission in our SC-FDMA model.

Figure 7 shows the performance of the Block Error Rate (BLER) in the presence of the clipping technique. It should be noted that clipping, by its nature, degrades the BLER as it generates distortions [7]. Since our constraints require us to maintain the BLER without degradation, in addition to clipping, filtering is performed to reduce the distortions generated by clipping. Ultimately, based on the results shown in Fig. 7, the BLER curve with the PAPR reduction technique remains aligned with the reference curve (theoretical BLER curve) which corresponds to the BLER of SC-FDMA System without any PAPR reduction.

5   Conclusion

NB-IoT is a dedicated technology for the Internet of Things, providing extensive coverage and various advantages. The NB-IoT technology utilizes SC-FDMA modulation, a close relative of OFDMA, for its uplink transmission. However, the high peak-to-average power ratio (PAPR) in SC-FDMA signals leads to the degradation of subcarrier orthogonality due to amplifier non-linearities, resulting in significant energy consumption from the battery at the transmitter.

In this article, we have studied and analyzed several commonly applied methods in OFDM, enabling us to adapt the clipping technique to SC-FDMA. After implementing and simulating the clipping technique, our results demonstrated a significant reduction in PAPR without degrading the signal's Block Error Rate (BLER). We observed that the PAPR decreased with the Roll-off Factor (RoF). Combining the clipping method with filtering techniques such as Root Raised-Cosine (RRC) or Raised-Cosine (RC) allowed us to achieve satisfactory results in terms of reduction gain and signal degradation correction.

In this article, our findings mainly focus on the clipping technique. Therefore, an extension of simulations for other types of clipping functions, such as Smooth Clipping or Deep Clipping, could be explored to leverage their unique properties and characteristics.

References

1. 3GPP. Technical Specification Group Radio Access Network; Study on provision of low-cost Machine-Type Communications (MTC) User Equipments (UEs) based on LTE (Release 13) (No. 36.888) (2016). Retrieved from https://www.3gpp.org/ftp/Specs/archive/36_series/36.888/
2. Cisco Systems. Cisco Visual Networking Index: Global Mobile Data Traffic Forecast Update. 2018-2023 White Paper (2019)
3. Owaid, M.H., Mohammed, S.J.: PAPR performance analysis of SC-FDMA and SC-FDMA-DSCDMA. In: 2022 8th International Conference on Contemporary Information Technology and Mathematics (ICCITM), Mosul, Iraq, pp. 284–289 (2022). https://doi.org/10.1109/ICCITM56309.2022.10031668.
4. Bebyrahma, A.M.K., Suryani, T., Suwadi.: Analysis of combined PAPR reduction technique with Predistorter for OFDM system in 5G. In: International Seminar on Intelligent Technology and Its Applications (ISITIA). Surabaya, Indonesia **2022**, 478–483 (2022). https://doi.org/10.1109/ISITIA56226.2022.9855274
5. Prasad, S., Arun, S.: Hanowa matrix based SLM technique for PAPR reduction in OFDM systems. In: International Conference for Advancement in Technology (ICONAT). Goa, India **2023**, 1–5 (2023). https://doi.org/10.1109/ICONAT57137.2023.10080797
6. The MathWorks, Inc. MATLAB version: 9.13.0 (R2022b) (2022). https://www.mathworks.com. Accessed 01 Jan 2023
7. Guel, D.: Etude de nouvelles techniques de réduction du facteur de crête à compatibilité descendante pour les systèmes multi porteuses. Université de Rennes, Thèse de doctorat (2009)

8. Guel, D., Palicot, J.: Analysis and comparison of clipping techniques for OFDM Peak-to-Average Power Ratio reduction. In: 2009 16th International Conference on Digital Signal Processing, Santorini, Greece, pp. 1–6 (2009). https://doi.org/10.1109/ICDSP.2009.5201128.

9. Guel, D., Palicot, J.: Clipping formulated as an adding signal technique for OFDM peak power reduction. In: VTC Spring: IEEE 69th Vehicular Technology Conference. Barcelona, Spain **2009**, 1–5 (2009). https://doi.org/10.1109/VETECS.2009.5073442

10. Li, X., Cimini, L.J.: Effects of clipping and filtering on the performance of OFDM. In: Proceedings of IEEE 47th Vehicular Technology Conference, vol. 3, pp. 1634–1638, 4-7 May (1997)

11. Li, X., Cimini, L.J.: Effects of clipping and filtering on the performance of OFDM. IEEE Commun. Lett. **2**, 131–133 (1998)

12. Ochiai, H., Imai, H.: Performance analysis of deliberately clipped OFDM signals. IEEE Trans. Commun. **50**, 89–101 (2002)

13. O'Neill, R., Lopes, L.B.: Envelope variations and spectral splatter in clipped multicarrier signals. In: Proceedings of Sixth IEEE International Symposium on Personal, Indoor and Mobile Radio Communications PIMRC'95., vol. 1, pp. 71-75, 27-29 (1995)

14. Panta, K., Armstrong, J.: Effects of clipping on the error performance of OFDM in frequency selective fading channels. IEEE Trans. Wireless Commun. **3**, 668–671 (2004)

15. Media Tek Inc., "PAPR on SC-FDMA". chez 3GPP TSG RAN WG1 Meeting, Anaheim 15th-22rd November 2015, California, USA (2015)

16. Islam, S.R., Kwak, D., Kabir, M.H., Hossain, M., Kwak, K.: The Internet of Things for health care: a comprehensive survey. IEEE Access **3**, 678–708 (2015)

17. Chen, M., Hao, Y., Li, L., Hu, L.: An efficient data transmission scheme for internet of things: a case study from E-Healthcare. IEEE Trans. Industr. Inf. **10**(2), 1397–1405 (2014)

Modelling of a Solar Photovoltaic Power Supply for a Wireless Access Point in a Rural Area

Thomas Djotio Ndié[1]([✉]), Alphonse Tabué Kamga[1], and Karl Jonas[2]

[1] University of Yaounde 1, National Advanced School of Engineering of Yaounde, Yaoundé, Cameroon
tdjotio@gmail.com, alphonse.kamga08@gmail.com
[2] University of Applied Sciences, Hochschule Bonn-Rhein-Sieg, Sankt Augustin, Germany
karl.jonas@h-brs.de

Abstract. The digital divide remains a major concern for rural areas in developing countries in general and for sub-Saharan Africa in particular. It is particularly characterized by the unavailability of energy resources on which the functioning and operation of network connectivity infrastructure depends. The constraints of availability of electrical energy, coupled with the difficulty of access, make it difficult to implement relevant and sustainable digital solutions in these hard-to-reach areas. We propose in this article, a model for solar photovoltaic power generation that allows for autonomous and continuous operation of a wireless access point (WAP) in areas where access to electrical power is difficult. Our approach first consists of designing the system and mathematically modeling the photovoltaic solar panel and the BUCK series chopper, as well as the P&O type MPPT control for the solar panel' maximum power point tracking. Finally, we simulate the operation of the system for appreciating its behavior in a possible real situation. For this final point, before the simulation process, we realized the system's global diagram consisted of the solar generator, adaptation stage (provided with the MPPT control of type P&O) and battery park. This simulation allowed us to study the behavior of the system in normal conditions but also in particular conditions reflecting the environment in which it will be deployed. The results of the simulation are satisfactory and allowed us to validate the model we proposed. We have successfully designed a solar photovoltaic power supply for the WiABox 2507 that takes into account all its energy constraints.

Keywords: wireless access point · photovoltaic generator · MPPT · DC-DC converter series · Pertub&Observ algorithm

1 Introduction

In a computer network, a wireless access point (WAP) is an intermediate device that uses radio waves for allowing wireless devices to access a wired network or the Internet. The access point can be a stand-alone gateway router directly connected to a network. It can also be directly integrated as part of the router itself. To use it in remote locations, it should be self-sufficient in electrical power, which would give it the distinction of being mobile. The source of electrical energy that powers it could be renewable, for example; in most cases it is a solar power supply.

A. Sere et al. (Eds.): AFRICOMM 2023, LNICST 587, pp. 113–130, 2025.
https://doi.org/10.1007/978-3-031-81570-6_8

Telecommunications/ICTs are slowly progressing in rural and remote areas of developing countries, especially in those with special public policies, initiatives and subsidies. In general, telecommunication/ICT services, such as basic telephony, short message services, videoconferencing and internet services, is almost absent [1, 2] in sparsely populated rural areas. Provided a range of digital applications and services to people in rural areas can significantly improve their economy, quality of life and reduce inequality. Examples include telephone and short message service (SMS), Internet services, e-(business, health, finance, culture, banking, learning, inclusion, government), telework, and Internet of Things/M2M services. In the current context where the whole world has been stricken by the CORONA VIRUS pandemic that affects the school system especially in rural areas, the proximity network services are an excellent tool to improve the living conditions in these areas.

This is one of the motivating reasons why the inception of the WiABox 2507 project [3, 4]. WiABox 2507 is a multi-band, broadband wireless access technology capable of operating in a dedicated frequency range to provide reliable and sustainable ubiquitous services in rural areas, mainly in developing countries [4]. Its objective is to realize an autonomous and sustainable wireless access point to provide proximity network services in a community. The constraints for a WiABox 2507 access node are as follows:

- Compatibility with WiBACK (Fraunhofer FOKUS' wireless backhaul technology) & current IEEE 802 standards
- Based on open infrastructure (soft and hardware) and integrates emerging paradigms like SDN, SDR, TV White Space.
- Ability to operate on a range of frequencies instead of dedicated frequencies.
- Enable the development of resilient, persistent and sustainable wireless mesh networks.
- Serve as optimized end-user support for critical and emergency remote applications for unconnected areas.
- Be able to operate without interruptions in areas with insufficient or no access to electrical power.

It is on this last point that this paper is focused. The goal is to propose a WAP that is autonomous in electricity, mobile, and therefore suitable for remote areas. The objectives are: (1) To model, design and realize a solar power system perfectly adapted to the WiABox 2507 technology to allow its use in remote areas. (2) Provide network support for the operation of IoT-based systems. (3) Develop low-cost equipment to make the system affordable. (4) Provide equipment that is easy to maintain, install, and use.

2 Modeling of the WiABox 2507 Power Supply System

2.1 System Description

Our photovoltaic power system for the WiABox 2507 will consist of a solar panel that converts solar energy into electricity, a rechargeable battery that stores the energy produced and a charge controller that controls the charge of the battery. When the WiABox 2507 is connected to this system, it uses the energy stored in the battery to operate.

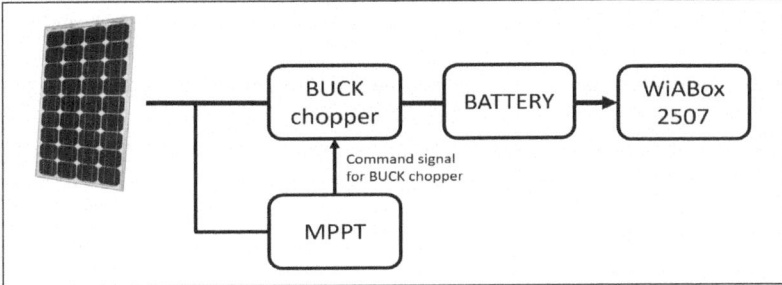

Fig. 1. Block diagram of the WiABox 2507 power supply system

Figure 1 shows the general structure of our autonomous photovoltaic system [5]. This structure is composed of four blocks: the solar panel, the charge controller (with a "Buck" type chopper and its MPPT control), the battery and the load, which in our case is the WiABox 2507.

The WiABox 2507 works with 12 V and calls for a maximum DC current of 02 amps when fully charged, that is a maximum power of 24 W. In order to guarantee an efficient, reliable and long lasting energy source it is recommended to adopt an autonomy of 04 days for our solar photovoltaic power system [6]. For that, we will need: (a) a monocrystalline solar panel of 210 watts-peak; (b) a storage battery of 72 A-hours (Ah) to have an autonomy of the system in average of 04 days; (c) a regulator/controller of load delivering a maximum current of 15 amperes (A), to easily convey the current coming from the solar panel for charging. The charge controller is equipped with a DC-DC converter, which is controlled by a pulse width modulation signal with a maximum power point tracking algorithm (MPPT). The system diagram is shown in Fig. 1.

2.2 Modeling of the Photovoltaic Solar Panel

A photovoltaic solar panel is composed of one or more photovoltaic solar cells whose function is to convert the power of solar radiation into electrical power. The cell behaves like a solar cell with a series resistance (Rs) and a shunt resistance (Rsh). These resistors will have some influence on the characteristic $I = f(V)$. The series resistance represents the internal resistance of the cell. It mainly depends on the resistance of the semiconductor used, the contact resistance of the collector gates and the resistivity of these gates [7].

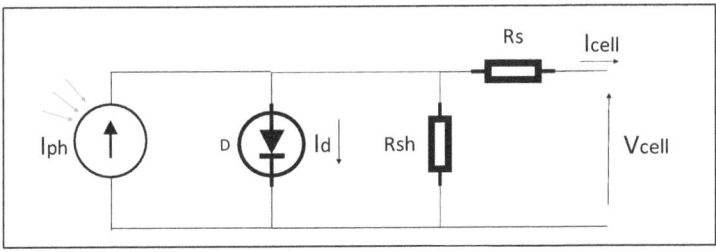

Fig. 2. Electrical diagram of a photovoltaic cell

The shunt resistance is due to a leakage current at the junction, it depends on the way it was made (Fig. 2);

This model uses a current generator to model the incident luminous flux, a diode for the phenomena of polarization of the cell and two resistors (series and shunt) [7] for the losses. This model is said to have five parameters, these parameters are the photo-current (Iph), the saturation current (I0), the ideality factor of the junction (A), the series resistance (Rs) and the shunt resistance (Rsh).

The physical study of a photovoltaic cell [8] allows us to obtain the current equation of the load:

$$I_{cell} = I_{ph} - I_d - I_{Rsh} \tag{1}$$

I_{cell}: Current delivered by the photocell.
I_{ph}: Photo current.
I_d: Current of the diode.
I_{Rsh}: Shunt current.

The resistance (Rsh) is higher so we can neglect the current IRsh so the equation is written:

$$I_{cell} = I_{ph} - I_d \tag{2}$$

We can deduce the current delivered by a cell:

$$I_{cell} = I_{ph} - I_0 \left[\exp\left(\frac{q(V_{cell} + R_S I_{cell})}{N_S AKT} - 1 \right) \right] - \frac{V_{cell} + R_S I_{cell}}{R_{Sh}} \tag{3}$$

With:

q [C]: Charge of the electron (1.602. 10–19 C).
Ns: Number of cells connected in series.
A: Ideality constant of the junction (1 < A < 2).
K [J/K]: Boltzmann constant (1.3805 .10–23 J/K).

The equations described above cannot represent the I-V characteristic of a PV module since they are specific to a single PV cell that represents the basic element of the panel, so we introduce the module-specific equation:

$$I_{PV} = N_p I_{ph} - N_p I_0 \left[\exp\left(\frac{q(V_{cell} + R_S I_{cell})}{N_S AKT} \right) - 1 \right] - N_p \frac{V_{cell} + R_S I_{cell}}{R_{sh}} \tag{4}$$

With Ns the number of cells connected in series in a module and, Np the number of cells connected in parallel in a module.

The characteristics of the solar photovoltaic panel that we will use are:

− Maximum power: 210 Wp
− Open circuit voltage: 32.5 V
− Maximum power point voltage: 28.3 V
− Short circuit current: 8.22 A
− Current at maximum power point: 7.41 A

– Operating temperature: −40 °C to +85 °C
– Efficiency: 15.44%.

• **Influence of temperature**

Temperature has a considerable influence on the behavior of the photovoltaic cell [9] and thus on its efficiency. This influence is mainly reflected by a decrease in the generated voltage (followed by a very slight increase in current). Figure 3 below shows the current-voltage (I-V) (a) and power-voltage (P-V) (b) characteristics of a photovoltaic module for one level of sunlight and several levels of temperature:

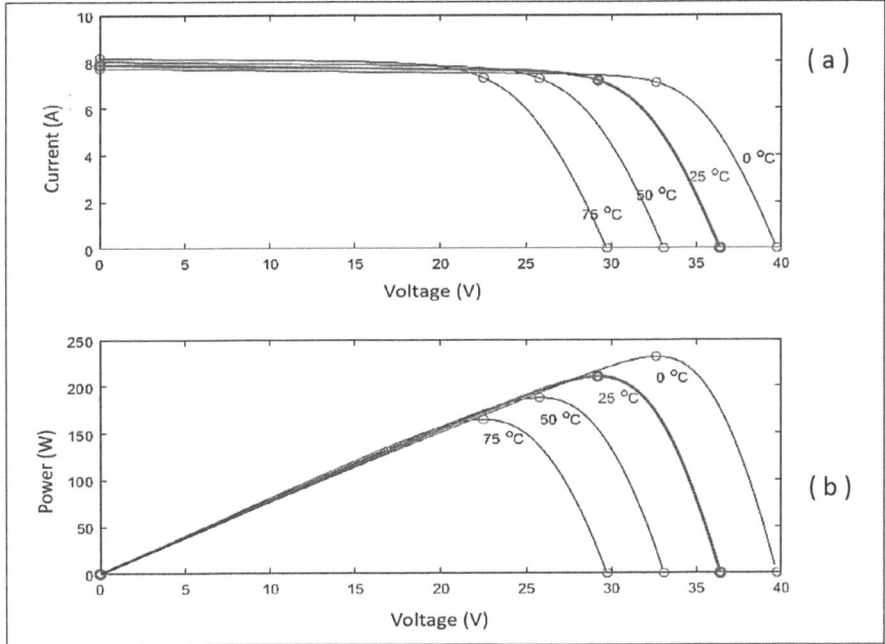

Fig. 3. (a) Influence of temperature on the current-voltage characteristic and (b) the power-voltage characteristic

We note a loss current of an order of magnitude estimated at 2.3mV/°C/cell. The short-circuit current increases slightly with the cell temperature (about 0.05% per degree Celsius).

• **Influence of solar radiation**

Here illustrated Fig. 4, we have varied the values of the sunlight level, kept the temperature constant, then, we have plotted the current-voltage (I-V) (a) and, power-voltage (P-V) (b) characteristics corresponding to each value. Photovoltaic cells exploit the photoelectric effect to produce direct current by absorption of solar radiation. This effect allows cells to directly converting the light energy of photons into electricity through a semiconductor material carrying electrical charges [10]. The efficiency of a photovoltaic cell or module is the ratio between the electrical energy produced by this cell or module and the light energy received on the corresponding surface [11]:

$$n[\%] = Pproduced[kW]/Pincident[kW]$$

Therefore, the actual efficiency varies continuously, particularly depending on the incident solar energy [12]. The brightness has a considerable influence on the performance of the cells. As shown in the graph in Fig. 4, the current increases proportionally with the irradiance (Fig. 4.a), while the open circuit voltage varies very little (Fig. 4.b). Thus, the greater the cloud cover, the lower the current generated.

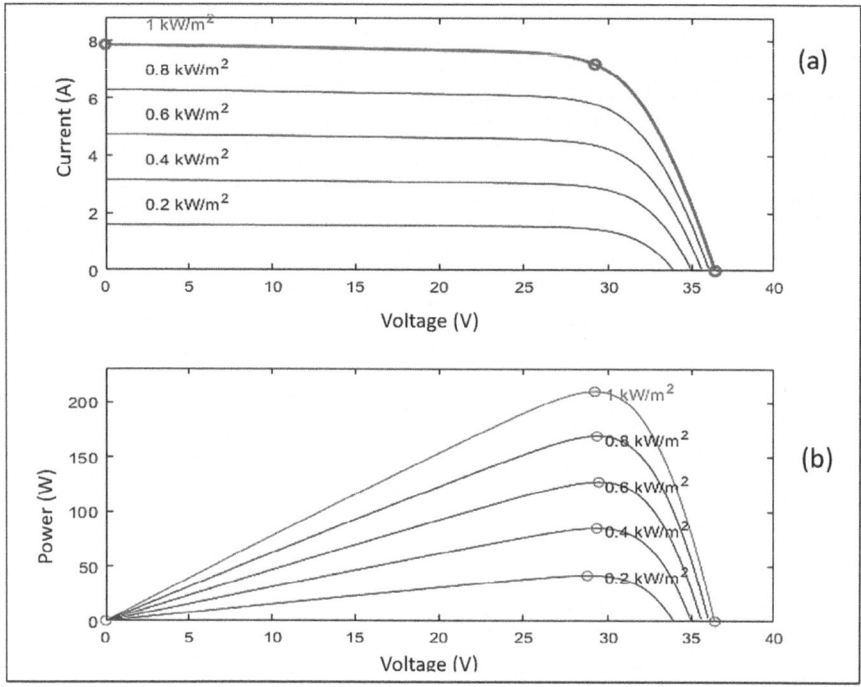

Fig. 4. (a) Influence of solar radiation on the current-voltage characteristic and (b) the power-voltage characteristic

From Eq. (4) we establish the Simulink model of the photovoltaic generator represented by the following Fig. 5:

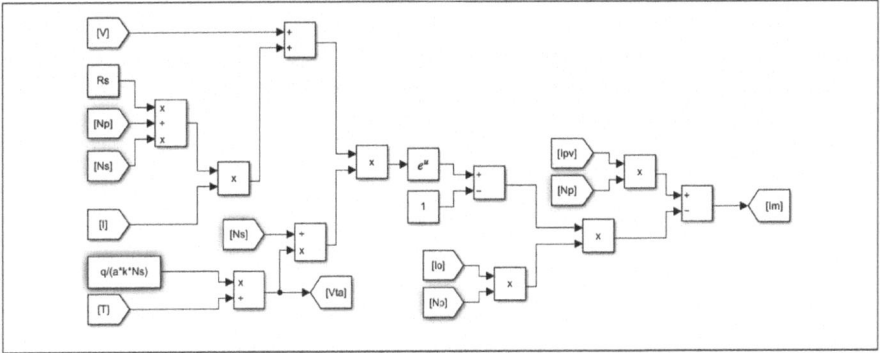

Fig. 5. Simulink model of the solar panel

2.3 Modeling the BUCK Chopper

A photovoltaic generator has non-linear current-voltage characteristics with a maximum power point (MPP) [1]. These characteristics depend on several parameters, the most important of which are the illumination level and the temperature of the photovoltaic cells. Moreover, depending on the characteristics of the load on which the GPV is delivering, we can find a very high discrepancy between the potential power of the photovoltaic array and the one actually transferred to the load in direct connection mode.

In order to extract the maximum power available at each moment at the terminals of the photovoltaic generator, and to transfer it to the load, the technique used classically is a matching stage between the photovoltaic generator and the load. There are two types of charge controllers: the PWM (Pulse Width Modulation) controller and the MPPT (Maximum Power Point Tracking) controller. We will use, for this work, the MPPT controller, which has a much higher efficiency than the PWM controller because, this stage plays the role of interface between the solar panel and the load. In addition, it has the advantage of ensuring, by a control action, the transfer of the maximum power supplied by the generator so that it is as close as possible to the maximum power available.

There are mainly three types of DC-DC converter: (a) the BUCK chopper used when the load voltage is lower than the voltage delivered by the solar panel, whose role is to convert its input voltage into a lower output voltage and keep it constant. (b) The BOOST chopper, used when the load voltage is higher than the voltage delivered by the solar panel, whose role is to convert its input voltage into a higher output voltage and keep it constant. (c) The BUCK-BOOST chopper used when the load voltage is lower or higher than the solar panel voltage, its role is to maintain the output voltage constant either by raising or by lowering the input voltage. The choice of one of these three choppers depends on the needs of the load in terms of voltage and current, as well as the specificities of the solar system. For our case, the BUCK and BUCK-BOOST chopper are indicated. The BUCK chopper has the advantage of a very good conversion efficiency, low electromagnetic noise, simplicity of the electronic circuit and a relatively low realization cost [13]. Nevertheless, the BUCK-BOOST chopper is more complex to realize, has a higher electromagnetic noise and is much more expensive. Our choice is therefore the BUCK chopper.

The BUCK chopper is a series type transistor DC-DC converter. The BUCK chopper consists of capacitors, inductor, diode and switch. It is designed for a power of 180 W corresponding to the nominal values I = 15 A, V = 12 V. Figure 6 shows the ideal circuit of the series chopper:

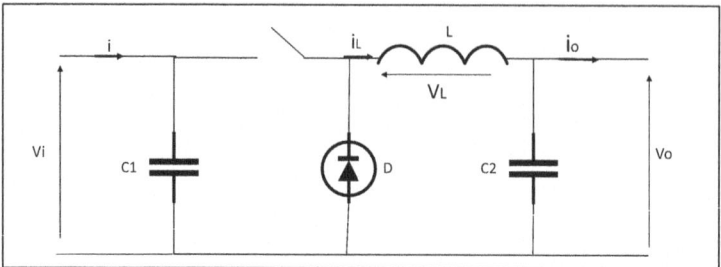

Fig. 6. Ideal circuit diagram of the series chopper

We note α, the duty cycle of the pulses that drive the switch and, *Te* the period of the pulses. Typically, the switch is a MOSFET or IGBT transistor, which are semiconductor devices in the "blocked-saturated" mode.

When the switch is closed for the duration αTe, a current flows through the circuit, but does not pass through the diode since it is inversely biased. The switch is driven at the switching frequency $fe = 1/Te$. The source *Vi* supplies power to the load and the inductor. During the time $t\varepsilon[\alpha Te, Te]$ the switch opens and the energy stored in the inductor drives the current flow in the freewheeling diode. The voltage across it is therefore zero.

- **Mathematical equivalent model**

In order to know the real behavior we have to make the representation of the equivalent circuit by the two states of the switch and then to draw the mathematical model linking the input/output variables. Figure 7 shows the equivalent circuit diagram of a devolving converter (series DC-DC converter) with the switch closed, while Fig. 8 represents the devolving converter with the switch open for $(1 - \alpha)Te$.

When we apply Kirchhoff's law to the above circuit, we get the following equations:

$$\begin{cases} i_{c1}(t) = C\frac{dV_i(t)}{dt} = i(t) - i_L(t) \\ i_{c2}(t) = C_2\frac{dV_o(t)}{dt} = i_L(t) - i_o(t) \\ V_L(t) = L\frac{di_L(t)}{dt} = V_i(t) - V_o(t) \end{cases} \tag{5}$$

The system of Eqs. (6) is deduced from Fig. 7 above.

$$\begin{cases} i_{c1}(t) = C\frac{dV_i(t)}{dt} = i(t) \\ i_{c2}(t) = C_2\frac{dV_o(t)}{dt} = i_L(t) - i_o(t) \\ V_L(t) = L\frac{di_L(t)}{dt} = V_o(t) \end{cases} \tag{6}$$

We therefore present a model that must faithfully reproduce the operating sequences and simulate both continuous and discontinuous conduction, and especially the transition

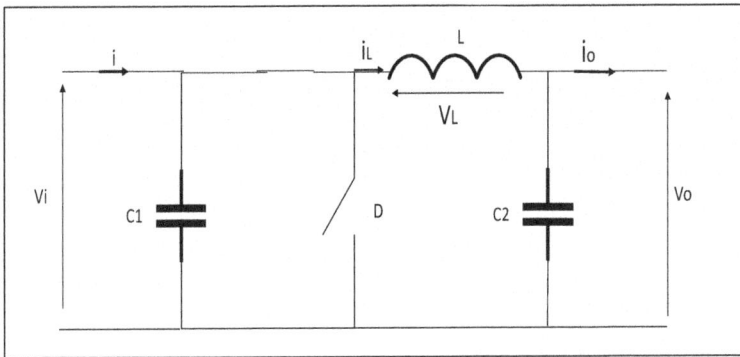

Fig. 7. Electrical diagram of the BUCK chopper in "closed" mode

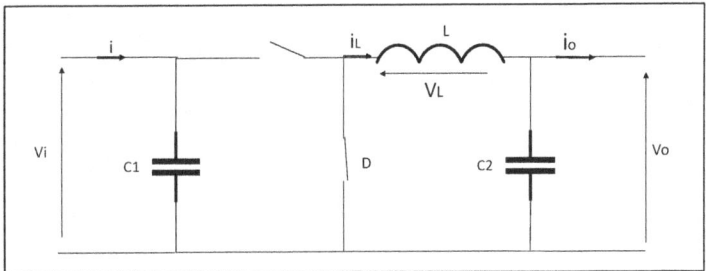

Fig. 8. Electrical diagram of the BUCK chopper in "open" mode

from one to the other [14]. For this, the nullity of the current *iL* must be verified during *toff*; and if it occurs, the current must be maintained at zero until the beginning of the next period when it must increase again.

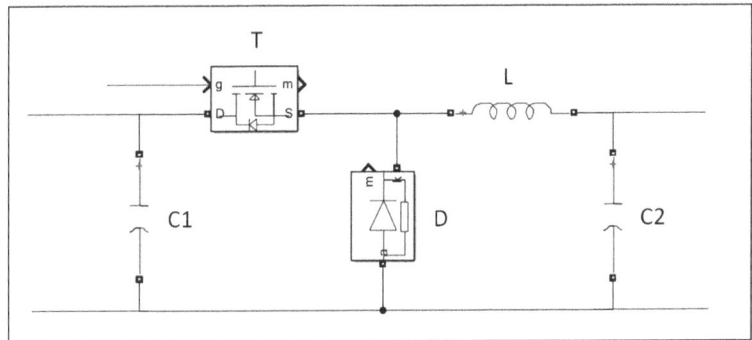

Fig. 9. Simulink model of the BUCK chopper

The Matlab-Simulink model proposed for this case precisely uses this detection of the current nullity. The identification of the conduction type is done by checking the nullity of the sum of the control signal K and the current iL. For continuous conduction, this sum is never zero, whereas for discontinuous conduction, this sum is zero between ßT and T. When the nullity of this sum is detected, a switch is switched in order to cancel the variation of the current iL and thus to maintain zero until the beginning of the next period. On the other hand, all models used for all components are relatively real. For example, the switch and diode models have a series resistance and leakage inductance, while the capacitor and inductor models have a series resistance. The simulation model of the BUCK chopper developed for this application is given, under the Simulink software, by Fig. 9 above. This simulation model is quite realistic because it takes into account the imperfections of the components it contains.

2.4 Modeling the MPPT Control Algorithm

There are several MPPT control algorithms, the choice of one of these algorithms depends on the specific requirements and constraints of the project. In the case of a simple PV installation, the "Pertub and Observe" (P&O) algorithm is an effective and economical choice [15]. This method is based on using a feedback loop to adjust the input voltage of a DC-DC converter to find the maximum power point of the solar panel. The principle of the Perturbation and Observation method is to perturb the generator's VPV voltage by a small amount around its initial value and to analyze the behavior of the resulting PPV power variation [16]. If a positive increment of the VPV voltage results in an increase of the PPV power, it means that the operating point is to the left of the maximum power point. If, on the contrary, the power decreases, it implies that the system has exceeded the MPP [17]. A similar reasoning can be done when the voltage decreases. Among the advantages of the P&O algorithm are its simplicity (thus easily implemented using microcontrollers), its high reactivity to variations in solar irradiance, its robustness and reliability [18].

Figure 10 shows the flowchart of the P&O algorithm as it is to be implemented in the control microprocessor. Its Simulink model is shown in Fig. 11.

The P&O electronics determine, from the externally imposed setpoints and the measurements taken from the PV generator and the loads, the conduction and blocking sequence of the switch and elaborate the logic signals necessary for its control according to the type of converter used. In the case of the PWM control, the switch state is varied at each rate that does not depend on the way the quantities of the systems interconnected by the power electronic converter evolve, this rate being essentially fixed according to the switching speed.

Knowing that any switching is equivalent to changing the potential of a system terminal seen as a current source by connecting it to another system terminal seen as a voltage source, the control by pulse width modulation (PWM) will thus consist in choosing a switching frequency of the switch and, to fix within the switching period, the conduction intervals of the switches connected to a terminal of the "current source", according to a reference signal which corresponds to the desired potential for this terminal. In digital form, this type of control is achieved by fixing the conduction intervals of the various switches on each period or each half-period of modulation, as shown in Fig. 12.

The output of the comparator can be generated as a rectangular voltage modulated in width (variable duty cycle: PWM signal) [19]. This is the result of the comparison

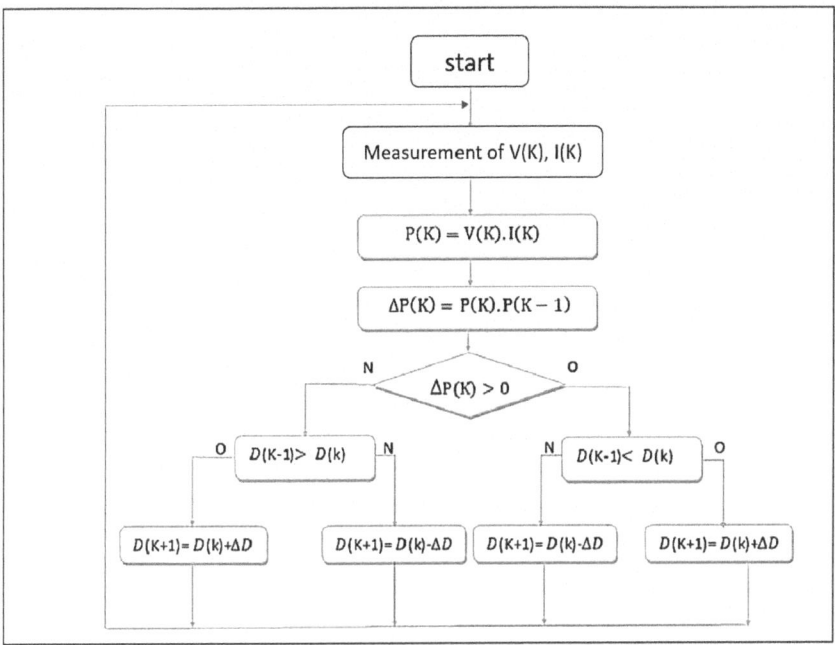

Fig. 10. Flowchart for finding the maximum power point using the P&O method.

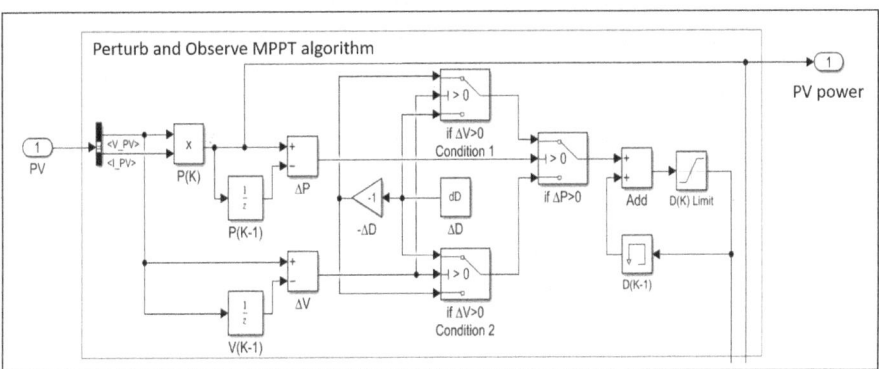

Fig. 11. Simulink model of the P&O algorithm

between the signal at the output of the integrator (Vref) and the one generated by a triangular generator with a frequency fixed by the converter operation. As the voltage Vref increases (decreases), the duty cycle α increases (decreases). The variations of the voltage Vref induce, for a given illumination and temperature, the displacement of the operating point on the power-voltage characteristic [19].

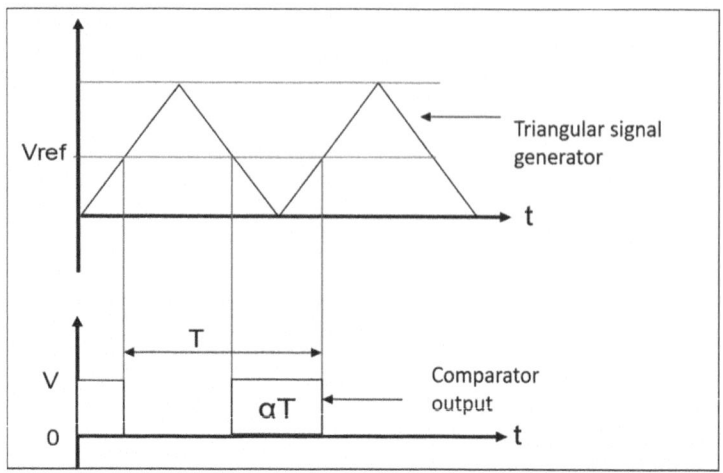

Fig. 12. Square-wave signal generation at the output of the comparator

3 Simulation and Analysis of Results

3.1 Overall System Diagram

Figure 13 represents the global schematic of our photovoltaic system; it is composed of a photovoltaic module with a power of 210 W-peak, a lithium-ion battery with a capacity of 72 A-hours (Ah) and a series chopper (BUCK) controlled by a P&O MPPT algorithm.

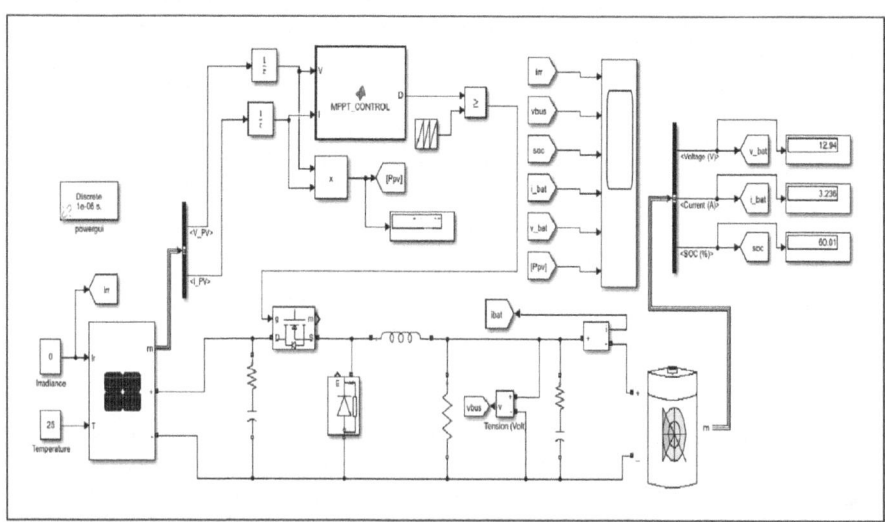

Fig. 13. Overall diagram of the Wiabox power system

To perform the simulation we used the mathematical model of all components of the WiABox 2507 power system. After having made the schematic of Fig. 13 and filled in the different values of the components, we started the simulation of our system.

3.2 Simulation Results

Several parameters must be taken into account to define the solar power supply required to cover an energy need. Apart from the choice of technology, the inclination and orientation of the solar panel, the temperature above the solar panel and the solar irradiation must be taken into account. The operation and profitability of a solar panel remains closely related to the rate of sunlight and the heat produced by the sun. In practice, the light intensity is the most important element in the operation and efficiency of a photovoltaic solar panel, more important than the heat. For the simulation of the system, we will study the behavior of the power system as a function of solar irradiation.

To carry out our simulation, we have considered a sample reflecting a variation of the solar irradiation in time. The Fig. 14 presents the curve of evolution of the sunshine in the time; we will use it for our simulation.

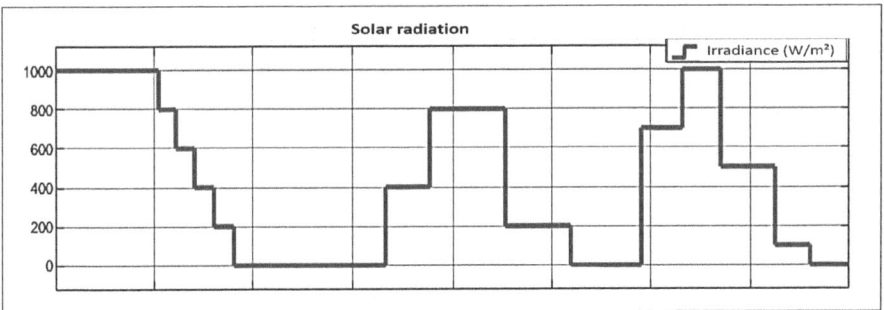

Fig. 14. Solar irradiance variation curve

Figure 14 illustrates a scenario representing the variation, in time and at constant temperature (25 °C), of the solar irradiation in a given location, reflecting a real case.

In Fig. 15 we can see the variation of the power of the photovoltaic solar panel as a function of the illumination. This is the power curve produced by the solar panel and transferred to the load through the charge controller. We can see that the controller constantly trying to extract the maximum power from the solar panel due to the many variations of the sunshine level. This is made possible thanks to the efficiency of the "Pertub & Observ" algorithm.

By zooming in on the plot of the power from the solar panel extracted by the charge controller, we can see the efficiency of the P&O algorithm, which tracks the point of maximum power to be extracted from the solar panel. We also observe that the response time of the algorithm following an abrupt change in the sunlight level is very favorable; it is around 0.025 s as shown in Fig. 16. Even under unfavorable weather conditions, the charge controller, using the P&O algorithm, always seeks to extract the maximum power from the solar PV array.

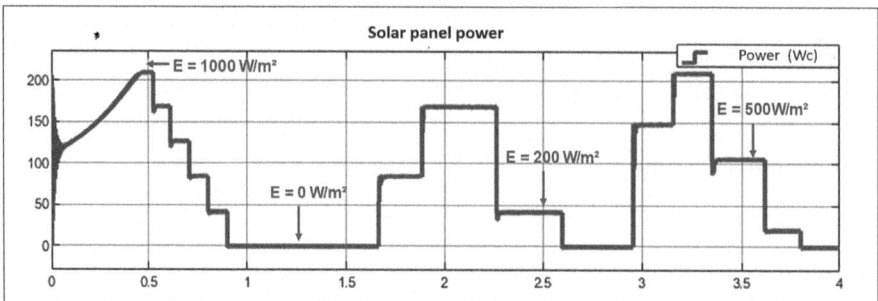

Fig. 15. Power of the solar photovoltaic panel

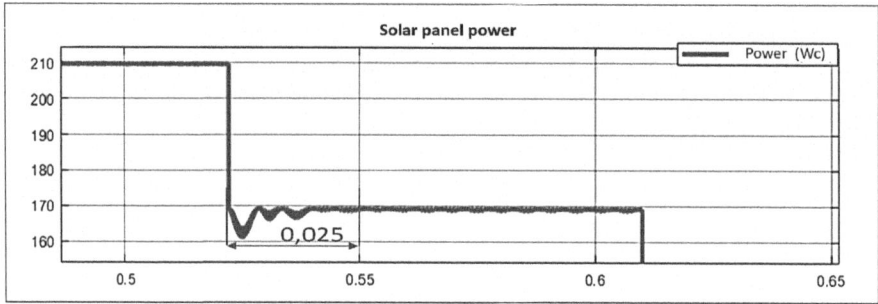

Fig. 16. Zoom on the curve of the power from the solar panel

Figure 17a shows the variation of the output voltage of the BUCK chopper as a function of the input power coming from the solar PV panel and the latter depends on the solar irradiation (Fig. 14). Figure 17b shows the variation of the voltage at the terminals of the battery supplied by the charge controller as a function of the amount of sunlight. We can see that Fig. 17a and Fig. 17b are identical; this is because the battery is directly connected to the charge controller, so they are equipotential.

The battery state of charge (SoC) is a relative measure of the amount of energy stored in a battery, defined as the ratio of the battery's charge at a certain time to its total capacity [20]. Accurate state-of-charge estimation is important because battery management systems use it to inform the user or the system itself of the remaining capacity until the next recharge to: (a) ensure proper battery operation; (b) implement control strategies and; (c) maximize battery life.

For the simulation, we used a Lithium-ion battery with 60% charge; Fig. 18 shows the result of the simulation of the charge and discharge of the battery as a function of the power from the solar panel (depending on the variation of sunshine). We notice that when the voltage at the terminals of the regulator is sufficient (i.e. higher than the voltage at the terminals of the battery bank), the battery is charged provided that its charge rate at this moment is not 100%. In the opposite case (the voltage at the terminals of the charge controller is lower than that at the terminals of the battery bank), the battery supplies energy to the load and to the controller, so naturally at this moment it discharges. This

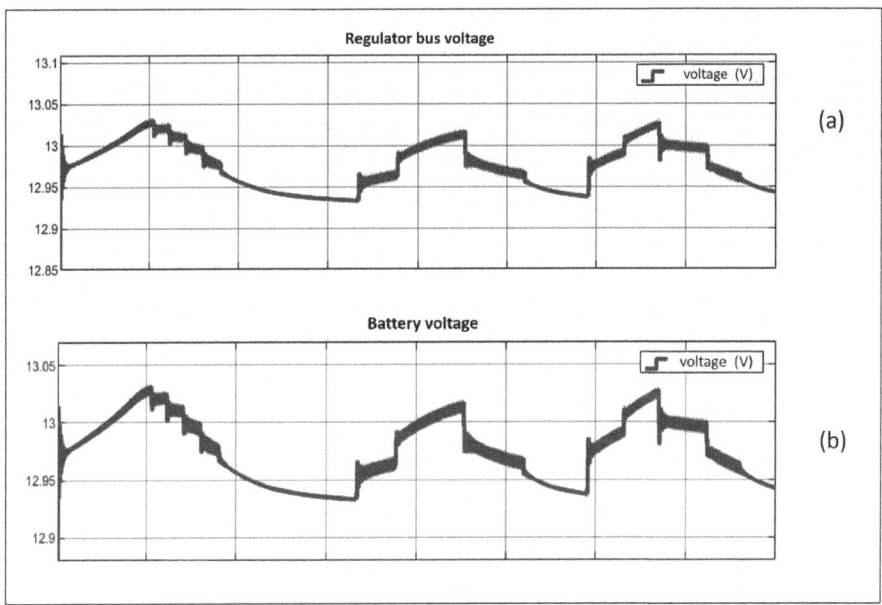

Fig. 17. (a) Variation of the output voltage of the BUCK chopper and (b) the battery voltage

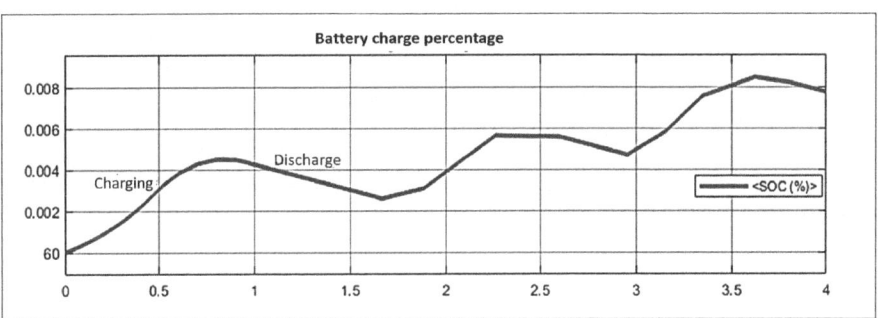

Fig. 18. Battery state of charge

second case occurs when the power from the solar generator is insufficient due to the level of sunlight.

The battery need to be recharged in order to store energy and release it when needed. Figure 19 shows the variation of the battery current as a function of sunshine (Fig. 14). We can see that this curve records negative and positive values; in fact, when the battery is in "CHARGE" mode, its current is negative, whereas when the battery is in "DISCHARGE" mode, its current is positive.

In Fig. 20, we see three zones (zone 1, zone 2 and zone 3). The zones 1 and 2 describe a phenomenon of regulation of the current of the battery following a brutal variation of this last due to the variation of the power of the solar generator (consequence of the

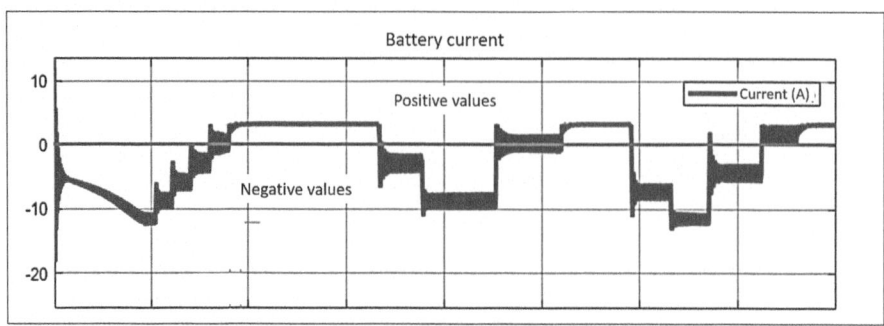

Fig. 19. Battery current as a function of solar radiation

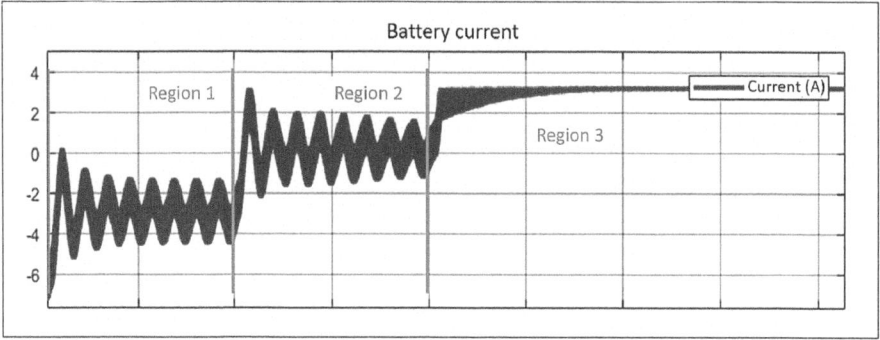

Fig. 20. Zoom on the battery current plot

variation of the sunning). We observe, on the zone 3, a stabilization of the current of the battery towards a fixed value.

4 Conclusion

This paper presents the design of a system that provides uninterrupted autonomous power to a wireless access point (WiABox 2507) in areas where electrical power is not readily available. The proposed solution integrates a power generation system operating through a P&O algorithm and a serial DC-DC converter. The objective of this approach was to improve the stability and efficiency of the system. To this end, the P&O algorithm was implemented in a BUCK converter and simulations with MATLAB software were done to validate the proposed model and demonstrate its efficiency.

Considering the requirements concerning the service continuity with respect to the availability of electrical energy at any time, this system is able to completely ensure this function even when the weather conditions are unfavorable. This system is designed to be used in various climatic environments (variation of temperature and humidity), for that, we could improve this work by studying the effects of the temperature on the performance of our power system; in particular at the level of the solar panel and battery park.

References

1. Dragomir, T.L., Petcut, F.M. et al.: Maximum power point determination for a photovoltaic panel using a Simulink model. In: 4th International Workshop on Soft Computing Applications (2010)
2. Ko, G., Routray, J.K., Ahmad, M.M.: ICT infrastructure for rural community sustainability. Community Dev. **50**(1), 51–72 (2018)
3. Djotio, T., Jonas, K.: Open-source firmware customization problem: experimentation and challenges. In: Intelligent Computing, pp. 306–317 (2019)
4. Djotio, T., Jonas, K.: A pedagogical approach for developing a firmware from open source code: case of WiAFirm, an OpenWRT-based firmware for WiABox appliance. Wiabox 2507 project initiative, step1: specification. Tandem Workshop Dakar, Sénégal - 15–16 March 2016
5. Abouda, S., Nollet, F., Chaari, A., Essounbouli, N., Koubaa, Y.: Direct torque control of induction motor pumping system fed by a photovoltaic generator. In: 2013 International Conference on Control Decision and Information Technologies (CoDIT) (2013)
6. Nazaripouya, H., Wang, Y., Chu, P. et al.: Optimal sizing and placement of battery energy storage in distribution system based on solar size for voltage regulation. In: 2015, IEEE Power & Energy Society General Meeting, pp. 1–5 (2015)
7. Sene, M., Samoura, A., Diouf, S., Diao, A., Mbow, C.: Electrical modeling of a silicon photovoltaic solar cell: comparative study of models characterizing the photovoltaic solar cell. Open J. Appl. Sci. **13**, 1787–1795 (2023)
8. Dey, B.K., Khan, I., et al.: Mathematical modelling and characteristic analysis of solar PV cell. In: IEEE 7th Annual (2016)
9. Fesharaki, V.J., Dehghani, M., et al.: The effect of temperature on photovoltaic cell efficiency. In: Proceedings of the 1st International Conference on Emerging Trends in Energy Conservation – ETEC; Tehran, Tehran, Iran, 20–21 November 2011
10. Ramalingam, K., Indulkar, C.: Chapter 3 - solar energy and photovoltaic technology. In: Distributed Generation Systems, Butterworth-Heinemann (2017)
11. Zhang, T., Wang, R.: High efficiency plants and building integrated renewable energy systems. In: Handbook of Energy Efficiency in Buildings, Butterworth-Heinemann (2019)
12. Chegaar, M., Hamzaoui, A., et al.: Effect of illumination intensity on solar cells parameters. In: TerraGreen 13 International Conference - Advancements in Renewable Energy and Clean Environment (2013)
13. Baharudin, N.H., Mansur, T.M.N.T., et al.: Performance analysis of DC-DC Buck converter for renewable energy application. In: Journal of Physics: 1st International Conference on Green and Sustainable Computing, 25–27 November 2017
14. Lang, Y., Ge, X., Gu, R., Zhang, Y.: The closed-loop design for buck chopper circuit. In: International Conference on Circuits, Devices and Systems (ICCDS) 5–8 September 2017
15. Hilali, A., Mardoude, Y., Ben Akka, Y., El Alami, H., Rahali, A.: Design, modeling and simulation of perturb and observe maximum power point tracking for a photovoltaic water pumping system. Int. J. Electr. Comput. Eng. (IJECE) (2022)
16. Ram, J.P., Babu, T.S., Rajasekar, N.: A comprehensive review on solar PV maximum power point tracking techniques. Renewable Sustain. Energy Rev. **67**, 826–847 (2017)
17. Piegari, L., Rizzo, R.: Adaptive perturb and observe algorithm for photovoltaic maximum power point tracking. IET Renewable Power Gener. **4**(4), 317–328 (2010)

18. Subudhi, B., Pradhan, R.: A comparative study on maximum power point tracking techniques for photovoltaic power systems. IEEE Trans. Sustain. Energy **4**(1), 89–98 (2012)
19. Kim, S.-H.: Pulse width modulation inverters. In: Electric Motor Control, DC, AC, and BLDC Motors, pp. 265–340, Butterworth-Heinemann (2017)
20. Hamdi, A., Behnam, M., Saeid, J., Amir, R., Ehsan, D.: Chapter 7 - Energy storage systems. In: Distributed Generation Systems, Design, Operation and Grid Integration, Butterworth-Heinemann, pp. 333–368 (2017)

Wireless Networks

FSO Transmission Link Performance Analysis for Enhancing Internet Infrastructure in Cote D'ivoire

Douatia Koné[1,2(✉)], Niangoran Medard Mené[1], and Aladji Kamagaté[1,3]

[1] Département Mathématiques-Physique-Chimie, Université Péléforo Gon Coulibaly, Korhogo, Côte d'Ivoire
douatiaben@gmail.com

[2] Direction de la Recherche et de l'Innovation Technologique, Ecole Supérieure Africaine des Technologies de l'Information et de la Communication, Abidjan, Côte d'Ivoire

[3] Département numérique et mathématiques, Agence National de Recherche, Paris, France

Abstract. Atmospheric free-space optical (FSO) transmission is one of the various types of wireless communication that are being developed today. This is an important alternative to consider for next-generation broadband to support high bandwidth. In this study we demonstrate the feasibility of using an FSO system in a 5G architecture operating in Côte d'Ivoire weather conditions, mainly in the following Korhogo, Man, Bouaké, Bondoukou, Man and Abidjan. Such an architecture requires high quality interconnection between the different parts of the network. To conduct this study, we collected meteorological data from January 2018 to December 2022 for each of these towns on the 'weather history' site. To characterize our propagation channel, we used the Gamma-gamma model. Attenuation levels caused by meteorological factors such as rain, fog, humidity and temperature were evaluated. Rain proved to be the most attenuating factor for FSO signals in Côte d'Ivoire, with attenuation levels of up to 5 dB/Km. The performance of these systems was analyzed in terms of signal-to-noise ratio and bit error rate. The results show that the rainy season is the least favorable time to deploy an FSO link, and that Man is the least favorable environment for such deployment. The Korhogo environment and the dry season are the most favorable for deploying an FSO connection. Similarly, for setting up an FSO connection, it is preferable to favor connection distances of less than 4.5 km.

Keywords: BER · FSO · Gamma-gamma distribution · SNR · Telecommunication · Côte d'Ivoire

1 Introduction

In an age of rapid digitalization and increasingly interconnected societies worldwide, the telecommunications play a fundamental role in the way we

A. Sere et al. (Eds.): AFRICOMM 2023, LNICST 587, pp. 133–154, 2025.
https://doi.org/10.1007/978-3-031-81570-6_9

communicate, share information and interact with our environment. However, behind the apparent ease of our telephone conversations, streaming videos, connected systems, autonomous vehicles and instantaneous messages, lie complex and profound issues that influence the way individuals, companies and nations are connected [1]. Particularly, Africa, as a continent undergoing rapid economic and digital growth, faces unique communication infrastructure challenges. Access to reliable broadband connectivity remains a major concern for many regions, due to geographical constraints, underdeveloped terrestrial infrastructures and the high costs associated with setting up traditional networks. According to a World Bank report, by 2021, 90% of the population in developed countries will have access to the Internet, while only 49% in developing countries [2]. Still according to the World Bank, in sub-Saharan Africa, only 36% of the population has Internet access, compared with 92% in North America, while in Côte d'Ivoire 45% of the population has Internet access. Innovative technologies are playing a crucial role in the search for solutions to bridge the digital divide. In this context, various systems are already in use in African states, notably in Côte d'Ivoire, where there are two main interconnection systems: wireless communication systems based on 3rd and 4th generation radio frequency (RF) technologies, and wired communication systems based on fiber optic technology [3]. Although these systems offer excellent performance, they are quite costly and difficult to deploy in certain regions due to the geographical profile of the area, especially in the case of fiber optics. Various technologies have been developed to overcome the limitations of existing technologies. Among these solutions, Free-Space Optics (FSO) technology is emerging as a promising alternative, capable of meeting connectivity needs at lower cost while overcoming traditional obstacles. By exploiting the fundamental principle of optical transmission through the free atmosphere, FSO systems promise high data rates on the order of fiber, low latency and rapid installation, making them an attractive solution for regions where the installation of wired infrastructure is difficult or impossible. Abu Jahid, Mohammed Alsharif and Trevor Hall present in a state-of-the-art analysis of FSO systems, the possibility of using FSO systems as a high-capacity backhaul connection system in 5th generation centralized architectures for the Internet of Things [4]. In [5], Yutao Shi and Al. present a method for improving the transmission capacity of a 5th generation network using a WDM-FSO interconnect. The main result of this work is to improve the mobility range of 5G wired and wireless communication systems through the joint use of the WDM-FSO link. However, changing weather conditions, such as heavy rainfall, high humidity, wide temperature variations and fog, can affect FSO signal quality, requiring sophisticated correction and attenuation mechanisms. Sherif Ghoname, Reba A. Fayed, Ahmed Abd EI Aziz, and Moustafa R. Aly have shown that humidity, fog and rain are important attenuation factors for the FSO link in Egypt. Their study shows that the attenuation levels caused by these factors can lead to a significant reduction in link margin for a transmission distance of 1 km [6]. It is in this context that a study carried out in Akure, Nigeria, presents the performance achieved by an FSO link in terms of link margin [7]. It shows that commercial systems operating at a wavelength of 1550 nm deliver excellent results in terms of link stability, with a link margin of over 0 dB for link distances of less than 10 km. In a previous study [8], it also analyzed the performance of a commercial FSO link operating at wavelength 1550 nm under Abidjan weather conditions. As a result, FSO systems could be perfectly deployed there, achieving excellent performance levels with BER of up to 10^{-13} for SNR values in excess of 50 dB.

In this paper, we aim to evaluate the influence of the meteorological seasons of a subtropical environment such as Côte d'Ivoire on the performance of a terrestrial FSO system, in particular for the environments of Korhogo, Man, Bouaké, Bondoukou, and Abidjan, which represent the main meteorological zones of Côte d'Ivoire. Mathematical models of the attenuation levels caused by rain, temperature, fog and humidity are analyzed and numerically simulated. Signal-to-noise ratio and bit error rate are considered as performance indicators, enabling a more general assessment of network link QoS. To characterize the turbulence of our propagation channel, we consider the Gamma-Gamma model [9], whose parameters are highly dependent on atmospheric and meteorological conditions [9,10]. Section 2 briefly describes the FSO technology and its modeling, while Sect. 3 discusses the influence of meteorological conditions on the FSO link. Section 4 presents the results combined with discussions and analyses. Section 5 concludes the paper.

2 FSO System for Telecommunication

FSO (Free Space Optics) systems are wireless communication technologies that use beams of light to transmit high-speed data through the open air, without the need for cables or physical wires. Unlike traditional technologies such as Wi-Fi, which use radio waves, FSO systems exploit light beams, usually in the visible light, infrared or mid-infrared range [11]. They operate between the 780 - 1600 nm wavelengths bands and use O/E and E/O converters. FSO systems work by using laser transmitters or LEDs to convert data into light signals. These light signals are then transmitted through the air to a remote receiver, where they are decoded into understandable data. These systems can be used for a wide range of applications, such as last-mile access in telecommunications networks where geographical conditions prevent the construction of a fiber-optic network. They can be used to link buildings or remote installations in urban or rural environments. Also, because of their independence from wired infrastructures, and ease of deployment, FSO systems can be used to rapidly restore communications in emergency situations when the fiber optic network fails, or the extension/development of an existing fiber optic network, or to provide high-speed connectivity for special events, trade fairs, etc. [12]. The main advantage of FSO systems is their ability to deliver very high data rates, ranging from several hundred megabits per second to several gigabits per second or even more, depending on conditions [13]. Because they use light rather than radio waves, FSO systems are not subject to electromagnetic interference from other wireless devices. Also, light beams are generally more difficult to intercept than radio signals, which can contribute to better data security [14]. The attractive features of FSO communications include licence-free operation, easy deployment which can be profitable for countries such as Côte d'Ivoire. Nevertheless, since their operating environment is the atmosphere, FSO systems can be affected by adverse weather conditions such as fog, rain, temperature, humidity or even air pollution. These factors can reduce the quality and range of the connection. So to determine their performances in a given environment, it's essential to understand the impact of each of these factors on the system, and to assess their intensity [9].

2.1   Network Architecture Design

Latest-generation communications network architectures are designed to meet the growing needs for connectivity, high throughput, low latency, and increased capacity. The fifth (5th) generation networks are also designed with this in mind. In order to provide efficient solutions to these needs and reduce deployment and operating costs, 5th generation networks rely heavily on network functions virtualization (NFV) and the decoupling of the control plane from the data plane. This enables network functions to be deployed and managed dynamically, allocating resources according to demand. This operating principle has given rise to a new, centralized architecture (called C-RAN for Cloud-Radio Access Network). In a C-RAN, the RAN's processing, control and management functions are centralized in a central data center (CU for centralized unit) or in network concentration points. Base stations (gNBs) in the field are reduced to relatively simple radio units (RUs), whose traffic management is handled by baseband units (BBUs) [14]. FSO technology is particularly well suited to this new network architecture, for the interconnection of RUs to the BBU (fronthaul connection), and/or as a secondary link for interconnection between the BBU and the CU (backhaul connection). Easy to deploy, it contributes in this architecture to reduce deployment and production time and costs, while enabling throughput levels of several Gigabytes per second [15]. Figure 1 shows a model of 5G architecture using FSO technology for the fronthaul interconnection and as a secondary link for the backhaul connection.

2.2   Analysis Method

When analyzing the performance of a telecommunication system, it is important to understand the intrinsic properties of its operating environment, in order to assess the level of losses the system may suffer as a result. For an FSO system, since the operating environment is the atmosphere, it is essential to model it accurately in order to assess its impact on system performance. The atmospheric channel is characterized by the presence of various meteorological factors (rain, fog, humidity, temperature) whose distribution varies over time. The method used to model our propagation environment must therefore be able to accurately describe the system's performance, taking into account the impact of these factors on it. Various propagation models exist for this purpose, but in

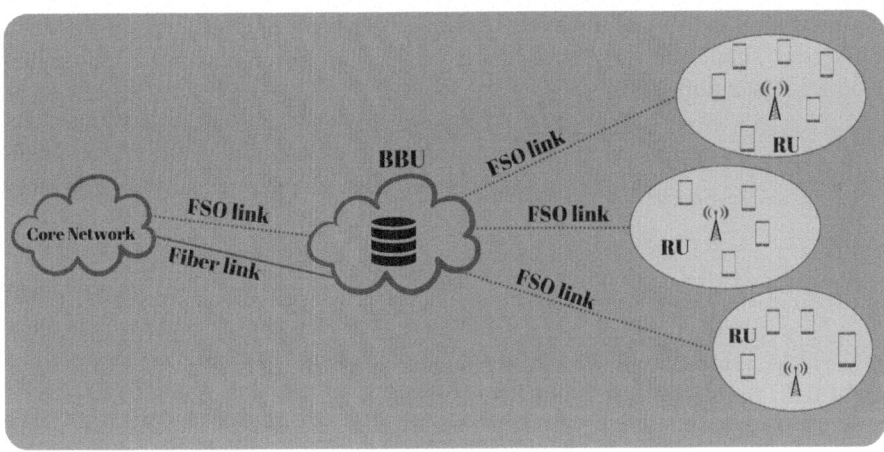

Fig. 1. 5G architecture using FSO technology for the fronthaul interconnection and as a secondary link for the backhaul connection

the FSO context the model generally considered is the gamma-gamma distribution model. The main advantage of this model is that it enables us to accurately describe the impact of atmospheric factors on the performance of an FSO system, whatever the nature (weak, medium, strong) of the atmospheric turbulence [16]. In this section we present the mathematical expression of this distribution and its role in the study of FSO system performance through the evaluation of SNR and BER.

2.3   Channel Modeling

Accurate modeling of the atmospheric channel in FSO systems is crucial for designing reliable links, estimating bit error rates (BER) and optimizing overall system performance for specific weather conditions. It is important to note that atmospheric channel modeling for FSO systems is often complex due to atmospheric variability and dynamics. Consequently, the used model must be capable of combining different parameters to account for the various physical phenomena involved in the propagation of optical signals in the atmosphere. In our case, in order to accurately account for the different scales of turbulence, we will use the gamma-gamma model. It can be used to describe atmospheric turbulence in low, moderate and high turbulence environments [17]. For this model, the distribution of irradiance as a function of atmospheric factors is given by Eq. 1 [17,18]:

$$\rho(I) = \frac{2(\alpha\beta)^{(\alpha+\beta)/2}}{\Gamma(\alpha)\Gamma(\beta)} I^{\frac{\alpha+\beta}{2}-1} K_{\alpha-\beta}(2\sqrt{\alpha\beta I}) \,, I \rangle 0 \tag{1}$$

K_v is the modified Bessel function of the second type, α and β are the effective numbers of small and large turbulence scales. The expressions for α and β are given by Eqs. 2 and 3 [18]:

$$\alpha = \left[exp\left(\frac{0.49\sigma^2}{1+1,11\sigma^{12/5}} \right)^{7/6} - 1 \right]^{-1}, \tag{2}$$

and

$$\beta = \left[exp\left(\frac{0.51\sigma^2}{1+0.69\sigma^{12/5}} \right)^{5/6} - 1 \right]^{-1}, \tag{3}$$

with σ^2 the atmospheric scintillation index, given by Eq. 4 [18,19]. For a horizontal link, the scintillation index is constant

$$\sigma^2 = 1,23C_n^2 k^{7/6} L_p^{11/6}. \tag{4}$$

where Lp is the link length, k the wave number ($k = \frac{2\pi}{\lambda}$) and C_n^2 the refractive index structure parameter [19].

2.4   Signal-Noise-Ratio (SNR)

Signal-to-Noise Ratio (SNR) is an essential communications metric that evaluates the quality of the transmitted signal in relation to the level of noise present in the transmission channel. It is a fundamental measure used to evaluate the performance and reliability of communication systems [18]. Its expression is given by Eq. 5 [18],

$$\gamma = \frac{P_u}{P_n} = \frac{\eta I}{2\sqrt{N_0}} \tag{5}$$

where P_u and P_n are respectively the useful power and the noise power, η represents the optical to-electrical conversion coefficient, and N_0 the mean noise optical power. For reliable and efficient communication, it is important to maintain an adequate SNR, especially in wireless communication systems. SNR management and enhancement are important aspects of communication system design and performance optimization [18,20].

2.5   Bit Error Rate (BER)

BER (Bit Error Rate) is a measure of the quality of data transmission in a digital communication system. It represents the probability of data bits being received erroneously in relation to the total number of bits transmitted. It's important to note that BER is closely related to the signal-to-noise ratio (SNR) in a communication system. A higher SNR generally leads to a lower BER, as a stronger signal to noise ratio enables better detection and recovery of data bits. The expression of BER as a function of atmospheric parameters is given by Eq. 6 [18,20],

$$BER = \frac{1}{2} \int_0^\infty p(I) erfc\left(\frac{<SNR>(I)}{2\sqrt{2}} \right) dI \tag{6}$$

where $erfc()$ is the complementary error function. To resolve this integral, the modified Bessel function of the second kind $K_v()$ in Eq. (1) is represented by the Meijer G function given by Eq. 7 [21]:

$$K_v = \frac{1}{2} G_{0,2}^{2,0} \left(\frac{x^2}{4} \middle| \begin{array}{c} - \\ (v-2), -(v-2) \end{array} \right) \tag{7}$$

and the complementary error function $erfc()$ in Eq. (6) is represented by the Meijer G function given by Eq. 8 [22]:

$$erfc(\sqrt{(x)}) = \frac{1}{\sqrt{x}} G_{2,0}^{1,2} \left(x \middle| \begin{array}{c} 1 \\ 0, 1/2 \end{array} \right). \tag{8}$$

Replacing Eq. 1 by its expression in Eq. 6, and using the relations given in Eq. (7) and Eq. (8), as well as using the solutions of the resulting integral given [23], we obtain the closed-form expression of the BER given by Eq. 9:

$$BER = \frac{1}{2} - \frac{1}{4\sqrt{\pi}\alpha\beta\Gamma(\alpha)\Gamma(\beta)} \frac{\eta}{\sqrt{N_0}} \times$$

$$H_{1,3}^{3,2} \left(\left(\frac{\eta}{2\sqrt{N_0}\alpha\beta} \right)^2 \middle| \begin{array}{c} (\frac{1}{2}, 1), (-\alpha, 2)(-\beta, 2) \\ (0, 1), (-\frac{1}{2}, 1) \end{array} \right). \tag{9}$$

2.6   Test Environment

Our operating environment Côte d'Ivoire. Côte d'Ivoire is a country with a surface area of 322,462 Km^2, and a population of 29,389,150. It is located in West Africa between the equator and the Tropic of Cancer. Côte d'Ivoire has a tropical climate, typical of the West African region. Because of its diverse geography, it has different climatic zones. The coast has an equatorial climate, while the interior of the country has a tropical climate with a rainy season and a dry season. The rainy season generally lasts from May to October. During this period, the country receives abundant rainfall, particularly in the south. July and August are often the wettest months. The dry season extends from November to April. During these months, the rainfall is much rarer, and the weather is generally warmer and drier. December to February are considered the driest months. Temperatures in Côte d'Ivoire vary according to region. In the coastal areas, temperatures are relatively moderate throughout the year, with averages around 25 to 30 °C (77 to 86 degrees Fahrenheit). In more inland and continental regions, temperatures can be higher, sometimes reaching 35 °C (95 degrees Fahrenheit) during the hot season [24]. Figure 2 shows the climate map of Côte d'Ivoire. In order to study the feasibility of deploying an FSO link to provide telecoms services in this environment, we consider five cities that perfectly represent the different meteorological characteristics of Côte d'Ivoire. The chosen cities chosen are Korhogo, Bouaké, Abidjan, Man and Bondoukou. For each of these cities, metrological data from 2018 to 2022 were obtained from the "weather-history" platform [25]. The analyzed parameters are visibility, temperature, humidity and precipitation data per hour. The values of these parameters were collected from the "weather history" platform. For our simulations, we considered a system operating at a wavelength of 1550 nm, as this is the wavelength commonly used in commercial FSO systems [17]. Numerical simulations of our system's performance are carried out using $MATLAB$ software.

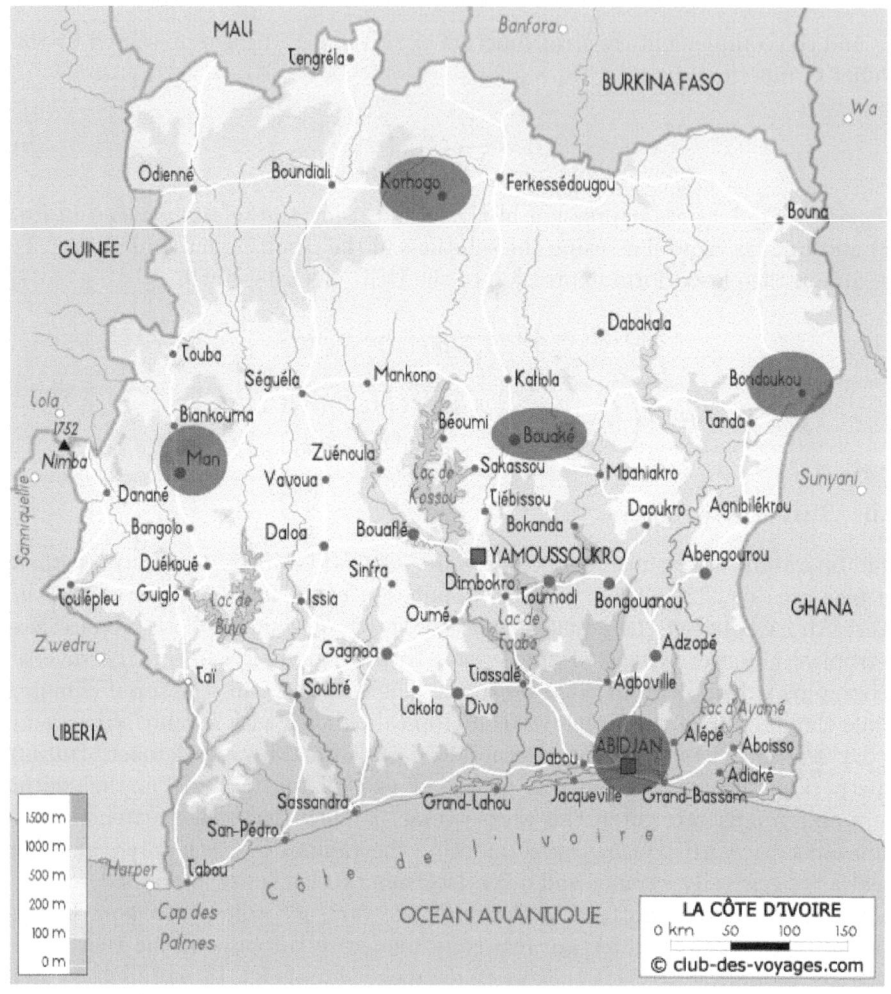

Fig. 2. Climatic map of Côte d'Ivoire

Korhogo in terms of population, Korhogo is the fourth most populous city in Côte d'Ivoire, and the largest city in the north of the country, with a population of 243,048 inhabitants in 2021 [26]. The climate is Sudanese (very hot and very dry). The climate is characterized by two main seasons. The long dry season from October to May precedes the rainy season marked by two rainfall peaks, one in June and the other in September. The December and January periods are marked by the harmattan, which causes temperatures to drop sharply. Korhogo is located at 380 m above sea level, with an average visibility distance of 10 Km [25].

Bouaké is Côte d'Ivoire second most populous city in terms with 536,719 inhabitants in 2021 [26], it covers an area of 72 Km^2. Bouaké has a tropical climate, with two main seasons: the rainy season from May to November and the dry season from November to May. This environment is located at 312 m above sea level, in the center of Côte d'Ivoire and has an average visibility range of 10 Km [25].

Abidjan is the largest city in Côte d'Ivoire in terms of population and surface area. It has a population of around 5 million inhabitants for a surface area of 422 Km^2 in 2021 [26]. In terms of climate, Abidjan enjoys an sub-equatorial climate, hot and humid. The rainfall is abundant over 1441 mm of water per year. This environment is located at 18 m above sea level in southern Côte d'Ivoire, on the shores of the Gulf of Guinea. It has an average visibility range of 10 Km [25].

Man is a large city in western Côte d'Ivoire and the capital of the Tonkpi region. It borders Liberia and has a population of around 200,000 inhabitants in 2021 [26] for a surface area of 64 Km^2. Man has a savannah climate with dry winters (Aw) according to the Koppen-Geiger classification. The average temperature in Man is 25°C and rainfall averages 1569 mm annually. This environment is located at 329 m above sea level. It has an average visibility range of 9 Km [25].

Bondoukou is a town in the north-east of Côte d'Ivoire, capital of the Gontougo administrative region of Gontougo, close to Ghana. It has a population of over 78000 inhabitants [26]. In Bondoukou, the rainy season is oppressive and cloudy. the dry season is humid and partly cloudy, and the climate is hot all year round. This environment is located at 343 m above sea level. It has an average visibility distance of 10 Km [25].

3   Weather Influence on FSO Link

3.1   Rain Influence on FSO Link

The rain is a meteorological phenomenon that occurs when water condensed in the atmosphere falls back onto the Earth's surface in the form of liquid water droplets. Rain generally occurs when warm, moist air rises into the atmosphere and cools, causing water vapour to condense into water droplets. These droplets then clump together to form water-laden clouds, and when they become heavy enough, they fall to the ground as rain. Raindrops cause scattering independent of the wavelength of the light beam; rain is said to be a non-selective scattering factor. According to ITU-R recommendations, the attenuation caused by rain in a given environment is described by Eq. 10 [25]

$$\beta_{pluie} = \alpha R^\rho. \tag{10}$$

The values of α and ρ depend on the precipitation rate per hour of the test environment. For an environment like Côte d'Ivoire where R<3.8 mm/h [23, 24], we have $\alpha = 0.509$ and $\rho = 0.63$ [18, 26].

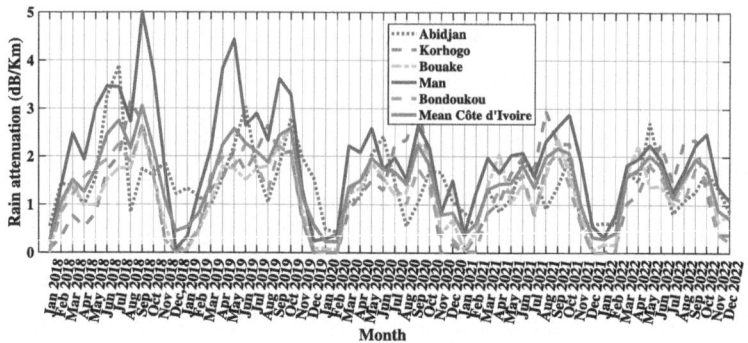

Fig. 3. Rain attenuation of the FSO link per month

Figure 3 shows the levels of rain attenuation per month on an FSO link from 2018 to 2022 in Abidjan, Bondoukou, Bouaké, Korhogo, and Man. The simulation parameter is the average precipitation rate per hour. For each of our test areas, its values have been collected on the "weather history" platform. The collected values are from 2018 to 2022. In general, the curves shown in Fig. 3 have the same appearance. They are characterized by two main trends. They show peak attenuations during the rainy season, mainly in July, August and September, followed by low attenuations during the dry season, especially in November, December and January. The Figure also shows that the environment with the highest rain attenuation is Man, with levels above the national average. The rainy season lasts an average of 9 months (February to November) in this environment. In 2018 and 2019, rain attenuation reached a maximum value of 5 dB/Km during the rainy season, compared with 3 dB/Km for the national average. Over the past three years, rain attenuation has decreased and now reaches a maximum value of 3 dB/Km. This can be explained by the decrease in rainfall due to climate change observed over this period. Maximum attenuations are observed during the months of May and September, which correspond in this area to the months with the highest rainfall rates [24, 27]. Abidjan is the second environment where rain attenuation is the highest during the rainy season. Its attenuation levels are generally lower than the national average, except in the high rainy season where they reach a maximum value of 2.6 dB/Km observed during the period from May to July [28]. In Korhogo, Bondoukou and Bouaké, attenuations are below the national average, except during the peak rainy season (July-August-September), where peak attenuations in Korhogo are above the national average. In the dry season, rain attenuation tends towards 0 in each of our environments. This is explained by the scarcity of rainfall during this period [25, 28]. These attenuation values are relatively low enough to block the FSO link in the context of telecommunication transmission for internet access [29]. Indeed, for an Internet connection, the recommended attenuation levels are those below 30 dB. So, in view of the overall attenuation levels observed, our test areas are excellent candidates for the deployment of an internet network using FSO technology [29].

3.2   Fog Influence on FSO Link

Fog is a meteorological phenomenon that occurs when small droplets of water suspended in the air reduce visibility at the Earth's surface. Fog generally forms when the air cools and its ability to retain moisture diminishes, causing water vapour to condense into tiny droplets [30]. The fog-forming process is often linked to specific weather conditions, notably night-time cooling and high humidity. When fog is dense, airborne water particles can scatter and disperse light from the optical beam, resulting in signal attenuation. Fog can act as an obstacle to optical beams, reducing the range and quality of transmission in an FSO system. The effects of fog on an FSO system depend on the intensity of the fog, the wavelength of the used optical beam, and the optical properties of the fog itself - fog is said to be a selective attenuating factor. Under conditions of intense fog, FSO transmission can become very limited, if not impossible. Equation 11 describes the attenuation caused by fog on a bond defined from Kim's experimental model for Mie scattering [30,31]

$$\beta_{brouillard} = \frac{3.91}{V} \left(\frac{\lambda}{\lambda_0} \right)^{-p} . \tag{11}$$

where V (Km) is the transmission distance, $\lambda_0 = 550$ nm is the visibility range reference wavelength, λ (nm) is the wavelength used for interconnection and p is the particle size distribution coefficient. The values of p described by the Kim model are given by Eq. 12 [18,30]

$$p = \begin{cases} 1.6 & ,V \rangle 50 \\ 1.3 & ,6 \langle V \langle 50 \\ 0.16V + 0.34 & ,1 \langle V \langle 6 \\ V - 0.5 & ,0.5 \langle V \langle 1 \\ 0 & ,V \langle 0.5 \end{cases} . \tag{12}$$

Figures 4 and 5 show the attenuation levels experienced by an FSO link in Abidjan, Bondoukou, Bouaké, Korhogo and Man, respectively, as a function of line-of-sight distance and month. For our simulations, we considered a transmitter using the 1550 nm wavelength, because it is more resistant to atmospheric attenuation factors than lower wavelengths. The simulation parameter is the average monthly variation in visibility distance. Its values were obtained from the "weather history" platform [25]. Figure 4 shows that the attenuation curves due to visibility distance for each of our test zones overlap. This reflects the small variation in sight distance between these zones. Overall, the levels of sight distance attenuation observed are low. The other main finding is that sight distance

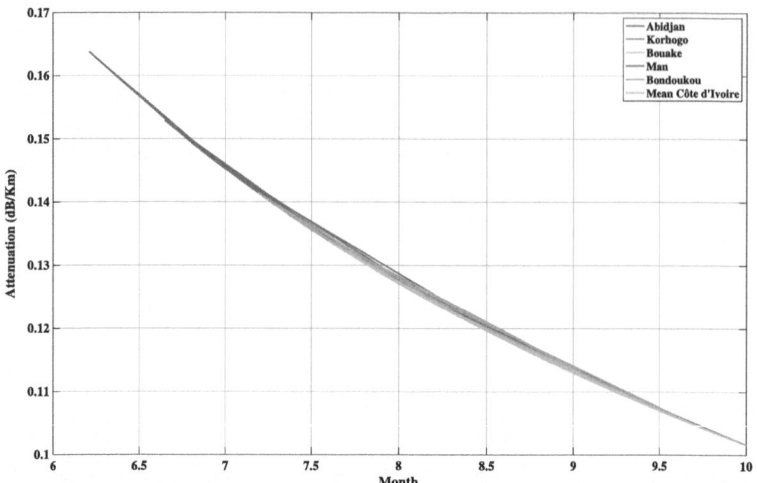

Fig. 4. Attenuation due to fog as a function of visibility distance

attenuation decreases as sight distance increases. With a visibility distance that can drop to 6.2 Km at an attenuation of 0.163 dB/Km, Man is the area with the lowest visibility distance and the highest level of sight distance attenuation. This might be due to the area's heavy rainfall and mountainous profile. These attenuation levels are relatively low enough to completely block the link in the case of Internet data transmission [29, 32].

In order to assess the monthly attenuation caused by fog on the FSO link in the Korhogo, Bouaké, Abidjan, Man and Bondoukou areas, we considered the average variation in visibility distance from January 2018 to December 2022 in each of our test areas as a simulation parameter. Numerical simulation of the attenuation caused during the month by fog is carried out using MATLAB numerical simulation software. Figure 5 shows the monthly attenuation curves caused by fog from January 2018 to December 2022. These curves have the same appearance as those in Fig. 3, which show the evolution of rain attenuation curves. In fact, as in Fig. 3, the curves shown in Fig. 5 have two general trends over the entire analysis period. High attenuation is observed during the rainy season (May to October) and low attenuation during the dry season, mainly from November to January. These observations reflect the important role played by rain in reducing visibility distance in our test area. The Man zone is the area with the highest levels of fog-induced attenuation. Fog-induced attenuation in this environment remains above the national average throughout the analysis period. In this environment, peak attenuation of 0.16 dB/Km is observed during August and September 2018. From 2019 onwards the peak value of attenuation due to fog drops to around 0.15 dB/Km, which can be explained by the lower monthly rainfall observed from this year onwards [27]. Contrary to the observation made for rain attenuation, the second zones with the highest fog attenuation

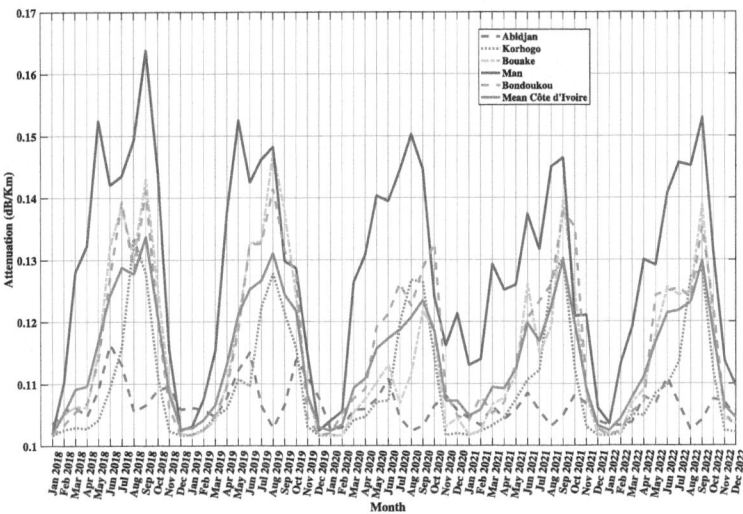

Fig. 5. Fog-induced attenuation of the FSO link for the wavelength 1550 nm

are Bouaké and Bondoukou, whose curves seem to overlap. This time, Korhogo and Abidjan have attenuation values below the national average. Bondoukou and Bouaké record attenuation peaks of around 0.142 dB/ Km during periods of heavy rain (August and September) [25]. This change in the ranking of cities with the highest attenuation is due to the fact that the presence of rain in some cases can reduce fog formation. Fog forms when the air is saturated with water vapor and cooled, causing moisture to condense into water droplets. When it rains heavily, the air is already saturated with moisture due to the rain, which means there is less potential for the additional condensation required to form fog droplets [33]. The Korhogo and Abidjan environments record levels of fog attenuation below the average trend. During the dry season, fog attenuation drops to around 0.1 dB/Km. The observed fog-induced attenuation and visibility values are low enough to prevent FSO transmission from working properly in these areas as part of the deployment of a fronthaul network for Internet access [14, 29].

3.3 Humidity Attenuation

Atmospheric humidity can also have an impact on free-space optical communication (FSO) systems. When humidity is high, the atmosphere contains a greater quantity of water vapor, which can lead to the absorption of infrared (IR) light used in FSO systems. Absorption of IR light by humidity can lead to attenuation of the optical signal, reducing the range and reliability of FSO communication [30]. In addition to light absorption, humidity can also lead to the formation of airborne water droplets, which act as obstacles to the optical beam. These droplets can scatter light and cause signal dispersion, resulting in fluctuations in the power of the optical signal received [29,32]. Equation 13 describes the absorption levels caused by humidity [30]

$$\left\{\begin{array}{ll} \sigma = e^{-A_i \times w^{1/2}} & \text{Si } w < w_i \\ \sigma = k_i \left(\frac{w_i}{w}\right) \beta_i & \text{Si } w > w_i \end{array}\right\}. \tag{13}$$

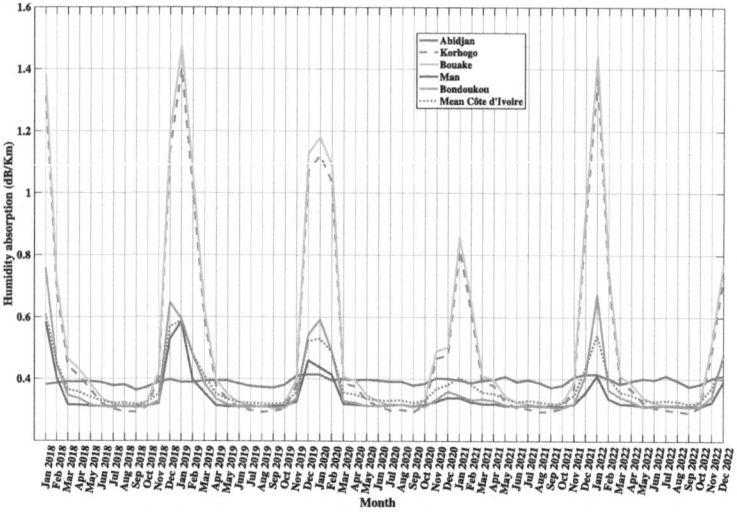

Fig. 6. Humidity-induced attenuation of the FSO link

With $\beta_i = 0.111$, $w_i = 1.1$, $k_i = 0.802$ and $w = \frac{1}{\rho_w} \int_{z_{sol}}^{z_t} \rho \times q_v \, dz$ the amount of precipitable water in the atmosphere. Figure 6 shows the monthly attenuation levels caused by fog in each of our test areas. To obtain it, we considered as simulation parameter the monthly specific humidity in Abidjan, Bondoukou, Bouaké, Korhogo, and Man. Its values from January 2018 to December 2022 were collected on the "historical-meteo" platform [25]. Our numerical simulations were carried out using Matlab. Generally speaking, the moisture attenuation curves for each of our environments follow the same pattern throughout the study period. For the Bondoukou, Bouaké, Korhogo and Man zones, two main trends are observed. We observe a period of low attenuation corresponding to the rainy season (May to October) and a period of high attenuation observed during the dry season, especially during the harmattan (November to March) [25]. This result can be explained by the fact that this period is characterized by a peak in specific humidity, mainly due to a sudden change in temperature between night and day. Indeed, it's very cold at night, but very hot during the day [25]. Humidity levels encountered during this period are generally of the order of 62% and are not high enough to lead to the formation of large raindrops. The particles thus present in the atmosphere are not dissipated by precipitation. This increases the water content of the atmosphere, resulting in high levels of specific moisture attenuation. The areas with the highest levels of attenuation, with peaks of around 1.4 dB/Km, are those of Korhogo and Bouaké, which are areas where harmattan is generally the most pronounced [34]. This value, higher than the national average of around 0.6 dB/Km, is observed during the month of January, which corresponds to the month of peak harmattan winds [25]. The Bondoukou area has the second highest attenuation levels, with peaks of around 0.6 dB/Km, again observed in January. It is followed by Man, which shows the same trends. As for the Abidjan area, attenuation levels vary slightly from month to month. Attenuation values in this zone seem constant at 0.4 dB/Km. This can be explained by the absence of harmattan winds in the south. As the Abidjan and Man zones are the ones with the most overcast periods during the year, humidity tends to be dispersed by rain, reducing its impact in terms of specific attenuation. During the rainy season, a sharp drop in attenuation due to specific humidity is observed in Bondoukou, Bouaké, Korhogo and Man. In Abidjan, the drop remains relatively small. This is explained by a balance in water content over the year, mainly due to evaporation of seawater. Overall, the attenuation levels observed, being well below 30 dB, should not prevent the FSO link from operating smoothly in our test areas as part of the deployment of a fronthaul network for Internet access [14, 29].

3.4   Temperature Attenuation

Atmospheric temperature can have an impact on free-space optical communication (FSO) systems. As the temperature rises, the ambient air heats up, which can lead to variations in air density and refractive index. These variations in refractive index can deflect the optical beam, resulting in light scattering and optical signal degradation. This phenomenon is known as atmospheric turbulence and can be characterized by the Richardson number (Ri), a parameter used to characterize atmospheric stability conditions as a function of vertical wind speed gradient and thermal stratification. For values of R_i below the threshold of 1, the environment is said to be unstably stratified (presence of cells with strong turbulence); for R_i above 1, the environment is said to be stably stratified (presence of cells with weak turbulence) [35]. Equation 14 illustrates its expression [35,36].

$$R_i = \frac{g\beta \triangle T L_c}{v^2}.$$ (14)

where β is the coefficient of thermal expansion $[K^{-1}]$, $\triangle T$ is the temperature difference between the hot wall temperature T_c and the reference temperature T_r [K], L_c is the characteristic length [m], and v is the fluid speed [m/s].

Figure 6 shows the variation in Richardson number over time for each of our test areas. To obtain it, we used as simulation variables the monthly temperature from January 2018 to December 2022 for Korhogo, Bouaké, Abidjan, Man, Bondoukou. The mathematical expression of the richardson number was numerically simulated using the $MATLAB$ system. The results described in Fig. 6

show that in each of our zones the Richardson number varies between 2.4 and 4. The Richardson number is a ratio between the stabilizing force due to thermal stratification and the destabilizing force due to vertical wind shear. When R_i is above a certain critical threshold of 1, the atmosphere is considered stable, i.e. thermal stratification predominates and there is little turbulence. Also, the values of R_i observed in our test zones suggest that they are zones of stable stratification [34,35]. The zones in which we observe the highest levels of R_i are Bondoukou, Bouaké and Korhogo, which correspond to the zones with the lowest attenuation amplitudes on the FSO link. These zones have their R_i above the mean value. The Man and Abidjan zones have the lowest R_i values, with levels below the national average. The best R_i values are observed during the dry season (November to April), which justifies the low attenuation values observed during this period. The low levels of R_i observed during the rainy season allow it to retain its status as the least favorable season to the operation of the FSO link. As our study areas are low-turbulence zones, it is possible to deploy an FSO link there as part of the establishment of an Internet network in these areas [17].

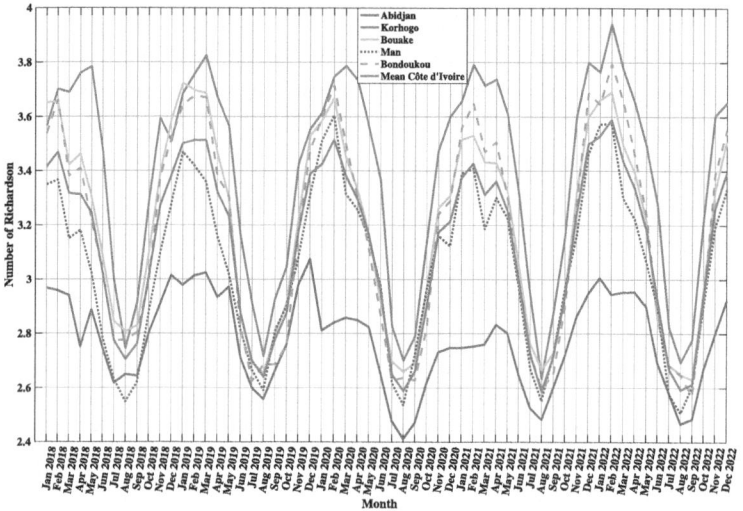

Fig. 7. Temperature-induced attenuation of the FSO link

4   Analysis and Discussions

4.1   Analysis

This section is devoted to analyzing the system's performance under the specific meteorological conditions of Korhogo, Bouaké, Bondoukou, Man and Abidjan. To do so, we analyze the values of the signal-to-noise ratio as a function of the transmission distance, and those of the bit error rate as a function of the signal-to-noise ratio. We use $MATLAB$ as our numerical simulation software. Simulation parameter values are given in Table 1.

Table 1. Operating parameters of FSO system

Operating parameters	Value
Transmitter Power	0.16 mW
Transmitter Efficiency	0.9
Receiver Efficiency	0.9
Wavelength	1550 nm
Electrical Bandwidth	1 Ghz
Laser Beam Divergence Angle	1 mrad
PIN Load Resistance	1 $K\Omega$
Dark Current	10 nA
PIN Responsivity	0.6 A/W

– **SNR vs Range**

The signal-to-noise ratio (SNR) is an essential indicator of link performance, giving us an idea of the quality of the received signal. For a transmitted signal operating at a wavelength of 1550 nm, at a transmit power of 0.1 dB and modulated according to the OOK-NRZ modulation scheme under the meteorological conditions of the selected areas, we obtain the results presented in Fig. 7, which shows the SNR variations as a function of the transmission distance of our FSO link. Figure 7 shows that the average SNR value evolves inversely with the link distance for each of our selected zones. For FSO link distances of less than 1 km, the SNR value varies between 170 dB and 50 dB. This indicates a good link quality for these transmission distances. For the FSO link distances between 1 Km and 4.5 Km, our environments maintain good SNR values, with a minimum value of 20 dB observed at Man. Beyond 4.5 Km, SNR values for Man fall below 20 dB, then to around 2 dB for a link distance of 10 Km, making Man the least favorable environment for FSO link deployment in terms of performance. The Abidjan, Bouaké and Bondoukou areas maintain SNR levels above 20 dB for a link distance of 6 Km. Korhogo, maintains SNR levels above 20 dB for link distances of up to 10 km. Korhogo is therefore the most favorable environment for deploying an FSO link. In view of these results, for the deployment of an FSO link in the general meteorological conditions of Côte d'Ivoire, distances less than 4.5 km should be favored. Indeed, for distances of less than 4.5 km, the link maintains the minimum 20 dB threshold required to establish a good Internet connection [37].

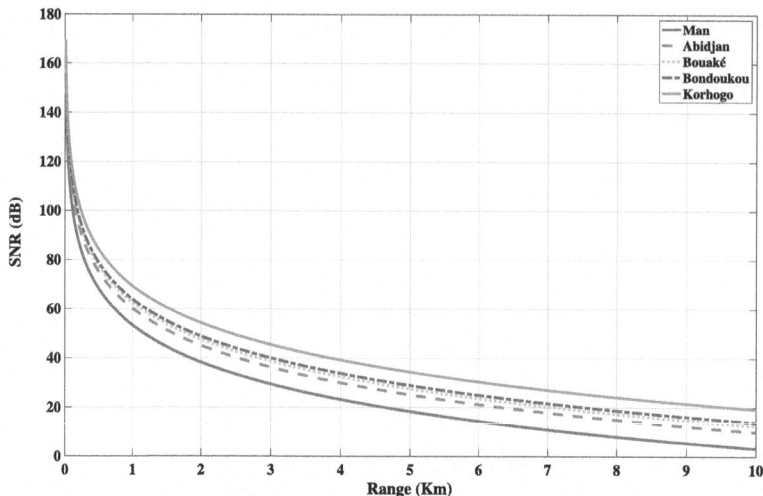

Fig. 8. SNR vs Range

– BER vs SNR

In order to evaluate the bit error rate (BER) of our system, we consider a signal modulated according to the On Off Keying Non-Return-to-Zero (OOK-NRZ) modulation scheme with a raised cosine impulse response filter [16] in the presence of atmospheric turbulence caused by weather conditions in Korhogo, Bouaké, Bondoukou, Abidjan, and Man. The BER values are shown in Fig. 9. Figure 9 shows the evolution of BER as a function of SNR in the meteorological conditions of Bouaké, Bondoukou, Man, Korhogo and Abidjan. The general shape of the curves shows that the BER decreases with increasing SNR. It shows that the highest value of the bit error rate for the FSO link in the general Ivorian meteorological context is observed in the Man area, and is of the order of 10^{-3}. This value is reached for an SNR value of 50 dB. This indicates fairly poor link performance in this environment. As BER is also dependent on atmospheric factors, these results could be explained by the high levels of attenuation observed in this environment. According to ITU-R S.579, atmospheric attenuation leads to an increase in BER through the induction of unwanted noise [38]. For a good link performance in telecommunication applications, we would need to find a method of reducing this value to at least 10^{-6} [39]. As for the Korhogo environment, it presents the best results in terms of BER, with values below 10^{-6} for SNR values above 20 dB, this can be explained by the low levels of attenuation observed in this environment. This suggests that the FSO link could be deployed for Internet telecoms applications in this area [39]. The Abidjan, Bouaké and Bondoukou environments show minimum BER values between 10^{-5} and 10^{-6} for SNR values between 35 dB and 50 dB. This also reflects the deployment potential of the FSO link for Internet telecommunication applications in this area [40]. In

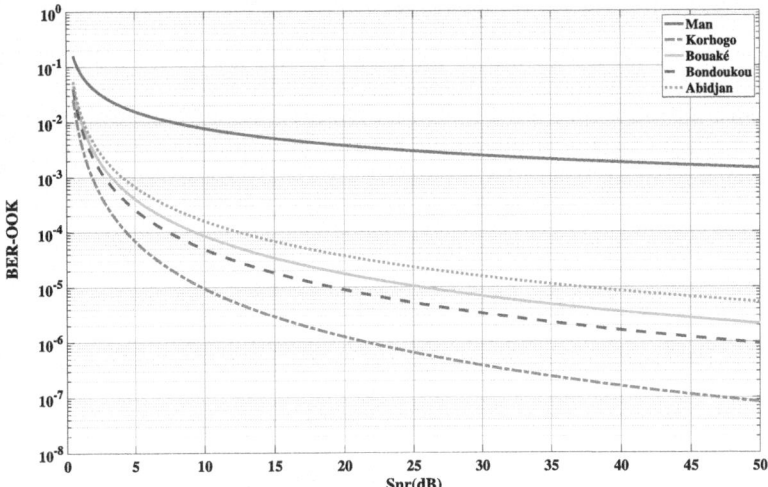

Fig. 9. BER vs SNR

view of this figure, Korhogo appears to be the most favorable environment for the deployment of an FSO link in Côte d'Ivoire, and Man the least favorable. Our results also show that for the use of an FSO system in our test areas as part of a Fronthaul interconnection for 5th generation networks, it is essential to integrate an autonomous error correction system into our architecture.

4.2 Discussion

It's worth pointing out that, compared with other contexts such as South Africa, where FSO technology has been used, Côte d'Ivoire has less restrictive characteristics for the connection. Indeed, in this environment, attenuation can reach 60 dB/Km, whereas in Côte d'Ivoire, the maximum threshold is 5 dB/Km [40]. The second main finding of this research is that rain is the main factor reducing FSO link quality in Côte d'Ivoire, and not fog as in London [41]. The rainy season is the least advantageous period for using an FSO link. In fact, during this period, the conditions favor the development of factors that lead to greater absorption, such as rain and fog. The stratification study revealed that Côte d'Ivoire is an environment with low turbulence instability. The results obtained in terms of reduction due to fog follow the same trend observed at Akure [8] and Kimberley in South Africa [40]. Indeed, the results obtained in these environments indicate that the reduction caused by fog decreases as the visibility distance increases, and that for a wavelength of 1550 nm, the maximum reduction is around 10 dB/Km [25]. The main difference in terms of visibility between our test areas and Akure and Kimberley is that, in Akure, visibility can reach 33.3 Km and 40 Km for Kimberly, while in Côte d'Ivoire, more precisely in Korhogo, Man, Bouaké, Bondoukou and Abidjan, the average visibility distance observed is 10

Km. For a mountainous setting such as Kimberly, the maximum degree of reduction observed is 0.11 dB/Km, while for Man it is 0.162 dB/Km [40]. Generally speaking, based on the results obtained, it can be stated that to achieve good results with an FSO connection in Côte d'Ivoire, it is advisable to favor connection distances of less than 4.5 km, and that the north presents the best profile for the deployment of an FSO link. However, for an excellent level of connectivity in a telecoms application, especially for a Fronthaul link, it is essential to find ways of improving link performance to reduce latency, and to use a stand-alone error correction system to improve the BER.

5   Conclusion

In a context where research into improving the performance of fifth-generation connectivity systems is booming, free-space atmospheric communication systems are taking root in telecommunications networks as a backhaul technology, offering exceptional throughput capabilities, low latency, high reliability and high cost-effectiveness. The aim of this study was to evaluate the performance of an FSO link in the context of setting up a telecommunications network in meteorological conditions such as Abidjan, Bouaké, Korhogo, Bondoukou and Man. The parameters taken into account included rain, fog, temperature and humidity. The analysis revealed that rain is the factor with the greatest impact on FSO link performance in each of our environments, and that the rainy season is the least suitable for its use in the Côte d'Ivoire meteorological context. Evaluation of the signal-to-noise ratio and the bit error rate in the presence of atmospheric attenuation factors showed that the link can continue to operate correctly over a distance of less than 4.5 km, with signal-to-noise ratio levels above 20 dB and bit error rate levels below 10^{-4} for Abidjan, Bouaké, Bondoukou, and below 10^{-6} for Korhogo. In terms of FSO link performance, the Man environment shows the weakest results, with BER levels above 10^{-3}. In order to improve the performance of the Ivorian Internet infrastructure using FSO technology, it is also essential to find techniques for improving the performance of this technology in the Ivorian environment. Some studies, notably that carried out by Abu Bakarr Sahr Brima, Edwin Ataro and Aladji Kamagate, have shown that acting on the polarisation state of light can have a significant impact on the performance of FSO systems [42]. In a forthcoming study, we intend to analyse the impact of using light polarisation states as a beam modulation scheme on improving the performance of FSO systems in Côte d'Ivoire.

References

1. Mheidly, N., Fares, M.Y., Fares, J.: Coping with stress and burnout associated with telecommunication and online learning. Front. Public Health **8**, 672 (2020)
2. World Bank data page. https://donnees.banquemondiale.org/?name_desc=true. Accessed 12 Aug 2023

3. Capri, R.: Telecommunications et croissance economique: Le cas de la telephonie Mobile en Cote D'ivoire. IOSR. J. Econ. Finan. (IOSR-JEF) **11**(2), 45–82 (2020)
4. Jahid, A., Alsharif, M.H., Hall, T.J.: A contemporary survey on free space optical communication: potentials, technical challenges, recent advances and research direction. J. Netw. Comput. Appl. **200**, 103311 (2022)
5. Shi, Y., Armghan, A., Ali, F., Aliqab, K., Alsharari, M.: Enriching capacity and transmission of hybrid WDM-FSO link for 5G mobility. Photonics **10**, 121 (2023). https://doi.org/10.3390/photonics10020121
6. Ghoname, S., et al.: Performance analysis of FSO communication system: Effects of fog, rain and humidity. In: 2016 Sixth International Conference on Digital Information Processing and Communications (ICDIPC). IEEE (2016)
7. Ajewole, M.O., Owolawi, P.A., Ojo, J.S., Adetunji, R.M.: Fog and rain attenuation characterization and performance of terrestrial free space optical communication in Akure, Nigeria. Aptikom J. Comput. Sci. Inf. Technol. **4**(3), 125–134 (2019)
8. Kone, D., Bamba, A., Kamagate, A.: FSO link based in Abidjan under weather conditions, in press (2023)
9. Andrews, L.C., Phillips, R.L.: Laser Beam Propagation Through Random Media, 2nd edn. Laser Beam Propagation Through Random Media (2005)
10. Ansari, I.S., Yilmaz, F., Alouini, M.S.: Performance analysis of FSO links over unified Gamma-Gamma turbulence channels. In: 2015 IEEE 81st Vehicular Technology Conference (VTC Spring), pp. 1–5. IEEE (2015)
11. Trichili, A., Cox, M.A., Ooi, B.S., Alouini, M.S.: Roadmap to free space optics. JOSA B **37**(11), A184–A201 (2020)
12. Estarán, J.M., Pointurier, Y., Bigo, S.: FSO SpaceComm links and its integration with ground 5G networks. In: Optical Fiber Communications Conference and Exhibition (OFC). San Diego, CA, USA 2019, pp. 1–3 (2019)
13. Sahoo, P., Yadav, A.: A comprehensive road map of modern communication through free-space optics. J. Opt. Commun., 000010151520200238. https://doi.org/10.1515/joc-2020-0238 (2020)
14. Hossain, M.F., Mahin, A.U., Debnath, T., Mosharrof, F.B., Islam, K.Z.: Recent research in cloud radio access network (C-RAN) for 5G cellular systems-A survey. J. Netw. Comput. Appl. **139**, 31–48 (2019)
15. Dhasarathan, V., Singh, M., Malhotra, J.: Development of high-speed FSO transmission link for the implementation of 5G and internet of things. Wireless Netw. **26**, 2403–2412 (2020)
16. Kiasaleh, K.: Channel estimation for FSO channels subject to Gamma-Gamma turbulence. In: Proceedings of the ICSOS, pp. 1–7 (2012)
17. Majumdar, A.K.: Advanced Free Space Optics (FSO). SSOS, vol. 186. Springer, New York (2015). https://doi.org/10.1007/978-1-4939-0918-6
18. Ghassemlooy, Z., Popoola, W., Rajbhandari, S.: Optical Wireless Communications: System and Channel Modelling with Matlab®. CRC press (2019)
19. Chaleshtory, Z.N., Gholami, A., Ghassemlooy, Z., Sedghi, M.: Experimental investigation of environment effects on the FSO link with turbulence. IEEE Photonics Technol. Lett. **29**(17), 1435–1438 (2017)
20. Zhang, H., et al.: February. Performance analysis of FSO system with different modulation schemes over gamma-gamma turbulence channel. In: 17th International Conference on Optical Communications and Networks (ICOCN2018), vol. 11048, pp. 191–197. SPIE (2019)
21. Gradstein, I.S., Ryzhik, I.M.: Table of Integrals, Series, and Products, 7th edn. (2007)

22. The wolfram functions site: ERFC functions. http://functions.wolfram.com/PDF/ Erfc.pdf. Accessed 12 Aug 2023

23. The wolfarm functions site: MeijerG functions. http://functions.wolfram.com/ PDF/MeijerG.pdf

24. Kottek, M., et al.: World map of the Köppen-Geiger climate classification updated (2006)

25. Weather data bank homepage. https://historique-meteo.net

26. Official open data portal CI. https://www.ins.ci/RGPH2021/RESULTATS %20DEFINITIFSRP21.pdf

27. Soro, G.E., et al.: "Estimation des pluies journalières extrêmes supérieures à un seuil en climat tropical: cas de la Côte d'Ivoire." Physio-Géo. Géographie physique et environnement **10**,211–227 (2016)

28. Kouadio, Y.K., Ochou, D.A., Servain, J.: Tropical Atlantic and rainfall variability in Côte d'Ivoire. Geophys. Res. Lett. **305**, 4 (2003)

29. KEENETIC ADSL présentation page. https://help.keenetic.com/hc/en-us/ articles/360002830880-ADSL-line-parameters. Accessed 12 Aug 2023

30. Forin, D.M., Incerti, G.: Free Space Optical Technologies: Trends in Telecommunications Technologies, ed. Bouras, Ch. J. (2010)

31. Yasir, S.M., Abas, N., Rauf, S., Chaudhry, N.R., Saleem, M.S.: Investigation of optimum FSO communication link using different modulation techniques under fog conditions. Heliyon, **8**(12), e12516 (2022)

32. Esmail, M.A., Fathallah, H., Alouini, M.S.: Outdoor FSO communications under fog: attenuation modeling and performance evaluation. IEEE Photonics J. **8**(4), 1–22 (2016)

33. Wallace, J.M., Hobbs, P.V.: Atmospheric Science: An Introductory Survey, vol. 92. Elsevier (2006)

34. Canut, G.: Intéraction Mousson/Harmattan, échanges de petite échelle (Doctoral dissertation, Université Paul Sabatier-Toulouse III) (2010)

35. Nauenberg, M.: Atmospheric refraction predictions based on actual atmospheric pressure and temperature data. Publ. Astron. Soc. Pac. **129**(974), 044503 (2017)

36. Grachev, A.A., Andreas, E.L., Fairall, C.W., Guest, P.S., Persson, P.O.G.: The critical Richardson number and limits of applicability of local similarity theory in the stable boundary layer. Bound. Layer Meteorol. **147**, 51–82 (2013)

37. Bouche-cousu blog, Wifi presentation page. https://bouchecousue.com/blog/ comment-lire-la-force-dun-signal-wifi/. Accessed 12 Aug 2023

38. Rec. UIT-R S.522-5. https://www.itu.int/dms_pubrec/itu-r/rec/s/R-REC-S.522- 5-199409-I!!PDF-F.pdf. Accessed 19 Aug 2023

39. Recommandation UIT-T G.997.1, série G: systèmes et supports de transmission, systèmes et réseaux numériques

40. Kolawole, O.O., Afullo, T.J., Mosalaosi, M.: Terrestrial free space optical communication systems availability based on meteorological visibility data for South Africa. SAIEE Africa Res. J. **113**(1), 20–36 (2022)

41. Nafees, M., Huang, S., Thompson, J., Safari, M.: Backhaul-aware user association and throughput maximization in UAV-aided hybrid FSO/RF network. Drones **7**(2), 74 (2023)

42. Brima, A.B.S., Ataro, E., Kamagate, A.: Performance enhancement of an FSO link using polarized quasi-diffuse transmitter. Heliyon **7**(11), e08248 (2021)

Lightweight Authentication System
for Software-Defined Wireless Sensor Networks

Amado Illy[1]([⊠]), Youssou Faye[2], and Tiguiane Yelemou[1]

[1] Université Nazi BONI, Bobo Dioulasso, Burkina Faso
amedilly65@gmail.com
[2] Université Assane Seck de Ziguinchor, Ziguinchor, Senegal
yfaye@univ-zig.sn

Abstract. Sybil attack consists to generate several false identities in order to bypass access control and thus produce false messages to seriously undermine the normal operation of Wireless Sensor Networks (WSN). It is considered one of the major threats to WSNs. The problem has been widely taken into account by researchers. However, detecting this attack and effectively countering it in the context of resource-constrained connected objects remains a challenge. In this paper, we propose a lightweight authentication system based on elliptic curve cryptography to counter this attack. This asymmetric encryption system uses smaller encryption keys than RSA and EL-Gamal, but offers the same level of security.

Keywords: Resource-constrained networks · Sybil attack · Authentication · Elliptic curves

1 Introduction

A Wireless Sensor Network (WSN) is a group of nodes which main function is to collect information about its environment and transmit it to a server for further processing. These nodes may be used in a multi-hop context, where each node plays the role of collector for its own environment and router for others neighboring peers. Ease of deployment of this type of network is an asset, enabling them to be easily integrated into a variety of application domains such as environmental monitoring, home automation, industry, etc. [1]. For reasons of concealment and cost, these nodes are often small in size. Their capacities, notably in terms of computing power, memory, storage and energy, are therefore limited. These constraints have a negative impact on the ability of these nodes to support robust security mechanisms or quality of service [2–4]. The aim of new proposals and protocols dedicated to (WSN) is to make a compromise between the security and quality of service provided by these solutions and the resource constraints of these nodes [5, 6]. In this context, an efficient security key management mechanism is a major asset for the smooth operation of these networks. In this paper, we propose an efficient authentication solution based on elliptic curve cryptography. This solution integrates efficient security key management to face Sybil attack. This protocol is less power-hungry and easy to

A. Sere et al. (Eds.): AFRICOMM 2023, LNICST 587, pp. 155–162, 2025.
https://doi.org/10.1007/978-3-031-81570-6_10

implement in WSN. The remainder of the manuscript is organized as follows. In Sect. 2, we present the Sybil attack and highlight previous work concerning proposed solutions to counter this attack. In Sect. 3, we present our lightweight authentication approach. In Sect. 4, we present results of a performance evaluation of our approach. Finally, we conclude in Sect. 5.

2 Related Works

In many cases, sensors in a network must cooperate to perform tasks. New sensors can use the identities of other legitimate sensors, defining Sybil attacks, which degrade data integrity, security and resources availability. Sybil attacks target routing mechanisms, resource allocation, data aggregation, privileged node election, distributed storage and misbehavior detection [7, 8]. While all ad hoc networks are vulnerable to Sybil attacks, WSNs can be protected using appropriate protocols. In the absence of a central authority, a Sybil attack is easy to carry out, unless large resources are used. However, detecting Sybil attacks is difficult. In the Sybil attack, malicious node has several identities and can appear in several places at the same time, and the probability of selecting such false sensors is high, leading to a reduction in the quality assurance provided by the multi-hop protocol [9]. As a rule, protocols assume a sensor have unique key, and since a central element of Sybil attacks is identity theft, authentication is the main defence. A trusted key server or base station can authenticate a sensor for other sensors on the network. If a unique key is used, the discovery of this key is critical for the whole network [10, 11]. In the field of WSN, the issue of Sybil attacks has been widely explored by researchers.

In [12], the authors propose a new strategy based on machine learning to detect spoofing attacks in wireless sensor networks. The proposed algorithm combines two classifiers to process and analyse instantaneous strength samples of the received signal to detect attacks. This solution is suitable in the context of WSN, but does not take into account all possible cases related to impersonation attacks. It is optimized for scenarios where the legitimate node and the malicious node are at the same distance or very close to each other in relation to the landmark.

Shantala Devi Patil et al. [13] have proposed a security solution to thwart imperson-ation attacks and node compromise in a WSN. They have implemented an authentication mechanism called PAW (Provisioning authentication on demand in WSN). This solu-tion is based on the authentication of external users wishing to access network resources. The proposed PAW system is divided into four phases: The preparation phase, carried out by the base station, which is the point of contact for external network users. The registration phase, in which users and cluster leaders register with the base station. In the authentication phase, a three-stage authentication is performed and a session key is established between the user and the cluster leader to secure data exchanges. In the final phase, a common session key is generated for the user and the cluster leader. Due to the resource constraints of WSN, this authentication solution is effective, but its complexity induces a high energy consumption. Authentication and establishment of the session key between the sensor nodes and the user is made up of several hash operations.

In [14], the authors proposed a protocol for sensor node authentication and key distribution. This solution makes it possible to combat impersonation attacks and mod-ification or replay of routing information in a WSN. The protocol consists of five steps:

The first consists of exchanging neighbor discovery information. The next step establishes a well-to-well relationship. The third step involves sharing group authentication keys, followed by initial node authentication. The final step involves re-authenticating the nodes. This solution can counter several types of attack, but its authentication process is very time-consuming. The number of messages exchanged in this protocol is high, generating high energy consumption.

Neha Badetia et al. [15] have proposed a distributed mechanism for authenticating nodes in WSN. Sensor nodes are logically arranged as a binary tree with the base station. A token is generated by the parent node for its child node. This token is then used by a child node for mutual authentication of the sensor nodes. This algorithm comprises two phases: a registration phase and an authentication phase. During the registration phase, each parent node generates a token for its child node, and these tokens are then used by the nodes for mutual authentication. The token contains the node's identity, public key, pseudo-random number and lifetime. This solution has a good level of security, but the amount of information stored in sensor nodes using this protocol is high. The nodes don't have enough resources and their storage capacity is limited.

Aishwarya Vardhan et al. [16] have proposed a mutual node authentication scheme that promotes secure exchange between sensor nodes. This solution combats identity theft attacks. It is based on double encryption of identification data, using both symmetric and asymmetric encryption algorithms. This solution offers an acceptable level of security, but the encryption mechanisms used generate high energy consumption. The asymmetric encryption algorithm is one of the most energy-intensive. The encryption process for this algorithm requires very high computing power.

Most of the proposed solutions, even if they provide acceptable security, are energy-intensive and provide significant system resources. They are thus unsuited to the context of resource-constrained networks.

3 Proposed Solution

In this section, first we present a network context and the threat and then the components of the solution.

3.1 Network Functional Architecture and Threat Presentation

3.1.1 Functional Architecture of the Network

Our architecture consists of an SDN controller, a base station and a set of nodes deployed in the observation environment. In our architecture, a sensor node collects data in its surrounding environment and transmits it to the base station. The base station receives the data collected in the field of observation. It uses the controller in the background to ensure the authenticity of the sensor nodes and the integrity of the data received. The controller is responsible for managing and authenticating each sensor node wishing to join the network.

3.1.2   Presentation of the Threat

In the sybbil attack, for the case of our architecture, a malicious node uses several identities simultaneously or non-simultaneously to disrupt network operation. By using multiple identities, an attacker can take control of the network and consequently carry out different types of attack. It can also bypass a decision on a particular agreement. Communications take place in a one-hop neighborhood, so it's not possible for an attacker to replay, and nodes won't need to decipher certain message fields to perform routing.

3.2   Our Solution Presentation

We propose an authentication system based on elliptic curve cryptography. This is an asymmetric encryption system, using smaller key sizes than other cryptographic algorithms, but offering the same level of security. The controller generates two keys for each node, a public key and a symmetric key, before deployment. Node identifiers are supplied by the provider. A range of identifiers is provided for a large number of nodes. This range of node identifiers will be stored at the base station before the nodes are deployed. The controller is also responsible for generating the elliptic curve parameters. Initially, the controller selects an elliptic curve EC over a finite field Fq and opts for a base point P with large order p (where p and q are prime numbers). The controller then makes it public to the base station, which in turn transmits it to all the sensor nodes in the network. The implementation of our authentication solution comprises three phases (see Fig. 1): first, registration phase, which consists of gathering the security identification information for each node. This information will be used during the authentication phase. The second, called the authentication phase, enables communication to be initiated between the sensor node and the controller based on the security credentials obtained. The third, called the re-authentication phase, requires sensor nodes that have been in standby mode for a long period to re-authenticate.

3.2.1   Registration Phase

Before launching the authentication process between two network entities, it is necessary for each part of the communication to go through a registration process in order to provide security credentials that will be used for the authentication phase. We will now illustrate the message flows exchanged during the registration and authentication phases. The registration phase takes place in three (03) stages.

Step 1: the sensor node sends a registration request to the controller via the base station. The message contains the symmetrical key, encrypted using the controller's public key. The encrypted message is concatenated with the node ID before being sent.

Step 2: on receipt, the base station checks the node's identity against the identity stored at its level. If this is the case, the base station forwards the encrypted message to the controller.

Step 3: After receiving the message from the base station, the controller first verifies the certificate, then decrypts the node's message using its private key to check the conformity of the key stored at its level. After verification, the controller will retransmit a new symmetrical key for the sensor node, which will be used during the authentication phase. This new key will be encrypted with the node's public key and transmitted to the base station, which in turn transmits it to the sensor node. On receipt, the node decrypts the message and checks that it has been registered when it has the new symmetrical key.

3.2.2 Authentication Phase

Step 5: when the node wants to authenticate, it generates a random number N1 using the elliptic curve parameter. It then encrypts this value using the new symmetrical key. The encrypted message is concatenated with the node ID, and the whole set is signed using the node's private key. It sends the set to the base station.

Step 6: on receipt, the base station checks the signature and the node ID. It then forwards the encrypted message to the controller.

Step 7: the controller decrypts the message and replies to the node, returning the N1 value concatenated with a new N2 value it generates. The message is encrypted using the new symmetrical key and transmitted to the base station.

Step 8: the base station transmits the encrypted message to the node.

Step 9: the node must send back the N2 value encrypted with the new symmetrical key to be authenticated.

Step 10: the base station transmits the encrypted message to the controller to complete the authentication process. By receiving the N2 value, the controller is certain that the node is not malicious and can be trusted.

3.2.3 Re-authentication Phase

This phase forces sensor nodes that have been in standby mode for a long time to re-authenticate (Table 1).

Table 1. Scoring table.

Symbols	Description
EpubC	Controller public key
EpubN	Node public key
EprivN	Node private key
CS	Symmetric key
ECso	New symmetric key
N1	Random number
IDN	Node identity
‖	Concatenation operator
Certif	Certificate

4 Analytical Evaluation

In this section, we present an analytical assessment of the security level of our protocol in the face of attacks and certain security constraints defined in WSNs.

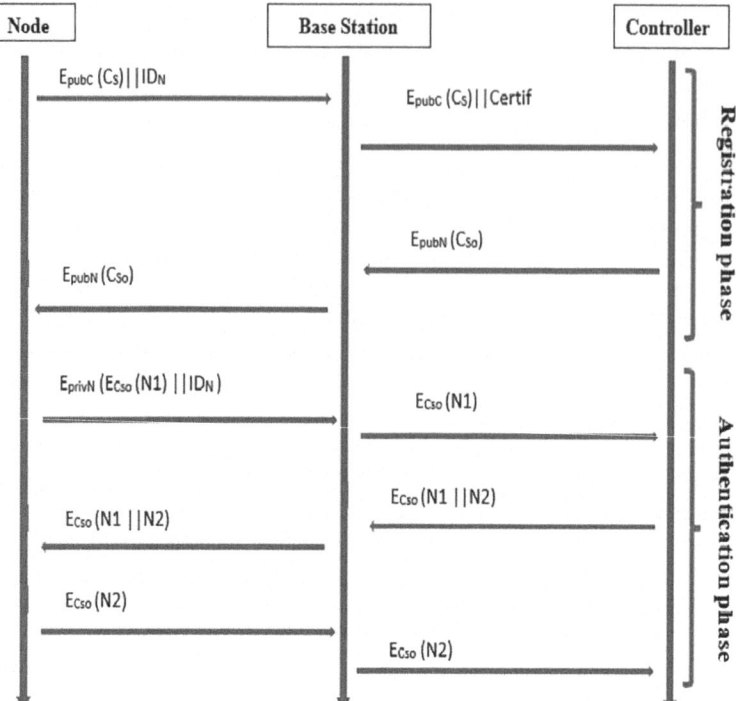

Fig. 1. Authentication system

4.1 Safety Analysis

This analysis is based on certain security constraints defined in WSN: access control, confidentiality and authentication.

Access control: the solution we propose prevents any element outside the system from accessing the network. For a node N wishing to join the network, it must necessarily go through a process of authentication and confidential data exchange. In our case, node N must send its authentication data to the controller via the base station. This authentication data is integrated into each node before it is deployed. If node N hasn't this authentication data, access control will fail and it will not be able to integrate into the network.

Confidentiality: this guarantees that information from a sensor node is only made accessible or revealed to its intended recipient. Our authentication system also ensures the confidentiality of authentication data exchanged between the node and the controller. Nodes have their own preliminary keys, such as the controller's public key, the base station's symmetrical key and their own public and private keys. When a node I wants to authenticate itself to the controller, it sends its authentication data encrypted with the corresponding public key. This mechanism guarantees the confidentiality of authentication data.

Authentication: our solution ensures the authentication of every node wishing to communicate in the network. The identity of each node is verified by the base station, and final authentication takes place at the controller. The elliptic curve parameters are used to generate unique keys for each node. These keys are used during the authentication process to ensure effective security.

4.2 Security Against Known Attacks

The different characteristics of WSNs expose them to numerous security threats [20, 21]. Denial of service and impersonation attacks are easier to carry out in this type of wireless, infrastructure-free network. In this section, we evaluate the security of our protocol against a few types of attack.

Attacks such as spoofing, modifying or replaying routing information fail against our protocol if the content of messages exchanged in the network is unknown. In our protocol, an attacker must not be able to usurp the identity, the public keys embedded in a node, or the values of the elliptic curve parameter. Since the usurpation of all this information is complex, our protocol offers an acceptable level of security against these types of attacks.

The proposed protocol is also resistant to sybil attacks, thanks to the verification of node identity by the base station. The nonces generated from the elliptic curve parameters remain secret and are transmitted securely between the node and the controller. It is very difficult to carry out such an attack against this protocol, if you don't know the random values generated by the node and controller.

5   Conclusion

With the rapid development of the Internet of Things (IoT), SDN technology is attracting increasing attention from researchers. Its centralized control improves device management efficiency and security. In this article, we have proposed a lightweight authentication system to combat identity theft attacks such as the sybil attack. This protocol is based on elliptic curve cryptography, which is an asymmetric encryption system that consumes less energy than others. In this contribution, a controller is responsible for managing and authenticating network nodes.

References

1. Gite, P., Chouhan, K., Murali Krishna, K., Kumar Nayak, C., Soni, M., Shrivastava, A.: ML based intrusion detection scheme for various types of attacks in a WSN using C4. 5 and CART classifiers. Mater. Today Proc. **80**, 3769–3776 (2023). https://doi.org/10.1016/j.matpr.2021.07.378
2. Numan, M., et al.: A systematic review on clone node detection in static wireless sensor networks. IEEE Access **8**, 65450–65461 (2020). https://doi.org/10.1109/ACCESS.2020.2983091
3. Lakshmi Narayanan, K., Santhana Krishnan, R., Golden Julie, E., Harold Robinson, Y., Shanmuganathan, V.: Machine learning based detection and a novel EC-BRTT algorithm based prevention of DoS attacks in wireless sensor networks. Wirel. Pers. Commun. **127**(1), 479–503 (2022). https://doi.org/10.1007/s11277-021-08277-7

4. Bala, P.M., Usharani, S., Abarna, V.: Detect the replication attack on wireless sensor network by using intrusion detection system. J. Phys. Conf. Ser. **1717**(1) (2021). https://doi.org/10. 1088/1742-6596/1717/1/012023

5. Dhanaraj, R.K., Jhaveri, R.H., Krishnasamy, L., Srivastava, G., Maddikunta, P.K.R.: Blackhole attack mitigation in medical sensor networks using the enhanced gravitational search algorithm. Int. J. Uncertain. Fuzziness Knowl.-Based Syst. **29**, 297–315 (2021). https://doi. org/10.1142/S021848852140016X

6. Batna, D., Constantine, D., Batna, D.: Protocoles pour la Sécurité des Réseaux de Remerciements (2018)

7. Patel, S.T., Mistry, N.H.: A review: sybil attack detection techniques in WSN. In: Proceedings of 2017 4th International Conference on Electronics and Communication Systems, ICECS 2017, vol. 17, pp. 184–188 (2017). https://doi.org/10.1109/ECS.2017.8067865

8. Zhang, K., Liang, X., Lu, R., Shen, X.: Sybil attacks and their defenses in the internet of things. IEEE Internet Things J. **1**(5), 372–383 (2014). https://doi.org/10.1109/JIOT.2014.234 4013

9. Newsome, J., Shi, E., Song, D., Perrig, A.: The Sybil attack in sensor networks: analysis & defenses. In: Third International Symposium on Information Processing in Sensor Networks, IPSN 2004, pp. 259–268 (2004)

10. Badetia, N., Hussain, M.: Distributed mechanism for authentication of nodes in wireless sensor networks. In: 2017 2nd International Conference for Convergence in Technology (I2CT), Mumbai, India, pp. 471–474 (2017). https://doi.org/10.1109/I2CT.2017.8226173

11. Furtak, J., Zielinski, Z., Chudzikiewicz, J.: Security domain for the sensor nodes with strong authentication. In: 2019 International Conference on Military Communications and Information Systems, ICMCIS 2019, no. D, pp. 1–6 (2019). https://doi.org/10.1109/ICMCIS.2019. 8842766

12. Pinto, E.M.D.L., Lachowski, R., Pellenz, M.E., Penna, M.C., Souza, R.D.: A machine learning approach for detecting spoofing attacks in wireless sensor networks. In: Proceedings - International Conference on Advanced Information Networking and Applications, AINA, vol. 2018-May, pp. 752–758 (2018). https://doi.org/10.1109/AINA.2018.00113

13. Patil, S.D., Patil, K.K.: Provisioning authentication on demand in wireless sensor networks: PAW. In: 2018 6th Edition of International Conference on Wireless Networks & Embedded Systems, WECON 2018 - Proceedings, pp. 116–121 (2018). https://doi.org/10.1109/ WECON.2018.8782063

14. Pathak, G.R., Edake, G.M., Patil, S.H.: Untraceability of sensor node authentication in wireless sensor networks. In: Proceedings - 2014 6th International Conference on Computational Intelligence and Communication Networks, CICN 2014, pp. 893–897 (2014). https://doi.org/ 10.1109/CICN.2014.188

15. Badetia, N., Hussain, M.: Distributed mechanism for authentication of nodes in wireless sensor networks. In: 2017 2nd International Conference on Convergence in Technology, I2CT 2017, vol. 2017-January, pp. 471–474 (2017). https://doi.org/10.1109/I2CT.2017.8226173

16. Vardhan, A., Hussain, M.: Dynamic and resilient protocol for mutual authentication of nodes in wireless sensor networks. In: 2017 International Conference on Advances in Computing, Communications and Informatics, ICACCI 2017, vol. 2017-January, pp. 2010–2015 (2017). https://doi.org/10.1109/ICACCI.2017.8126140

17. Mishra, A.K., Tripathy, A.K., Puthal, D., Yang, L.T.: Analytical model for sybil attack phases in internet of things. IEEE Internet Things J. **6**(1), 379–387 (2019). https://doi.org/10.1109/ JIOT.2018.2843769

18. Al-Naeem, M.A.: Prediction of re-occurrences of spoofed ACK packets sent to deflate a target wireless sensor network node by DDOS. IEEE Access **9**, 87070–87078 (2021). https://doi. org/10.1109/ACCESS.2021.3089683

A K-Means Based Approach for Optimal Gateway Deployment in LoRaWAN-SIM

Thomas Djotio Ndie[1]([✉]), Antoine Junior Tsagmo Denkeng[2], Karl Jonas[3], and Roblex Nana Tchakouté[1,2,3]

[1] Bonn-Rhein-Sieg University of Applied Sciences, Rheinbach, Germany
tdjotio@gmail.com, nanatchakouteroblex@gmail.com
[2] Faculty of Sciences, University of Yaounde 1, Yaounde, Cameroon
juniortsagmo@gmail.com
[3] National Advanced school of Engineering of Yaounde 1, Yaounde, Cameroon
karl.jonas@h-brs.de

Abstract. **LoRa** is a technology that enables low-energy wireless communications over very long distances. Under these conditions, the simulation of LoRa projects becomes essential. Indeed, it allows on the one hand to virtually model and evaluate the performance of projects in the field and, on the other hand, to anticipate the optimization of the often expensive costs during the implementation of these projects. In this paper, we revisit the issue of simulation for LoRaWAN networks. Our research has led us to conclude that a LoRaWAN simulator's relevance can be assimilated to the problem of better gateway placement with the best exploitation of their parameters. Our approach consists of first studying some of the existing simulators with the aim of proposing a generic architecture model for such a tool and then, proposing recommendations for the selection of relevant simulators. To validate our model, we used the K-means machine learning technique to solve the problem of bad gateway locations in the LoRaWAN-SIM simulator. From our prototyped **K-LoRaWAN-SIM** simulator, we observed a gain of 10 gateways compared to the LoRaWAN-SIM simulator considered as our reference prototype. In fact, the results obtained with 25 gateways are close to those obtained with 35 gateways in LoRaWAN-SIM.

Keywords: Internet of Things · LPWAN · LoRa Technology · Simulation

1 Introduction

Considering the growth of the world's population, the main future challenges are intrinsically linked to energy management, natural resource monitoring, pollution control, the efficiency of environmental protection infrastructures, disaster prevention, medical monitoring and smart agriculture; to name but a few [1]. At the heart of these issues is the Internet of Things (IoT) and, LoRa technology is part of it. In such a context, the simulation of LoRaWAN networks becomes very important, as it can be used to observe the virtual behavior of the network

© ICST Institute for Computer Sciences, Social Informatics and Telecommunications Engineering 2025
Published by Springer Nature Switzerland AG 2025. All Rights Reserved
A. Sere et al. (Eds.): AFRICOMM 2023, LNICST 587, pp. 163–178, 2025.
https://doi.org/10.1007/978-3-031-81570-6_11

with the aim of getting as close as possible to the real world for decisions and actions to be applied. LoRaWAN is considered very promising due to its open accessibility, simplicity and flexibility both technologically and commercially [2]. A good understanding of the constraints inherent to this technology is necessary for the modeling and realization of a simulator in the field. An LPWAN simulator is a software that allows giving an overview of the real operation of an LPWAN network under specific conditions.

LoRa devices operate in ISM (Industry, Science, Medicine) bands that are subject to interferences [3]. Uplink messages are sent by nodes to the network server and are relayed by one or more gateways Downlink messages are sent by the network server to a single terminal and are relayed by a single gateway [3]. For some sensitivity thresholds, the gateway decodes the signal more easily than for others. Any packet with a sensitivity below the minimum sensitivity will not be detected by the gateway and will be considered lost.

LoRaWAN supports spread factors (SF) between 7 and 12, which allow for a trade-off between range and data rate. SF7 has the shortest range and highest data rate; SF12 is the exact opposite. The SF value is assigned when a new node connects to the base station. Since the SF symbols are orthogonal, the same gateway can receive different transmissions with different SFs on the same channel simultaneously, although in real-life scenarios this is not always the case [4]. The base station sends an acknowledgment frame (ACK) to the node when it receives a successful transmission. However, if a node does not receive an ACK frame, it retransmits the previous data until a successful ACK occurs [5].

However, in this panorama of upcoming challenges, to our humble knowledge, the academic community and individuals do not have clear information and guidance on the appropriate simulator(s) for the work they have in mind. Indeed, a number of open-source network simulators have been developed in recent years; but, most of them were developed for specific research purposes (first generation). Therefore, they tend to focus on a specific aspect. They are often limited by a number of assumptions. They also cannot properly capture the operation of the entire LoRaWAN protocol stack and therefore cannot properly simulate a real-world network. For this reason, our attention is mainly focused on the so-called second generation simulators. Our research has also led us to conclude that the relevance of a LoRaWAN simulator resides in the problem of placing gateways with the best exploitation of their characteristics in the simulator. The contributions made in this paper are to (1) - Propose a generic model of a LoRaWAN simulator architecture and suggest recommendations for relevant selection of a simulator. (2) - Propose an optimal solution for the gateway deployment problem in a LoRaWAN network, applied to the LoRaWAN-SIM simulator case. To validate our model, we used the K-means machine learning technique to solve the gateway placement problem in the LoRaWAN-SIM simulator. From our prototyped K-LoRaWAN-SIM simulator, we observed a gain of 10 gateways compared to the LoRaWAN-SIM simulator considered as our reference prototype. Indeed, the results obtained with 25 gateways in K-LoRaWAN-SIM are close to those obtained with 35 gateways in LoRaWAN-SIM.

The rest of this paper is organized as follows: Sect. 2 is devoted to works related to LoRa simulators and suggests an argued recommendation. In Sect. 3, we propose a generic architecture model for a LoRaWAN simulator. In Sect. 4, we also propose a solution to the gateway deployment issue in LoRaWAN-SIM based on the K-Means algorithm. Before concluding, we present our experiments and interpretations of the results in Sect. 5.

2   Related Research and Suggestions

2.1   State of Research on LoRaWAN Simulators

The research question on LoRa technology simulators has already been addressed in the literature by Silva and al. [6] and Christos Bouras and al. [1]. They produced surveys presenting respectively LoRaWAN simulations of the NS3 Module only and, the LoRa simulators (too specific), mostly of the first generation. However, these works are limited today because they do not take into account more complete or complex simulations of LoRa networks. This hampers users in their simulation projects. Contrary to these surveys, we focus in this paper on more complete simulators so-called second generation. Indeed, their varied functions allow us to better simulate real-world constraints, which makes them more relevant.

Indeed, we have gone through some works that have been interested in different LoRa network simulators, capable of performing useful evaluations. We can quote without being exhaustive: *NS3* [6], [7], *LoRaSim* [8], *LoRaFREE* [9], *LoRaEnergySim* [10], *LoRaWAN_Simulator* [11], *IoT-MAB* [12], *LoRaWAN-SIM* [13] and *FLoRa* [14]. However, many of these simulators are deployed for specific research purposes. They are generally oversimplified and contain a number of assumptions that affect the accuracy of their results. Here, we will only present simulators that are in line with a logic of completeness of functionality.

2.2   Recommended LoRa Simulators

The LoRaWAN network simulation model illustrated in Fig. 1, consists of the set of steps that any simulator should necessarily take into account for its operation. Indeed, a user must be able to model his network, specify the traffic model and, the routing algorithms that can be used. He must be able to obtain performance measurements of the simulated network. [1]. This model suggests an abstract or generic architecture for LoRaWAN simulators. From this model could be derived different architectures that could lead to the implementation of simulation tools in the field.

Ideally, the expected recommendation would be to propose simulators to users according to their sector of activity (e.g. medical monitoring, intelligent agriculture, environmental monitoring). Unfortunately, current simulators are not yet at this level of development. Nevertheless, there are some that are trying to address these issues. Figure 2 presents the general architecture of a LoRaWAN

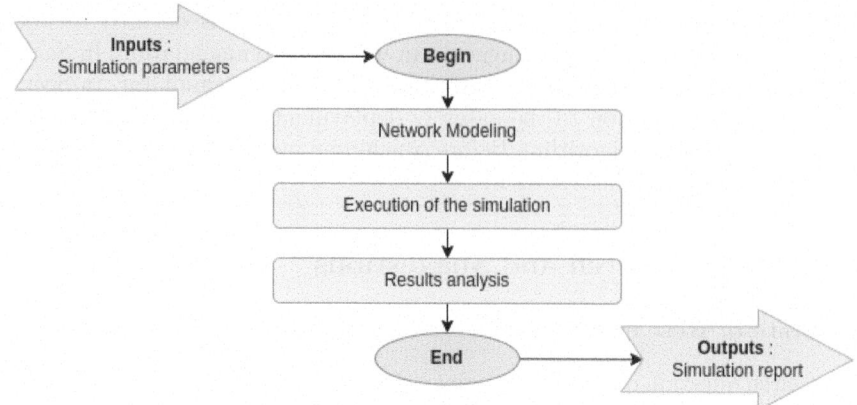

Fig. 1. LoRaWAN simulator model

network [11]. The gateway is used to transfer messages from the end nodes to the network server. In a LoRaWAN network, end nodes are not tied to a specific gateway. The data transmitted by an end node is received by multiple gateways. Each gateway forwards the packet received by the end node to the network server via a link (cellular, Ethernet, satellite or Wi-Fi).

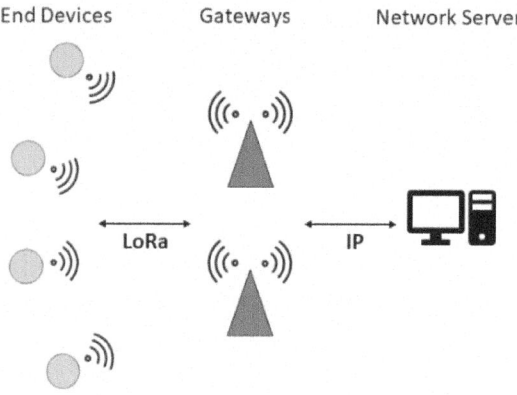

Fig. 2. Architecture of the LoRaWAN network

The NS3 Simulator. NS3 is a popular simulator for Internet systems, which supports LoRaWAN simulations. It is intended for teaching and research purposes with the goal of simulating a wide variety of networks. It includes over 700 different simulation scenarios. It supports a wide range of protocols and wireless network simulations as well. It is written in C++ and Python and, makes use of class A of the LoRaWAN specifications for its terminals [7], [6]. This is the least energy-consuming class compared to classes B and C. It is free and open source, available under the GNU GPLv2 license, and maintained by a vibrant global community.

LoRaWAN_Simulator. LoRaWAN_Simulator [11] is a working environment implemented in MATLAB. It is developed to characterize the behavior of LoRaWAN networks, taking into account physical, media access control, and network aspects. The wide variety of parameters it handles allows it to stand out as one of the most complete simulators currently available in the field. The points that make it special are: the accuracy of its physical layer for the examined settings, support for multiple gateways, modeling of half and full duplex gateways, the ability to enable or disable receive windows, consideration of uplink/downlink interference, and the impact of different coding rates in interference and noise limited scenarios.

IoT-MAB. IoT-MAB [12] is a SimPy-based simulator developed in Python 3. It uses machine learning techniques to enable LoRa devices to use innovative learning techniques to simulate the intelligent allocation of distributed resources in a LoRa network. Its goal is to introduce artificial intelligence into LoRa networks for better management of network resources. However, its handling and use are not easy.

LoRaFREE. LoRaFREE [9] is a more comprehensive SimPy simulator than LoRaSim. Unlike LoRaSim, it takes into account a packet error model, imperfect orthogonality of spreading factors, fading impact, and duty cycle limitation at the device and gateway level. LoRaFREE supports two-way communication by adding downlink capability and retransmission strategy in case of confirmable uplink transmissions. LoRaFree also extends LoRaSim's energy consumption profile to consider the energy consumed at the time of reception. In addition, this simulation environment is capable of simulating the timing of synchronized transmissions.

LoRaWAN-SIM. The LoRaWAN-SIM simulator [13] is completely written in Perl. It is designed primarily to evaluate confirmed transmissions, unconfirmed transmissions, and, large device simulations that include multiple gateways. It consists of two major modules that run sequentially. Based on a time-slicing approach, it has also been shown to be interesting for evaluating the optimal data collection time in LoRa networks.

The important remark is that the vast majority of LoRa simulators currently available are only used to evaluate the metrics of a LoRaWAN network. To our humble knowledge, (1) many of them are not yet specialized for specific areas of our daily life (for example simulators dedicated to medicine, precision agriculture, environmental monitoring and others); (2) only 03 of these simulators (NS3

Module, LoRaWAN_Simulator, and LoRaWAN-SIM) would be fairly suitable for use in complex applications such as the smart city. Although LoRaWAN-SIM has caught our attention, in its version at the time of writing this article, it does not yet allow an optimal deployment of gateways.

3   Proposal of an Ideal Simulator Model

We define an ideal or generic simulator as one that would accept a high number of (1) simulation settings as input and, (2) simulation results or data as output. Such a simulator is characteristic of a high level of network manageability on the one hand and, on the other hand, of a high level of understanding of the said network with as much detail as possible.

3.1   Properties of an Ideal Simulator

These are essential metrics for the proper functioning of the network in a massive IoT:

- A large number of nodes (High Nber of ED): greater than or equal to 1000
- A large number of gateways (High Nber of GW): greater than or equal to 10
- Rate of packets delivered (Delivery ratio)
- Rate of packets received (Reception ratio)
- Downlink and ACK (Downlink & ACK)
- Evaluation of energy consumption (Energy evaluation)
- Collisions evaluation
- Imperfect orthogonality of SF (SF Orthogonality)
- Adaptive data rate implementation (ADR)
- A large number of results returned (Nber of Returns): greater than or equal to 10.

3.2   Mathematical Model of an Ideal Simulator

Let P_R = our set of user parameters and the results that a simulator can offer. Let SimI denote the ideal simulator, $S = \{s_1, s_2, ..., s_n\}$ a set of simulators, and $Sim(s_i)$ a function that takes a simulator s_i as parameter and returns the total number of parameters and results in P_R. *n = total number of simulators in our study.* We model this ideal simulator by :

$$SimI = argmax(Sim(s_i)) \; ; \; 1 < i < n$$

$$Sim(s_i) = \sum_{j=1}^{m} P_j \; ; \; \text{With } P_j = \begin{cases} 1 \; if \;\; s_i \;\; has \;\; the \; P\_R_j \\ 0 \; if \; not \; (The \; P_j \;\; are \quad\quad equal) \end{cases}$$

Let us recall here that we are not trying to evaluate the relevance of a parameter in relation to another, but rather the presence or not of a parameter in the simulator.

4   Optimal Gateway Deployment

4.1   Issue Focus: Poor Deployment of Gateways

From our previous study, we found that the simulation question essentially raises 2 important concerns: the optimal placement and deployment of gateway nodes, so that the results obtained during simulation minimize errors during actual network deployment. In other words, the goal is to provide a means to determine the optimal positions of the gateway nodes for efficient network operation. Indeed, a good placement of gateway nodes inevitably leads to an optimal coverage of the area to be monitored, and consequently, to an economy of the global number of these gateway nodes. We have chosen the LoRaWAN-SIM simulator as the basic framework for experimenting with this problem of optimal positioning of gateway nodes for deployment that would ensure good network performance. As presented in the previous section, LoRaWAN-SIM is described as a package formed of two modules: one for selecting the parameters and the other for launching the actual simulation.

When using LoRaWAN-SIM, we found that the gateway and sensor nodes are completely generated randomly in a plot. The problem with this is that the network implements a haphazard arrangement of gateways. As a result, this non-optimal arrangement of the gateways has consequences on the network's overall performance. Indeed, their bad placement does not allow optimal coverage and could affect the quality of service (QoS) of the network. This is what motivates us to look for a technique to propose an approach that will allow a better disposition of the gateways that will optimize the network performances.

4.2   Motivations

We wish to offer the possibility to generate during the simulation, a network whose distribution of sensor and gateway nodes will be closer to reality. The node placement model should be economical in the number of gateway nodes needed to provide better QoS performance during network operation.

4.3   Resolution Approach

To solve this problem of finding the best gateway layout, we propose a solution based on machine learning, particularly clustering algorithms. These clustering algorithms allow to partition of the data into subgroups, or clusters, in an unsupervised way [15].

Among these unsupervised learning methods, we can distinguish hierarchical approaches; centroid methods (K-means and K-medoids), and, density approaches (DBSCAN). We have chosen the K-means algorithm because our data (points in the plane) are numerical and unlabeled. Our proposed approach allows for a more intelligent grouping of gateways in the network into node groups.

The K-Means Algorithm: K-means is an iterative algorithm that partitions the data set into K distinct subgroups (clusters). It tries to make the intra-cluster data points as similar as possible while keeping clusters as distant as possible [16]. It assigns data points to a cluster such that the sum of the squared distance between these points and the centroid of the cluster is at a minimum. The manual approach shows limitations in determining the optimal positioning of gateway nodes in the simulators studied above, especially in the context of a massive IoT network.

$$arg\ min \sum_{k=1}^{K} \sum_{\vec{x}_i \in C_k} d(\vec{x}_i, \mu_k)^2$$

However, it is difficult to find the exact cluster centers, so we use a heuristic.

Algorithm 1. K-means clustering algorithm

Require: dataset X of nodes coordinates, number of groups $K \in N$
Ensure: k groups centers coordinates for gateways
1: $I \leftarrow \infty$
2: take K arbitrary centres $c_k \in D$
3: **repeat**
4:     Initialize all k groups to empty $G_k \leftarrow \varnothing$
5:     **for** $i \in 1, ..., N$ **do**
6:         $k^* \leftarrow argmin_{k \in 1,...,K} d(x_i; c_k) G_{k^*} \leftarrow G_{k^*} \bigcup x_i$
7:     **end for**
8:     Re-compute the centers: $c_k \leftarrow$ centre of gravity of G_k
9:     $I \leftarrow I_W$
10:     Calculate I_W
11: **until** $I - I_W < threshold$

4.4   Architecture of K-LoRaWAN-SIM

Here, K-means is included in the first module to solve the target problem. Figure 3 depicts the workflow that models the proposed enhanced simulator architecture named **K-LoRaWAN-SIM**.

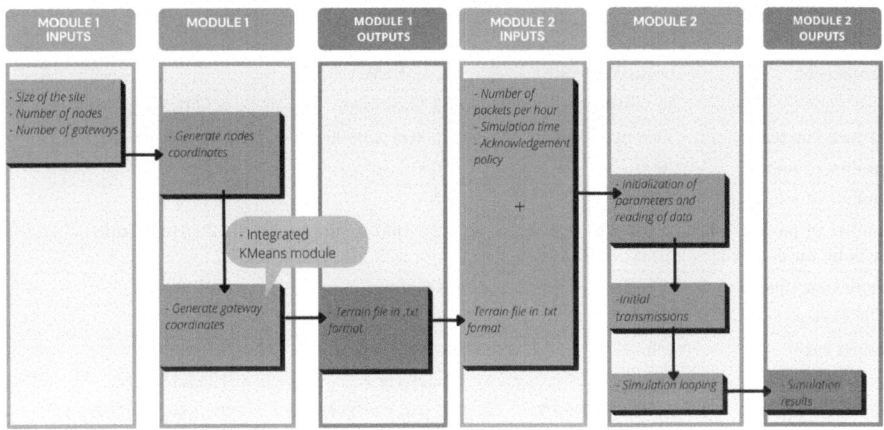

Fig. 3. Workflow of K-LoRaWAN-SIM

5 Experiments and Results (Case of LoRaWAN-SIM)

5.1 Experimental Protocol

Working Environment

- **Working machine:** a PC running Ubuntu 20.04.3 LTS 64-bit OS, with an Intel processor Core^{TM}i5-9300HF CPU @ 2.40GHz × 8 and 16 GB of RAM.
- **Programming language:** we implemented our K-Means learning module with the scikit-learn library in Python3, which we then coupled with LoRaWAN-SIM initially developed within Perl 5.30.

Simulation Settings: The different parameters used for our experiments are recorded in Table 1. These settings are independently used first in the LoRaWAN-SIM simulator version we took as a reference, and then in our developed prototype K-LoRaWAN-SIM simulator.

Our example use case consists in simulating a typical scenario of environmental monitoring applications such as air quality monitoring in a target area by a massive IoT network. To illustrate this, we have chosen an experimental framework with an area of nearly 9Km2 (assimilated to a community) in which we have dispersed nearly 3000 nodes, interconnected by a variable number of gateways.

Methodology for Results Validation: The choice of the minimum number of gateways (35 and 9) used to launch the network was made each time following numerous experiments in the **LoRaWAN-SIM** and **K-LoRaWAN-SIM** simulators.

The optimal choice of gateways: We first performed about ten runs and each time we observed the state of the network connectivity, i.e., if all the nodes

Table 1. Simulation parameters: In order to make our results reproducible.

Parameters	LoRaWAN-SIM	K-LoRaWAN-SIM	
	35 Gateways	35 Gateways	9 Gateways
Site size (meters)	3000 m x 3000 m	3000 m x 3000 m	3000 m x 3000 m
Number of nodes	3000	3000	3000
Number of gateways	35	35	9
Number of packets sent per hour for each ED	12 : 1pkt/5min	12 : 1pkt/5min	12 : 1pkt/5min
Simulation time(sec)	10000 sec	10000 sec	10000 sec
ACK Policy	2	2	2
Coding rate	4/5	4/5	4/5
Bandwidth (BW)	125 KHz	125 KHz	125 KHz
Path Loss Model	$L_{pl}(d_0) = 95dB$, $d_0 = 40m$, $\gamma = 2.08$, $\sigma = 3.57$	$L_{pl}(d_0) = 95dB$, $d_0 = 40m$, $\gamma = 2.08$, $\sigma = 3.57$	$L_{pl}(d_0) = 95dB$, $d_0 = 40m$, $\gamma = 2.08$, $\sigma = 3.57$
Receiver sensitivity (per SF for BW125)	$[-124, -127, -130, -133,$ $-135, -137]$dBm	$[-124, -127, -130, -133,$ $135, -137]$dBm	$[-124, -127, -130, -133,$ $-135, -137]$dBm
Power & consumption T_x	2dBm, 0.0396 mW; 7dBm, 0.099 mW; 14dBm, 0.2508 mW	2dBm, 0.0396 mW; 7dBm, 0.099 mW; 14dBm, 0.2508 mW	2dBm, 0.0396 mW; 7dBm, 0.099 mW; 14dBm, 0.2508 mW
Consumption R_x	0.15 mW	0.15 mW	0.15 mW

of the network were well connected by all the gateways. We then gradually reduced the number of gateways in the LoRaWANSIM use case to 35 gateways. We concluded that this was the minimum number needed to cover all nodes in the network. Finally, to highlight the effectiveness of our K-means based optimization algorithm in terms of minimizing the number of gateways (due to a good layout from now on), we proceeded to progressively decrease the number of gateways in the K-LoRaWAN-SIM use case down to 9 gateways. We managed to achieve the same results in terms of coverage and network connectivity.

Validation of simulation results: We generated 10 instances per simulation for each set of parameters and took the average of these results to populate tables. For example, for the values of *the average energy consumed by a node*, we took the sum of the average energies of each run and divided it by the number of times we performed these runs. In order to confirm the choice of the average, we have evaluated the standard deviation (σ) on the obtained results in order to corroborate that there is not too much variability in the obtained results. e.g.:

- For the energy, we have about one standard deviation of $\sigma = 2mJ$
- For the ratio, we have about a standard deviation of $\sigma = 0.2\%$

5.2 Experimental Results, Comparisons and Discussions

Analysis and Interpretation of Results: Figures 4, 5 and 6 illustrate the graphs of the different configurations relative to the Table 1. It can be seen that the last two propose a better arrangement of gateways than the first one.

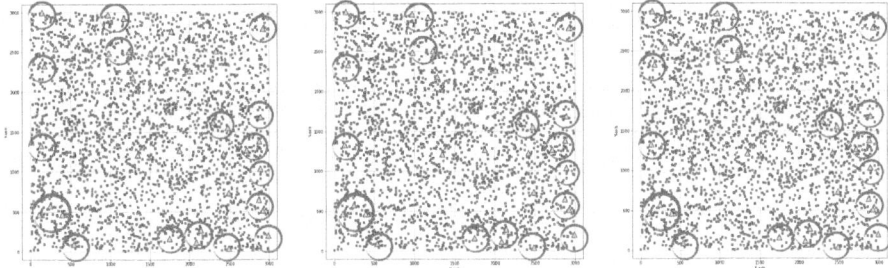

Fig. 4. $9km^2$, 3000 ED, 35 GW without K-means

Fig. 5. $9km^2$, 3000 ED, 35 GW with K-means

Fig. 6. $9km^2$, 3000 ED, 9 GW with K-means

The energy consumption is represented by the diagrams in Fig. 7. This low value obtained is consistent with the expected good energy performance of the network. The packet delivery and reception rates are represented by the diagrams in Fig. 8. The high value obtained is a good indicator of good performance of the ratio of sending and receiving packets in our network. These two figures are only the representation of the results of the output of simulations quantified in Table 2.

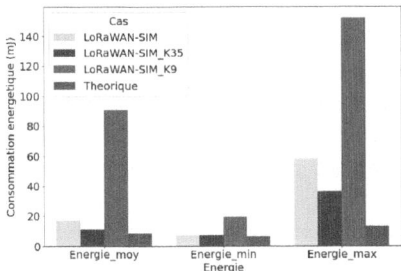

Fig. 7. Energy consumption

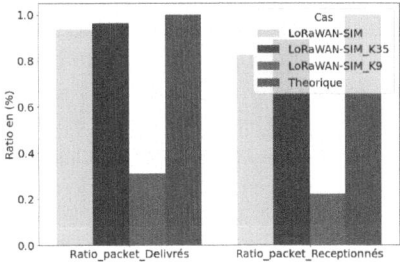

Fig. 8. Ratio of delivered/received packets

However, we observe that there is a relationship between the poor performance of the 3rd experiment (4th column of Table 2) and the reduced number of gateways. Similarly, there is a relationship between the very high energy consumption and the poor packet delivery and reception ratio. We say that the numbers in the 4th column of Table 2 justify the energy consumption for this set of parameters. **The massive data traffic to the only available gateways affects the operation of the entire network by decreasing the quality of service (QoS) including minimizing the network throughput**. This large amount of retransmission is the cause of the increase in energy consumption resulting in a rapid depletion of the batteries. The very high number of lost packets cannot guarantee a good QoS either.

Table 2. Summary of observations

Parameters	LoRaWAN-SIM	K-LoRaWAN-SIM		
	35 Gateways	35 Gateways	9 Gateways	Theorics Val
Average energy consumed by the node (mJ)	16,72881	11,06441	90,46371	8,2764
Minimum energy consumed by the node (mJ)	6,86721	6,95059	19,15122	6,3162
Maximum energy consumed by the node (mJ)	58,33216	35,90506	151,81651	13,2858
Total number of single transmission	102395	102170	156541	99000
Total number of retransmissions	115860	44620	1122483	0
Total number of transmissions	214747	146163	1173782	99000
Total number of packets acquired	95887	98542	48299	99000
Total number of packets delivered	176177	129769	258842	99000
Total number of lost packets	3508	627	105241	0
Ratio of packets delivered	0,93650	0,96449	0,30854	1
Ratio of packets received	0,82353	0,88784	0,22052	1

Consequently, we are looking for a compromise to reduce the number of gateways while maintaining good performance.

Trade-Off Between Gateway Reduction and Performance: We have found the compromise of the number of gateways per experiment: We performed many executions and each time we observed the packet delivery and reception ratios because this information is a function of the network energy consumption. It also allows us to characterize the network from the number of retransmissions recorded. As a standard, the desired packet delivery and reception ratios are respectively at least 90% and 80%. To this end, we have gradually increased the number of gateways in the K-LoRaWAN-SIM use case to 25, the average number representing the best compromise sought at the outset. This represents a reduction of 10 gateways compared to the LoRaWAN-SIM reference tool and, in addition, provides good performance in terms of adequate QoS in the network. We make the following observation: the new set of settings passed to the K-LoRaWANSIM simulator provides quite good results in output. We have indeed found the desired compromise that satisfies us both on the number of gateways used and on the network performance (see Table 3, Figs. 10 and 11). We can then say that compared to LoRaWANSIM, K-LoRaWAN-SIM has even more advantages, especially the reduction of the number of gateways needed and the good performance for the network (Fig. 9).

Discussions. Compared to **LoRaWAN-SIM**, the proposed tool **K-LoRa-WAN-SIM** takes into account the gateway centralization parameter with the aim of providing better performances.

The optimization brought by the **K-means** to this simulator has a global impact on the network settings, such as: the global energy consumption of the

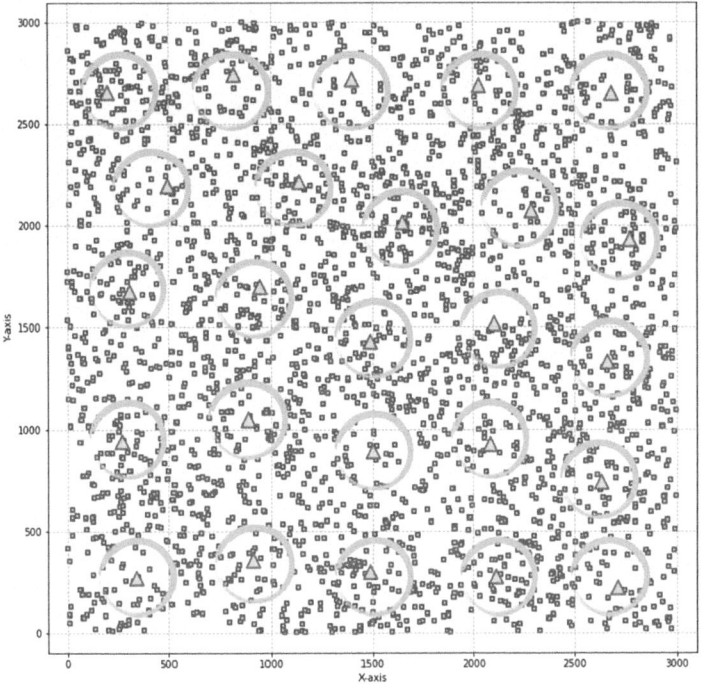

Fig. 9. $9km^2$, 3000 ED, 25 GW with K-means

Table 3. Summary of observations

Parameters	LoRaWAN-SIM	K-LoRaWAN-SIM			
	35 Gateways	35 Gateways	9 Gateways	25 Gateways	Theorics Val
Average energy consumed by the node (mJ)	16,72881	11,06441	90,46371	16,74796	8.2764
Min energy consumed by the node (mJ)	6,86721	6,95059	19,15122	8,94078	6.3162
Max energy consumed by the node (mJ)	58,33216	35,90506	151,81651	37,18431	13.2858
Total number of single transmission	102395	102170	156541	102120	99000
Total number of retransmissions	115860	44620	1122483	128367	0
Total number of transmissions	214747	146163	1173782	227080	99000
Total Number packet Acquity	95887	98542	48299	95712	99000
Total number of packets delivered	176177	129769	258842	185467	99000
Total Number of losts packets	3508	627	105241	3409	0
Ratio of packets delivered	0,93650	0,96449	0,30854	0,93724	1
Ratio of received packets	0,82353	0,88784	0,22052	0,81675	1

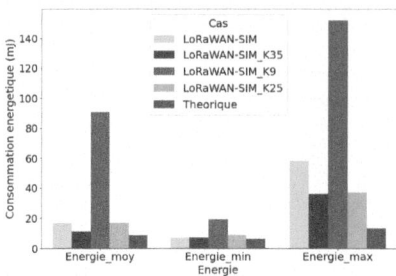

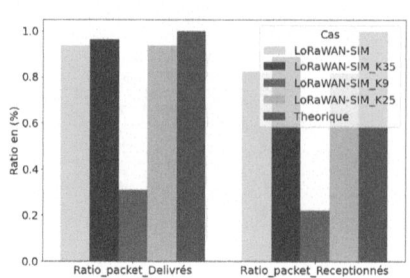

Fig. 10. Energy consumption

Fig. 11. Ratio of delivered/received packets

network, the data collection time, the transmission reliability, the reduced number of gateways in the network, the transmission speed (packet delivery rate). Indeed, a better positioning of gateways allows us to use good spreading factors, which are important settings to maintain an acceptable level of power consumption of the sensor devices, to have a larger coverage, a good quality of service, just to mention a few. On the other hand, our prototype takes just a little longer to generate the simulation results (5 s longer on average). **K-LoRaWAN-SIM** is accessible at the URL **https://github.com/antoinetsagmo/K-LoRaWAN-SIM**.

6   Conclusion and Future Work

LPWAN technologies are gaining more importance in almost every area of life in this increasingly connected world. This paper presents the best LoRa simulators in the literature to our humble knowledge. However, **LoRaWAN-SIM**, an open-source simulator has caught our attention thanks to its ease of use and the numerous results it provides. Following the experiments, in particular by visualizing the layout of the gateways generated by the tool, we realized that the essential problem of simulation in a LoRaWAN network can be assimilated to that of bad placement of gateways. We provided a solution based on the K-means machine learning technique.

K-LoRaWAN-SIM is available online at **https://github.com/antoinetsagmo/K-LoRaWAN-SIM**. It allowed us to conduct experiments and compare the results with those of the LoRaWAN-SIM reference tool available at **https://github.com/deltazita/LoRaWAN-SIM**. This new LoRa network simulator offers the possibility to realize a better placement of gateway nodes in the network. It also allows realizing an interconnection guaranteeing a better coverage with a minimal number of gateway nodes while keeping a correct level of performance and quality of service. We have seen that K-LoRaWAN-SIM provides almost identical results to the basic LoRaWAN-SIM tool while saving about ten gateways on the following test parameters: energy consumption, total number of unique transmissions, the total number of lost packets, the ratio of delivered and received packets, etc.

In the future, we are interested in scaling up. Indeed, for execution time constraints, we did not simulate large networks corresponding to real-life scenarios for applications that can cover a geographical area on the scale of a city for example. This type of scenario has the characteristic of generally requiring a very large number of sensor nodes.

Acknowledgements. This work was carried out in the WiCoNet laboratory of the Ecole Nationale Supérieure Polytechnique and UMMISCO of Computer Science Department of Yaoundé 1 University.

References

1. Bouras, C., Gkamas, A., Salgado, S.A.K., Kokkinos, V.: Comparison of LoRa simulation environments. In: Barolli, L., Hellinckx, P., Enokido, T. (eds.) Advances on Broad-Band Wireless Computing, Communication and Applications, pp. 374–385, Cham (2020). Springer International Publishing
2. Sinha, R.S., Wei, Y., Hwang, S.-H.: A survey on LPWA technology: LoRa and NB-IoT. ICT Express **3**(1), 14–21 (2017)
3. Ayoub, W., Samhat, A.E., Nouvel, F., Mroue, M., Prévotet, J.-C.: Internet of mobile things: Overview of LoRaWAN, DASH7, and NB-IoT in LPWANs standards and supported mobility. IEEE Commun. Surv. Tutorials **21**(2), 1561–1581 (2019)
4. Croce, D., Gucciardo, M., Tinnirello, I., Garlisi, D., Mangione, S.: Impact of spreading factor imperfect orthogonality in LoRa communications. In: Piva, A., Tinnirello, I., Morosi, S. (eds.) Digital Communication. Towards a Smart and Secure Future Internet, pp. 165–179, Cham (2017). Springer International Publishing
5. Tiago Afonso Antunes de Figueiredo. Lorawan performance evaluation (2019)
6. Silva, J., Flor, D., de Junior, V.A., Bezerra, N., Medeiros, A.: A survey of LoRaWAN simulation tools in ns-3. J. Commun. Inf. Syst. **36**(1), 17–30 (2021)
7. Reynders, B., Wang, Q., Pollin, S.: A LoRaWAN module for ns-3: Implementation and evaluation. In: Proceedings of the 10th Workshop on Ns-3, WNS3 '18, pp. 61–68, New York, NY, USA (2018). Association for Computing Machinery
8. Bor, M.C., Roedig, U., Voigt, T., Alonso, J.M.: Do LoRa low-power wide-area networks scale? In: Proceedings of the 19th ACM International Conference on Modeling, Analysis and Simulation of Wireless and Mobile Systems, MSWiM '16, pp. 59–67, New York, NY, USA (2016). Association for Computing Machinery
9. Abdelfadeel, K.Q., Zorbas, D., Cionca, V., Pesch, D.: Fine-grained scheduling for reliable and energy-efficient data collection in LoRaWAN. IEEE Internet Things J. **7**(1), 669–683 (2020)
10. Callebaut, G., Ottoy, G., van der Perre, L.: Cross-layer framework and optimization for efficient use of the energy budget of IoT nodes. In: 2019 IEEE Wireless Communications and Networking Conference (WCNC), pp. 1–6 (2019)
11. Marini, R., Mikhaylov, K., Pasolini, G., Buratti, C.: LoRaWANSim: a flexible simulator for LoRaWAN networks. Sensors **21**(3) (2021)
12. Ta, D.-T., Khawam, K., Lahoud, S., Adjih, C., Martin, S.: LoRa-MAB: a flexible simulator for decentralized learning resource allocation in IoT networks. In: 2019 12th IFIP Wireless and Mobile Networking Conference (WMNC), pp. 55–62 (2019)
13. Zorbas, D., Caillouet, C., Hassan, K.A., Pesch, D.: Optimal data collection time in LoRa networks–a time-slotted approach. Sensors **21**(4) (2021)

14. Slabicki, M., Premsankar, G., Di Francesco, M.: Adaptive configuration of LoRa networks for dense IoT deployments. In: NOMS 2018 - 2018 IEEE/IFIP Network Operations and Management Symposium, pp. 1–9 (2018)
15. Jain, A.K.: Data clustering: 50 years beyond k-means. Pattern Recogn. Lett. **31**(8), 651–666 (2010). Award winning papers from the 19th International Conference on Pattern Recognition (ICPR)
16. MacQueen, J., et al.: Some methods for classification and analysis of multivariate observations. In: Proceedings of the Fifth Berkeley Symposium on Mathematical Statistics and Probability, number 14 in 1, pp. 281–297. Oakland, CA, USA, (1967)

Assessing the Impact of Web Caching on Resource Utilization in Low Capacity Networks

J. A. Okuthe[✉]

Walter Sisulu University, Potsdam, East London 5200, South Africa
jokuthe@wsu.ac.za

Abstract. Caching web objects closer to hosts for reuse can improve the performance of services that rely on the Internet. However, in recent times a large portion of the Internet traffic delivery is through HTTPS where Transport Layer Security (TLS) provides end-to-end encryption ensuring data integrity, authenticity, privacy and confidentiality between the Web server and client. Encrypted traffic is not malleable to caching and reuse by the network, since each session is unique. Nonetheless, by deploying a cache system that operates over encrypted communication channels using an initial key exchange protocol and a hash function between the cache server and the clients, we implemented HTTPS Web caching configuration in an active community network environment. Results obtained from the study showed a 64.03% drop in the local loop bandwidth utilization and a reduction of the Web traffic component from 95.49% to 52.54%. In addition, there was a 44.1% decline in the local loop traffic volume. Although the LAN traffic volume is not a major area of concern due to the existence of a 1Gbps Ethernet capacity, the resulting 4.01% reduction in LAN traffic volume is a positive contribution from the study.

Keywords: Bandwidth · Proxy Caching · Encryption · Traffic Volume

1 Introduction

Web caching can improve the performance of Web-based systems by storing Web elements in locations that are closest to the host [1]. The reasoning behind this strategy is that temporal locality implies objects stored nearer to recently accessed items have a high chance of being required in the near future. Therefore, Web caching enables the possibility of fulfilling some host requests for Web objects locally resulting in improved response time. Furthermore, lowering of both network bandwidth utilization and workload on the content provider's servers occur when Web caching is adopted.

Although Web caching would be complete when local replication of Web objects occurs, the cache is limited in size. Therefore, a selection of objects to store locally is necessary. The objects requested frequently and not changed often end up being the best candidates for caching. Typically, organizational caching policies aligned to

© ICST Institute for Computer Sciences, Social Informatics and Telecommunications Engineering 2025
Published by Springer Nature Switzerland AG 2025. All Rights Reserved
A. Sere et al. (Eds.): AFRICOMM 2023, LNICST 587, pp. 179–193, 2025.
https://doi.org/10.1007/978-3-031-81570-6_12

unique business strategies dictate which objects are selected for caching [2]. In general, the optimal cache replacement policy targets the best use of available cache capacity with the goal of improving cache hits and reducing server loads. Some of the common cache replacement policies include least recently used and least frequently used [3]. An alternative strategy is the size based web replacement policy that avoids caching of large objects.

In our previous study, a high proportion of Web traffic was evident after the optimization of DNS service [4]. In mitigation, we enabled proxy caching on the community network's gateway router. Since a majority of Web communication is through HTTPS which ensures end-to-end encryption, the implemented cache configuration operates over encrypted communication channels using an initial key exchange protocol and a hash function between the router and clients [5]. A 32GB Micro SD card stores Web objects for reuse. Adoption of the cache replacement policy shipped with the gateway routed including storage duration and Web object size is ensures efficient migration of proxy caching server within the community network environment.

2 Related Work

2.1 Benefits of Web Caching

The benefit of Web caching is in most instances improved user experience due to reduced network bandwidth utilization and improved response time [6]. Yang [7] established that Web caching improves the network latency by up to 26%. In low bandwidth network relying on modems, Cao [8] found that the average latencies experienced by clients reduces by over 23% through Web caching adoption. Work undertaken by Mahdavi [9] in the collaborative web caching environment showed that bandwidth usage per request was reduced by 1.32, 1.35, and 1.4 times for 8KB, 16KB, and 32KB cache sizes, respectively. The corresponding throughput improvement was 1.3, 1.32, and 1.35 times for 8KB, 16KB, and 32KB cache sizes. The study examined the performance of LCW, FIFO and LRU cache replacement strategies. Results showed that the Least Cache Worthiness (LCW) performs better followed by LRU and then FIFO. For a cache size of 20MB, the hit ratios were 0.23 for LCW, followed by 0.17 for LRU, and lastly 0.14 for FIFO.

In the Simultaneous Proxy Evaluation (SPE) architecture [10] where a live workload evaluation of multiple proxies is undertaken, OOPS required only 21.5% of the bandwidth of the pass through proxy. Squid used 21.0% of the bandwidth whereas Apache required 17.0% of bandwidth used when there is no web caching in place. The effectiveness of Web caching reported in the hybrid web caching architecture [11] indicates that Web caches in the local access network perform better than regional and national level ones. A different approach to Web caching adopted in the server side web caching strategy [12] showed a significant reduction in the number of cache misses which resulted in reduced bandwidth utilization and faster response time. Besides bandwidth conservation and response time improvement, the other contribution of Web caching is reduced workload on the content providers' servers [13].

Recent work on the potential of web caching has focused on networks involving Internet of Things (IoTs) [14–16] which allow many mobile based applications like smart homes, electric grids, transport, and digital health to exist. The large number of connections associated with IoTs produce massive amounts of data that require alternative caching solutions. Possible ways of addressing these challenges include the use of content identifiers rather than the host identifier where the nodes communicate through content name instead of the host address [17]. Content-based naming allows for the implementation of in-network caching feature [18] avoiding extra add-ons to the network layer. Placing replica content across the network can help improve caching efficacy in the IoT environment [19]. Requests for content need not travel across the entire network to find the content source. Instead, caching nodes along the request path provide the required resources.

2.2 Caching HTTPS Objects

A large portion of the Internet traffic delivery is through HTTPS in which the Transport Layer Security (TLS) provides end-to-end encryption to ensure data integrity, authenticity, privacy and confidentiality [5]. Encrypted traffic is typically not malleable to caching and reuse by the network, since each session is unique to the Web server and client [20]. The split-TLS Web caching strategy [5] uses an untrusted cache service deployed as a gateway for the client. To enforce cache trust by clients, a certificate is installed on the client Trusted Root Certification Authority Store. The cache server then becomes a trusted agent by the client as root Certification Authority (CA) and any certificate signed by the server is trusted and valid. The cache server forwards traffic back and forth between the client and the Web server using two separate TLS connections [5]. One connection from itself to the client and the other between itself and the Web server. The downside to the split-TLS scheme is that the cache server has full access to traffic sent between the client and the Web server.

In a cache system that operates over encrypted communication channels [21], an initial key exchange protocol and a hash function exchange between the cache server and the client occurs. The client receives the encrypted Web content from the cache server, and later gets the encrypted decryption keys from the Web service provider. Alternatively, the cache server can send the decryption key to the client alongside the Web content. The cache server manages the encrypted Web content and corresponding decryption keys. Hence guaranteeing privacy and confidentiality since the generation of keys is a process that is independent from Web content transfer and therefore the cache server has no access the Web content [21].

2.3 Web Caching Schemes

The demand for Internet content has risen in recent years. Although servers have largely improved in terms of processing power and storage capacity, network backhauls and local loops have not kept pace resulting in poor Web services [22]. For this reason, Web caching and prefetching offer effective solutions for user access latency and high network bandwidth utilization [23]. For a single user, Web caching can typically be achievement by the client Web browser. On a local area network, users obtain Web caching services from the middle layer between the client and the Web server as part of a proxy as illustrated in Fig. 1. Optimal performance proxy caches are located near the network gateway to minimize bandwidth usage across the Internet infrastructure. Proxy servers cache many objects from several servers. This enables reuse of Web objects.

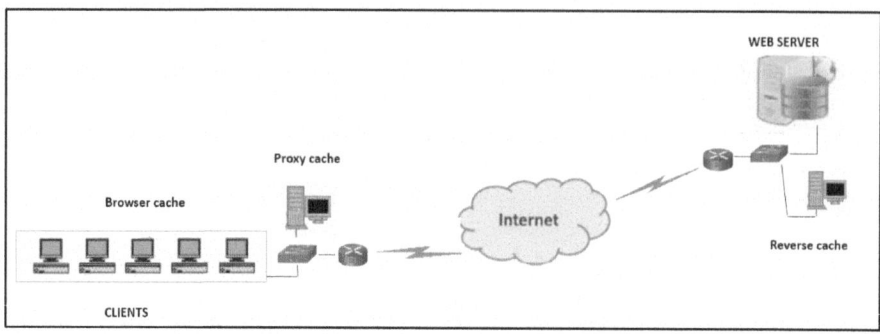

Fig. 1. Web caching service categories

When the implementation of Web caching service is next to a specific Web server instead of clients, reverse caching occurs since Web objects are stored away from clients and located closer to the Web server [24].

The proxy level caches are typically located closer to network gateway to reduce the bandwidth utilization over Internet connections and store objects from different web servers. This helps facilitate sharing of web resources. Proxy caching deployment has minimal interruption on the networking environment and is therefore the preferred configuration [25]. It achieves the economy of scale by offering services to several hosts and does not rely on the provisioning of Web servers. Consequently, end-to-end transparency during configuration change is not required since the implementation takes place within a local setting.

3 Network Environment

The implementation of proxy caching occurred on the gateway router within the community network. Figure 2 shows the topology of the community network. A 32GB Micro SD card stores Web objects for reuse. The cache system configuration adopts encrypted communication channel communication between clients and Web servers allowing the with the gateway router acting as the cache server to store and forward Web objects.

The retention of the Web object size at 500 MB and cache refresh timeout of 3 days remained in force. Enabling secure SSL channels between the gateway router and hosts on the LAN ensures security and privacy. While data collected at the router interface provides the characteristics of traffic flow to and from the Internet, the mirroring port on the LAN switch is a retrieval point for packet movement within the LAN. Packets sourced from the two capture points are dumped to disk for offline analysis.

The collection of traffic flow from both the ingress router interface and a mirroring port on the LAN switch used N-Top Deep Packet Inspection (nDPI) software [27]. To obtain exhaustive network status activity, nDPI performs traffic characterization based

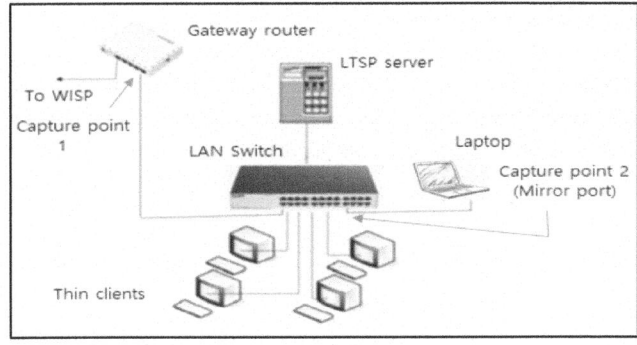

Fig. 2. Community network environment

on both MAC and IP addresses allowing recognition of IP and non-IP traffic. Additional flow information attainable from active interfaces include throughput statistics as well as Layer 4 and Layer 7 protocol activities.

4   Network Resource Utilization

4.1   Pre Web Caching

Before activating proxy caching on the gateway router, collection of control data was from both the router's ingress port and the mirroring port on the LAN switch occurred. The first instance of data collection was when the local loop capacity stood at 1 Mbps, the second occasion took place immediately after the bandwidth enhancement from to 10 Mbps [26]. A third data collection happened one month after the bandwidth upgrade to 10 Mbps [26]. The final pre-Web caching data collection took place after DNS service optimization [4]. Reported results include bandwidth utilization, traffic composition and traffic volume metrics at the four pre-Web caching measurement milestones.

Bandwidth Utilization
Table 1 shows the bandwidth utilization for the four measurement instances as 1 Mbps, 8.13 Mbps, 9.57 Mbps and 7.07 Mbps respectively. These were, before bandwidth upgrade, immediately following upgrade, one month after the upgrade and pre-DNS service optimization.

Table 1. Pre-Web Caching Bandwidth Utilization

Milestone	Before upgrade	Immediately after upgrade	One month after	After DNS service optimization
Bandwidth utilization (Mbps)	1.00	8.13	9.57	7.07

Traffic Composition and Traffic Volume

The composition of the monthly traffic collected at the router interface for the four measurement instances appears in Table 2. The highest proportion of local loop traffic is consistently web-based except one month after the bandwidth upgrade. The maximum contribution from web traffic is 95.49 and occurs after DNS optimization. The lowest proportion of 43.26% arises one month after the bandwidth upgrade.

Table 2. Percentage distribution of the top five applications

Application	Web	DNS	ICMP	NetBIOS	Unknown	Total traffic (GB)
Before upgrade	91.63	2.7	0.00	0.03	0.29	1.17
Immediately after upgrade	49.42	45.28	4.63	0.03	0.64	5.86
One month after upgrade	43.26	56.14	0.04	0.03	0.56	6.69
After DNS optimization	95.49	4.11	0.24	0.00	0.16	6.91

LAN Traffic

The analysis of data captured from the switch mirroring port immediately after the bandwidth upgrade shown in Fig. 3 indicate that SSL accounts for 48.83% of the total LAN traffic. The contribution from Google is 39.38%, Cloudflare 5.69% and Amazon 1.32%. The total LAN traffic is 25.97GB. Table 3 depicts the LAN traffic composition for the four data capture instances.

4.2   Post Web Caching

After enabling proxy caching on the gateway router, data collection takes place from both the router's ingress port and the mirroring port on the LAN switch for the duration of three months starting from 1st day of July to 30th day of September 2021. Results from the data analysis provided the updated bandwidth utilization, traffic composition and traffic volume.

Bandwidth Utilization

The weekly router interface traffic graph with proxy caching enabled is shown in Fig. 4. The maximum incoming traffic rate is 13.7 Mbps while the outgoing is 1.75 Mbps.

Traffic Composition and Traffic Volume

Figure 5 depicts the composition of local loop traffic. The highlighting of this information appears in Table 4. The highest proportion of traffic traversing the community network

Application	Duration	Sent	Received	Breakdown	Total	
Total	236:15:24	3.21 GB	22.76 GB	Sent Rcvd		25.97 GB
Amazon	47:06:14	85.35 MB	257.49 MB	Sent Rcvd	342.84 MB	1.32 %
ApplePush	02:45:20	3.14 MB	14.59 MB	Sent Rcvd	17.73 MB	0.07 %
Cloudflare	27:34:16	152.36 KB	1.29 MB	Sent Rcvd	1.44 MB	5.69 %
DHCP	06:41:12	7.01 MB	7.01 MB	Sent Rcvd	14.02 MB	0.05 %
DNS	34:38:53	36.31 MB	61.54 MB	Sent Rcvd	97.65 MB	0.38 %
Facebook	04:15:03	13.61 MB	97.68 MB	Sent Rcvd	111.29 MB	0.43 %
Google	73:24:28	1.15 GB	9.19 GB	Sent Rcvd	10.34 GB	39.38 %
HTTP	04:15:35	17.98 MB	149.06 MB	Sent Rcvd	168.84 MB	0.65 %
ICMP	04:12:19	0 Bytes	2.61 MB	Rcvd	2.61 MB	0.01 %
IGMP	01:25:11	105.23 KB	0 Bytes	Sent	105.23 KB	0.0 %
LLMNR	04:53:23	5.22 MB	0 Bytes	Sent	5.22 MB	0.02 %
MDNS	03:46:54	5.22 MB	0 Bytes	Sent	5.22 MB	0.02 %
Microsoft	01:02:38	4.18 MB	6.26 MB	Sent Rcvd	10.44 MB	0.04 %
NetBIOS	16:36:29	26.11 MB	0 Bytes	Sent	26.11 MB	0.1 %
Office365	05:11:05	10.44 MB	41.78 MB	Sent Rcvd	52.22 MB	0.2 %
SNMP	83:07:47	54.39 MB	0 Bytes	Sent	54.39 MB	0.21 %
SSDP	42:14:25	171.41 MB	0 Bytes	Sent	171.41 MB	0.66 %
SSL	73:24:28	0.63 GB	12.05 GB	Sent Rcvd	12.68 GB	48.83 %
UPnP	05:54:12	64.93 MB	0 Bytes	Sent	64.93 MB	0.25 %
Unknown	92:37:56	392.27 MB	20.15 MB	Sent Rcvd	412.92 MB	1.59 %
WhatsAppVoice	01:02:36	123.47 KB	0 Bytes	Sent	123.47 KB	0.0 %
WindowsUpdate	01:25:12	1.29 MB	1.29 MB	Sent Rcvd	2.58 MB	0.01 %
Yahoo	02:47:24	2.08 MB	8.31 MB	Sent Rcvd	10.39 MB	0.04 %
YouTubeUpload	00:36:39	2.34 MB	5.45 MB	Sent Rcvd	7.79 MB	0.03 %
eDonkey	00:36:38	6.23 MB	9.35 MB	Sent Rcvd	15.58 MB	0.06 %

Fig. 3. LAN traffic composition one month after bandwidth upgrade

is web-based at 52.54% followed closely by DNS with a contribution of 28.71%. The traffic volume through the router interface is 6.98 GB.

LAN Traffic
The analysis of data captured from the switch mirroring port shown in Fig. 6 and summarized in Table 5 indicate that. DNS accounts for 0.34% of the total LAN traffic. The contribution from Google is 55.58%, SSL 26.68% and Amazon 2.85%. The total LAN traffic is 18.65GB.

4.3 Comparison

The configuration of proxy caching on the gateway router was to mitigate the high proportion of the web component of the local loop traffic. To highlight the impact of web caching with respect to bandwidth utilization, traffic composition and traffic volume a comparison between pre and post Web caching is necessary.

Bandwidth Utilization
Table 6 shows the bandwidth utilization against the corresponding local loop capacity before bandwidth upgrade, immediately after bandwidth upgrade and one month

Table 3. LAN traffic composition prior to proxy caching activation

Application	SSL	Google	Apple	DNS	Microsoft	Facebook	Total traffic (GB)
Distribution (%) Before upgrade	4.76	41.52	0.01	0.65	0.83	0.0	20.18
Distribution (%) Immediately after	39.5	33.6	16.6	0.0	2.4	1.1	24.58
Distribution (%) One month after	48.83	39.38	0.07	0.36	0.04	0.43	25.97
Distribution (%) After DNS activation	11.98	32.22	0.09	0.18	42.95	0.0	19.43

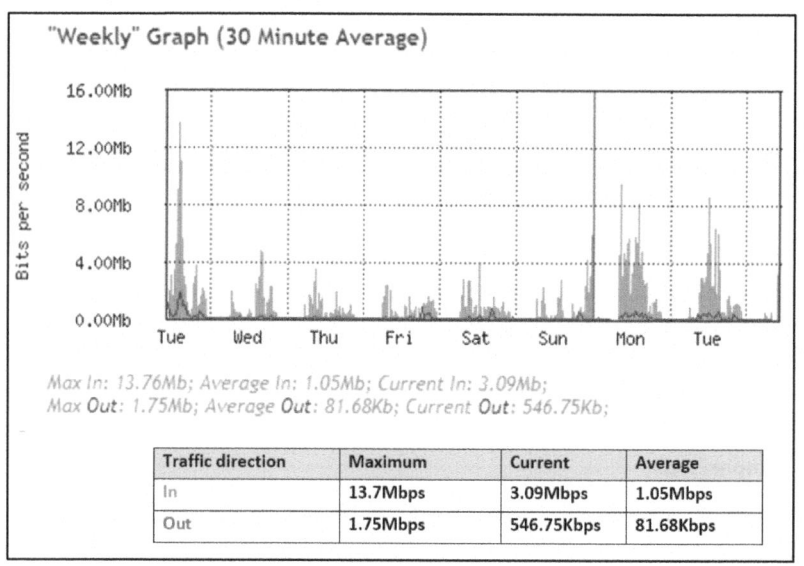

Fig. 4. Weekly Router Traffic Statistics – 10th August 2021

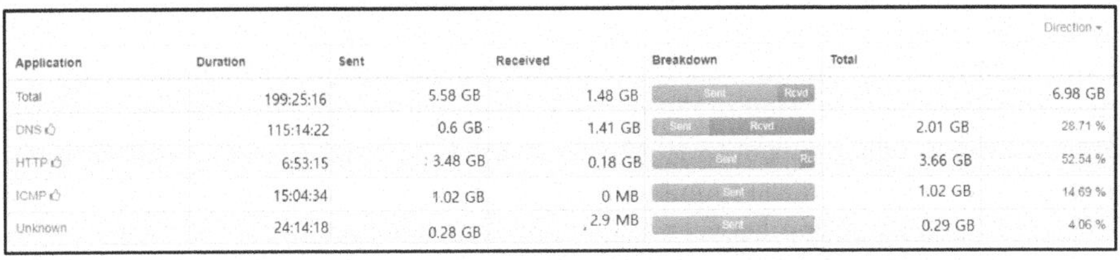

Application	Duration	Sent	Received	Breakdown	Total	Direction
Total	199:25:16	5.58 GB	1.48 GB	Sent Rcvd		6.98 GB
DNS	115:14:22	0.6 GB	1.41 GB	Sent Rcvd	2.01 GB	28.71 %
HTTP	6:53:15	3.48 GB	0.18 GB	Sent Rc	3.66 GB	52.54 %
ICMP	15:04:34	1.02 GB	0 MB	Sent	1.02 GB	14.69 %
Unknown	24:14:18	0.28 GB	2.9 MB	Sent	0.29 GB	4.06 %

Fig. 5. Router interface traffic composition and traffic volume - August 2021

Table 4. Tabular view of router interface traffic composition after proxy caching activation

Application	Web	DNS	ICMP	NetBIOS	Unknown	Total traffic (GB)
Distribution (%)	52.54	28.71	14.69	0.00	4.06	6.98

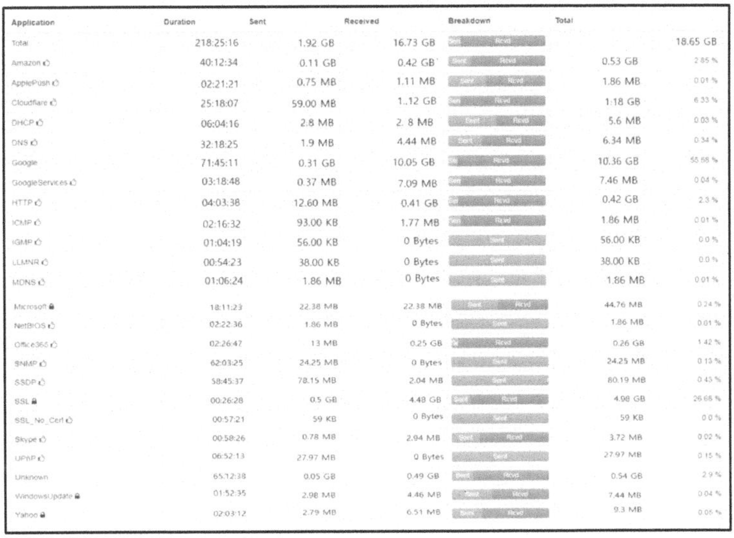

Application	Duration	Sent	Received	Breakdown	Total	
Total	218:25:16	1.92 GB	16.73 GB	Sent Rcvd		18.65 GB
Amazon	40:12:34	0.11 GB	0.42 GB	Sent Rcvd	0.53 GB	2.85 %
ApplePush	02:21:21	0.75 MB	1.11 MB	Sent Rcvd	1.86 MB	0.01 %
Cloudflare	25:18:07	59.00 MB	1..12 GB	Sent Rcvd	1:18 GB	6.33 %
DHCP	06:04:16	2.8 MB	2. 8 MB	Sent Rcvd	5.6 MB	0.03 %
DNS	32:18:25	1.9 MB	4.44 MB	Sent Rcvd	6.34 MB	0.34 %
Google	71:45:11	0.31 GB	10.05 GB	Sent Rcvd	10.36 GB	55.68 %
GoogleServices	03:18:48	0.37 MB	7.09 MB	Sent Rcvd	7.46 MB	0.04 %
HTTP	04:03:38	12.60 MB	0.41 GB	Sent Rcvd	0.42 GB	2.3 %
ICMP	02:16:32	93.00 KB	1.77 MB	Sent Rcvd	1.86 MB	0.01 %
IGMP	01:04:19	56.00 KB	0 Bytes	Sent	56.00 KB	0.0 %
LLMNR	00:54:23	38.00 KB	0 Bytes	Sent	38.00 KB	0.0 %
MDNS	01:06:24	1.86 MB	0 Bytes	Sent	1.86 MB	0.01 %
Microsoft	18:11:23	22.38 MB	22.38 MB	Sent Rcvd	44.76 MB	0.24 %
NetBIOS	02:22:36	1.86 MB	0 Bytes	Sent	1.86 MB	0.01 %
Office365	02:26:47	13 MB	0.25 GB	Sent Rcvd	0.26 GB	1.42 %
SNMP	62:03:25	24.25 MB	0 Bytes	Sent	24.25 MB	0.13 %
SSDP	58:45:37	78.15 MB	2.04 MB	Sent	80.19 MB	0.43 %
SSL	00:26:28	0.5 GB	4.48 GB	Sent Rcvd	4.98 GB	26.68 %
SSL_No_Cert	00:57:21	59 KB	0 Bytes	Sent	59 KB	0.0 %
Skype	00:58:26	0.78 MB	2.94 MB	Sent Rcvd	3.72 MB	0.02 %
UPnP	06:52:13	27.97 MB	0 Bytes	Sent	27.97 MB	0.15 %
Unknown	65:12:38	0.05 GB	0.49 GB	Sent Rcvd	0.54 GB	2.9 %
WindowsUpdate	01:52:35	2.98 MB	4.46 MB	Sent Rcvd	7.44 MB	0.04 %
Yahoo	02:03:12	2.79 MB	6.51 MB	Sent Rcvd	9.3 MB	0.05 %

Fig. 6. LAN traffic composition after proxy caching activation

Table 5. Tabular view of LAN traffic composition after proxy caching activation

Application	Google	SSL	Amazon	Office 365	DNS	Unknown	Total traffic (GB)
Distribution (%)	55.58	26.68	2.85	1.42	0.34	2.9	18.65

after upgrade bandwidth upgrade. Also indicated is the bandwidth utilization after DNS service optimization. The last data set reflects the bandwidth utilization after the activation of proxy caching. Before the upgrade, the local loop bandwidth was 1 Mbps. Subsequently, its enhancement to 10 Mbps occurred. After DNS service optimization, a second upgrade of the local loop bandwidth to 40 Mbps took place. Table 6 gives a glimpse of the relationship between bandwidth utilization and local loop capacity. A visual representation of this information appears in Fig. 7.

Table 6. Bandwidth utilization and local loop capacity

Milestone (Mbps)	Before upgrade	Immediately after upgrade	One month after upgrade	After DNS service optimization	After proxy caching
Bandwidth utilization	1.00	8.13	9.57	7.07	13.76
Local loop capacity	1.00	10	10	10	40

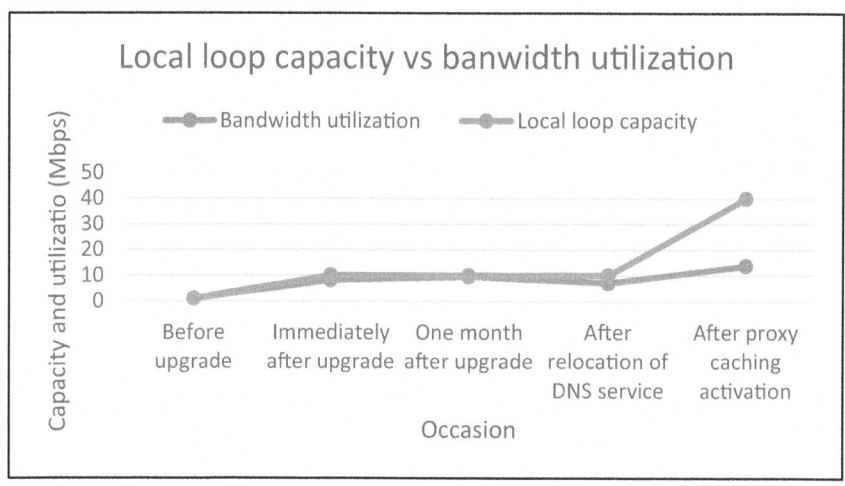

Fig. 7. Bandwidth utilization versus local loop capacity

Before the local loop capacity upgrade, the bandwidth utilization had peaked to the maximum capacity of 1 Mbps. When an upgrade to 10 Mbps occurred, bandwidth utilization increased to 8.13 Mbps. However, one month after the upgrade, bandwidth utilization rose to 9.57 Mbps. The optimization of DNS service helped reduce bandwidth utilization to 7.07 Mbps. As expected, the second bandwidth upgrade to 40 Mbps resulted in the increase of bandwidth utilization to 13.76 Mbps.

Traffic Composition

Table 7 shows the composition of local loop traffic before and after proxy cache configuration. The visual amplification of this information appears in Fig. 8.

Table 7. Router interface traffic composition after and before proxy caching activation

Application	Web	DNS	ICMP	NetBIOS	Unknown
Distribution (%) - After	52.54	28.71	14.59	0.00	4.06
Distribution (%) - Before	95.49	4.11	0.24	0.00	0.16

The deployment of a proxy cache on the gateway router resulted in a drop of the Web traffic from 95.49% to 52.54%. However, the DNS traffic component increased from 4.11% to 28.71%. Similarly, the unknown traffic flow proportion increased from 0.16% to 4.06%.

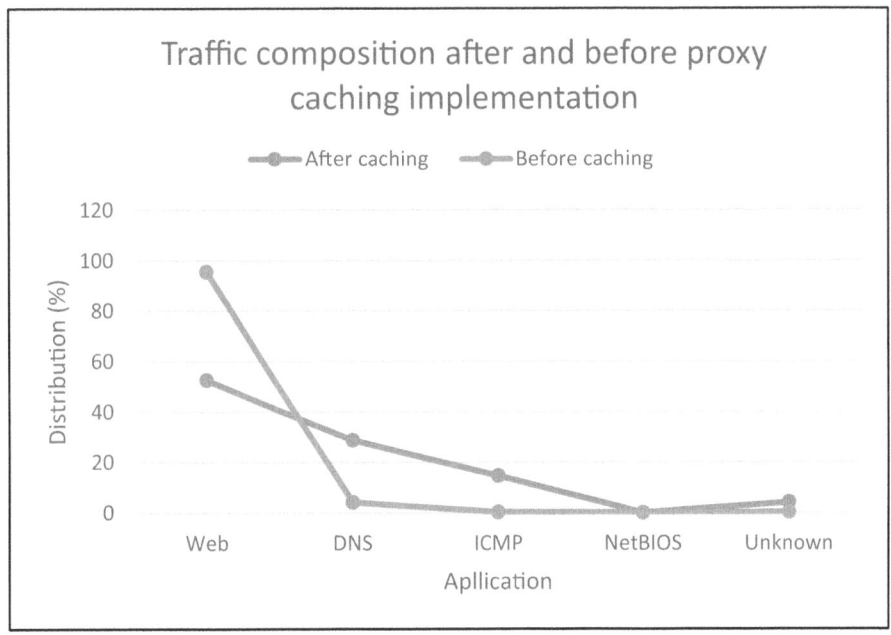

Fig. 8. Router interface traffic composition before and after proxy cache activation

The implementation of proxy caching led to an increase in the ICMP traffic portion from 0.24% to 14.59%. Only outgoing ICMP and Unknown packets from the LAN were noticeable with no evidence of incoming ICMP and Unknown packets as reflected in Fig. 6.

Traffic Volume

Table 8 shows the total local loop traffic volume as well as the LAN traffic volume before, immediately and one month after the bandwidth upgrade. Data collected after DNS service optimization and activation of proxy caching are also given.

Table 8. Local loop traffic volume and LAN traffic volume

Milestone	Before upgrade	Immediately after upgrade	One month after upgrade	After relocation of DNS service	After proxy caching
Local loop (GB)	1.17	5.86	6.69	6.91	6.98
LAN (GB)	20.18	24.56	25.97	19.43	18.65

The initial local loop and LAN total traffic were 1.17 GB and 20.18GB respectively. Both local loop and LAN traffic increased when bandwidth upgraded to 10 Mbps occurred. While the local loop traffic continued to rise one month after the bandwidth upgrade, DNS service optimization and proxy cache activation, the LAN traffic began to decline as shown in Fig. 9.

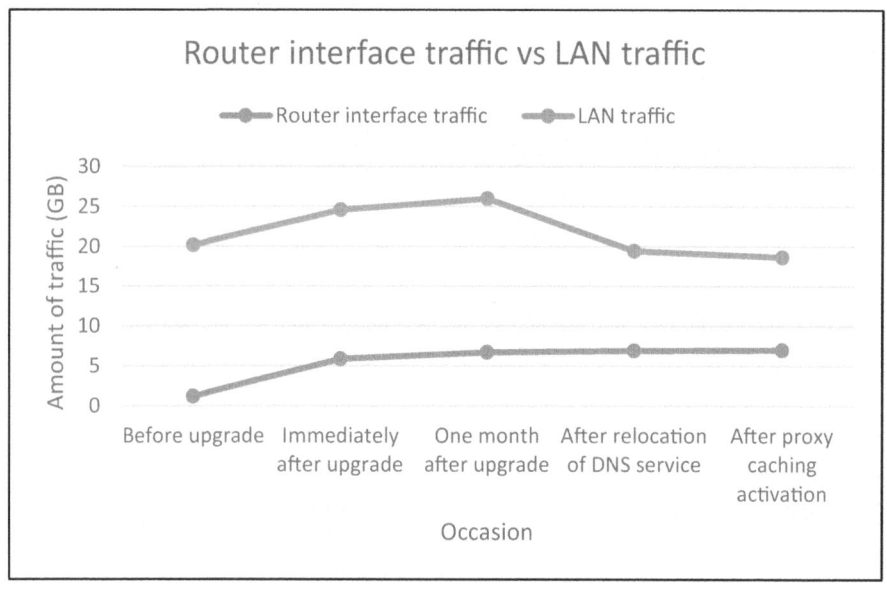

Fig. 9. Local loop traffic volume and LAN traffic volume comparison chart

The trend for the local loop traffic and LAN traffic are identical before bandwidth upgrade, immediately after upgrade and one month after the upgrade. The optimization of DNS service and activation of proxy caching resulted in a downward trend for the LAN traffic volume.

5   Discussion

Proxy caching activation on the gateway router resulted the bandwidth utilization increased from 7.07 Mbps to 13.76 Mbps represents a 94.6% surge. Prior to the implementation of proxy caching, the local loop capacity had been enhanced from 10 Mbps to 40 Mbps a 300% rise. The initial bandwidth upgrade from 1 Mbps to 10 Mbps which is a 900% escalation resulted in an increase of bandwidth utilization from 1 Mbps to 9.57 Mbps depicting a growth of 860%. Therefore, the activation of proxy caching resulted in a lower increase in bandwidth utilization. If the local loop capacity enhancement undergoes normalization to 100% through division by nine, the increase in bandwidth utilization before proxy caching activation would be 860% divide by nine resulting in 95.56%. Similarly, normalizing the second local loop upgrade to 100% through division by three gives the increase after the implementation of proxy caching to 94.6% divide by three resulting in 31.53%. This implies that the activation of proxy caching reduced the rate of increase in bandwidth utilization from 95.56% to 31.53% representing a 64.03% drop.

Before the activation of proxy caching, the Web component of the local loop traffic was 95.49%. This reduced to 52.54% after proxy caching configuration on the gateway router representing a 42.95% decrease. The main reason for implementing Web caching was to reduce the high proportion of the local loop Web traffic component. Therefore, the realization of this objective is evident.

During the initial bandwidth capacity enhancement from 1 Mbps to 10 Mbps representing an increase of 900%, the total router interface traffic grew from 1.17 GB to 5.86 GB which is a 400% rise. The subsequent bandwidth upgrade from 10 Mbps to 40 Mbps a 300% escalation led to an increase of the local loop traffic volume from 6.91 GB to 6.98 GB representing 1.01% rise. Normalizing the bandwidth capacity upgrade to 100%, the percentage increase in local loop traffic volume would be 400% divide by nine giving 44.44%. Using a similar reasoning, normalizing the subsequent local loop upgrade to 100% results in the increase in local loop traffic volume being 1.01% divided by three. This gives 0.34%. Therefore, implementing Web caching resting a drop of the local loop traffic volume from 44.44% to 0.34% representing a 44.1% reduction.

Despite the LAN traffic volume not being a major area of concern because of Ethernet capacity of 1Gbps, it is evident that the implementation of proxy caching leads to a decrease in the LAN traffic volume from 19.43 GB to 18.65 GB. This is a 4.01% reduction and occurs even though the local loop bandwidth underwent a 300% hike from 10 Mbps to 40 Mbps and therefore an increase in LAN traffic was expected.

6   Future Work

To gain better understanding of the full impact of proxy caching, it would be useful to reconfigure proxy caching on the LTSP server. This would provide data that can help establish the optimal configuration of the proxy caching within the community network environment. In addition, the implementation of reverse caching strategies in a simulated infrastructure would further assist in the investigation and quantification of the benefits of Web caching with respect to both bandwidth conservation, reduction of Web traffic and lowering of traffic volume.

7 Conclusion

Web caching is a recommended strategy for reducing bandwidth utilization and both local loop Web traffic component and traffic volume. In low capacity network environments, the main service provision constraint is the local loop. Therefore conserving local loop resource is a pleasant intervention.

References

1. Chandrakar, R., Varshney, S.: A comprehensive survey on importance of web caching and pre-fetching. Int. J. Sci. Res. **5**(6), 1009–1016 (2016)
2. Selcuk, K., Li, W.S., Luoand, Q., Hsiung, W.P., Agrawal, D.: Enabling dynamic content caching for database-driven web sites. ACM SIGMOD **30**(2), 532–543 (2001)
3. Podlipnig, S., Böszörmenyi, L.: A survey of Web cache replacement strategies. ACM Comput. Surv. **35**(4), 374–398 (2003)
4. Okuthe, J., Terzoli, A.: Assessing the impact of DNS configuration on low bandwidth networks. In: Saeed, R.A., Bakari, A.D., Sheikh, Y.H. (eds.) 14th EAI International Conference, AFRICOMM 2022, pp. 76–86. Springer, Cham (2023)
5. Al-Dailami, A., Ruan, C., Bao, Z., Zhang, T.: QoS3: secure caching in HTTPS based on fine-grained trust delegation. Secur. Commun. Netw. **7**, 1–16 (2019)
6. Cao, P., Irani, S.: Cost-aware WWW proxy caching algorithms. In: USENIX Symposium on Internet Technologies and Systems (1997)
7. Mockapetris, P., Dunlap, K.J.: Development of the domain name system. In: SIGCOMM 1988: Symposium proceedings on Communications architectures and protocols, August 1988, pp. 123–133 (1988)
8. Cao, P., Zhang, J., Beach, K.: Active cache: caching dynamic contents on the web. In: Proceedings of IFIP International Conference on Distributed Systems Platforms and Open Distributed Processing (1998)
9. Mahdavi, M., Shepherd, J., Benatallah, B.: A collaborative approach for caching dynamic data in portal applications. In: Proceedings of the 15th Australasian Database Conference, vol. 27, pp. 181–188 (2004)
10. Davison, B.D., Wu, B.: Implementing a web proxy evaluation architecture. In: Proceedings of the 30th International Conference for the Resource Management and Performance Evaluation of Enterprise Computing Systems (CMG), Las Vegas, NV (2004)
11. Lam, H.K., Truong, N.X.: Performance analysis of hybrid web caching architecture. Am. J. Netw. Commun. **4**(3), 37–43 (2015)
12. Ramu, K., Sugumar, R.: Design and implementation of server side web proxy caching algorithm. Int. J. Adv. Res. Comput. Commun. Eng. **11**(2), 1–14 (2012)
13. Gupta, M., Garg, A.: Content delivery network approach to improve web performance: a review. Int. J. Adv. Res. Comput. Sci. Manag. Stud. **2**(12), 374–385 (2014)
14. Al-Ward, H., Tan, C.K., Lim, W.H.: Caching transient data in information-centric internet-of-things (IC-IoT) networks: a survey. J. Network Comput. Appl. **206**, 103491 (2015)

15. Hamid, A., Din, I.U., Fasee, U., Muhammad, T., Murad, K., Mohsen, G.: ELC: edge linked caching for content updating in information-centric internet of things. Comput. Commun. **156**, 174–182 (2020)

16. Serhane, O., Yahyaoui, K., Nour, B., Hussain, R., Kazmi, S.M.A., Moungla, H.: PbCP: a profit-based cache placement scheme for next-generation IoT-based ICN networks. Comput. Commun. **194**, 311–320 (2022)

17. Nour, B., et al.: A survey of internet of things communication using ICN: a use case perspective. Comput. Commun. **142**, 95–123 (2019)

18. Rezaeifar, Z., Wang, J., Oh, H., Lee, S.B., Hur, J.: A reliable adaptive forwarding approach in named data networking. Future Gener. Comput. Syst. **96**, 538–551 (2019)

19. Wu, H., Fan, Y., Wang, Y., Ma, H., Xing, L.: A comprehensive review on edge caching from the perspective of total process: placement. Policy Deliv. Sens. **21**(15), 5033 (2021)

20. Leguay, J., Paschos, G.S., Quaglia, E.A., Smyth, B.: CryptoCache: network caching with confidentiality. In: 2017 IEEE International Conference on Communications (ICC), Paris, France, pp. 1–6 (2017)

21. Emura, K., Moriai, S., Nakajima, T., Yoshimi, M.: Cache-22: a highly deployable encrypted cache system. In: 2020 IEEE International Symposium on Information Theory and Its Applications (ISITA), pp.465–469 (2020)

22. Sulaiman, S., Shamsuddin, S.M., Abraham, A., Sulaiman, S.: Web caching and prefetching: what, why, and how? IEEE Xplore (2008)

23. Krishnamurthy, B., Jennifer, R.: Web Protocols and Practice, 1st edn, pp. 407–441. Addison Wesley, Upper Saddle River (2003)

24. Wang, J.: A survey of web caching schemes for the internet. ACM Comput. Commun. Rev. **25**(9), 36–46 (1999)

25. Zeng, D., Wang, F., Liu, M.: Efficient web content delivery using proxy caching techniques. IEEE Trans. Syst. Manag. Cybern. **34**(3), 270–280 (2004)

26. Okuthe, J.A., Terzoli, A.: Quantifying the shift in network usage upon bandwidth upgrade. In: E-Infrastructure and E-Services for Developing Countries, pp. 340–354. Springer, Cham (2022)

27. Becchi, M., Franklin, M., Crowley, P.: A workload for evaluating deep packet inspection architectures. In: IEEE International Symposium on Workload Characterization, pp. 79–80. Seattle, Washington, USA (2008)

Channel Allocation Based K-Medoids in a Wireless Mesh Network

Thomas Djotio Ndie[1(✉)], Paulin Melatagia Yonta[2], Ismaël Samaye[2], and Karl Jonas[3]

[1] National Advanced School of Engineering of Yaounde, Yaounde, Cameroon
tdjotio@gmail.com
[2] University of Yaounde 1, Yaounde, Cameroon
paulinyonta@gmail.com, samayeismael@gmail.com
[3] Bonn Rhein Sieg Univerty, Sankt Augustin, Germany
karl.jonas@h-brs.de

Abstract. Wireless mesh networks (WMNs) are considered one of the most promising approaches to power networks using non-physical connection media that require high bandwidth and coverage. Because of its qualities in terms of bandwidth and coverage, they face quality of service problems such as throughput due in some cases to poor channel allocation. The channel allocation issue in a WMN is similar to a graph edge coloring problem which is an NP-complete problem. In order to solve this problem, various approaches have been proposed, some based on graph theory, some on conflict graph theory, and others using message exchange for synchronization on communication channel between nodes. In this paper, we present K-MEDAL, an approach to channel allocation in WMNs based on K-medoids algorithm. For our simulation, we used a testbed composed of 33 static nodes randomly arranged over an area of $1000Km^2$ in the NS-2 simulator. The K-medoids algorithm allowed us to build small network clusters to reduce the complexity of the channel allocation problem. Compared to other solutions found in the literature, the K-MEDAL approach shows out a 2 to 3 times increase in both the throughput distributed over the active links of a cluster and the aggregate throughput per cluster.

Keywords: Wireless mesh network · K-medoids · channel allocation · network cluster

1 Introduction

Recent advances in wireless technology have led to the emergence of a new class of network called Wireless mesh networks (WMNs). These networks aim to solve problems such as coverage area and quality of service in terms of bandwidth encountered by single access point networks. A WMN is similar to an ad-hoc

© ICST Institute for Computer Sciences, Social Informatics and Telecommunications Engineering 2025
Published by Springer Nature Switzerland AG 2025. All Rights Reserved
A. Sere et al. (Eds.): AFRICOMM 2023, LNICST 587, pp. 194–207, 2025.
https://doi.org/10.1007/978-3-031-81570-6_13

network with the difference that the mobility of some network elements is limited or almost nil. It consists mainly of three types of nodes: mesh gateways (MG), mesh routers (MR) and mesh clients (MC). The function of MG is to allow interconnection of the mesh network with other networks. the MRs constitute the backbone of the network by allowing communications between different network clients. A MC is any terminal equipment that can connect to a MR in order to communicate with other clients. It should be noted that in a WMN, communications (requests and responses) are made by multi-hop through MR to MG. Figure (1) shows an architecture of a WMN.

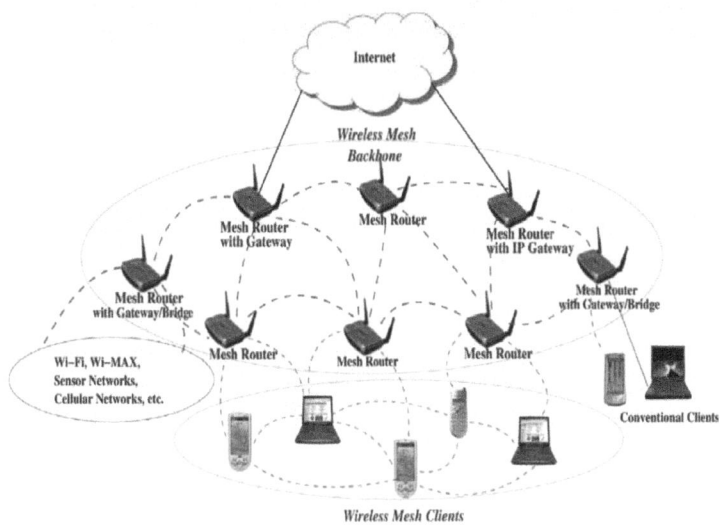

Fig. 1. Network architecture [1]

In a WMN, MRs are connected to each other by radio waves (channels) that are assigned to each router interface according to the number of interfaces. From this channels allocation between MR interfaces, can raise up interference problems which are disturbances (noise) that appear when a MR communicates with another. Interference can be internal when a MR interface interfere with each other or, external when it is produced by other neighboring MR. Since the number of channels used for communication is limited for a frequency, the challenge here will be to find a strategy that allows for interference minimization. Various approaches to solve the interference issue have been proposed in the literature. Some of them are based on graph theory using the solution of the graph edge coloring problem [4] or, conflict graphs [3]. Others are based on messages synchronization technique on the communication channel [5]. Unfortunately, these different solutions are not adapted to large networks with a large number of nodes and, are also not tolerant for certain network constraints, in particular the scalability control of a mesh network. Thus, the question that emerges is to find an approach that allows an efficient channel allocation that minimizes interference and adapts to the network's evolution.

In our paper,we propose K-MEDAL, a solution to the problem of channel allocation in a mesh network, based on k-medoids, an artificial learning method. It has the particularity of taking into account large networks made up of a large number of nodes. Indeed, these methods offer good properties to allow decision making based on static or evolving data. Artificial learning techniques are classified into three main categories which are: supervised learning in which the data passed to the learner is labeled; unsupervised learning in which the learner places the labels on the data himself and; reinforcement learning in which the learner observes his environment, makes decisions based on a maximum cumulative value. Specifically, we have used the K-medoids algorithm, an unsupervised learning technique, to contribute to channel allocation issue in a WMN. Our approach avoids considering the network as a whole. Instead, it focuses on the formation of sub-networks by constructing small network clusters and then applying channel allocation policies based on the interference between nodes in a cluster. To the best of our knowledge, this approach presents better results in terms of throughput, compared to the solution of [6] which uses the clustering principle according to the node's degree.

The rest of the paper is organized as follows: Section 2 presents related works on channel allocation in a WMN. Section 3 presents K-MEDAL, our K-medoids based approach. Section 4 presents the implementation and evaluation of our model. We conclude and propose future work in Sect. 5.

2   Related Worrk

Manos Delakis et al. [3] proposed a model for channel allocation in an experimental network deployed in the city of Heraklio. They used a model based on multipoint link conflict graphs to model internal interference. A multipoint link conflict graph (MPLCG) is a graph in which a vertex represents a set of interfaces that communicate with each other. From the MPLCG we can have a model that represents the internal interference in each node. This approach has the advantage of allowing internal interference modeling. However, the solution has some limitations in that it only works with directional antennas and, more importantly, the construction of the conflict graph is difficult when the number of nodes increases. Stefan Pollak et al. [4] in their work implemented a centralized two-phase algorithm for channel allocation in a WMN. First, a random channel allocation is made to nodes taking into account their expected loads and the interference effect of other links. Then, the algorithm tries to resolve the interference in the network using steps similar to the first. The difference here is that the channel assignment and routing paths are based on the results of the first phase. Note that the second phase only stops when a change is no longer needed. The advantage of this approach is that it allows channel allocation to take into account loads on links. in contrast, requires a large number of channels and a limited number of nodes. In their work Stefan Bouckaert et al. [5] present a simple but efficient channel selection scheme for dynamic mesh networks, based on the exchange of control messages. This scheme is able to perform channel configuration almost instantaneously, in a fully distributed manner and with minimal overhead. The Frequency Selection based on Message Exchange (FRESME) protocol is implemented with the IEEE 802.11b/g protocol for channel allocation. It is capable of rapid distributed channel selection in multi-channel and multi-interface mesh networks. The FRESME protocol is limited by the fact that the approach requires node synchronization, which incurs significant overhead on the network, and scaling is very complicated for networks with large nodes.

Sadeq Ali Makram et al. [6] worked on an allocation model in a mesh network based on the clustering approach by building small clusters of subnets. In their approach, instead of considering the network as a whole, they preferred to divide it into smaller clusters and manage the channel assignment locally in each cluster. The goal of clustering is to minimize the complexity of channel assignment into smaller, more manageable local problems. For cluster formation, they use the number of neighbors directly connected to a node and, depending on this value, the node will be elected the cluster head of nodes that are connected to it. This approach also allows reusing channels between clusters in order to minimize interference. It should be noted that the solution has some shortcomings: (1) the approach causes a lot of internal interference because only one channel is assigned to all nodes in a cluster; (2) the method used for cluster formation is not optimal because it can have multiple clusters, which can be difficult to manage.

After presenting these related works on channel allocation, we compare them according to the criteria that a good channel allocation algorithm proposed in [3] should fulfill.Indeed, the authors of [3] argue that a channel allocation algorithm must guarantee: (1) interference control and, (2) network scaling. Looking at Table 1, we can see that the solutions we just outlined do not meet these criteria both on interference control and network scalability. The table is filled with the following two values:

No: indicates that the proposed solution does not meet the criteria.
Yes: indicates that it does.

Table 1. Comparative table of different approaches

TECHNIQUES	INTERFERENCES		Connectivity	Diversity of channels	Load balancing	distributions	Extensibility	stability
	Intra-flow	Inter-flow						
MPLCG [4]	Yes	Yes	Yes	Yes	No	Centralized	No	No
FRCA [5]	No	No	No	No	No	Centralized	No	Yes
FRESME [6]	Yes	No	No	No	No	Centralized	No	No
CCA [7]	No	Yes	Yes	No	Yes	Locally	No	No

In this section, we have presented works dealing with the solution of the channel allocation problem in a mesh network. We highlighted the advantages that each of them proposes in a specific context for WMNs. We have also noticed some criteria that are not fulfilled by these approaches in terms of channel management, node management or network scalability. The main common limitation of these different approaches is the number of nodes used for their implementations, which do not support scaling.

3   Channel Allocation by K-Medoids

In this section, we propose K-MEDAL which consists of two main steps: the first one consists of forming clusters and, the second consists of making an allocation of channels to different network.

3.1   Constraints on Nodes

Our model must satisfy a number of conditions. We assume that wireless mesh routers have the following characteristics:

- Each mesh router has at least 3 interfaces.
- All mesh routers are fixed.
- The mesh routers are randomly distributed in the target area.
- Each mesh router has a fixed position along the x-axis and y-axis.
- Each mesh router can communicate with other nodes in the network.

3.2   Network Model

We used a graph to model the network. The WMN is a graph defined by $G = (V, C, E)$ with :

- $V = \{V_1, V_2, \ldots, V_n\}$ being the set of nodes;
- $C = \{C_1, C_2, \ldots, C_n\}$ being the set of available channels;
- $E = \{(v_i, u_j, c_r)|v_i, u_j \in V \wedge c_r \in c\}$ being the set of wireless links between nodes v_i and its neighbors u_j on channel c_r. [6].

3.3   Step 1 :Cluster Model

The allocation of channels requires a definition of a set of sub-networks from the formation of clusters such that $G = \{G_1, G_2, ..., G_K\}$ with :
$G_i = \{V_1, V_2, \ldots, V_n\}$ and **n** the number of nodes in the cluster G_i and **K** is the number of cluster. We apply the K-medoids algorithm to form the clusters. A node will be assigned to a cluster according to its position relative to the cluster head that is closest to it. Cluster heads are first randomly selected and then calculated. Clusters are formed with respect to the interference range of the centroids in each cluster. A node will belong to a cluster if that node is within the interference range of centroid. We specify that a wireless mesh router is characterized by two metrics which are: the transmission range and the interference range. The transmission range is the maximum distance a node can transmit,

while the interference range is the distance at which any node within that radius
can disrupt the source node's communication.

We used the following phases for clusters formation. The K-medoids algorithm
forms clusters based on the Euclidean distance between them and nodes of the
interference range of the centroids of each cluster. The process consists of the
following phases:

- **Phase 1: Initial grouping**

  In this phase of the algorithm, we define the number of clusters, We then
  perform a random selection of the centroids of clusters and subsequently
  each node is assigned to a cluster according to its distance from the nearest
  centroid.

- **Phase 2: Re-clustering and recalculation of centroids**

  Following the initialization phase of the centroids, we compute the centroids of
  each cluster. If a cluster **k** has **n** nodes then the centroid μ_k will be calculated
  as follows: the coordinate pair: (1) allows us to calculate the average of the
  coordinates of nodes in the cluster to find the new centroid and then the Eq.
  (2) allows a reallocation of nodes in clusters according to the new calculated
  centroids.

$$\mu_k = \left(\frac{1}{n} \sum_{i=1}^{n} V_i x \ , \ \frac{1}{n} \sum_{i=1}^{n} V_i y \right) \tag{1}$$

$$V_i \in G_k \ , \ if \ \forall j \ |V_i - \mu_k| = min_j |V_i - \mu_j| \ and \ V_i \in PI_{\mu_k} \tag{2}$$

PI_{μ_k}: : is the interference range of the centroid μ_k

- **Phase 3: Choice of the centroid**

  After cluster formation, the node with the coordinates calculated in phase
  2 is selected. If no node has these required coordinates then a node with
  coordinates closest to those of the calculated centroid is searched for.

The pseudo-code of our clustering algorithm is given below. Note in this pseudo-
code that the exit condition of the loop is that the computed centroids are the
same for two consecutive iterations.

3.4   Step 2: Channel Allocation in and Between Clusters

After dividing the network into subnets, we proceed to the channel allocation
phase for different nodes within and between clusters. The channel allocation
comprises three phases. The phase 1 is the definition of channels for inter-cluster
connections. The phase 2 is the division of the remaining channels by the number
of defined clusters. In phase 3, the channel allocation is done within and between
clusters.

Algorithm 1: *Algorithm $K - MED - WMN$*

Input: Let K be the number of clusters
Let $G = (V, E)$ be the WMN
Output: $G = \{G_1, G_2, ..., G_K\}$the set of clusters
begin
    1.Initial formation of G_k by initialization of centroids
    while *the centroids of step $n + 1$ are not the same as those of step n* **do**
        2.calculation of centroids and reformation of clusters.
        3.centroids calculation and cluster reformation.
        4.Choice of centroids .
    end
end

- **Phase 1: Selection of channels for inter-cluster connections**
  In this phase we define the number of channels that will be used for inter-cluster connections. We take all available channels **C** minus the channels that will be used for inter-cluster connections.

- **Phase 2: Distribution of channels in clusters**
  Having defined the number of channels that will be used for inter-cluster connections, we now need to allocate the remaining channels according to the number of clusters for intra-cluster connections. Equation (3) allows us to define the number of channels that will be used for inter-cluster connections. Assuming that the frequency band has some **C**, channels, and that we have defined the number of channels for inter-cluster connections $C_{inter\_cluster}$ we divide the remainder of the subtraction $C - C_{inter\_cluster}$ by the number of clusters to get the number of channels in each cluster.

$$C_G = \frac{C - C_{inter\_cluster}}{K} \tag{3}$$

C_G :Number of channels for each cluster.
C: Number of possible channels
$C_{inter\_cluster}$:Number of channels defined for inter-cluster
K : The number of clusters.

- **Phase 3: Channel allocation within and between clusters**
  As we already have the number of channels allocated to each cluster and the number of channels for inter-cluster connections, we proceed with the allocation. In this allocation we ensure that a node has a different channel on each interface.

The pseudo code of our channel allocation algorithm is given below. The algorithm assigns channels to nodes according to the clusters that were formed by the K-MED-WMN algorithm.

Algorithm 2: *Algorithm $K - MEDAL$*

Input: Let $G = \{G_1, G_2, ..., G_K\}$ be the set of clusters formed
Let $C = \{C_1, C_2, ..., C_n\}$ be the set of available channels
Output: Mesh network with efficient channel allocation

1 **begin**
2   **for** *each Cluster G_i* **do**
3   **while** $G_i \neq \emptyset$ **do**
4   **for** *each $l_i \in E$ from G_i* **do**
5             $l_i = c_i \in C_{G_i}$
6   **if** V_i *is a border node such that V_i et V_j are linked by l_{ij}*
            then
7                $l_{ij} = c_j \in C_{inter\_cluster}$
8   **end**
9   **end**
10   **end**
11   **end**
12 **end**

The operating principle of the k-MEDAL algorithm is as follows:

– At the level of line 5, each link of a cluster will be assigned one of the possible channels for its cluster.
– On line 6, if node V_i is a border node, i.e. it is between two clusters and is connected to the neighbouring cluster by node V_j via the link l_{ij} . Then the link V_j through link l_{ij}. Then the link l_{ij} will be assigned a channel defined as inter-cluster channel.

Figure (2) below shows an example of allocation model between two clusters (cluster 1 and cluster 2) for which two channels have been defined for inter-cluster connections and the rest of the channels are used for intra-cluster connections.

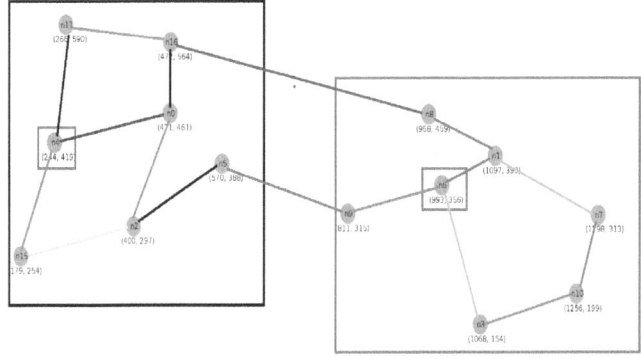

Fig. 2. Assigning channels to clusters in an WMN

In this section we described our k-MEDAL model for channel allocation, which supports networks composed of large numbers of nodes. It also aims at reducing interference in the network while ensuring good cluster formation. In the next section, we simulate and evaluate k-MEDAL.

4   Simulation and Results

We conducted our simulation in NS-2 with 33 static nodes randomly placed in a 1000 Km^2. The physical layers are configured to simulate the IEEE 802.11a standard, the simulation has a duration of 300 s. A Constant Bit Rate (CBR) traffic is attached to a connection with some important parameters such as the packet size and the time interval between two packets. The transmission rate of an exchange is 2.4 Mbps. The choice of the number of clusters was made by trial and error, to our humble knowledge there is no formal method to define this number. To do this we started with two, then three, then four clusters. We noticed that each time the number of clusters increased, the values of metrics were also better. Capturing with the NAM tool allows us to have on Fig. (3), an illustration of the k-MED-WMN algorithm presented in Sect. 3. On this Fig. (3) we have the formation of the following 04 clusters: cluster 1 of green color, cluster 2 of red color, cluster of yellow color and cluster 4 of black color.

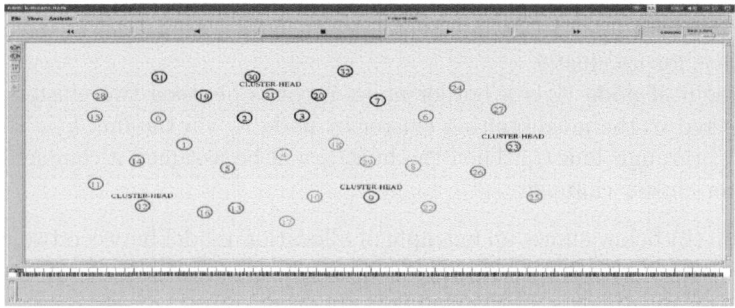

Fig. 3. Capture of the k-MED-WMN simulation (Color figure online)

We compared the experimental results of the K-MEDAL approach with those of the CCA approach [6]. Just to recall, CCA [6] also uses cluster construction to assign channels to nodes in a mesh network. The simulation scenario is based on the following two traffic models: (1) a single-hop traffic model and (2) a multi-hop traffic model.

4.1 Probability of Packet Loss

The probability of packet loss in our case here is defined by Eq.(4) [6] :

$$P = 1 - \left(\frac{r\left(l_{v,u}^{a}, t\right)}{s\left(l_{v,u}^{a}, t\right)} \right) \tag{4}$$

On this equation(4) the loss probability is computed as follows: is computed $r\left(l_{v,u}^{a}, t\right)$ by a node (**u** or **v**) on the channel; **a** as a function of time over the number of packets sent $s\left(l_{v,u}^{a}, t\right)$ by a node (**u** or **v**); on the channel **a** as a function of time in each cluster. We can observe on Fig. (4) that the packet loss probability is similar in both approaches in cluster 1 and slightly higher in clusters 2 and 3 for K-MEDAL, this means that the K-MEDAL algorithm has a weakness on this point.

4.2 Distributed Throughput on Active Links in a Cluster

Distributed throughput on the active links in a cluster is the overall throughput that can be achieved on a connection between nodes when they are exchanged. The aim is to make a comparison on the distribution of the throughput on links of each cluster. To do this we proceeded as in the comparison of the packet loss probability, taking links in each cluster with the best results and comparing them with those of links of the K-MEDAL approach. It can be seen from Fig. 5 that the K-MEDAL approach shows much better results compared to the On-demand CCA approach.

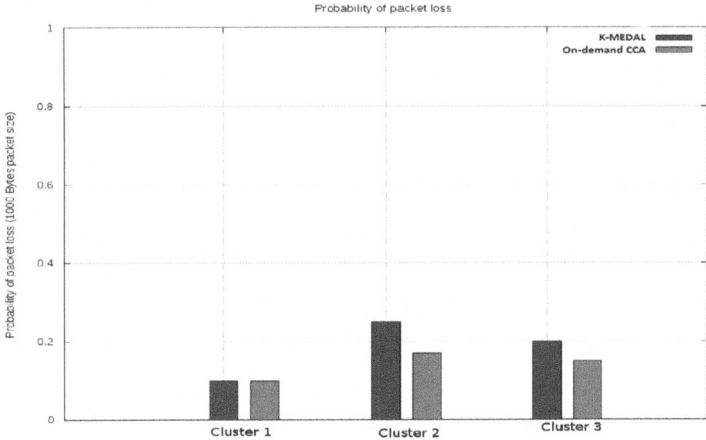

Fig. 4. Probability of packet loss

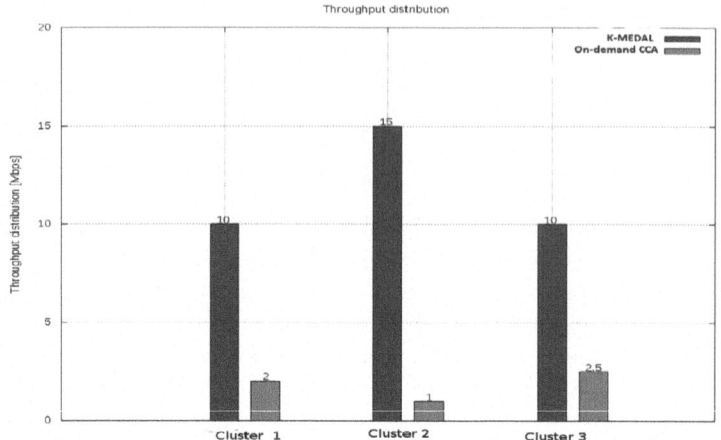

Fig. 5. Distributed throughput on active links in a cluster

4.3   Aggregate Throughput per Cluster

The aggregate throughput per cluster is the overall throughput that can be achieved in all clusters. The evaluation of the aggregate throughput of each cluster shows that the K-MEDAL approach has an aggregate throughput 2 to 3 times higher than the On-demand CCA approach. Figure 6 on a possible case simulated on the aggregate throughput confirms the advantage of the K-MEDAL approach compared to On-demand CCA.

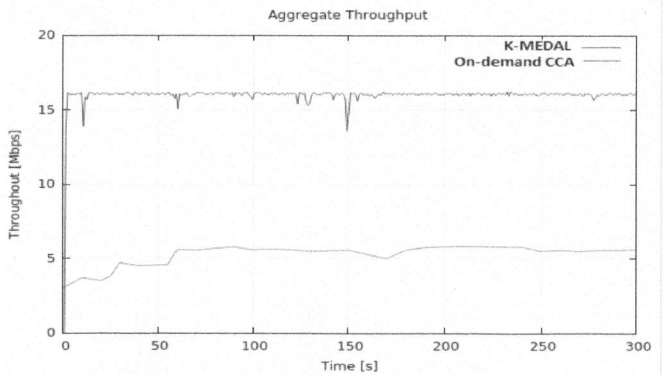

Fig. 6. Aggregate throughput per cluster

5   Discussion

After having implemented and tested our solution, we compare it according to the criteria mentioned in [3], to other existing approaches discussed in the Sect. 2. An overview is shown in Table 2. We see that the K-MEDAL approach fulfils several criteria of a good channel allocation algorithm compared to others.

Table 2. Comparison of the different existing approaches and the k-Medoids-al approach

TECHNIQUES	INTERFERENCES		Connectivity	Diversity of channels	Load balancing	distributions	Extensibility	stability
	Intra-flow	Inter-flow						
MPLCG [4]	Yes	Yes	Yes	Yes	No	Centralized	No	No
FRCA [5]	No	No	No	No	No	Centralized	No	Yes
FRESME [6]	Yes	No	No	No	No	Centralized	No	No
CCA [7]	No	Yes	Yes	No	Yes	Locally	No	No
K-MEDAL	Yes	Yes	Yes	Yes	No	Hybrid	Yes	Yes

In WMNs, VoIP is one of the main applications for voice communication. In order to provide a good quality of service (QoS), the mesh network must have a good throughput distributed over the links and an aggregated throughput for the available bandwidth. This necessarily requires a good channel allocation. In our work, we have proposed a channel allocation model using the K-medoids method called K-MEDAL. From the implementation and evaluation, we found that the K-MEDAL approach improves metrics such as: distributed throughput over the active links in a cluster and, aggregate throughput per cluster. This is an important result for wireless communications, if we consider the application in a wireless community network. Despite some cases of packet loss observed in K-MEDAL, we believe that compared to others, our proposed model can provide good voice communication in a WMN.

6   Conclusion

The problem of channel allocation in WMNs has been receiving a lot of attention due to the need to satisfy a good quality of service. In this paper we have presented, implemented and evaluated K-MEDAL, an approach that allows channel allocation in a WMN, using the K-medoids algorithm for the division of the network into sub-networks or clusters. We have shown that this approach allows cluster formation by taking into account the position of nodes and their neighbors at the same time. Our experimental results showed that this method of channel allocation compared to other methods significantly reduces internal and external interference and improves the saturation and overall throughput in the network.

However, it should be noted that our approach has some limitations: (1) several continuous cluster formations are needed to have a good network configuration; (2) the number of clusters is done by trial and error; (3) the channel load balancing constraint according to the traffic in the network is not taken into account. Therefore, our future work will propose a model based on artificial learning algorithms to find the best possible cluster configuration for a candidate network. In particular, we will focus on the study of different clusters formations produced by K-MEDAL and will take into account the load balancing according to the traffic observed in the network.

Acknowledgements. This work was supported by UMMISCO, WiCoNet and the University of Yaounde I.

Author's Contributions. Ismael SAMAYE conceived, designed and directed this research.Thomas DJOTIO NDIE and Paulin MELATAGIA YONTA have investigated, implemented and wrote the paper. All authors reviewed and approved the final manuscript.

Funding. This work has no funding.

Availability of Data and Materials. No data or models were generated during the study. However, a code wrote in C and OTCL languages was used to implement the simulation.

References

1. Akyildiz, I.F., et al. Wireless mesh networks: a survey. Comput. Netw. **47**, 445–487 (2005)
2. Ishmael, J., Bury, S., Pezaros, D., Race, N.: Deploying rural community wireless mesh networks. IEEE Internet Comput. **12**(4), 22–29 (2008). https://doi.org/10.1109/MIC.2008.76
3. Al Islam, A.A., Islam, M.J., Nurain, N., Raghunathan, V.: Channel assignment techniques for multi-radio wireless mesh networks: a survey. IEEE Commun. Surv. Tutorials **18**, 988–1017 (2015)
4. Delakis, M., Siris, V.A.: Channel assignment in a metropolitan wireless multi-radio mesh network. In: 2008 5th International Conference on Broadband Communications, Networks and Systems, pp. 610–617. IEEE (2008)
5. Pollak, S., Wieser, V., Tkac, A.: A channel assignment algorithm for wireless mesh networks with interference minimization. In: 2012 5th Joint IFIP Wireless and Mobile Networking Conference (WMNC), pp. 17–21. IEEE (2012)
6. Bouckaert, S., Letor, N., Blondia, C., Moerman, I., Demeester, P.: Distributed on demand channel selection in multi channel, multi interface wireless mesh networks. In: IEEE GLOBECOM 2007-IEEE Global Telecommunications Conference, pp. 5086–5091. IEEE (2007)
7. Makram, S.A., Gunes, M., Kchiche, A., Krebs, M.: Dynamic channel assignment for wireless mesh networks using clustering. In: Seventh International Conference on Networking (ICN 2008), pp. 539–544. IEEE (2008)

8. Tragos, E.Z., Fragkiadakis, A., Askoxylakis, I., Siris, V.A.: The impact of interference on the performance of a multi-path metropolitan wireless mesh network. In: 2011 IEEE Symposium on Computers and Communications (ISCC), pp. 199–204. IEEE (2011)

9. Arbin, N., Suhaimi, N.S., Mokhtar, N.Z., Othman, Z.: Comparative analysis between k-means and k-medoids for statistical clustering. In: 2015 3rd International Conference on Artificial Intelligence, Modelling and Simulation (AIMS), pp. 117–121. IEEE (2015)

10. Chen, Z., Zhou, J., Chen, Y., Chen, X., Gao, X.: Deploying a social community network in rural areas based on wireless mesh networks. In: 2009 IEEE Youth Conference on Information, Computing and Telecommunication, pp. 443–446. IEEE (2009)

11. Karunaratne, S., Gacanin, H.: An overview of machine learning approaches in wireless mesh networks. IEEE Commun. Mag. **57**(4), 102–108 (2019)

12. Houaidia, C., Van den Bossche, A., Idoudi, H., Val, T., Azzouz Saidane, L.: Impact des interférences dans un réseau sans fil multi-sauts (2014)

13. Morissette, L., Chartier, S.: The k-means clustering technique: General considerations and implementation in Mathematica. Tutorials Quantitat. Methods Psychol. **9**(1), 15–24 (2013)

14. Sun, Y., Peng, M., Zhou, Y., Huang, Y., Mao, S.: Application of machine learning in wireless networks: Key techniques and open issues. IEEE Commun. Surv. Tutorials **21**(4), 3072–3108 (2019)

E-health

Digitization of Patient Records in Maxillofacial and Stomatology Surgery: A Case Study of the Maxillofacial and Stomatology Surgery Unit at Sominé Dolo Hospital in Mopti, Mali

Seydou Golo Barro[1,2(✉)], Aly Abdoulaye Guindo[1], Thioukany David Thera[3], Irénée Bamogo[1], and Cheick O. Bakayoko[4]

[1] Virtual University of Burkina Faso, Master e-Health and Telemedicine, Ouagadougou, Burkina Faso
seydou_golo@yahoo.fr
[2] Nazi Boni University, Bobo-Dioulasso, Burkina Faso
[3] Hôpital Sominé DOLO de Mopti, Sevare, Mali
[4] University of Science, Technology, Bamako, Bamako, Mali

Abstract. In healthcare facilities, data is collected and stored for traceability and subsequent use. The objective of this work is to develop an application for data collection and analysis in maxillofacial surgery. After a preliminary study on the needs. We used the UML language (Unified Modeling Language) to model the system. The 2TUP (Two Tracks Unified Process) process was used for analysis and design. The database created was implemented in Microsoft Access; Power BI was used for statistical analysis and data visualization. We have developed an Access data collection application and a Power BI application allowing easy and reliable visualization of the activity balance. Five hundred and fifty-eight (558) scanned patient records. Average age 30.44. Sex ratio 3.20 in favor of men. 419 patients consulted in emergency. Traumatic pathologies were more frequent 69.89%. 410 patients were operated on, 547 patients were satisfied with the surgical results. 3 theses were realized with the database. Our solution allows you to store, manage, share, and make statistical analyses dynamically and instantly of patient data in maxillofacial surgery and stomatology. The results have improved medical information management, clinical decision-making, and care planning.

Keywords: Numérisation dossier patient · Analyse et Colette de données · Application de chirurgie maxillo-faciale

1 Introduction

The medical approach is built upon patient observation and the monitoring of their condition [1]. In our daily medical practice, the recording of hospitalized, operated, or consulted patients, as well as various pathologies and procedures, is carried out manually, with the inherent risks of errors, omissions, and redundancies [2]. The hospital

A. Sere et al. (Eds.): AFRICOMM 2023, LNICST 587, pp. 211–226, 2025.
https://doi.org/10.1007/978-3-031-81570-6_14

information system is a computerized system designed to facilitate the management of medical and administrative information within a hospital. It can improve and enhance the quality and efficiency of healthcare services [3].

Patient record data in healthcare facilities serve as a written record of clinical, biological, diagnostic, and therapeutic information obtained during a patient's medical journey. It is a tool for reflection, synthesis, planning, care traceability, and even research [4].

In a study evaluating Mali's Health Information System (HIS), it was found that the health information system in place in basic healthcare structures (Community Health Center, district level: Referral Health Center, and central services) collected data on paper before transferring it to electronic formats [5].

We have observed that computerized patient data in our hospitals, if they exist, are very superficial. They do not support adequate decision-making for policymakers, let alone provide specialists with the ability to address various research questions, both for student theses and articles for scientific publications. It is unfortunate that we repeatedly need to refer to the same patient records to extract a small part for specific needs. It is clear that all these processes do not harness the tremendous potential of Information and Communication Technologies (ICT), which are more necessary than ever to hope for a significant improvement in the healthcare system, particularly in computerized patient data [6].

The ease with which ICT can collect patient data, structure it, order it, analyze it, and distribute this information to geographically distant users on a wide range of computers makes it an obvious candidate for a technological solution for patient data collection and analysis systems [7]. Given the scarcity of patient data collection and analysis applications in our hospitals that take into account the specificity of each medical specialty, we propose to develop an application for collecting and analyzing patient data in maxillofacial and stomatology surgery. Specifically, we will focus on the Maxillofacial and Stomatology Surgery Unit at Sominé Dolo Hospital in Mopti, Mali. This will lead to the creation of a medical records database, enabling rapid cross-sectional record retrieval and statistical calculations to facilitate decision-making in maxillofacial and stomatology surgery. We asked ourselves how decision-making in maxillofacial and stomatology surgery could be facilitated by the use of patient data collection and analysis tools. We believe that using ICT tools for patient data collection and analysis can enhance the quality and reliability of rapid decision-making they enable. The goal of our work was to develop a patient data collection and analysis tool and create a computerized patient database to facilitate decision-making in maxillofacial and stomatology surgery at Sominé Dolo Hospital in Mopti.

2 Materials and Methods

2.1 Study Setting

Our study framework was the Sominé DOLO Hospital in Mopti which is the only second reference medico-surgical facility in the 5th Administrative Region of Mali. It is located in the administrative area of Sevaré on the edge of the national road 6 (RN6).

2.2 Existing Study

To be able to give an opinion on the existing system, we first sought to know and evaluate it; by analyzing. We analyzed workstations, patient records, and records (emergency room, operating room and hospitalization), as well as circulating information. This analysis enabled us to confirm that:

- At the end of each month and/or on request, the statistics are done manually before being sent to the hospital's health information system manager.
- And data collection during theses and scientific papers was also manual.

2.3 Criticism and Suggestions

We have identified the difficulties associated with the manual collection and analysis of patient data and propose a computerized solution for the collection and analysis of patient data.

2.4 Méthode de Résolution Problème

Modeling language. For modeling, we chose UML (Unified Modeling Language) is a unified object-oriented modeling language. It is a graphic formalism resulting from notations used in different methods of objects [8].

Analysis and design method. There are a multitude of analysis methods, among which we can mention SADT (Structured Analysis and Design Technique), MERISE (Method of Study and Realization Computer for Business Systems) and 2TUP (Two Tracks Unified Process). For our study, the method chosen is the 2TUP process. The process is structured around three essential phases:

- a technical branch.
- a functional branch.
- a phase of implementation [9, 10].

2.5 System Modelling

Use Case Diagram. Table 1 illustrates the identification of use cases and description of use cases.

Table 1. Identification and description of use cases

Actor	Use case	Description
Cashier and/or Secretary medical	Manage admissions	It allows you to manage different patient admissions
	Create a folder administrative	It allows you to create an administrative file. It allows you to generate a unique patient identifier: IdPatient

(continued)

Table 1. (*continued*)

Actor	Use case	Description
Cashier	Pay for the medico surgical procedure	It allows you to pay for procedures (medical-surgical and nursing care) after or before the patient has benefited from these medical-surgical procedures
Doctor specialist or Generalist or the internal	Update patient file	It allows the patient file to be updated during and after hospitalization
	Manage patient file data	It allows you to access patient data, make modifications, add information, or delete the record
	Create a new medical record	It allows the user to create a new patient record in the application This involves collecting all the information in a patient file from admission to discharge
Doctor specialist or generalist	Perform analyzes statistics	It allows statistical analysis and visualization of patient data in the form of a table, disk, histogram, radar, sunbeam, etc
Male nurse	Create a nursing file	Allows you to create a nursing care record
	Update the nursing file	It allows daily updating of the nursing file during the patient's hospitalization
Cashier, Secretary medical, Doctor specialist, generalist, Internal and admin	Authentication	It allows you to grant or not access to the application to a user
	Manage appointments	It allows you to see the available consultation days, make an appointment, make changes, or cancel an appointment
Admin	Managing rights in a hospital	The system analyst in a hospital allows you to manage user access rights according to their access levels in a hospital

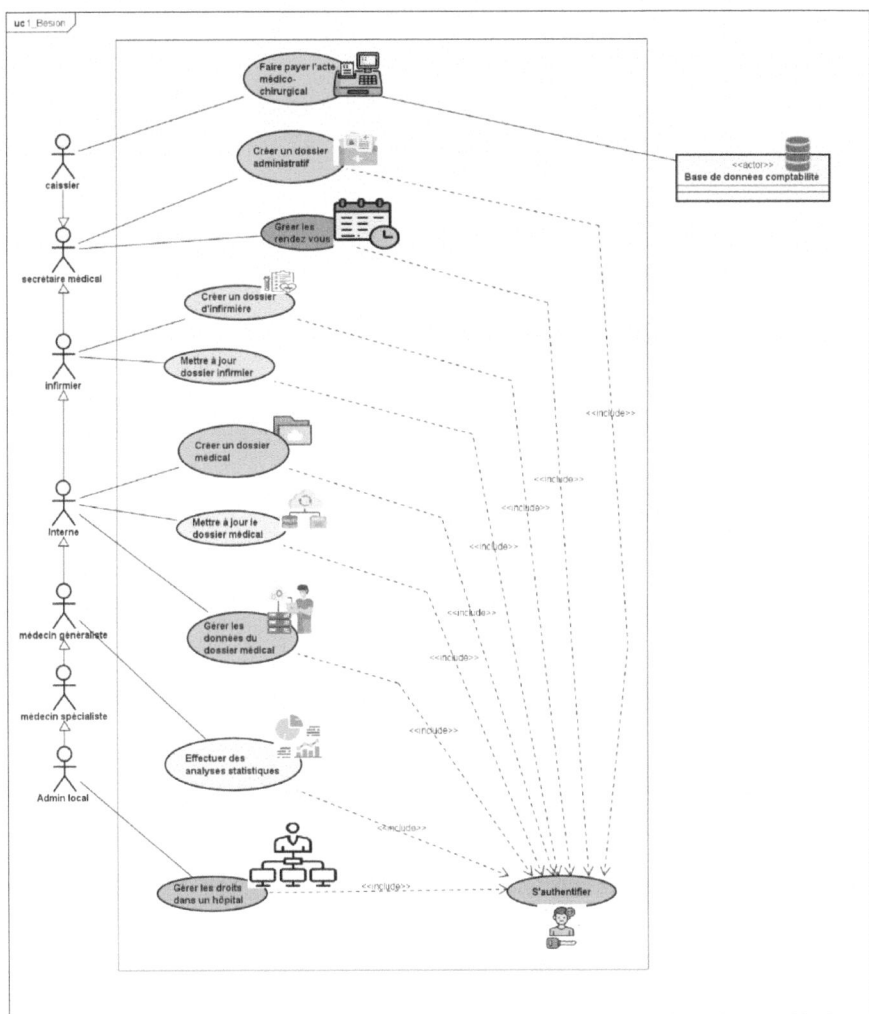

Fig. 1. Use case diagram

The use case diagram is illustrated by (Fig. 1).

Sequence Diagram. Sequence diagrams are the graphical representation of interactions between actors and the system in chronological order [11]. The (Fig. 3 and Fig. 4) illustrates sequence diagrams of normal use cases respectively <<Save a Consultation>> and <<perform statistical analysis statistiques>> (Fig. 2).

Class Diagram. La (Fig. 4) identifies and describes classes.

Package Diagram. Splitting the class diagram into a package makes it possible to group classes according to their functionality or domain, making system design clearer and more organized [12]. The (Fig. 5) shows the package diagram.

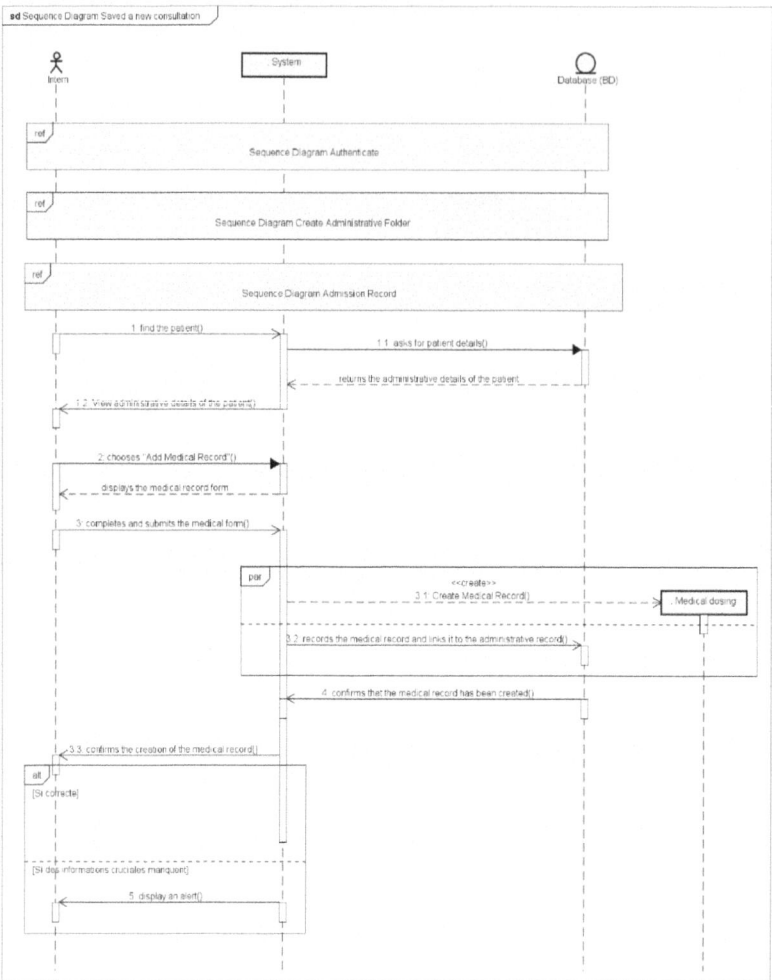

Fig. 2. Use Case Sequence Diagram <<Save a Consultation>>

Deployment Diagram. The deployment diagram is a static view that is used to represent how system components are distributed and their relationships between them [12, 13]. The latter is illustrated by the (Fig. 6).

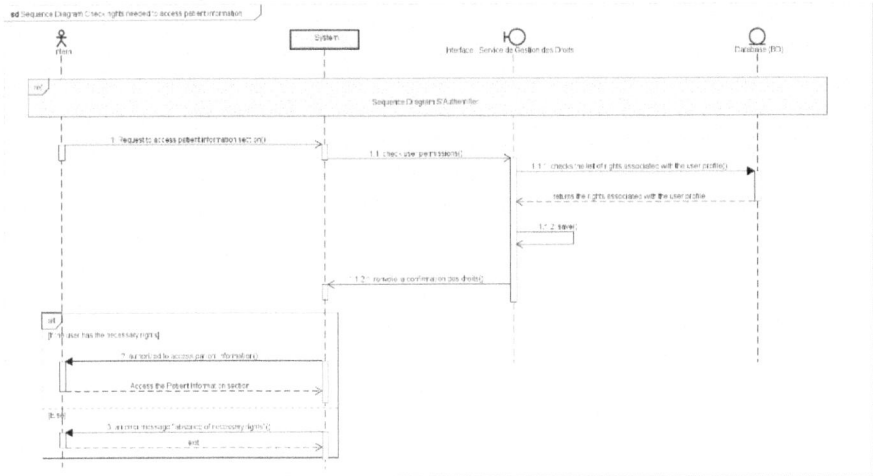

Fig. 3. Sequence Diagram Check rights needed to access patient information

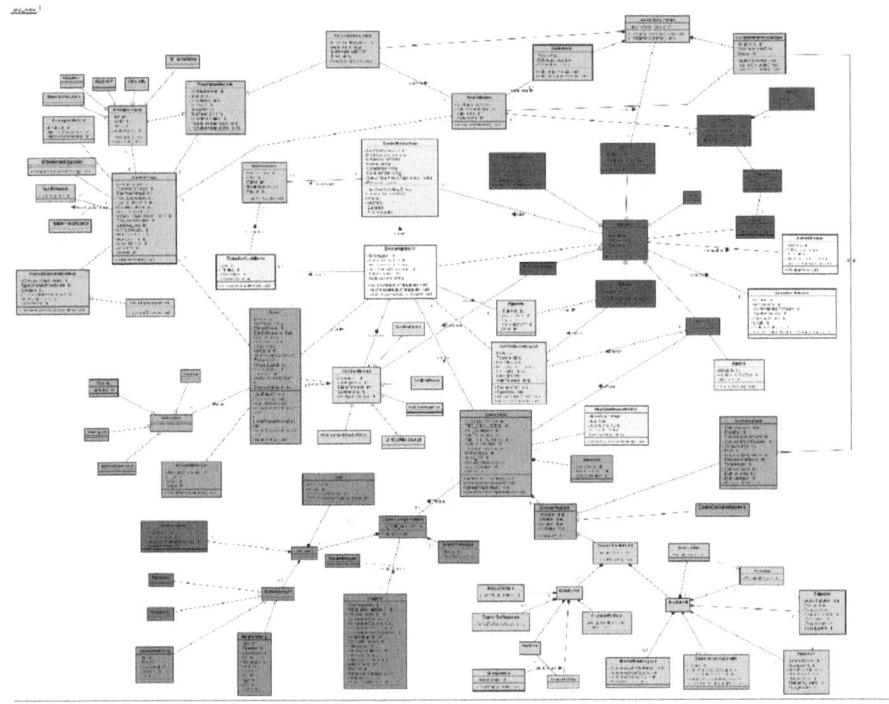

Fig. 4. Class diagram

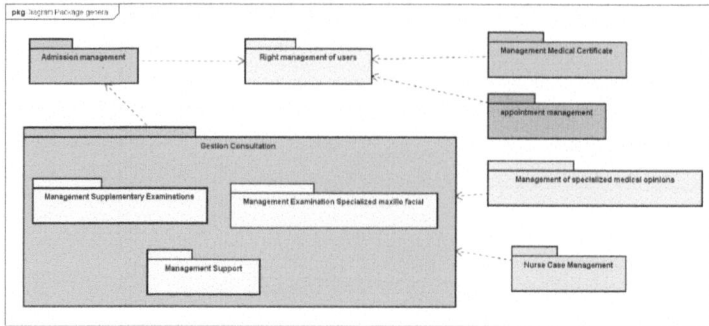

Fig. 5. Package diagram

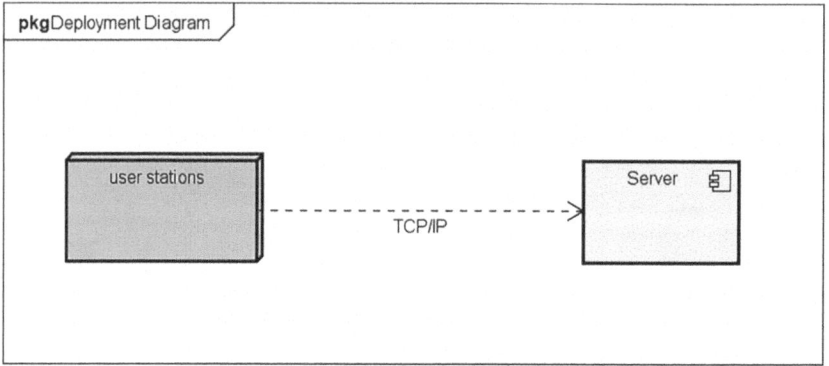

Fig. 6. Deployment diagram

2.6 Technologies Used

Data Collection. We chose Microsoft Access – relational then that it is easy to use and also it is part of the Office range that is essential for any user whether he is a student or professional [14, 15]. After the implementation of the database on Microsoft Access 365; we created forms to facilitate the recording, consultation and management of patient data.

Statistics and data analysis. With our solution we studied several parameters namely: age, sex, socio-economic level, number of patients per diagnosis, by type of intervention, by results of interventions, number of interventions per technique, number of research work by type, by student (theses and thesis) and or by doctor making requests concerning any activity in the department of maxillofacial surgery of stomatology: consultation, operating room, hospitalization and scientific research.

Power BI is a self-service business intelligence platform developed by Microsoft that enables the analysis, transformation and visualization of interactive data, providing advanced analytics and engaging visualizations. It mainly uses DAX (Data Analysis Expressions) for calculations and data modeling, as well as M Query for data transformation and SQL for database queries. By connecting to different data sources, Power BI aggregates data from EMR systems, SQL databases, and other sources, facilitating a comprehensive analysis of medical information. Power BI offers advanced security features, ensuring the privacy of sensitive medical information, as well as collaboration and sharing features, enabling healthcare professionals to work together and make decisions based on reliable, real-time data. In addition to its mobility through mobile applications, Po-wer BI can be integrated with other tools and processes, providing a scalable, automated and extensible solution for data management. For our solution, we chose Power BI to analyze and display our patient record data in maxillofacial surgery and stomatology and it does so in a visually understandable way, thanks to graphical visualizations, interactive dashboards and data segments [16].

For the above reasons; in our solution you expect to combine the power of these two Microsoft applications namely: Access 365 to create our future database that will be dynamically linked to Power BI. Through a Power BI dashboard, we will be able to use tables and graphs, dynamic cross-sections to make decisions in maxillofacial surgery and stomatology. We planned to make these tools functional in the maxillofacial surgery and stomatology unit of the Sominé Dolo hospital in Mopti.

Validation test and application evaluation. Verification and validation of all steps before proceeding to testing.

In order to evaluate the functionality of our application, we will collect patient data from the maxillofacial surgery and stomatology unit of the Sominé Dolo Hospital of Mopti from March 2016 to June 2023. Were included in our test all patients admitted to the unit of maxillofacial surgery and stomatology of the hospital Sominé Dolo of Mopti which we will find the medical record. Patients with incomplete records will be excluded.

We intend to extract data from three medical theses in this database.

3   Résultat

3.1   Patient Data Collection Access Application

Presentation of Some Interfaces. <<Authentication>> interface: It allows users to authenticate to access their personal spaces by entering their username and valid password. As the (Fig. 7).

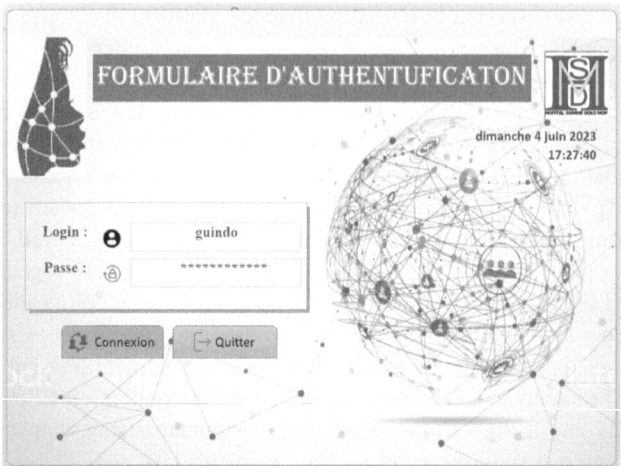

Fig. 7. Authentication

Interface «Home» once the health staff (the cashier or the medical or internal secretary or the doctor) has authenticated; according to its level of access, it accesses its space shown by the (Fig. 8) Next. It can perform the following tasks among others: Saves a new consultation (Fig. 9); follow up and update a patient record (Fig. 11) manage patient data (Fig. 10) and perform statistical analyses (Fig. 12).

Fig. 8. Authentication

Interface "Main interface for saving a new consultation" (Fig. 9).

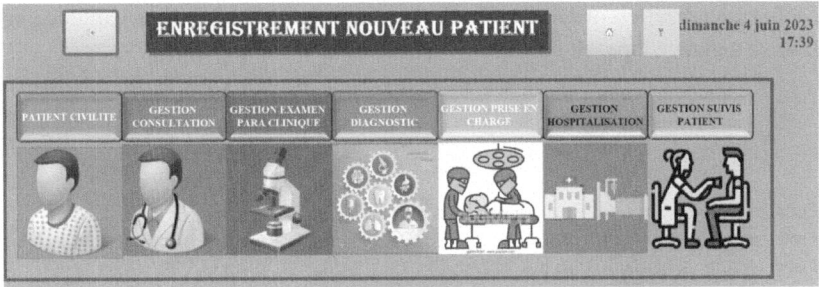

Fig. 9. Main interface for saving a new consultation.

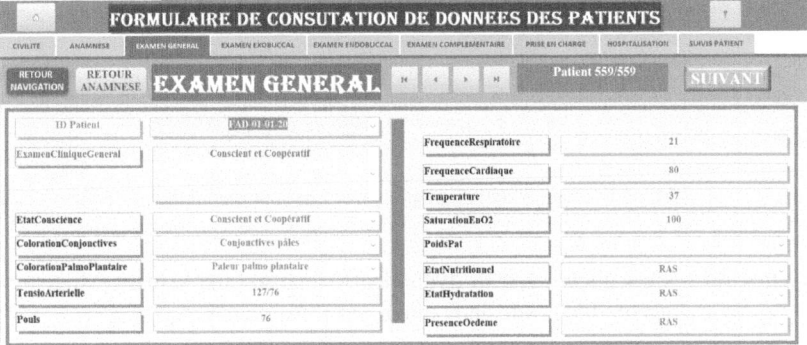

Fig. 10. Consultation of medical data (medical file)

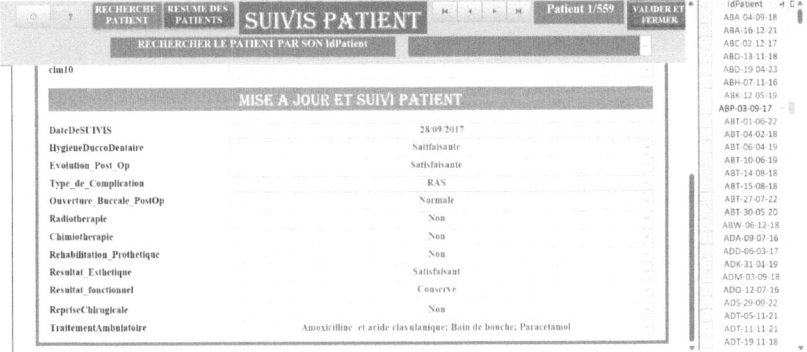

Fig. 11. Patient Tracker Interface for Folder Update

3.2 Power BI Application for Business Balance Visualization

From the <<Home>> interface of the Access application, we can access the Power BI application; in order to perform statistical analyses and display the data of the patient record. Once (the doctor) has authenticated, he can access his space on different terminals (desktop, laptop, tablet or smartphone). They can perform tasks such as:

Global visualization of all quantitative and qualitative patient data variables in the database at a glance through its dashboard illustrated by (Fig. 12).

Fig. 12. Overall statistical analysis of patient record data

A click on a view allows you to dynamically analyze and visualize statistics by pathology, causal agent, diagnostic and patient. As illustrated by the (Fig. 13).

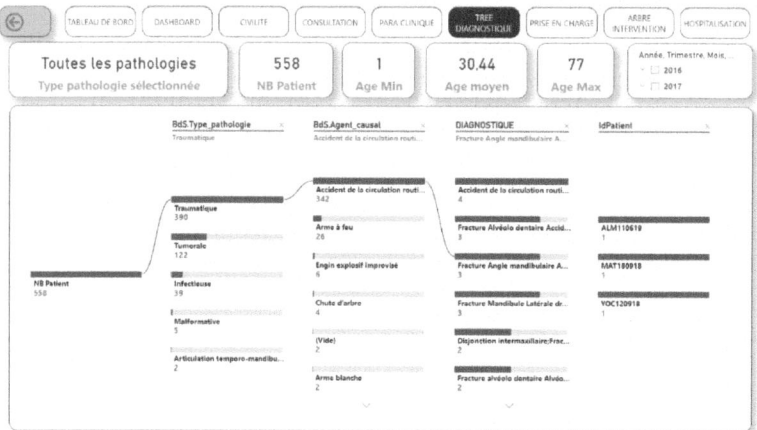

Fig. 13. Statistical analysis of patient record data by type of pathology

Clicking on a "type of pathology" (traumatic example) and a "type of causal agent" (firearm example) allows you to dynamically analyze and visualize the statistics of the pathology and causal agent (Fig. 14).

Fig. 14. Statistical analysis of patient record data by causal agent type

3.3 Summary of the Main Results of the Statistical Analyses

Between the 2016 and 2023 patient records, 558 patient records were saved. The age of the patients ranged from 1 to 77 years, with an average of 30.44 years. Men were the majority, with 425 male patients versus 133 female patients with a sex ratio of 3.20 in favor of men. Farmers were the dominant profession among patients, with 164 patients, followed by housewives with 89 patients. The level of education was predominant among out-of-school 316 patients, followed by secondary level 106 patients, primary 89 patients, Superior 25 patients. The majority of patients (89.61%) had their management funded by their fa-mille. Emergency consultations accounted for the majority of cases (419 patients), followed by outpatient consultations (138 patients). Traumatic pathologies were the most frequent (69.89%), followed by tumor pathologies (21.86%), infectious pathology (6.99%), malformative pathology (0.9%) and pathologies of the temporo-mandibular joints (0.36%). We recorded 2 patients with facial paralysis, 3 patients with non-cancerous salivary pathologies. CT scans were the most commonly performed imaging exam (53.05%), followed by X-rays of the lower faces and maxillae with right and left scrolls (10.57%). The majority of patients were blood type (O) and rhesus positive (40.14%), followed by (21.86%) blood type (B) and rhesus (+), (20.61%) were san-guin group and rhesus (A+). Of the patients who underwent surgery, 410 were operated on in an emergency situation, compared with 144 patients who were operated on after the programme. General anesthesia with orotracheal intubation was predominant (43.19%), followed by general anesthesia with nasal intubation (39.78%), local anesthesia (11.29%). The average duration of surgery was 3 h with extremes between (less than 1 to 8 h). The most common route was the endo-oral translesional route alone (99 patients), followed by the endo-oral and exo-oral route (96 patients), and the exo-oral route alone (78 patients). The majority of patients were medically discharged (98.3%), some deaths (0.9%), transfers to other services (0.36%) and (0.36%) discharge against medical advice. During the postoperative follow-ups 547 of our patients were satisfied with the surgical results, insufficient results in 8 patients, 3 failures were observed in our series. The scientific activity of the maxillofacial unit in 2023 included 3 general medical theses respectfully on ballistic trauma, road traffic accident trauma and odontogenic tumors.

3.4 Security Policies

We have adopted some good practices to ensure the security of digitized data, namely to secure access to digitized data by limiting its access to authorized persons. This by implementing so-called authentication controls; our data is regularly backed up to the cloud since we use the OneDrive of MS office 365 to minimize data loss in the event of a system failure or cyber-securityattacks; access permissions are granted according to the user's needs. Its access authorisations are reviewed regularly to ensure that users only have access to the data they need. This is done through the retrieval of connection histories; users are trained and made aware of good security practices, such as securing their passwords and using Wi-Fi networksSecure fi to avoid the risk of hacking and regular updating of software to fix security vulnerabilities and vulnerabilities.

4 Discussion

The objective of this work was to digitize the patient file data in maxillofacial surgery and stomatology at the Sominé Dolo Hospital in Mopti, Mali, in order to facilitate clinical decision-making. The results obtained highlighted the effectiveness of the patient data collection and analysis tool as well as the computerized database created. In addition, the Power BI application allowed a user-friendly and reliable visualization of the unit's activity balance.

At present, several computer applications specialized in the management of medical records have been studied. For example, the Cake Framework model MVC was used to explore the activity within the maxillofacial and aesthetic surgery department of Ibn Tofail Hospital, CHU Mohamed VI, Marrakech. Although efficient, it allows free text entry in certain fields, which can complicate the analysis of qualitative variables [2]. The eMe-diNexus app in India enables complete digitization of patient records and offers telemedicine features, but its limited geographical availability and telemedicine regulations can be obstacles [17]. Anatomage offers 3D scanning and pre-operative planning solutions, but their high cost can be prohibitive [18]. Other applications like Cinz@n in Mali [19], DHIS2 in West Africa [20], Epic Systems and CareCloud offer medical records management features, but they are not specifically specialized in maxillofacial surgery and stomatology [21, 22].

In our solution, we opted for efficient modeling of patient record data to minimize redundancies, input errors, and facilitate statistical analyses of qualitative variables. Thus, only first and last names and quantitative variables require manual entry, while other information is selected from drop-down lists. This approach improves data quality and facilitates research in maxillofacial surgery and stomatology.

Statistical analyses revealed several important elements. First, the male predominance among patients is consistent with other studies in the field [2, 23, 24]. Traumatic pathologies were the most frequent, followed by tumor and infectious pathologies, thus emphasizing the importance of trauma and tumor management in this specialty. The frequent use of computed tomography (CT) and radiographs demonstrates the importance of imaging in the diagnosis and planning of interventions. The high level of patient satisfaction with the surgical outcomes is a testament to the effectiveness of the interventions performed within the unit.

The digitization of the patient record has significantly improved the management of medical information, promoting better coordination of care and providing a reliable source of information for health planning and policy. The introduction of the patient data collection and analysis tool as well as the Power BI application greatly facilitated clinical decision making. Dynamic dashboards enabled professionals to quickly visualize activity data, leading to better resource management and more informed decisions.

However, our work has limitations, including Microsoft Access's limited ability to handle large amounts of data and its level of security. In addition, our solution currently only covers the maxillofacial and stomatology surgery unit, and does not support other hospital services and specialties. We plan to correct these limitations by developing a web version of our solution.

This study showed that the digitization of the patient record in maxillofacial surgery and stomatology offers many benefits for medical data management, clinical decision making, and research in this area. Effective data modelling and the use of tools such as Power BI have contributed to the improvement of medical practice within the unit. However, challenges remain for wider implementation and continuous improvement of the solution.

5 Conclusion

The digitization of the patient record in maxillofacial surgery allows a better management of medical data, their centralization, their accessibility and their sharing between the different health professionals involved in the management of the patient. It provides quick and easy access to all the patient's medical information, facilitating diagnosis, management, planning and scientific research. It also reduces the costs associated with patient record management, such as storage, transportation and paper records management costs. Finally, the digitization of the patient record in maxillofacial surgery allows a better traceability of the patient's medical information, which improves the quality and safety of care, and thus contributes to the satisfaction of the patient and all health professionals involved in its management. In addition to the ergonomics it offers, this application provides an innovative solution to facilitate decision-making in maxillofacial surgery and stomatology at Sominé Dolo Hospital from. Mopti.

References

1. Lievre, A., Moutel, G.: Le Dossier Médical: Concepts et Evolutions (Droits des Patients et Impact Sur la Relation Soignants-Soignés) (2010). www.ethique.inserm.fr
2. Karimi, F.E., Hattab, N.M.: Application informatique de la gestion du dossier médical en chirurgie maxillo-faciale et esthétique, p. 3

3. Nabila, S., Katia, R., Sonia, M.K.: Le système d'information hospitalier, un préalable pour la mise en place d'un système d'information sanitaires: Cas du CHU de Tizi-Ouzou, p. 86

4. dossier_du_patient_-_fascicule_1_reglementation_et_recommandations_-_2003.pdf. Consulté le: 11 septembre 2023. https://www.has-sante.fr/upload/docs/application/pdf/2009-08/dossier_du_patient_-_fascicule_1_reglementation_et_recommandations_-_2003.pdf

5. Sacko, P.M.A.: Evaluation du Systeme d'Information Sanitaire (SIS) du Mali: cas du District de Bamako, p. 79

6. Bagayoko, C.: Mise en place d'un système d'information hospitalier en Afrique francophone: cinz@n, étude et validation du modèle au Mali, These de doctorat, Aix-Marseille 2, 2010. Consulté le: 9 mars 2023. https://www.theses.fr/2010AIX20680

7. Brelstaff, G., Moehrs, S., Anedda, P., Tuveri, M., Zanetti, G.: Internet patient records: new techniques. J. Med. Internet Res. 3(1), E8 (2001). https://doi.org/10.2196/jmir.3.1.e8

8. Solnon, C.: Modélisation UML

9. 2TUP: définition et explications, Techno-Science.net. https://www.techno-science.net/definition/670.html. consulté le 6 mars 2023

10. Gislain, Z.N.T.: Gestion de l'inventaire en utilisant le QR code, Mémoire soutenu en vue de l'obtention du diplôme de Master professionnel en Réseaux, Télécommunications et Systèmes - 2021 2020. 10/gestion-de-l-inventaire-en-utilisant-le-qr-code/

11. Villalobos, J.: Fédération de composants : une architecture logicielle pour la composition par coordination (2003)

12. Booch, G., Christerson, M., Jonsson, P., Overgaard, G., Graham, I.: Les bases de la conception Orientée Objet

13. IFT6825 Génie logiciel - UML. http://www.iro.umontreal.ca/~dift6825/UML.htm. consulté le 11 septembre 2023

14. Jack, P.: Introduction aux bases de données avec ACCESS — Wikiversité. https://fr.wikiversity.org/wiki/Introduction_aux_bases_de_donn%C3%A9es_avec_ACCESS. consulté le 12 septembre 2023

15. Vidéo de formation Access - Support Microsoft. https://support.microsoft.com/fr-fr/office/vid%C3%A9o-de-formation-access-a5ffb1ef-4cc4-4d79-a862-e2dda6ef38e6. consulté le 12 septembre 2023

16. maggiesMSFT, Power BI documentation - Power BI. https://learn.microsoft.com/en-us/power-bi/. consulté le 23 mai 2023

17. Études de cas médicaux et discussion | Nouvelles médicales Inde | eMediNexus. https://www.emedinexus.com/. consulté le 9 mars 2023

18. Table de dissection virtuelle - Plateforme d'anatomie 3D - Table d'anatomie. https://anatomage.com/. consulté le 9 mars 2023

19. Bagayoko, C.O.: Mention: Santé publique et Recherche Clinique, p. 142

20. DHIS2: DHIS2. https://dhis2.org/. consulté le 9 mars 2023

21. Epic | ...With the patient at the heart. https://www.epic.com/. consulté le 12 septembre 2023

22. Our Software | Epic. https://www.epic.com/software/. consulté le 12 septembre 2023

23. Bouguila, J., Zairi, I., Khonsari, R.H., Jablaoui, Y., Hellali, M., Adouani, A.: [Epidemiology of maxillofacial traumatology in Tunis]. Rev. Stomatol. Chir. Maxillofac. 109(6), 353–357 (2008). https://doi.org/10.1016/j.stomax.2008.04.009

24. Konsem, T., et al.: [Epidemiology of maxillo-facial traumatism s sequels at stomatology and maxillo-facial surgery service of Yalgado Ouedraogo University Hospital Center]. Odonto-Stomatol. Trop. Trop. Dent. J. 39(156), 66–72 (2016)

Design of an Electronic Health Record Module in the Pediatrics Department of the Ouahigouya Regional University Hospital Center

Seydou Golo Barro[1,2](✉), Irénée Bamogo[1], and Aly Abdoulaye Guindo[1]

[1] Virtual University of Burkina Faso, Ouagadougou, Burkina Faso
seydou_golo@yahoo.fr
[2] Nazi BONI University, Bobo Dioulasso, Burkina Faso

Abstract. In Burkina Faso, most existing hospital information systems are limited to managing administrative and financial aspects. Computerized tools for managing medical data (clinical, paraclinical, therapeutic, etc.) are almost non-existent. Our goal was to setup a basic HIS in which will be integrated as first module, the very one that is lacking in Burkina Faso's hospitals, a computerized patient records module. The design of this module as well as the hospital information system within which it will be deployed was based on a study of the businesses identified in Ouahigouya regional university hospital center and the interactions of patients with this hospital center. The pediatrics department has been taken as a model for the design of the module. This basic hospital information system with its embedded computerized patient records module has been deployed into the pediatrics department. The designed module allows almost complete digitization of commonly used paper supports (consultation record, medical record, treatment and monitoring sheet) with the resulting advantages (time saving, ease of access to data and statistical reports draw up). This was a very new experience in a reference healthcare center, which can respond to the identified problem.

Keywords: Hospital Information System · Electronic Health Record ·
eXtensible Markup Language · Enterprise Resource Planning · Business Process
Model and Notation · Unified Modeling Language

1 Introduction

1.1 Context

In hospitals, there are some factors that affect the quality of data that are fed back to decision makers. These factors come from the limits and disadvantages of paper supports, because data management are essentially based on these one. Indeed, in Burkina Faso, like the other countries of the French-speaking sub-region [1], few hospitals have an hospital information system (HIS) equipped with an electronic health record module. Most existing systems in these countries are limited to financial management and/or data

© ICST Institute for Computer Sciences, Social Informatics and Telecommunications Engineering 2025
Published by Springer Nature Switzerland AG 2025. All Rights Reserved
A. Sere et al. (Eds.): AFRICOMM 2023, LNICST 587, pp. 227–246, 2025.
https://doi.org/10.1007/978-3-031-81570-6_15

entry [2, 3]. As a reminder, an Hospital Information System (HIS) is a computer system designed to facilitate the management of all medical and administrative information within an hospital [4].

1.2 Problematic

With the large amounts of data that must be processed daily in hospitals, the limits and disadvantages of paper supports (consultation record, medical record, nursing record, treatment and monitoring sheet) are well known. Not only these limitations have analytical implications for decision makers who are at the top of the national health system, but at the lowest level of the ladder, they seriously affect the quality of patient care by the healthcare providers. And this, healthcare providers are the first ones to feel it.

The following observation illustrates the challenges faced by healthcare providers in hospitals clinical departments because of the disadvantages of the paper support. For example, having a patient history and other previous clinical and paraclinical data for the management of a new episode of illness is never easy. Indeed, these data are scattered in health notebooks, sometimes multiple and poorly preserved, or in files stored in the archives and covered in dust and difficult to access in the shortest possible time. Thus, with each new consultation, this obliges healthcare providers to collect the same data again in the consultation register and to completely reconstitute a new medical file, for patients to be readmitted to hospital. This process that we encounter in most clinical departments of hospitals in Burkina Faso has the following repercussions:

– On the efficiency of healthcare providers: the complete reconstruction from scratch of the patient care scenario (collection of administrative data, collection of complaints, collection of the same medical history, prescription of permanent validity test, etc.) delays the patient care due to the time devoted to recreating the medical record; the scattering of previous medical data across multiple files stored in archives, and sometimes in multiple, poorly maintained or unavailable health notebooks, make it difficult for healthcare personnel to easily reconstruct the patient's medical history;
– On the patient: the re-prescription of exams whose results remain valid for the patient's entire life (such as blood type and hemoglobin electrophoresis) obliges the patient to spend money again for the same exams if healthcare personnel are not able to access previous results (unavailable health notebook or no notification of these exams results in the health notebook), resulting in a financial impact;

Then, when it comes time to compile data for statistical purposes, the following factors negatively impact the quality of the transmitted data, compromising the quality of data to the higher authorities of the system:

– Incompleteness of data due to non-reporting of important items;
– Data sometimes illegible due to poorly written handwriting style of some healthcare agents;
– Inconsistency of some data attributable to human error;

The use of a computerized system for managing patients' medical data helps to address these problems [5].

1.3 Objectives

General Objective. The general objective was to design an Electronic Health Record (EHR) module in a clinical department of a reference healthcare center in Burkina Faso, which takes into account the specific needs of the target users. This clinical module should address the problems posed by paper-based records.

Specific Objectives. The specific objectives were as follows:

– Design an EHR module that meet the definition of the International Organization for Standardization (ISO) based on the paper-based records to be digitalized and the business processes characterizing the target clinical department.
– Deploy this EHR module within the target clinical department.
– Evaluate the implementation of this module.

2 Methodology

We present in the following subtitles the framework of our work, then essential and critical aspects on which it seemed essential to us to look into by way of preparations for our design project: the method of unique patient identification, the modeling of our EHR, the standards and references to be used.

2.1 Project Framework

The Ouahigouya Regional University Hospital Center is a reference healthcare center in the northern region of Burkina Faso. The pediatrics department of this center was the site where we set up and implemented our EHR module.

The management of patients' medical data is exclusively done using paper supports. The pediatrics department includes an emergency unit, a hospitalization unit, a neonatology unit, and a Nutritional Recovery and Education Center. The pediatric emergency unit receives urgent cases, referred patients, evacuated and transferred patients, every day of the week, 24 h a day. Seventh year medical students participate in patient care and continuity of care. They are the first point of contact for the service with patients received in this unit. Physicians and physician assistants provide outpatient consultations and also visit patients in the hospitalization unit.

The entire process of collecting and managing patients' medical data relies exclusively on paper-based system, including consultation registers, hospitalization registers, medical records, nursing records, treatment and monitoring sheets, medical test order, prescriptions, and hospitalization discharge summaries.

2.2 Norms and References

The content of the medical record generated by our EHR module must reflect the terminological characteristics of medical language. To achieve this, we have defined norms and references to be used.

Types of Data. Our EHR module will be designed to manage textual data and icono-graphic data (images). Textual data will be stored in the form of structured data, while iconographic data (images) will be stored in the form of semi-structured data (a string of characters encoded in base64 format).

Terminological References. The terminologies used in filling out certain items will be based on predefined lists of terms specific to different domains of healthcare:

- The terminology of symptoms is based on a list of validated terms derived from medical vocabulary;
- At the level of diagnoses, two entities should be distinguished:

  - The diagnoses suggested at the hypothesis stage (diagnostic hypothesis) may sometimes include imprecise terms, as they may include "groups or families of pathologies" that will need to be refined later. The terminology used at this stage is based on a merged list of terms from the common medical vocabulary and a disease dictionary;
  - The final or definitive diagnoses: they result from refining or adjusting the diagnostic hypothesis after confirmation medical exams. These diagnoses have a higher level of precision and can be coded. The terminology of the diagnoses used at this stage is based on the International Classification Diseases, 10th revision (ICD-10);

- The terminology of medications is based on the International Nonproprietary Name (INN), also known as the common or generic name of the medication;

2.3   The Unique Patient Identification Method

Our EHR module has been designed to assign a unique identifier to patients. The chosen identification method uses a simplified version of the one implemented by Barro et al. [6] in Burkina Faso. The algorithm takes as input a string of characters resulting from concatenating strict identification traits (last name, first name(s) and date of birth) and complementary identification traits (mother's maiden name and first name(s), father's name(s) and last name). The steps of this algorithm are as follows:

- Processing of the data: All data are converted to uppercase (last names and first names). Accented characters are replaced by their unaccented equivalents. If there is more than one first name (for the patient, his mother or his father), these first names are organized in alphabetical order.
- Hashing: The resulting string of characters is hashed using the SHA 512 algorithm.
- Selection of the first 8 characters of the string resulting from this hashing.

2.4   The EHR Characteristics

Architecture. The International Organization for Standardization (ISO) defines the EHR as "a repository of information regarding the health status of a subject of care, in computer processable form, stored and transmitted securely and accessible by multiple authorized users, having a standardized or commonly agreed logical information model that is independent of EHR systems and whose primary purpose is the support of continuing, efficient and quality integrated health care" [7]. The literature reports three types of Electronic Medical Record (EMR) structures, according to Hayrinen et al. [8]:

– Time-oriented EMR: data is presented in chronological order;
– Problem-oriented EMR: notes are taken for each problem assigned to the patient, and each problem is described according to subjective information, objective information, evaluations, and the plan of care (SOAP structure);
– Source-oriented EMR: the content of the record is organized according to the method by which the information was obtained, for example, visit notes, radiography reports, and blood analyses. In each section, data is presented in chronological order;

EMR systems typically combine these three types [8]. To ensure that our clinical module generates an EHR that meets the ISO definition and structures the data according to the types described above, we designed it with the following concept. We conceive the EHR as a unique object that should integrate a summary of all patient data (administrative, clinical, paraclinical, therapeutic, and medical history information). Its content should not be fixed but should be continuously updated and evolved through the addition of new data resulting from all medical events that occur during the patient's life. The entire patient history should be contained within this object. It should be attached to one and only one patient and should contain a unique instance for the patient owner. The variety of data to be grouped within the EHR requires organization. We proposed to structure our EHR according to the organizational tree presented in the Fig. 1:

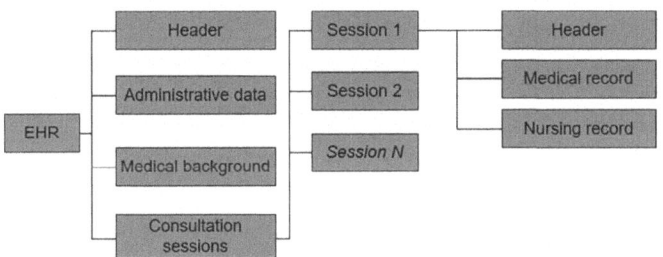

Fig. 1. The EHR Organizational tree

The data in the EHR is divided into four main sections: header section, administrative data section, medical background section, and consultation session section. Consultation sessions correspond to the medical events experienced by the patient, such as consultations and medical procedures. The data within a session is further divided into sub-sections, such as heard, medical record, nursing record, and so on. Consultation sessions are arranged chronologically, and the data is sourced from the various healthcare providers and services that the patient has received care from, so that the complete medical history of the patient is contained within this single object. Such a synthetic object allows for both a temporal (evolution over time) and transversal (interdepartmental) analysis of the data.

The XML Format. To implement the architecture and concept we plan to adopt for our EHR, the disaggregated data provided to our clinical module will be processed and compressed into a single data format using XML [9]. The advantages of this concept are those inherent in the XML document format:

– When the EHR formatted in XML is retrieved as a single block from the database, it becomes an object that can be queried and manipulate using XPath and XQuery [10];
– As XML is the standard data exchange format between information systems [9], any information system or application, regardless of its nature and execution environment, can easily browse and extract specific data from this EHR formatted in XML;

Figures 2 and 3 provide an overview of the XML structure of our EHR. For better presentation and readability, we are formatting this document using an XSL style sheet.

```
<root version="1.0" xmlns:xsl="http://www.w3.org/1999/XSL/Transform">
    <idDossier></idDossier>
    <idHopital></idHopital>
    <dateCreation></dateCreation>
    <dateDerniereModification></dateDerniereModification>
    <profil>
        <nom></nom>
        <prenoms></prenoms>
        <sexe></sexe>
        <dateNaissance></dateNaissance>
        <statutMatrimonial></statutMatrimonial>
        <profession></profession>
        <carteIdentite></carteIdentite>
        <niveauInstruction></niveauInstruction>
        <mutuelles></mutuelles>
        <assurance></assurance>
        <nomPere></nomPere>
        <prenomsPere></prenomsPere>


            <chirurgicaux></chirurgicaux>
            <gynecoObstetriques></gynecoObstetriques>
            <vaccinaux></vaccinaux>
        </personnels>

        <familiaux>
            <ascendants></ascendants>
            <collateraux></collateraux>
            <descendants></descendants>
        </familiaux>
    </antecedents>
    <sessions>
        <session></session>
    </sessions>
</root>
```

Fig. 2. XML structure of the EHR (version 1.0).

2.5 The Hospital Information System Architecture

Our EHR module will be designed as a component of a Hospital Information System (HIS). To do this, we needed to lay the foundation of a basic HIS, of which the EHR will

```
<session>
    <idSession></idSession>
    <idHopital></idHopital>
    <service></service>
    <dateEnregistrement></dateEnregistrement>
    <dateDerniereModification></dateDerniereModification>
    <modeEntree></modeEntree>
    <modePec></modePec>
    <ficheTetu></ficheTetu>
    <ficheReferenceEvacuation></ficheReferenceEvacuation>
    <etatSession></etatSession>
    <rendezVous></rendezVous>
    <structureProvenance>
        <type></type>
        <departement></departement>
        <province></province>
        <region></region>

        <hypothesesDiagnostiques></hypothesesDiagnostiques>
        <resumeSyndromique></resumeSyndromique>
        <examensParacliniques></examensParacliniques>
        <resultatsExamens></resultatsExamens>
        <traitements></traitements>
        <iconographie></iconographie>
        <commentaires></commentaires>
    </dossierMedical>
    <dossierInfirmier>
        <evaluationEtat></evaluationEtat>
        <patientARisque></patientARisque>
        <traitementsAdministres></traitementsAdministres>
        <surveillance></surveillance>
        <actesPoses></actesPoses>
        <commentaires></commentaires>
    </dossierInfirmier>
</session>
```

Fig. 3. XML structure of the "session" node

be one of the first components. Other modules may be added later to eventually form a complete HIS.

The proposed HIS model will be an Enterprise Resource Planning (ERP) model [11], as it is a model that allows us to establish the plan of an information system and ensure perfect integration and interoperability of its subsystems [1]. An ERP system consists of a set of modules that work together, relying on a common database to support all of its features. It offers the advantage of providing a highly structured approach to managing organizational resources. We have adopted a patient-centered process approach [12].

To build the plan of our HIS, we considered the interactions of the patient with the different services identified within the hospital and analyzed the sequences of activities that occur within them. Following this analysis, we proceeded to model the processes that we were able to identify.

To have a detailed and visually appealing representation of the business processes that occur within the different services, we have constructed Business Process Model and Notation (BPMN) diagrams [13]. BPMN is a modeling language used to represent an organization's business processes through a graphical representation. This language is designed for the analysis and design of business processes that involve the interaction of different systems. BPMN is complementary to the Unified Modeling Language (UML), which focused more on the analysis and design of information systems. Figure 4 shows BPMN diagram that describe the processes that occur in the emergency unit of the pediatrics department.

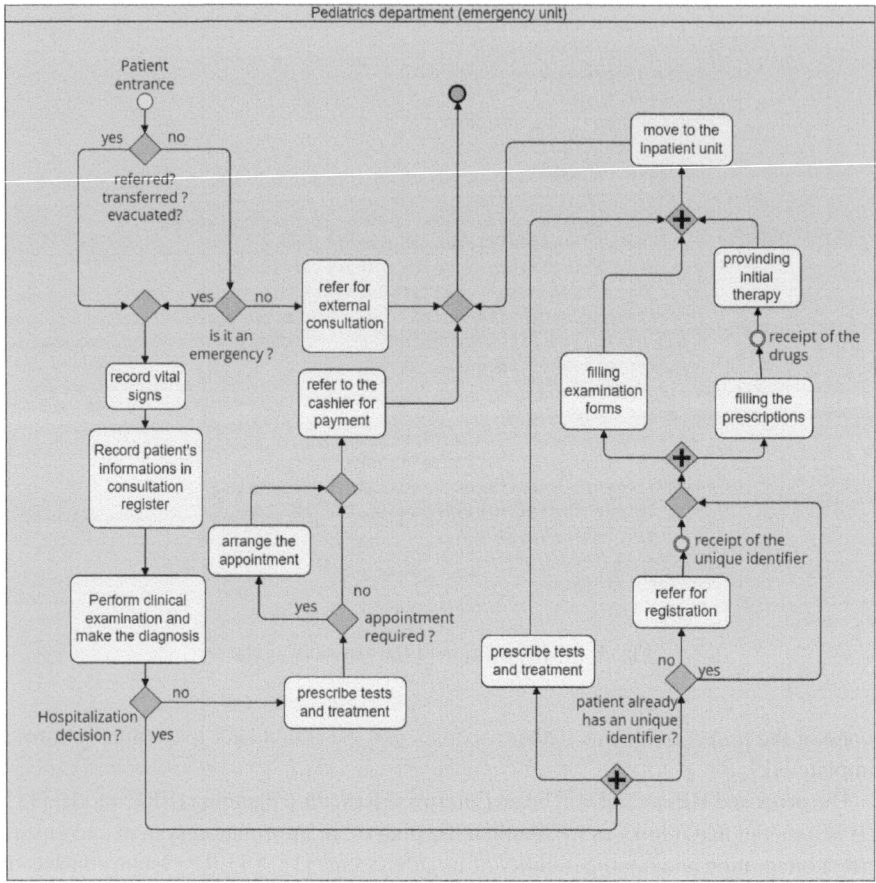

Fig. 4. Businesses processes in pediatric emergency unit

The HIS is a stack of independent modules that are connected to a common database. For each department to be included in the HIS, a module will be designed. However, for the scope of this project, only two modules will be designed: the EHR module intended for clinical departments, and a basic system administration module that will handle user management. Figure 5 presents the network architecture of the HIS.

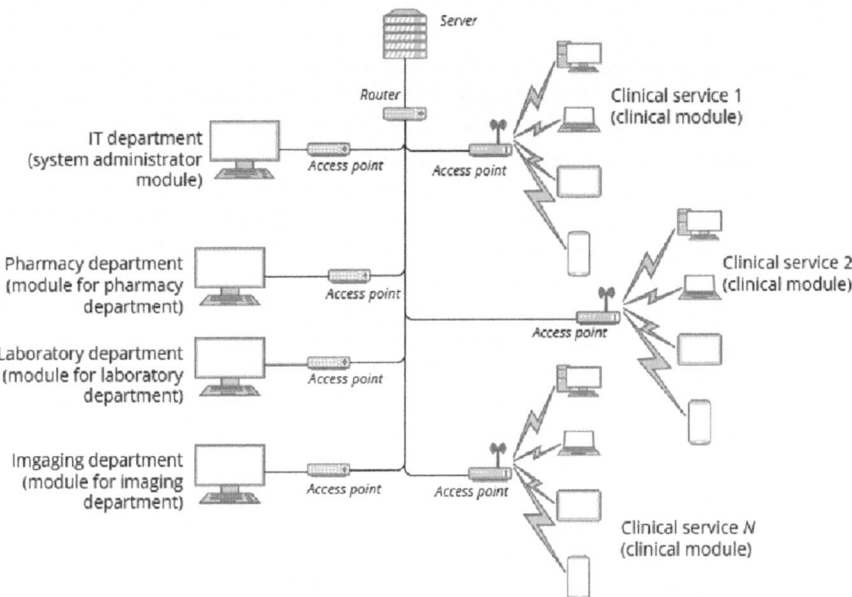

Fig. 5. The HIS network architecture

2.6 The EHR Module Architecture

Our EHR module is a web-based application that adopts a 3-third architecture [14], with the following layers: presentation layer, processing layer, and data access layer. We used the "MVC" design pattern provided by Symfony [15] Framework to build this module according to this architecture. Figure 6 shows the 3-third architecture adopted for our EHR module.

2.7 Database Modeling

The database modeling of our system was done as follow. Based on the consultation and hospitalization records, medical and nursing records, as well as monitoring and treatment sheets, we established a data dictionary and identified the entities involved in the processes of the pediatrics department, as well as the relationships and cardinalities between these entities. We used the Looping [16] modeling tool to construct the graphical representation of our conceptual data model. Figure 7 shows this conceptual data model. Depending on the type of value to be assigned to the properties, the types of data used are: Varchar, Int, Date, Datetime, Logical (Bool), Text. The properties of the entities correspond to the fields (columns) of the database tables. Some fields are intended to receive composite data (semi-structured data). We used JSON and XML objects to organize these data. The data type corresponding to these objects at the database level is the CLOB (Character Large Object) type, also designed as TEXT.

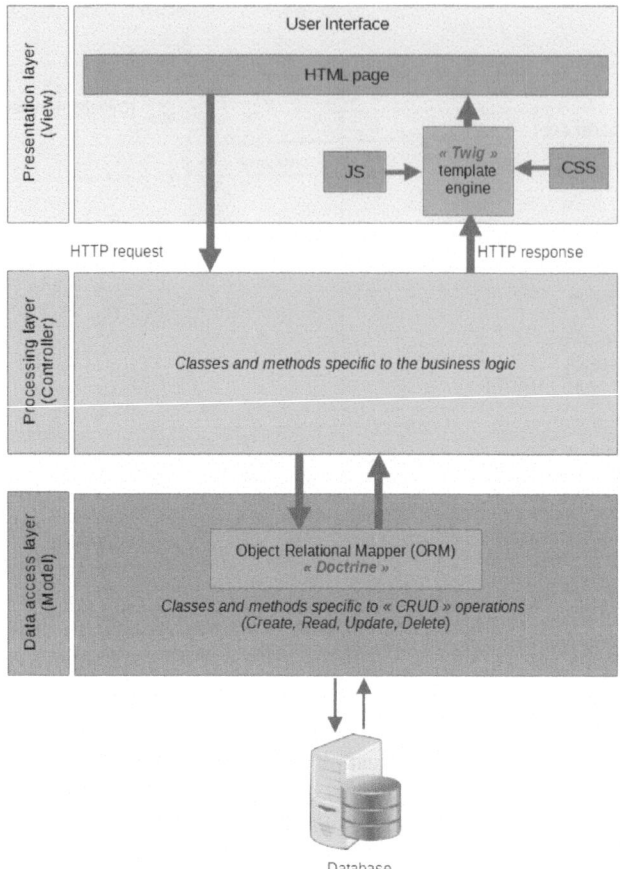

Fig. 6. Three-third architecture of the clinical module

2.8   UML Modeling

In this subsection, we present the following UML diagrams, which respectively describe the functional and dynamic characteristics of our module:

- The use case diagram (Fig. 8)
- The sequence diagram of two main scenarios (Fig. 9, Fig. 10)

2.9   Technologies and Development Environment

The development tools and technologies we used are as follow:

- Back-end languages. We used PHP as the main scripting language, and JavaScript for certain AJAX [17] requests.
- Front-end technologies: HTML, JavaScript, and CSS were used for the visual rendering of the graphical interfaces. In Symfony, the template engine used for assembling and constructing HTML pages is Twig [18];

- Web server: We used WampServer [19] as the application server;
- Database: we used PostgreSQL [20] as the database management system;
- Development environment: we used Visual Studio Code [21] as code editor;

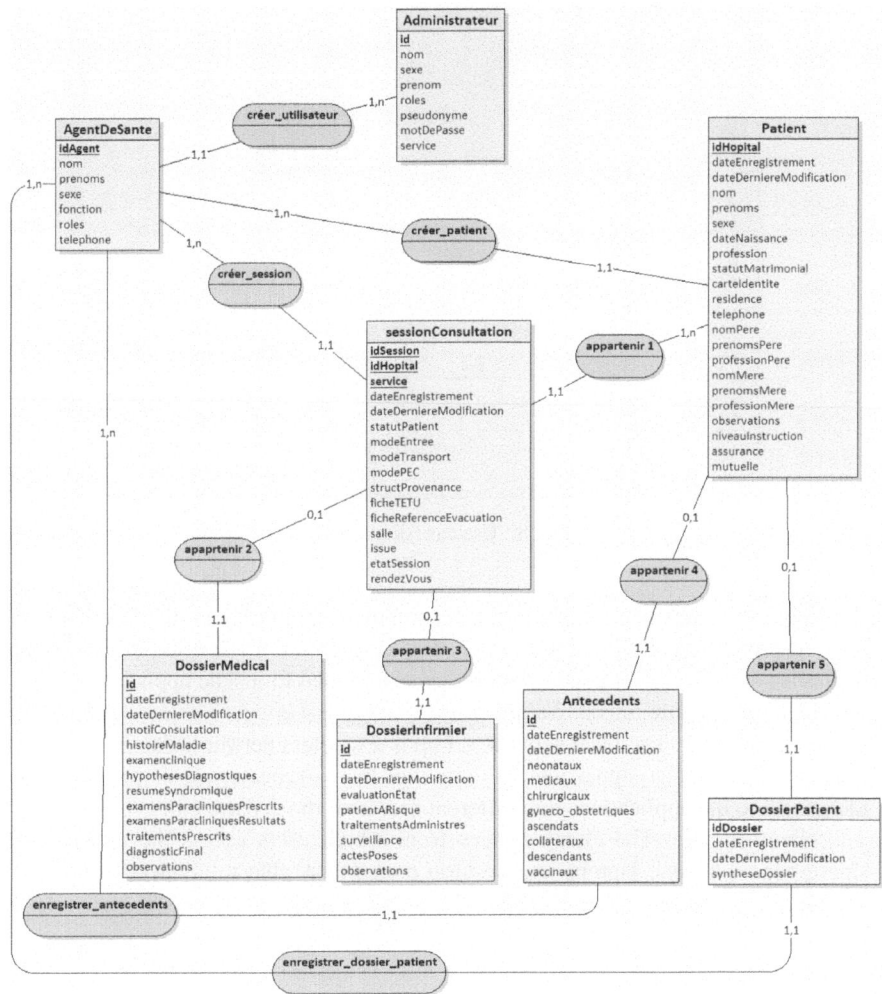

Fig. 7. Conceptual data model of the clinical module

2.10 Deployment of the Module

Our basic HIS and the clinical module it integrates were deployed within the pediatrics department after setting up and configuring a secure wireless local area network (Wi-Fi). The components of the entire system implemented are:

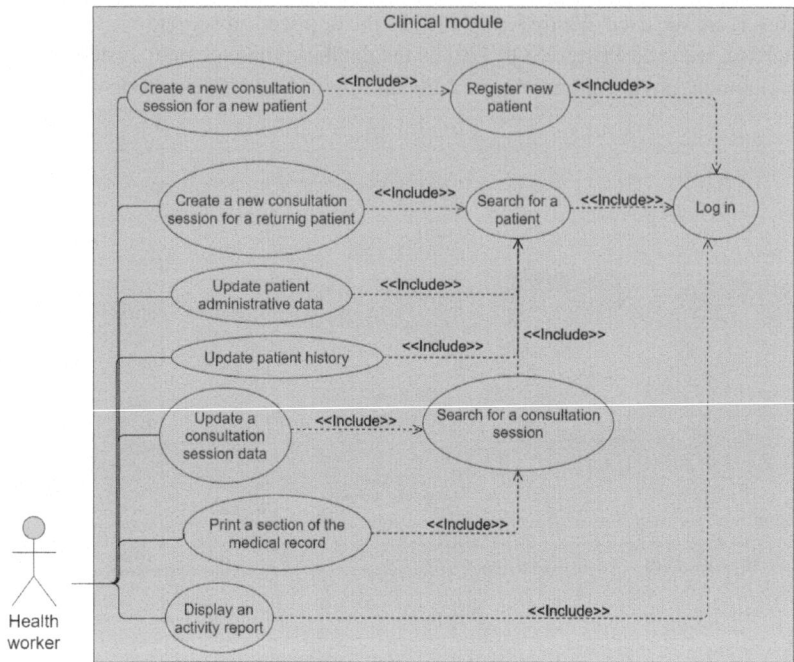

Fig. 8. Use case diagram

- The server: the server used is a desktop computer equipped with the Windows 10 operating system, configured as a server. It was installed in one of the rooms of the pediatrics department. A fixed IP address was assigned to it. The application server on which our module runs is WampServer;
- The local network: The local network set up is a wireless network. The access point used emits a low range signal, which is amplified by two repeaters, so that it is possible to connect to the application from different rooms of the department;
- The client devices: The client devices from which users access the module are smartphones, tablets, laptops and desktop computers (able to connect to the wifi signal);

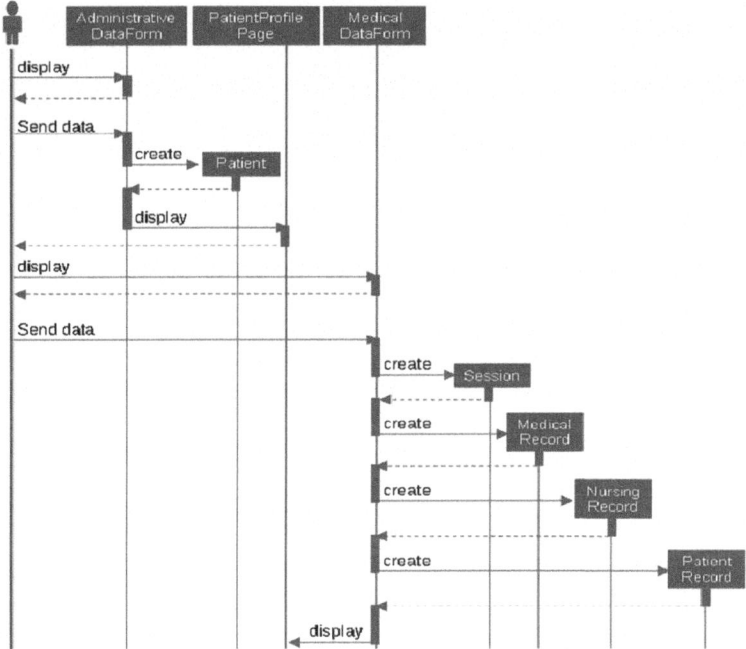

Fig. 9. Sequence diagram: create a new consultation session for a new patient

3   Results

3.1   The Generated EHR

Our EHR module called *"iDossier"* allows generating an EHR as presented below in its version 1.0. In accordance with our concept and the structure we have defined in our methodology, the EHR presented in the illustrations below is a unique XML object, loaded from the database, and then formatted using an XSL style sheet.

This XML document, attached to one and only one patient, contains all the patient's data (history, administrative, clinical, paraclinical, and therapeutic data), collected for each episodes of illness. Any intervention on the patient's data (recording a new episode of illness, recording or updating clinical, paraclinical, or therapeutic data) results in an update of this synthetic XML document, either by adding new nodes (new data) or by modifying nodes (updating data).

This single document allows for both a vertical observation of data (within a single department) and a cross-sectional observation (across different departments). It is possible to navigate within this file by expanding the nodes. Since it is an XML document, XQuery or XPath queries can be used to extract and cross-reference data as needed (Figs. 11, 12, 13 and 14).

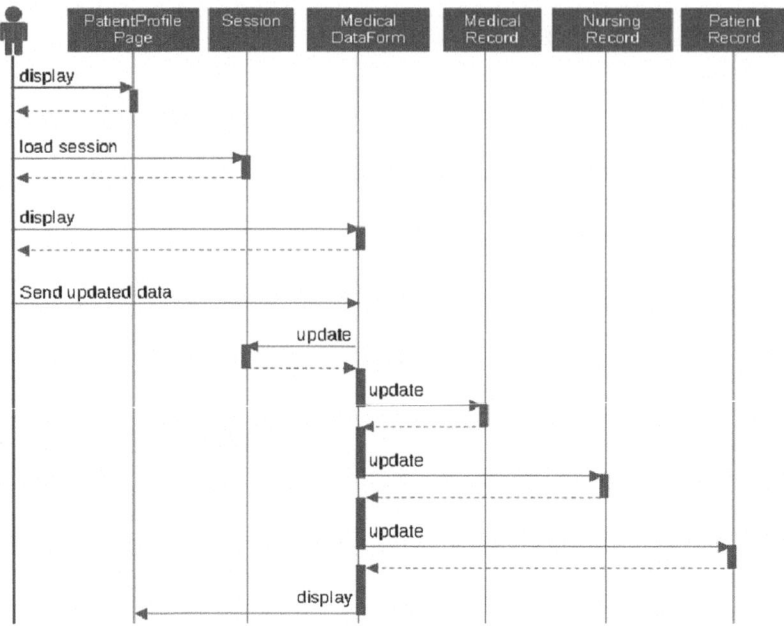

Fig. 10. Sequence diagram: update a consultation session

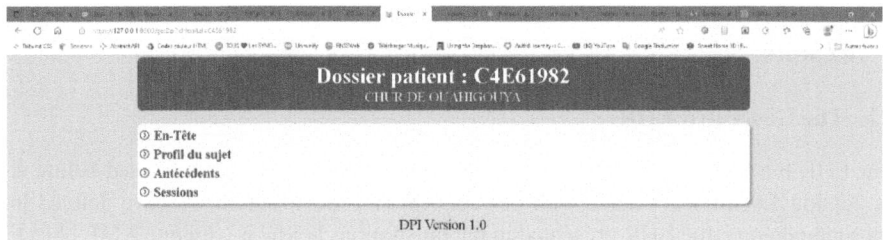

Fig. 11. The Electronic Health Record, with its four sections "header", "subject profile", "histories" and "sessions".

3.2 Implementation of the Module in the Pediatrics Department

The implementation of the module within the pediatrics department began on January 9th 2023. The first users involved were seventh year medical students and physicians. The routine that we put in place is as follow:

- In the emergency unit, all patients received (outpatients and patients to be hospitalized) are first recorded. This is immediately followed by the collection and recording of "medical data". This recording generates a digital version of the medical record in its entirety. The treatment and vital signs grid, constituting a part of the nursing record, is also generated for patients to be hospitalized;
- In the hospitalization unit, updates to the medical records of hospitalized patients during visits are made directly in their digital medical record;

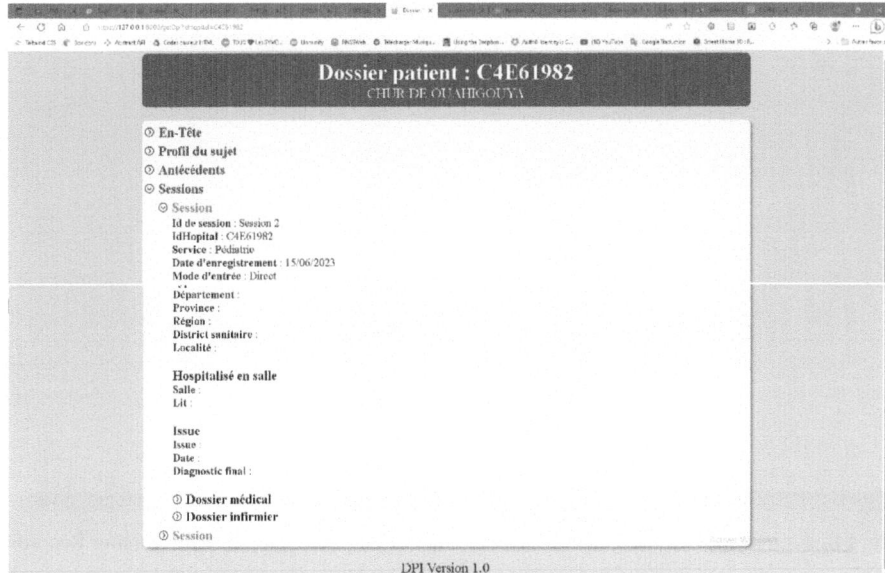

Fig. 12. An overview of a "consultation session" node, containing the corresponding consultation header data and the "Medical Record" and "Nursing Record" nodes, which respectively contain the data from the medical record and nursing record attached to the current episode of illness.

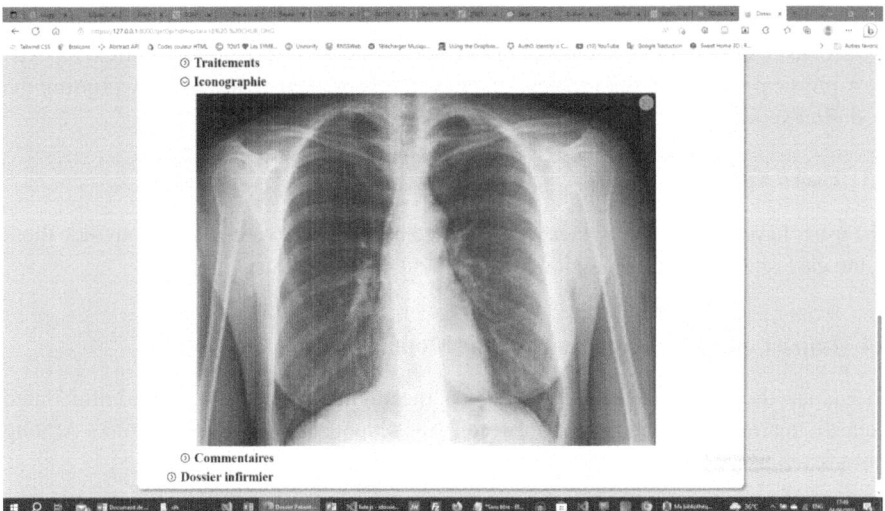

Fig. 13. An overview of the "Iconography" node. This node belongs to the "Medical Record" node and displays the iconographic data (imaging, printed examination report captures, and other photographs).

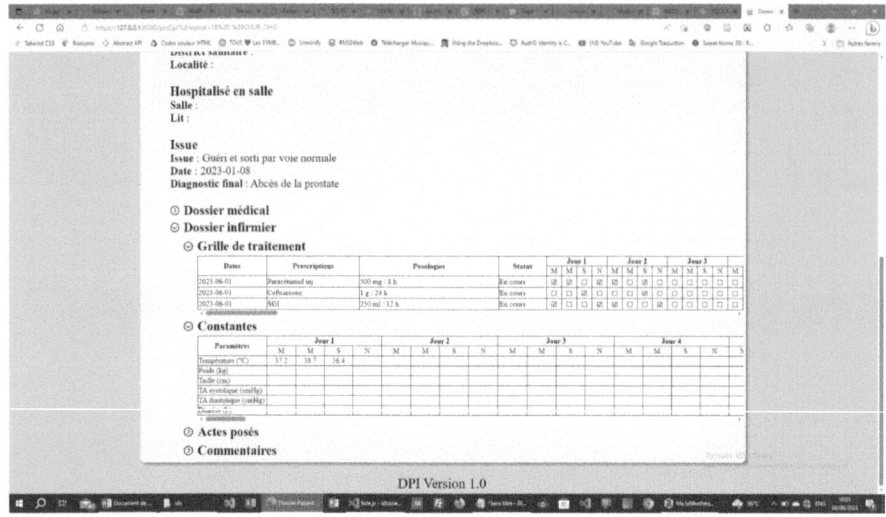

Fig. 14. An overview of the "Treatment grid" and "Vital signs grid" in the "Nursing Record" node.

– Interacting with the data from mobile devices (smartphones and tablets) allows users to be mobile during their tasks and instantly access these data from the patient's bedside;
– The statistics functionality offers tables that allow real-time notification of the received pathologies. The data available makes it easy to generate statistical reports;
– A physical version of the medical record can be obtained at any time by printing the digital version;

3.3 Users Adoption

The users have adopted the system put in place because we were able to convince them of the ease and benefits that digital management of patient data can bring.

3.4 Impact and User Experience of the Module

To evaluate the impact and user experience of the module among users, we administrated a questionnaire to the users who numbered 7 (the seventh year medical students). Among these seven users:

– All of them (7/7) said that the user interface is user-friendly;
– Five users (5/7) said that the functionalities meet all their needs;
– Only two users (2/7) said that the module offers them a time-saving benefit;
– All of them (7/7) said that searching for and accessing patient data is easy;
– Six users (6/7) said that using the module is easy;

3.5   Difficulties and Limitations

Lack of a Performant Network Infrastructure. The Ouahigouya Regional University Hospital Center does not have a usable network infrastructure for the implementation of our module. Some local networks exists, but they are intended for other purposes.

Logistical Difficulties. The local network was not steady. This sometimes caused interruptions or difficulties in connecting and accessing the module. During power outages, the absence of an uninterruptible power supply required the server to be manually restarted when power was restored.

Difficulties Related to a Lack of Training. The time we had for users training was insufficient. The difficulties in using the module were due to gaps resulting from this lack of prior training and practice.

4   Discussion

4.1   Technology Used

Our EHR module is based on web technologies. This type of technology is mature, proven, and offers ease of use and deployment [1]. For users, there are no constraints in terms of terminal compatibility. Any terminal (smartphone, tablet, laptop, and desktop computer), as long as it has a web browser that meets current standards, can be used to access the module.

Some systems have been designed as desktop applications. This is the case, for example, with MEDCAB in Cameroon [22]. While a desktop application requires each user to have a computer, the same is not true for a web application like ours. In the scenario we have established, tablets and smartphones were sufficient and much more practical for recording, updating, and consulting patient data, both in the reception and treatment room of the emergency unit and at the bedside of patients in the hospitalization unit.

4.2   Deployment of the Module

Setting up an HIS requires a network infrastructure that allows for the interconnection of the different departments of the hospital. The context of our work did not provide this framework. The HIS integrating our EHR module was thus deployed on a computer that served as a server, installed within the pediatrics department itself. In the context of the experimental implementation of the module, such a deployment may be sufficient, but the data cannot be shared with other departments.

4.3   Functional Coverage

A complete HIS integrates a set of modules and functionalities intended to meet the needs of the departments within the hospital [23]. Our HIS is in its embryonic stage and integrates only the bare essentials. The clinical module, which was designed based on the common needs in the pediatrics department of Ouahigouya regional university hospital center, includes only the functionalities related to the most commonly observed processes in the pediatrics department. The module as well as the HIS that houses it have been designed to easily accommodate future developments.

4.4 Users Adoption

All staff in the pediatrics department recognized the difficulties in managing and exploiting data related to paper-based records. Physicians, health assistants, nurses, as well as 7th-year intern trainees, embraced the implemented computer system. Other studies dealing with the implementation of EHRs in healthcare centers also mention good adherence by healthcare staff [1, 24, 25].

4.5 User Experience

The negative points identified in the user experience evaluation are mainly that the module does not offer a time-saving advantage compared to paper-based supports (5 of the 7 users). The reasons for this negative feedback were mainly the inability to provide users with adequate training beforehand. Indeed, the conditions for a good training on the use of the module were not met. The time allocated for training was only 3 h, just enough to present the interfaces and the functioning mode of the module. There was not really a training session. In addition, one of the users had not been able to attend the very short training session.

4.6 Challenges

In the implementation of our EHR module, we noted challenges that hindered the proper functioning of the system put in place. These included the absence of a performant network infrastructure, instability of the local wireless network setup, frequent power outages, and insufficient user training. Studies related to the implementation of EHRs in developing countries have also identified these same challenges [26, 27]. The malfunctions attributable to poor quality of the local network and power outages were not only causing frustration among users but also leading to parallel use of physical records. It is therefore crucial to address these challenges in order to fully harness the potential that an EHR can bring. To tackle these challenges, the commitment of hospital leaders and healthcare authorities in the country to EHR implementation should be one of the primary determinants. These leaders and authorities should prioritize EHR implementation programs. It is through the determination of these leaders that solutions to the various barriers we have observed in our EHR implementation will emerge. According to *Odekunle et al.*, facilitating factors for EHR implementation in Sub-Saharan African countries include implementation planning through the definition of realistic goals, initial and ongoing user training, financial support from authorities, and the adoption of an appropriate system [26].

5   Conclusion

Based on a systematic study of the needs and business processes of the pediatrics department of Ouahigouya regional university hospital center, we designed and implemented the embryo of an HIS integrating an EHR module. The processes that run in this department are standard processes found in most clinical departments and other hospitals. The result we have achieved can therefore be transposed to other clinical departments and, consequently, to other hospitals. Our work is a first experimental local implementation of its kind in a reference healthcare center in Burkina Faso. The multilateral monitoring we carried out during this implementation allowed us to identify the essential factors for a successful integration of digitalization within our healthcare centers. It remains that the first responsible parties of these centers and health authorities need to be more involved in supporting this integration through concrete measures.

References

1. Bagayoko, C.: Mise en place d'un système d'information hospitalier en Afrique francophone: cinz@n, étude et validation du modèle au Mali, These de doctorat, Aix-Marseille 2, 2010. Consulté le: 7 septembre 2022. https://www.theses.fr/2010AIX20680

2. Aubain, D., Les logiciels libres SIH une solution pour le démarrage de ce type de projet dans les hôpitaux des pays du Sud en particulier, avr. 2016

3. Ly, O., et al.: Utilisation des Applications du Systeme d'Information Hospitaliere (SIH) des Hopitaux et Centres de Sante de Reference (CSREF) de Bamako et de Kati Au Mal, Revue Malienne de Science et de Technologie, vol. 1, no. 24 (2020)

4. Degoulet, P.: Les systèmes d'information hospitaliers. In: Venot, A., Burgun, A., Quantin, C. (eds.) Informatique médicale, e-Santé: Fondements et applications, pp. 307–330. Springer, Paris (2013). https://doi.org/10.1007/978-2-8178-0338-8_12

5. Menachemi, N., Collum, T.H.: Benefits and drawbacks of electronic health record systems. Risk Manag. Healthc. Policy **4**, 47–55 (2011). https://doi.org/10.2147/RMHP.S12985

6. Barro, S.G., Ugon, A., Nana, N.R., Staccini, P.: Patient's unique identifier for efficient and secure monitoring of pregnant women in Burkina Faso. In: Mantas, J., Hasman, A., Househ, M.S., Gallos, P., Zoulias, E., Liaskos, J. (eds.) Studies in Health Technology and Informatics. IOS Press (2022). https://doi.org/10.3233/SHTI210931

7. ISO/TR 20514:2005(en), Health informatics — Electronic health record — Definition, scope and context. https://www.iso.org/obp/ui/#iso:std:iso:tr:20514:ed-1:v1:en. consulté le 10 septembre 2023

8. Häyrinen, K., Saranto, K., Nykänen, P.: Definition, structure, content, use and impacts of electronichealth records: a review of the research literature. 26 septembre 2014

9. Chituc, C.-M.: XML interoperability standards for seamless communication: an analysis of industry-neutral and domain-specific initiatives. Comput. Ind. **92-93**, 118–136 (2017). https://doi.org/10.1016/j.compind.2017.06.010

10. XPath and XQuery Functions and Operators 3.1. https://www.w3.org/TR/xpath-functions-31/. consulté le 8 septembre 2023

11. Addo-Tenkorang, R., Helo, P.: Enterprise Resource Planning (ERP): A Review Literature Report (2011). https://doi.org/10.13140/2.1.3254.7844

12. Sebai, J., Yatim, F.: Approche centrée sur le patient et nouvelle gestion publique : confluence et paradoxe. Santé Publique **30**(4), 517 (2018). https://doi.org/10.3917/spub.185.0517

13. Chinosi, M., Trombetta, A.: BPMN: an introduction to the standard. Comput. Stand. Interfaces **34**(1), 124–134 (2012). https://doi.org/10.1016/j.csi.2011.06.002
14. Hussain, A., Sharma, P.K.: Deployment of web application in LAN based 3 tier architecture. IJSRCSEIT 341–345 (2019). https://doi.org/10.32628/CSEIT195661
15. Symfony: Symfony, High Performance PHP Framework for Web Development. https://symfony.com/what-is-symfony. consulté le 24 septembre 2022
16. Looping - Modélisation Conceptuelle de Données. https://www.looping-mcd.fr/. consulté le 11 décembre 2022
17. AJAX Introduction. https://www.w3schools.com/xml/ajax_intro.asp. consulté le 11 décembre 2022
18. Symfony: Creating and Using Templates (Symfony Docs). https://symfony.com/doc/current/templates.html. consulté le 11 décembre 2022
19. WampServer: WampServer. https://www.wampserver.com/. consulté le 11 décembre 2022
20. PostgreSQL Global Development Group: PostgreSQL, PostgreSQL, 11 décembre 2022. https://www.postgresql.org/. consulté le 11 décembre 2022
21. Visual Studio Code - Code Editing. Redefined. https://code.visualstudio.com/. consulté le 11 décembre 2022
22. Kamadjeu, R., Tapang, E., Moluh, R.: Designing and implementing an electronic health record system in primary care practice in sub-Saharan Africa: a case study from Cameroon. Inform. Primary Care **13**, 179–186 (2005). https://doi.org/10.14236/jhi.v13i3.595
23. Nøhr, C.: Evaluation of electronic health record systems. Yearb. Med. Inform. **15**(01), 107–113 (2006). https://doi.org/10.1055/s-0038-1638481
24. Tubaishat, A.: Evaluation of electronic health record implementation in hospitals. CIN Comput. Inform. Nurs. **35**(7), 364 (2017). https://doi.org/10.1097/CIN.0000000000000328
25. Antwi, F.M.: A case study on impact of electronic health records system (EHRS) on healthcare quality at asamankese government hospital. In Review, preprint (2022). https://doi.org/10.21203/rs.3.rs-2023326/v1
26. Odekunle, F.F., Odekunle, R.O., Shankar, S.: Why sub-Saharan Africa lags in electronic health record adoption and possible strategies to increase its adoption in this region. Int. J. Health Sci. (Qassim) **11**(4), 59–64 (2017). Consulté le: 9 septembre 2023. https://www.ncbi.nlm.nih.gov/pmc/articles/PMC5654179/
27. Acquah-Swanzy, M.: Evaluating electronic health record systems in Ghana: the case of Effia Nkwanta Regional Hospital. Master thesis, UiT Norges arktiske universitet (2015). Consulté le: 3 juin 2023. https://munin.uit.no/handle/10037/8080

Emergency Severity Index (ESI), A More Suitable System for Emergencies in Burkina Faso

Roland M. Tougma[1], Boureima Zerbo[2]([✉]), Désiré Guel[1]([✉]), and P. Justin Kouraogo[1]

[1] Université Joseph KI ZERBO, Ouagadougou, Burkina Faso
guel.desire@gmail.com
[2] Université Thomas SANKARA, Ouagadougou/Saaba, Burkina Faso
bzerbo@gmail.com

Abstract. The triage system an emergency department must prioritize the patients' needs above all else. Additionally, it enables improved care organization based on client type, institutional mission, and available resources. In order to conduct effective triage, the Orientation and Reception Nurse (ORN) should employ a reliable, valid, and reproducible tool that considers the specificities of both pediatric and adult patients in prehospital medicine, as well as the national healthcare. The aim is to assess the validity and reliability of existing triage systems in emergency care, with the ultimate objective of developing an emergency triage system tailored to Burkina. To achieve this, our focus will be on identifying reliable and valid triage systems, which will serve as a basis for proposing or adapting a suitable triage system for Burkina Faso.

Keywords: Emergency Severity Index (ESI) · Electrocardiogram (ECG) · Pulse Oxymetry · Healthcare · patient · triage

1 Introduction

Triage is a critical process in emergency departments (EDs) that involves assessing and prioritizing patients based on the severity of their condition and the available resources. Its primary objective is to ensure that critical patients receive timely and suitable care, while efficiently managing limited. Triage systems have been developed and implemented in various countries, including several African nations. Burkina Faso does not have an official triage system for patients, it will be discussed after the review to propose a triage system in Burkina Faso. By implementing an effective triage system in Burkina Faso, healthcare providers can deliver prompt and appropriate care to patients, ultimately saving lives and enhancing overall operations within the emergency department.

© ICST Institute for Computer Sciences, Social Informatics and Telecommunications Engineering 2025
Published by Springer Nature Switzerland AG 2025. All Rights Reserved
A. Sere et al. (Eds.): AFRICOMM 2023, LNICST 587, pp. 247–255, 2025.
https://doi.org/10.1007/978-3-031-81570-6_16

2 Research Methodology

In our comprehensive literature review, we considered the most recent updated versions of various triage systems and prioritized studies that provided analytical data. The implementation of these triage systems has been reinforced in China and numerous other countries, largely due to the impact of COVID-19 [1–3]. We performed a systematic review using a broad search strategy to identify all studies evaluating the performance of triage systems in emergency care against any reference standard that approximates the actual patient emergency, specifically in the African zone where resources (material and personnel) are particularly limited. Given the absence of an official triage system in Burkina Faso, our approach relied on observational methods. After a thorough review of valid and reliable triage systems around the world, such as the Emergency Severity Index (ESI) [4] and the Canadian Triage and Acuity Scale (CTAS) [5], there's also the Manchester Triage System [6], not forgetting the Australasian Triage Scale (ATS) [7] and the Pediatric Emergency Care Applied Research Network (PECARN) [8]. Closer to home, South Africa offers the South African Triage Score (SATS) [9], while Malawi opts for the Emergency Triage, Assessment and Treatment (ETAT) [10]. Better still are systems based on Artificial Intelligence [1]. We found that the triage methods used in Burkina Faso's health centers were closer to the ESI model. However, it is important to note that the health environment in Burkina Faso lacks material and human resources. With the aim of adapting an established practice, we have customized the ESI model to incorporate the collection of patients' vital signs and medical history, thus providing a triage framework suited to our specific context.

3 Related Work

Several triage systems have been created worldwide to help emergency services optimize care, such as ESI [4, 13], CTAS [5], MTS [6], ATS [7], PECARN [8]. Each attempt to tropicalize triage procedures according to resources and local context, such as intelligent systems [1, 11] or MEWS [12], SATS [1, 11, 14]. In Africa, there have been significant advancements in triage systems in emergency departments in recent years like SATS [9], ETAT [10], MEWS [12] or ESI [13]. These advancements aim to enhance the efficiency and efficacy of patient care; particularly in resource-limited environments. Here are some examples of triage systems that have been developed within African emergency departments:

3.1 South African Triage Scale (SATS)

South African Triage Scale (SATS) [9] is widely utilized as a triage system not only in South Africa but also in several other African countries. Its primary objective is to ensure that patients receive appropriate and timely medical care based on the severity of their condition. SATS employs a combination of physiological parameters, presenting complaints, and clinical judgment to assign patients into one of four triage categories: emergency, very urgent, urgent, and non-urgent. One of key strengths of the South African Triage Scale (SATS) is the simplicity and ease of use [14]: SATS is intentionally designed to be a simple and user-friendly triage system [14]. It allows for a rapid assessment of patients and appropriate allocation of resources based on their needs. Note also that SATS is culturally appropriate [15, 16].

However, like any triage system, SATS has both strengths and weaknesses. In some instances, due to the system's simplicity, patients with potentially serious conditions may be assigned a lower priority [17, 18], resulting in delayed care. Additionally, the subjectivity of individual assessors can influence the triage outcomes [17, 19].

3.2 Emergency Triage, Assessment, and Treatment (ETAT)

ETAT [20] is a systematic approach widely employed in emergency medical settings to prioritize patient care and optimize resource allocation [10]. It follows a standardized set of guidelines and protocols, reducing variability in care and improving quality and safety. ETAT can be effectively implemented across diverse emergency settings, encompassing hospitals, clinics, and mobile healthcare services, with adaptations specifically tailored to pediatric emergencies [21].

An invaluable asset of the ETAT is that ETAT facilitates effective communication among healthcare professionals involved in the emergency response. However, we noted that different healthcare professionals may interpret a patient's condition differently, leading to inconsistencies and errors in patient management [22]. Furthermore, challenges arise from limited availability of healthcare providers, as well as shortages in essential equipment and medications, which can impact the ability to deliver timely and comprehensive care. Therefore, a comprehensive evaluation of patients becomes crucial in addressing their complete healthcare needs [22].

3.3 Emergency Severity Index (ESI)

The Emergency Severity Index (ESI) [4] is an algorithm used for classifying patients into distinct acuity levels, enabling effective triage decisions and resource allocation. It considers both adult and pediatric triage and employs four decision points (A, B, C, and D) to assign patients to one of five triage levels.

We give below the four-decision points witch can be reduced to four key questions represented in Fig. 1: **A**: Does this patient require immediate intervention to be saved? **B**: Is this a patient who should not wait? **C**: How many resources will this patient need? **D**: What are the patient's vital signs?

4 Emergency Severity Index Like Triage System in Burkina Faso (ESI)

The utilization of a level 5 scale is not widely implemented across all emergency departments in Burkina Faso. Consequently, the assessment of severity levels is subjectively determined by the personnel receiving the patients. Upon arrival, the patient has direct access to the examination room [23]. If this room is already occupied, the patient is placed on the waiting bench in the corridor. There is no reception service as such that's but also, the triage system currently used in our health centers looks more like ESI [4]. Taking into consideration the practices of emergency physicians and aiming to enhance

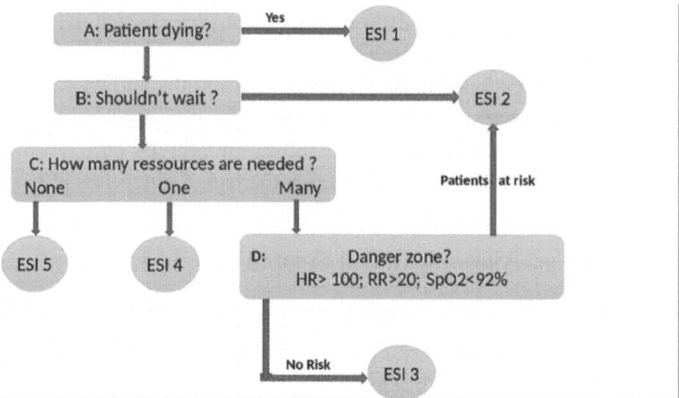

Fig. 1. ESI algorithm

the system, we have adopted the ESI as our triage system. We have implemented the ESI algorithm, with the exception that we propose the automatic collection of vital signs (within milliseconds). Another advantage lies in the simplicity of its algorithm, alongside our efforts to provide access to vital signs and patient medical histories. These contributions mark the current stage of our thesis.

4.1 Vital Signs Acquisition Scheme Design

The solution is to design a tool that automatically detects vital constants (D of the ESI algorithm) shown in Fig. 2. This sensor of physiological data such as oxygen level, pulse, ECG, pressure (Fig. 3), are automatically detected and displayed on the screen with the possibility to print. This module is suitable for ambulances and fire departments and makes the printed data available at the same time as the patient is admitted to the hospital.

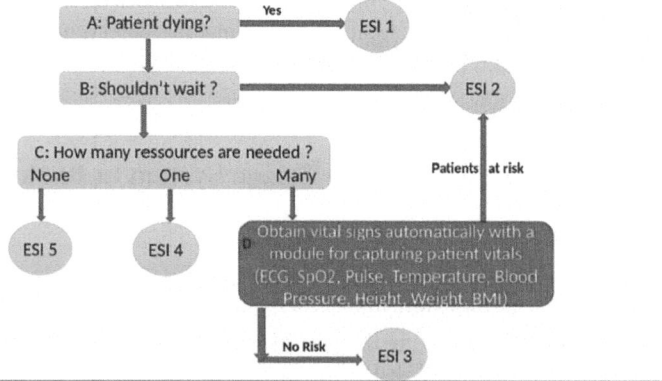

Fig. 2. ESI algorithm adapted in Burkina Faso

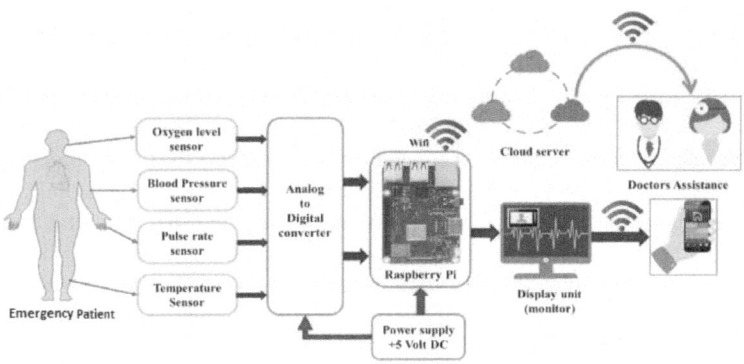

Fig. 3. Automatic vital signs capture process

4.2 Medical History Obtaining Process

Equipped with a Wi-Fi module, data collected by the patient is automatically synchronized with the monitor and the electronic medical record based on the International Classification of Diseases version 11 (ICD11) [28] and taking into account interoperability standards used in the healthcare field [29]. If there is no connection, patient data can be printed out and updated at a later date. To validate our tests, we developed an electronic patient health record. It should be noted that this idea is supported and defended by the Burkina Faso Ministry of Health, which wishes to set up a patient health record valid in Burkina Faso's health centers. This helps also to enhanced communication: ours works facilitate effective communication among healthcare professionals involved in the emergency response by using a common language terminology and unique patient identifier (Patient ID), it ensures clear and concise communication, leading to better coordination and teamwork.

5 Results and Discussion

In order to validate our findings, we conducted a comparative study on measurement speed within emergency department. The objective was to compare our newly developed automated vitals capture tool with the current manual method used by the hospital. To assess the time required for vital signs measurement using the manual method, we visited 10 healthcare facilities and recorded the duration of each measurement for 55 patients. During our visits, we identified that 5 measuring devices were faulty, representing 10% of the study population, and thus we excluded these patients from our analysis. The number of patients considered in this study is 50. The measurement time of the manual method (for the most part several minutes (Mn)) compares with our so-called automatic method, which takes a few milliseconds (mis) to take vital signs of 50 patients.

5.1 Results

We proceeded by analyzing the time required for measuring the constants. The data was obtained nearly instantaneously, in milliseconds. The doctor or nurse in charge took the saturometer or blood pressure monitor to measure the patient's vital signs, and we timed the process. It should be noted that in some cases, the device is faulty, and we either have to shake it, charge the batteries or go to another department to take a printout. In such cases, we don't take the time into account, as it becomes abnormally long, and we therefore consider them as outliers. The table below compares the measurement time for each constant. The data includes the average measurement time for each vital sign, both for all 50 patients and for each method (automatic and manual). The total number of patients is 50, and the average measurement time is computed by summing the duration for each patient and dividing it by the total number of patients, i.e., 50. For instance, the average weight measurements are calculated using the following formula:

$$\text{Average Weigth} = \sum_{n=1}^{50} \left(\frac{Duration\,for\,each\,patient}{50} \right)$$

$Average_{weight} = 13800$ ms *for Manual method*
$Average_{weight} = 5,18$ ms *for Automatic method*

The other data in the table are obtained using the same formula and are listed in the table below:

Methods	weight measurement time in milliseconds	Size measurement time in milliseconds	Temperature Measurement tine in milliseconds	Pouls Measurement tine in milliseconds
Manual method (MM)	138000	257520	435780	299460
Automatic method (AM)	5, 18	5,20	5,9578	4,8958
Time saved (TS) = MM-AM	137994,8436 = 2,28 mn	257514,793 = 4,29 mn	435774,042 = 7,26 mn	299455,076 = 4,99 mn
Methods	Oxygene saturation (SpO2) measurement time in milliseconds	Electrocardiogram (ECG) measurement time in milliseconds	Blood Pressure Measurement tine in milliseconds	Body Mass Index (BMI) Measurement tine in milliseconds
Manual method (MM)	1187880	519660	355920	137520
Automatic method (AM)	5,9578	4,7734	7,550446809	3,7316
Time saved (TS) = MM-AM	1187874,044 = 1,97 mn	519655,225 = 8,66 mn	355912,45 = 5,93 mn	137516,25 = 2,29 mn

We present the differences between the two measurement methods through the following graphs.

Figures 4 and 5 summarize the difference in measurement between the two methods: one is fast, stable and predictable (brown), while the other (blue) is slow (average measurement time is 6 minutes for Oxygen saturation (SpO2) and temperature (see table)) and unpredictable because it is manual. This time is invaluable for attending to other patients. Beyond the speed of measurement, these two graphs tell us that automatic measurement is reliable and valid no matter who measures it, whereas manual measurement

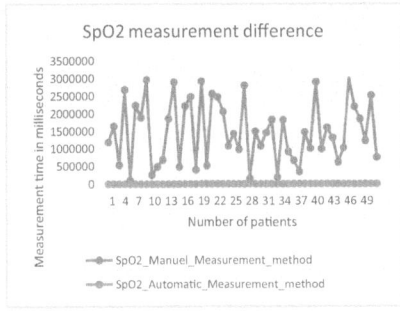

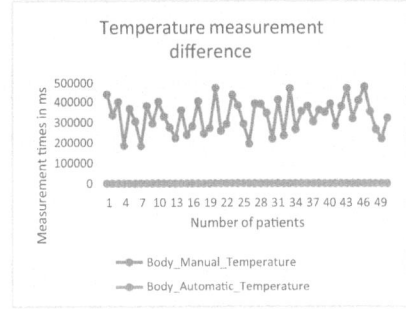

Fig. 4. SpO2 Measurement difference   **Fig. 5.** Temperature measurement difference

requires a minimum of experience (the more experience you have, the more accurate your measurement). This is why the curve for manual measurement varies.

5.2 Strengths and Weaknesses

This literature review is based on a comprehensive and systematic search and has attempted to include as many relevant studies as possible. This study is a synthesis that aims to find a more pragmatic approach to sorting systems in Burkina Faso in order to propose a system that can be easily used. After observation, we noted that some centers resemble the ESI sorting model in practice. In view of the fact that study data on the validity [24] and reliability of the ESI [25] sorting system [26] was available, we opted for a model that could be adopted in Burkina Faso. As a major contribution, ESI does not tell you how to obtain vital signs, so we have proposed a tool to automatically capture vital signs and make them available for emergencies. We're also aware that a patient's medical history is essential for proper care, which is why we've integrated the patient's electronic health record. This record retrieves data on the patient's vital signs during the consultation. However, this remains a proposal that needs to be accepted and adapted by Burkina Faso's healthcare stakeholders. This study does not take into account the optimization of resources, which is why we have to take this into account in the rest of this article.

6 Conclusions

Triage is essential, as it is the only option for managing patient flow in the emergency room. It's important to note that there are many triage tools available worldwide. Each tool is well adapted to the area of action, medical policies and available resources. This is why we chose to adapt the ESI triage system to Burkina Faso, given its ease of use and good inter- and extra-judge correlation [27, 28]. We proposed a rapid solution for obtaining vital signs and patient consultation histories.

6.1 Strengths and Weaknesses

After proposing methods for measuring vital signs and medical histories based on the Internet of Medical Objects, the next stage of our work will focus on optimizing healthcare resources in a world where there is a real shortage of them.

References

1. Lee, J.-T.: Prediction of hospitalization using artificial intelligence for urgent patients in the emergency department. Sci. Rep. (2021)
2. Liu, Y., et al.: Development and validation of a practical machine-learning triage algorithm for the detection of patients in need of critical care in the emergency department. Sci. Rep. 11 (2021)
3. Chen, Y., Ismail, R., Cheema, M.R., Ting, D.S., Masri, I.: Implementation of a new telephone triage system in ophthalmology emergency department during COVID-19 pandemic: clinical effectiveness, safety and patient satisfaction. Eye 36, 1126–1128 (2022)
4. Wuerz, R.C., Travers, D., Gilboy, N., Eitel, D.R., Rosenau, A., Yazhari, R.: Implementation and refinement of the emergency severity index. Acad. Emergency Med. (2008)
5. Ding, Y., Park, E., Nagarajan, M., Grafstein, E.: Patient prioritization in emergency department triage systems: an empirical study of the Canadian triage and acuity scale (CTAS), 28 April 2018
6. Dewitte, K.: Audit of a computerized version of the Manchester triage system and a SIRS-based system for the detection of sepsis at triage in the emergency department (2022)
7. Hodge, A., Hugman, A., Varndell, W., Howes, K.: A review of the quality assurance processes for the Australasian Triage Scale (ATS) and implications for future practice (2013)
8. Nakhjavan-Shahraki, B.: Pediatric emergency care applied research network (PECARN) prediction rules in identifying high risk children with mild traumatic brain injury. Eur. J. Med. (2017)
9. Rosedale, K.: The effectiveness of the South African Triage Score (SATS) in a rural emergency department: original article. South Afr. Med. J. 101(8) (2011)
10. King, C.: Paediatric emergency triage, assessment and treatment (ETAT) – preparedness for implementation at primary care facilities in Malawi. Nat. Libr. Med. (2021)
11. Liu, Y., et al.: Development and validation of a practical machine-learning triage algorithm for the detection of patients in need of critical care in the emergency department. Sci. Rep. 11 (2021)
12. Kruisselbrink, R.: Modified early warning score (MEWS) identifies critical illness among ward patients in a resource restricted setting in Kampala, Uganda: a prospective observational study. Nat. Libr. Med. (2016)
13. Mirhaghi, A.: The culture of care interfacing internal validity of emergency severity index 42, P297–298 (2016)
14. EMSSA: The South African Triage Scale (SATS) (2017)
15. Dixon, J.: Using the South African triage scale for prehospital triage: a qualitative study. BMC Emerg. Med. 125 (2021)
16. Dalwai, M.: Reliability and accuracy of the South African triage scale when used by nurses in the emergency department of Timergara Hospital, Pakistan: research. Afr. J. (2014)
17. Mould-Millman, N.-K.: Validity and reliability of the South African triage scale in prehospital providers. BMC Emerg. Med. (2021)
18. Rominski, S.: The implementation of the South African Triage Score (SATS) in an urban teaching hospital, Ghana. Afr. J. Emerg. Med. 4, 71–75 (2014)

19. Markussen, D.L.: Validation of a modified South African triage scale in a high-resource setting: a retrospective cohort study. Scand. J. Trauma Resusc. Emerg. Med. 31, 13 (2023)
20. World Health Organization: Emergency Triage Assessment and Treatment (ETAT) course. Training Mater. (2005)
21. Crouse, H.L.: Impact of an Emergency Triage Assessment and Treatment (ETAT)-based triage process in the paediatric emergency department of a Guatemalan public hospital. Paediatr. Int. Child Health 36 (2015)
22. Twomey, M.: Limitations in validating emergency department triage scales 24(7), 477–479 (2007)
23. Study of the management of medical emergencies at the Centre Hospitalier National Yalgado Ouedraogo
24. Elshove-Bolk, J.: Validation of the Emergency Severity Index (ESI) in self-referred patients in a European emergency department. Med. J. 24, 170–174 (2007)
25. Tanabe, P., Gimbel, R., Yarnold, P.R., Kyriacou, D.N., Adams, J.G.: Reliability and validity of scores on the emergency severity index version 3. Acad. Emerg. Med. (2008)
26. Esmailian, M.: Inter-rater agreement of emergency nurses and physicians in emergency severity index (ESI) triage. Emerg (Tehran) 4 (2014). https://pubmed.ncbi.nlm.nih.gov/264 95372/
27. Friedman, R.: The use of and satisfaction with the emergency severity index. J. Emerg. Nurs. 38, 120–126 (2012)
28. World Health Organization: Publication of ICD-11 2022 (2022)
29. Torab-Miandoab, A., et al.: Interoperability of heterogeneous health information systems: a systematic literature review. Nat. Libr. Med. (2023)

Cybersecurity and Privacy

The State of Data Breaches in the African Cyberspace: A Trend Analysis Using Social Media and Research Literature

Jabu Mtsweni[1,2], Muyowa Mutemwa[1(✉)], Mfundo Masango[1], Samson Chishiri[1], and Siwe Moyakhe[1]

[1] Council for Scientific and Industrial Research (CSIR), Information and Cyber Security Centre, Pretoria, South Africa
{mmutemwa,mmasango1,schishiri,smoyakhe}@csir.co.za
[2] Stellenbosch University, Military Academy, Stellenbosch, South Africa

Abstract. Cybersecurity attacks are classified in the top 10 global risks by the World Economic Forum in 2023. The common cyber-incidents that affect businesses, governments, and individuals across the globe are data breaches. Recent reports indicate that these incidents are on the rise, with an estimation of over 12 billion personal records breached, impacting on individual's privacy and organization's reputation. Comprehensive insight on data breaches in Africa is not readily available as reporting of these incidents by victims is not mandatory in many African countries, and available trends tend to be limited and scattered. This paper aims to provide a contextual understanding of data breach trends in Africa using social media data (current) and research literature (past). The data from social media, including news websites, were collected over a 3-month period tracking data breaches in the African content, whilst the research literature focused on prominent data breaches in African countries between 2020 and 2023. The research results indicate the data breaches trend that is on the rise in Africa with Nigeria showing higher engagements on social media, whilst South Africa being the data breach haven with a large exposure of personal data online. The impact of data breaches on customers and businesses in Africa is determined as being negative and unabated. This paper recommends practical and evidence-based security controls to minimize data breaches.

Keywords: Cybersecurity · Information Security · Data breach · African Cyberspace · Cyber Attacks

1 Introduction

Data is growing faster and, in more places, than we think [1]. This is fueled mainly because organizations sometimes do not even know their entire data universe. Data breach, leakages, and/or exposure are bound to happen, and this is supported by the 59% of data breaches observed globally in 2022 alone [1]. As such, it is agreed by various experts that data breaches are becoming more common and have been on the rise for

A. Sere et al. (Eds.): AFRICOMM 2023, LNICST 587, pp. 259–273, 2025.
https://doi.org/10.1007/978-3-031-81570-6_17

several years, and this trend isn't slowing down. As countries take steps to implement data protection laws, it is evident, at least based on [2], that African countries are lagging behind on data protection laws with only a handful of African countries having robust data protection laws [2].

In South Africa, the increasing trend in data breaches is also observed through data breach notifications to the Information Regular. By June 2023, the Information Regulator in South Africa had received over 1,021 data breach notifications, which is double the number that was reported in the previous five months of the same year [3]. In February 2023, the Nigerian Data Protection Bureau (NDPB) announced that it was investigating over 110 companies over allegations of privacy and data breaches [4]. The Communications Authority of Kenya (CAK) reported that the number of cyber threats had more than doubled in the financial year 2021–2022, attributing this to the growth of internet users as well as digital transformation in the country [5].

These events clearly indicate that cyber incidents, particularly data breaches pose a serious threat to the African cyberspace and its users. These incidents are no longer merely a technological issue but have a direct impact on business reputations and personal privacy. Nevertheless, the research-based understanding of data breach trends in Africa is still limited to business reports and newspapers articles.

This study, therefore, seeks to understand the trend of data breaches in Africa using social media analysis as well as research literature reviews. This is done to contextualize the phenomenon from different perspectives using current and historical reports and data, which may provide comprehensive insights and research-based evidence on the scale of this scourge including its impact as well as possible mitigations.

The rest of this paper is structured as follows; Sect. 2 covers the general global data breach trends to lay the foundation for focusing on the African cyberspace. Section 3 describes the research objectives and approach that underpin the research presented in this paper. In Sect. 4, we cover the first phase of the analysis focusing on the social media data analysis and complementing this with the research literature analysis of data breaches in Africa in Sect. 5, which is phase 2 of the research study. Section 6 provides a discussion and implications of data breaches in the African cyberspace taking into consideration the two-phased analyses. The research paper is concluded with recommendations to decision-makers in Sect. 7.

2 Global Data Breach Trends

On a global scale, cybersecurity attacks, including data attacks are ever increasing, and this is caused in part by the rising number of software and hardware vulnerabilities reported and recorded on the National Vulnerability Database (NVD). Figure 1 shows that in the last five (5) years the disclosed number of vulnerabilities have been on the increase. The severity of the vulnerabilities that are classified as critical or high, does not always translate to the impact as also being severe. This is because exploiting a vulnerability depends on several factors such as the environment wherein the vulnerability is found, the human factor, availability of an exploit code, and value of the digital asset.

According to [6], the increase over the years in the number of vulnerabilities could mean that researchers are discovering more vulnerabilities; or that there is a high number

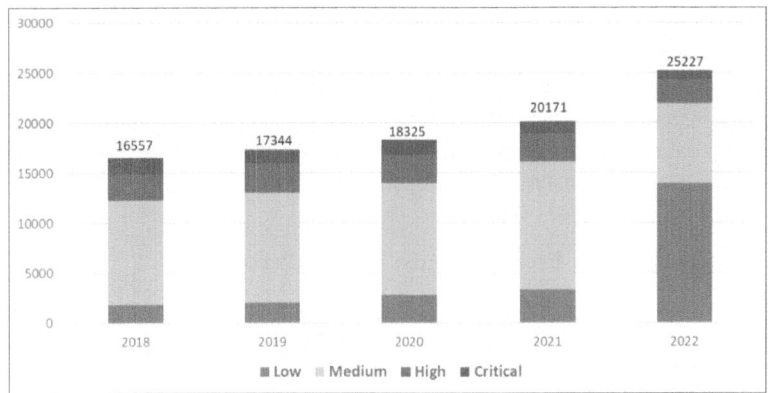

Fig. 1. Vulnerabilities per year since 2018.

of software or hardware that is released with vulnerabilities. This has a direct impact on the trend of data breaches and other cyber incidents. According to [7], threat actors are becoming successful with data breaches through the exploitation of disclosed vulnerabilities found in different software and hardware, including security tools. As such there seems to be a direct link between the number of disclosed vulnerabilities and the rate of data breaches.

The following two subsections give a high-level look at data breach trends seen on a global scale as discussed in Subsect. 2.1 and in the African scale as discussed in Subsect. 2.2 below.

2.1 Cybersecurity Data Breach Trends: Global Perspective

According to the Verizon Data Breach Investigations Report (DBIR) of 2023 [8], Business Email Compromise (BEC) amounted to 50% of social engineering attacks. DBIR also shows the presence of ransomware in 24% of data breaches. One of the major factors seen in the report is that 74% of data breaches was due to a human factor, of which 84% of that human factor element originated from external sources, largely driven by a financial gain. The DBIR lists the three major techniques by which organization were breached, which are: *stolen credentials, phishing attacks,* and the *exploitation of both disclosed and zero-day vulnerabilities.*

According to the Sophos Survey [9], over the years cyber-criminals have been developing and sharing tools through ransomware-as-a-service and this has resulted in more organizations across the world being hit with ransomware-related data breaches. The survey states that 66% of organizations across the world had experienced a ransomware breach between 2020 and 2023. The survey report further states that between the years 2020 and 2023, there was a noticeable reduction in the number of breaches related to ransomware as was the case in 2021, however, in general the trend graph has shown an aggregated steady increase of data breaches over that same period. From the Sophos survey report [9] looking at the year 2023, Singapore was the country with the highest rate of ransomware attacks with 84% of organizations in that country experiencing a ransomware breach. In contrast, the United Kingdom had the lowest surveyed rate of 44% ransomware breaches. What was noticeable is that South Africa had the biggest increase in the number ransomware breaches between 2020 and 2023. What the survey also suggest is that 30% of the organizations that had experienced a ransomware breach also had their data stolen and used as extortion, thus contributing to 46% of organizations that were forced to pay ransomware to regain access to their data.

2.2 Cybersecurity Data Breach Trends: African Perspective

According to African Cyberthreat Assessment Report [10], the main driver for the African internet penetration is attributed to mobile devices being connected to the internet. However, this internet penetration also comes with cybersecurity challenges.

According to the Africa Cyber Security Outlook [11], the most common cybersecurity data breaches experienced by African in 2022 were Business Email Compromise (BEC) with 26%, ransomware breaches with 17%, data leakage with 16%, denial of service with 13%, insider threat with 11% and supply chain attacks with 5%. Furthermore, according to [11], the top three attacks seen in the Eastern Africa region were ransomware attacks, followed by BEC and lastly data leakages.

In the Western Africa region, the top three attacks that were observed were Denial-of-Service (DoS) and/or Distributed DoS, followed by BEC and data leakage. In Southern Africa, the top three cyber-attacks seen were BEC, followed by data leakages and 1 ransomware. The following are two examples of data breach techniques used to compromised organizations in the African region. The first is Business Email Compromise (BEC), where threat actors gain access to an enterprise' email servers using social engineering techniques, then send malicious emails to their targets. Such emails contain malicious attachments, links to malware and malicious domains. In addition to sending out malicious emails, threat actors are also able to edit and change payment or banking details thereby resulting in immediate financial damage.

According to [10], majority of the threat actors responsible for carryout BEC scams were found in West Africa. The Interpol's African Cybercrime Operations Desks discovered that Nigeria region was high on the list of hosts for threats actors in the African region. Hosting such BEC threat actors is not the only challenge, the African continent has also experienced BEC attacks, which have results in financial losses. Although in comparison to other regions around the world, the Africa region is the least targeted region for BEC scams with 0,74%, of which South Africa alone accounts for more than half of the target recipients of BEC scams on the continent. This may, however, be because the formal tracking and monitoring of such attacks in Africa is generally limited. The second example of data breaches in Africa is banking trojans and stealers. Banking trojans and stealers is a type of trojan that is installed on a victim's machine disguised as a game or useful software with the hope of monitoring a victim as they type in sensitive information such as usernames, passwords, credit card details, and other personal information. Examples of such trojans include spyware and rootkits. According to Trend Micro [10], Morocco was the most affected African country with 18,827 detections, followed by South Africa with 6,560 detection and Nigeria with 5,366 detections. The Trend Micro report [10] further reveals that the two most prevalent bank trojans and stealers seen in the Africa region is Zbot with 67.67% of detections, followed by Fareit with 15,39% of detections.

According to [10], one of the biggest challenges in the African region is the lack of reported cases of data breaches. Of the 20 countries surveyed across the African continent, only over two-thousand cases had been reported compared to a much larger number seen by security tools deployed across the continent. In addition to the 42 countries surveyed [10], only half of these countries had a mechanism for organizations and individuals to report cybercrime. However, according to the United Nations Conference on Trade and Development [11], 39 of the 54 countries on the African continent have legislation in place that deals with reporting of cybercrime, but implementation is still a challenge. Out of the 15 remaining Africa countries, 2 countries are still drafting their legislations while 13 have not even started.

This section has shown based on literature review that the world and the African content still has some mileage to cover at legislation and technical levels to reduce the increasing trend of data breaches.

3   Research Objective and Approach

The main research objective for this paper is to understand and contextualize the state of data breaches in the African cyberspace through timely social media engagements and research literature reviews. The research approach adopted to realize this objective was multi-pronged, influenced by the timely manner of data on social media, but also by the research that has been done over time in this domain by other researchers and news reporters.

The primary data collection for this study focused on the scrapping of public social media data and news websites over a 3-month period (May–July 2023) focusing on reports and engagements around data breaches in Africa. The data collection process was aided by a custom data breach tracker focusing on all African countries guided by case-insensitive keywords such as "data breach", "data leak", and "data exposure". The public data collected from social media and other websites were analyzed using the Topic Analytics feature found in Talkwalker[1] and qualitative analysis with the specific focus on the data collected over the research period, engagements, potential reach, unique authors, distribution of engagements across the different African countries, popular themes on data breaches, grouping of similar stories as well as sentiment of data breaches.

Phase 2 of the data analysis was supported by the research literature review analysis and data collected through a desktop study of the prominent data breaches in Africa that have occurred between 2018 and 2023. The data was then analyzed using a simple matrix to understand the organizations affected, period of the breach, data compromised, number of data records compromised, attack vectors, and breach impact. It is acknowledged that the social media and research data used for the trend analysis in this paper is not exhaustive, mainly because data attacks are forever evolving. However, the analyzed data was found sufficient to provide qualitative and quantitative insights on the trend of data breaches in the African cyberspace.

---

[1] https://app.talkwalker.com/

4 Understanding Data Breaches in Africa: Social Media Trend Analysis

In this section, we present and discuss the analysis of data breach trends in Africa using social media posts and engagements. The analysis is structured into the overview of the results, themes discovered, trend analysis of results over the 3-month period, distribution of data breach posts and engagements per country, sentiment analysis, and future trend forecasting.

Between May–July 2023, over 1,944 tweets related to data breaches were collected and analyzed, authored by 1,207 unique authors resulting into 1,858 engagements on social media and news websites with a potential reach of 45.9 million users, based on views, followers, retweets, and engagements scores. Data breach stories that are similar were grouped together and this resulted in a total of over 178 unique data breaches conversations over the research period across Africa. However, this does not necessarily mean 178 data breaches occurred in Africa in 3 months because some of the data was on data breaches that may have occurred in the past and authorities were either investigating or providing updates on breaches that have occurred before May 2023 when the data collection period started.

Fig. 2. Top themes on data breach posts and engagements on social media and news websites.

Figure 2 shows the top themes as per the data collection over 3 months. The common themes associated with data breach are data, breach, ransomware, cybersecurity, privacy, data protection, data security, and phishing. These themes are correlating with the data found in literature (as highlighted in Sect. 2) on attack types and techniques in various data breaches in African and rest of the world.

On analysis of the themes over the period of the study, it was evident that the data breaches trend was increasing across all different themes supporting claims that data breaches in Africa are on an upward trend (see Fig. 3).

Focusing on the total results collected over 3 months, the data breach trend in the African cyberspace indicates an upward trajectory using the stream graph as show in Fig. 4.

In addition, a prediction of 274 data breach results over a 7-day period suggests a trend in the African cyberspace that is not decreasing. This is done using the Talkwalker forecasting feature [12].

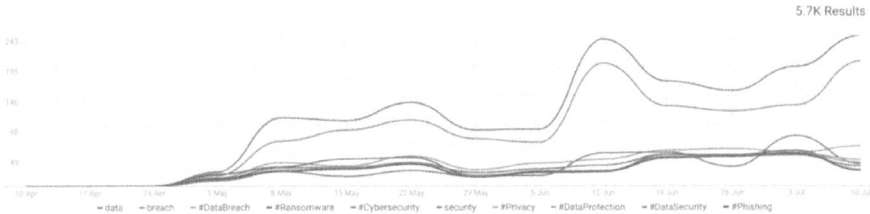

Fig. 3. Data breach theme analysis over time.

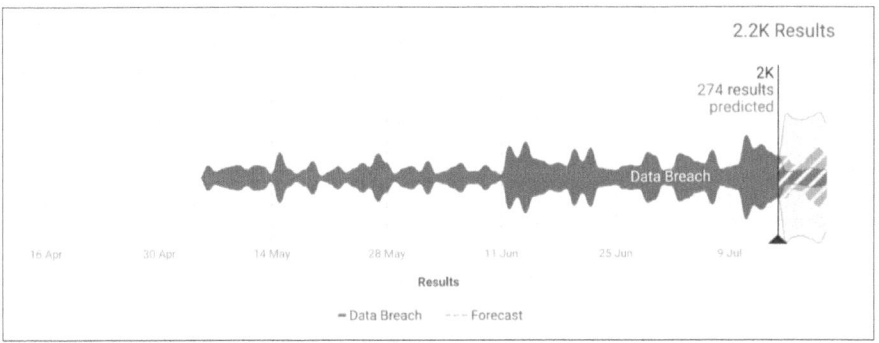

Fig. 4. Data breach trend analysis over 3-months with a forecast

When drilling into the African countries affected by these results Fig. 5 depicts that most of the data breach stories emanate from Nigeria (36%), followed by Kenya (16%) and South Africa (15%). These results are congruent with the observations in literature (see Sect. 2) as well as global trend reports.

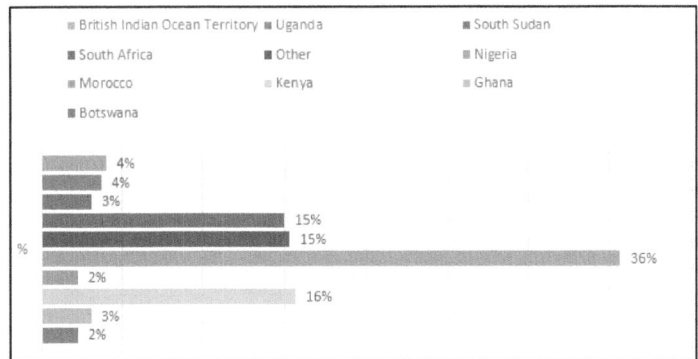

Fig. 5. Data breach posts share across the African continent (over a 3-month period)

Figure 6 demonstrate the trends of data breach stories over a 3-month period and clearly shows that as more data collection was done, it became evident that data breach stories were more on an increase. The increase over the period of the study was caused by different data breach events such as the news of the Nigerian Data Protection Commission (June 2023) announcing the investigation of financial institutions, universities, and insurance companies for data breaches as well as the South African Department of Justice being fined 5 million rands by the Information Regulator for a data breach that occurred in 2021.

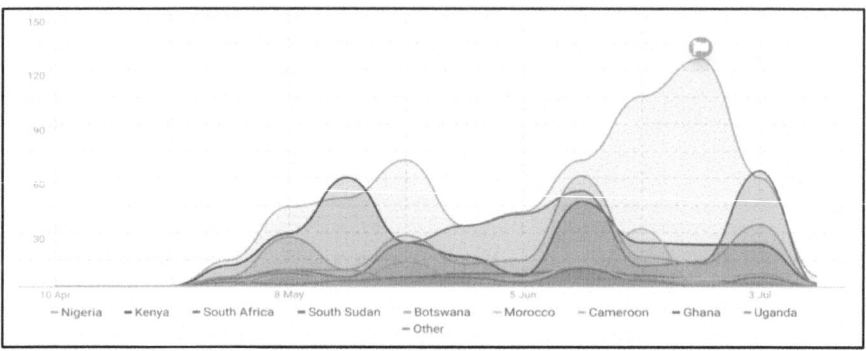

Fig. 6. Data breach peak trends over 3 months in African countries.

In understanding the potential impact of data breaches in the African cyberspace on business and citizens, sentiment analysis of the social media and news website data was done. Figure 7 depicts the sentiments through engagements by possible customers, clients, stakeholders, and organizations that have been affected by the data breaches. The sentiments are split up into 3 categories, namely positive, neutral, and negative. From the analysis, it is evident that the data breaches have a negative impact on affected parties with over 62% of the posts attracting negative sentiments. The trend line also suggests that as data breach posts increase so are the negative sentiments, albeit we observed a slight decline in month#3.

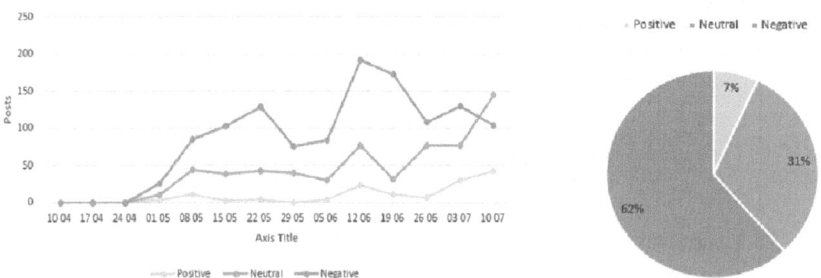

Fig. 7. Sentiment analysis of tweets across different Africa countries

The sentiments key drivers around data breaches during this reporting period were mostly influenced by potential loss of revenue, loss of customers, loss of trust, data theft, financial losses by customers, breach of users' privacy, exposure of users to cyber-crime, reputational harm, data exposure by employees, and regulatory fines. These key drivers indicate, to a large extent, potential impact of data breaches on organizations and individuals and are aligned to what is already reported in literature and other countries outside the African continent. In analyzing the individuals' posts, the extent of data breach impact was also evident in individual stories such as the one cited in Fig. 8.

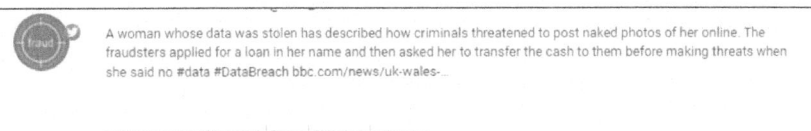

Fig. 8. Impact of data breaches on individuals

In wrapping up the analysis of phase 1, the data breach events in the top three countries over the reporting period are summarized in the subsections that follow. It should be noted that the subsections only deal with data breach engagements over 3 months, and that the engagements do not only deal with the actual data breaches, but also other stories related to the data breaches in the specific countries as collected from social media and news websites.

4.1 Nigeria

The data breach stories that were observed related to Nigeria during the research period relate to:

The Nigeria Data Protection Commission. The commission announced that it was investigating three deposit money Banks, Babcock University, Leadway Insurance, and other suspects over alleged data breaches, and this was accompanied by a possible loss of revenue by this companies amounting to 2% of their profits. This obviously has direct impact on the cited business and as such expected to generate heightened engagements on social media [13]. This story had a potential reach of over 2.8 million.

Houbi Data Breach Fix. This story was reshared in Nigeria reporting on the fix that a cryptocurrency company based in Seychelles conducted after a leak of contact details of just under 5.000 users.

Strange Ways Employees Expose Data. The awareness story on how users could leak data accidentally was also well shared and engaged on social media. Several tips were shared in this regard.

4.2 Kenya

In Kenya, most of the data breach related stories were influenced by the following events during the reporting period:

New Mega Africa Ltd and Absa data breach case. This data breach story was popular in Kenya during the reporting period where the court barred the Absa bank from auctioning the property of New Mega Africa over unpaid loans. This is due to a pending Sh1.5 billion data breach lawsuit that the firm had initially won where Absa was alleged to have leaked confidential of New Mega Africa to third parties that led to their credit rating diminishing. The bank is currently appealing the order [14].

Equity Bank Kenya Data Breach. The Kenyan Equity Bank was on the spot after a client lost Ksh300,000 in 17 min following a major data breach. The bank indicated that they are investigating the matter, even though indications are that the bank has had numerous data fraud and data breach complaints [15].

Dismissal of a Data Breach Complaint: The Court in Kenya dismissed the complaint by Wamae & Allen against the Office of the Data Protection Commissioner (ODPC) that one of their former employees had shared personal and sensitive data with other former employees. The case was dismissed due to the reasons that the data was already in public and that data subjects does not include juristic persons as per the data protection laws in Kenya.

4.3 South Africa

Between May–July 2023, South Africa had over 283 data breach related stories that when analyzed based on similarities resulted into 33 unique data breach stories. The topical data breaches engagements during the period of the study involved the following stories:

Half a Million Customers Data Breach. A data leak of over half a million customers data at Incredible Connection, HiFi Corp, Rochester, Russell's, Sleepmasters, Bradlows and Everyshop made headlines in South Africa during the research period [16]. The group that owns all these companies was compelled by the Protection of Personal Information (POPIA) regulation in South Africa to publicly notify data subjects of the data breach. The impact of the breach was the exposure of personal information of customers on a publicly accessible hacker, but at a cost. It was not clear at the time of the research study how the data breach occurred.

Showmax Subscribers Online Data Breach. The other data breach that created engagement on social media in South Africa during the period of the research study was the leakage of login details of more than 27 000 Showmax subscribers online [17]. In this data breach, customers' emails and passwords were compromised, and Showmax in a statement indicated that this was an external incident and none of their database systems were breached [17].

Department of Justice Data Breach Fine. The other data breach related story that made the most social media engagement headlines was the Department of Justice fine of R5 million by the South African Information Regulator for not taking the necessary measures to correct security gaps after a data breach in 2021 [18].

The qualitative analysis of the social media data provided in this subsection clearly demonstrate that the awareness of data breaches in Africa has increased and data breaches posts are common across different countries, further confirming that data breaches are on the rise in the African continent.

The next section delves into understanding the data breaches in Africa using research literature focusing on the period between 2020 and 2023 to triangulate the data breach global and social media trends with research literature.

5   Understanding Trend of Data Breaches in Africa Using Research Literature

This section details data breaches in Africa between January 2018, and July 2023. Table 1 presents the attack type, country, and impact of the data breach. Within the African continent, a trend analysis of cyber-attacks reveals that various types of attacks, including ransomware, DDoS, insider-threats, and others, have been observed in data breach incidents. It is noted that the information available regarding the identified data breaches was either limited or not disclosed by the organizations, however, it can be noted that one (1) data breach was indicated as a ransomware attack [18], another data breach was indicated to be a DoS/DDoS attack [19], four (4) data breaches were indicated to be hacking incidents [20–23] and one (1) data breach was classified as a malware attack [24].

The analysis of these data breaches shows some alignment and correlation with the data analyzed in the previous section, particularly with the data breach on Equity Bank that seems to have a wider impact in East Africa.

Each of the analyzed data breach may have resulted in the extraction of different types of data from the affected organization, such as personally identifying information of customers, stakeholders, employees, and even executive board members' personal information.

The financial impact of these data breaches extends beyond the volume of data lost; organizations also suffer reputational damage and face additional penalties imposed by regulators in African countries.

The process of gaining unauthorized access to an organization's network is a timely process and the time to gain access varies based on the type of attack being used by the external actor [25]. Different attack vectors are utilized to identify possible points of entry. Some common attack vectors include ransomware, social engineering with BEC, insider threats, open-source intelligence [25].

The data breaches discussed above could explained as a triangle that identifies 3 main key components that could be used as a root cause analysis (see Fig. 9).

The people component can be identified as a possible point of entry to the organization. The people component has access to the data component and is recognized as a resource within the organization by the technology component which will implement less security restrictions as the compared to security restrictions that need to be implemented for an external actor. According [26], people are viewed as being high risk within cyber-attacks as they become an immediate internal threat actor.

The organizational triangle identifies the people component as employees that have access to internal assets within the organization, the data is all the information that is

Table 1. Summary of prominent and selected data breaches in Africa (2020–2023)

Country	Organization	Types of attacks	Impact	Year-Month
South Africa	Department of Justice	Ransomware	Financial Reputation damage Regulatory fine	2021-Sep
Senegal	Senegalese Government Websites	DoS/DDoS	Reputation damage	2023-May
Rwanda	Equity bank	Hacking	Financial Reputation damage	2021-Jul
Uganda	MTN Airtel	Hacking	Financial Reputation damage	2020-Oct
South Sudan	Bank of South Sudan	Hacking	Financial Reputation damage	2023-Apr
Morocco	IKEA	Malware	Reputation damage Data Breach	2022-Nov
Kenya	Naivas	Hacking	Reputation damage Data Breach	2023-May

Legend	
	Hacking
	DoS/DDoS
	Ransomware
	Malware

collected, processed, and stored within the organization and the technology component controls, implements, and manages access to the data component within the organization.

The data breaches discussed in this section all touch on the 3 key components of the organizational triangle. For instance, the analysis of the Department of Justice data breach, the technology component was compromised as licenses for the tools were not renewed within a proper time frame [18], thus access to the data component was not adequately controlled or monitored by the technology component.

The Moroccan data breach, a possible compromise through the human component, thus bypassing the technology component and allowing for access to the data component. [27], discusses different attack vectors that were used during the COVID-19 pandemic.

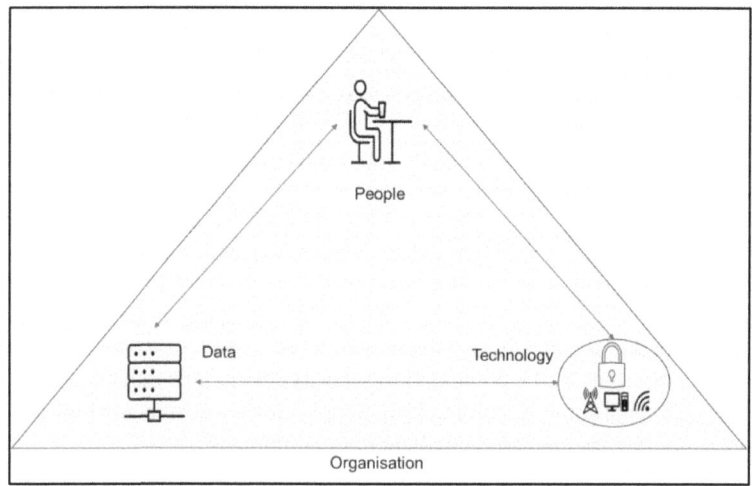

Fig. 9. Organizational Triangle

These attack vectors exposed flaws in both the people and technology components of the organizational triangle.

6 Discussion and Implications

This research study demonstrates that data breaches in Africa are topical in government and businesses. From the analysis done based on social media and research data, it is evident that data breaches have also become part of legal disputes as well as law enforcement activities in Africa, where perpetrators are arrested (e.g., Equity Bank data breach) or organizations fined (e.g., Department of Justice in South Africa).

The trend analysis shows that data breaches are on the rise from the incidents and awareness point of view across the different African countries with Nigeria leading from the awareness point of view and South Africa prominent in the number of actual data breaches. Kenya has demonstrated the real harm of data breaches on users, as well as how data breaches do not only impact one country but could also be impactful across boarder as observed with the Equity Bank breach. Other countries may be having low engagement and data on breaches, but this does not necessarily mean they are not experiencing them or are immune from cyber-attacks. In Africa, it is evident that many data breaches are not reported, possibly due to less robust data protection laws and lack of business and user awareness. Using expert knowledge, we have demonstrated in this paper that data breaches are triggered by the organizational triangle that focus on people, data, and technology. It is clear that people are the weakest link, but when security controls in people or processes are not strong, data breaches will occur through various techniques such as ransomware attacks, business email compromise, phishing, malware attacks and in some instances accidental data leakages and exposure by business and individuals.

It is also evident from the analysis that detailed information about the data breaches in Africa are limited to what is reported on the news websites and social media. Most organizations that fall victim to data breaches do not even share threat intelligence so that other organizations could be aided not to suffer the same data breaches. The lack of reporting and sharing plays into the hands of malicious actors because they can repeat the same data breach attacks without much effort.

The impact of data breaches on customers and businesses in Africa is determined as being negative, and unabated. And based on the data analysis, it is apparent that data breaches can have serious financial, reputational, legal and privacy implications. As such decision makers need to ramp-up the practical implementation of data protection laws as well as data protection awareness campaigns to protect organizations and users from malicious actors, thus promoting national security.

7 Conclusion and Recommendations

This research paper provides a contextual understanding of data breach trends in the African cyberspace using social media and research literature analysis. Close to 2,000 data points were collected on social media and news posts using specially crafted key-words over a 3-month period to understand the trend over time. The results indicate that data breaches are common African countries and data breach incidents are no longer superficial or distant but are real and impacting on businesses and individuals.

The following practical and evidence-based recommendations are made by the authors for African government and organizations to arrest the increasing rate of data breaches in the public and private sector. Robust legislation: we recommend implementation of strong legislative laws that could be used as a hindrance to threat actors. These legislative laws could be used to guide individual citizens, government departments and the private sectors on how to report cybercrime. The laws could also be used by the African governments to penalize negligent organization that fail to implement the minimum-security controls, thus at the very least circumventing a data breach. Specifically related to BEC, multifactor authentication could aid in reducing the high number of data breaches observed. Employee awareness training and phishing simulation can also be used as forms for countermeasures. Phishing simulations allow for organizations to measure users' responsiveness towards identifying phishing emails that are sent to their mailboxes. Based on the organizational triangle, the phishing simulations that are conducted within each organization are also meant for the continuous assessment of the knowledge and operational use of the security controls by the employees. Other common best security practices such as regular patching of software, user awareness training, and deployment of NextGen security tools are encouraged. Consistent period data risk assessments are recommended, including privilege user activity monitoring and activity management. Lastly, it is also no longer sufficient at minimum to install security tools, but these security tools also need to be periodically patched and updated to prevent data breaches caused by the same tools.

References

1. Rubrik Zero Labs. https://www.rubrik.com/content/dam/rubrik/en/resources/report-review/rpt-rubrik-zero-labs-global-report.pdf. Accessed 05 Sept 2023
2. DLA Piper. https://www.dlapiperdataprotection.com/. Accessed 05 Sept 2023
3. ITWeb Homepage. https://www.itweb.co.za/content/j5alrMQAJOQMpYQk. Accessed 18 Sept 2023
4. Niametrics Homepage. https://nairametrics.com/2023/02/14/nigeria-data-protection-bureau-says-110-companies-under-investigation-for-data-breach/. Accessed 18 Sept 2023
5. TechArena HomePage. https://www.techarena.co.ke/2023/04/13/kenya-airports-authority-suffers-data-breach-from-notorious-hacking-group/. Accessed 14 Aug 2023
6. Skybox Security. https://www.skyboxsecurity.com/resources/report/vulnerability-threat-trends-report-2023/. Accessed 18 Sept 2023
7. The Record Homepage. https://therecord.media/zyxel-says-a-threat-actor-is-targeting-its-enterprise-firewall-and-vpn-devices. Accessed 14 July 2023
8. Verizon. https://www.verizon.com/business/resources/reports/dbir/. Accessed 18 Sept 2023
9. Sophos. https://www.sophos.com/en-us/whitepaper/state-of-ransomware/. Accessed 13 Sept 2023
10. Interpol. https://www.interpol.int/content/download/16759/file/AfricanCyberthreatAssessment_ENGLISH.pdf. Accessed 13 Sept 2023
11. KMPG. https://kpmg.com/za/en/home/insights/2022/09/africa-cyber-security-outlook-report-2022.html. Accessed 13 Sept 2023
12. Talkwalker platform. https://www.talkwalker.com/blog/summer-2022-release. Accessed 15 July 2023
13. Daily Trust. https://dailytrust.com/banks-telcoms-oil-firms-to-lose-2-revenue-for-data-breach-fg/. Accessed 12 July 2023

14. Business Daily Africa. https://www.businessdailyafrica.com/bd/corporate/companies/court-bars-absa-from-auctioning-firm-in-sh1-5bn-data-breach--4285810. Accessed 15 July 2023
15. KDB. https://mambomseto.co.ke/equity-bank-on-the-spot-once-again-after-client-loses-300k-in-17-minutes/. Accessed 15 July 2023
16. Mybroadband. https://mybroadband.co.za/news/security/494239-half-a-million-customers-hit-by-incredible-hifi-corp-and-everyshop-data-breach.html. Accessed 13 July 2023
17. Showmax. https://stories.showmax.com/za/important-notice-security-incident-affecting-user-credentials. Accessed 13 July 2023
18. News24. https://www.news24.com/news24/tech-and-trends/news/department-of-justice-fined-r5m-for-not-beefing-up-cyber-security-after-2021-data-breach-20230705. Accessed 13 July 2023
19. Reuters. https://www.reuters.com/world/africa/senegalese-government-websites-hit-with-cyberattack-2023-05-27/. Accessed 10 July 2023
20. The East African. https://www.theeastafrican.co.ke/tea/business/rwanda-jails-8-kenyans-equity-bank-hacking-case-3463908. Accessed 10 July 2023
21. MTN, Stanbic & others in Uganda. https://myjoyonline.com/hackers-break-into-mobile-money-system-to-steal-billions-from-airtel-mtn-stanbic-and-others-in-uganda. Accessed 10 July 2023
22. The City Review. https://cityreviewss.com/anonymous-takes-down-boss-website-wants-exchange-rate-below-40k/. Accessed 10 July 2023
23. Business Daily. https://www.businessdailyafrica.com/bd/opinion-analysis/columnists/naivas-data-breach-a-wake-up-call-for-firms-to-comply--4223182. Accessed 10 July 2023
24. SC Magazine. https://www.scmagazine.com/brief/threat-intelligence/ikeas-kuwait-morocco-franchises-hit-by-vice-society-ransomware-gang. Accessed 10 July 2023
25. Hammouchi, H., Cherqi, O., Mezzour, G., Ghogho, M., El Koutbi, M.: Digging deeper into data breaches: an exploratory data analysis of hacking breaches over time. Procedia Comput. Sci. **151**, 1004–1009 (2019)
26. Krause, T., Ernst, R., Klaer, B., Hacker, I., Henze, M.: Cybersecurity in power grids: challenges and opportunities. Sensors **21**(18), 6225 (2021)
27. Susukailo, V., Opirskyy, I., Vasylyshyn, S.: Analysis of the attack vectors used by threat actors during the pandemic. In: IEEE 15th International Conference on Computer Sciences and Information Technologies (CSIT), pp. 261–264 (2020)

Advancing Mobile Money Payments Through Blockchain and Interoperability Protocols

Edem Kodjo Agbezoutsi[1] [iD], Pascal Urien[1(✉)], and Toundé Mesmin Dandjinou[2]

[1] 19 Place Marguerite Perey, 91120 Palaiseau, France
{kodjo.agbezoutsi,pascal.urien}@telecom-paris.fr
[2] Université Nazi BONI, 01 BP 1091 Bobo-Dioulasso, Burkina Faso

Abstract. Currently, mobile network operators (MNOs) manage their own Mobile Money (MM) transaction solutions, making them responsible for managing transaction databases and their interaction with customers. The goal of integrating Mobile Money transactions onto the Blockchain is to improve trust in the Mobile Money system. In this paper, we propose a Mobile Money payment protocol based on Blockchain technology, called "Mobile Money Using Blockchain (2MUB)". This protocol aims to improve the security, speed, interoperability and trust of financial transactions by using the advantages of Blockchain technology while offering an intuitive user experience. We discuss various aspects of this protocol, including advantages for users, potential challenges, and opportunities for its large-scale adoption, particularly in developing countries where Mobile Money is a real economical fact. Account management of users using approved BIP (Bitcoin Improvement Proposal) standards allows for revealing only the minimal transaction data necessary for traceability in an enhanced version of this protocol. However, this may increase the size of transaction data on the Blockchain to some extent. In addition to improving trust in the MM ecosystem, it also addresses the problem of interoperability by federating Mobile Money solutions in the ecosystem. Finally, we present the results of a case study to demonstrate the effectiveness of our protocol in a real-world environment, such as Burkina Faso.

Keywords: Security · Blockchain · Payments · Mobile Money · USSD · traceability · trust · protocol

1 Introduction

The Internet is now accessible in most parts of the world, with an estimated 60% of the population being connected in 2021 [1], totaling 4.5 billion people online. However, there is an unequal distribution of network coverage across continents. The disparity in Internet access, known as the digital divide, is a significant challenge, particularly in developing countries. This divide is particularly prominent in rural areas where Internet coverage remains limited.

The USSD technology using the 2G channel of GSM is advantageous for the development of Mobile Money. Mobile Money does not require Internet connection (3G and

© ICST Institute for Computer Sciences, Social Informatics and Telecommunications Engineering 2025
Published by Springer Nature Switzerland AG 2025. All Rights Reserved
A. Sere et al. (Eds.): AFRICOMM 2023, LNICST 587, pp. 274–287, 2025.
https://doi.org/10.1007/978-3-031-81570-6_18

higher channels) for its implementation and operation, but instead uses the USSD/GSM channel, which constitutes an advantage for countries whose GSM coverage is much higher than mobile internet.

Mobile Money plays an important role in monetary transactions in developing countries. It allows access to financial services even in remote rural areas. However, it has shortcomings such as the presence of multiple operators, a lack of federation and interoperability between Mobile Money solutions, a lack of trust in operators, and an uniqueness of the database at the Mobile Money operator.

In an increasingly digital world, the use of mobile payment systems is on the rise, particularly in developing countries. However, interoperability between different mobile payment systems remains a significant challenge. That's why we propose a Mobile Money payment protocol based on blockchain technology, called "Mobile Money Using Blockchain (2MUB)". This protocol aims at improving the security, speed and interoperability of financial transactions by using the advantages of blockchain technology while providing an intuitive user experience. We will discuss various aspects of this protocol, including the benefits for users, potential challenges, and opportunities for its large-scale adoption, particularly in developing countries where Mobile Money is an economic reality. Here we will present the results of a case study to demonstrate the effectiveness of our protocol in a real-world environment, such as Burkina Faso.

To address the limitations of current Mobile Money solutions, we proposed in our previous work [2, 3] the use of blockchain to enhance trust within the Mobile Money ecosystem. In our earlier research, we explored the traceability and federation of mobile payment solutions using blockchain technology. We described how blockchain services can be leveraged to improve transparency and security in Mobile Money transactions, presenting a concrete example of implementing blockchain for the federation of Mobile Money providers in Africa. We also examined the advantages of this federation, such as interoperability, accessibility, competition and innovation, along with the challenges involved in establishing an efficient Mobile Money federation. The objective of this study is to provide a detailed definition of the protocol enabling Mobile Money payments supported by blockchain services.

A major challenge in blockchain transactions is the transaction per second (TPS) limit. TPS is closely tied to the consensus algorithm for validating transactions and mining blocks. Initially, Ethereum and Bitcoin had TPS of 15 and 7 respectively [4], both using proof of work (POW) consensus. Currently, Ethereum has adopted proof of stake (POS) consensus, which allows for faster block mining and improved ecological sustainability. This has enabled Ethereum to reach a TPS of 160,000 [5]. To compare, Visa and MasterCard can process around 1700 TPS and PayPal 200 TPS. In 2019, Orange Money Burkina recorded 15 million transactions per day, equivalent to 174 TPS. In 2020, this increased by 23% to 18.45 million transactions, or 214 TPS. With a requirement of about 600 TPS for federation of three Mobile Money platforms in a country like Burkina Faso, Ethereum can handle the TPS load. Hence, using the Ethereum blockchain to improve the Mobile Money ecosystem is a crucial aspect of our contribution.

This paper is organized in five sections. Section 2 (related works) describes, in practice and research, how interoperability is conceived and deployed. Section 3 discusses the contribution blockchain could bring to the Mobile Money ecosystem. The Mobile

Money payment protocol on the blockchain is described in Sect. 4 and illustrated by transactions recorded on Ethereum test blockchain. Section 5 presents management of user accounts and the overall architecture.

2 Related Works

Interoperability has become a concern with the rise of Mobile Money in developing countries due to the diversity of solutions offered by different providers. in [6] interoperability in Mobile Money refers to the ability for customers to transfer money between accounts at different Mobile Money Operators (MMOs) as well as between accounts at Mobile Money schemes and bank accounts. Leading countries in Mobile Money such as India, Kenya, Tanzania and Rwanda have each adopted a solution that suits their economic environment and laws.

In 2008, the Reserve Bank of India issued guidelines for interoperability among prepaid payment instrument providers [6]. These guidelines aimed to facilitate money transfers between different digital wallets through the regulator-provided Unified Payments Interface (UPI) [7]. However, this central model may lead to integration complexities and only bank-backed mobile wallets with valid customer information are eligible to participate. The study in [8] proposes three options for customer detail lookup during processing, including a central database, a peer-to-peer query, and a hierarchical lookup. The peer-to-peer option is initially considered the most suitable for the Indian market, but this may change as the system size increases. Other options in the Indian landscape include the Mobile Payment Foundation of India model for interoperability in a highly regulated financial environment.

In Kenya, the Mobile Money market is well established in the African region and provides person-to-person money transfer services to low-end unbanked customers. Interoperability is not mandatory in Kenya's National Payments System regulations. However, payment service providers are allowed to make their own interoperable arrangements. The Central Bank of Kenya has left it to the market to decide how providers interoperate but has proposed a framework for easier interoperability [9]. So far, interoperability in Kenya has happened through bilateral agreements between Mobile Money providers rather than a common central system [10, 11]. A common central system, however, could improve coordination, customer experience and faster implementation of interoperability compared to private switches or bilateral agreements. This is also the case in Burkina Faso.

In Tanzania, there are 4 mobile network operators offering Mobile Money services to subscribers. It's one of the world's most successful Mobile Money markets with 25% of the population being active users, transacting 2 billion dollars per month in 2014 [12]. According to a study, Tanzania launched Account to Account (A2A) interoperability in 2014 and the regulatory environment allowed providers to freely choose the best technical model for their interests, resulting in providers opting for bilateral point to point integrations for interoperability [3].

Rwanda has a mature and competitive Mobile Money market with various providers offering similar services such as balance maintenance, deposits, withdrawals, and fund transfers. However, there is currently no central clearing and settlement system for

Mobile Money providers to offer interoperability. A study in [13] reviewed the regulation of Mobile Money in Rwanda and suggested a light-handed regulatory approach. New regulations in Rwanda require interoperability before integration can occur, but it is currently limited to transactions through agents. Interoperability between the banking system and Mobile Money is also available, but it requires a physical visit to a bank branch. The next step would allow for remote payment from one provider's account to another.

The study in [14] suggested using blockchain technology to create a prototype system for Mobile Money interoperability that is based on a decentralized shared ledger. This would ensure non-repudiation, protect data privacy, and authenticate the origin of the data. But these authors don't propose a protocol doing so.

In [6] authors develop the ideas which create the interoperability between Mobile Money providers. "As we have demonstrated in our contributions [2], they take into account the MMOs and banking institutions that are integral parts of the ecosystem and perform Mobile Money transaction operations between them." These proposals are supported by the laws and regulations in place within the economic area. The proposals' schemes are as follows:

- bilateral agreements between schemes and banks;
- neutral processor between schemes, and between schemes and banks;
- commercial processor between schemes, and between schemes and banks;
- using a bank and a national Automated Clearing House (ACH) to interface with other banks;
- direct connectivity to national ACH for all schemes and banks;
- commercial processor for bank interface, bilateral between schemes.

Overall, interoperability in Mobile Money is a complex issue that varies across countries. Different solutions and models are being explored to enhance interoperability, improve coordination, and provide seamless money transfer services for customers.

3 Mobile Money and Blockchain: A Better Future

3.1 Mobile Money

The trend of mobile payment, known as Mobile Money, is rapidly growing in developing countries. It involves transactions made by using a mobile device, and can be credited to a bank card, the operator's bill, or an electronic wallet. The electronic wallet can be funded through cash deposits from an agent, merchant, or bank transfer, and is tied to the customer's SIM card number, which is managed by the Mobile Network Operator (MNO). Mobile Money is implemented using Unstructured Supplementary Service Data (USSD) technology, which enables the sending of short commands from a mobile device to the Global System for Mobile Communications (GSM) network via the signaling channel. Unlike SMS, USSD operates on a session-oriented connection rather than a store-and-forward architecture and has a maximum text message length of 160 bytes [15]. This ease of deployment and use, even for non-literate populations, makes USSD [14] a key factor in the growth of Mobile Money.

USSD command uses numeric codes with the prefix '*' and the suffix '#'. Specifically, a user enters command like "*xxx#" and accesses to a pop-up menu which can be navigated through the phone keys. A Mobile Money transfer usually consists of 4 steps; registration, encashment, transfer and withdrawal [2].

3.2 Blockchain's Contribution

Blockchain can be used in different sectors and can meet different needs. Blockchain is applied to almost every field we can think of, such as banking [7] [8, 17], finance [8, 9], electoral voting [16, 17], education [18, 21], insurance [20] [21], agriculture [24], health [22], to name a few. The areas of application remain very broad and are not limited to what has been mentioned above. The technology's key features and uses focus on security, fraud prevention, traceability, and trusted third-party concerns. Our solution tackles the challenges of Mobile Money by integrating two primary elements: *tracing transactions and federating Mobile Money solutions through the use of blockchain technology.* Our proposal is a blockchain-based Mobile Money payment protocol that provides increased security by eliminating a central point of failure and reducing the risk of corruption or hacking. Furthermore, the decentralized system offers greater user flexibility by enabling transactions anytime, anywhere, without relying on a centralized infrastructure.

4 Enhancing Mobile Money Transactions with Ethereum Blockchain

4.1 Mobile Money Protocol for Blockchain

We introduced in [2] a *Mobile Money Protocol for Blockchain*, described by Fig. 1.
Actors involved in a transaction using this version of the protocol are as follows:

- **Customer A:** the initiator of the transaction, transferring an amount to Customer B.
- **Customer B:** the recipient of the transaction initiated by Customer A.
- **MNOA (Mobile Network Operator A):** it plays a central role in the transaction system as the custodian of the accounts for Customer A and Customer B.
- **The controller:** it plays a crucial role in monitoring communication exchanges and transactions within the economic space. Its primary responsibility is to store all data related to each transaction to enhance trust between customers and the MNO.
- **Central Bank:** it is responsible for ensuring the stability of the currency in the economic context.
- **Blockchain:** a technology used to record and secure transactions in a decentralized manner.

1. The transaction session is initiated by Customer A through his mobile device interface by entering the command *999*2#.
2. The MNO receives the command from Customer A interpreted as a request for a money transfer from account A to account B to be recorded in the blockchain.

3. Exchanges occur between the customer making the payment and the MNO in order to gather information that will be stored in an *InfoRx.json* file (as seen in the left part of Fig. 2. The MNO generates a random number *(RandomNum)* with 256 bits of entropy.

4. The MNO generates an Ethereum RequestTx transaction specifically for Customer A. This transaction is assigned the identifier IdReqTx. The data field of this transaction comprises the concatenation of the SHA256 hash of the content of the InfoRx.json file with the random number. In other words, it is represented as hash(InfoRx.json ∥ RandomNumber).

5. The MNO then posts RequestTx on the blockchain, using its Ethereum address as the destination account.

6. The MNO initiates an SMS notification to Customer A, seeking validation or rejection of the transaction request. Simultaneously, a copy of the transaction data is dispatched to a legacy controller or regulator for further processing and oversight.

7. The MNO verifies the information contained in InfoRx, including Customer A's identification and authentication, the necessary balance for transferring the specified value of X, and Customer B's identifying information.

8. The MNO transfers the amount X from account A to account B by creating the Ethereum transaction TransfTx (identified as IdTransfTx). The data field of this transaction is the hash value of the InfoTx.json file, which contains information such as IdReqTx, RandomNum, and the status of the transaction (Yes/No), as shown in the right part of Fig. 2

9. The MNO posts the TransfTx transaction to the blockchain, using its Ethereum address as the destination account.

10. The MNO finally provides complete information to the legacy controller/regulator. It sends SMS confirmations to both the receiver and sender, including the transaction identifier (IdTransfTx), the status of the transaction (Yes/No), and the RandomNumber. This enables them to retrieve and verify the transaction on the blockchain.

For each transaction, the MNO creates a mapping table between the information IdReqTx and IdTransfTx, and shares it with the legacy regulator/controller. This entity guarantees to customers the authenticity of every blockchain transaction performed by the MNO. It verifies the information provided by the MNO and stored in the blockchain, and sends a warning if there is an issue.

The current version of our protocol involves transactions between accounts of the same operator, and records data on the blockchain in hashed form [25].

In order to improve this protocol and to add interoperability between accounts while also providing non-compromising information to users and allowing authorized actors to track transactions, we introduce a user account management system based on BIP standards. This mapping of Mobile Money accounts to BIP 32 addresses will al low for improved tracking and management of the transactions.

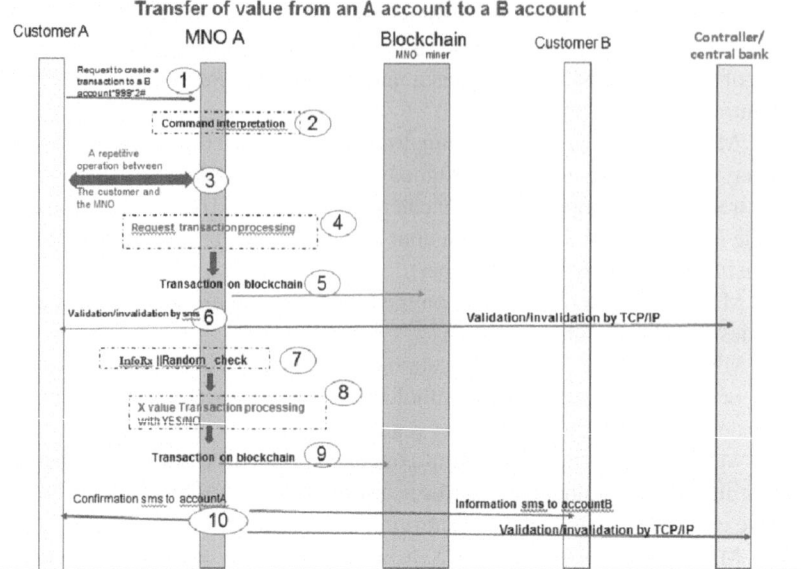

Fig. 1. Sequence diagram of Mobile Money transaction

"InfoRx":{	"InfoTx":{ "IdReqTx":
"Op Code": "2",	"0xe75def95df7aee86fef20fb0bbb9ec1ebc23be4ceea9017
"Source number": "76 17 82 65",	0fe9455abd22f4f7f"},
"Destination number": "74 43 38 19",	
"Transfer amount": "50000 CFA",	"RandomNum":{ "Random Number":
"MNO id": "0011"	"C4483BACC2DE4BA1852387A96D7FC"},
}	"StatusTx": { "transaction valid":"Yes" }

Fig. 2. InfoRx.json Request Transaction Information (left part), InfoTx.json Transaction Information (right part)

5   User Account Management and Expert Architecture

The ownership of tokens, cryptocurrencies, and other assets on the blockchain is managed using cryptographic keys, addresses, and digital signatures. These keys are not stored in the blockchain network, but instead are generated and stored by users in a wallet (either physical or logical) which operates in a similar manner to a traditional customer account. Next section explains how customer accounts are managed by sponsoring entities such as MNOs and banks.

5.1   Organization of Users' Account

In our contribution, the blockchain is at the center of transaction operations, so user accounts are managed either by the MNO (this is the classic case, as these are basically Mobile Money accounts) or by a partner bank or by an institution capable of financially guaranteeing the franchises with the regulating central bank. This management for end-users is possible thanks to their infrastructures participating in the blockchain. A Mobile Money account is under the control of a sponsoring actor, because all accounts are associated with SIM identifiers managed by MNO.

During registration operation, a customer account is created and associated with the use of blockchain services. A wallet that operates on the blockchain does not contain funds, an account or wallet in the blockchain system manages key pairs that enable transactions to be created (unlocking funds assigned to it, or locking funds to another account).

A sponsoring actor performs the process by generating the keys associated with the customer's Mobile Money wallet. At the current stage of research and recommended best practices, the management of a customer's wallet will be carried out according to the BIP32 [26] standards. Thus, the operator generates a daughter key pair for the customer from its master key, which will constitute the root for the generation of several other key pairs and addresses associated with future customer transactions. From the customer root, two key branches A and B are initially generated. The A branch is used, when the client uses his mobile phone for transactions with USSD commands, and the B branch when the client goes through a TCP/IP application. The BIP32 standards are used to avoid escalation attacks. The procedures of BIP32 are briefly described in the section dedicated to the Hierarchical Deterministic (HD) Wallet.

From a seed, the sponsoring actor derives key branches that will correspond to the accounts of the customers; a second possibility consists in generating a seed for the account of each customer. This will allow the sponsoring actor to have control over the accounts of the clients under his sponsorship in order to solve any problems that may arise (i.e. when the sender has the wrong recipient and the operator has to cancel the transaction operation).

At the end of this procedure, the sponsoring actor responds to the customer by means of an "account status sms" (successful creation; failed creation with reasons: authentication problem, server unavailability). A wallet is created for the customer, who can access it through an application using the TCP/IP channel on the network (Branch A) and also through the classic USSD Mobile Money application (Branch B). To carry out a transaction via a TCP/IP application, the customer receives an ID and password by SMS, allowing him to access his account. The management of his account is dynamic and data (ID and password) change every access request from the customer to his online account, to increase security.

5.2 Architecture of the Mobile Money Ecosystem Using the Blockchain

We plan three deployment scenarios in order to test our contribution, which we can be illustrated by Fig. 3:

- **Scenario 1** corresponds to use the current MNO Mobile Money architecture and a gateway to access Blockchain. This is the actual situation in Mobile Money ecosystems. Thus, the customer-MNO segment set-up remains unchanged, except that instead of having a MNO database, it is rather a blockchain infrastructure that validates Mobile Money transactions and federates the Mobile Money solutions of the same ecosystem. The channel is of course USSD.

- **Scenario 2** is associated to the use of the open-source tools of the [27] project on segment 1: Customerr-MNO. This is the case in a laboratory test environment where we replace the MNO with elements from the OSMOCOM project. Thus, the MNO will no longer be a black box. The channel is of course the USSD as in scenario 1.
- **Scenario 3** is related to the use of an application that could directly access the blockchain through the TCP/IP channel to perform transactions in the blockchain. The use of the TCP/IP channel will guarantee a high level of transparency. This channel allows each actor to create, verify all Mobile Money transactions made via USSD on the blockchain. This TCP/IP channel offers greater security than the USSD channel.

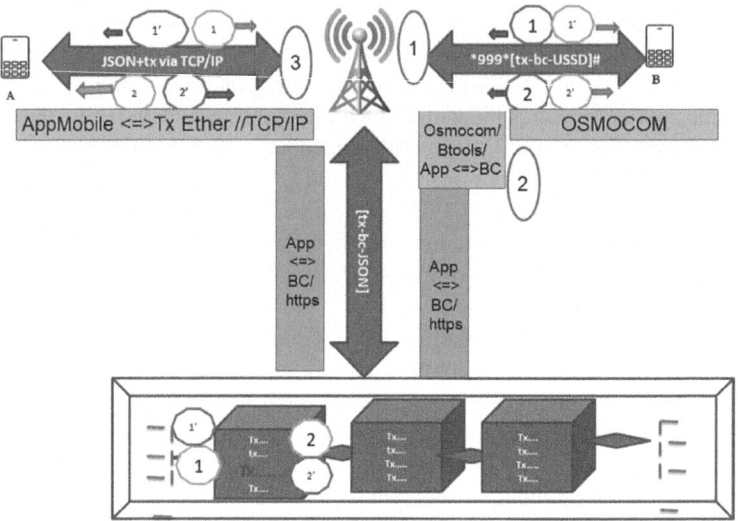

Fig. 3. Three scenarios for experimental architecture

6 Mobile Money Interoperability by 2MUB

6.1 Interoperability DAP

Interoperability requires a compensation system. Many thoughts have been proposed with different architectures. Our contribution is based on a Decentralized Autonomous Platform (DAP) that manages compensation rules in compliance with regulations in the economic space.

The components of our Decentralized Autonomous Platform are as follows:

1. **Smart Contracts:** self-executing agreements between parties with terms of the agreement directly written into code.
2. Blockchain technology: a secure, decentralized, and tamper-proof ledger for storing data.

3. **Cryptocurrency or tokens:** a digital asset used to incentivize and reward users for participating in the platform. This point will be further developed in future work.
4. **User interface:** a way for users to interact with the platform and access its services. Here, we always retain the USSD Mobile Money interface which is a key factor for the adoption of Mobile Money, even by non-literate individuals.
5. **Backend infrastructure:** servers, databases, and other technology that support the platform's functionality. And decentralized governance system: a mechanism for making decisions and managing the platform in a democratic and transparent manner.

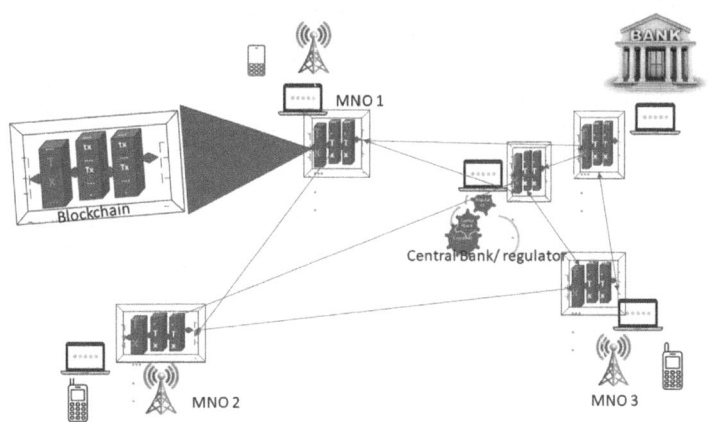

Fig. 4. The Mobile Money ecosystem in blockchain context

Figure 4 provides an insight into the involvement of actors in the Mobile Money ecosystem in the deployment, by showcasing the blockchain nodes (previously introduced in [2]).

6.2 Compensation-Based Interoperability in Smart Contracts

For a transaction between account A of MNO 1 and account B of MNO 2, the operators first have each a credited account in the compensation chamber with a guarantee to secure the transactions for a given period. This operation is transparent to the users. Then, the compensation between the operators takes place as in a banking system.

We achieve interoperability between user accounts and the federation of Mobile Money Operators (MMOs) through a smart contract.

The compensation operations between the MMOs, as outlined in Fig. 5 corresponding to the code of the smart contract, occur through the following steps:

- **Operation identification:** Mobile Money operators identify financial operations they want to compensate, based on criteria such as date, amount, beneficiary, etc.
- **Compliance verification:** Mobile Money operators verify the compliance of the operations to be compensated with internal policies and rules.

- **Fund transfer:** Mobile Money operators perform fund transfers to compensate the operations. This transfer can be made by wire transfer, check or other means of payment.
- **Compensation confirmation**: Mobile Money operators confirm compensation by exchanging confirmation messages.

```solidity
pragma solidity >=0.7.0 <0.9.0;

contract MobileMoneyCompensation {
    address public operator1;
    address public operator2;
    // structure pour stocker les opérations à compenser
    struct Operation {
        uint256 amount;
        address beneficiary;
        uint256 date;
        bool verified;
        bool compensated;
    }
    // tableau pour stocker les opérations
    Operation[] public operations;

    constructor(address _operator1, address _operator2) public {
        operator1 = _operator1;
        operator2 = _operator2;
    }
    // ajouter une opération à compenser
    function addOperation(uint256 _amount, address _beneficiary, uint256 _date) public {
        operations.push(Operation({
            amount: _amount,
            beneficiary: _beneficiary,
            date: _date,
            verified: false,
            compensated: false
        }));
    }

    // vérifier la conformité de l'opération
    function verifyOperation(uint256 _operationId) public {
        Operation storage operation = operations[_operationId];
        require(!operation.verified, "Lopération a déjà été vérifiee.");
        require(msg.sender == operator1 || msg.sender == operator2,
        "Seul l'opérateur peut vérifier l'opération.");
        operation.verified = true;
    }

    // effectuer le transfert de fonds pour compenser l'opération
    function compensateOperation(uint256 _operationId) public {
        Operation storage operation = operations[_operationId];
        require(operation.verified, "L'opération n'a pas été vérifiée.");
        require(!operation.compensated, "L'opération a déjà été compensée.");
        require(msg.sender == operator1 || msg.sender == operator2,
        "Seul l'opérateur peut compenser l'opération.");
        operation.compensated = true;
        operation.beneficiary.transfer(operation.amount);
    }

    // enregistrer les détails de la compensation
    function recordCompensation(uint256 _operationId) public {
        Operation storage operation = operations[_operationId];
        require(operation.compensated, "L'opération n'a pas été compensée.");
        require(msg.sender == operator1 || msg.sender == operator2,
        "Seul l'opérateur peut enregistrer la compensation.");
    }
}
```

Fig. 5. Mobile Money Compensation Smart Contract Code

- **Recording:** Mobile Money operators record compensation details in their respective systems.
- **Liquidation:** Liquidation is the final step of compensation, where funds are transferred to the appropriate beneficiary accounts.

This code defines a smart contract called MobileMoneyCompensation (see Fig. 5) which allows adding operations to be compensated, verifying them, compensating them, and recording the compensation details. Mobile Money operators are identified using their Ethereum addresses.

7 Conclusion

In this paper, we proposed an improvement to the Mobile Money payment protocol using blockchain technology. This upgrade takes into account the presence of multiple mobile network operators (MNOs) and the involvement of banks as Mobile Money providers. The main challenge associated with this multiplicity of actors is the interoperability between customers of different providers. To solve this problem, we proposed the use of a decentralized application (DAP) through the design of smart contracts to define rules and protocols. We also examined the use cases of this approach in Mobile Money ecosystems such as India, Tanzania, etc. 2MUB allows an improvement of transactions traceability and increases trust in the Mobile Money ecosystem.

In perspective, our next works will involve developing the ability to support our Mobile Money transactions on a cryptocurrency that is not a standard cryptocurrency (such as bitcoin, Ethereum, or altcoin), but rather a digital form of the currency in the zone. Thus, for each monetary zone where Mobile Money is deployed on the blockchain, there will be two forms of the same currency: digital in the form of cryptocurrency and physical. Later, it will be a matter of showing in detail how we use the BIP32/39/44 standards to manage Mobile Money user accounts on the blockchain.

References

1. '60% of the World's Population Is Now Online — DataReportal – Global Digital Insights'. Accessed 12 Oct 2022. https://datareportal.com/reports/6-in-10-people-around-the-world-now-use-the-internet#:~:text=As%20we%20revealed%20in%20our,total%20population%20is%20now%20online.&text=More%20than%20330%20million%20people,the%20start%20of%20April%202021
2. Agbezoutsi, K.E., Uriene, P., Dandjinou, T.M.: Towards blockchain services for mobile money traceability and federation. In: 2019 3rd Cyber Security in Networking Conference (CSNet), pp. 14–20 (2019). https://doi.org/10.1109/CSNet47905.2019.9108970
3. Agbezoutsi, K.E., Urien, P., Dandjinou, T.M.: Mobile money traceability and federation using blockchain services. Ann. Telecommun. 76(3), 223–233 (2021). https://doi.org/10.1007/s12243-021-00840-4
4. Zhang, S., Lee, J.-H.: Analysis of the main consensus protocols of blockchain. ICT Express 6(2), 93–97 (2020). https://doi.org/10.1016/j.icte.2019.08.001
5. '160 000 transactions par seconde (TPS) - Ethereum (ETH) et ChainLink (LINK) pourraient faire mieux que VISA', CryptoActu. Accessed 14 Jul 2021. https://cryptoactu.com/160000-transactions-par-seconde-tps-ethereum-eth-chainlink-link-visa/

6. Dick, C.: A2A InteroperAbIlIty Making Mobile Money Schemes Interoperate. Consult Hyperion Gunnar Camner, GSMA. https://www.gsma.com/mobilefordevelopment/wp-content/upl oads/2014/03/A2A-interoperability_Online.pdf

7. Lakshmi, K.K., Gupta, H., Ranjan, J.: UPI based mobile banking applications – security analysis and enhancements. In: 2019 Amity International Conference on Artificial Intelligence (AICAI), pp. 1–6 (2019). https://doi.org/10.1109/AICAI.2019.8701396

8. Kumar, S.B.R., Rabara, S.A., Martin, J.R.: A system model and protocol for mobile payment consortia system. In: 2009 International Conference on Test and Measurement, pp. 438–442 (2009). https://doi.org/10.1109/ICTM.2009.5413011

9. Interoperability in Branchless Banking and Mobile Money | Blog | CGAP. Accessed 02 Feb 2023. https://www.cgap.org/blog/interoperability-in-branchless-banking-and-mobile-money

10. Writer, S.: Kenya's Central Bank gives mobile money interoperability thumbs up. ITWeb Africa. Accessed 02 Feb 2023. https://itweb.africa/content/6GxRKMYJBl1qb3Wj

11. Why is mobile money interoperability important for Kenya?. Financial Sector Deepening Kenya. Accessed 02 Feb 2023. https://www.fsdkenya.org/blogs-publications/blog/why-is-mobile-money-interoperability-important-for-kenya/

12. The impact of mobile money interoperability in Tanzania · 2020. 3. 16. · interoperability in Tanzania that is the focus of this publication. After more than a decade of mobile - [PDF Document]', vdocuments.mx. Accessed 05 Jan 2023. https://vdocuments.mx/the-impact-of-mobile-money-interoperability-in-2020-3-16-interoperability-in.html

13. Argent, J., Hanson, J.A., Gomez, M.P.: The Regulation of Mobile Money in Rwanda. https://www.theigc.org/sites/default/files/2013/08/Argent-Et-Al-2013-Working-Paper.pdf

14. Mvula, F., Phiri, J., Tembo, S.: A Blockchain based Mobile Money Interoperability Scheme. IJACSA **11**(1) (2020). https://doi.org/10.14569/IJACSA.2020.0110117

15. Al-juaifari, M.K.R.: Secure SMS mobile transaction with peer to peer authentication design for mobile government. Am. J. Eng. Res., 7 (2015)

16. Gupta, P.: End to end USSD system. TATA Tele Service Limited, INDIA, July, vol. 7, p. 2010 (2010)

17. Popova, N.A., Butakova, N.G.: Research of a possibility of using blockchain technology without tokens to protect banking transactions. In: 2019 IEEE Conference of Russian Young Researchers in Electrical and Electronic Engineering (EIConRus), pp. 1764–1768 (2019). https://doi.org/10.1109/EIConRus.2019.8657279

18. Hanifatunnisa, R., Rahardjo, B.: Blockchain based e-voting recording system design. In: 2017 11th International Conference on Telecommunication Systems Services and Applications (TSSA), pp. 1–6 (2017). https://doi.org/10.1109/TSSA.2017.8272896

19. Thuy, L.V.-C., Cao-Minh, K., Dang-Le-Bao, C., Nguyen, T.A.: Votereum: an Ethereum-Based E-Voting system. In: 2019 IEEE-RIVF International Conference on Computing and Communication Technologies (RIVF), Danang, pp. 1–6. IEEE, Vietnam (2019). https://doi.org/10.1109/RIVF.2019.8713661

20. Nguyen, Q.K.: Blockchain - a financial technology for future sustainable development. In: 2016 3rd International Conference on Green Technology and Sustainable Development (GTSD), pp. 51–54 (2016). https://doi.org/10.1109/GTSD.2016.22

21. Liu, Q., Guan, Q., Yang, X., Zhu, H., Green, G., Yin, S.: Education-industry cooperative system based on blockchain. In: 2018 1st IEEE International Conference on Hot Information-Centric Networking (HotICN), pp. 207–211. IEEE, Shenzhen (2018). https://doi.org/10.1109/HOTICN.2018.8606036

22. He, X., Alqahtani, S., Gamble, R.: Toward privacy-assured health insurance claims. In: 2018 IEEE International Conference on Internet of Things (iThings) and IEEE Green Computing and Communications (GreenCom) and IEEE Cyber, Physical and Social Computing (CPSCom) and IEEE Smart Data (SmartData), pp. 1634–1641. IEEE, Halifax, NS, Canada (2018). https://doi.org/10.1109/Cybermatics_2018.2018.00273

23. Nath, I.: Data exchange platform to fight insurance fraud on blockchain. In: 2016 IEEE 16th International Conference on Data Mining Workshops (ICDMW), pp. 821–825. IEEE, Barcelona, Spain (2016). https://doi.org/10.1109/ICDMW.2016.0121

24. Wu, H.-T., Tsai, C.-W.: An intelligent agriculture network security system based on private blockchains. J. Commun. Netw. **21**(5), 503–508 (2019). https://doi.org/10.1109/JCN.2019.000043

25. Mutambaie, M.K.: Blockchain Technology – The Next Computing Paradigm Shift, South Africa, p. 7 (2024)

26. bitcoin/bips32. Bitcoin (2022). Accessed 29 Mar 2022. https://github.com/bitcoin/bips/blob/274fa400d630ba757bec0c03b35ebe2345197108/bip-0032.mediawiki

27. 'Overview - OsmocomBB - Open Source Mobile Communications'. Accessed: Jul 2022. https://osmocom.org/projects/baseband

Blackhole Attack Detection and Countermeasure Solution in RPL

Fatiè Daoud Idriss Siéba, Hamadoun Tall, Amado Illy,
and Tiguiane Yélémou(✉)

Université Nazi BONI, Bobo-Dioulasso, Burkina Faso
tyelemou@gmail.com

Abstract. The Routing Protocol for Low-power and lossy networks (RPL) is proposed by the Routing Over Low-power and Lossy Networks (ROLL) team to meet the routing requirements of the Internet of Things. Since its introduction into our daily lives, the Internet of Things (IoT) has led to a considerable increase in the number of devices used for this purpose. Unfortunately, this increase has been accompanied by the emergence of a number of attacks affecting this equipment and network operation. The RPL protocol, for example, is subject to a blackhole attack aimed at isolating part of the network. Effective solutions are struggling to emerge due to the resource constraints of the connected objects used in these networks. In this paper, we present a lightweight and effective method for detecting blackhole attacks by the victim node itself, and propose countermeasures.

Keywords: blackhole attack · RPL

1 Introduction

The quick development of communication technologies and microelectronics has led to the emergence of miniature devices capable of communicating without a wired link. Most of these devices are characterised by their small size and limited resources (CPU, on-board power, memory). As a result, these nodes cannot support traditional routing protocols. This is why the Routing Over Low-power and Lossy Networks (ROLL) team of the Internet Engineering Task Force (IETF) proposed the Routing Protocol for Low-power and lossy networks (RPL) in March 2012 through RFC 6550 [1]. RPL allows nodes far from the sink to use intermediate nodes to transmit their data.

In its description, RPL has numerous security mechanisms that enable it to effectively face to external attacks. Unfortunately, most of these mechanisms are not sufficiently specified and therefore not implemented. This makes the protocol vulnerable to both internal and external attacks. The blackhole attack is one of the attacks to which this protocol is exposed. In this attack, a malicious node acting as an intermediary rejects messages sent to the sink node. This means that

A. Sere et al. (Eds.): AFRICOMM 2023, LNICST 587, pp. 288–295, 2025.
https://doi.org/10.1007/978-3-031-81570-6_19

packets coming from the downstream part of the sink and using this malicious node cannot reach the sink. This creates an isolation of this part of the network.

In this paper, we propose a mechanism for detecting this malicious behaviour by the victim node itself and an approach for thwarting the attack. Our approach does not involve any nodes other than the victim nodes. It is therefore less complex than most approaches involving additional nodes or the use of specific messages. The rest of our paper is organised as follows. In Sect. 2, we present a brief state of the art on RPL security. Our contribution is presented in Sect. 3. In Sect. 4, we conclude with some perspectives.

2   Related Works

RPL is a distance vector and source routing protocol. It is the preferred routing protocol for low-resource equipment. Because of the limited resources (CPU, on-board energy, memory) of sensor nodes, it is difficult to implement traditional security mechanisms in these networks. As a result, this protocol is vulnerable to a number of attacks. The authors of [2–4] propose a classification of these attacks as follows: resource attacks, topology attacks and traffic attacks. Figure 1 summarises these categories and the attacks belonging to them. as well as the attacks belonging to these categories.

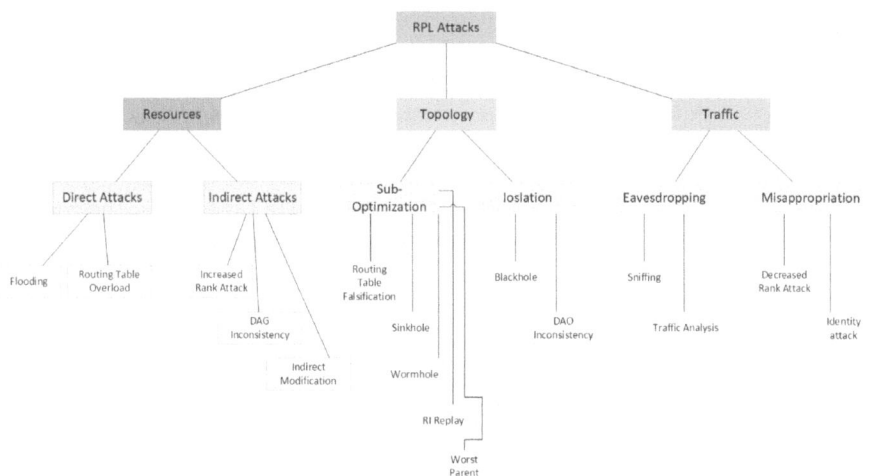

Fig. 1. Taxonomy of attacks against RPL networks [2].

In this paper, we are going to look at topology attacks. The aim of topology attacks is to affect the transmissions of certain network nodes. They can be divided into sub-optimisation attacks and isolation attacks. Sub-optimisation attacks concern the construction of the network and directly affect the network topology. The network does not converge optimally and the nodes do not use the best paths for their transmissions. Most of these attacks involve communicating incorrect control messages or inducing a node to choose a non-optimal parent. A malicious node may also delay the transmission of data messages to the destination. Path reversal is also used for espionage purposes.

Isolation attacks aim to prevent a node from transmitting its packets to a destination. They consist of retaining all or part of the victim's packets. These attacks can take place during topology construction by withholding control messages [5,6] or during the data transmission phase by simply deleting packets received from nodes downstream of the sink. Several authors have carried out work to counter these attacks. Verma et. Al [7] propose Ensemble Learning based Network Intrusion Detection System (ELNIDS). ELNIDS is an IDS based on artificial intelligence. This IDS uses learning to combat sinkhole, blackhole, selective forwarding, sybil, clone-ID, flooding and local repair attacks. The IDS uses the following modules: the sniffer, the sensor events/traffic repository, the feature extraction module, the analysis engine, the signature database and the alarm/attack notification manager. Although the test results highlight its performance, this evaluation was carried out on matlab and concerns only the overall binders.

Self-Organizing Map IDS for RPL Protocol Attacks was proposed in [8]. The solution uses artificial intelligence and more specifically Self-Organizing Maps (SOM), which was proposed by T. Kohenen. This method provides a simplified representation of a high-resolution map based on self-learning [8]. Various modules are used to produce this map. The IDS detects flooding, sinkhole and DODAG version number attacks. It all starts with data from various simulations in real-life situations. This data is provided as input to a module called 'aggregator'. This module takes six (06) parameters: message type (DIO/DIS/DAO), source IP address, destination IP address, current DODAG version value, current source node rank and Unix timestamp [8]. This input will give six (06) output parameters: the ratio of DIS messages, the ratio of DIO messages, the ratio of DAO messages, the ratio of version number changes, the ratio of rank changes and the energy consumption at the destination node. The ratios are calculated on the basis of the different messages having a common destination during a given period [8]. The output data is then passed on to a normalization module called the 'nomalizer', which is responsible for normalizing the data. After normalization, the data is then passed to the trainer module to build the maps. The downside of their assessment is the lack of data on the time taken to detect the attack, as well as the false positive and false negative rates.

Hybrid of Anomaly-Based and Specification-Based IDS for IoTs Using Unsupervised OPF Based on MapReduce Approach was proposed in [9]. This solution counters selective forwarding, sinkhole and wormhole attacks by combining an Anomaly Agent-Based IDS (AA-IDS) and several Specification Agent-Based IDSs (SA-IDSs) [10]. SA-IDSs are implemented at router node level, while AA-IDS is implemented at root node level. The role of SA-IDSs is to collect traffic information and help unmask malicious nodes. Once the data has been collected, it is transmitted to the root node. The root node is responsible for distributing the received data using an algorithm called Optimum-Path Forest without assistance. This algorithm groups the data into clusters, enabling the root node to perform anomaly detection. To classify nodes as malicious or not, the root node relies on the analyses of the AA-IDS and SA-IDSs. The IDS can be extended to cover attacks such as the Blackhole and decrease rank attacks. The downside of this solution is the high energy consumption of the router nodes and the root node, due to the tasks they perform.

Game Theory IDS was proposed in [11]. This IDS has a decentralized localization and combines signature-based detection with anomaly-based detection. Signature-based detection is used to detect known attacks on the RPL protocol, while anomaly-based detection is used to detect unknown attacks. In order to detect attacks, the system initializes a game between the two (02) IDSs and the attackers using Nash Equilibrium Game Theory. Nash Equilibrium is used in this solution to determine a state of equilibrium. This state of equilibrium enables the system to activate the anomaly detection technique to identify new attack signatures [11]. With the combination of these two (02) IDS types, the solution can counter flooding, sinkhole, blackhole, sybil and wormhole attacks.

In [12], Ribera et al. propose a solution for detecting blackhole and greyhole attacks using the heartbeat protocol. Their solution is based on the lightweight heartbeat protocol (LHP) proposed by Wallgren et al. in [13]. The solution in [13] is based on sending ICMPv6 ECHO messages at regular time intervals and waiting for a response from the receiving node. Any absence of response indicates a blackhole attack. Ribera et al. propose a solution with the same operating principle as LHP, the only difference being that messages are based on the User Datagram Protocol (UDP). According to the authors, this change enables a shorter detection time. Evaluation of their solution against normal operation shows only a 0.23% increase in CPU usage, 0.01% in TX transmission rate, and 0.06% in RX reception rate.

In [14], Lightweight Trust-Aware RPL is proposed by D. Airehrour et al. to combat blackhole and selective forwarding attacks. When these attacks are carried out, malicious nodes have a higher packet loss rate than normal nodes. Thus, the solution makes it possible to determine the reliability of nodes through trust values based on this characteristic of the attacks. The system works on the basis of the Minimum Rank with Hysteresis Objective Function (MRHOF). This function selects paths with low metrics, using hysteresis. Hysteresis will reduce the rate of disconnections due to small metric changes. Lightweight Trust-Aware RPL can detect complex blackhole attacks and control the frequency of rank changes. As a result, throughput and packet loss can be improved. Nevertheless, the solution has two drawbacks: high power consumption due to promiscuous mode, and unintentional packet rejection by some nodes due to errors that could be assimilated to a blackhole attack [14].

In [15], IOULIANOU et al. offer an intrusion detection system called Security Framework for RPL-Based IoT Networks (SRF-IoT) to combat blackhole and rank attacks. In its implementation, two networks are created. The first is a monitoring network featuring the SFR-IDS, and the second is the supervised network. The solution is based on the success rate of messages sent by each node, through a sniffing of packets sent across the network and other metrics that the SRF-IDS provides to the various nodes within its reach. This task is performed by the SRF-IDS to optimize the energy consumption of the network nodes being monitored. These metrics (node ip address, verified IP flag and number of packets sent) are sent to the nodes to enable them to choose the best parent by calculating a confidence value. Nodes with a value below a certain threshold are blacklisted. Although the solution is effective in detecting and isolating malicious nodes, it does entail the creation of large storage tables for neighborhood entries.

3   Our Solution

In this section, we present our approach to dealing with the blackhole attack. First, we present our mechanisms for detecting the attack. Then we propose a countermeasure solution. Unlike the majority of existing approaches, our approach uses only victim nodes with traditional RPL mechanisms for both detecting the attack and resolving it.

Principle of the Blackhole Attack Detection Solution. The solution we propose enables a malicious node to be detected in an RCSF using the various child nodes. In normal operation, a parent node receives messages from its child nodes and forwards them to the sink. In normal operation, some messages may not be transmitted for various reasons (poor quality radio links, a node that is far away and therefore unreachable, sabotage by a malicious parent node, etc.). The blackhole attack on the RPL protocol consists of a malicious parent node not retransmitting messages received from its children to the sink. Our solution enables a child to know whether or not its message is being retransmitted to the sink by its parent node. To this end, each node must operate in promiscuous mode and have two (02) counters: C1 and C2. Counters C1 and C2 are used respectively to count the number of messages sent by the node and the number of these messages retransmitted by its parent. The promiscuous mode in our situation allows the node to detect messages that are retransmitted by the parent node to the next node towards the sink. The malicious parent node in charge of sending their messages to the sink silently rejects them. Each node increments its C1 counter each time a data packet is sent. After sending, it listens to its parent. The data messages sent by the latter are intercepted and processed to determine whether the source address is its own. A comparison function is implemented to perform this task. Once the address has been obtained, the node compares this value with its own address. If the source address of the intercepted message is not its own, the message is simply dropped. If the source address is that of the node which sent the message, C2 is incremented. From the C1 and C2 counters, it will then be able to determine the rate of packets retransmitted to the sink with a ratio of C2/C1. To take into account the different causes of packet loss, the retransmission rate threshold for determining the malicious node is set at

50%. The choice of this threshold value is justified by the operating mode of the blackhole attack as well as other retransmission problems that may intervene. Taking these parameters into account, the child node can formally identify a malicious parent node.

Description of the Principle of the Detection Solution. Our proposed solution to the blackhole attack is based on the statistical results generated by the nodes through the C1 and C2 counters. This solution will allow a child node that detects that its parent is malicious to initiate a search procedure for a new parent. In addition to these counters, we are implementing a blacklist on each node to store the address of the malicious parent. Using the statistics provided by C1 and C2, when a child node determines that its parent is malicious, the first step is to activate the blacklisting function for the malicious parent's address. Once this has been done, the second step is to initiate a procedure to choose the new best parent. For this choice, the node will choose the second best parent that it has stored in its neighbourhood table. This operation will save resources compared to a global repair procedure. Once the new parent has been chosen, communications resume and the nodes in the subnetwork concerned reset their counters without removing the malicious parent from the blacklist cache. Our solution works as shown in the flowchart in Algorithms 1 and 2.

Algorithm 1. Malicious node detection

Require: $C1 = 0, C2 = 0, R = 0, i = 0$
  while $i < 11$ **do**
    if $next_h op! = NULL$ **then**
      node.child.sendto(next_hop)
      ++C1
      $listento(next\_hop)$
      if transfered_source_address=node.child.address **then**
        $+ + C2$
      end if
      $+ + i$
    end if
  end while
  $R = C2/C1$
  if $R < 0.5$ **then**
    print ("malicious node")
  end if

---

4   Conclusion

Threats to WSNs are on the increase. The nodes involved in these networks are highly vulnerable. Their low capacity (CPU, memory, on-board energy) makes it difficult to apply traditional security mechanisms. This paper highlights a number of attacks on RPL. We are particularly interested in the blackhole attack.

Algorithm 2. Blacklisting and new parent selection

if $R < 0.5$ **then**
   printf ("malicious node")
end if
blacklist(next_hop.id)
init_DIS_send
if $parent.id = next\_hop.id$ **then**
   reject(next_hop.id)
else
   select(parent.id)
end if
sent_DAO_send(parent.id)

This attack consists of a parent node preventing its child nodes from transmitting data to the sink. A number of solutions have been proposed to deal with this attack. Most of these solutions use IDS or cryptographic protocols. Due to the nature and complexity of some of these solutions, expected performance is mixed. Our contribution to securing RPL covers two aspects (detection and countermeasure). Detection is achieved through simple calculations based on a system of two counters and a ratio to determine a malicious parent. Countermeasure uses a blacklist and a mechanism to search for a new parent when the malicious parent is detected. The countermeasure principle uses RPL's own new parent search mechanism. This limits the additional resource-intensive operations required to counter the blackhole attack. For future work, we are planning real-life tests to confirm the performance of our approaches.

References

1. Brandt, A.,et al.: RFC 6550: RPL: IPv6 routing protocol for low-power and lossy networks (2012)
2. Almusaylim, Z.A., Alhumam, A., Jhanjhi, N.Z.: Proposing a secure RPL based internet of things routing protocol: a review. Ad Hoc Netw. **101**, 102096 (2020)
3. Boudouaia, M.A., Ali-Pacha, A., Abouaissa, A., Lorenz, P.: Security against rank attack in RPL protocols. IEEE Netw. **34**(4), 133–139 (2020)
4. Kamble, A., Malemath, V.S., Patil, D.: Security attacks and secure routing protocols in RPL-based internet of things: survey. In: 2017 International Conference on Emerging Trends & Innovation in ICT (ICEI), pp. 33–39. IEEE (2017)
5. Sokat, B.: Blackhole attacks in IoT networks. Ph.D. thesis, Izmir Institute of Technology (Turkey) (2020)
6. Mayzaud, A.: Monitoring and Security for the RPL-based Internet of Things. Ph.D. thesis, Université de Lorraine (2016)
7. Verma, A., Ranga, V.: ELNIDS: ensemble learning based network intrusion detection system for RPL based internet of things. In: 2019 4th International conference on Internet of Things: Smart innovation and usages (IoT-SIU), pp. 1–6. IEEE (2019)

8. Kfoury, E., Saab, J., Younes, P., Achkar, R.: A self organizing map intrusion detection system for RPL protocol attacks. Int. J. Interdiscipl. Telecommun. Netw. (IJITN) **11**(1), 30–43 (2019)
9. Bostani, H., Sheikhan, M.: Hybrid of anomaly-based and specification-based ids for internet of things using unsupervised OPF based on MapReduce approach. Comput. Commun. **98**, 52–71 (2017)
10. Simoglou, G., Violettas, G., Petridou, S., Mamatas, L.: Intrusion detection systems for RPL security: a comparative analysis. Comput. Secur. **104**, 102219 (2021)
11. Sedjelmaci, H., Senouci, S.M., Taleb, T.: An accurate security game for low-resource IoT devices. IEEE Trans. Veh. Technol. **66**(10), 9381–9393 (2017)
12. Ribera, E.G., Alvarez, B.M., Samuel, C., Ioulianou, P.P., Vassilakis, V.G.: Heartbeat-based detection of blackhole and greyhole attacks in RPL networks. In: 2020 12th International Symposium on Communication Systems, Networks and Digital Signal Processing (CSNDSP), pp. 1–6. IEEE (2020)
13. Wallgren, L., Raza, S., Voigt, T.: Routing attacks and countermeasures in the RPL-based internet of things. Int. J. Distrib. Sens. Netw. **9**(8), 794326 (2013)
14. Airehrour, D., Gutierrez, J., Ray, S.K.: A trust-aware RPL routing protocol to detect blackhole and selective forwarding attacks. J. Telecommun. Digital Econ. **5**(1), 50–69 (2017)
15. Ioulianou, P.P., Vassilakis, V.G., Shahandashti, S.F.: A trust-based intrusion detection system for RPL networks: detecting a combination of rank and blackhole attacks. J. Cybersecur. Priv. **2**(1), 124–153 (2022)

Social Engineering Attacks on the Cyber-Physical System: Human Cyber and Physical Impacts*

Robert Makila Beni(✉)📷

Université Nouveaux Horizons, Lubumbashi Route Kasapa 2465, Democratic Republic of the Congo
robert.makila@unhorizons.org

Abstract. Technological advancements have created new issues in IT security. Cyber-physical infrastructures, which mix physical elements with interconnected IT systems, have emerged as a major trend in industries such as transportation, energy, health, and public safety. However, the integration of the physical and digital worlds has generated new security threats, including social engineering attacks. Cybercriminals employ social engineering to trick users and obtain personal information or access privileges to computer systems. Social engineering attacks are frequently carried out using communication channels such as social networks, e-mails, and phone conversations. This study intends to investigate how social engineering attacks can be carried out in a cyber-physical-human environment. We will investigate the impact of cyber-physical-human infrastructures, cybercriminals' attack strategies, the effects of these attacks, and measures of prevention. The significance of this research stems from the fact that cyber-physical infrastructures are increasingly being employed in crucial scenarios where a breach in security could have fatal implications. It is therefore critical to understand the dangers associated with these infrastructures and to put adequate safeguards in place to protect them against social engineering attacks.

Keywords: Social Engineering · Cybersecurity · Cyber-physical Systems · Cyber-Physical-Human Systems · Human Factor · Industrial control systems

1 Introduction

Cyber-physical system (CPS) social engineering attacks are a rising worry. In order to get unauthorized access to sensitive data or systems, these assaults take advantage of human nature. Social engineering techniques can be used to persuade individuals to divulge private information, download malicious software,

---

* Université Nouveaux Horizons.

© ICST Institute for Computer Sciences, Social Informatics and Telecommunications Engineering 2025
Published by Springer Nature Switzerland AG 2025. All Rights Reserved
A. Sere et al. (Eds.): AFRICOMM 2023, LNICST 587, pp. 296–311, 2025.
https://doi.org/10.1007/978-3-031-81570-6_20

or access dangerous websites, all of which can jeopardize the security of CPS. Attackers frequently try to stop or slow down information flow, add unauthorized modifications to instructions or commands, send false information about how a system is operating, change ICS software and configuration settings, interfere with the operation of equipment protection systems, and also with the operation of safety systems.

The word has faced multiple malware attacks affecting industries with significant impacts : 1.In 1988, a Password attack on a programmable logic controller, causing a denial of service in the manufacturing plant, years after civil nuclear, chemical, energy, transport, water, food and health sectors also were targeted [3]. 2.The maroochy water services attack, causing a release of 265.000 gallons of untreated sewage [10]. 3.In 2016, an attack occured on ukrainian power grids, 30 stations were attacked depriving electricity to approximately 225.000 customers [10]. 4.The Pipedream recently launched in 2022, a disruptive and devastating attacks mutilple vital industrial devices [15]. Social engineering exploiting the human vulnerabilities is the reason thinking of the scenario on cyber-physcal infrastructures where he is an actor.

2   Related Studies

2.1   Human Factor, Cyber Hygiene, Cyber-Physical Systems, and Industrial Control Systems in the Context of Cybersecurity Master's Thesis Master of Engineering Cybersecurity 2023 , South-Eastern Finland University of Applied Sciences

This study investigates the cybersecurity risks of vital infrastructure systems, including human factors and operational technology (OT). The study proposes that the risk of cyberattacks can be mitigated by active learning, best practices, cultural change, fatigue and stress management, insider threat prevention, knowledge and skills development, personal safety, societal safety, and safety management [20].

The study also identifies the following OT best practices for reducing cyberattacks: Create and enforce a cyber hygiene policy - Implement cybersecurity awareness campaigns for employees and top management - Employ strict security policies - Implement an intrusion prevention and detection system (IPS/IDS) - Manage and control authorization and user accounts - Segment networks - Discover, identify, classify, and prioritize OT assets -Prevent OT threats - Implement physical security measures - Provide end-user awareness and training - Remove, disable, and rename unnecessary OT assets - Restrict the roles of temporary personnel -Secure remote access - Secure physical access - Keep software up to date, including operating systems, applications, and firmware - Use a web application firewall (WAF) - Implement virtual patch management. The study also recommends that CPS/ICS staff participate in cyber-exercises, such as penetration tests, phishing drills, ransomware drills, malware drills, DDoS drills, and incident response drills. These exercises can help staff to learn how to cooperate and communicate effectively during a cyberattack, investigate attacks, and recover from attacks [20].

2.2 Looking Back to Look Forward: Lessons Learnt from Cyber-Attacks on Industrial Control Systems

There has been a variety of cyberattacks since the 1980 s that target industrial control systems (ICS), some of which have had an effect on parts of critical national infrastructure (CNI) [21].

Although there are restrictions on who can access information on ICS-focused hacks, especially in a CNI context, this paper gives a thorough summary of those that have been publicly disclosed. In order to better understand attack vectors, threat actors, impact, and targeted sectors and locations, cyber-security practitioners can identify and analyze previous ICS-focused cyberattacks. This is important for the ongoing creation of comprehensive risk management strategies [21].

2.3 A History of Cyber Incidents and Threats Involving Industrial Control Systems

Malicious cyber attackers have been focusing on industrial control systems that oversee vital infrastructure assets for a long time. The majority of these incidents don't receive as much media attention as those involving enterprise (information technology) systems, therefore neither their specifics nor the dangers they pose are as well understood [10].

An examination of publicly documented cyber events involving vital infrastructure assets is provided in this chapter. The occurrences listed below are by no means all of them. However, the report highlights the rising trends in the volume and complexity of cyberattacks and offers useful insights into the dangers and vulnerabilities facing industrial control systems [10].

2.4 Industrial and Critical Infrastructure Security: Technical Analysis of Real-Life Security Incidents

Modern Information Technology (IT) components are being actively incorporated into industrial enterprises' critical infrastructures and their rigid Operational Technology (OT) architectures. However, as OT systems gradually grow more interconnected, they have subtly changed into enticing targets for various adversarial forces. This study presents a comprehensive and current survey of the most common threats and assaults against critical infrastructures, including Industrial Control Systems, as well as the communication protocols and devices used in these contexts [22].

This study shows that assaults on critical infrastructure increase in frequency due to the proliferation of cheap tools and methods that can help either the early or late stages of an attack. Furthermore, the investigation reveals that certain OT-specific network protocols and devices have flaws in their design and execution that might easily allow adversaries to have a decisive impact on physical operations [22].

- The authors provide a thorough study and discussion of the significant ICS and critical infrastructure (CI) security incidents to date. This makes it possible to get a full picture of the strategies, tactics, and practices used by the attackers. The events are further classified based on the types of vulnerabilities that take advantage of the level of the ICS that is affected, their results, and potential mitigation techniques [22].
- A comparison of all popular communication protocols used in the context of ICS and CI with regard to security features. This talk also goes into detail about the flaws in protocols that have been identified by the pertinent literature, which leads to frequent attack types and significant obstacles to achieving a higher level of security.
- An examination and discussion of the flaws found in academic research on ICS-specific devices, as well as how these flaws are used to subvert CI and ICS control mechanisms [22].

3   Literature Review

3.1   Social Engineering

Social engineering is a non-technical attack that uses human interaction to deceive victims into disclosing personal information or acting in ways that are harmful to themselves or an organization [2].

The direct communication between the perpetrator and the victim is the foundation of social engineering. Instead of using brute force, the attacker will typically attempt to persuade the target to compromise themselves.. The attack cycle gives these criminals a constant way to deceive you [6, 7].

Social Engineering Attack Cycle:

1. *Preparation.* The attacker will conduct background research on you or a larger organization in which you are connected. This data can be obtained through a variety of means, including social media, public records, and direct observation [2, 5].
2. *Infiltration.* The attacker will cultivate trust before establishing a relationship or initiating an engagement. Email, phone calls, and in-person meetings can all be used to do this [2].
3. *Exploitation.* Once trust and a vulnerability have been created, the attacker will use the victim to further the attack. This can be accomplished by asking sensitive information, installing malware, or enticing the victim to engage in other dangerous behavior [2].
4. *Disengagement.* The assailant abruptly ceases contact with the victim following his malicious activity and vanishes [2].

Types of Social Engineering Attacks:

1. *Phishing.* is a sort of cyber attack in which the adversary sends an email or text message that looks to be from a genuine source [1,2], such as a bank or credit card firm. The email or text message will frequently include a link that, when clicked, would redirect the victim to a false website that appears to be the actual one. The attacker can take the victim's personal information if they enter it on the bogus website [5,7]

2. *Vishing.* also known as voice phishing, the victim is duped into providing sensitive information over the phone by using emotions and fear [6].

3. *Smishing.* also known as SMS phishing, the victim is duped into supplying personal information over SMS [6].

4. *Baitware.* is a sort of attack in which the attacker leaves a USB drive or other electronic device in a public location. When the victim plugs in the device, malware is frequently installed on their computer [2,5].

5. *Tailgating.* An attack in which the attacker accompanies a legitimate employee into a secure location. Once inside, the attacker has the ability to steal sensitive data or install malware [2,5].

6. *Pretexting.* is the act of impersonating someone in order to obtain information that will permit access. Pretexting is a form of social engineering attack in which the attacker fabricates a fake situation to acquire the victim's trust. For example, the attacker could impersonate a government official or a representative of a respectable organization in order to deceive the victim into disclosing sensitive information [2,6].

7. *Dumpster Diving.* is the process of searching for information in someone else's waste [2,5].

8. *Eavesdropping.* an attacker listens or reads a conversation without authorization; he can also intercept any type of communication [1,2].

9. *Reverse Social Engineering.* the attacker makes himself so important that the victim seeks his advise before or after the attacker provides the information required [5].

10. *Piggybacking.* the purposeful or unintended facilitation of an authorized person [2].

11. *Shoulder sniffing.* He peers over someone's shoulder to obtain sensitive information such as a PIN or a password [2,5].

3.2   Cyber-Physical Systems

A cyber-physical infrastructure (CPI) is an integrated system that combines computation, networking, and physical processes. CPIs are becoming more popular because they provide a number of benefits, including increased efficiency, productivity, and safety.

Types of CPS:

- *Smart grids.* which utilize sensors and networking to monitor and control the flow of electricity [1].

- *Smart transportation systems.* Smart transportation systems monitor and control traffic flow using sensors and networking [1].
- *Smart buildings.* employ sensors and networking to monitor and control energy consumption, lighting, and other functions. [1]
- *Industrial control systems.* Industrial control systems monitor and control industrial processes through the use of sensors and networking [1].

Cyber-Physical Infrastructure Vulnerabilities:

- *Cyberattacks.* Cyberattacks have the potential to disrupt or disable CPIs [1]. For example, a cyberattacker could take control of a smart grid and trigger a power outage.
- *Physical attacks.* Physical attacks can be used to disrupt or deactivate CPIs as well [1]. An attacker, for example, could damage a smart transportation system by destroying its sensors or networking equipment [4].

Social Engineering Attacks on Cyber-Physical Systems: Social engineering attacks are a sort of attack that uses human interaction to deceive victims into disclosing personal information or acting in ways that are harmful to themselves or an organization [1]. As cyber-physical systems (CPS) become more interconnected and reliant on software and networks, they are increasingly being attacked by social engineering attacks.
Here are some examples of CPS social engineering attacks:

- *Attack 1.* In 2010, an attack known as "Stuxnet" damaged numerous nuclear installations in Iran. Hackers from the United States have recently carried out a number of cyber-attacks on Iran [9].
- *Attack 2.* Two examples of hacking ICS assaults that can be used to spy on individuals are DuQu and Flame. In 2012, Flame, for example, targeted and discovered numerous ICS networks in the Middle East. The primary purpose of this spyware was to obtain confidential information from businesses, such as addresses and keys inputted [9].
- *Attack 3.* An attacker hacked a computer at a water filtering plant in Pennsylvania (USA) and utilized it as its own spam and pirated software distribution systems [9].

CPS will become more vulnerable to social engineering attacks as they become more linked and reliant on software and networks. Organizations must be aware of the hazards of social engineering attacks and take precautions to defend themselves.

4   Materials and Methods

4.1   Case 1:

To assess the impact of the information technology agent's phishing awareness, a phishing assault test was carried out on June 24 at 12:41, specifically targeting the network administrator of a corporation with cyber-physical infrastructures categorized as smart buildings. The attack was prepared using the knowbe4 phishing tool to pretend to be an Insider IT using the email address it@companyname.domain. With an inoffensive link leading to a 404 not found page, the content explicitly requested a password change owing to a suspected breach. A second email was also sent to the attacker, robert.makila@unhorizons.org, to preview and check the efficacy of the scenario and ensure that it was delivered (Fig. 1).

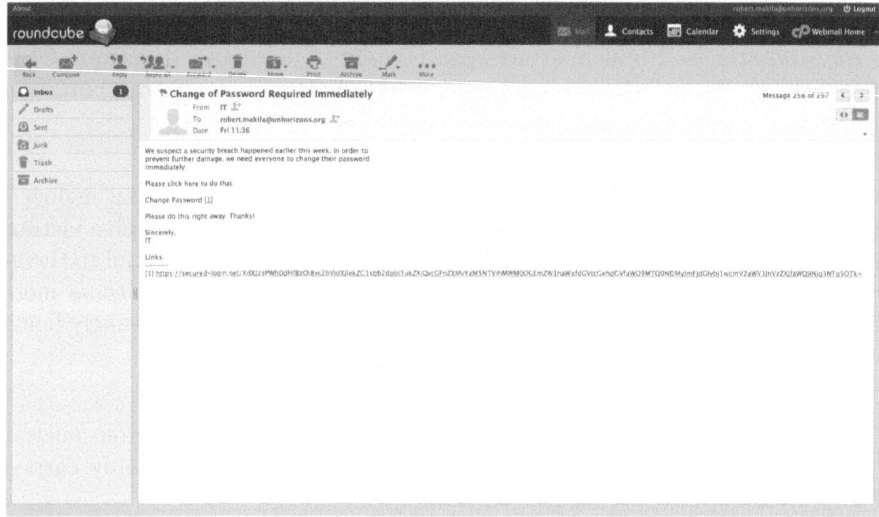

Fig. 1. Case 1 Phishing Attack Content.

4.2   Case 2:

Major CPS/ICS occurrences with a clearly defined attack history from 2000 to 2022 have been the subject of data collecting. A thorough examination of the first intrusion method to distribute or allow the malware to spread in the targeted systems is brought out from the historical narrative or scenario. Data is divided into two categories (cyber and physical) with the obvious purpose of determining the effect of social engineering approaches on cyber-physical systems. A strategy based on a cyber-physical-human assessment (Table 1).

The result demonstrates that ICS cyber attacks can be successful through a variety of delivery methods, including social engineering, insider attacks, and physical access. This suggests that a holistic approach to security is needed to mitigate ICS cyber attacks.

The Table 2 shows that social engineering, particularly spear-phishing, is the most common delivery method used in ICS cyber attacks apart from Directory

Table 1. Physical incidents table.

Ref	Name	Delivery Methods	Year
R [10]	Maroochy Water Service Breach	**Insider Attack**	2000
R [10]	Turkish Pipeline Explosion	**Physical access**	2008
R [10,11]	Stuxnet (Iran)	**Social Engineering : Tailgating, USB Stick**	2010
R [11,12]	Duqu	**Social Engineering : Tailgating, USB Stick**	2011
R [11–13]	Flame	**Social Engineering : Tailgating, USB Stick**	2011
R [3]	Shionogi	**Insider Attack**	2011
R [12]	Gauss	**Social Engineering : Tailgating, USB Stick**	2012
R [3]	Turbine control system	**Social Engineering : Tailgating, USB Stick**	2012
R [10,15]	Triton / Trisis	**Physical access**	2017

Table 2. Cyber incidents table.

Ref	Name	Delivery Methods	Year
R [10]	Night Dragon	**Social Engineering : Spear-Phishing**	2010
R [10]	Gas Pipeline	**Social Engineering : Spear-Phishing**	2012
R [10]	Shamoon	**Social Engineering : Spear-Phishing**	2012
R [3]	Niagara AX	**Directory Traversal**	2012
R [10]	Target Stores	**Social engineering : Phishing**	2013
R [10]	New York Dam	**Internet Accessible Device**	2013
R [10]	Havex	**Social engineering : Phishing**	2013
R [10,15]	German Steel Mill	**Social engineering : Spear-Phishing**	2014
R [10,15]	Dragonfly/Energetic Bear.1	**Social engineering : Spear-Phishing**	2014
R [10]	BlackEnergy	**Social engineering : Spear-Phishing**	2014
R [10,15]	Ukraine Power Grid1	**Social engineering : Spear-Phishing**	2015
R [10]	Kemuri Water Attack	**Vuln. on the Internet-facing payment App. server**	2016
R [10]	Shamoon 2	**Social engineering : Spear-Phishing**	2016
R [10]	Ukraine Power Grid2	**Social engineering : Spear-Phishing**	2016
R [10]	CRASHOVERRIDE / Industroyer	**Social engineering : Spear-Phishing**	2017
R [10]	APT33	**Social engineering : Spear-Phishing**	2017
R [10]	NotPetya	**Social engineering : Spear-Phishing**	2017
R [10]	Dragonfly/Energetic Bear.2	**Social engineering : Spear-Phishing**	2017
R [3]	Wolf Creek	**Social engineering : Phishing**	2017
R [19]	Samsam - Transportation	**Remote Desktop Protocol**	2018
R [18]	Norsk Hydro	**Social engineering : Spear-Phishing**	2019
R [3]	Oil producers attack	**Social engineering : Spear-Phishing**	2020
R [3]	Israeli Water Facilities	**Internet Accessible Device**	2020
R [3]	Honda	**Social engineering : Spear-Phishing**	2020
R [16]	Florida wanter plant attack	**Watering Hole**	2021
R [17]	Kojima industries attack	**Social engineering : Spear-Phishing**	2022
R [15]	Pipedream	**Social engineering : Spear-Phishing**	2022

traversal, Internet accessible device, phishing, watering hole and remote desktop. This is because spear-phishing attacks are targeted and personalized, making them more likely to be successful (Table 3).

5 Data Analysis and Results

5.1 Case 1:

Table 3. Case 1 Result table.

Target	Action	Time
Network Admin	Click	**Within the first 8 h of the attack**

The network administrator clicked on the simulated malicious link within the first 8 h of the attack, the attacker could gain access to the network and launch further attacks. The network administrator could then be used to spread malware to other devices on the network, steal sensitive data, or disrupt operations.

The human in a cyber-physical system can also make use of social engineering concepts as an insider. Insider attacker knows the infrastructure , can be able to not trigger the IDS alert, is trusted because he belongs to the targeted workers of the organization.

someone that has knowledge of the organization's information and intentionally negatively impacts the enterprise's integrity. In most cases, malicious insiders are former employees, contractors, or business partners, employees that never follow the information technology procedures and rules. employee whose computer is infected with malware. The attacker in the similar way of insider, used the insider email schema to build trust with the victim (Fig. 2 and 3).

5.2 Case 2:

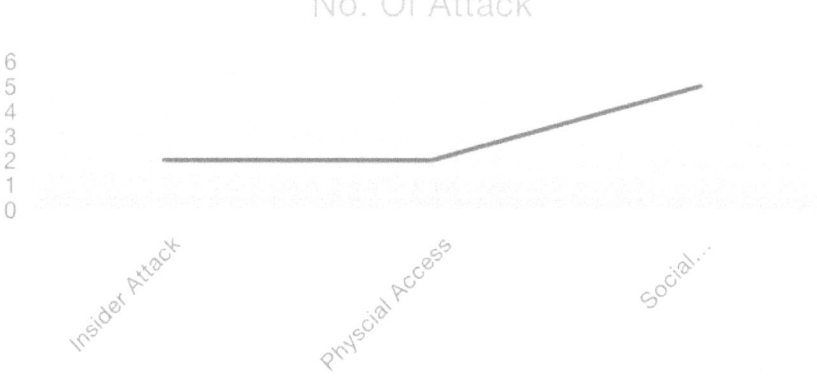

Fig. 2. Physical Incidents Result

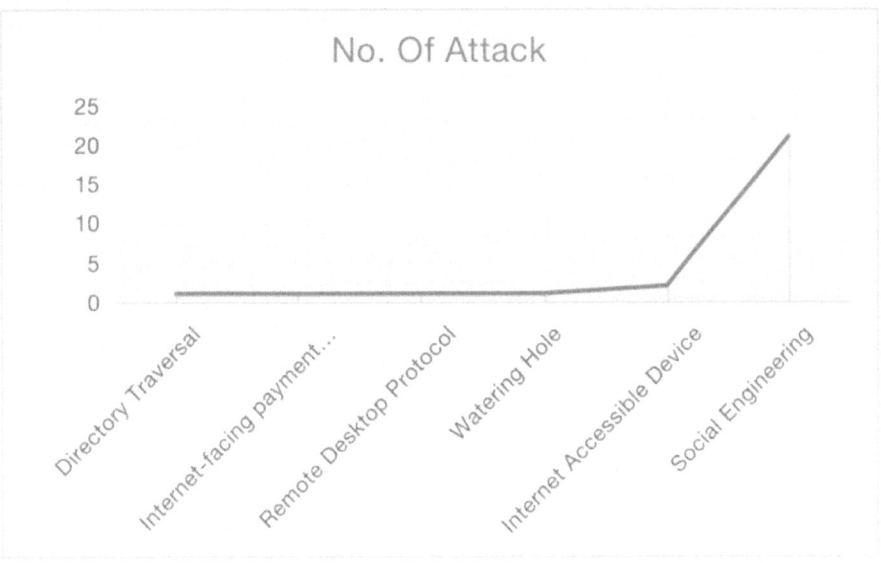

Fig. 3. Cyber Incidents Result

6   Discussion

6.1   Cyber and Physical Impact

Case 1 :
Targeting the Network Administrator is an attack with significant impact, as long as he stores very sensible information of the IT infrastructure (Password, etc.).

The attacker employed social engineering attack techniques to make the attack successful by appealing to the IT Administrator's emotions by posing an urgent scenario and requesting that he changes the password due to a security breach. In order to make the victim accept the pretext and think the source was an insider, the attacker also employed impersonation when sending the email with a reliable email account (the same domain name with the victim).The victim was unable to think whether or not to click the link . A phishing attack, which has been demonstrated in this study to be destructive on getting access to the internal network and the hacker can change data, break the confidentiality and integrity of the system after having access to the system.

Case 2 :
After gathering major incidents in the cyber-physical systems from 2000 to 2022, with a clear history of what exactly happened. One aspect and difficulty of conducting this study is that certain attacks remain unclear in their history, some companies hide information or deny attacks. we have been able to distinguish

cyber and physical incidents based on the prior delivery method used to conduct the attack. And results are significant in terms of social engineering attack aspects. The weakest component of the cyber-physical systems is the human. The reason that attackers used social engineering attacks in order to deliver malicious code or malware into the victim's system. This investigation has found the following results (Table 4):

Types of attacks :

- Physical attacks 25 %,
- Cyber attacks 75 % ;

Mode of attack : Social engineering :

- Physical attacks 55.5 %,
- Cyber Attacks 77.7 %,
- Cyber-Physical 58.3 %;

Average attack :

- Physical attacks 3 ,
- Cyber attacks 4.5.

Table 4. Cyber and Physical Impact table.

Statistics	Attack	Success rate
Rates : Physical attack	Physical	**25%**
Rates : Cyber attack	Cyber	**75%**
Mode : Physical attack	Social Engineering	**55.5%**
Mode : Cyber Attack	Social Engineering	**77.7%**
Mode : Cyber-Physical	Social Engineering	**58.3%**
Average : Physical Attack	Physical	**3**
Average : Cyber Attack	Cyber	**4,5**

Social engineering is the most common mode of attack for all these two types of attacks (Fig. 4 and (Table 5)).

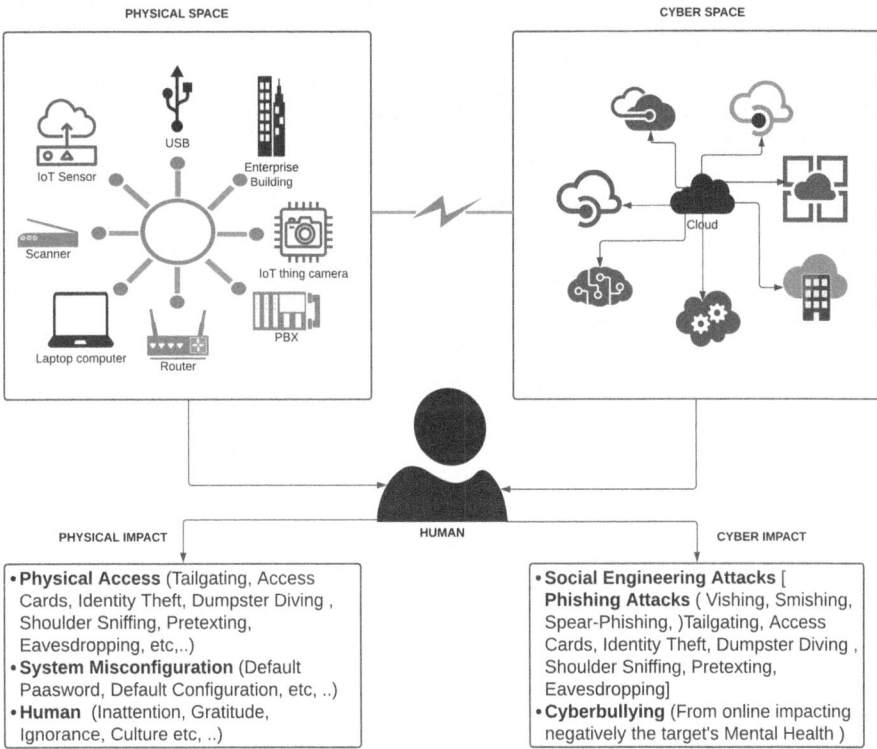

Fig. 4. Cyber and Physical Impact.

Table 5. Social Engineering : Cyber and Physical Impact with security goals table.

Attacks	Security goals affected	Cyber Impact	Physical Impact
Phishing, Vishing, Smishing, Spear Phishing, etc. ..	**Confidentiality, Integrity, Availability, Authentication**	- Malicious Injection - Sensitive Data Manipulation - Disclosure of sensitive information such as passwords, credits card number, - Malware Installation - Abuse of privilege	- Device dysfunction - Data loss integrity - Financial loss - Loss of reputation - Loss of production and revenue.
Pretexting, Impersonation, Tailgating, Diversion Theft, Baiting, Piggybacking, Reverse social engineering, etc. ...	**Confidentiality, Integrity, Availability**	- System disruption - Unauthorized Access. - Malware Installation	- Corporate espionage -Identity theft - Data Leakage - Trade secret disclosure
Eavesdropping	**Confidentiality**	- Information disclosed such as Password, Digital Signature	- Information disclosed such as physical address, reports, financial statement, Decision reports.
Shoulder Sniffing	**Confidentiality**	- Password, sensitive information are taken	- Important documents, evidence, information are disclosed

6.2 Social Engineering : Cyber and Physical Impact with Security Goals

6.3 Impact on Human and Good Security

Data Breaches. Social engineering attacks can be used to get sensitive data, such as consumer information, employee information, or intellectual property. This information can then be utilized for harmful objectives like identity theft, fraud, or industrial espionage [5, 8].

Disruptions to Critical Systems. Social engineering attacks can be used to disrupt critical systems such as electricity grids, transportation systems, or water systems. This can result in fatalities, property destruction, and economic upheaval [8].

Physical Harm. In some circumstances, social engineering attacks can cause physical harm to someone. An attacker, for example, could employ social engineering to deceive someone into opening a door or entering a building, where they could be attacked [4, 9].

Loss of Trust. Successful social engineering attacks can destroy trust between individuals, organizations, and governments. This can make collaboration on critical problems like cybersecurity and national security more challenging [9].

6.4 Consequences on Economics and Politics

Social engineering attacks can also have a huge economic and political impact. A data breach, for example, could cause a loss of trust in a firm or organization, resulting in a drop in sales or investment. A system outage could result in economic consequences such as lost production or infrastructure damage [9]. A physical attack could also result in the loss of life or major property damage, both of which could have a huge impact on a community or region [7, 9].

Economic Losses. Social engineering attacks can result in economic losses such as lost productivity, infrastructure damage, and reduced investment [7, 9].

Political Instability. Discord and instability within a country or region can be sown via social engineering attacks. This can make achieving political goals like peace and prosperity more challenging [7, 9].

7 Measures for Prevention

Employee Education. Employees should be taught how to recognize and report suspicious emails and phone calls . They should also understand the dangers of social engineering attacks and how to defend themselves. Being cautious with the information disclosed online, particularly on social media, to suspicious emails, imposters, phishing, etc. ... [5]

Security Measures. such as firewalls, intrusion detection systems, updating programs with the most recent security updates, using strong passwords [5], update them on a frequent basis and data encryption, can aid in the protection of cyber-physical systems against social engineering attempts [4,8].

Maintaining Resilience. Cyber-physical systems should be built to withstand social engineering attacks. This can be accomplished by employing redundant systems and situating essential systems in secure regions [5,8].

The novel approach to mitigating CPS cyber attacks based on human, cyber and physical aspects that have been outlined addresses all three of these delivery methods. By implementing a comprehensive security program that includes also Background checks, Firewalls, Intrusion detection and response systems, Encryption, Access Control and video surveillance and Physical barriers can significantly reduce the risk of a successful CPS cyber attack.

8   Limits and Perspectives Research on Social Engineering Attacks on Cyber-Physical Systems

There are several limitations to study on CPS social engineering attacks. One limitation is that replicating real-world attacks in a laboratory setting might be challenging. This work is crucial for the development of appropriate security mechanisms to safeguard CPS from these threats.

Understanding the Psychology of Social Engineering. what makes people vulnerable to social engineering attacks and how to develop effective responses.

Improving Security Awareness. attempting to increase CPS users' security awareness so that they can better identify and resist social engineering attempts.

The study of social engineering attacks on CPS is still in its early phases, but it is a significant area of study that has the potential to enhance CPS security.

9   Conclusion

Social engineering is a non-technical attack that uses human interaction to deceive victims into disclosing personal information or acting in ways that are harmful to themselves or an organization. As cyber-physical systems (CPS) become more interconnected and reliant on software and networks, they are increasingly being attacked by social engineering attacks. The basic notion behind social engineering on CPS is to use the human factor to obtain access to or control of a CPS. This can be accomplished through several strategies such as phishing, tailgating, and pretexting.

References

1. Jean-Paul, A.Y., Ola, S., Hassan, N.N., Nesrine, K., Ali, C., Mohamad, M.: Cyber-physical systems security: limitations, issues and future trends. Microprocessors Microsyst. **77**(103201), 1–15 (2020)
2. Breda, F., Barbosa, H., Morais, T.: Social engineering and cyber security. In: 11th International Technology. Education and Development Conference on Proceedings, pp. 4204–4211. IATED, Valencia, Spain (2017)

3. Thomas, M., Alexander, S., Sam, M., Miriam, S., Benjamin, G.: Looking back to look forward: lessons learnt from cyber-attacks on industrial control systems. Int. J. Crit. Infrastruct. Prot. **35**(100464), 1–18 (2021)
4. Solange G,.: Cybersecurite , Securite Informatique et Reseaux. 5th edn. Dunod, France (2016)
5. AqibHafiz, R.S., Jyoti.: social engineering attacks and prevention: a mirror review. Think India J. **22**(16), 2530–2536 (2019)
6. Ansh, M., Dev, V., Harsh, S., Jay, K., Dharmil, G.: A review of social engineering attacks and their mitigation solutions. Int. J. Eng. Tech. Res. **10**(10), 215–220 (2021)
7. Al-Mhiqani, M.N., Ahmad, R., Yassin, W., Hassan, A., Abidin, Z.Z., Ali, N.S., Abdulkareem, K.H., : Cyber-security incidents: a review cases in cyber-physical systems. Int. J. Adv. Comput. Sci. Appl. **9**(1), 500–508 (2018)
8. Ajeet S. , Anurag J.: Study of cyber attacks on cyber-physical system. In: 3rd International Conference on Internet of Things and Connected Technologies (ICIoTCT) on Proceedings, pp. 686–690. Elsevier, Jaipur (India) (2018)
9. Amit, K., Sreenath, N.: Cyber physical systems: analyses, challenges and possible solutions. Internet Things Cyber-Phys. Syst. **1**, 22–33 (2021)
10. Hemsley, K., Fisher, R.: A history of cyber incidents and threats involving industrial control systems. In: ICCIP 2018. IAICT, vol. 542, pp. 215–242. Springer, Cham (2018). https://doi.org/10.1007/978-3-030-04537-1_12
11. Eric, D.K., Joel, T.: Industrial Network Security (Second Edition), Securing Critical Infrastructure Networks for Smart Grid, SCADA, and Other Industrial Control Systems, 2nd edn. Syngress-Elsevier, USA (2014)
12. Paulo, S., Jana, S., Andrew, R.: Introduction to Cyber-Warfare: A Multidisciplinary Approach. Elsevier, USA (2013)
13. Rosenberg, J.: Embedded security, Rugged Embedded Systems: Computing in Harsh Environments. Elsevier, USA (2017)
14. Fayi, S.Y.A.: What Petya/NotPetya ransomware is and what its remidiations are. In: Latifi, S. (ed.) Information Technology - New Generations. AISC, vol. 738, pp. 93–100. Springer, Cham (2018). https://doi.org/10.1007/978-3-319-77028-4_15
15. Malik, M.I., Ibrahim, A., Hannay, P., Sikos, L.P.: Developing resilient cyber-physical systems : a review of state-of-the-art malware detection approaches, gaps, and future directions. Computers **12**(4), 79,1–26 (2023)
16. Few, C., Thompson, j., Awuson-David, K., Al-Hadhrami, T.: A case study in the use of attack graphs for predicting the security of cyber-physical systems. In: 2021 International Congress of Advanced Technology and Engineering (ICOTEN) on Proceedings, pp. 1–7. IEEE, Yemen (2021)
17. Md, H.R., Thorsten, W., Mohammed, S.: Manufacturing cybersecurity threat attributes and countermeasures: review, meta-taxonomy, and use cases of cyber-attack taxonomies. J. Manuf. Syst. **68**, 196–208 (2023)
18. Oueslati, N.E., Mrabet, H., Jemai, A., Alhomoud, A.: Comparative study of the common cyber-physical attacks in industry 4.0. In: 2019 International Conference on Internet of Things. Embedded Systems and Communications (IINTEC) on Proceedings, pp. 1–7. IEEE, Tunis, Tunisia (2019)
19. Hasssan, N.: Ransomware Revealed. Apress, Berkeley (2019)
20. Tuomala V.: Human factor, cyber hygiene,cyber-physical systems, and industrial control systems in the context of cybersecurity. Master thesis, South-Eastern Finland University of Applied Sciences, pp. 1–92 (2023)

21. Miller, T., Staves, A., Maesschalck, S., Sturdee, M., Green, B.: Looking back to look forward: Lessons learnt from cyber-attacks on industrial control systems. Int. J. Crit. Infrastruct. Prot. **35**(100464), 1–19 (2021)
22. Makrakis, G.M., Kolias, C., Kambourakis, G., Rieger, C., Benjamin, J.: Industrial and critical infrastructure security: technical analysis of real-life security incidents. IEEE Access **9**, 165295–165325 (2021)

Proposal of Honeypot-Based Data Mining Methods for the Discovery of Intrusions in Big Data Databases

Koffi Kanga[1]([✉]), Beman Hamidja Kamagaté[2], Raogo Kabore[3], and Souleymane Oumtanaga[4]

[1] ESATIC (Ecole Supérieure Africaine des TIC: Republic of Côte d'Ivoire), Abidjan, Côte d'Ivoire
Kanga.koffi@esatic.edu.ci

[2] Laboratory of Information, Communication Sciences and Technologies, (Ecole Supérieure Africaine Des TIC), LASTIC-ESATIC, Abidjan, Cote d'Ivoire, 18bp, 1501 Abidjan, Côte d'Ivoire
beman.kamagate@esatic.edu.ci

[3] Communication Sciences and Technologies (Ecole Supérieure Africaine Des TIC), LASTIC-ESATIC, Abidjan, Cote d'Ivoire, 18bp, 1501 Abidjan, Côte d'Ivoire
raogo.kabore@esatic.edu.ci

[4] Computer Science and Telecommunications Research Laboratory (Institut Nationale Polytechnique Houphouet Boigny), LARIT - INPHB, Yamoussoukro, Côte d'Ivoire

Summary. In this paper we propose a data mining technique for the discovery of intrusions in big data. To achieve our objective, we first reviewed the different data mining works and tools to our knowledge for the extraction of data from big data. Secondly, we chose a honeypot (honeyD) from a set (of honeypots) based on well-defined criteria. Thirdly, we combined this honeypot (honeyD) with different classification algorithms (decision trees and clustering such as k-means, DBSCAN to identify possible intrusions into the databases) in a functional architecture in which, we have presented and explained the role of each of its components. The implementation of our proposal shows that the combination of the honeypot with these different clustering algorithms gives convincing results which make it possible to detect possible intrusions in the data big databases.

Keywords: Intrusion detection · computer security · data mining · big data

1 Introduction

Talking about data mining methods for detecting intrusions in big data databases using honeypots deserves explanation.

Indeed, data mining is a set of techniques allowing extracting data or knowledge in the form of models allowing to describe the current behavior and/or to predict the future behavior of the system [2]. To do this, data mining makes use of statistical techniques, databases, data analysis and artificial intelligence.

© ICST Institute for Computer Sciences, Social Informatics and Telecommunications Engineering 2025
Published by Springer Nature Switzerland AG 2025. All Rights Reserved
A. Sere et al. (Eds.): AFRICOMM 2023, LNICST 587, pp. 312–332, 2025.
https://doi.org/10.1007/978-3-031-81570-6_21

As for big data, it is a concept that became popular in 2012 to reflect to the fact that companies are faced with increasingly large volumes of data to process, which present a strong commercial and marketing challenge. Several definitions exist in the literature [3], but we retained the one which stipulates that it is a set of technologies, architectures, tools and procedures allowing an organization to very quickly capture, process, analyze large quantities and heterogeneous and changing content, then extract relevant information at an affordable cost.

For the storage of this variety of data, big data makes use of four (4) families of DBMS called NoSQL (Key-value oriented database, document-oriented database, column-oriented database and graph-oriented database).

As for a honeypot, it would be defined according to the context of use. Thus, in the literature honeypots are defined as a means of attracting attackers, while others consider them as tools to detect intrusions.

In [6], a honeypot is defined as an effective counter -measure to prevent unauthorized use of critical information systems in networks. In the remainder of our paper, we adopt the following definition: "A honeypot is a secure resource which is set up and which has the objective of attracting hackers with the aim of not attacking or compromising them"

Furthermore, an intrusion is any use of a computer system for purposes other than those intended, generally due to the acquisition of privileges in an illegitimate manner.

For intrusion detection, it consists of analyzing the information collected in search of possible attacks by security audit mechanisms.

As for an intrusion detection system, it would be a set of tools and methods used to detect and report abnormal activities produced in a computer system. Thus, an IDS aims to protect a system from malicious activities coming from known or unknown sources. This protection is provided automatically to ensure the confidentiality, integrity and availability of the systems. Cannady et al. I in [7] states that an IDS has two detection approaches: anomaly-based detection and signature-based detection [7].

Today, the digital revolution with its corollary of exponential data growth, capturing these large volumes of data from various sources to be processed at a high and acceptable speed would be a wish; but securing this data seems even better. However, this security requires the implementation of a set of tools and processing methods (MAPREDUCE algorithm, Machine Learning, Deep Learning, etc.) based on data mining techniques in the big data databases.

The remainder of our paper is organized as follows:

- Sect. 2, we present the state of the art
- Sect. 3, we identify our problem
- Sect. 4, we illustrate our contribution and in
- Sect. 5, we present an implementation of our contribution
- Sect. 6 is devoted to a discussion and we will end with a conclusion in Sect. 7. In this section, we will identify some perspectives

2   State of the Art

2.1   Intrusion detection

In a computer system, intrusion detection involves two (2) approaches. The first is to look for signatures of known attacks while the second is to define normal system behavior and look for what does not fit into that behavior.

2.1.1   Signature Approach [8]

The signature approach consists in defining attack scenarios and searching for traces of these scenarios in the system. This system could contain big data databases and system audit (log) files.

- **The search for patterns**: this IDS-based method makes use of data from a database containing a set of signatures. In this set, each signature contains information about the protocols and ports used by a specific attack and a pattern to recognize suspicious packets.
- **Generic search**: it is suitable in the case of virus signatures. We look in the executable code for commands that are potentially dangerous, such as unreferenced and detected DOS commands, email broadcasts, instructions linked to known attacks.
- **Protocol analysis**: this is a method based on a flow conformity check and an observation of suspicious fields and parameters. This approach makes it possible to detect unknown attacks.
- **Integrity Check**: it takes a photo of all the files on a system and generates an alert in the event of corruption of one of the files.
- **Heuristic analysis and** anomaly detection: this approach carries out intelligent analysis which facilitates the detection of suspicious activity or any other anomaly.

2.1.2   Behavioral Approach [8]

The basic principle of the behavioral approach is to construct a reference model of the behavior of the monitored entity (user, machine, service, application) to which the observed behavior can be compared. If the latter is too far from the reference, an alert is issued to report the anomaly.

- **Probabilistic analysis**: this approach is sometimes described as **Bayesian**: Bayesian networks make it possible to model situations in which causality plays a role, but where knowledge of all the relationships between phenomena is incomplete, so that it is necessary to describe them in a probabilistic way. Thus, for each element of the profile, the probability of each event likely to occur subsequently is specified. The indications obtained progressively on the state of the modeled system influence the confidence granted to a given proposition.
- **Statistical analysis**: in this approach, the profile is established by observing the value of certain parameters of the system considered as random variables. For each system parameter, a statistical model is used to establish the distribution of the corresponding random variable. Once the model is established, a distance vector is calculated between the stream of observed events and the profile. If the distance exceeds a certain threshold, an alert is issued.

- **Immunology**: builds a model of normal behavior of services (and not users). Here we observe a service for a long enough time in good conditions to build a complete behavior model.
- **graphs**: The goal is to highlight properties and the relationships between these properties. The advantage of this approach is that it makes it easier to process rare events.

2.2 Architecture and Intrusion Detection Honeypot

2.2.1 Intrusion Detection Architecture [9]

Intrusion detection architectures can be classified into three categories:

- **Centralized architecture:** In this architecture, all intrusion detection data is collected and analyzed from a centralized location. This can include data from different endpoints such as firewalls, IDSs, IPSs, anti-virus software. This architecture is generally used in fixed networks and enterprises.
- **Distributed and cooperative architecture:** In this architecture, the data is shared between the nodes for a global analysis of the security of the network. Alerts are generated if an intrusion is detected by multiple nodes. This architecture is generally used in wireless sensor networks and ad hoc networks.
- **Hierarchical architecture:** In this architecture, certain nodes are designated as monitoring nodes to collect and analyze intrusion detection data. In Table 1 below, we make a comparison of these architectures.

Table 1. Comparative table of IDS architectures

Comparison criterion	Centralized architecture	Distributed and cooperative architecture	Hierarchical architecture
Global overview	Yes	Yes	Yes
Centralized alert management	Yes	No	Yes
Ability to detect threats	Yes	Yes	Yes
Single point of failure	Yes	No	Yes
Reliability	Yes	Medium to high	Medium to high

2.2.2 Honeypots for Intrusion Detection [9]

In [9], the authors present the honeypots according to their implementation environment and their level of interaction. So, for the implementation environment, they present the production and research honeypot. The production honeypots are used to detect attacks from the outside while the research honeypots are used to study the activities of hackers.

According to the level of interaction, the authors present:

– **Low Interaction Honeypots**

They would be easier to install, configure, deploy and maintain due to their fairly simple design. They are best known for their powers of detecting unauthorized connections. Since the functionalities offered by these honeypots are limited, the level of attack risk also seems limited. This type of honeypot is not designed to discover new attacks, but rather to monitor and analyze the network environment of the place where they are installed.

– **Medium Interaction Honeypots**

These honeypots offer more functionality than those in the previous category and therefore their interaction levels are relatively higher. They require more attention during installation and configuration. However, the configuration must always take into consideration network security when the honeypot is attacked.

– **High Interaction Honeypots**

These honeypots provide more information about attacks, but consume more time during installation, configuration and maintenance. They also present a very high level of risk because they give attackers greater control over the operating system. Moreover, these honeypots are often installed in an uncontrolled portion of the network (e.g. absence of a firewall) and it is often necessary to strengthen the security of the rest of the network in order to minimize the risk that the honeypot be used as a starting point for an attack.

2.2.3   Data Mining Methods [10]

We distinguish two Data mining techniques:

Techniques Supervised

They produce prediction models, which from the values of a set of predictor variables (input values), predict the value of a target variable or variable to be explained (output value). They include three classes of techniques:

- Estimation: brings together the techniques which make it possible to define the link between a set of predictor variables and a target variable of numerical type.
- Classification: brings together the techniques which make it possible to define the link between a set of predictor variables and a categorical target variable, most often Boolean.
- Forecasting: similar to estimation and classification except that the results relate to the future.

Unsupervised Techniques

They produce clustering models, which from the values of a set of variables, they classify the current object in a class (cluster), the classes are unknown in advance. In this category, there are three classes of techniques:

- Description: gathers the techniques which make it possible to describe the links between the various variables of the concept.
- Grouping (clustering): groups the techniques which make it possible to create classes of data similar between them and different from the data of another class (that is to say, the intersection between the classes must always be empty).
- Association: gathers the techniques which make it possible to describe the links between the values of the various variables of the concept by producing for example a model of rules of association.

2.2.4 Algorithm Types

- Association rule detection algorithm: This algorithm uses data mining techniques to identify association rules between system activities and intrusions. It can detect intrusions that have similar patterns to previous intrusions, but it may be sensitive to variations in data and false alarms.
- Behavior Detection Algorithm: This algorithm uses behavior monitoring techniques to identify abnormal user and system behavior. It can detect intrusions that have never been seen before, but it can be sensitive to variations in normal behavior and false alarms.
- Correlation algorithms: use correlation techniques to detect relationships between different security events and identify potential attacks.
- Model-based algorithms: build a model of normal behavior and detect anomalies by comparing real data to this model.
- Neural network-based detection algorithm: This algorithm uses neural networks to identify anomalous activity in the data (Table 2).

Table 2. Comparative table of data mining algorithms

Big data database family	Association rule detection	Behavior detection	Correlation detection	Detection based on neural networks	Model-based detection
Key-value	No	Yes	No	Yes	No
Document oriented	No	Yes	No	Yes	Yes
Column oriented	Yes	Yes	Yes	Yes	Yes
Graphs	No	No	Yes	Yes	No

2.3   Intrusion Detection Tools [10]

In the literature, several intrusion detection tools exist. In this part we present the most representative ones to our knowledge in terms of their mode of operation and their different architectures.

2.3.1   SNORT

SNORT is an Open Source Network Intrusion Detection System (NIDS), capable of analyzing real-time traffic on IP networks.

SNORT is able to perform real-time network traffic analysis and is equipped with different intrusion detection technologies such as protocol analysis and pattern matching, it can detect many types of attacks such as: malware, buffer overflows, port scans and sniffing.

● Operating Mode

The "offline" sniffer mode which simply reads the packets circulating on the network and displays them continuously on the screen. It is a question of listening to the network, by typing one or more lines of commands which will indicate to SNORT the type of result to be displayed.

The "packet logger" mode which logs packets to disk. This mode is in all respects similar to the previous one, except that the logs are no longer displayed on the screen, but are entered directly into a log file.

The more configurable NIDS mode, which allows to analyze the traffic on the network following rules defined by the user and to establish actions to be carried out according to the cases.

● SNORT Architecture [11, 12]

The essential components of the SNORT architecture are:

− **Packet Decoder**: it captures data packets from network interfaces, prepares them to be pre-processed or sent to the detection engine.
− **Pre-processor**: these are components used with SNORT to improve the possibilities of analysis and recomposition of captured traffic. They receive the packets, reprocess them and send them to the detection engine.
− **Detection Engine**: This is the most important component of SNORT. Its role is to detect any intrusions that exist in a packet. To do so, the search engine is based on the rules of SNORT. Indeed, this engine consults these rules and compares them one by one with the data packet. If there is compliance, the detector records it in the log file and/or generates an alert. Otherwise the packet is dropped.
− **Logging and Alerting System:** it allows to generate alerts and log messages according to what the detection engine has found in the analyzed packet.
− **Output modules** (or plugins): allows the intrusion generated by the alert and notification system to be processed in several ways (sends to a log file, generates an alert message to a Syslog server, or stores this intrusion in a database) (Fig. 1).

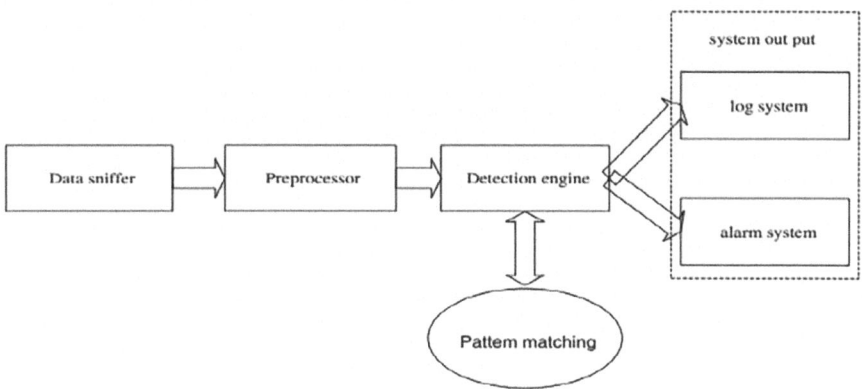

Fig. 1. Simplified architecture of SNORT [11]

2.3.2 Meerkat [13]

Suricata is an open-source intrusion detection system (IDS) that helps detect attacks and anomalies on computer networks. It is capable of processing high-speed data streams using hardware or software acceleration technologies to improve performance. It is based on a multi-threaded architecture and uses detection rules written in Lua language. It can be used in detection, prevention or network analysis mode. It supports a variety of network protocols, such as TCP, UDP, HTTP, DNS and SLL, it can detect anomalies and suspicious behavior in the data of these protocols. It uses different detection mechanisms, including basic signatures, behavior analysis, and protocol rules. It can also use network analysis tools to identify trends and attack patterns. It can integrate with existing security tools such as Security Management Systems (SIEM) for comprehensive analysis.

- **Operating Mode**

  Suricata's mode of operation is based on a layered architecture that enables efficient processing of network data. It consists of several layers, each playing a specific role in detecting intrusions.

- **Packet capture**: The first layer is responsible for capturing network packets using technologies such as LIB PCAP or PF_RING. The packets are then forwarded to the next layer for analysis.
- **Protocol analysis**: The second layer is responsible for analyzing network protocols such as TCP, UDP, HTTP, DNS and SSL. It uses mechanisms such as base signatures, behavior analysis, and protocol rules to detect anomalies and suspicious behavior.
- **Intrusion detection**: The third layer is responsible for detecting intrusions using the information collected by the previous layers. It uses network analysis tools to identify trends and attack patterns.
- **Notification**: The last layer is responsible for the notification of alerts and detected incidents. Alerts can be sent by email, SMS or via a web interface. It can also integrate with existing security tools such as Security Management Systems (SIEM) for comprehensive analysis (Fig. 2).

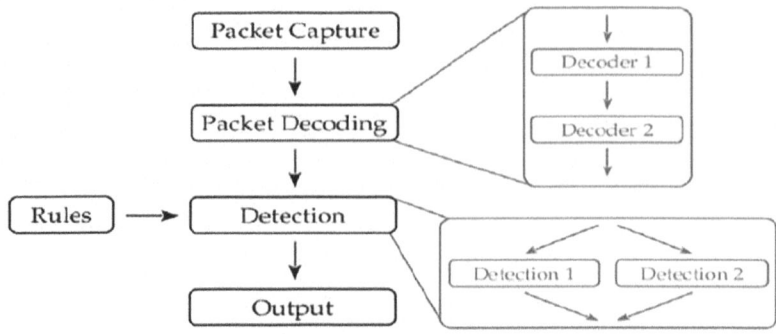

Fig. 2. SURICATA architecture

2.3.3 OSSEC (OpenSource Security)

It is an open-source intrusion detection system (HIDS) that helps monitor activities on operating systems and networks. It uses signature-based detection techniques to detect known intrusions and behavior-based detection to detect unknown intrusions. It can also use log analysis tools to identify trends and attack patterns. It is based on a client-server architecture and makes it possible to centralize the security data of several systems; which facilitates the management of alerts and decision-making. It supports a large number of operating systems, such as Windows, Linux, MacOs, and BSD (Fig. 3).

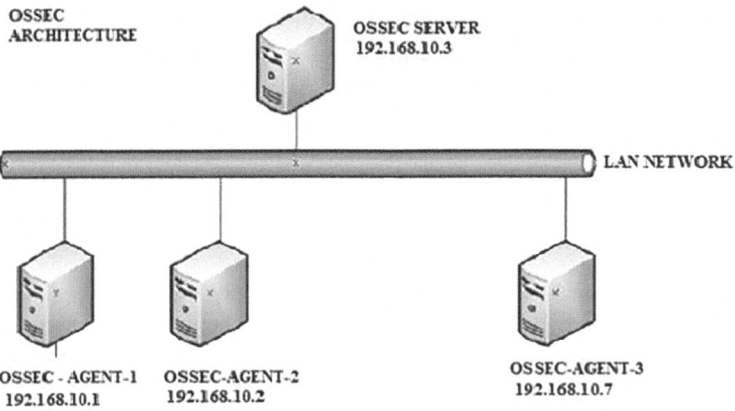

Fig. 3. Architecture of OSSEC [14]

- **Operating Mode**

OSSEC's mode of operation is based on client-server architecture. It consists of several components that work together to detect intrusions and anomalies on systems and networks. These are:

- **Agent**: this component consists of agents installed on the systems and networks to be monitored. They collect security information, such as event logs and security alerts, and send them to the OSSEC server for analysis.
- **Server**: The **server component** is responsible for analyzing the data collected by the agents. It uses signature-based detection rules and machine learning algorithms to identify anomalies and suspicious behavior. It generates alerts in the event of intrusion detection.
- **Console**: The OSSEC **console component** is a web interface that allows you to manage alerts, rules and configurations. It also allows you to view analytics data and generate reports.
- **Notification**: this component of OSSEC is able to notify administrators in the event of intrusion or anomaly detection via email or SMS notifications. It can also integrate existing security tools such as security management systems (SIEM) for comprehensive analysis.

2.4 Other Intrusion Detection Tools (IDS)

It is important to note that this list is not exhaustive and that new software is developed regularly, so it is important to keep researching the latest technology to ensure that you are using the best tool. For these other forms of tools, we classify them into 3 (three) categories. These are:

- Network Based Tools (NIDS): Bro, Tripwire, McAfee Network Security Platform, Symantec DeepSight IDS, Prelude-IDS, SELKS
- Host Based Tools (HIDS): McAfee Host Intrusion Prevention System, Wazuh, AppArmor, SELinux, ClamAV
- IDS hybrid tools: OSSEC, AIDE, Tripwire

Table 3. Advantages and disadvantages of other IDSs

	Benefits	Disadvantages
NESTS	Alarm in case of anomaly Multiple positioning Real Time Execution	Signatures to be updated, Traffic absorption. Inoperative for encrypted streams Management of false positives, Expertise desired
HIDS	Station protection Real-Time Execution	Ineffective against attacks on multiple hosts. Different configurations depending on the systems used
Hybrid	Reduction of false positives Real Time Execution Ensures the correlation of events	More sources, more difficult management and interpretation of alarms

For comparison, we present the advantages and disadvantages of these 3 categories in Table 3.

3 Problematic

From this literature review, it appears that excellent research work has been carried out. This work resulted in the implementation or use of IDS. Others use data mining techniques and methods to highlight malicious activity. The question that arises at the moment would be to know what result would we obtain if we proceeded to set up an environment using data mining tools coupled with honeypots?

4 Contribution

In this part, we make the choice of honeypot based on well-defined criteria. This choice will be coupled with a data mining technique which is itself selected according to equally defined criteria. Thus presented, our contribution is the combination of a honeypot with different data mining techniques in an architecture whose components and roles will be presented.

4.1 Choosing the Type of Honeypot

4.1.1 Selection Criteria

In order to choose the type of honeypot best suited to our needs, we define the selection criteria according to the objectives set. To do this, we have:

- **The relevance of the data collected**: The honeypot must be able to collect the data relevant to our analysis.
- **Event log collection**: The honeypot must be able to collect real-time event logs for further analysis.
- **Scalability**: In the case of big data, it is important to choose a honeypot that can evolve according to the growth of the data.
- **Data security**: It is important to ensure that the selected honeypot can protect collected data and event logs from unauthorized access.
- **Big data database configuration**: A honeypot that can be configured to connect and collect data from big data databases.

   By taking into account these aforementioned selection criteria, we will be able to make an informed choice for the type of honeypot that will best suit our needs.

4.1.2 Evaluation of the Different Types of Honeypots

The identified honeypots are classified according to the level of interaction: low, medium and high.

The Relevance of the Data Collected: In general, honeypots with a high level of interaction are considered to be the most suitable in terms of the relevance of the data collected. This is due to their ability to more realistically simulate target environments for attackers. Honeypots with a lower level of interaction can also be used to collect useful data, but they may be less efficient in terms of the relevance of the data collected.

Event Log Collection: Highly interacting honeypots are best suited for event log collection. They can capture and record a large amount of information about malicious interactions with the system. Low interaction level and medium interaction level honeypots also collect event logs, but less in a comprehensive and detailed way.

Scalability: Low-level interaction honeypots are the most suitable for scalability, as they are generally simpler and lighter to manage. High-interaction honeypots can be more difficult to manage and use due to their increased complexity. Medium-level interaction honeypots fall somewhere in between in terms of ease of management and use.

Data Security: When it comes to security, high interaction level honeypots are considered the most secure, followed by medium interaction level honeypots and finally low interaction level honeypots. High interaction honeypots are considered the most secure because they mimic a real system or application hence the attention required for configuring and securing the system. Unlike the other types of honeypot mentioned.

Big Data Database Configuration: Honeypots with a high level of interaction are the most suitable for configuring big data databases. They offer large data storage and processing capacity. Honeypots with low levels of interaction are generally considered the least effective, as they lack the functionality needed to process the enormous amounts of data. As for honeypots with a medium level of interaction, they generally have a greater variety of functionalities for processing data.

4.1.3   Choice and Justification

Table 4. Summary of the strengths and weaknesses of the different types of honeypots according to the criteria

Criteria	Low Level Honeypot	Mid -Level Honeypot	High Level Honeypot
Relevance of the data collected	Low to medium	Medium to high	High
Collecting event logs	Medium to high	High	High
Scalability	High	Medium to high	Medium to high
Data security	Average	High	High
Configuring the big data database	Low to medium	Average	High

As established in the table, high-level honeypots best meet the various criteria set out. Our choice then fell towards a honeypot with a high level of interaction (HoneyD) (Table 4).

4.2   Choice of Data Mining Methods

4.2.1   Selection Criteria

In order to choose the data mining method best suited to our needs, it is important to define the selection criteria according to the objectives set. To do this, we have:

Accuracy: Accuracy refers to the ability of the data mining method to correctly detect database intrusions. The higher the accuracy, the fewer false alerts generated by the method.

Prediction Time: Prediction time refers to the time required for the data mining method to process the data and produce results. For effective intrusion detection, it is important to choose a method that is capable of processing data in real time.

Scalability: In the case of big data, it is important to choose a model that can evolve according to the growth of the data collected.

4.2.2   Evaluation of the Different Types

Classification and clustering are two popular techniques used in data mining to solve pattern recognition and data grouping problems. Although they have similar goals, they differ in terms of accuracy, prediction time and scalability.

Accuracy: When it comes to accuracy, classification is considered more accurate than clustering. This is because the classification is supervised and uses feedback to correct errors, thereby maximizing the accuracy of predictions. Clustering, on the other hand, is an unsupervised process and does not use feedback to correct errors, which can lead to lower prediction accuracy.

Prediction time: In general, classification takes longer than clustering to make predictions because it has to perform deeper analysis of the data to determine the relationships between variables. Clustering, on the other hand, is faster because it does not require such in-depth data analysis.

Scalability: Clustering is often considered more scalable than classification because it can process larger amounts of data in a short time. Classification, on the other hand, can become slower and less efficient as the amount of data increases, which can make it difficult to use for large data sets.

4.2.3   Choice and Rationale

Finally, we opt to combine the two techniques to benefit from the advantages of each of them and obtain more precise and reliable results (Table 5).

Table 5. Summary table

Criteria	Classification	Clustering
Precision	High	Moderate
Prediction time	Moderate to high	Fast
Scalability	Low to moderate	High

4.3 Choice of Data Mining Models

4.3.1 Classification

The different types of classification algorithms are:

– **Regressions**: such as logistic regression, which predicts the probability of belonging to a given class using a regression function.
– **Decision trees**: such as C4.5 and ID3, which use a tree structure to separate data into smaller subgroups and classify data based on different conditions on the features.
– **Nearest neighbors**: such as KNN, which classifies an observation according to its k nearest neighbors.
– **Bayesian classification**: such as Naïve Bayes, which uses probability theorems to predict the class of an observation.

4.3.2 Clustering

The different types of clustering algorithms are:

– K-means: It is an algorithm that partitions a data set into k groups based on their geometric proximity.
– Density-based clustering (DBSCAN): This is an algorithm that finds clusters by identifying regions of high density in the data.

4.4 Solution Design

In this part, we will design our new intrusion detection architecture and present its components.

4.4.1 Presentation of the Solution

Our solution offers a particular approach for intrusion detection in big data databases. It incorporates the use of honeypots to collect information on potentially malicious activity, combined with classification and clustering algorithms to identify malicious behavior. This method enables fast and effective detection of intrusions and dangerous activities, thus minimizing the risks to databases. The algorithms used are trained on representative data to guarantee their reliability. To implement such a solution, we have identified several key steps, namely: setting up a honeypot, collecting and preparing data, training algorithms and intrusion detection.

4.4.2 Functional Architecture

The functional architecture of our solution is as follows (Fig. 4):

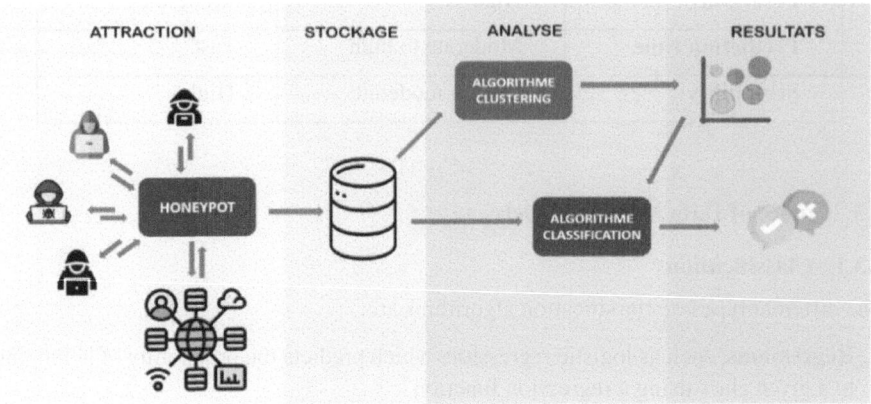

Fig. 4. Functional architecture of the solution

a) Attraction area

This entry area includes:

- Attackers such as hackers.
- A honeypot with a high level of interaction which serves as a trap for potential attackers. It collects information on attack techniques and intruder behaviors to help better understand and prevent threats.

  b) Storage area
  c) Analysis area

  This input area includes:

- Clustering algorithm: it groups suspicious activities into different groups based on their similar characteristics using data collected by the honeypot.
- the Classification algorithm: it analyzes the data collected by the honeypot and the groups formed by the clustering algorithm to determine whether they represent a threat or not. By using the information from the clustering for a more detailed analysis, it thus reinforces the precision of its results and minimizes false positives.

d) Results area

It corresponds to the area where the results of the different analyses of our clustering and classification algorithms are stored.

5   Implementation

5.1   Presentation of the Tools

For the implementation of our solution, we made use of the tools presented in Table 6 below:

Table 6. Implementation tools

TOOLS	PRESENTATION
Python	It allowed us to write machine learning programs faster and more efficiently using Scikit-learn, Pandas, Numpy.
Google Colab	It allowed us to write and run code in Python, document our code that supports math equations, import external datasets, have free cloud services with free GPU, integrate Numpy , Pandas, Scikit-learn.
Ubuntu	It served as our host OS for installing our honeypot.

5.2   Implementation Approach

In order to solve the problem of intrusion detection in big data databases, we use classification and clustering algorithms. This choice is motivated by a study, we want to compare these different algorithms to make a better proposal for a classification method and/or technique.

5.2.1   Collecting Data with the Honeypot (Honeyd)

Data Collection is Done Using the HoneyD Tools
It allowed us to log connection attempts and malicious queries to the simulated NoSQL-like database. It also allowed us to collect information on the modus operandi of the attackers. This information helps with accuracy in predicting intrusions.

5.2.2   Clustering and Classification

The steps of our analysis are as follows:

– Importing modules and loading data

   In this step we load the data as well as the different python libraries that will allow us to use the data. We have the **KDD Cup 99 datasheet** to train our model. This datasheet includes information about attacks.

5.2.3 Data Processing

This analysis step consists of understanding and visualizing the data to assess their quality and relevance for the model. It involves correcting errors and inconsistencies, transforming data to fit algorithms, and determining the most important variables to include in the model. It also helps uncover correlations between variables, hidden trends and patterns present in the data.

– **Scaling qualitative attributes**

  Encoding consists of giving codes to column values that are text.

– **Reduction or selection of features**

  Feature selection involves choosing the most relevant variables to include in the model. We use principal component analysis (PCA). This step reduces the dimensions of the dataset for better analysis.

5.3 Application of Clustering Algorithms

After these steps we select the parameters associated with each clustering algorithm.

5.3.1 Dbscan

• Choice of parameters

  We use the grid method for the choice of parameters (distance and minimum points).

• Application of DBSCAN (Fig. 5)

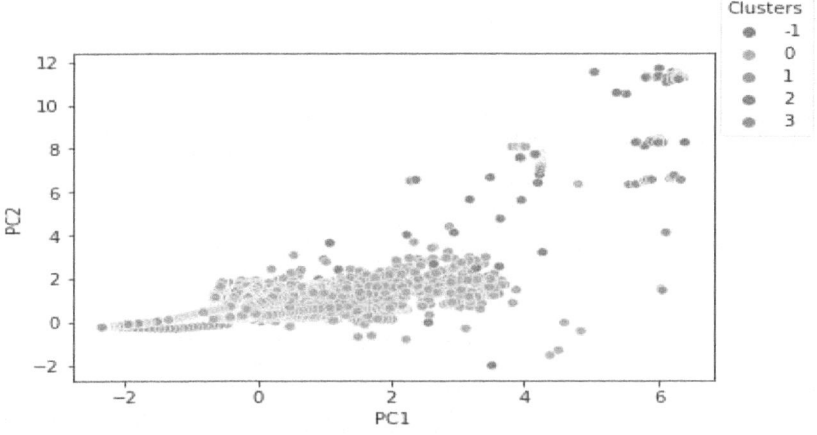

Fig. 5. dbscan algorithm results

We obtain 5 clusters, one of which consists of outliers.

5.3.2 K-Means

- Choice of parameter K (number of clusters)

The parameter K represents the number of clusters to form, we use the Elbow method to find the number of clusters to form (Fig. 6).

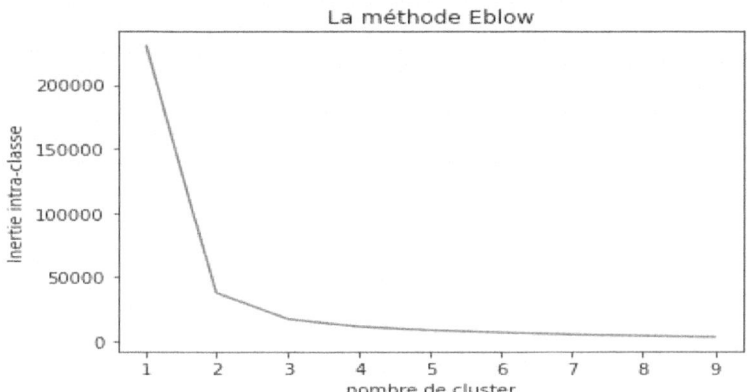

Fig. 6. Result after applying the Elbow method

The elbow of the graph represents the number of clusters, here the value of K is therefore **3.**

- Application of K-MEANS

Here is presented the different cluster shapes using K-means (Fig. 7).

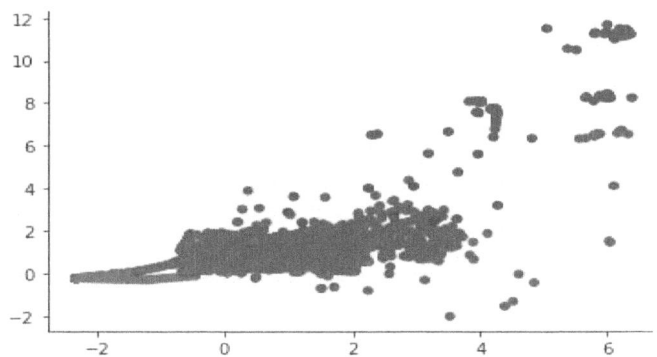

Fig. 7. Result after application of the K-means method

5.4 Application of Classification Algorithms

We use in the rest of our approach the clusters obtained after application of the clustering algorithms for the training of the classification models. And here are the different results obtained (Table 7).

Table 7. Results after classification

Methods	Regression	Naives Bayes	Decision tree	K-NN
K-means	95.49%	89.98%	99.60%	99.37%
BDBSCAN	89.57%	90.71%	97.60%	96.52%

Comments

The use of the honeypot (honeyD) associated with the different classification algorithms allows us to note that the decision trees and the KNN respectively give satisfactory results of 99.6% and 99.37% while the dbscan results are less important than the k-means.

6 Discussion

Our study aimed to propose a data mining method based on the use of honeypots in Big Data databases to improve the detection of computer attacks. We explored several data mining techniques, including classification, anomaly detection, and clustering, to extract relevant information from the data collected by honeypots.

For the application of our approach, we performed our simulations using the Honeyd tool to create an environment of vulnerabilities to attract potential attackers. We also used NoSQL databases to manage the collected data and apply data mining techniques. Our results showed that the use of honeypots (honeyD) in Big Data databases is an effective method to detect computer attacks. In particular, the clustering technique combined with the classification algorithm made it possible to identify abnormal traffic present in the database.

However, the need to have a well-designed Big Data infrastructure to manage the massive data collected by honeypots and also the need to update them regularly to remain relevant in the face of new threats could improve the security of the infrastructures.

Furthermore, our study showed that the use of honeypots in Big Data databases was a promising method to improve the detection of computer attacks by exploiting data mining techniques.

7 Conclusion and Prospects

In this work, our aim was to propose honeypot-based data mining methods for the discovery of intrusions in Big Data databases. Our major concern was how to detect different intrusions into different big data database categories using honeypots and data mining techniques. The main objective of this study was therefore the establishment of a framework for securing data from big data. In order to achieve this objective, we first carried out a state of the art in order to present the different works from the field of intrusion detection. Then we presented the different honeypots and made a classification by functionality in order to make a choice to apply to the different types of big data database. Then we studied the different data mining techniques to highlight the different intrusions. All this allowed us to implement an intrusion detection architecture that integrates the use of the honeypot (Honeyd) to collect information on potentially malicious activities, combined with classification algorithms such as regression, decision, and clustering such as k-means, DBSCAN to identify possible intrusions into databases.

As a follow-up to this intrusion detection work, we could set up an expert system dedicated to intrusion detection based on honeypots to feed the system's knowledge base.

References

1. Mahamadou, B., Diday, E.: Data mining report Analysis of indebtedness by level of development of countries. Docplayer.fr. Consulted on 11 November 2022
2. Sellami, L.: Data Mining Approach for Intrusion Detection, p. 15. Accessed 11 November 2022
3. Big Data: Big Data Definition. https://www.lebigdata.fr/definition-big-data. Accessed 10 Dec 2022
4. https://www.universitylib.com/introduction-to-big-data/
5. Oracle: What is Big Data? Oracle.com. https://www.oracle.com/fr/big-data/what-is-big-data/. Accessed 17 Dec 2022
6. Iyad, K., Malek, S.: A dynamic honeypot design for intrusion detection. IEEE ACS/International, Washington, DC, USA, Consulté le 8 janvier 2023. ISBN: 0-7803-8577-2
7. Portokalidis, G., Bos, H.: SweetBait: Zero-hour worm detection and containment using honeypots. J. Comput. Netw. Special Issue Secur. Self-Protect. Self-Healing Syst., Consulté le 11 janvier 2023
8. David, D., et al.: HoneyStat: local worm detection using honeypots. In: Proceedings of the 7th International Symposium on Recent Advances in Intrusion Detection (RAID), pp. 39–58. Consulté le 11 février 2023
9. Zpitzner, L.: Honeypots: Tracking Hackers, Addison Wasley Professional, Septembre 2002. ISBN - 0321108957
10. Fekolkin, R.: Intrusion detection & prevention system: overview of snort & suricata. Internet Security, A7011N, Lulea University of Technology, pp. 1–4.
11. Chi, R.: Intrusion detection system based on snort. In: Liu, X., Ye, Y. (eds.) Proceedings of the 9th International Symposium on Linear Drives for Industry Applications, Volume 3, pp. 657–664. Springer, Heidelberg (2014). https://doi.org/10.1007/978-3-642-40633-1_82
12. Réseaux et Sécurité Informatique: Les IDS/IPS SNORT (eventus-networks.blogspot.com). Consulté le 10 July 2023
13. Ghafir, I., Prenosil, V., Svoboda, J., Hammoudeh, M.: A survey on network security monitoring systems. In: 2016 IEEE 4th International Conference on Future Internet of Things and Cloud Workshops (FiCloudW), Vienna, Austria, pp. 77–82 (2016). https://doi.org/10.1109/W-FiCloud.2016.30
14. Singh, A.P., Singh, M.D.: Analysis of host-based and network-based intrusion detection system. Int. J. Comput. Netw. Inf. Secur. 6(8), 41–47 (2014)

15. Zpitzner, L.: Honeypots: Tracking Hackers. Addison-Wesley Professional (2002). ISBN - 10: 0321108957
16. Majorczyk, F.: Detection of behavioral intrusions by diversification of COTS: application to the case of web servers" thesis, Doctorate in Computer Science, University of Rennes I, 2008, 182p. Consulted on 16 November 2022
17. Bouzayani, H.: Quantitative model for intrusion detection. An IDS-HONEYPOT collaborative architecture, Master's thesis, University of Quebec in Outaouais (UQO), 81p. (2012)
18. Diallo, A.: State of the art and prospects for a solution against DoS, final dissertation, Master in Software Engineering. Assane SECK University of Ziguinchor UFR Sciences et Technologies, 84p. (2020)
19. Rania, D.: "Network intrusion detection system based on the KNN classification algorithm" end-of-study project, Master in Information Systems Security, SAAD DAHLAB University of Blida 1, 2019, p. 63

Potential Cyber Threats to the National Elections in the Digital Age in Africa

Thuli Mkhwanazi[1,2]($\boxtimes$), Avuya Shibambu[1,2], Vhuthu Nefale[1,2], Jabu Mtsweni[1,2], Jackie Phahlamohlaka[1,2], Muyowa Mutemwa[1,2], and Norman Nelufule[1,2]

[1] Council for Scientific and Industrial Research (CSIR), Pretoria, Brummeria 0184, Russia
tmkhwanazi@csir.co.za
[2] Defence and SecurityCluster, Information and Cybersecurity Centre (ICSC), Brummeria 0184, Russia

Abstract. This paper is a theoretical review following a systematic literature review aimed at providing insightful information and advisory regarding potential cyber threats to national elections in Africa in the digital age. It therefore, focuses on potential cyber threats to the general elections process in Africa. It highlights the importance of cybersecurity in relation to the digital and traditional electoral process. The paper delves into different types of cyber ills, citing examples from past instances worldwide including Africa, emphasizing the need for robust cybersecurity measures. It also discusses the possible impacts of cyber threats on the electoral process and its stakeholders. This paper offers mitigation techniques to ensure a safe and secure national general election, particularly in the cyberspace.

Keywords: Cybersecurity · Vulnerabilities · Cyber threats · Electoral Process · National Elections

1 Introduction

It is evident across different countries that the cyberspace is now playing an instrumental role in influencing national and local government elections for good or bad, and this is common in low-income, middle-income, and high-income countries. Cyberspace is therefore seen as the equalizer across countries when it comes to elections, and this is irrespective of whether countries have adopted digital applications such as e-voting or not.

Recently, Nigeria experienced over 12 million cyber-attacks during the 2023 Presidential Election [1] and suspicions of cyber spies infiltrating Kenyan networks long before the elections of 2022 were also reported by Reuters in 2023, however the Kenyan officials dismissed the allegations from this report [2, 3]. Regardless of the dismissal of the information by the Kenyana officials, a thesis by [4], corroborated that fake news and disinformation in campaigns has always given negative reflections on the cybersecurity measures of the country hosting elections [4]. In the above-mentioned thesis, it was also mentioned that in Brazil, fake news dominated the Brazilian presidential race including

A. Sere et al. (Eds.): AFRICOMM 2023, LNICST 587, pp. 333–350, 2025.
https://doi.org/10.1007/978-3-031-81570-6_22

politicians making claims of the fraudulent nature of the electronic voting system [4]. The false claims of vulnerabilities about the vote counting machines in the United States of America were also made by the presidential candidate in the previous elections and these claims ended up in courts and some cases are still ongoing [5-7].

It is considering the above-mentioned events that this study was conducted. The rest of the paper is structured as follows: Sect. 2 provides a brief description of the research process followed; Sect. 3 provides a high-level overview of current cyber threats and vulnerabilities that may impact on the General Election process; Sect. 4 reviews past cyber incidents that affected the election process in various countries; Sect. 5 presents potential cyber threats in the general election and discusses each; Sect. 6 discusses cyber vulnerabilities in the general election which are different from cyber threats; Sect. 7 delves into the impact of the cyber attacks on the election stakeholders; Sect. 8 discusses mitigation factors as this paper's major offering; and Sect. 9 concludes this paper.

2 Research Approach

The research presented in this paper followed a systematic literature review using popular research databases such as Scopus, Web of Science and Google Scholar. According to [8], a systematic literature review is a research approach that involves a comprehensive and structured analysis of existing academic publications and other relevant sources on a specific topic or research question. The primary goal of a systematic literature review is to provide a thorough and unbiased summary of the current state of knowledge in a particular field or area of study. In this research, we adopted the following steps in reviewing the potential cyber threats in national elections in the digital age focusing mostly on the threats influenced by the cyber space; (1) planning, (2) selection (3) extraction, and (4) execution These steps are demonstrated in the sections that follow.

3 Overview of Cyber Threats, Vulnerabilities and Attacks in General Elections

The proliferation of digital technologies comes with opportunities and benefits to improve electoral processes, such as ease of communication through social media and websites with voters, an increased uptake and awareness of voter registration, the ability for political parties to campaign far and wide with limited resources, casting of votes using electronic machines, digital counting of votes, including the live (instant) dissemination of election results. However, in as much as digital technologies provide benefits, there are increasing malicious actors who take advantage of vulnerable and insecure digital technologies in cyberspace to further their nefarious objectives in the election process.

It is reported by the European Union Agency for Cybersecurity (ENISA) that most countries in the European Union (EU) have "either postponed or discontinued the use of electronic voting, citing high threats and risks". According to the EU Cybersecurity Agency and ENISA, a high-level of cybersecurity is key for safeguarding the whole election lifecycle [9] to ensure:

- Democracy and human rights protection
- Critical assets protection
- Basic security protection
- Election integrity security

There are innumerable cyber threats and vulnerabilities that may affect an electoral process. These vulnerabilities emanate before, during, and after elections, and may be evident in the cyberspace as well as in the physical realm. This is mostly because cyber is cross-cutting. Typical examples of cyber-attacks against elections include that of the Kenyan Election in 2022. It was reported by Reuters that cyber spies infiltrated Kenyan networks in 2019 [2, 3] at least three years before the elections. Another research study highlights the influences of social and mainstream media influences on the 2016 United States (US) Elections [10]. In 2020, it was also reported that a cybersecurity hacker was spotted online selling personal information of over 200 million voters in the US with voter registration data of 186 million [6, 7, 11, 12] and it is suspected that most of this data was sourced through various spear phishing campaigns.

Generally, the election life cycle constitutes several categories of cyber entities that are vulnerable to election threats. The common vulnerabilities and threats to elections can generally be classified under various categories of the election lifecycle (see Fig. 1).

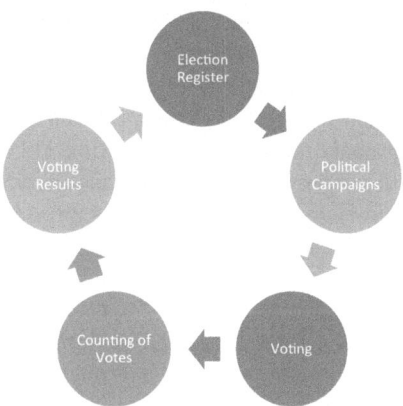

Fig. 1. South African Election Lifecycle

The next sub-sections discuss the Election Lifecycle and its associated cyber-ills in the context of South Africa (SA) (see Fig. 1).

Election register or voters' roll: In SA, elections are conducted by the Independent Electoral Commission (IEC), and eligible voters are SA citizens who are 18 years and older who reside inside or outside SA. According to the IEC, in 2019, a total of 26 million voters were registered with over 17 million casting their votes. Comparing to 1999, the voters registration roll had increased by 8.5 million in 2019. The voters' roll is "gold" to political parties, marketing companies, cyber criminals, and other nation-states. In SA, the voters' roll is online where anyone can check if they or anyone else are registered or not, using an Identity (ID) number. This also technically means the election voters' roll is susceptible to potential cyber-attacks as well as cyber-criminal activities such as phishing and data breaches.

Political campaigns: According to the IEC, there are over 1500 political parties registered in SA with about 321 parties registered for National Elections [13]. The Western Cape province has the highest number (333) of political parties registered at a Municipal Level. All the political parties compete for 400 seats in Parliament and other seats at Provincial levels. Based on the vast proliferation of political parties in SA, the public political campaigning process is indeed susceptible to cyber interference and manipulation.

Voting: In SA, voting is still manual and no electronic voting is allowed. However, there are digital devices used at the voting stations to confirm the voters' roll and account for those who have voted. A manual register is also used. However, because the voting system is not centralized, possibilities of voting manipulation are a possibility, albeit very minimal with the controls in place. However, disinformation surrounding the voting process should not be ignored.

Counting and Results: In SA, voting results are released as they are confirmed per voting districts and provinces. The results are also released on the IEC website and at the IEC Results Information Centre. The manipulation of the voting results is seen as low risk from a cyber perspective, since the counting of votes is a manual process that involves different stakeholders including political parties. The main cyber threat is the dissemination of fake results and fake news online surrounding the voting results. This has an impact on the integrity of election results.

General Elections present an undeniable opportunity for cybercriminals, political opponents, propagandists, and foreign nation states driven by various motives. While monetary gain remains a primary incentive for cybercrime [14-16], political events like the general elections create a vast cyber threat landscape encompassing power, control, influence, ideology promotion, and even terrorism. As a result, it is imperative for all stakeholders involved in the 2024 General Elections to take proactive and meticulous measures to mitigate cyber threats before, during, and after the elections. Maintaining heightened vigilance and implementing robust cybersecurity measures is crucial in safeguarding the integrity and security of the electoral process.

The next section delves into selected international countries' use cases of past election interference through cyber means.

4   Selected Use Cases of Elections Interference Through Cyber Incidents

The use cases in this section demonstrate that cyber threats and attacks against national elections are no longer something that is discussed by researchers and cyber experts, but it is real and happening across different nations, developed and/or developing. The use cases are presented according to the years that they were reported in.

4.1 United States of America: Democratic Party 2016 Presidential Election Cyber Hacks

On the 2nd of June 2017, the Russian President, Vladimir Putin conceded for the first time that any US presidential election-related hacking attacks may have emanated from Russia [17]. However, he denied the responsibility that the hackers were Russian state-sponsored hackers.

4.2 President Macron and the National Front (France) Targeted by Hackers

On the 25th of April 2017, the security firm Trend Micro published a report stating that the Fancy Bear Russian hacking group was targeting President Macron and his election campaign [18]. According to Trend Micro, they discovered four new fake web domain names that were very similar to the domain names of the Presidential Macron election campaign. The results from the Trend Micro investigations suggested the aim of the hackers was to try to trick careless campaign workers into accidentally compromising their email accounts. In an interview on the 25th of April 2017, President Macron's digital campaign manager, Mounir Mahjoubi confirmed that there were cyber-attacks on the campaign, however they were not successful [18]. On the 5th of May 2017, two days before the elections and during the last hours of the election campaigns, President Macron's election campaign was hacked and about 14.5 gigabytes of emails, personal and business documents were posted to the text-sharing site spanning over 70 thousand files [19, 20]. On close examination of the files leaked, President Macron's election campaign stated that there was a mixture between fake and authentic documents "to create confusion and misinformation".

4.3 SA Local Government Elections (2019)

During the 2019 Local Government Elections in SA, the proliferation of misinformation was observed on social media with the assumed intention to influence and/or interfere with free and fair elections. According to a study by Baldassaro which collected over 400 000 tweets from the political mainstream during the election campaign season and election day [21], it was determined that out of these many tweets, at least about 10 dodgy web domains were disseminating misinformation to over 1 million users, and some of the tweets linked to these domains were also shared by top politicians online.

4.4 Kenya Presidential Election Disinformation and Network Hacks (2022)

During the tightly contested Kenya's Presidential Election in August 2022, disinformation campaigns were widely distributed because of hyped social media engagements in different African countries including SA. Before the election results were officially released, prominent and verified social media users spread false results about who had won the election. As already highlighted in the introduction section, the global news reporter in Reuters released a story in May 2023 claiming that the Chinese-Sponsored Cyber spies called Backdoor Diplomacy [2, 3] infiltrated Kenyan networks from 2019 until 2022 and breached the finance ministry, the president's office intelligence agency and others, seeking sensitive information on the Kenyan government. These claims, as per Reuters, are based on the analysis of the hacking data and sources who investigated cyber breaches in Kenya [2]. However, Chinese authorities have disputed these claims as "baseless".

4.5 Brazilian Electronic Voting System Questioned in the Presidential Election (2022)

Brazil fully implemented an electronic voting system in the year 2000 and has been seen as a success for many years because it made voting easier for people and prevented fraud. However, from 2018 until the elections in 2023, the system has been called into question. In 2020, the electoral courts' systems in Brazil suffered multiple Distributed Denial of Service (DDoS) attacks with over 5 million access attempts received from overseas countries during the vote counting process and this delayed the release of the results for hours [22].

4.6 Millions of Cyber-Attacks in Presidential Election in Nigeria (2023)

The Nigerian Guardian reported in March 2023 that the over 12.9 million cyber-attacks were recorded during the Presidential Election [1, 23]. The Ministry of Communications and Digital Economy in Nigeria confirmed these cyber-attacks and indicated that they were mostly blocked and originated within and outside Nigeria. The ministry further indicated that there has been a large increase in the cyber threats to the Nigerian cyberspace. It was reported that networks and websites were mostly targeted with over 6 million attacks on the Presidential Election Day, increasing from about 1.5 million attacks on regular days.

By delving into the above historical cyber incidents, this section shed light on the vulnerabilities and risks that electoral processes face in the digital age, emphasizing the importance of strengthening cybersecurity measures to safeguard the democratic process. The next section aims to provide a comprehensive understanding of the specific challenges, threats and vulnerabilities that may impact the 2024 General Elections.

5   Potential Cyber Threats in the General Elections

In conducting a systematic literature review to identify potential cyber threats to general elections, we initially performed comprehensive searches across reputable online databases such as IEEE Xplore, ACM Digital Library, Scopus, and Google Scholar. The search keywords employed included "cyber threats," "election security," "voting systems," "electoral fraud," "phishing attacks," "hacking," "disinformation," and "election interference." We filtered the search results by focusing on peer-reviewed articles, reports, and studies published between 2015 and 2021, giving priority to research specifically related to cyber threats in the context of general elections. After a thorough review, the selected literature provided insights into a range of potential cyber threats, including but not limited to voter registration system breaches, social media manipulation, and election result manipulation. Some of the cyber threats were identified through social media intelligence, previous experience, as well as technical learnings from other elections such as those discussed in Sect. 4.

The threats are grouped into the following four main categories in Fig. 2:

- Political Disinformation Campaigns
- Election Data Breaches
- Phishing Attacks
- Service Disruptions.

The list presented in Fig. 2 is not exhaustive but gives an overview of the most prevalent and common cyber threats in SA and other countries.

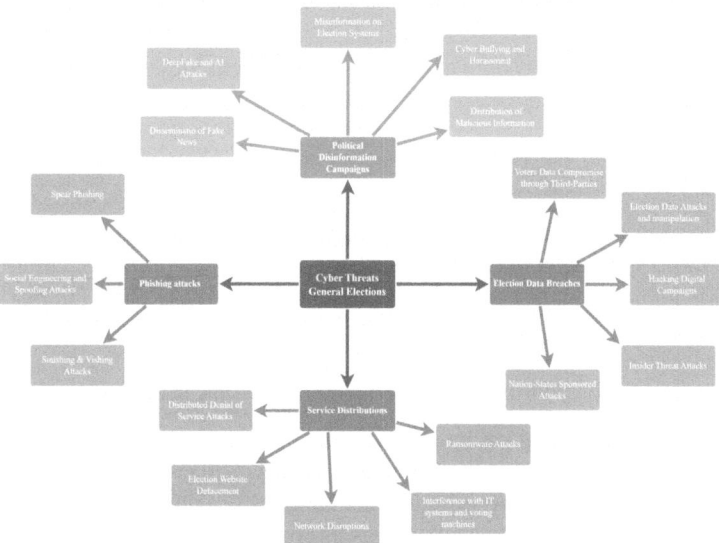

Fig. 2. Potential Cyber Threats to General Elections

The following subsections explain the potential cyber threats to general election.

5.1 Disinformation Campaigns

As the cyber threat landscape incessantly advances, it results in a new range of cyber threats that target human weaknesses more than the Information and Communication Technologies (ICT) that humans use. A relevant example of the above-mentioned cyber threats is Information Confrontation, which is a recent and trending type of cyberattack where adversaries make use of Information Weapons to influence politics or gain power [3, 6, 12, 21, 24-26]. As such, Information Confrontation is a cognitive cyber-attack or threat whereby information is purposefully misrepresented and made public by an adversary group or state actor using digital ICT, to sway public opinion on political or social matters. An example of information confrontation is disinformation.

Disinformation campaigns involve deliberate spreading of false information with the intent to deceive and manipulate. Disinformation aims to influence public opinion. In this instance, disinformation may be used by political opposition actors to manipulate voting or voter turnout.

Similar and related to disinformation is misinformation. These two concepts differ in terms of intent and the spread of false or misleading information. Misinformation may be unintentional, whereas disinformation involves deliberate efforts to deceive or manipulate. Misinformation refers to false or inaccurate information shared unknowingly by individuals who believe the information is true. An example of misinformation would be the public (potential voters) spreading disinformation either through word of mouth or social media platforms, believing it to be true. Misinformation can be the result of misunderstandings, misinterpretations, or the dissemination of outdated or incorrect information.

While the above concepts both encompass various activities, their focus is often on influencing the human mind.

5.2 Data Breaches

Voter registration databases contain the personal information of registered voters. A breach of these systems could result in the theft, manipulation, or deletion of voter data. SA has a Protection of Personal Information Act (POPIA), that is in place, while cybersecurity researchers endeavor on developing tools to assist with POPIA compliance [27].

Data breaches before, during, and after elections can come in myriad ways, including:

- **Election Data Attacks** to voting systems could alter vote counts, modify candidate preferences, steal identities, or manipulate results. Safeguarding the security and integrity of electronic voting systems, including implementing secure transmission protocols and robust auditing mechanisms, is crucial to prevent any manipulation of election results.
- The **Compromise of Voters Data** can come in multiple ways, mainly through third parties such as marketing companies, service providers, political parties, private companies, and government entities. In SA, we have already observed political parties sourcing voters' personal information from marketing companies and using the data to target voters in certain areas via short-messaging-services. Furthermore, hackers may use publicly available data sources to scrap and combine various data points to monetize voters' data such as identity, home addresses, email addresses, phone numbers or voting districts.
- **Hacking Digital Campaigns** for sensitive political information has been observed in local and international elections [4, 5, 14, 19, 20, 28]. With the growing digitalization of campaigns, adversaries have discovered fresh avenues to interfere with, disrupt, and steal vast amounts of information from political opponents. These include email addresses of political party staff members or donors, as well as personal documents obtained from campaign resources such as networks and websites.
- **Insider threats** includes individuals within the electoral process who have authorized access to sensitive systems or information, such as election officials, IT staff, or political party members, may exploit their positions or misuse their privileges for personal gain or to disrupt the electoral process and critical IT systems. These insiders may

engage in data manipulation, unauthorized disclosure of confidential information, or intentional disruption of critical systems.

- **Foreign-sponsored attacks** are prevalent before, during, and after the elections. The conflict between Russia/Ukraine and SA's position provides a threat for nation-sponsored cyber hackers within and outside the country to disrupt the Elections using the cyberspace. Generally, state sponsored attacks focus on stealing classified information from government and intelligence services, as observed in Kenya.

5.3 Phishing Attacks

Phishing attacks or threats in local and international elections refer to a type of cyber-attacks where malicious actors attempt to deceive persons involved in the electoral process, such as voters, political campaign staff, politicians, or election officials to gain unauthorized access to sensitive information or manipulate the election outcome. Phishing attacks are typically carried out through fraudulent emails, text messages, or websites that imitate legitimate sources, such as political organizations, government agencies, or social media platforms. It has been observed in the US that phishing attacks have been prevalent in 2016 and 2018 Presidential Elections [29]. These phishing attacks have been targeting political campaigns as well as candidates online. In 2022, phishing attacks were detected targeting county workers managing elections [29].

Phishing attacks in the 2024 General Elections may come in different ways such as:

- **Spear phishing**, which is more targeted at a specific individual, large groups, politicians, or departments within an organisation using continuous communication over an extended period. Therefore, political parties, candidates, or election officials may be targeted through spear phishing to gain unauthorised access to their accounts or systems or for impersonation of misleading campaign information [29].
- **Smishing attacks** are gaining prominence in the digital age particularly in a country such as SA where mobile phone adoption is over 100%. Smishing can be easily defined as a combination of the words "SMS" and "phishing". It is a form of phishing attack that involves the use of text messages (SMS) to deceive and exploit individuals for various intents including revealing sensitive information.

The consequences of successful phishing attacks in elections can be severe and detrimental to the nation's democracy. They can compromise the integrity of the voting process, erode public trust, and impact the legitimacy of election results.

5.4 Service Disruptions

The threat of service disruption is real on different fronts in Africa. For instance, load-shedding, crime, vandalism, social unrests, and protests are all potential non-cyber threats that are well documented and have been experienced before in the previous elections. Disruptions to Information Technology (IT) systems associated with the elections can never be ignored as a cyber threat. IT service disruptions in elections can have significant consequences, affecting the integrity, efficiency, and trustworthiness of the electoral process. These disruptions can arise from various sources, including technical failures, cyber-attacks, or even deliberate sabotage.

It can be noted from this section that cyber threats against elections are plentiful, and the list provided here is not exhaustive, but provides an indication of what authorities may need to pay attention to for better cyber preparedness before, during and after the general elections.

6   Cyber Vulnerabilities against General Elections

There is a difference between threats and vulnerabilities. Generally, threats come from external and internal sources such as cyber attackers and insiders. It is almost impossible to eliminate cyber threats. On the other hand, vulnerabilities may emanate because of weaknesses in cybersecurity systems, lack of security controls (logical and physical), lack of security awareness in voters, lack of monitoring of social media platforms, and outdated or legacy IT systems.

This section highlights some of the cyber vulnerabilities that may impact General Elections (see Figure 3). The categorized cyber vulnerabilities in Fig. 3 are not exhaustive but cover the most common vulnerabilities based on external information.

1. Vulnerable Electoral IT Systems
2. Lack of Cybersecurity Risk Assessments
3. Lack of Security Incidents and Events Monitoring
4. Lack of Security Awareness
5. Lack of Technical Cybersecurity Skills
6. Lack of Cybersecurity Response Plans

Fig. 3. Cyber Vulnerabilities against General Elections

Below, we discuss at high-level some of these vulnerabilities that authorities need to be aware of (see Fig. 3).

Vulnerable Electoral IT Systems: vulnerable IT systems are a common trend across the digital landscape, and systems used in elections for voter registrations are no different. These systems could be vulnerable in the following ways:

- Outdated systems as well as legacy systems can be an easy target for malicious actors.
- Weak access controls without multi-factor authentication, and unaudited access rights can make it easier for cyber hackers to infiltrate IT systems that may lead to data breaches, manipulation of data and system configurations.
- Insecure network infrastructure that has weak or poorly configured security measures could be a vulnerability that may impact electoral IT systems and can expose election systems to data interceptions through attacks such as Man-in-the-Middle attacks.

- Lack of secure coding practices in locally developed systems, such as voter registration portals, could also be a vulnerability that introduces threats that may lead to data breaches impacting on the integrity of the elections.
- Third-party vulnerabilities, in cases where the election authority is relying on external service providers for the development or hosting of their IT systems.

These vulnerabilities may be exploited by insiders and outsiders to undermine the integrity, confidentiality, and availability of electoral IT systems. Vulnerabilities need to be assessed, tracked, and patched where technically feasible or isolated.

Lack of Cybersecurity Assessments: it is best practice to regularly conduct technical and non-technical security assessments and penetration testing against critical IT systems for the elections. An oversight in this regard could expose the IT systems to cyber threats. For such critical IT systems, it is important that technical cybersecurity assessments are done on a regular basis, at least monthly, particularly in the build-up towards elections because vulnerabilities are introduced almost daily for the common IT systems. Non-technical security assessments could be done at least every six months.

Lack of Security Incidents and Events Monitoring: it is a common security maxim that you cannot protect what you do not know or monitor. And it is now well known that African countries such as SA are a "heaven" for cyber criminals[1], and as such lack of security monitoring on critical applications, networks, data leakages, and other events could be a vulnerability that may lead to cyber threats being realized. The Nigerian government made some inroads in this regard by deploying resources before and during the elections to monitor and block cyber-attack attempts, and as reported above, monitored over 12 million events that were all blocked as per the ministry's claim.

Lack of Security Awareness: it has been determined by the Verizon Data Breach Report that 75% of data breaches are caused by human-error, misconfigurations, and social engineering. The lack of security awareness and culture by users, in the context of elections, voters, election officials and politicians, is a serious vulnerability. This vulnerability can realize the cyber threat relating to election data attacks as well as voters personal information leakages. Lack of security awareness raises the threat of phishing, smishing, and vishing attacks, and any breach related to voters' information, election officials, and politicians could have an impact on the elections, even if the leakages and data attacks do not happen directly through the election IT systems and databases.

Lack of Cybersecurity Skills: technical cybersecurity skills are crucial in ensuring a proper cybersecurity posture. The lack of skilled cybersecurity experts could be a vulnerability to General Elections as any potential breaches and incidents may not be reacted upon timeously. The lack of technical skills could lead to risks such as ineffective incident detection and response, limited ability to assess and mitigate systems vulnerabilities, insufficient knowledge of emerging threats, limited ability to incident response and recovery, and too much reliance on third-parties or service providers which could expose the election processes to third-party cyber threats.

Lack of Cybersecurity Response Plans: inadequate cybersecurity response plans and backup procedures and lack of robust disaster recovery plans could result in data loss or prolonged system downtime during elections in the event of a cyber-attack, system

---

[1] https://www.itweb.co.za/content/KzQenvjyBo2qZd2r.

failure, or natural disaster. This is seen as a critical vulnerability in any IT system and should be mitigated following best practices.

Lack of Incident Response Plans: it is impractical to aim to eliminate all cyber threats and vulnerabilities, and as such, a lack of plans to respond and recover from cyber incident could be more devastating to the election regime. This could lead to issues such as prolonged system down time, increased reputational damage, failure to preserve evidence for cyber investigations, and inability to learn from previous incidents.

The next section explores the significant impact that the discussed cyber threats and vulnerabilities would impose on the various stakeholders involved in the electoral process.

7 Impact of Cyber Attacks on Election Process Stakeholders

The consequences of hackers realizing a cyber threat or exploiting a cyber vulnerability within the election context can have enormous implications. They can compromise the integrity of the voting process, erode public trust, and impact the legitimacy of election results. These threats and vulnerabilities have multi-dimensional impact that covers processes, people, and technology.

Over and above the technical impact imposed by the identified cyber threats and vulnerabilities, the non-technical impacts on the election process are discussed below.

7.1 Psychological

The identified cyber threats to General Elections have the potential to induce significant psychological consequences on both individuals and the broader society [13]. The perceived existence of cyber threats can elicit fear, anxiety, and a pervasive sense of distrust among voters, thereby undermining their confidence in the electoral process. Consequently, these psychological reactions can contribute to voter apathy and reduced voter turnout as individuals may feel disheartened or skeptical about the integrity of the elections. The psychological impact can manifest as heightened political polarization, increased hostility, and a deterioration of social cohesion. Moreover, targeted cyber-attacks directed at political candidates or parties can instill a sense of vulnerability and insecurity, resulting in heightened stress levels and diminished psychological well-being among the affected individuals. Taking proactive measures to address these concerns will safeguard the psychological well-being of individuals, uphold the legitimacy of the electoral process, and preserve the democratic values that underpin a fair and inclusive society.

7.2 Financial Liabilities

Cyber-attacks on the electoral process can result in significant financial liabilities for various stakeholders involved. The financial impact can include costs associated with incident response, investigation, remediation, and restoration of affected systems. Additionally, there may be expenses related to legal actions, fines, and penalties imposed by regulatory authorities. Cyber-attacks can also lead to economic losses due to disrupted campaign activities, decreased voter trust, reduced donor contributions, and potential lawsuits. Moreover, the need to enhance cybersecurity infrastructure and implement preventive measures further adds to the financial burden.

7.3 Legal Consequences

In the context of SA, the implementation of the (POPI Act which came into effect on the 1st of July 2021, holds significant implications for political parties in SA. If the Information Regulator identifies a political party's failure to adequately protect citizens' or members' personal identifiable information (PII) and neglect of established POPIA minimum security measures, the party may face legal consequences. This could entail initiating legal proceedings against the political party, potentially resulting in penalties, fines, and other punitive measures enforced by the information regulator [27].

7.4 Social Unrest

In July 2021, SA as a nation experienced social unrest known as the July 2021 riots, the Zuma unrest or Zuma riots. The unrests occurred in SA's KwaZulu-Natal and Gauteng provinces from the 9th to the 18th of July 2021 [30]. The cause of these unrests was sparked by the imprisonment of former President Jacob Zuma for contempt of court. It is believed that members of the public or citizens felt the former president was being treated unfairly by his political party.

7.5 Reputational Damage

On February 24, 2023, SA was added to the "grey list" by the Financial Action Task Force (FATF), designating it as a jurisdiction under heightened monitoring due to concerns over compliance with the FATF 40 Recommendations and the effectiveness of its anti-money laundering (AML) and counter-terrorist financing (CTF) system, as highlighted in the 2021 FATF mutual evaluation report. This classification subjects the country to increased financial scrutiny by international bodies. In this context, any instability arising from the national elections could potentially erode the remaining confidence in SA, both domestically and internationally. Furthermore, there is a risk of post-election unrest, which could further exacerbate the negative impact on the country's stability and reputation.

7.6 Divisions Among Different Groups

Division among different groups can be a significant concern. The country's diverse population encompasses various ethnic, political, and social groups, each with their own interests and ideologies. This diversity can create fertile ground for cyber threats, as different factions may attempt to exploit existing divisions and manipulate public opinion through disinformation campaigns, targeted hacking, or social engineering. Divisions based on race, political affiliation, or socioeconomic factors can be weaponized by hacktivists to undermine trust in the electoral process and destabilize democratic institutions, making it crucial to address these divisions and promote unity in safeguarding the electoral system.

7.7 Legislative Paralysis

Legislative paralysis could exacerbate the vulnerabilities and risks faced by the electoral process. Legislative paralysis refers to the inability or delay in passing necessary laws and regulations to address emerging cyber threats effectively. Without comprehensive legislation in place, the country's electoral system might lack the necessary safeguards to protect against cyber-attacks, disinformation campaigns, or manipulation of election results. This paralysis can hinder the implementation of robust cybersecurity measures, leaving the electoral process susceptible to interference and compromising the integrity of the elections. Urgent and proactive action from lawmakers is essential to mitigate potential cyber threats and ensure a fair and secure democratic process.

7.8 Disruption of Election Operations

Ransom attacks can paralyze the IT systems essential for conducting elections. This includes voter registration databases, voting machines, result reporting systems, or communication platforms used by election officials and political campaigns. Such disruptions can hinder voter registration, delay voting processes, or prevent the timely reporting of accurate election results. In some cases, ransomware attacks may involve the manipulation or tampering of election data. Attackers may alter voter registration records, voting tallies, or result reporting systems, leading to inaccuracies, or casting doubt on the integrity of the election outcome. This can undermine public trust and confidence in the electoral process.

   While achieving absolute security in the cyber environment is an unattainable goal, there are several cybersecurity controls that can be implemented to enhance protection. The next section provides an in-depth exploration of proactive cybersecurity measures that can be adopted to effectively mitigate potential cyber threats and attacks.

8   Mitigation Techniques Against Cyber Threats and Vulnerabilities

8.1 Mitigation Against Political Disinformation Campaigns

- Regularly monitor, detect and analyse online misinformation and disinformation.
- Develop a rapid response plan in collaboration with tech-companies to deal decisively and close to real-time with false and/or misleading information.
- Develop a clear communication plan that could be used by the election authority and government communication agencies for engagement with political parties on dealing with cyber disinformation, public awareness and education campaigns educating voters about misinformation and potential impact.
- Media to work together with the election authorities to provide guidance on how to identify and verify reliable sources of information.
- Collaborate with the social media platforms to enhance content moderation of election posts including algorithms to detect, flag or remove false information.
- Foster international collaborations and cooperation on information sharing and threat intelligence.
- Establish legal and regulatory frameworks that addresses disinformation campaigns during elections.

8.2 Mitigation Against Election Data Breaches

- Implementing appropriate encryption mechanisms for sensitive data at rest and in transit could help protect the confidentiality and integrity of electoral information.
- Deploy multi-factor authentication (MFA). This will enhances security, protect against password-based attacks, increases accountability, safeguards voter data, deters fraudulent activities, and promotes compliance with security standards.
- Conducting extensive security vetting on insiders and third parties to minimize insider threat attacks as well as third-party breaches such as contractors.
- Implementing backup, restore, and recovery plans which can help ensure data and systems are regularly backed up and can be restored in case of a cyberattack or data loss, thus minimizing the impact and downtime.

8.3 Mitigation Against Phishing Attacks

To mitigate the risk of phishing attacks, it is critical that election officials, campaign staff, and volunteers are trained or made aware about cybersecurity best practices, such as identifying phishing emails, avoiding suspicious downloads, and reporting potential threats that could reduce the risk of successful phishing attacks. It is important for the political parties to appoint a cybersecurity specialist as part of their campaigns to ensure that there is political party members' awareness training. These cybersecurity specialists could work alongside law-enforcers to report, and where possible, take down cybersecurity threat attempts.

8.4 Mitigation Against IT Service Disruptions and Attacks

Preventing and mitigating service disruptions and attacks against IT systems for elections and associated government services requires proactive measures such as:

- Implementing strong cybersecurity measures, including firewalls, encryption, intrusion detection systems, and regular security updates, helps safeguard IT systems from cyber threats.
- Conducting regular maintenance and testing (vulnerability and penetration assessment) of voting machines, registration systems, and other critical IT infrastructure ensures their reliability and identifies potential issues in advance.
- Developing comprehensive contingency plans can help election authorities respond to IT disruptions effectively. This includes backup systems, redundancy measures, and clear protocols for handling technical failures or cyber incidents.
- Engaging IT professionals, cybersecurity experts, and technology vendors can provide valuable insights, assistance, and guidance in identifying and mitigating potential IT service disruptions and security issues. These professionals and experts could be on a retainer basis to avoid delayed procurement process during an incident.
- Developing comprehensive incident response plans enables a swift and coordinated response in the event of targeted attacks or advance persistent threats. For incident response, the NIST Cyber Incident Response Cycle [31] is recommended:

    o Preparation

o Detection & Analysis
o Containment, Eradication & Recovery
o Post-incident Activity

9 Conclusion

Over the years, the cyber space has evolved significantly with the digital transformation changing every sector. With the positive changes that came along with it, negative implications also emerged, including increasing cyber threats and vulnerabilities. This paper gave a highlight of potential cyber threats to the General Elections in the digital era. An introduction of why this is important, and a high-level view of the potential cyber ills was given. The paper went into more detail highlighting different types of cyber threats and vulnerabilities that could impact General Elections in Africa focusing on the South African context, and some examples of instances where cyber-attacks were lodged to disrupt electoral processes in various parts of the world. This sheds some light on the reality of the global cybersecurity challenges and emphasizes the importance of having a strong cybersecurity backbone to safeguard General Elections. The possible impacts of cyber threats to the electoral process and its stakeholders were discussed. This helps with highlighting why the cyber threats identified in this report need to be taken into consideration. Potential mitigation techniques that can be employed by election process stakeholders to try and hinder malicious actors from disrupting the electoral process were outlined. The paper is closed-off by suggesting mitigation techniques that may enhance the security of General Election.

References

1. Opanuga, J.: Nigeria records 12.9 million cyberattacks during presidential election. The Guardian Newspapers, Nigeria, pp. 1–2, 14 March 2023
2. Reuters, "Kenyan Official Dismisses Reuters Report on Chinese Hack as 'Propaganda," US News and World Report, Nairobi, pp. 1–2, 25 May 2023
3. Maweu, J.M.: "'Fake Elections'? Cyber Propaganda, Disinformation and the 2017 General Elections in Kenya," African Journalism Studies, vol. 40, no. 4. Taylor and Francis Inc., pp. 62–76, 2 October 2019. https://doi.org/10.1080/23743670.2020.1719858
4. A. Christiansen, "How are cybersecurity threats, in the form of disinformation campaigns, reflected on the security measures they inspire?," Report, Malmo University, Sweden, 2023
5. Fidler, D.P.: "The U.S. Election Hacks, Cybersecurity, and International Law," In: AJIL Unbound, Cambridge University Press, pp. 337–342 (2016). https://doi.org/10.1017/aju.2017.5
6. Dawood, Y.: Combatting foreign election interference: canada's electoral ecosystem approach to disinformation and cyber threats. Election Law J. Rules Polit. Policy 20(1), 10–31 (2021). https://doi.org/10.1089/elj.2020.0652
7. Stedmon, N., Security, C., Factors, H.: The impact of cyber security threats on the 2020 US elections. http://maristpoll.marist.edu/wp
8. Okoli, C.: A guide to conducting a standalone systematic literature review. Commun. Assoc. Inf. Syst. 37, 1–33 (2015). http://aisel.aisnet.org/cais/vol37/iss1/43
9. Ryan, A., Van Geel, O., Pennings, F., Tirtea, R., Follmer, V.: Lection cybersecurity: challenges and opportunities, US, February 2019. https://www.enisa.europa

10. Eady, G., Paskhalis, T., Zilinsky, J., Bonneau, R., Nagler, J., Tucker, J.A.: Exposure to the russian internet research agency foreign influence campaign on Twitter in the 2016 US election and its relationship to attitudes and voting behavior. Nat. Commun. **14**(1) (2023). https://doi. org/10.1038/s41467-022-35576-9

11. Holovkin, B.M., Tavolzhanskyi, O.V., Lysodyed, O.V.: Corruption as a cybersecurity threat in the new world order. Connections **20**(2), 75–87 (2021). https://doi.org/10.11610/Connec tions.20.2.07

12. Olaniran, B., Williams, I.: Social media effects: hijacking democracy and civility in civic engagement, pp. 77–94 (2020). https://doi.org/10.1007/978-3-030-36525-7_5

13. Love, J., Mamabolo, S.: 2022 IEC annual report, South Africa, June 2022. Accessed 19 August 2023. https://www.elections.org.za/content/

14. Ablon, L.: Data thieves: the motivations of cyber threat actors and their use and monetization of stolen data (2018). www.rand.org

15. Wessels, M., van den Brink, P., Verburgh, T., Cadet, B., van Ruijven, T.: Understanding incentives for cybersecurity investments: development and application of a typology. Digit. Bus. **1**(2) (2021). https://doi.org/10.1016/j.digbus.2021.100014

16. Goldman, Z.K., Mccoy, D.: Economic espionage deterring financially motivated cybercrime (2016). http://cseweb.ucsd.edu/savage/papers/WEIS2012.pdf

17. Higgins, A.: Maybe private Russian hackers meddled in election, Putin says, The New York Times, New York, pp. 1–2, 1 June 2017. Accessed 15 August 2023. https://www.nytimes. com/2017/06/01/world/europe/vladimir-putin-donald-trump-hacking.html

18. CBS, Russia-linked hackers targeting French election, security firm says, 2017 CBS Interactive Inc., Paris, pp. 1–2, 25 April 25 2017, Accessed 19 August 2023. https://www.cbsnews. com/news/russia-hacked-french-election-trend-micro-report-fancy-bear-pawn-storm/

19. Hansen, I., Lim, D.J.: Doxing democracy: influencing elections via cyber voter interference. Contemp. Polit. **25**(2), 150–171 (2019). https://doi.org/10.1080/13569775.2018.1493629

20. Auchard, E.F.B.: French candidate Macron claims massive hack as emails leaked, Reuters, Frankfurt City, Germany, pp. 1–2, 05 May 2017. Accessed 12 August 2023. https://www.reu ters.com/article/us-france-election-macron-leaks-idUSKBN1812AZ

21. Baldassaro, M.: Identifying and tracking disinformation during the May 2019 South Africa Elections, Harvard: Harvard Law School, October 2024

22. Paraguassu, L.: Brazil court to probe Bolsonaro for attacks on voting system, Reuters, Brazil, pp. 1–2, 03 August 2021. Accessed 10 August 2023. https://www.reuters.com/world/ame ricas/attacked-by-bolsonaro-brazils-top-judges-say-electronic-voting-is-free-fraud-2021-08-02/

23. Mohammed, K.H., Mohammed, Y.D., Solanke, A.A.: Cybercrime and digital forensics: bridging the gap in legislation, investigation and prosecution of cybercrime in Nigeria. Int. J. Cybersecur. Intell. Cybercrime **2**(1), 56–63 (2019). https://doi.org/10.52306/02010519zjrk 2912

24. Fujiwara, T., Müller, K., Schwarz, C.: The effect of social media on elections: evidence from the United States (2023)

25. Baptista, J.P., Gradim, A.: Understanding fake news consumption: a review. Soc. Sci. **9**(10), 1–22 (2020). MDPI AG, https://doi.org/10.3390/socsci9100185

26. Tenove, C., Fellow, P.R.: Digital threats to democratic elections: how foreign actors use digital techniques to undermine democracy (2018)

27. Moabalobelo, T., Ngobeni, S., Molema, B., Phantsi, P., Dlamini, M., Nelufule, N.: Towards a privacy compliance assessment toolkit. In: IEEE IST-Africa Conference Proceedings, Pretoria, South Africa, pp. 1–8. IEEE, May 2023

28. Garnett, H.A., James, T.S.: Cyber elections in the digital age: threats and opportunities of technology for electoral integrity. Election Law J. Rules Polit. Policy **19**(2), 111–126 (2020). https://doi.org/10.1089/elj.2020.0633

29. Suzuki, Y.E., Monroy, S.A.S.: Prevention and mitigation measures against phishing emails: a sequential schema model. Secur. J. **35**(4), 1162–1182 (2022). https://doi.org/10.1057/s41 284-021-00318-x
30. Africa, S., Sokupa, S., Gumbi, M.: Report of the expert panel into the July 2021 Civil unrest, Pretoria, November 2021. Accessed 15 Aug 2023.
31. Cichonski, P., Millar, T., Grance, T., Scarfone, K.: Computer security incident handling guide : recommendations of the national institute of standards and technology, Gaithersburg, MD, August 2012. https://doi.org/10.6028/NIST.SP.800-61r2

Intersection of Electronic Security and Digital Forensics: Data Protecting Techniques and Uncovering Data Clues

Norman Nelufule[✉], Boitumelo Nkwe, Daniel Shadung, Kele Masemola, Tanita Singano, Japhtalina Mokoena, Zamo Ngubane, and Ntombizodwa Thwala

Defence and Security Cluster, Council for Scientific and Industrial Research (CSIR), Information and Cybersecurity Centre (ICSC), Brummeria, Pretoria 0184, Republic of South Africa
nnelufule@csir.co.za

Abstract. With the current era of technology, protecting data and infrastructure has become more of a concern as sensitive information is being stored on Digital platforms. The various new technologies being developed make it harder to secure electronic data as malicious actors keep utilizing the latest tips and tools to perform attacks. These latest technologies also display gaps within digital forensics as there are not a lot of tools that can assist in the investigation of cyber incidents and properly preserve digital evidence after an incident has been detected. For example, as more individuals and organizations migrate their data and infrastructure to cloud platforms, new skills and forensic tools are required to extract evidence from the cloud. This study presents various electronic security measures and case studies of security breaches where the use of Digital Forensics assisted with the investigation and the subsequent results assisted the organization affected or educated other institutions to be aware of techniques used by malicious actors. Keeping abreast with the latest tools and techniques will ensure that effective security measures are implemented to prevent security breaches. The continuous adaptation in technologies will assist in ensuring that investigators are able to perform forensically sound.

Keywords: Digital Forensics · Digital Evidence · Data Protection · Electronic Security

1 Introduction

The Fourth Industrial Revolution (4IR) represents the current era of technological advances, that is characterized by the convergence of digital, physical, and biological technologies in producing, accessing, and managing big data. The evolution of industrial revolution technologies has a long history as depicted in Fig. 1. As we increasingly rely on the electronic systems to create and store sensitive information, data protection tools and systems becomes an integral part of safeguarding individuals' privacy, ensuring business continuity, maintaining national security, and fostering trust in the digital

A. Sere et al. (Eds.): AFRICOMM 2023, LNICST 587, pp. 351–367, 2025.
https://doi.org/10.1007/978-3-031-81570-6_23

world. At the intersection of electronic security and digital forensics, the 4IR has both advantages and disadvantages. The 4IR brings cutting-edge technologies like artificial intelligence (AI), machine learning (ML), and big data analytics, which can be exploited to develop more sophisticated and proactive cybersecurity solutions. These solutions can be deployed to detect patterns, detect anomalies, and predict the potential digital security breaches, thereby bolstering electronic security measures [1–3]. With advancements in digital forensics tools and techniques, organizations can investigate and analyze cyber incidents more efficiently. Digital forensics can also help in locating the source of a security breach, aiding in developing appropriate response strategies and mitigating future security risks.

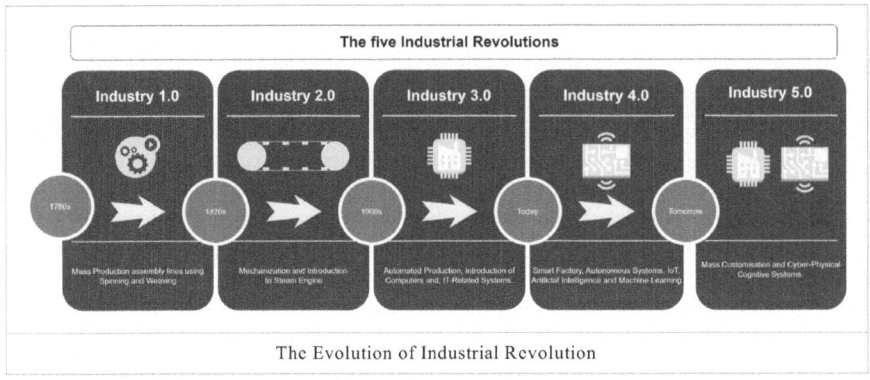

The Evolution of Industrial Revolution

Fig. 1. The Illustration of the Evolution of Industrial Revolution.

Despite bringing advantages, the 4IR also enhances the capabilities of cyber attackers to develop more tools for security breaches. Cybercriminals can exploit advanced technologies to launch more sophisticated attacks, making it challenging to detect and respond to threats effectively [1, 4–11]. As the 4IR empowers defenders with tools and technologies, it also enhances the capabilities of cybercriminals. In [12], it was discussed that cybercriminals can exploit advanced technologies to launch more sophisticated and targeted attacks, making it challenging to detect and respond to threats effectively. [13] mentioned that cybercrimes suspects are also escaping traceability due to the anti-forensic tools that helps them to avoid detection.

The rapid pace of technological advances in the 4IR requires continuous training and upskilling for security professionals and digital forensic investigators [12, 13]. Maintaining expertise in emerging technologies can be resource-intensive for the organizations. Training and awareness are key components so that users of technology can understand the pros and cons of those technologies. Such training and awareness sessions should incorporate the legal aspects of cybersecurity, data breaches, cybercrimes, cyberlaws, and digital forensics to enhance knowledge and capability on how to legally deal with cyber incidents. This is important as electronic security and digital forensic can intersect during cyber incidents investigations and some cases may end up in court to litigate suspect. In [14], it was discussed that the intersection of electronic security and digital forensics can raise complex legal and ethical questions, such as data ownership, chain of custody, and the use of artificial intelligence in decision making processes during digital forensics investigations. These are the main components that specialist should understand and master, since digital evidence acquired without following these crucial steps can be dismissed in a court law. This work aims to outline some of the advantages that are offered by enabling electronic security for the purpose of protecting data, detecting data clues, and enhancing the identification and extraction of digital evidence. This paper also aims to explore by means of systematic review, various electronic security measures and case studies of security breaches where the use of Digital Forensics assisted with the investigations. These concepts will cover the intersection of electronic security tools and digital forensic investigations. The remainder of this work is presented as follows: Sect. 2 presents the background of digital forensic, Sect. 3 presents the methodology adopted in this work, Sect. 4 presents the analysis and findings, and Sect. 5 presents the conclusion.

2 Background

In the 1940s, no one thought that computers can fall victims of cyber-attacks due to the size and complexity of the first working digital computing device tested in 1943 [15]. This computer was also referred to as monster machine, and access to this monster machine was limited and there was no network to connect two computers to each other. The notion of a computer virus was established way back in 1949 when John von Neumann realized that written computer program has a potential to reproduce themselves [15]. In the 1970s, the history of computer security was established during a research project that was gaining access to the internet and developing remote computer network access [15]. Around 1979, a 16-year-old Kevin Mitnick got arrested for hacking crimes that he has been committing for years [15]. In the year 1987, Andreas Luning and Kai Figge contributed to the first computer antivirus, leading to the birth of cybersecurity tools and electronic security [15]. Around 1996, after the world experienced the internet, many viruses began to surface with more sophisticated methods including polymorphism creating a new challenge for cybersecurity companies. Early 2000s after emailing and social media was established, cyber threats began to multiply [15].

Digital forensic emerged during the 1980s after the personal computers were introduced and they stated gaining popularity in the 1990s after the FBI hosted the first International Law Enforcement Conference on Computer Evidence in the United States [16]. Since the advent of 4IR, digital forensic has become a necessity and many countries do not have skills and expertise to combat the high rate of crimes as analyzed in [16–18] This historical background of cybercrimes and digital forensics can also be summarized as shown in Table 1.

2.1 Digital Forensic Techniques

Digital forensics procedure is described as the use of computing resources and the juristic investigative approaches to preserve, collect, and examine digitally acquired evidence [19]. This process demands that appropriate legal procedures are followed to ensure that

Table 1. Table of timelines in cybercrimes

Year of Event	Description of Event
1978	First cybercrime in Florida involving the unauthorized and erasure of data from a computing system. During these period cybercrimes were resolved according to the existing laws in the absence of federal laws of cybercrimes
1983–1984	Canada passed the legislation to deal with cybercrimes, the US also passed the Federal Computer Fraud and Abuse Act
1990–1992	UK passed the British Computer Misuse Act. First paper on cybercrime by Collier and Spaul
2002–2005	Best practices for computer forensic paper awarded to the Scientific Working group on Digital Evidence. ISO 1725 was published for the competence of testing and calibration laboratories
2005 and beyond	Various cybercrimes related regulations were discussed and adopted

there is legal search authority, chain of custody, use of validated digital forensic tools, repeatability, reporting, and potentially expert testimony in a court of law. The process is carried out by a digital forensic expert who is trained in the field and certified to use the required tools to produce credible digital evidence admissible in a court. According to the National Institute of Standards and Technology (NIST), the digital forensic investigation framework can be summarized graphically as in Fig. 2 [20]. In this figure, the process starts at evidence collection phase, then proceeds to examination phase which include, choice, the identification, and correlation subphases, from examination phase it proceeds to analysis phase which includes the construction and analysis of acquired evidence, the analysis phase is followed by the generated report. This process can also be repeated to ensure admissibility of digital evidence in court.

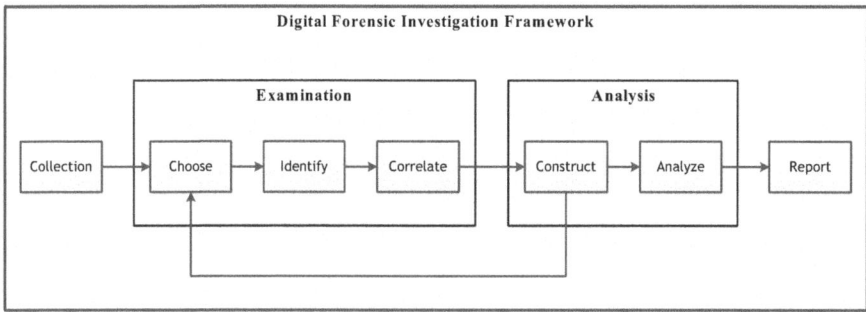

Fig. 2. An overview of Digital Forensic Investigation Process

The warrant of search in digital forensic investigation is a crucial step. In [17], the authors of the "Search and Seizure of Digital Evidence by Forensic Investigators in South Africa" looked at the digital forensics landscape from a South African perspective and identified that there are no set standards or procedures followed by cyber security professionals. However, there are several international Digital forensics and international standards that digital forensics professionals can follow to ensure that their evidence is handled in a manner that can be admissible in court [17]. Some of the standards that were identified in the research paper are summarized in Table 2.

Table 2. Table of Summary of Digital Forensic Standards followed in South Africa

Standard	Description
Principles of the Association of Chief of Police Officers (ACPO)	In 1997, The ACPO drafted the "Good Practice Guide for Computer-Based Electronic Evidence". This guide outlines four principles for collecting and managing digital evidence • 1st Principle: Investigators should not alter data that may be used in court • 2nd Principle allows investigators to access original data only in exceptional situations and if they are competent to do so • 3rd Principle requires investigators to record all processes applied to digital evidence • 4th Principle requires investigators to follow all legal principles during the analysis of digital evidence
ISO 27037: Security Techniques	Guidelines for identification, collection, acquisition, and preservation of evidence. Digital forensic investigators should do the following: • Minimize the handling of original evidence • All actions taken should be documented • Any changes to the data should be accounted for • Local laws and regulations of evidence should be followed • Investigators should not take actions beyond their level of competence
The ISO/IEC DIS 27037	Standard specifies that all processes in digital forensic investigations should be auditable, repeatable, reproducible, and justifiable. This process has the following goals: • All processes and results should be able to be evaluated by independent forensic investigators • The same results should be obtained when the same procedures and methods are used • Digital forensic investigators should be able to validate all actions and methods used. All the recommended phases should be by investigators which are identification, collection, acquisition, and preservation of evidence • The ISO/IEC DIS 27037 The guidelines and procedures for incident investigations are outlined in the ISO/IEC 27043 Standard on Information Technology. Follows the principle of the Daubert test that states that test outlines factors to ensure the integrity of evidence, including that theories and techniques used by experts should have been tested, subjected to peer review, and enjoy widespread acceptance

The standards summarized in Table 2, guides the sequence of events that should be adhered to during digital evidence collection in cybercrime investigations.

2.2 The Role of Digital Forensic Investigation in Uncovering Clues

Digital forensics plays a critical role in investigating cyber incidents and uncovering clues to identify perpetrators [21–24]. This process entails collecting, preserving, and analyzing digital evidence that will help digital forensics experts to understand the nature and scope of cyberattacks, support legal actions against cybercriminals, and help organizations strengthen their cybersecurity defenses [13, 24–26]. Digital forensics is becoming a broad concept, with various types of forensic investigations involved. These types include but are not limited to mobile, computer, server, networks, emails, database, cloud, etc. some of the most well-known types of digital forensic are depicted in Fig. 3. It is important for someone who intends to be a certified digital forensic examiner to master at least all the types listed below as these are the most useful types of forensics used to uncover digital clues during a cyber incident investigation.

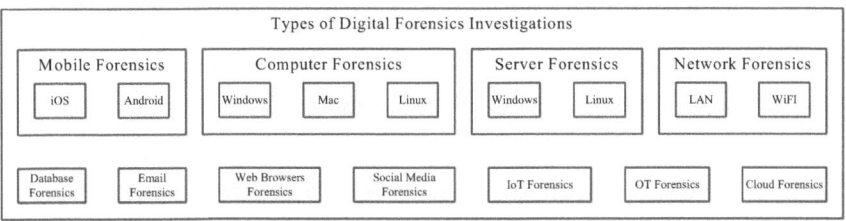

Fig. 3. An overview of the main types of Digital Forensics

Evidence Collection and Preservation

Digital forensic investigations require swift collection and preservation of digital evidence from affected systems and networks to ensure that it remains unaltered and credible. This process involves forensic imaging of storage media, capturing network traffic and maintaining the chain of custody to ensure the admissibility of evidence in legal proceedings [27–33].

Chain of custody is described as the method of tracking, managing, and preserving the timeline and chronological order of how digital evidence is handled by forensics experts during an investigation [34]. The purpose of this process is to ensure that the integrity of the evidence in question is not tampered with by a person who is not authorized to handle any case or incident-related evidence. The evidence must be preserved to ensure its admissibility in a court of law. When there is insufficient documentation in the chain of custody report, the evidence runs the risk of being deemed inadmissible in a court of law.

Cyber Incident Analysis

Digital forensics experts examine the preserved evidence to construct the sequence of events leading up to and during the cyber incident. They conduct network forensics to retrieve network logs from firewalls and packet tracers and use them to trace and analyze packets. Database logs are also used to view all database transactions that took place. From the Wireless forensics, wireless traffic can be collected and analyzed to retrieve any anomalies on the traffic. Data can be captured through continuous monitoring, during an attack or from captured log data. On the Memory forensics, a lot of information can be gathered from temporary storage such as usernames and passwords.

From the Email forensics, email headers can be used to investigate the email origin, server hopes and its destination, and Malware forensics can also be conducted and analyzed to determine its origin and impact.

This analysis of digital evidence can uncover digital clues, indicators and patterns that may link the attack to specific threat actors. Further analysis may often involve collaboration with intelligence agencies and international partners such as Interpol and other agencies to pursue criminals outside the national jurisdiction area.

Legal Support

Digital forensics findings often serve as critical evidence in legal proceedings. Investigators are expected to present their findings in a clear, reliable, and concise manner that can be understood by legal professionals and the courts to institute criminal prosecution of alleged cybercriminals [14, 22, 35]. This process will also undergo severe cross-examination by the defense council.

Incident Response Improvement

Understanding how the incident occurred and the techniques used by attackers can guide organizations in strengthening their security posture to prevent similar incidents in the future by studying past incidents, security professionals can identify trends, emerging threats, and vulnerabilities to better prepare for future attacks.

Data Recovery

In some cases, cyber incidents may result in data loss or data manipulation. Digital forensics can assist in recovering lost or altered data, which is especially important in cases involving ransomware attacks or data breaches. In a ransomware attack, the attacker encrypts the data and renders it unusable and demand ransom in bitcoin before they decrypt the data, however digital forensic tools can recover the encryptions that can be used to decrypt the data.

3   Methodology

This work adopts a systematic review approach based on cybersecurity incidents related to the South African landscape and beyond as guided by [36–41]. The detail of the proposed approach includes framing, literature searches and assessment. The research materials and literatures data were collected from IEEE Explore, Web of Science and Scopus indexing databases. In addition to these materials, reports and cases were also used to assess some of the digital forensic technologies adopted and used in some of the successful cases in South Africa. The impact of the exposure of vulnerable systems such as financial institutions and metropolitans were discussed. The role of digital forensics in pursuing and arresting perpetrators has been explained and presented in a tabular form.

3.1 Scoping

The scope of focus on this article includes literature related to electronic security technologies, electronic evidence, digital forensic investigations, and any other combination of electronic security and digital forensics.

3.2 Framing

The rapid advancements in technology have created security gaps that cybercriminals can exploit to launch sophisticated attacks. This has created a need for cybersecurity and digital forensic specialists to constantly update their security and investigation tools to keep up with the attacks. This study uses systematic review to highlight some of the security measures that have been effective in preventing cyberattacks. Furthermore, real-world cases where digital forensics was instrumental in successfully bringing perpetrators to book are presented.

3.3 Literature Search and Assessment

This study used IEEE Explore, Web of Science and Scopus indexing databases to collect data. The search strings used were: "electronic security measures" OR "electronic security tools" OR "data breaches in South Africa". The first step was to filter out irrelevant papers by looking at the keywords from the paper titles. Paper abstracts were then read to identify relevant papers and discard irrelevant ones. Once all the irrelevant papers were filtered out, full text reading of the remaining papers was done.

4   Discussion, Analysis and Findings

4.1   Electronic Security Measures

There are various electronic security measures that are employed to protect data and information systems from unauthorized access, data breaches, and cyberattacks. These measures aim to ensure that there is data confidentiality, data integrity, and data availability regularly. Some of the essential electronic security measures used to safeguard data and information systems are summarized in Table 3.

In 2016, Standard Bank faced a cyber-attack in which cybercriminals attempted to steal funds by targeting the bank's internal systems. However, due to the bank's robust electronic security measures in place, including multi-factor authentication, anomaly detection, and real-time security monitoring and incidence response, the attackers' attempts were thwarted. The security measures in place helped identify and block suspicious transactions, preventing cybercriminals from gaining unauthorized access to customer accounts and sensitive data [20].

In 2018, First National Bank (FNB), also faced a phishing attack where cybercriminals attempted to deceive customers into disclosing their login credentials and personal information. FNB's strong electronic security measures, including email filtering, spam detection, and user awareness, helped the bank to detect and block the phishing emails before they reached a significant number of customers. This proactive approach prevented potential data breaches and protected customers from falling victim to the scam [20].

Table 3. Table of Summary of Electronic Security Measures

Data Security Measure	Description
Firewalls	The barrier between an organization internal network and external internet that monitors, and controls incoming and outgoing network traffic based on policies
Patch Management	The application of regular software updates and patches for addressing known security vulnerabilities in operating systems, applications, and other related software
Encryption	The conversion of data into a coded format that can only be deciphered with a unique encryption key
Backup and Disaster Recovery	The process of continuous data backups to ensure that data is available in case of data loss due to cyber incidents or hardware failures
Multi-Factor Authentication (MFA)	Demands the user to provides multiple forms of identification before gaining access to a system or data
Physical Security Measures	This is controlled access to data centers and server rooms, video surveillance, and environmental controls. It complements electronic security to protect the physical infrastructure hosting information systems
Security Monitoring and Incidence Response	Deploying of security monitoring tools to allow the organization to detect and respond to security incidents promptly, minimizing the impact of potential data breaches

4.2 Digital Forensics Success Cases in South Africa and Abroad

There are several successful cases wherein perpetrators were found and charged, and some of the money recovered. However, the success rate is very low compared to the high rise of cybercrimes incident reported annually. South Africa is currently rated number six (6) in the world in terms of cybercrimes incidents (Table 4).

Table 4. Summery of Cases Solved Using Digital Forensics

Digital Forensic Case	Description
Swift Banking System Attacks (2016) [42]	Society for Worldwide Interbank Financial Telecommunication (SWIFT) experienced cyberattacks targeting the messaging system used for international financial transactions. The insights gained from digital forensic analysis helped financial institutions identify and mitigate the risks associated with similar attacks, leading to strengthened security measures within the global financial community
VBS Mutual Bank Heist (2018) [43]	Venda Building Society (VBS) Mutual Bank in South Africa experienced a high-profile cyber heist where cybercriminals siphoned off millions of rands from the bank's systems. The investigation into the incident involved a collaboration between law enforcement agencies and digital forensics experts. The analysis of all the digital evidence, including network logs and communication trails, investigators were able to trace the stolen funds back to specific individuals involved in the heist. Subsequently, several suspects were arrested and prosecuted for their roles in the cyber-attack
Orion Data Leak (2019) [44]	Millions of South Africans' personal information was exposed in a data leak event involving the business Orion in 2019. Working closely with law enforcement and digital forensics teams, the South African Banking Risk Information Centre (SABRIC), a banking sector group dedicated to combating cybercrime, investigated the incident. The cybercriminals responsible for the data leak were found and caught through thorough analysis of digital evidence and collaboration with international partners, which resulted in their successful prosecution

(*continued*)

Table 4. (*continued*)

Digital Forensic Case	Description
Experian Data Breach (2020) [45]	In 2020, Experian, a global credit reporting company with operations in South Africa, experienced a data breach that affected millions of South African citizens. The breach occurred when a suspected fraudster posed as a legitimate client and obtained access to Experian's database. The attacker then stole personal information, including names, identification numbers, and contact details of individuals. Experian promptly disclosed the breach and worked with law enforcement agencies to investigate the incident. This breach underscored the importance of protecting vast databases containing sensitive personal information

4.3 Convergence of Electronic Security and Digital Forensics

The nature of electronic security and digital forensics was outlined in detail in [46], as building a cybersecurity program that comprises of the following levels: *Architecture, Passive defense, active defense, intelligence and offensive.* The purpose of these levels is to ensure that the implemented security controls to prevent low level incidents from occurring in an operational environment. In the case of an incident taking place within an environment, then the organization will have to initiate incident response steps which are defined as an approach that handles and manages the state of the system after it was infiltrated and containing the environment with the hope of recovering it to its pre infiltration state. How Digital forensics can be used within the scope of cybersecurity is investigating crimes and internal policy, violations, reconstructing security incidents, troubleshooting operational problems, and recovering from accidental system damage. The following are goals of Digital Forensics Incident response (DFIR) in the cybersecurity space:

- Swift and effective in responding to security events.
- Investigate incidents with a systematic procedure.
- Minimize damage to the organization including preventing data loss, protecting systems, mitigating business disruption, and reducing compliance risks.
- Recover rapidly and complete from security incidents by Identifying the root cause, eradicating the threat across all organizational systems.
- Facilitate the effective prosecution of attackers by law authorities and provide evidence for legal actions taken by the organization.

4.4 Emerging Threats and the Need to Stay Ahead of Cybercriminals

Emerging threats in the cybersecurity landscape present significant challenges to organizations and individuals alike. Cybercriminals continually evolve their tactics, techniques, and procedures (TTPs) to exploit vulnerabilities and evade traditional security measures.

To effectively combat these threats, continuous innovation and adaptation are essential to stay ahead of cybercriminals. Table 5 summarizes these emerging threats and how they can be tackled.

Table 5. Table of Emerging Threats

Threat Type	Solution
Changing Technology	The technology landscape is continuously evolving with the introduction of new devices, applications, and services. Each new advancement brings its own set of security challenges. To address these evolving threats, cybersecurity professionals must constantly update their knowledge and adapt their strategies to protect against emerging risks
Nation-State Threats	State-sponsored cyberattacks pose significant challenges as they are highly organized, well-funded, and persistent. To counter nation-state threats, continuous innovation is vital to develop advanced threat intelligence, strengthen defense mechanisms, and promote international collaboration
AI threats attacks	Cybercriminals leverage AI to automate attacks, evade detection, and personalize phishing campaigns. Cybersecurity professionals must innovate by incorporating AI into their defense strategies to proactively detect and respond to AI-powered threats
Zero Day Exploits	Zero-day vulnerabilities, unknown to vendors, are lucrative for cybercriminals. They can exploit these vulnerabilities before patches are available and remain hidden

4.5 Challenges and Future Directions

The rapid growth in the development of generative artificial intelligence tools also has a negative impact on the cybersecurity field. Criminals can now create more sophisticated malware that can be very difficult to detect. Social media companies are also upgrading their security features, mobile companies are also not left behind in upgrading the security features. Some of the main challenges and future suggestions are listed in Table 6.

Table 6. Table of Challenges and Future Directions

Digital Forensic Type	Description of Challenges
Cloud Forensic	Security has been upgraded in some of the cloud applications, with multi-factor authentication required to gain access to the cloud data. Digital forensic specialists should explore more tools to uncover the keys to unlock the multi-factor authentication
Sophisticated Cyber threats	Cyber criminals are always ahead of cybersecurity and digital forensic specialists. With the advent of technology, cybercriminals are now able to use Artificial Intelligence tools to develop more sophisticated malware. This means that cyber specialists and digital forensic examiners should always improve their knowledge and tools
Data Privacy and Legal Concerns	Digital forensics involves handling sensitive data which raises privacy concerns and legal challenges related to data protection, and chain of custody [47]. Investigators should navigate through acceptable legal frameworks and ensure that they comply with privacy regulations during their investigation process
Encryption and Anonymization	The growing use of encryption and anonymization techniques by cybercriminals hinders digital forensics investigations. The continuous use of dark web computers makes it difficult for investigators to identify the suspects
Lack of Skilled Personnel	Adequate funding, skilled personnel, and training are essential to ensure effective cybersecurity and digital forensics capabilities
International Collaboration	Cybercrime investigation often transcends national borders, and this requires international collaboration among law enforcement agencies and digital forensics teams. Differing legal jurisdictions, lack of consulate relationships, and challenges in sharing evidence can impede investigations

5 Conclusion

The advantages of utilizing Digital Forensics when handling cyber incidents were stated as there is a correlation with the security of electronic data and digital forensics due to the constant development of technologies in the current era. Various security measures that can be implemented to prevent security breaches, cyberattacks and unauthorized access to certain data were addressed. There is a direct correlation between Digital forensics and incident response and as such collaboration between security professionals and Forensics investigators is necessary to solve incidents that occur in the environment effectively. Securing electronic data and the use of Digital Forensics in investigating and resolving an incident is presented in this paper.

Various case studies were used to display the impact of effective implementation of security measures to prevent breaches and preserve evidence for investigation once an incident has been detected, these case studies helped provide awareness to educate other institutions or individuals about some of the methods used by malicious actors. Challenges with Security and Forensics were presented, and future works included the advancement and adaptation of these techniques and technologies for users and organizations to implement effective controls to secure their data and for investigators in Forensics to develop the skills necessary to preserve, analyze and document electronic evidence obtained. Continued research and understanding of the latest technologies are the only way to stay abreast of what is going on as technology evolves and understanding how to effectively deal with each technology or incident that may occur.

References

1. Renold, A.P.: Survey of evidence collection methods for Internet of Things forensics. In: Proceedings of the 1st IEEE International Conference on Networking and Communications 2023, ICNWC 2023. Institute of Electrical and Electronics Engineers Inc. (2023). https://doi.org/10.1109/ICNWC57852.2023.10127407
2. Castiglione, A., Cattaneo, G., De Maio, G., De Santis, A., Roscigno, G.: A novel methodology to acquire live big data evidence from the cloud. IEEE Trans Big Data 5(4), 425–438 (2019). https://doi.org/10.1109/TBDATA.2017.2683521
3. Choo, K.-K.R., Esposito, C., Castiglione, A.: Evidence and forensics in the cloud: challenges and future research directions. IEEE Cloud Comput. 4(3), 1–6 (2017)
4. Li, S., Qin, T., Min, G.: Blockchain-based digital forensics investigation framework in the Internet of Things and social systems. IEEE Trans. Comput. Soc. Syst. 6(6), 1433–1441 (2019). https://doi.org/10.1109/TCSS.2019.2927431
5. Tiwari, A., Mehrotra, V., Goel, S., Naman, K., Maurya, S., Agarwal, R.: Developing trends and challenges of digital forensics. In: 2021 5th International Conference on Information Systems and Computer Networks, ISCON 2021. Institute of Electrical and Electronics Engineers Inc. (2021). https://doi.org/10.1109/ISCON52037.2021.9702301
6. Silvarajoo, V.R., Yun Lim, S., Daud, P.: Digital evidence case management tool for collaborative digital forensics investigation. In: 2021 3rd International Cyber Resilience Conference, CRC 2021. Institute of Electrical and Electronics Engineers Inc., January 2021. https://doi.org/10.1109/CRC50527.2021.9392497
7. Lee, S., Kim, H., Lee, S., Lim, J.: Digital evidence collection process in integrity and memory information gathering. In: First International Workshop on Systematic Approaches to Digital Forensic Engineering (SADFE 2005), Taipei, Tawan. IEEE, February, pp. 1–12 (2005)
8. Bennett, D.: The challenges facing computer forensics investigators in obtaining information from mobile devices for use in criminal investigations. Inf. Secur. J. 21(3), 159–168 (2012). https://doi.org/10.1080/19393555.2011.654317
9. Maheswari, K.U., Shobana, G.: The state of the art tools and techniques for remote digital forensic investigations. In: 2021 3rd International Conference on Signal Processing and Communication, ICPSC 2021, pp. 464–468. Institute of Electrical and Electronics Engineers Inc., May 2021. https://doi.org/10.1109/ICSPC51351.2021.9451718
10. Pourvahab, M., Ekbatanifard, G.: Digital forensics architecture for evidence collection and provenance preservation in IaaS cloud environment using SDN and blockchain technology. IEEE Access 7, 153349–153364 (2019). https://doi.org/10.1109/ACCESS.2019.2946978

11. Hemanth, J., Pelusi, D., Chen, J.I.-Z. (eds.): Intelligent Cyber Physical Systems and Internet of Things. Engineering Cyber-Physical Systems and Critical Infrastructures, vol. 3. Springer, Cham (2023). https://doi.org/10.1007/978-3-031-18497-0

12. Li, K.-C., Gupta, B.B., Agrawal, D.P.: Recent Advances in Security, Privacy, and Trust for Internet of Things (IoT) and Cyber-Physical Systems (CPS), 1st edn. CRC Press, Parkway (2021)

13. Yaacoub, J.P.A., Noura, H.N., Salman, O., Chehab, A.: Advanced digital forensics and anti-digital forensics for IoT systems: techniques, limitations and recommendations. Internet Things 19 (2022). https://doi.org/10.1016/j.iot.2022.100544

14. Van Nguyen, T., Truong, T.V., Lai, C.K.: Legal challenges to combating cybercrime: an approach from Vietnam. Crime Law Soc. Change 77(3), 231–252 (2022). https://doi.org/10.1007/s10611-021-09986-7

15. Chadd, K.: The history of cybercrime and cybersecurity, 1940–2020. Cybercrimes Mag., 1–5 (2020). https://cybersecurityventures.com/the-history-of-cybercrime-and-cybersecurity-1940-2020/

16. Pieterse, H.: The cyber threat landscape in south africa: a 10-year review. Afr. J. Inf. Commun. 28 (2021). https://doi.org/10.23962/10539/32213

17. Nortjé, J., Myburgh, D.C.: Forensic investigators in South Africa. PER/PELJ 2019 (2019). https://doi.org/10.17159/1727

18. Van Niekerk, B.: An analysis of cyber-incidents in South Africa. Afr. J. Inf. Commun. (AJIC) (20) (2017). https://doi.org/10.23962/10539/23573

19. Avoine, G., Hernandez-Castro, J.: Security of Ubiquitous Computing Systems: Selected Topics. Springer, Cham (2021).https://doi.org/10.1007/978-3-030-10591-4.

20. Dimitriadis, A., Ivezic, N., Kulvatunyou, B., Mavridis, I.: D4I - digital forensics framework for reviewing and investigating cyber attacks. Array 5, 100015 (2020). https://doi.org/10.1016/j.array.2019.100015

21. Pollitt, M., Caloyannides, M., Novotny, J., Shenoi, S.: Digital forensics: operational, legal and research issues. In: De Capitani di Vimercati, S., Ray, I., Ray, I. (eds.) Data and Applications Security XVII. IFIPIFIP, vol. 142, pp. 393–403. Springer, Boston (2004). https://doi.org/10.1007/1-4020-8070-0_28

22. Nance, K., Ryan, D.J.: Legal aspects of digital forensics: a research agenda. In: Proceedings of the 44th Hawaii International Conference on Systems and Sciences, Kauai, HI, USA. IEEE, February 2011

23. Yaacoub, J.-P.A., Noura, H.N., Salman, O., Chehab, A.: Digital forensics vs. anti-digital forensics: techniques, limitations and recommendations, March 2021. http://arxiv.org/abs/2103.17028

24. Jansen, A.: Digital records forensics: ensuring authenticity and trustworthiness of evidence over time. In: 5th International Workshop on Systematic Approaches to Digital Forensic Engineering, SADFE 2010, pp. 84–88. IEEE Computer Society (2010).https://doi.org/10.1109/SADFE.2010.20.

25. Horsman, G., Lyle, J.R.: Dataset construction challenges for digital forensics. Forensic Sci. Int. Digit. Investig. 38 (2021). https://doi.org/10.1016/j.fsidi.2021.301264

26. Casino, F., et al.: Research trends, challenges, and emerging topics in digital forensics: a review of reviews. IEEE Access 10, 25464–25493 (2022). https://doi.org/10.1109/ACCESS.2022.3154059

27. Chow, K.P., et al.: Digital evidence search kit. IEEE, Taipei, Taiwan (2005)

28. Dewald, A.: Characteristic evidence, counter evidence and reconstruction problems in forensic computing. In: Proceedings - 9th International Conference on IT Security Incident Management and IT Forensics, IMF 2015, pp. 77–82. Institute of Electrical and Electronics Engineers Inc., August 2015. https://doi.org/10.1109/IMF.2015.15

29. Yadav, D., Mishra, M., Prakash, S.: Mobile forensics challenges and admissibility of electronic evidences in India. In: Proceedings - 5th International Conference on Computational Intelligence and Communication Networks, CICN 2013, pp. 237–242 (2013). https://doi.org/10.1109/CICN.2013.57

30. Zhao, Z.: A framework to analyze reliability of digital evidences in computer systems. In: Proceedings - 2015 6th International Conference on Intelligent Systems Design and Engineering Applications, ISDEA 2015, pp. 21–25. Institute of Electrical and Electronics Engineers Inc., April 2016. https://doi.org/10.1109/ISDEA.2015.15

31. Moussa, A.F.: Electronic evidence and its authenticity in forensic evidence. Egypt. J. Forensic Sci. 11(1) (2021). https://doi.org/10.1186/s41935-021-00234-6

32. Azemović, J., Mušić, D.: Methods for efficient digital evidence collecting of business processes and users activity in eLearning environments. In: IC4E 2010 - 2010 International Conference on e-Education, e-Business, e-Management and e-Learning, pp. 126–130 (2010). https://doi.org/10.1109/IC4E.2010.92

33. Nikkel, B.J.: Improving evidence acquisition from live network sources. Digit. Investig. 3(2), 89–96 (2006). https://doi.org/10.1016/j.diin.2006.05.002

34. Alenezi, A., Atlam, H.F., Alsagri, R., Alassafi, M.O., Wills, G.B.: IoT forensics: a state-of-the-art review, challenges and future directions. In: COMPLEXIS 2019 - Proceedings of the 4th International Conference on Complexity, Future Information Systems and Risk, pp. 106–115. SciTePress (2019). https://doi.org/10.5220/0007905401060115

35. Khan, A., Wiil, U.K., Memon, N.: Digital forensics and crime investigation: legal issues in prosecution at national level. In: 5th International Workshop on Systematic Approaches to Digital Forensic Engineering, SADFE 2010, pp. 133–140 (2010).https://doi.org/10.1109/SADFE.2010.8

36. Schryen, G.: Writing qualitative is literature reviews—guidelines for synthesis, interpretation, and guidance of research. Commun. Assoc. Inf. Syst. 37, 286–325 (2015). https://doi.org/10.17705/1cais.03712

37. Kitchenham, B., Pearl Brereton, O., Budgen, D., Turner, M., Bailey, J., Linkman, S.: Systematic literature reviews in software engineering - a systematic literature review. Inf. Softw. Technol. 51(1), 7–15 (2009). https://doi.org/10.1016/j.infsof.2008.09.009

38. Oosterwyk, G., Brown, I., Geeling, S.: A synthesis of literature review guidelines from information systems journals. Kalpa Publ. Comput. 12, 250–260 (2019)

39. Khan, K.S., Kunz, R., Kleijnen, J., Antes, G.: Five steps to conducting a systematic review. J. R. Soc. Med. 96, 118–121 (2003). http://www.ncbi.nlm.nib.gov/entrez/query/

40. Siddaway, A.P., Wood, A.M., Hedges, L.V.: How to do a systematic review: a best practice guide for conducting and reporting narrative reviews, meta-analyses, and meta-syntheses. Annu. Rev. Psychol. 70, 747–770 (2019). https://doi.org/10.1146/annurev-psych-010418

41. Okoli, C.: A guide to conducting a standalone systematic literature review. Commun. Assoc. Inf. Syst. 37, 1–33 (2015). http://aisel.aisnet.org/cais/vol37/iss1/43

42. Michelle Liu, X.: A risk-based approach to cybersecurity: a case study of financial messaging networks data breaches. Coast. Bus. J. 18(1) (2021)

43. Motau, T.: The Great Bank Heist Investigator's Report to the Prudential: Venda Building Society (VBS), Johannesburg (2018)

44. Orion, P.: Complainant versus orion pharmaceutical email and website. Code Pract. Rev., 1–4 (2020)

45. Experian ® Data Breach Resolution: Data Breach Industry Forecast 2020, Johannesburg (2020)
46. Salfati, E., Pease, M.: Digital Forensics and Incident Response (DFIR) Framework for Operational Technology (OT) (2022). https://doi.org/10.6028/NIST.IR.8428
47. Moabalobelo, T., Ngobeni, S., Molema, B., Phantsi, P., Dlamini, M., Nelufule, N.: Towards a privacy compliance assessment toolkit. In: IEEE IST-Africa Conference Proceedings, Pretoria, South Africa, pp. 1–8. IEEE, May 2023

Emerging Phishing Attack Trends: A South African Case Study

Jabu Mtsweni[1,2], Precious Maduma[1], Vhuthu Nefale[1], Alex Ramantswana[1], Mfundo Masango[1], and Muyowa Mutemwa[1]([⊠])

[1] Council for Scientific and Industrial Research (CSIR), Information and Cyber Security Centre, Pretoria, South Africa
{pntuli1,vnefale,aramantswana,mmasango1,mmutemwa}@csir.co.za
[2] Military Academy, Stellenbosch University, Stellenbosch, South Africa

Abstract. Phishing is a common type of cyber-attack, that uses fraudulent emails or text messages to trick victims into revealing personal information that could further be used to commit actual cyber-crimes. Phishing attacks are prevalent in the cybersecurity space and are becoming complicated and varied as new technologies enter the market. As generative artificial intelligence platforms also become prevalent, we note that phishing attacks become even easier to craft. These attacks pose a real threat and challenge for businesses and individuals, particularly as digital transformation transcends into all spheres of our daily lives. Existing phishing or spam detection techniques do not always evolve as fast as the attack vectors emerge. Further, reporting of phishing emails or fraudulent text messages by users is not engrained in the business culture. The modus operandi of attackers before COVID-19 have changed with new phishing and smishing attack vectors emerging as the different technologies get adopted by users. The objective of this paper is to use phishing data collected from two anonymous South African organizations to technically examine the emerging phishing attack trends. We analyze and map the emerging phishing attacks using thematic analysis, payload analysis, and perceived objectives of the attack which include promoting spam emails, harvesting personal information, hacking into organizations' networks and so on. The paper contributes by developing technical and strategic guidelines on how phishing attacks could be mitigated through a cyber-resilience culture.

Keywords: Cybersecurity · Phishing · Smishing · Spam Emails · Email Security

1 Background and Introduction

1.1 Introduction

Emails are the most preferred mode of communication for businesses today. At the same time, 97% of companies are being targeted email-based phishing attacks [1]. According to Trend Micro, in one year (2020–2021), close to 700 million phishing attacks were detected in Africa with South Africa sharing a third of these attacks. The Interpol report

A. Sere et al. (Eds.): AFRICOMM 2023, LNICST 587, pp. 368–382, 2025.
https://doi.org/10.1007/978-3-031-81570-6_24

[2] released in 2021 indicates that the main cyberthreats in Africa are online scams perpetuated by fake emails or text messages that claim to be from legitimate sources and are used to siphon personal information from individuals to commit cyber-fraud. The same report also highlights that Business Email Compromise (BEC) are rife in Africa. These BEC attacks are quite common and are a serious threat to all organizations of any type [3].

Recent research suggest that these types of attacks have increased significantly during the COVID-19 pandemic and with the adoption of many technologies to enable remote work, these attacks are not abating [3], and over 90% of organizations are getting spoofed, meaning that some of the existing security solutions are not aiding in winning the battle.

Figure 1 depicts a Google trend on the topic of "phishing" in South Africa since 2018, which also indicates that phishing is on the upward trajectory (79% on 22 July 2023) compared to (27% on 18 August of 2018) in terms of search interest over time, and this represents a percentage increase of over 193% [4]. These stats were closely comparable with the world-wide picture, confirming that phishing attacks are a serious challenge across the board.

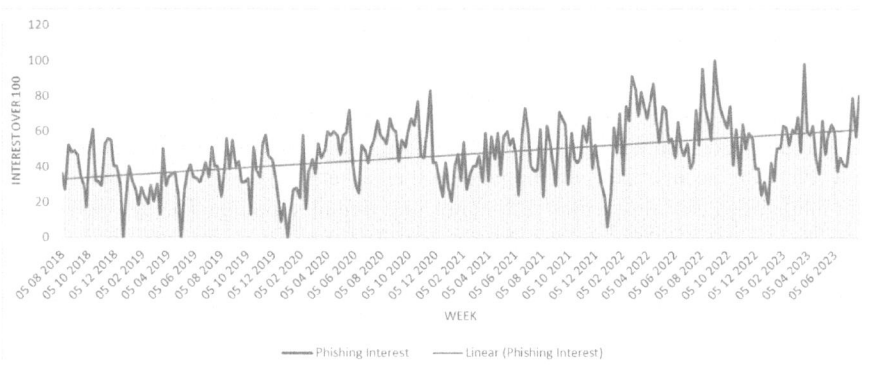

Fig. 1. Google search phishing trends over 5 years

What is also of note is that the types of phishing attacks have moved to text-messages on social media platforms such as WhatsApp, voice messages, as well as video content on social media platforms such as YouTube and TikTok. Of great concern is the maturity of Generative Artificial Intelligent (AI) tools that makes it simpler for anyone, even with no technical skills to generate fraudulent emails that are crafted in any language with limited grammatical and spelling errors, making them even more believable.

What is also evident is that there is a lack of investment in cybersecurity in Africa, but this is costing African countries billions of dollars every year according to [5].

1.2 Background

In this section, we provide background information on phishing and definitions of terminologies used in this research. In general, phishing attacks start with preparation, followed by execution, and finally exploitation [6]. All these phases evolve as emerging techniques and technologies evolve.

Social Engineering. This is a general term that defines all cybersecurity attacks that rely on human interaction to trick the target into revealing sensitive information either through clicking on a link, opening a malicious email attachment, and/or freely giving information to unauthorized individuals. This type of attack makes humans ignore or forget any precautions before performing a computer related action. The purpose of such messages is to gain access, reveal sensitive information, execute malware, or cause damage to computer systems.

Phishing. This is a type of a social engineering attack that involves sending fraudulent emails or text messages that are meant to give the victim the assurance that they are from a legitimate source, such as a bank or credit card company.

Smishing. Is an attack that involves sending fraudulent text messages to a target with the same intention as phishing e-mails.

Vishing. This attack is different from phishing or smishing in that it uses voice or videos claiming to be an authorized pre-approved trusted person from a reputable and reliable organization (e.g., insurance company or bank) with the hope of tricking the intended victim into revealing sensitive information, such as passwords of pin codes.

Phishing attacks occur in a systematic and planned manner. In [6], a phishing taxonomy is proposed and is aligned to the emerging attack trends. This is shown in Fig. 2 below. Phishing occurs via a communication media, targeting a device of interest such as a mobile device using various techniques like e-mail spoofing. The taxonomy also shows the countermeasures against phishing attacks.

What is lacking in the taxonomy are the phishing intentions or objectives because they are not always common across different attacks. In this study, we attempt to address this aspect. What further makes circumventing phishing attacks difficult lies mostly in the design of the emailing system architecture, where an email can originate from any source using a myriad of tools and platforms and be transported to the destination via different intermediaries. At the same time, email can be transported via legitimate paths carrying payloads that may look innocuous, until obliviously activated by the target.

Figure 3 explains the process of email communication from the sender's email client to the recipient's email client through various email servers. Attackers can use email communications to spread malware by exploiting email security vulnerabilities.

Malware can be sent via email attachments, links or images and can infect one or more devices by spreading ransomware attacks, crashing victims' systems, providing hackers remote device access, steal victim's personal data, destroy files, or add victim's account malicious ad system [7]. Attackers also use phishing emails to trick victims into clicking malicious links or downloading malware-infected attachments.

1.3 Structure of the Paper

The rest of the paper is structured as follows: Sect. 2 discusses the research methodology adopted for this paper. In Sect. 3, the related research work is analyzed and synthesized

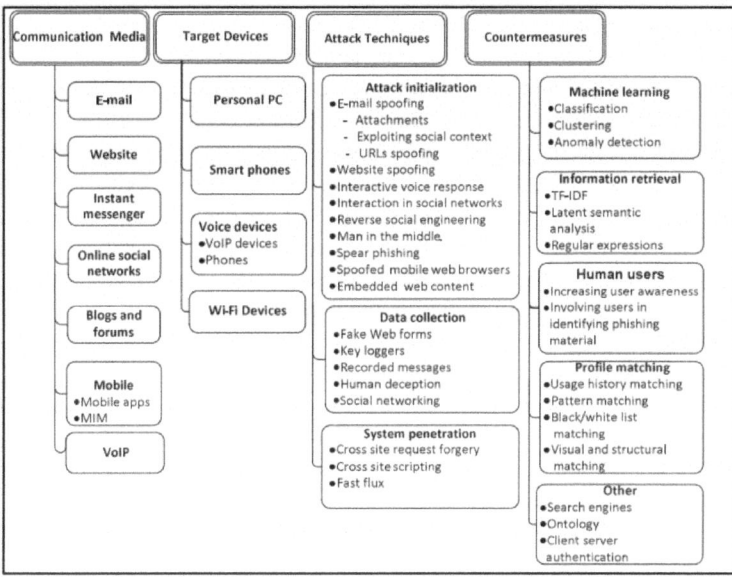

Fig. 2. Phishing attacks taxonomy [6]

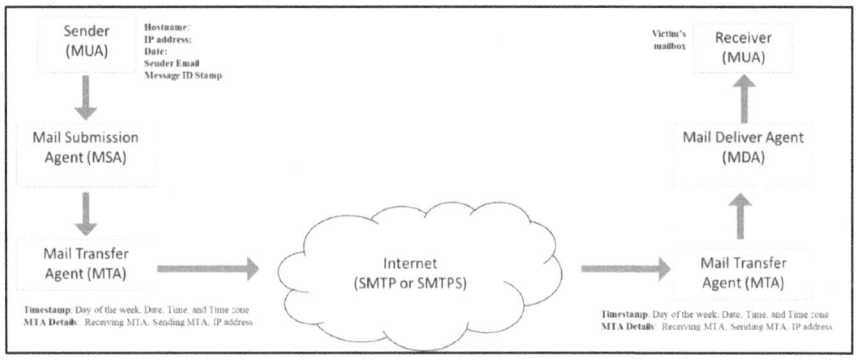

Fig. 3. Email communication system

in relation to our research objective. Section 4 details the data collection process and sampling followed in this study. Section 5 describes the payload attack analysis with selected examples, and Sect. 6 highlights the thematic analysis that provided the emerging phishing attack trends. Section 7 provides technical and strategic guidelines for mitigating phishing attacks, and the paper is concluded with a summary in Sect. 8.

2   Research Methodology

The research conducted for this paper followed a Design Science Research (DSR) approach [8]. The DSR was chosen because it is found to be suitable for research of this nature that deals with a technical subject covering the whole research lifecycle, including clear problem identification. In addition, DSR tends to accommodate both quantitative and qualitative research methods and can be applied as a problem-driven and solution-driven research approach and can also allow researchers to end-up with different types of artefacts, such as tools, frameworks and/or processes.

This study adopts the research literature review as the first step in fully understanding the challenges in relation to phishing attacks in a general context. A case study approach [9] is adopted to specially focus the research on South Africa. A case study is a widely used approach in research and business for performing in-depth analysis of a subject, which for the purposes of this is a country (South Africa). And there has been several research studies relying on case studies to understand phishing, malware, and intrusion detection datasets.

The South African case study is chosen purely because of readily available (recent) data of phishing emails from two anonymous organizations in South Africa, which could be a challenge to source from other environments due to sensitivity and datedness of such data [10]. In addition, social media engagements on phishing were easily accessed and contextualized with a South African context.

In analyzing the phishing data (from email gateways), payload analysis techniques were employed to identify the patterns and relationships between the data sets at technical level. This was critical in understanding the phishing attack trends from the research data set. Payload analysis refers to technical and statistical techniques for analyzing the payload in events (e.g., phishing email). This technique is used in intrusion detection systems, spam-filters, anti-virus software, and other security tools [11]. Payload analysis may include investigating source of the email, IP (Internet Protocol) address locations, and links or attachments for malicious content. Identifying the features of the payload assists in understanding the objective of the phishing attack [10].

Using phishing data from social media and email-gateways, thematic analysis was also applied. Thematic analysis is qualitative-based and allows for manual identification of themes and patterns within data [12].

3 Related Work: Phishing Attacks

Prior studies have looked closely at attack vectors, social engineering strategies, and technical defenses in the context of phishing attacks. To shed light on the human-centered aspects of this common cybersecurity threat, this study seeks to delve deeper into the psychological factors influencing user susceptibility to phishing.

Phishing is an active research topic across the globe, with varying titles such as social engineering, phishing attacks, business email compromise, and spam. In the table below, we show a selected list of related works spread between 2010–2023. Our research complements these studies by providing a comprehensive analysis of phishing attacks using multiple sources of data (Table 1).

4 Data Collection and Sampling

This paper relied on data collected through "Phish Alert", where users voluntarily report phishing emails at the organization and from an e-mail gateway detecting phishing emails. In total, over 600 phishing emails were collected from two large organizations in

Table 1. Summary of Related Work

Authors	Title	Year	Contribution
Williams, Hinds, & Johnson [13]	Exploring susceptibility to phishing in the workplace	2018	Authority, urgency, and context impact users' susceptibility to phishing
L'Huiller et al. [14]	Latent semantic analysis and keyword extraction for phishing classification	2010	Use of latent semantic analysis and text mining for characterization of phishing attacks
Pejic-Bach, Jajic, & Kamenjarska [15]	A Bibliometric analysis of phishing in the Big Data Era: high focus on algorithms and low focus on people	2023	Results indicate that real-time data collection and development of effective algorithms are essential in combating phishing attacks
Sharma & Bashir [16]	An analysis of phishing emails and how the human vulnerabilities are exploited	2020	Words used in emails are targeting users' emotional tendencies and triggers for phishing attacks
Burita, Matoulek, Halouzka & Kozak [17]	Analysis of phishing emails	2021	Contribute to the understanding of phishing emails, while adding to the knowledge base on education and training in phishing email defense
Parker & Flowerday [18]	Contributing factors to increased susceptibility to social media phishing attacks	2020	Identify the factors that contribute to an increased susceptibility to social media phishing attacks and propose a model to reduce this susceptibility

South Africa. After pre-processing the data, and removing obvious false positives, the final data for analysis had 587 e-mails.

In addition, phishing reports were collected from social media with the focus on South Africa. This data provides an overview of emerging phishing trends reported by the public on social media. A total of over 415 tweets using the keywords "phishing attacks" (*case insensitive and no-exact match) were collected between 23 June 2023 – 29 July 2023. The analysis is presented in Sect. 6.

5 Payload Attack Analysis

In this section, we highlight the payload attack analysis that was conducted to understand the emerging phishing and smishing attacks. This is done using a multi-prong approach and tools to analyze collected phishing emails. The emails are analyzed using tools such as emails header analyzer to determine origins of the email, path of the email, if it was detected by the existing email server that received it, and if it had any attachments or URLs and whether they were malicious or not, and if anti-virus tools were able to detect it or not.

The payload attack analysis is critical as it gives us insights into emerging techniques used by attackers, as well as payloads that are generally included in the emails and objectives of those payloads. The objective of the payload analysis is to also pick up weaknesses within email security specifically related to phishing and how these weaknesses can be mitigated.

5.1 Tools

The following tools were used for the payload analysis, and they are briefly described.

- **Email Header Analyzer**[1] – this tool was used to extract and analyze email header fields and values to give comprehensive insights on various elements such as source, email servers, network hops, and so on.
- **Whois** – this is the Internet record listing that identifies who owns a domain and IP address blocks.
- **AbuseIPDB**[2] – this is a service used to report and query IP addresses for abuse or other malicious activities.
- **VirusTotal**[3] – it is a Google service used to analyze suspicious files, domains, IPs, and URLs to detect malware and other breaches.
- **Browserling**[4] – we used this as an online browser sandbox that lets one securely open a website in an isolated environment.
- **Splunk SIEM** (Security Incidents and Events Monitoring) - in this context, this tool was used for data ingestion and visualization of phishing data.
- **EML Analyzer**[5] – this tool was used in combination with the Email Header Analyzer to extract email headers, domains, URLs, and attachments within an EML file. EML analyzer also automatically submits contents for relevant checks, for example, URLs are submitted to Virus Total, AbuseIPDB and others.

5.2 Payload Analysis

In this section, we discuss the findings of the analyses performed on the dataset of phishing emails. The summary of the email data points only from two (2) email gateways is tabulated in Table 2 below.

---

[1] https://www.gaijin.at/en/tools/e-mail-header-analyzer/.

[2] https://www.abuseipdb.com/.

[3] https://www.virustotal.com/.

[4] https://www.browserling.com/.

[5] https://eml-analyzer.herokuapp.com/.

It can be noted there were only 43% of unique email senders with all emails originating from 20 countries. Some of the emails came from the same source, however, targeting different recipients within the two organizations studied. This clearly indicates that spear phishing is also a common attack in many of the phishing emails in South Africa. The trend suggests that phishing emails in South Africa equally exploit both URLs (Uniform Resource Locator) and attachments as payloads.

Table 2. Table captions should be placed above the tables.

	Email Senders	Country of Origin	IP Addresses	URLs in Emails	Attachments in Emails
Totals	587	587	587	280	299
Unique	250	20	190	118	156
%	100%	100%	100%	48%	51%

Email Header Analysis. According to the analysis, 52% of the emails analyzed failed the SPF check. A sender policy framework (SPF) record is a type of DNS TXT record that lists all the servers authorized to send emails from a particular domain [19]. This implies that the email servers from which the phishing emails originated are not permitted to send emails on behalf of the domain. This can be seen as an indication that the domains have been spoofed.

Figure 4 depicts the distribution of the country of origin of the emails based on the sender's email address and message-id. The analysis indicated that 43% of the emails are sent through the United States of America (USA) with South Africa accounting for 32%. South Korea appeared 11% followed by Germany at 3%. From this analysis, it is evident that phishing attacks in South Africa originate from USA servers, and this is not surprising since most of the Internet Service Providers that were analyzed included Google, Microsoft Corporation, and Amazon Technologies, amongst others. All these organizations offer several different internet services that allow for hosting of phishing sites and replaying of emails.

The analysis further revealed at least 56% of the URLs found in 48% of the emails were detected as malicious. Furthermore, on average, only 3.6% of the anti-malware tools found in VirusTotal detected 56% of the URLs in selected e-mails as malicious. This is a concern as this means that if the phishing email gets to the user and the user can open the link, then a larger breach could happen. In addition, the analysis revealed that 57% of the e-mails had attachments. From the analysis, the top 3 identified file extensions that were attached to flagged emails are the Portable Document Format (PDF), which is the leading flagged file extension within the analyzed email data set, followed by docx, which is a Microsoft Word Open Extensible Markup Language (XML) format document file, and lastly zip, which is a file extension for a compressed archive file.

During the analysis of phishing email headers, it was noted that the "Reply-to" headers field are often not the same as the "From" header field. This is due to spoofing of domains and attackers wanting to get the response to the email instead of the email

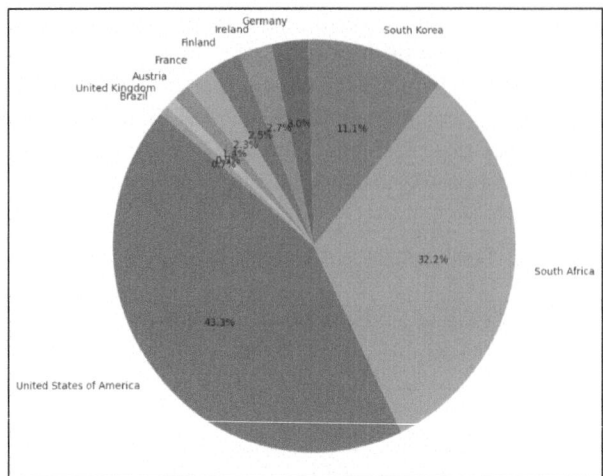

Fig. 4. Distribution of emails per country of origin

being sent to the spoofed email account. It was also noted that emails that pass the SPF alignment check (reply-to domain and from domain headers match) are due to attackers owning that domain, as registering a domain is quite simple.

Figure 5 depicts the top 10 Blocked URL Classifications that were sandboxed. A contrast can be drawn to indicate that most of the blocked URLs are firstly classified as *phishing* as they were requesting for user information or user credentials, the second classification is *dangerous file extension*, the attachments possibly had underlying code or an attached executable which was picked up during the sandboxing process. The third classification of the URLs is *malware*, which is described as a malicious program or code that is harmful to systems. The URLs could be redirected to download, install, or execute the malicious code or program once the user has clicked on the URL contained in e-mail.

The next section focuses on thematic analysis to describe the emerging phishing trends in South Africa using the message title in the email subject as well as content from the social media data.

6   Emerging Phishing Trends

Using the phishing data collected from various sources as well as data from social media collected over a 30-day period, this section discusses the trends of emerging phishing and smishing attacks.

Based on the thematic analysis as shown in Fig. 6, we observed that in South Africa, most of the phishing engagements on social media centers around *banking scams, flight bookings, smishing via SMS, cloned websites, stolen pin-codes, bogus holiday accommodation, impersonating attacks, ransomware attacks, hacked accounts, fake support online, cyber-crime, use of QR codes to circumvent anti-phishing tools* and many others. The smishing attacks using SMS/MMS consist of a combination of more than just a

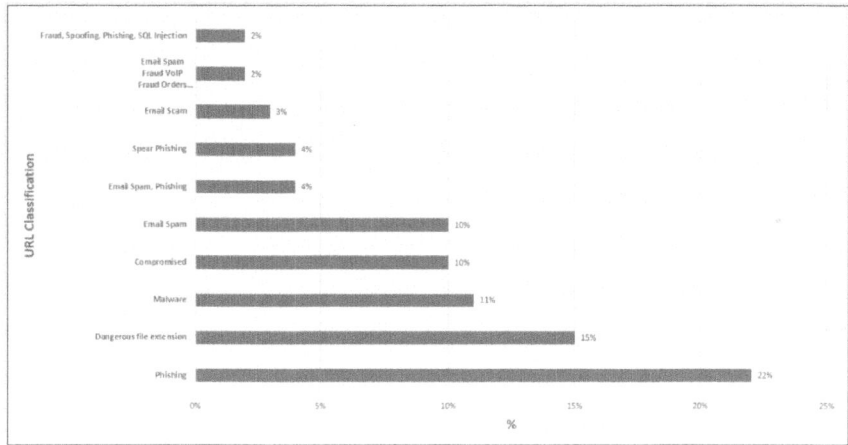

Fig. 5. Top 10 Block URL Classifications

Fig. 6. Social media posts on phishing

malicious URL link that has a payload, this requires legitimizing the contents of the message and making it seem like an actual message from a reputable actor such as a financial or insurance institute.

Figure 7 depicts the common email subjects used by attackers to entice a user to viewing the email as a legitimate email. The email subjects can also be spoofed by an attacker based on information they gathered when doing reconnaissance in the organizations. Based on the analysis, the trends in South Africa suggest that most email subjects focus on the following subjects: *banking, insurance policies, credit cards, purchase orders, bank statements, request for quotations, echo sign signature requests, contract management, shipment, invoicing, payments, mobile rewards, billing, and reminders of different kinds.*

It is evident that phishing attacks tend to be well aligned with the operations of organizations studied. For instance, one organization part of the case study adopted the online signing of documents, and phishing attacks also adapted to this new way of work.

In addition, we have observed that the request for quotations, which when responded to gives away a lot of sensitive information, are used by hackers to extract personal and business information from users.

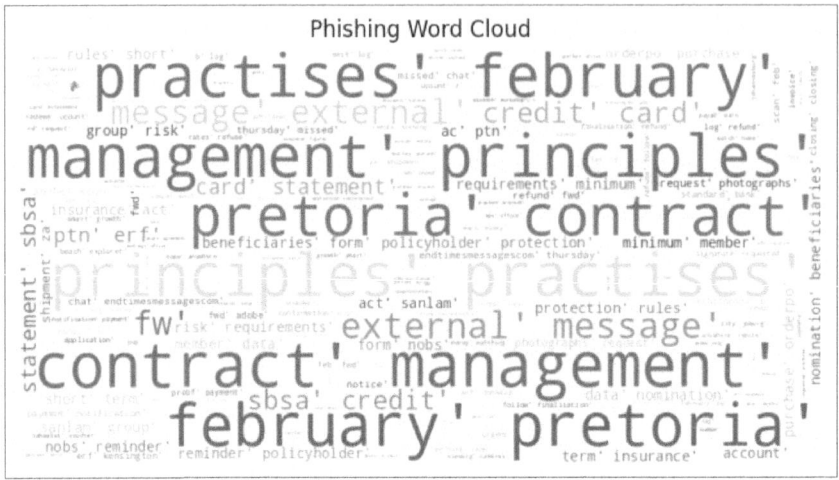

Fig. 7. Common email subjects

Based on the social media data, the analysis shows that raising awareness via social media on phishing is growing in South Africa. Figure 8 depicts the top 10 accounts that have tweeted regarding phishing. Based on the analysis, the South Africa Police Services are leading the engagements about phishing, followed by the South African Government and lastly within the telecommunications and banking sectors, Vodacom and Nedbank formed part of the list as the largest organizations in South Africa promoting anti-phishing campaigns. Additionally, we observed cybersecurity awareness campaigns against phishing by different institutions advising their users what to do and not do when using electronic services.

In this subsection, we also demonstrate that our analysis is aligned to what is already in literature. According to the literature, phishing attacks are indicated to be on the rise. And based on the literature, the following phishing trends are being observed at a global level. Some of these trends were observed in the analysis of the data collected for this research study.

- **Brandjacking.** This is a type of cyberattack in which an attacker impersonates a brand or company to trick victims into sharing personal information or downloading malware, and this can also be done either via email or social media [20].
- **URL Spoofing.** This is the type of attack in which an attacker creates a legitimate-looking phishing web address to trick users into clicking on it and visiting a malicious website. URL spoofing is often used in phishing attacks to trick users into revealing sensitive information or downloading malware.
- **Smishing.** This is a type of phishing attack performed on mobile text messages. And in our analysis of literature and collected data, it is evident that this is an emerging

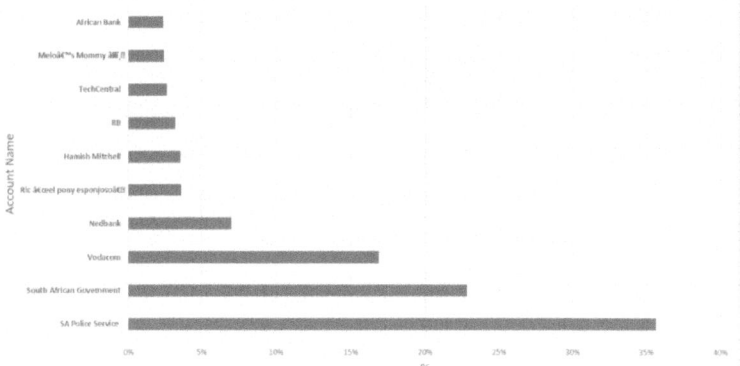

Fig. 8. Top 10 accounts with largest reach

trend, especially for mobile banking and mobile phone rewards targeting users of online banking and mobile phone users.

- **COVID-19 Spoofed Emails** [21]. Although, COVID-19 has mostly been tamed across the world, cybercriminals still attempt to impersonate government agencies, healthcare orgs, and financial institutions with the aim to steal personal or financial info or introduce malware into corporate networks.
- **E-mail Metadata Spoofing** [22]. Metadata Spoofing refers to an attack pattern in which an adversary changes a resource's metadata, such as a file, directory, or repository, to present a malicious resource as legitimate or trusted. The goal of a metadata spoofing attack is to trick the victim into believing that a malicious resource such as an email is from a trusted source. And this technique is also used to trick anti-phishing tools.

7   Technical and Strategic Guidelines

Email attackers have been introducing new attack vectors to run successful phishing campaigns. One aspect that the attackers focus on is the medium, which is the way the phishing attack is delivered, either through the internet, short message service (SMS)/multimedia messaging service (MMS) or voice. These attacks always have an associated to vector such as email, social networks, websites just to name a few.

This section proposes recommendations related to technical and strategic guidelines (see Fig. 9). To combat phishing and phishing attacks, effective countermeasures, such as cybersecurity awareness training and incorporating technologies to filter, block, or warn about emails or suspicious SMS, are needed. The authors of this paper therefore provide the recommendations summarized in Fig. 9 to minimize phishing attacks and their impact.

Domain-Based Message, Authentication, Reporting and Conformance (DMARC) Enablement. It is recommended that email users, especially enterprises consider enabling DMARC to counter spoofed emails [1]. DMARC authentication acts as a strong protection against phishing assaults and email fraud, fostering trust in email

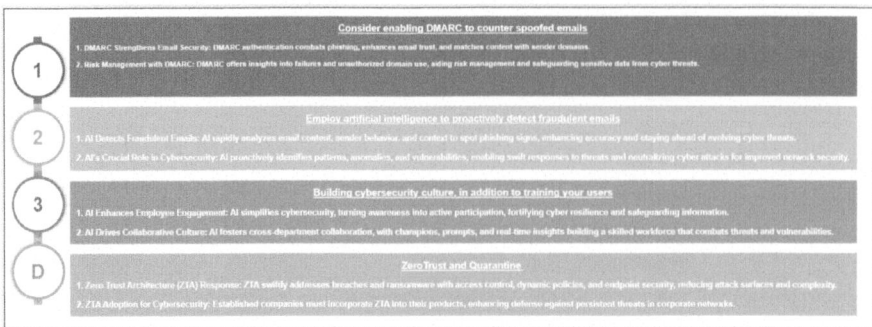

Fig. 9. Technical and strategic guidelines

communications, according to [1]. DMARC does this by matching email content with sender domains and by authenticating messages using cryptographic techniques. Additionally, DMARC offers organizations vital information to manage potential risks and unauthorized domain use through valuable insights into email authentication failures and enforcement actions. Adopting DMARC stands out as a crucial preventative action for protecting sensitive data and email integrity in the face of growing cyber threats.

Artificial Intelligence (AI) Employment. The second is to employ AI enabled security tools to proactively detect fraudulent emails. AI enabled security tools can detect subtle signs of phishing attempts by rapidly analyzing email content, sender behavior, and contextual cues using machine learning algorithms and pattern recognition techniques. This approach not only improves the accuracy of detecting malicious emails, but it also enables organizations to stay ahead of ever-changing cyber threats. Because of AI's ability to learn and adapt, the digital landscape gains a strong defense against fraudulent emails, protecting sensitive information, and improving overall email security.

Build a Cybersecurity Culture. The third recommendation is to build a cybersecurity culture, in addition to training email users. By simplifying difficult terminology and enabling employees and the cybersecurity team to move from awareness to actionable actions. It directs staff members toward particular security procedures, making cybersecurity an active element of daily operations as opposed to a passive idea. Employees become frontline defenders against threats because of this transition, which also strengthens the organization's cyber resilience. As a result, sensitive information and crucial systems are better secured, hence strengthening overall cybersecurity posture [23].

Zero Trust Architecture (ZTA) [24]. This strategic guideline focusses on the use of quarantine and sandboxing. Related to social engineering attacks, a proactive approach of preventing compromised user accounts from gaining access to organizational data and information or executing ransomware attacks is the ZTA. With this approach the aim is to verify the trust relationship of an account or asset before granting access. Assets that are not trusted can be quarantined. And in addition, attachments and URLs can have their trust status verified by sandbox environments. Making use of security technologies that can execute or open attachments, and URL links in a sandboxed environment, could assist with malicious detections before the emails are delivered to users.

Lastly, organizations could take proactive measures to protect their brand by monitoring social media and online activity for signs of brandjacking and taking legal action against attackers when necessary [25].

8 Summary and Conclusion

The prevalence of email-based phishing attacks has become a significant issue, with over 97% of companies being targeted, particularly in Africa where cyber threats such as online scams and Business Email Compromise (BEC) have become rampant. The use of Generative AI tools has further exacerbated the problem by enabling the creation of sophisticated fraudulent emails. Despite the surge in phishing attacks, there remains a lack of investment in cybersecurity across the continent, resulting in substantial financial losses.

To combat these threats, this paper has demonstrated that in South Africa phishing attacks are continuing to be on the rise, new techniques are being used by the attackers taking advantage of daily operations of the organizations' studied. This paper suggests technical and strategic guidelines based on the payload and thematic analysis, and these include implementing DMARC, utilizing AI for detection, fostering a cybersecurity culture, and adopting a Zero Trust Architecture.

References

1. Mimecast: Cyber Risk Command the C-suite's focus: the state of email security 2023. Mimecast (2023)
2. Interpol: African Cyberthreat Assessment Report: Interpol's key insight into cybercrime in Africa. Interpol (2021)
3. Saud Al-Musib, M., Al-Serhani, F.M., Humayun, M., Jhanjhi, M.H.: Business email compromise (BEC) attacks. Mater. Today Proc. **81**(2), 89 (2023)
4. Google Trends: Google Trends: Phishing. Google, 31 July 2023. https://trends.google.com/trends/explore?date=today%205-y&geo=ZA&q=%2Fm%2F027b9k&hl=en-GB. Accessed 03 Aug 2023
5. IT-Online: Trend Micro tackles rising cybercrime in Africa. IT-Online, 30 June 2022. https://it-online.co.za/2022/06/30/trend-micro-tackles-rising-cybercrime-in-africa/. Accessed 06 Sept 2023
6. Aleroud, A., Zhou, L.: Phishing environments, techniques, and countermeasures: a survey. Comput. Secur. **68**, 160–196 (2017)
7. Proofpoint US: What Is Email Security? - Defining Security of Email, 23 July 2023. https://www.proofpoint.com/us/threat-reference/email-security. Accessed 20 Aug 2023
8. Weber, S., Beck, R., Gregory, R.: Combining design science and design research perspectives–findings of three prototyping projects. In: 45th Hawaii International Conference on System Science (HICSS) (2012)
9. Yin, R.: Case Study Research - Design and Methods, SAGE Publisher, Thousand Oaks (2009)
10. Verma, R., Zeng, V., Faridi, H.: Poster: data quality for security challenges: case studies of phishing, malware and intrusion detection datasets. In: Proceedings of the 2019 ACM SIGSAC Conference on Computer and Communications Security, CCS 2019 (2019)

11. Maestre, V., Sandovol, O.A., Garcia, V.L.: Alert correlation framework for malware detection by anomaly-based packet payload analysis. J. Netw. Comput. Appl. **97**, 11–22 (2017)
12. Joffe, H.: Thematic Analysis. Wiley, Hoboken (2011)
13. Williams, E., Hinds, J., Joinson, A.: Exploring susceptibility to phishing in the workplace. Int. J. Hum. Comput. Stud. **120**, 1–13 (2018)
14. L'Huillier, G., Hevia, A., Weber, R., Ríos, S.: Latent semantic analysis and keyword extraction for phishing classification. In: EEE International Conference on Intelligence and Security Informatics: Public Safety and Security (2010)
15. Pejić-Bach, M., Kamenjarska, T., Jajić, I.: A bibliometric analysis of phishing in the big data era: high focus on algorithms and low focus on people. Procedia Comput. Sci. **219**(1), 91–98 (2013)
16. Sharma, T., Bashir, M.: An analysis of phishing emails and how the human vulnerabilities are exploited. In: Advances in Human Factors in Cybersecurity: AHFE 2020 Virtual Conference on Human Factors in Cybersecurity, USA (2020)
17. Burita, L., Halouzka, P., Kozak, P.: Analysis of phishing emails. AIMS Electron. Electr. Eng. **5**(1), 93–116 (2021)
18. Parker, H.J., Flowerday, S.V.: Contributing factors to increased susceptibility to social media phishing attacks. South Afr. J. Inf. Manag. **22**(1), 1–10 (2020)
19. Görling, S.: An overview of the Sender Policy Framework (SPF) as an anti-phishing mechanism. Internet Res. **17**(2), 169–179 (2007)
20. Thakur, K., Hayajneh, T., Tseng, J.: Cyber security in social media: challenges and the way forward. IT Prof. **21**(2), 41–49 (2019)
21. Saleous, H., et al.: COVID-19 pandemic and the cyberthreat landscape: research challenges and opportunities. Digit. Commun. Netw. **9**(1), 211–222 (2023)
22. Jalda, C.S., Nanda, A.K., Pitchai, R.: Spoofing e-mail detection using stacking algorithm. In: 8th International Conference on Smart Structures and Systems (ICSSS) (2022)
23. Mwin, E.N., Mtsweni, J., Chimbo, B.: Conceptual mapping of the cybersecurity culture to human factor domain framework. In: Future of Information and Communication Conference, Switzerland (2023)
24. Pönkänen, P.: Zero trust guidelines for enterprises. JAMK Univ. Appl. Sci. (2023)
25. CISA: COVID-19 exploited by malicious cyber actors. CISA, 8 Apr 2020. https://www.cisa.gov/news-events/cybersecurity-advisories/aa20-099a. Accessed 20 Aug 2023
26. Violino, B.: Phishing attacks are increasing and getting more sophisticated. Here's how to avoid them, 23 February 2023

5G Network Security: Unraveling Vulnerabilities and Innovating Defense Mechanisms

Mamoon M. Saeed[1], Elmustafa Sayed Ali[2]([✉]), Othman O. Khalifa[3], and Rania A. Mokhtar[4]

[1] Department of Communications and Electronics Engineering, Faculty of Engineering, University of Modern Sciences (UMS), Sana'a, Yemen
[2] Department of Electrical and Electronics Engineering, Red Sea University (RSU), Port Sudan, Sudan
elmustafasayed@gmail.com
[3] Department of Electrical and Computer Engineering, International Islamic University Malaysia, Kuala Lumpur, Malaysia
[4] Department of Computer Engineering, College of Computers and Information Technology, Taif University, P.O. Box 11099, Taif 21944, Saudi Arabia

Abstract. Rapid developments in cellular communications are accompanied by rising privacy and security worries. Many people refrain from participating in activities like social networking, shopping, transactions, and conducting a lot of business because network security and user privacy are major concerns in our daily lives. However, there is now a greater need for a private, highly secure business. This was accompanied by an increase in the requirements for it due to the growing hazards and programmers in our daily activities. The Fifth Generations (5G) groups are rapidly developing, as evidenced by the fact that the number of supporters is increasing by several times per second around the world in light of the ongoing revelations. According to statistics, 80% of people worldwide claim to use 5G mobile phones, and the percentage has been steadily rising for a very long time. A high level of security is also necessary because the 5G network serves as the basis for the 5G network. From there, this article gives an overview of some of the different 5G network vulnerabilities that can occur. Additionally, certain recent advancements in 5G security have revealed several flaws that still exist, allowing experts to concentrate on and fix these flaws.

Keywords: security · 5g · vulnerabilities · evolved packet core · network access security

1 Introduction

Today's news focuses on advancements in the 5G wireless network. The development and acquisition of more dependable and realistic technologies are becoming increasingly popular. As a result, the specialists focus on looking into and solving any issue or backlog that existed as recently as the fourth generation of flexible correspondence.

A. Sere et al. (Eds.): AFRICOMM 2023, LNICST 587, pp. 383–392, 2025.
https://doi.org/10.1007/978-3-031-81570-6_25

The organization is more vulnerable to new threats and vulnerabilities as a result of the transition from the first single confirmation to the shared verification in the 5G/LTE Advanced (LTE-A) networks [1, 2]. Customers who demand quick information access, little lag time, high throughputs, and high information rates are catered to by the LTE-A network. These various factors urge researchers to carry out further studies and work to fortify and safeguard LTE-A security from gatecrashes. As a result, this inquiry evaluates the most recent developments in LTE-A security while also pointing out any problems the LTE-A organization may truly have and that it has to address [3].

As seen in the Figure, the Home Network, Serving Network, and Mobile Station (MS) were all involved in the 5G security process.

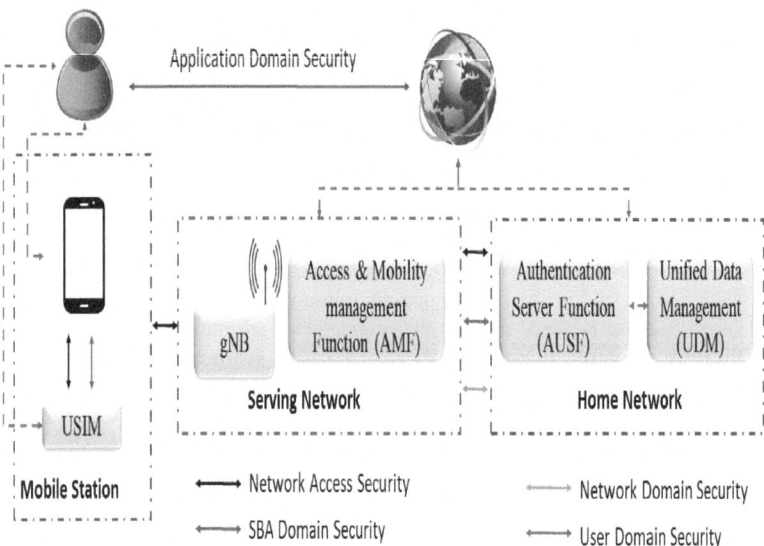

Fig. 1. 5G security architecture.

2   5G Security Design

The plan for 5G and Evolved Universal Terrestrial Radio Access Organization (E-UTRAN) and Evolved Packet Core are the two main components of an organization called Evolved Packet Core (EPC). Few overviews have been undertaken to help with LTE-A security, identify potential issues, and show progress being made in LTE-A security. Nevertheless, as illustrated in Fig. 2, the Third Generation Partnership Project (3GPP) has specified five tiers that comprise the LTE-A security framework.

- *Network Access Security:* protecting the radio access interface from threats and ensuring the organization's entrance for mobile clients.
- *Security of Network Domain:* protects against assaults on wireline connections and ensures that convenient backhaul center points safely exchange client and flagging data at flexible backhaul frameworks.

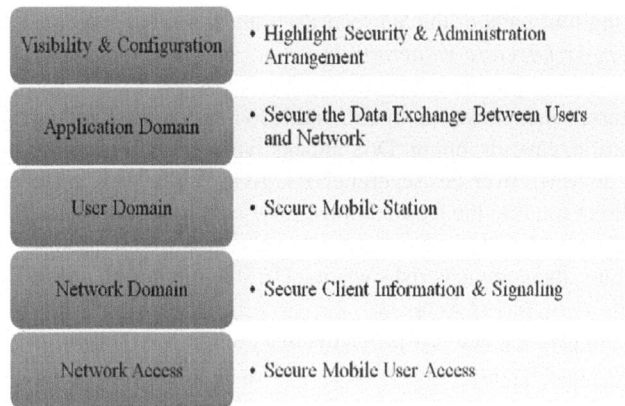

Fig. 2. 5G security Layers.

- *Security of Client Domain:* Access to the mobile station is secure.
- *Security of Application:* This permits programs from the customer and company to think about securely transferring data.
- *Perceivability and Safety Configuration:* gives users access to data on organizational strategy and activated security features. The layers [4] are displayed in Fig. 1.

3 Vulnerabilities on 5G Security

The information provided by the author in [5] led to a thorough research focus on 5G network security attacks. The attacks were categorized into groups, and they discussed how they had an impact on 5G companies. As indicated in Fig. 3, this section addresses the assaults and the dangers they represent to LTE-A. Based on the review by [5], they offered a comprehensive research focus on 5G network security attacks. They classified the attacks as groups and described how they affected 5G companies. This section examines the assaults and the risks they pose to 5G, as shown in Fig. 3.

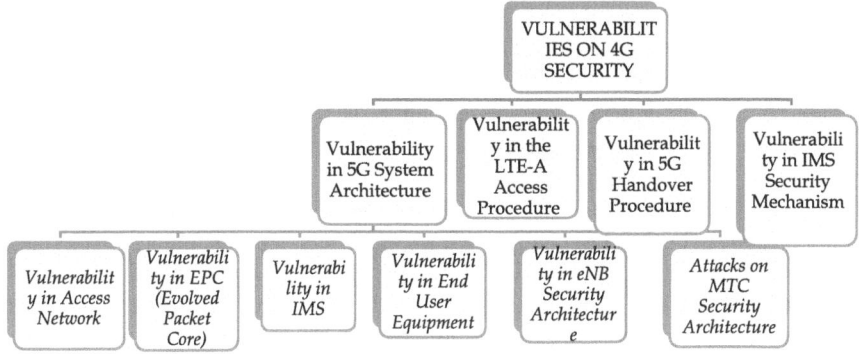

Fig. 3. Vulnerability in 5G System.

The following four parts of the 5G security framework may have vulnerabilities.

A. *5G System Architecture Vulnerability*

Additional security problems are caused by the 3GPP LTE-A networks' flat IP-based architecture, which makes them vulnerable to attacks such as IP address spoofing, insertion, alteration, eavesdropping, DoS attacks, viruses, worms, spam emails, etc. In the flat design, an MME oversees several eNBs, giving malevolent attackers on the all-IP network a direct route to the base stations. Low-cost base stations called eNBs have made it simple for attackers to gain access so they can create their rogues. Due to various mobility situations, there are new risks when a UE shifts from one end to another [6, 7].

B. *Vulnerability in Access Network*

The authors in [5] look at a few problems that compromise the security of 5G organizations, such as discovering or locating the IMSI, or International Mobile Subscriber Identity, which is an essential component of 5G businesses. Finding the IMSI causes the client's information to be disclosed, which results in the client's security being violated.

The client is also at significant risk because it is possible to track the client's whereabouts by obtaining the area ID and PDA ID. Assaults like RF sticking, spoofing, and sniffing are also more common in access organizations and are widely used in real-layer attacks and DDOS attacks [8, 9]. The two attacks are crucial for 5G businesses because they drain the CPU and stop it from responding to service requests.

A botnet that can obtain and use the victim's data can be controlled by a DDOS attacker. There are other types of network intrusions as well, such as replay attacks and eavesdropping attacks, however, 5G has lately completely stopped them.

C. *Vulnerability in EPC (Evolved Packet Core)*

Regarding 5G, significant worries continue to exist. Because the HSS (Home Subscriber Server) is the hub of EPC networks and maintains the endorser's information, such as IMSI, attacks like DOS and DDOS will overwhelm the HSS (Home Subscriber Server), cause it to use up more resources, affect the behavior of client equipment, and have an impact on SGW (Serving Gateway). It has been documented that insiders can control base stations and shut them down [5].

D. *Vulnerability in IMS*

The biggest threat to IMS is an SIP-related attack, like an SIP flood attack. Resource depletion, DOS attacks, and the initiation of other IMS attacks like SMS and VOLTE-A could all result from this attack. VoLTE-A voice over LTE. Attacks against VOLTE-A could reflect poorly on the LTE-A organization and tie it to the outmoded circuit switch architecture. Attacks with VOLTE-A, SIP flooding DOS, quiet calls, VOLTE-A spamming, mocking, and phishing are a few examples. Additionally, significant attacks are launched against SMS, a component that is essential to any portable aid and is dependent on the IMS design. Attacks on aberrant charging in VOLTE-A are another type of attack, as seen in Fig. 3.

The attacker can get the data for free from VOLTE-A administrators, which could result in a DOS attack. Three potential methods of informational attacks against VOLTE-A were mentioned in some studies. The first is a free charging attack that uses IP caricature to access the information; the second is an extortion charging attack that connects to a spam server and provides false information to the victim to drastically increase the cost. The ongoing VOLTE-A attack is dishonest because it can give the IP bundle time to live, releasing the packages after they have been accounted for. TCP/SYN flooding and SQL injection attacks are two other IMS attacks. Various clients can connect to an LTE-A network, allowing harmful attacks, worm attacks, spam emails, information modification, and the acceptance of a variety of credit cards for banking [10], according to [8].

E. Vulnerability in End User Equipment

This type of assault contaminates the client's devices with malware and botnets, dramatically raising the risk to the client's security. The former can be used to steal any kind of information from the victim, including SMS, email, and much more, whilst the latter can be used by attackers to exploit mobile users by starting attacks on the organization, such as DOS assaults, SMS attacks, and strange charge attacks. According to [1, 11], the LTE-A network, which is divided into three angles, has several potential faults.

The first is the internal network, which manages the entry and central businesses. The second is the outer network, which signals oncoming threats from the outside. Attacks coming from the client's equipment make up the third viewpoint. Furthermore, as depicted in Fig. 4, the architect created a building with six categories of LTE-A weaknesses. Additionally, by the LTE-A security engineering section, the designer categorizes the assaults into five different groups based on the LTE-A networks' five tiers [1].

F. eNB Security Architecture Vulnerability

Both the links between the UE and the eNB and the backhaul between the eNB and the EPC, make data and conversations susceptible to being intercepted and eavesdropped [12]. The current eNB security mechanism is unable to thwart various protocol attacks, including eavesdropping attacks, MitM attacks, masquerading attacks, and compromising subscriber access lists, as a result of a lack of strong mutual authentication between the UE and the eNB and the eNB's inadequacy as a trusted party.

G. Attacks on MTC Security Architecture

The MTC lacks security protocols for 3GPP networks, non-3GPP access, and communication between MTC applications and MTC devices. Additionally, there are no security mechanisms for communication between ePDGs and MTC devices. Since MTC devices usually need to have minimal capabilities in terms of both energy and computing resources, they are particularly vulnerable to a variety of attacks. These dangers include bodily harm, network intrusions, credential theft, and protocol attacks. When many MTC devices seek network access simultaneously, there may be signaling overhead between an HSS and the MME due to simultaneous authentication [13, 14].

H. Vulnerability in the LTE-A Access Procedure

The EPS-AKA program has no privacy protections. In other instances, the Globally Unique Temporary Identity system was unable to give the IMSI, therefore it had to be released (GUTI). It is unable to exchange messages with the active MME or retrieve the IMSI from it. Because the MME must send the UE's requests to the HSS/AuC before the UE has been validated by the MME, DoS attacks cannot be stopped. Only after getting a RES can the MME authenticate the UE.

The SN must go back to the HN to request a new set of When the UE stays in the SN for an extended amount of time and utilizes the entire set of its AVs for authentication, the SN must contact the HN to request a fresh set of authentication vectors. The result is bandwidth usage and authentication signaling cost on the SN and HN. Numerous issues with the EAP-AKA protocol exist, such as user identity leakage, vulnerability to MitM attacks, sequence number (SQN) synchronization, and higher bandwidth usage [15–17]. The EAP-AKA or EAP-AKA' is recycled by the LTE-A system to offer secure access authentication.

I. 5G Handover Procedure Vulnerability

The current eNB can generate new keys for several target eNBs by chaining the current key with those parameters because the key chaining architecture is in use. An attacker will be able to obtain the keys for the following sessions after compromising the present eNB. By transmitting an LTE-Aring handover request message between eNBs or an S1 path switch acknowledgment message from an MME to a target eNB, a malicious eNB might prevent the NCC value from refreshing. The target eNB and the UE won't establish a security link, thus the UE must start a fresh handover operation [3, 15, 18–20].

J. Vulnerability in IMS Security Mechanism

Complexity of the system and energy use in UE The EPS AKA for LTE-A access authentication and the IMS AKA for IMS authentication are the two AKA protocols that an IMS UE is required to implement. IMS AKA is vulnerable to MitM attacks, has poor SQN synchronization, and uses more bandwidth. The registration request is received by the core network (I-CSCF/S-CSCF/HSS) from the P-CSCF/MME and is used to implement access authentication. However, by flooding the I-CSCF/S-CSCF/HSS with legitimate packets that contain inaccurate IMSI/IMPI, an attacker could conduct a DoS attack [21–24].

4 Improvements in Security Aspects of 5G Network

This section describes the improvements that have been made to 5G organization security from various studies and sum them up as current contributions in Table 1 to provide a summary and comprehend how the improvements on LTE-A security have been done.

The weaknesses and improvements of the 5G/LTE-A network security are discussed in this article, along with the ongoing audits that have been performed on this organization from various angles. As a result, this will provide analysts who must look into and analyze this sector with enough knowledge.

Numerous security improvements have been found and added to 5G networks after thorough investigation and analysis. Implementing improved encryption methods and protocols to safeguard data in transit is one notable advance. Stronger encryption measures made possible by these developments make it far more difficult for unauthorized parties to intercept and decipher sensitive data.

The use of improved authentication and access control systems is a crucial component of the security upgrades in 5G networks. This minimizes the danger of unauthorized access and potential cyberattacks by ensuring that only authorized devices and users may connect to and access the network. Additionally, advances in network slicing have made it possible for various network segments to be isolated inside the 5G infrastructure, guaranteeing that any compromise in one segment would not affect the security or functionality of other parts. This isolation improves the network's overall security posture and lessens the effects of any potential intrusions.

Table 1. Related Works for Improvements on Security Aspect of 5G Network

Dataset	Best Accuracy Achieved & Author	Category	Number of actions (classes)
KTH	97.6% [Ziaeefard et al.']	General purpose Action recognition	6
Weizmann	100% [yangwang et al. 09; Lin et al. 09; Zeng and Ji et al.]	General purpose Action recognition	10
IXMAS	89.4% [Xinxiao Wu et al.']	Motion Acquisition	13
UCF Sports	93.5% [Simon Ones et al.']	Sports action	150
HAHA	56.8% [Andrew Gilbert et al.']	Movies	12
i3DPost Multi-View	80% [Michael B. Holte et al.']	Motion Acquisition	12
HMDB-51 (II)	Oh et al.	Movies	51
UCF-101 (IV)	Soomro et al.	Sports	101
Sports-1M (IV)	Karpathy et al.	Sports	487
ActivityNet (II)	Heilbron et al.	Human activities	203
NTU RGBD (II)	Shahroudy et al.	Human activities	60

The overall effects of these security upgrades have been encouraging. On 5G networks, researchers have noticed a sharp decline in security incidents and successful cyberattacks. Various known vulnerabilities and threats have been successfully mitigated by the strengthened access control, authentication, and encryption systems, creating a more secure environment for data transmission. However, it's crucial to remember that ongoing research and awareness are needed to keep ahead of potential security issues due to the permanence of cyber threats and the growth of technology. To maintain the security of 5G networks and successfully counter new threats, industry players, researchers, and regulatory agencies must continue to work together.

5 Conclusions

To identify the gaps or difficulties that must be overcome to achieve a higher level of security and prevent attackers from stealing or monitoring any private data or shutting down the 5G organization, this article aims to compile several issues relating to recent LTE-A network security flaws. It also maintains the level of development necessary to enable the security of the 5G network.

References

1. Ahlawat, A., Kumar, S.: Investigating various possible attacks and vulnerabilities in LTE-A (2018)
2. Saeed, M.M., et al.: Survey of privacy of user identity in 5G: challenges and proposed solutions. Saba J. Inf. Technol. Netw. (SJITN) **7**(1) 2019
3. Saeed, M.M., Saeed, R.A., Saeid, E.: Preserving privacy of paging procedure in 5thG using identity-division multiplexing. In: 2019 First International Conference of Intelligent Computing and Engineering (ICOICE). IEEE (2019)
4. Mukhtar, A.M., Saeed, R.A., Mokhtar, R.A., Ali, E.S., Alhumyani, H.: Performance evaluation of downlink coordinated multipoint joint transmission under heavy IoT traffic load. Wirel. Commun. Mob. Comput. **2022**, Article no. 6837780 (2022). https://doi.org/10.1155/2022/6837780
5. He, L., Yan, Z., Atiquzzaman, M.: LTE-A/LTE-A-A network security data collection, and analysis for security measurement: a survey. IEEE Access **6**, 4220–4242 (2018)
6. Saeed, M.M., et al.: A comprehensive review on the users' identity privacy for 5G networks. IET Commun. **16**(5), 384–399 (2022)
7. Macaulay, T.: The 7 deadly threats to 5G: 5G LTE-A security roadmap and reference design, vol. 25, p. 2017 (2013)
8. Pathak, P.H., et al.: Visible light communication, networking, and sensing: a survey, potential and challenges. IEEE Commun. Surv. Tutor. **17**(4), 2047–2077 (2015)
9. Saeed, M.M., et al., A novel variable pseudonym scheme for preserving privacy user location in 5G networks. Secur. Commun. Netw. 2022, 7487600 (2022)
10. DeMarinis, N.: On LTE-A Security: Closing the Gap Between Standards and Implementation. Worcester Polytechnic Institute (2015)
11. Saeed, M., et al., Preserving privacy of user identity based on pseudonym variable in 5G. Comput. Mater. Contin. **70**(3), 5551–5568 (2022)
12. Saeed, M.M., Saeed, R.A., Saeid, E.: Identity division multiplexing based location preserve in 5G. In: 2021 International Conference of Technology, Science and Administration (ICTSA). IEEE (2021)
13. Yan, X., Ma, M.: A privacy-preserving handover authentication protocol for a group of MTC devices in 5G networks. Comput. Secur. **116**, 102601 (2022)
14. Gupta, S., Parne, B.L., Chaudhari, N.S.: SRGH: a secure and robust group-based handover AKA protocol for MTC in LTE-A networks. Int. J. Commun. Syst. **32**(8), e3934 (2019)
15. Shaik, A., et al., Practical attacks against privacy and availability in 5G/LTE-A mobile communication systems (2015)
16. Elfatih, N.M., et al.: Internet of vehicle's resource management in 5G networks using AI technologies: current status and trends. IET Commun. **16**, 400–420 (2022). https://doi.org/10.1049/cmu2.12315
17. Wu, S., et al.: Identifying security and privacy vulnerabilities in 5G LTE-A and IoT communications networks. In: 2021 IEEE 7th World Forum on Internet of Things (WF-IoT). IEEE (2021)
18. Masud, M.: Survey of security features in LTE-A handover technology. System **1**(2) (2015)
19. Bitsikas, E., Pöpper, C.: Don't hand it over vulnerabilities in the handover procedure of cellular telecommunications. In: Annual Computer Security Applications Conference (2021)
20. Bikos, A.N., Sklavos, N.: LTE-A/SAE security issues on 5G wireless networks. IEEE Secur. Priv. **11**(2), 55–62 (2012)
21. Wang, D., Liu, C.: Model-based vulnerability analysis of IMS network. J. Netw. **4**(4), 254–262 (2009)

22. Saeed, M.M., et al.: A comprehensive review on the users' identity privacy for 5G networks. IET Commun. **16**, 384–399 (2022). https://doi.org/10.1049/cmu2.12327
23. Tu, G.-H., et al.: New security threats caused by IMS-based SMS service in 5G LTE-A networks. In: Proceedings of the 2016 ACM SIGSAC Conference on Computer and Communications Security (2016)
24. Lu, Y.-H., et al.: Ghost calls from operational 5G call systems: IMS vulnerability, call DoS attack, and countermeasure. In: Proceedings of the 26th Annual International Conference on Mobile Computing and Networking (2020)
25. Suliaman, A.G., Alkattan, Z.M.T.: Survey on vulnerability of 5G/LTE-A network security and improvements (2021)
26. Li, C.-Y., et al.: Transparent AAA security design for low-latency MEC-integrated cellular networks. IEEE Trans. Veh. Technol. **69**(3), 3231–3243 (2020)
27. Parameshachari, B., Panduranga, H., liberata Ullo, S.: Analysis and computation of encryption techniques to enhance the security of medical images. In: IOP Conference Series: Materials Science and Engineering. IOP Publishing (2020)
28. Miyim, A.M., Wakili, A.: Performance evaluation of LTE-A networks. In: 2019 15th International Conference on Electronics, Computer and Computation (ICECCO). IEEE (2019)
29. Yu, W., et al.: Survey of public safety communications: user-side and network-side solutions and future directions. IEEE Access **6**, 70397–70425 (2018)
30. Muthana, A., et al.: Enhancing privacy of paging procedure in LTE-A. Int. J. Eng. Sci. Invent. **7**(2), 42–50 (2018)
31. Ferrag, M.A., et al., Security for 5G and 5G cellular networks: a survey of existing authentication and privacy-preserving schemes. J. Netw. Comput. Appl. **101**, 55–82 (2018)
32. Liu, F., Peng, J., Zuo, M.: Toward a secure access to 5G network. In: 2018 17th IEEE International Conference on Trust, security and Privacy in Computing and Communications/12th IEEE International Conference on Big Data Science and engineering (TrustCom/BigDataSE). IEEE (2018)
33. Saeed, R.A., Saeed, M.M., Mokhtar, R.A., Alhumyani, H., Abdel-Khalek, S.: Pseudonym mutable based privacy for 5G user identity. J. Comput. Syst. Sci. Eng. **29**(1), 1–14 (2021). https://doi.org/10.32604/csse.2021.015593Muthana
34. Jover, R.P., Lackey, J., Raghavan, A.: Enhancing the security of LTE-A networks against jamming attacks. EURASIP J. Inf. Secur. **2014**(1), 1–14 (2014)
35. Hussein, S.: Lightweight security solutions for LTE-A/LTE-A networks, Paris 11 (2014)
36. Sulaiman, A.G., AlDabbagh, S.: Modified 128-EEA2 algorithm by using HISEC lightweight block cipher algorithm with improving the security and cost factors. Indones. J. Electr. Eng. Comput. Sci. **10**(1), 337–342 (2018)
37. Premchander, T.: Survey on vulnerability of 5G/LTE-A network security and improvements
38. Liyanage, M., et al.: Leveraging LTE-A security with SDN and NFV. In: 2015 IEEE 10th International Conference on Industrial and Information Systems (ICIIS). IEEE (2015)
39. Mohapatra, S.K., et al.: Comprehensive survey of possible security issues on 5G networks. Int. J. Netw. Secur. Appl. **7**(2), 61 (2015)
40. Cheema, A., et al.: Prevention techniques against distributed denial of service attacks in heterogeneous networks: a systematic review. Secur. Commun. Netw. **2022**, 8379532 (2022)
41. Ekene, O.E., Ruhl, R., Zavarsky, P.: Enhanced user security and privacy protection in 5G LTE-A network. In: 2016 IEEE 40th Annual Computer Software and Applications Conference (COMPSAC). IEEE (2016)

42. Saeed, M.M., Saeed, R.A., Azim, M.A., Ali, E.S., Mokhtar, R.A., Khalifa, O.: Green machine learning approach for QoS improvement in cellular communications. In: 2022 IEEE 2nd International Maghreb Meeting of the Conference on Sciences and Techniques of Automatic Control and Computer Engineering (MI-STA), pp. 523–528 (2022). https://doi.org/10.1109/MI-STA54861.2022.9837585

43. Davids, C., et al.: Research topics related to real-time communications over 5G networks. ACM SIGCOMM Comput. Commun. Rev. **46**(3), 1–6 (2018)

44. Elmustafa, S.A., et al.: Machine learning technologies for secure vehicular communication in internet of vehicles: recent advances and applications. Secur. Commun. Netw. **2021**, Article no. 8868355 (2021). https://doi.org/10.1155/2021/8868355

45. Alsaqour, R., Ali, E.S., Mokhtar, R.A., Saeed, R.A., Alhumyani, H., Abdelhaq, M.: Efficient energy mechanism in heterogeneous WSNs for underground mining monitoring applications. IEEE Access **10**, 72907–72924 (2022). https://doi.org/10.1109/ACCESS.2022.3188654

Author Index

The manufacturer's authorised representative in the EU is Springer
Nature Customer Service Centre GmbH, Europaplatz 3, 69115 Heidelberg,
Germany. If you have any concerns regarding our products, please
contact ProductSafety@springernature.com

Printed and bound by CPI Group (UK) Ltd, Croydon, CR0 4YY

27/04/2026

02097845-0007